P9-EDU-049

COMPARATIVE ECONOMIC SYSTEMS
Models and Cases

The Irwin Series in Economics
Consulting Editor   Lloyd G. Reynolds   *Yale University*

COMPARATIVE ECONOMIC SYSTEMS

Models and Cases

Edited by
MORRIS BORNSTEIN
Professor of Economics
The University of Michigan

AMBROSE LUTHERAN COLLEGE
LIBRARY

 Fourth Edition 1979

RICHARD D. IRWIN, INC. Homewood, Illinois 60430

CAMROSE LUTHERAN COLLEGE
LIBRARY

© RICHARD D. IRWIN, INC., 1965, 1969, 1974, and 1979

All rights reserved. No part of this publication may be
reproduced, stored in a retrieval system, or transmitted,
in any form or by any means, electronic, mechanical,
photocopying, recording, or otherwise, without the prior
written permission of the publisher.

ISBN 0-256-02152-X
Library of Congress Catalog Card No. 78–059216
Printed in the United States of America

5 6 7 8 9 0   6 5 4 3 2

PREFACE

This book, like the three previous editions, is about the organization, operation, and performance of economic systems, both in theory and in practice. It deals with alternative methods of determining the bill of goods to be produced, the allocation of resources to produce it, and the distribution of the resulting income. These are some of the most vital questions of our time—urgent issues for all economies, both capitalist and socialist, both developed and underdeveloped. The book explores various alternative answers by analyzing different economic systems and comparing them with each other.

This collection of readings is primarily intended for use in college courses in comparative economic systems. It is somewhat unorthodox because it is specifically designed to serve either as collateral reading in conjunction with one of the textbooks in the field, or as the core around which a comparative economic systems course can be organized. With the latter purpose in mind, I have prepared editorial notes for each division, section, and article in the book which integrate the various parts and selections and which place them in an overall conceptual framework. With few exceptions, the selections are articles reprinted in their entirety, rather than isolated excerpts. As a result, they present the author's full argument and at the same time are of an appropriate length for student reading assignments.

The selections in this volume are the fruit of an extensive search of the literature over a number of years in connection with my courses in comparative economic systems at The University of Michigan. They include "classic" articles by the most distinguished figures in the field, as well as lesser known, often overlooked articles by other authors. In many cases, the articles are from out-of-print volumes or less accessible journals. All of them can be read with understanding and profit by students in courses in comparative economic systems which require only principles of economics as a prerequisite. In a few instances, very technical passages, references to foreign-language sources, or supplementary statistical tables have been omitted.

This book covers the principal topics included in most college courses in comparative economic systems, although it is impossible in a volume of reasonable size to include all of the topics treated by different instructors in a field so broadly defined. This book excludes certain topics which are covered by relatively few instructors—for example, primitive economies—as well as other topics on which a considerable variety of material is readily available in inexpensive paperback form, such as the U.S. economy, Marxism, and problems of less developed countries.

Part I of the book provides a conceptual framework by explaining the scope and method of comparative economic systems. Part II presents theoretical analyses of the market economy and of regulated capitalism, followed by case studies of France and Japan which give a broader view of capitalist regulated market economies to readers familiar primarily with the U.S. economy. The selections in Part III include articles on different theoretical models of market socialism, as well as a case study of Yugoslavia. Three selections discuss workers' self-management of enterprises, a subject of great interest to students. Part IV, on the centrally planned economy, contains basic theoretical articles and case studies of the USSR, Eastern Europe, and China, which explain both the prototypical "Soviet model" and its modification in other countries. Part V compares economic systems from various standpoints, including enterprise management, unemployment, and inflation. It concludes with a multidimensional comparison of East and West Germany.

Although the material is presented in this sequence, the selections are chosen and the book is constructed so that the chapters can logically and conveniently be assigned in several different orders and combinations to fit the individual instructor's approach to the subject.

More than half the material in this edition did not appear in the Third Edition. This reflects the rapid development of the literature in comparative economic systems. I wish to thank the many persons who made suggestions for the new edition. The cooperation of authors and publishers who granted permission to reprint selections included in the book is appreciated. Finally, I am grateful to my wife, Reva, for her encouragement and forbearance during the preparation of the book.

December 1978   Morris Bornstein

CONTENTS

part I

Comparing Economic Systems

An analytical framework for comparing economic systems is essential in the study of economic systems—both economic models and actual economies. The most common bases of comparison are (1) the ownership of the means of production and (2) the methods of resource allocation. The means of production may be owned privately (individually), as in capitalism, or publicly (collectively), as in socialism. In turn, resources may be allocated by markets through the use of prices, as in a decentralized market economy, or by administrative commands expressed in real (physical) terms, as in a centrally planned economy. Various combinations of these two dimensions are possible, and Parts II, III, and IV of this book are concerned, respectively, with capitalist market economies, socialist market economies, and centrally planned economies.

The following selections discuss the methodology of comparing economic systems. The first provides an overview of the subject matter and some of the current issues in the field. The second suggests ways of classifying economic systems from the standpoint of decision making. The third explains possible objectives of economic policy and the instruments which can be used to pursue them.

1

THE COMPARISON OF ECONOMIC SYSTEMS: AN INTEGRATION*

Morris Bornstein

A logical way to begin the study of any subject is to consider what it comprises and how it may sensibly be analyzed, including some of the pitfalls. This is especially important in the case of comparative economic systems, because it is one of the broadest and most complex fields within economics, involving theoretical tools, institutional description, and social and political aspects. It is therefore not surprising that the literature is extensive and varied and that different writers take different approaches to the same questions. This essay provides a comprehensive and integrated view of the subject, to serve as a general analytical framework for the various theoretical models and case studies of different economic systems which follow.

The task of this paper is to integrate various approaches to the comparison of economic systems. The first section briefly considers the concept of an economic system. The second examines various ways of comparing economic systems. The third reviews some of the current issues in the field. The final section presents some conclusions. Throughout, the discussion focuses on an examination of the scope and method of the field, rather than a review of the principal literature on the many subjects composing it.

---

* Adapted from Morris Bornstein, "An Integration," in *Comparison of Economic Systems: Theoretical and Methodological Approaches,* ed. Alexander Eckstein (Berkeley and Los Angeles: University of California Press, 1971), pp. 339–55. Copyright © 1971 by The Regents of the University of California; reprinted by permission of the University of California Press. The present version omits references to other papers in *Comparison of Economic Systems: Theoretical and Methodological Approaches,* which examine a number of these questions in more detail and sometimes from a different viewpoint.

Thus, although specific works are cited for illustrative purposes at various points, the paper is a methodological, rather than a bibliographic, essay.

I. CONCEPT OF AN ECONOMIC SYSTEM

One may begin with the concept of a *system*, of which an economic system is a type. A general definition is that a system refers to a collection of "objects, ideas, or activities united by some regular form of interaction or interdependence." Thus, two dimensions are involved: what is being organized, and how the components are related to each other.

A more sophisticated and complex definition is as follows: The *participants* in a system may be individuals or different groupings of individuals. Through the *interactions* of participants, the actions of one participant simultaneously or sequentially affect other participants. Orders and rules govern these interactions. *Orders* are dated messages calling for a specific response from the participant(s) to whom they are addressed. *Rules* are messages stipulating (or constraining) for an indefinite period the actions of (a set of) participants under specified conditions. *Organizations* consist of a set of participants who regularly interact, according to rules and orders, to accomplish a set of activities constituting the purpose of the organization. The *motivation* of a participant is a function which associates with each course of action the utility of its outcome to him. Such motivations govern responses to orders and rules within organizations. Thus, the study of a system involves the analysis of the interaction of organizations, including the composition of the organizations, the orders and rules signalling action, and the motivations affecting the participants' responses to these signals.

An *economic system*, in turn, involves the interaction of organizations of participants engaged, according to rules and orders, in the production, distribution, and use of goods and services. It may be viewed as the set of arrangements by which the community determines (1) what shall be produced ("the bill of goods"); (2) how it shall be produced, including (*a*) the institutions and instruments to be used and (*b*) the pattern of resource allocation; and (3) how the resulting personal income and claims to goods and services shall be distributed (and redistributed) among households.

II. BASES OF COMPARISON OF SYSTEMS

Economic systems may be compared in regard to three main aspects. (1) What forces influence the system, determining its character? (2) What is the nature of the system? How does it operate? What are the nature and extent of state intervention in economic life? (3) How well does the system perform, in regard to its own goals and in regard to additional goals which are esteemed by others if not, or more than, by the system itself? Thus, we wish to know (1) what makes systems similar or different, (2) what the similarities or differences in systems are, and (3) what differences in performance are associated with differences in systems. These three aspects will be discussed in turn in some detail.

Forces Influencing the Economic System

These forces are so numerous and their relationship so complex that a comprehensive discussion is beyond the scope of this paper. Instead, it is convenient to group them into three main categories, each of which subsumes a number of elements: (1) the level of economic development, (2) social and cultural factors, and (3) the "environment." Although these categories are not necessarily exhaustive, they illustrate how different kinds of forces shape the nature and performance of economic systems.

Level of Economic Development. The level of economic development can be measured and compared by various indicators, including the level of per capita income, the rate of growth of per capita income, the share of investment in GNP, the share of primary, secondary, and tertiary activities in total employment or GNP, and so forth.[1] Whichever measures are used, it is clear that economic growth alters the size and structure of the economy, and that these changes in turn modify the economic system.

Thus, economic growth and development in the United States in the last 50 or 100 years has been responsible for many changes in the economic system, for instance in the nature and extent of government intervention to deal with problems of market power arising from the emergence of large firms and trade unions; problems of external diseconomies, such as water and air pollution; and problems of scientific discovery of a character and magnitude affecting survival, such as the utilization of nuclear energy.

Another example is the current economic reforms in Eastern Europe which seek to adapt the economic system to changes in the nature of the economy. This process has frequently been described as a shift from a more centralized system in the "extensive" phase of economic development, to a less centralized system in the "intensive" phase. In the earlier period, the tasks of "economic construction" were socialization of the means of production, a sharp increase in the rate of investment, rapid structural change, and revision of the income distribution. In this period, resource allocation was dominated by physical planning and administrative rationing. In contrast, the intensive phase is characterized by emphasis

---

[1] For an extended treatment of the subject, with a wealth of empirical data, see Simon Kuznets, *Modern Economic Growth: Rate, Structure, and Spread* (New Haven, Conn.: Yale University Press, 1966).

on greater efficiency in the use of given resources, greater responsiveness to household demand for consumer goods and services, and greater emphasis on competitiveness in international trade. This phase is seen to require a more decentralized economic system, involving greater reliance on market forces rather than administrative allocation, more need for scarcity prices, greater enterprise autonomy, and more emphasis on incentives instead of commands.

Although these examples illustrate how changes in the level of development affect the nature of the economic system, it is clear that a given level or pattern of economic development is not uniquely associated with a specific economic system. Rather, different countries at approximately the same stage of economic development exhibit a great variety of economic systems. Thus, it is not very satisfactory to classify countries into such groups as "West," "East," and "South," because some of the Communist countries in "East" are no more developed than some of the non-Communist countries in "South."

Instead, an "exclusion principle" seems useful. Although a given level of development can accommodate more than one economic system, certain levels of development may be incompatible with particular economic systems. One reason may be that the level of development alters the system. Another is that the system eschews a level or pattern of development which is incompatible with (i.e., threatens) the system. Thus, tribal or oligarchic societies may resist economic changes which will disrupt the traditional social structure.

The level of economic development is also related to the economic system in several other ways. First, it is part of the environment in which the system operates and which affects the system's performance. Second, it influences the culture, which also shapes the economic system. Finally, one of the aims of the system may be to alter the level of development. These propositions are developed further in subsequent sections.

Social and Cultural Forces. Many aspects of society and culture influence the economic system. One is social stratification, based on race, occupation, income, wealth, religion, or other factors; another is the customs, traditions, values, and beliefs of society. By way of illustration, I shall examine the influence of ideology, which has received considerable attention in the literature of comparative economic systems.

An ideology is a set of ideas and values guiding individuals (and organizations composed of them) in interpreting their environment, choosing goals in regard to maintaining or changing the environment, and selecting the means to achieve these goals. An economic ideology is a set of ideas related to economic action. Ideology may affect the economic system in various ways. It influences both the ends and the means of the system: what its goals are, including the priorities among them; the institutions and instruments of the system and the patterns of their use; and attitudes about changes in goals and institutions and instruments. Thus, ideologies may maintain or alter systems.

However, there are a number of difficulties in identifying the influence of ideology on the economic system. First, although a single consistent ideology is sometimes ascribed to a pure model of an economic system (e.g., "rapid industrialization through comprehensive central planning based on public ownership"), in actual real-world economies there are various interest groups with different ideologies about the ends or means of the system. Second, ideologies may be misleading. The ideology may seek to rationalize what is being done rather than constitute its true motivation. Or the aim may be to deceive—to conceal what is being done by describing it in completely different terms. Thus, the explicit ideology may not be the normative guide to action. Rather, the effective ideology may be implicit in the nature and operation of the economic system, from which it must be deduced, as has been suggested for the Soviet Union.[2] Third, there is a time gap between an ideology and the economic system to which it relates. An ideology can lag behind changes in the economy which it is supposed to guide, or an ideology may lead the system it aims to change. The gap is narrowed in the former case when outdated ideas are finally abandoned, and in the latter case when ideology succeeds in changing the system.

In conclusion, ideology does not determine the economic system in the sense that a single consistent ideology unambiguously and effectively shapes the economic system. Rather, different ideologies—some explicit, some concealed—influence economic institutions, policies, actions, and results. For this reason, one may prefer to account for the effect of ideology in terms of more specific concepts like perception, attitudes, norms (preference functions), institutions, and patterns of behavior, through which ideologies are expressed and operate.

Environment. The natural environment of an economic system includes such elements as the size (in area and population), location (topography, climate, access to the sea), and natural-resource endowment of the economy. These features affect the nature of the economic system indirectly in various ways. For example, they help determine the level and character of economic development. They also affect ideologies and other aspects of culture—for instance, attitudes toward the need to emphasize national unity of geographically diverse and distant regions, the desirability or feasibility of a high degree of self-sufficiency, and the like.

Another aspect of environment is contact with other economic systems which is a source of transmission of ideology and information about

---

[2] See, for instance, Morris Bornstein, "Ideology and the Soviet Economy," *Soviet Studies*, vol. 18, no. 1 (July 1966), pp. 74–80.

alternative arrangements and their results. An economic system may change as a result of its contact with another system. For example, a country may modify some facets of its economic system, such as its foreign-trade arrangements, in order to accommodate international economic relations with a country having a different system. Or it may change important aspects of the economic system—indeed, even the system itself —because a powerful neighboring state insists upon it.

Thus, while an economic system operates in an environment which affects its performance, the system itself may be influenced directly or indirectly by its environment.

To analyze how these various forces—the level of development, social and cultural factors, and the environment—influence economic systems, is to study how economic systems change. It is an investigation of the dynamic process, as distinct from either interspatial (transnational) comparisons at a given time or intertemporal comparisons of the economic system of the same country at different times (e.g., the United States in 1928 versus 1968). For some purposes, it is convenient to classify these forces of change into exogenous factors, such as new technology and developments in world politics, and endogenous factors, such as the effect of increasing affluence in creating new interest groups or ideologies capable of modifying the economic system.

Nature and Operation of Economic Systems

The nature and operation of an economic system may be analyzed in terms of its social preference function, its institutions and instruments, and its patterns of resource allocation and income distribution. These three aspects are, of course, related. The social preference function determines which institutions and instruments are used in which patterns of resource allocation and income distribution to pursue which social aims. And the most useful focus of analysis for all three aspects is the nature and degree of state intervention in economic life.

Social Preference Function. The social preference (or utility or welfare) function expresses the community's effective aggregate preferences regarding the ends and means of economic activity. In analyzing and comparing systems, we wish to consider both how the community's decisions are reached and what these decisions are.

In regard to the first aspect, three mechanisms may be distinguished: (1) individual preferences expressed through individual choice in markets (consumer sovereignty); (2) individual preferences expressed through the political process, either by direct voting on certain issues or by indirect voting through the selection of legislators and government officials; and (3) the preferences of a ruling group not selected through the electoral process. Several questions must then be investigated. What is the relative importance of each of these mechanisms in determining the community's preference on such matters as the composition of output, the distribution of income, and so forth? How does each of these mechanisms formulate its respective preference function? What is the resulting preference function generated by each mechanism? Finally, how are the several preference functions integrated into a single (consistent?) community preference function?

In addition, we wish to compare the resulting community preferences in regard to the objectives of economic policy, the choice of institutions and instruments to achieve these aims, and the combination of these institutions and instruments in particular patterns of resource allocation and income distribution. The community's objectives will include goals in regard to the level of employment, price stability, per capita consumption, the rate of growth of national income, the distribution of income and wealth, the balance of payments, and so forth. These objectives may be expressed more precisely in specific economic policies and in quantitative terms as "targets."

Institutions and Instruments. *Institutions* may be defined as relatively fundamental organizational arrangements for conducting production and distribution. They are often prescribed by law and not altered as easily as instruments. Examples of institutions include firms, households, markets in which firms exchange with other firms and with households, banks, trade unions, and government economic agencies. Each of these institutions in turn has various types and subtypes. For instance, government economic agencies may be concerned with planning, regulation, redistribution (e.g., social security), or the provision of public goods. An important aspect of any institution is the motivation of its participants, because different participants may have different motivations, with their relative strength and interaction determining the motivation of the institution as such.

The institutional distinction most often made in the study of economic systems concerns the ownership of the means of production. The variants of *private* ownership include individual, partnership, cooperative, and corporate enterprises. When the means of production are *socially* owned, they may be operated by departments of government at different levels (e.g., federal, state, local), by autonomous public boards, or by the personnel of the enterprise ("workers' management"). In all of these cases, private and social, the actions of the enterprise may be restricted by other institutions, using some of the instruments noted below. However, the trend in the study of economic systems is to downgrade the significance of ownership as a critical element in the nature and operation of economic systems, on the ground that it is less important than the pattern of resource allocation and income distribution. Thus, it is now commonly held that "capitalism" and "socialism" are not very useful classifications of economic systems, and that these distinctions are more of ideological or political significance. Nevertheless, although ownership is not decisive in determining the character of the economic system, it is significant both as a factor in income distribution (an important feature of any system) and as a source of power in the formulation of the community's preference function.

Instruments refer to the tools used by the state when it intervenes to (attempt to) achieve social goals in the economic sphere. In comparison with institutions, instruments are more often subject to quantitative expression, are more easily and more frequently altered, and are used by only one kind of institution (government agencies). At least five types of instruments may be distinguished. (1) *Fiscal* instruments include taxes, subsidies, transfer payments, and government purchases. (2) *Monetary* instruments involve changes in interest rates, reserve ratios, and credit rationing; government lending and borrowing; management of existing debt; and control of consumer credit. (3) Altering *exchange rates* is another instrument. (4) Among *direct controls* are production assignments, allocation orders, fixing of prices and wages, and allocation of foreign exchange. Finally, (5) *changes in the institutional framework*—e.g., in property rights or rules for the operation of markets—may be considered another type of instrument.[3]

Thus, the comparison of systems involves the study of the prevalence and operation of various institutions, as well as the purposes for which, and manner in which, the state uses the possible instruments of economic policy to direct the economic activity of these institutions toward social goals.

Patterns of Resource Allocation and Income Distribution. The interaction of institutions and instruments generates the pattern of resource allocation and income distribution in the system. Three complementary approaches to the analysis of these patterns appear in the literature, each stressing somewhat different elements of the same economic processes.

Centralization versus decentralization involves the delineation of different hierarchies and the relationships among and within them, including (1) the locus at which different decisions are made on such matters as investment, current production, the decision rules applicable to a given unit, and changes in the hierarchical structure; and (2) the flow of information, involving the form, content, purpose, and routing of "messages." Although the choices along the centralization-decentralization continuum in the two cases are related, they need not be identical. For

---

[3] A comprehensive analysis of these instruments is presented in E. S. Kirschen and others, *Economic Policy in Our Time* (Amsterdam: North-Holland Publishing Company, and Chicago: Rand McNally, 1964), vol. I. (For a brief summary, see Selection 3 in this book, pp. 35–40.)

example, the flow of information could be more centralized than the decision-making process, as when the central authorities collect a great deal of information only in order to make it available to autonomous units which use it for decentralized decisions.[4]

Command versus exchange contrasts resource allocation in physical terms via administrative orders with resource allocation in response to money flows and prices in markets. Money and prices may be used in a command economy, but they perform only "secondary allocation," helping to implement plans drawn up through physical planning techniques. Although it is intended that money flows should supplement administrative orders, in practice they often conflict with them, inducing "violations" of the plan.

Planning versus the market focuses on the manner and extent of state intervention in the economy through "planning." This approach is concerned with such questions as the following: What is the coverage, in scope and detail, of the plan? How is the plan prepared—by what techniques and with what participation by lower units? How seriously is the plan implemented, and what instruments and adjustment mechanisms are used? In addition, one must be aware that some areas of government intervention may be outside the scope of what is customarily included in the "plan," and such extra-plan activities may reinforce or conflict with the plan.

In all three approaches, it is essential to investigate both the formal and the informal mechanisms and their relationship in actual operation, not merely official descriptions or theoretical models of the processes.

To summarize this section briefly: An economic system consists of a particular set of arrangements in regard to a social welfare function, institutions and instruments, and patterns of resource allocation and income distribution. Any specific economic system—whether a model or an actual case—represents a unique combination of these three related aspects. To compare the nature and operation of different systems, we must compare them in detail in all three respects, as systems are likely to be more similar or different in one respect than another. Next we want to associate differences in the nature of the system with differences in performance.

Performance of Economic Systems

One may argue that the ultimate purpose of comparing economic systems is to find ways of improving the performance of a given system (in the light of its social preference function). For this purpose, we want

---

[4] This example was suggested by Oldřich Kýn.

to compare the results of different systems, operating in similar or different environments, in regard to various performance criteria which are deemed important.

The criteria commonly considered include the following:

1. The level of output. (The objective ordinarily is a high or full-employment level, although the quantitative expression of this target depends upon assumptions or goals regarding labor force participation rates and the length of the work week.)
2. The rate of growth of output.
3. The composition of output (the shares of consumption, investment, and military programs; collective vs. individual consumption; and so forth).
4. Single-period ("static") efficiency.
5. Intertemporal ("dynamic") efficiency.
6. Stability (of output, employment, prices).
7. Economic security of the individual (security of income and/or of employment).
8. Equity (involving both an "appropriate" degree of inequality of income and wealth, and equality of opportunity).
9. Economic freedoms (of property, consumption, occupational choice).
10. A balance-of-payments situation which is satisfactory in the light of the country's economic structure.
11. Adaptability to change (in the preference function, the environment, etc.)

Other criteria may be derived from these. For example, the level of per capita consumption, sometimes suggested as an index of welfare, is a combination of 1, 3, and the size of the population. Similarly "economic justice" usually refers to goals in regard to 7, 8, and sometimes 9.

As is well known, some of these objectives are complementary, i.e., mutually reinforcing; for example, the higher the rate of growth, the greater the level of output (in the next period). Others may be competitive, i.e., mutually conflicting; for example, price stability may conflict with a high level of output and a high rate of growth.

Thus, for an aggregate evaluation of an economic system's performance it is necessary to have a utility or welfare function according to which the different criteria can be assigned appropriate weights. Different preference functions will assign different weights to the various performance criteria. The prevailing community preference function may differ in this respect from the function of some part of the community (which may be a majority or a minority of the population) which is given little weight in, or is overruled by, the prevailing function. The function prevailing in one community (i.e., country) may differ from that in another community, or in the same community at another time. It may also differ from that of the analyst of systems, who must recognize when he is using his own preference function to evaluate the system(s) he is studying.

Thus, the comparative evaluation or ranking of different economic systems will depend on (1) the performance of the systems in regard to the various criteria considered, and (2) the preference function(s) assigning weights to the several criteria. The latter is essentially a value judgment, somehow formulated for the community as a whole, but the former is more nearly subject to objective scientific measurement.

Two steps are required for empirical comparisons of performance. First, each of the various criteria must be defined as precisely as possible to permit quantitative measurement. This is easier for some criteria than for others. For example, Lorenz curves can show the degree of inequality in the distribution of income and wealth. National accounts depict the level and composition of output. Statistics on employment (unemployment) and personal income provide a measure of economic security. Variations in output, employment, and prices indicate the degree of (in)stability of the economy. Efficiency is more difficult to quantify, but the extent of idle resources may furnish some measure of single-period efficiency, and calculations of aggregate factor productivity offer an indication of intertemporal efficiency. It is even possible to quantify some of the differences in economic freedoms, for example to use the respective shares of output produced by private and public enterprises as some index of freedom of enterprise.

Once the criteria have been defined carefully, the next step is to measure the performance of the economies to be compared, in as uniform a way as possible. This involves many well-known problems of international comparisons, such as differences among countries in the availability, reliability, coverage, and methodology of data. Although such calculations are usually difficult and complex, they yield the final product toward which the comparison of economic systems is directed. They show the difference in performance—the merit of which is to be assessed in the light of one or more preference functions, and the causes of which are to be explained by the analysis of the nature and operation of the system.

III. SOME CURRENT ISSUES

The aim of the preceding sections has been to present a comprehensive view of the comparison of economic systems, showing the unity and coherence of the various parts of the subject. However, scholars in the field do not agree on all aspects of the methodology for studying economic systems. In this section, I shall consider four current methodological issues, suggesting how they should be resolved. I shall discuss in turn (1) the model versus the case approach; (2) the study of economic systems versus the study of economic development; (3) the comparative systems versus the comparative economics approach; and (4) the disciplinary versus the interdisciplinary approach.

Models versus Cases

Models of economic systems are simplified abstractions presenting the main institutional features and operating characteristics of different types of economic systems. They are often inspired by one or more important real-world economies, although they purport to represent general types rather than specific economies. A *case study* deals with an actual economy, which typically incorporates features from various pure models, as a result of such influences as the level of economic development, social-cultural forces, and environmental circumstances. Thus, each specific case has its own unique combination of social preference function, institutions and instruments, and patterns of resource allocation and income distribution.

The model approach to the study of systems has been criticized on the ground that it is concerned with oversimplified abstractions from reality; for example, that it is not useful to consider a pure centrally administered economy, simply because none has ever existed or is likely to exist. A second objection is that it is not possible to measure and compare the performance of models, while this can be done in regard to case studies. As a result, it is argued, the comparison of models is especially vulnerable to ideological biases in interpretation and assessment.

In turn, the case approach has been challenged on the ground that the reality of an actual economy is so complex that any case must be considered selectively, in the light of some conception of the critical variables —i.e., a model. Furthermore, it is a common pitfall to identify a case, explicitly or implicitly, as—in some sense and to some degree—representative of a group of countries with common characteristics. For example, often the United States is chosen as an example of capitalism, the Soviet Union as an illustration of socialism, France as a case of indicative planning, and so forth. The unsophisticated reader—student, citizen, or politician—may then erroneously assume that the features and results of the prototype country generally characterize the entire group, and that a comparison of the relative merits of the prototypes, according to one or more performance criteria, reveals the relative merits of the "families" the prototypes are supposed to represent. This may lead to incorrect conclusions because other countries in the group may differ from the prototype in important respects; and the relative performance (merit) of the two groups will therefore depend on which member is selected as the prototype, as well as which performance criteria are chosen for comparison. In short, intragroup differences are frequently so great that prototypes are not or cannot be representative. Intragroup differences may even exceed intergroup differences in regard to certain characteristics or performance criteria.[5]

The model and case approaches should, however, be viewed as complementary rather than competitive. Models provide a framework for selecting and comparing cases. In turn, the comparison of cases with the models they are supposed to illustrate should lead to the revision and improvement of the models, for example the elaboration of various models of centrally planned socialism, or of market socialism, with different ownership arrangements and different combinations of command and exchange. In this respect, the West and East European economies offer especially promising case studies which can suggest various intermediate models between the traditional model of regulated capitalism inspired by the United States and the classic model of centrally planned socialism suggested by the Soviet Union. Hopefully, these intermediate models will generate a number of testable hypotheses about the operation and performance of economic systems to guide subsequent case studies.

Economic Systems versus Economic Development

The issue here is the extent to which the comparative study of economic systems should include the less developed countries and primitive economies. For this purpose, *less developed countries* are defined as those with low per capita income levels, which are associated with differences —from the more developed countries—in various aspects of economic structure. These aspects include the distribution of national income by sector of origin, the type of enterprise, the structure of the labor force, factor shares and the size distribution of income, patterns of income use, and foreign-trade proportions. One striking characteristic of many less developed countries is the coexistence of an important "traditional" sector in agriculture alongside a "modern" industrial sector. *Primitive economies,* on the other hand, refer to isolated, nonmonetized tribal societies in which economic activity is guided chiefly by tradition and custom, rather than exchange or command. Although this definition may suggest some overlap with the traditional sector in the "dual" economy, the difference is that in the dual economy the traditional sector is in contact with and is being changed by the modern sector, whereas the primitive economy lacks such strong links to a parallel modern sector. With these distinctions in mind, I find myself in agreement with the position that the study of comparative

---

[5] Some relevant empirical evidence may be found in George J. Staller, "Fluctuations in Economic Activity: Planned and Free Market Economies, 1950–1960." *American Economic Review,* vol. 54, no. 4 (June 1964), pp. 385–95; George J. Staller, "Patterns of Stability in Foreign Trade: OECD and COMECON, 1950–1963," *American Economic Review,* vol. 57, no. 4 (September 1967), pp. 879–88; and Frederic L. Pryor, *Public Expenditures in Communist and Capitalist Nations* (Homewood, Ill.: Richard D. Irwin, Inc., 1968).

economic systems may fruitfully include the less developed countries but not primitive economies.

The major reason for including the less developed economies is that the level or stage of economic development is one of the forces affecting the nature of the economic system, as well as the conditions (environment) in which it performs. Moreover, there are large and interesting intragroup differences among the less developed countries,[6] and it is desirable to investigate how these differences in the level of development are associated with the nature and performance of economic systems. Finally, there are interesting questions about the interaction of the modern and traditional sectors in the less developed countries which do not arise in the study of more developed economies.

On the other hand, the study of primitive economies may reasonably be excluded because it is not very useful to compare cases where great differences exist in material technology and the stock of useful knowledge, because the resulting differences in the economic activities of society cannot be attributed in significant measure to differences in the economic system. That is, "intra-epochal" comparisons are desirable, but "interepochal" comparisons are not very relevant. Of course, this position does not mean that the study of primitive societies is pointless or without interest. Rather, it suggests that the subject be considered part of economic anthropology, instead of comparative economic systems.[7]

Comparative Systems versus Comparative Economics

The *comparative systems* approach encompasses the study of the entire economic system, with the broad scope indicated above in Section II and with emphasis on the relationship among the various parts of the system. In contrast, the *comparative economics* approach is a partial or sectoral view which compares economies in relation to certain components, for example, labor markets, the nature and operation of large enterprises, agricultural organization, or the conduct of foreign trade.

It seems clear that these should be considered complementary rather than alternative approaches. On the one hand, the sectoral approach needs a view of the entire system, because the characteristics of a given sector in

---

[6] Kuznets believes that the variety in economic systems is probably greater among the less developed countries than among the more developed countries, because the common technology in the dominant modern component in the latter dictates considerable similarity in economic structure, organization, and goals.

[7] Some recent examples of economic anthropology are Manning Nash, *Primitive and Peasant Economic Systems* (San Francisco: Chandler Publishing Company, 1966), and *Tribal and Peasant Economies: Readings in Economic Anthropology*, ed. George Dalton (New York: Anchor Books, 1967).

a particular country are determined by the system of which it is a part. On the other hand, sectoral comparisons enhance our understanding of the respective systems as a whole. Thus both approaches—and a synthesis of the results—are necessary. (If a comprehensive label embracing both the comparative systems approach and the comparative economics approach is deemed useful, "comparative economic studies" may serve the purpose.)

There are, however, some reasons for believing that it may be more fruitful to emphasize the sectoral approach in future research in the field. Most past research has stressed the systems approach, and a substantial (though by no means complete) body of "system-focused" literature is now available. Thus, at the margin the returns from research are likely to be greater in selected comparative sectoral studies. These studies can also help illuminate differences and similarities *within* the usual groupings of countries—such as East and West. Finally, such studies will hopefully enrich the U.S. economics curriculum by introducing a comparative dimension into courses in public finance, labor, industrial organization, and so forth. As a rule, these courses now deal solely with the U.S. economy, leaving consideration of the respective aspects of other economic systems to courses labeled "comparative economic systems" or "economic development."

Disciplinary versus Interdisciplinary Approach

To what extent can the comparative analysis of economic systems, along the lines suggested above, be performed exclusively with the tools ordinarily found in the economist's tool box? Or must considerable use be made of the concepts and techniques of other disciplines, notably history, anthropology, political science, sociology, and psychology?

Perhaps more than other branches of economics, the comparison of economic systems requires a multidisciplinary or—better still—interdisciplinary approach. Some aspects of the subject may need this approach to a greater extent than others. For example, the comparison of ideologies involves other disciplines much more than does the comparison of growth rates.

In this field, as in others, it is incumbent upon the investigator to use all of the relevant tools. In some cases, he may acquire and use them himself. In others, the most satisfactory solution will be to secure the collaboration of appropriate scholars in other fields who possess the additional disciplinary skills. Illustrations include joint work by economists and political scientists on government resource-allocation decisions, by economists and psychologists on enterprise management, and by economists and sociologists (or anthropologists) on social-cultural forces shaping the economic system. Fortunately, current trends in other social-science disciplines are favorable to such collaboration. The comparative method has long been used in anthropology,[8] and in recent years systematic comparative studies have received increasing attention in both political science and sociology. Thus, comparative politics is concerned with transnational analysis of "the social configuration, the interest group universe, political parties, ideological attitudes as they shape and condition political behavior, and elite structure."[9] Comparative sociology is devoted to cross-societal studies of kinship, family, and marriage; polity and bureaucracy; social stratification and mobility; ecology, urban sociology, and demography; and cultural value orientation.[10] The potential for mutual assistance and cross-fertilization between these fields and comparative economic studies is clear and exciting.

IV. CONCLUSION

The scope of comparative economic studies is broad, encompassing three main aspects. First, the field deals with the factors influencing economic systems, including the level of economic development, social and cultural forces, and the "environment." A second aspect is the nature and operation of systems, involving social preference functions, institutions and instruments, and patterns of resource allocation and income distribution. Third, the subject is concerned with the performance of systems, both empirical measurement of results for various performance criteria and aggregate evaluations in the light of the weights assigned to the various criteria by one or more social preference functions.

The broad scope of the field in turn accommodates—indeed requires— a variety of research methods and analytical approaches, disciplinary and interdisciplinary.

Finally, comparative economic studies make a unique contribution to economics as a whole, by providing the perspective to overcome the parochialism inherent in economic thinking—on both theoretical and policy questions—based on the experience of a single economic system. The comparison of systems enriches the analyst's understanding of his own system, sharpening his appreciation of its merits and demerits and suggesting organizational and operational changes to improve its performance.

---

[8] Cf. A. R. Radcliffe-Brown, "The Comparative Method in Social Anthropology," *Journal of the Royal Anthropological Institute of Great Britain and Ireland*, vol. 81 (1951), parts I and II, pp. 15–22.

[9] Roy C. Macridis and Bernard E. Brown, "Introductory Essay," in *Comparative Politics: Notes and Readings*, ed. Roy C. Macridis and Bernard E. Brown, rev. ed. (Homewood, Ill.: The Dorsey Press, 1964), p. 4.

[10] Cf. Robert M. Marsh, *Comparative Sociology* (New York: Harcourt, Brace & World, 1967).

2

CLASSIFYING ECONOMIC SYSTEMS*

Egon Neuberger

> *Because of the many dimensions involved, there are various approaches to the classification of economic systems. In this selection, Neuberger proposes and explains four criteria: (1) the locus of decision making, (2) the motivation of the decision maker, (3) the information on which the decision is based, and (4) the mechanism coordinating the decisions of different decision makers.*

What criteria should be applied? The criterion most generally used is property relationships—that is, one asks who owns the means of production. Any good Marxist will tell you that, once you have the answer to this crucial question, you can easily place any system into its proper pigeonhole. A difficulty with this approach is that all 20th-century economic systems would have to be squeezed into either of two categories: capitalism (means of production owned by private capitalists) or socialism (means of production owned by society, or by the state as its representative). An insistence on using the single criterion of property relationships would force us to lump the United States, France, Denmark, and Nazi Germany under capitalism, and the Soviet Union, Communist China, Yugoslavia, and Albania under socialism. This would make for some very uncomfortable bedfellows indeed.

We must seek a less Procrustean classification of economic systems. Surely, a multidimensional approach is needed. Let us consider the following four key structures in any economic system: decision making, motiva-

---

* Excerpted from Egon Neuberger, "Comparative Economic Systems," in *Perspectives in Economics: Economists Look at Their Fields of Study*, ed. Alan A. Brown, Egon Neuberger, and Malcolm Palmatier (New York: McGraw-Hill Book Company, 1971), pp. 252–66. Copyright © 1971 by McGraw-Hill, Inc. Used with permission of McGraw-Hill Book Company. Egon Neuberger is Professor of Economics at the State University of New York (Stony Brook).

tional, informational, and coordination structures.[1] This will enable us to focus on four questions: (1) What is the locus of decision making? (2) What motivates a decision maker to reach a particular decision? (3) What information does he need to reach a decision? (4) What mechanism coordinates the decisions of several decision makers? Let us note that decision making, not property, has been moved to the center of the stage.

THE DECISION-MAKING STRUCTURE

In dealing with the locus of decision-making power, one must consider the level of the economy at which decisions are made, the types of decisions made there (for example, the decision on how many houses are to be built in a tract is more important than the decision on the colors to be used for interior decoration), and the legal or extralegal sanctions (property rights, tradition, or bureaucratic position) provided to protect the right of a decision maker, or a group of decision makers, to make decisions.

What is our reason for placing ownership in a secondary position, making it merely one of several sanctions provided to protect the right of a decision maker to make a decision? The answer is that ownership rights, in themselves, may signify very little. They may mean anything from complete control over the owned object to virtually no control at all. For example, they may range from the almost absolute control you have in the decision to save or spend the dollar in your wallet to the almost zero control a child of three has over the same dollar deposited in his name by his parents in a savings bank. In addition, ownership is by no means the sole sanction behind a decision maker's right to dispose freely of some object. The native chieftain who rules a tribe by virtue of tradition may have both the decision-making power and the ability to reap many benefits from the tribe's property without having actual ownership over anything. The same can be said of a high functionary in a socialist state, or of a top executive in many United States corporations.

The most important question concerning a decision-making structure is the degree of its centralization or decentralization. While much has been written about this question, no fully satisfactory treatment exists. Of the many important issues here, we shall attempt to clarify only two. Instead of the simple dichotomy between centralization and decentralization, we shall deal with four basic types of decision-making structures—complete centralization, administrative decentralization, manipulative decentraliza-

---

[1] This classification has been developed more fully by the author in Egon Neuberger and William Duffy, *Comparative Economic Systems: A Decision-Making Approach* (Boston: Allyn and Bacon, Inc., 1976). It does not represent a consensus among students of comparative economic systems. Classification of economic systems is one of the issues at the frontier of the study of methodology in this field.

tion, and complete decentralization. And we shall discuss shifts in decision making in cases where there are more than two levels in a hierarchy.[2]

It is easy to define *complete centralization* in the abstract. This exists when a unique, central, monolithic authority in an economic system makes all the decisions. No national economic system based on such complete centralization has ever existed. The cost and difficulty of obtaining the necessary information and the problem of assuring that everyone in the economic system does what he is told provide effective barriers against such centralization. The only conceivable way such a system could be made to operate is by means of a cybernetic revolution, where the information and control problems are solved by information technology and automation.

Administrative decentralization provides for the formulation of basic decisions by the central authority, but for the delegation of the responsibility to implement the decisions and the right to make the necessary subordinate decisions to lower-level authorities. The control over the actions of lower-level authorities is achieved by placing limitations on their freedom of action—for example, by commanding them to do something, forbidding them to do something else, or setting rules by which they must guide their decisions. A textbook case of administrative decentralization is the army. The army clearly represents the ultimate in a hierarchical, command organization, with all the important decisions being reached at the top of the pyramid, and so may appear to represent complete centralization. However, no commander worth his salt spells out for his subordinates the precise manner in which his commands are to be implemented—for example, a division commander is not likely to tell the company commander which squad to send out on patrol.

For the third type of decision-making structure we have coined the name *manipulative decentralization*. This is similar to administrative decentralization, but in this case the central authorities do not place explicit limitations on the freedom of action of lower-level authorities. Instead, they control their actions by affecting the environment within which these actions take place. For example, they may manipulate prices, bonuses, taxes or subsidies, or access to credit.

The fourth type of decision-making structure is *complete decentralization*. This provides for the dispersal of basic decision-making power among a number of independent decision-making centers. In the extreme case— again virtually nonexistent—each of these centers would have complete freedom of decision. The textbook case of complete decentralization is

---

[2] These ideas are based on Egon Neuberger and Frederic L. Pryor, A *New Conceptual Framework for Analyzing Economic Systems* (unpublished paper, International Development Research Center, Indiana University, 1969), which develops other aspects in greater depth and deals with many issues that could not be included here.

pure competition, where each entrepreneur has complete freedom to make his decisions and there is no higher organ to control his actions in any way. Paradoxically, in the case of pure competition it is obvious that all this freedom actually amounts to very little real power. This is because the invisible hand of the market serves as a demanding taskmaster. Thus, situations of oligopoly—where a few sellers divide the market—or of "countervailing power"—where strong buyers face strong sellers across a market—offer better examples of complete decentralization in the economic sphere.

The fundamental difference between administrative and manipulative decentralization, on the one hand, and complete decentralization, on the other, is between the delegation of authority to lower echelons merely to make decisions that implement the basic decisions reached by higher echelons, in the former, and the dispersal of decision-making power among independent decision-making organs, in the latter. In the one case, circumscribed rights are granted to subordinates and can be taken away at the discretion of the superior. In the other case, by rights of ownership, custom, or law many independent organs possess power which they cannot be deprived of, except by major changes in these sanctions. In view of this, we would argue that the most significant watershed lies between complete decentralization and administrative or manipulative decentralization, rather than between centralization and decentralization.

Another crucial issue arises when we consider shifts in decision-making power in a system that has more than two levels of authority. In a three-level hierarchy, the definition of decentralization, whether administrative or manipulative, is no longer clear. In this case, there are 12 possible shifts in decision-making power:

	1	2	3	4	5	6	7	8	9	10	11	12
Central units	−	−	−	+	+	+	−		+		−	+
Intermediate units	−		+	−		+	−	+	+	−	+	−
Primary units (enterprises)	+	+	+	−	−	−	+		−		−	+

Let us define *decentralization* as a shift of decision-making power from the top toward the bottom of the hierarchy (that is, where the power of the highest unit decreases (−) and the power of the lowest unit increases (+)). It should be clear that there are three kinds of decentralization (columns 1, 2, and 3), the most thorough being seen in column 1 and the least thorough in column 3. *Centralization* is, of course, defined by the reverse process, as in columns 4, 5, and 6. The most thorough centralization appears in column 4, the least thorough in column 6.

Semidecentralization occurs when there is a downward shift in decision-making power between any two adjoining levels. The two cases of semi-decentralization are seen in columns 7 and 8. *Semicentralization* is the reverse phenomenon and is pictured in columns 9 and 10.

Positive-intermediation occurs when the intermediate decision-making units gain power at the expense of the highest and lowest units, as in column 11. *Negative-intermediation* occurs when the intermediate units lose power at the expense of the highest and lowest units, as in column 12.

THE MOTIVATIONAL STRUCTURE

A decision maker bases his decisions, either consciously or subconsciously, on his perception of the circumstances surrounding the particular choice facing him; the goals he is pursuing; the incentive structure linking his goals and the various alternative decision outcomes available to him; and the type, amount, and quality of information at his disposal or obtainable with further effort and expense.

There exists no generally acceptable theory of human motivation. By combining elements of many different theories of motivation, we can indicate some of the important aspects of this problem. At very low levels of income, physiological needs, such as hunger and thirst, and a desire for security against natural or man-made disasters are likely to be the dominant motivational variables. The economic system must satisfy these needs or use coercion as a substitute. As income rises, material incentives, in their role of satisfiers of physiological needs, and coercion will begin to decrease in importance. Their place is taken by the desire for self-esteem and recognition, for furthering the goals of the organization to which one belongs or for exercising influence over the goals and operation of the organization. To the extent that material incentives represent recognition of the individual's importance and of the significance of his contribution to the organization, they remain crucial motivational elements even at very high income levels. How else is one to explain the extremely high salaries paid to executives in some United States companies when the lion's share of the additional $100,000 of income ends up with the Internal Revenue Service?

Given this range of possible motivational variables, the economic system may be structured in such a way as to accept the objectives of the participants as given or to try to remold them. Most economic systems, including those of the United States and the Soviet Union, use the first approach. The motivational structure of the system is adapted to providing the participants in the economic process with appropriate incentives, principally in the form of positive material benefits, but also in the form of ego-satisfying, nonmaterial rewards. Negative incentives in the form of coercion have been used in systems such as the antebellum South or slave labor camps under Hitler and Stalin. However, no modern economic system has been based primarily on coercion.

While most economic systems accept the objectives of the participants as given, some systems use the second approach. They attempt to remold the value structure of the participants in such a way as to make them place a low value on selfish motives, particularly with respect to material benefits. Mao Tse-tung's attempt in the Great Proletarian Cultural Revolution to remold the value structure of the Chinese people is an extreme example.

THE INFORMATIONAL STRUCTURE

Another major input into decision making is information. Information has been gaining importance recently because of changes both in economic systems and in information technology. We will define information very broadly to include the collection, transmission, processing, storage and retrieval, and analysis of economic data; the communication of orders or other signals; and the feedback necessary for evaluating decisions taken as a result of the signals. As we move from a subsistence economy to a traditional economy, from that to a market economy or centrally planned economy, or even to the extreme of a cybernetic economy, the importance of information in the economic system rises very greatly. The larger the number of participants in the economic process, the greater the division of labor, the more complex the technological processes, and the wider the assortment of goods and services an economic system produces, the more information-intensive the economic process becomes. Information becomes more essential not only for the system as a whole but for every participant in the economic process.

The amount of information entering into the decision-making process varies greatly among decision makers in the same economic system, with those nearer the center of economic power requiring and obtaining more information than those at the periphery. It also varies greatly among decision makers with similar positions but operating under different economic systems.

The three major types of informational signals are prices; data on physical units of inputs, outputs, capacities, and the like; and commands. Data on physical units and commands are hallmarks of Soviet-type central planning, while prices are hallmarks of the market system. However, each type of informational signal can be found in both centrally planned and market systems.

Information may be generated with a given organization or received from outside the organization. It may be obtained by horizontal channels —for example, from customers or rival businesses—or by vertical channels —for example, as commands from higher echelons or as data on levels of output and unused capacities transmitted from a firm to its ministry. Information may consist merely of scattered bits of data used to support an action based on intuition, or it may be generated by a well-established system of information collection and analysis, using the latest instruments of information technology.

Three indirect indicators of the degree of informational centralization may be found in an economic system: (1) horizontal channels of information; (2) reliance on price changes, manipulation of incentives, and generalized monetary and fiscal policy; and (3) limitations on the types of messages that can be demanded by the center and sent from the center to the enterprises. All three correspond to informationally decentralized systems.

The way an economic system is organized with respect to the demand it places on informational inputs to decision making, the channels of information that are established, and the ability of decision makers to obtain high-quality information in a reasonable time and at a reasonable cost—these are important factors in determining the efficiency of the system.

THE COORDINATION STRUCTURE

Decisions of many separate decision-making units are coordinated in three ways: by tradition, by a market, or by a plan.

Tradition

This coordinating mechanism may be best explained by the following description of the Trobriand Island economic system:

> Every man knows what is expected from him, in virtue of his position, and he does it, whether it means the obtaining of a privilege, the performance of a task, or the acquiescence in a *status quo*. He knows that it has always been thus, and thus it is all around him, and thus it always must remain. The chief's authority, his privileges, the customary give and take which exist between him and the community, all that is merely, so to speak, the mechanism through which the force of tradition acts. For there is no organized physical means by which those in authority could enforce their will in a case like this. Order is kept by direct force of everybody's adhesion to custom, rules and laws, by the same psychological influences which in our society prevent a man of the world doing something which is not "the right thing." The expression "might is right" would certainly not apply to Trobriand society. "Tradition is right, and what is right *has* might"—this rather is the rule governing the social forces in Boyowa, and I dare say in almost all native communities at this stage of culture.[3]

---

[3] Bronislaw Malinowski, *Argonauts of the Western Pacific* (New York: E. P. Dutton & Co., 1922), pp. 158–59.

A Market

The "invisible hand," as the coordinating mechanism in the market, consists of three major elements: every individual is motivated by self-interest; he obtains the commodities and services he requires through exchange with others; and by his pursuing his self-interest, in competition with others, the welfare of society is maximized. Some quotations from Adam Smith illustrate these points:

> It is not from the benevolence of the butcher, the brewer, or the baker that we expect our dinner, but from their regard to their own interest. We address ourselves, not to their humanity but to their self-love, and never talk to them of our own necessities but of their advantages.[4]

While humans obtain most of what they need by means of exchange— "Give me that which I want, and you shall have this which you want"— this does not happen with other species: "Nobody ever saw a dog make a fair and deliberate exchange of one bone for another with another dog."[5] The most important, but by no means most obvious, aspect of the market is that, according to Smith, a man pursuing his own self-interest is

> . . . led by an invisible hand to promote an end which was not part of his intention. Nor is it always the worse for the society that it was no part of it. By pursuing his own interest he frequently promotes that of the society more effectually than when he really intends to promote it.[6]

Or again,

> Every individual is continually exerting himself to find out the most advantageous employment for whatever capital he can command. It is his own advantage, indeed, and not that of the society, which he has in view. But the study of his own advantage naturally, or rather necessarily, leads him to prefer that employment which is most advantageous to the society.[7]

A Plan

The third major coordinating mechanism is a plan. One of the earliest examples of planning is told in the Biblical story of Joseph, who prepared Egypt for seven lean years by gathering grain and storing it in the warehouses of the Pharaoh during seven fat years. A more recent example is the centrally planned economic system introduced by another Joseph, Joseph Djugashvili, better known as Stalin.

---

[4] Adam Smith, *The Wealth of Nations* (London: J. M. Dent & Sons., Ltd., 1910), p. 13. [First published 1776–78.]

[5] Ibid., pp. 12–13.

[6] Ibid., p. 400.

[7] Ibid., p. 398.

According to its adherents, the major advantages of a plan as the coordinating mechanism are (1) the possibility of ex ante coordination, which enables a given objective to be attained more smoothly and more speedily, and (2) the reduction of uncertainty as to the actions of competitors, suppliers, and buyers, which makes for more rational investment decisions and may help in internalizing external economies.

In addition to requiring a coordination mechanism, an economic system must provide mechanisms for assuring that decisions are implemented. Implementation in a traditional society is based on voluntary adherence to custom, or, if need be, on the enforcement of custom by such means as ostracism. In a market system, implementation takes place through the operation of the price system. In a planned system there are many possible mechanisms for enforcing the decisions of the planners. The usual one is by informational messages in the form of commands from superiors to inferiors. But this role could theoretically be performed by a cybernetic system transferring information from one machine to another, by the setting of prices by planners, by the use of coercion, or possibly even by the willing cooperation of all the participants. All of these implementing mechanisms, of course, contain motivational or informational components, and could be dealt with as aspects of the motivational and informational structures. Closely connected with implementing mechanisms are the economic policies—monetary, fiscal, or antitrust—adopted by the government in any given economic system.

3

THE OBJECTIVES AND INSTRUMENTS OF ECONOMIC POLICY*

Etienne S. Kirschen
and
Lucien Morissens[1]

This selection shows how a country's economic system can be analyzed in terms of the objectives of economic policy and the instruments used to pursue them. The principal objectives include full employment, price stability, economic growth, improvement in the balance of payments, satisfaction of collective needs, and modification of the distribution of income and wealth. To accomplish these goals, governments use instruments of public finance, monetary and credit measures, direct controls, alteration of the exchange rate, and even changes in the basic institutional framework. The authors

* Excerpted by permission from *Quantitative Planning of Economic Policy*, ed. Bert G. Hickman (Washington, D.C.: Brookings Institution, 1965), pp. 111–33. Material originally published in E. S. Kirschen and others, *Economic Policy in Our Time* (Amsterdam: North-Holland Publishing Company, 1964), is reprinted by permission of the North-Holland Publishing Company. Etienne S. Kirschen is Professor and Director, and Lucien Morissens is Professor, at the Department of Applied Economics of the Free University of Brussels.

[1] Much of the substance of the present paper is drawn from *Economic Policy in Our Time* (Amsterdam: North-Holland Publishing Company, 1964), by E. S. Kirschen (Belgium), J. Bénard (France), H. Besters (Germany), F. Blackaby (United Kingdom), O. Eckstein (United States), J. Faaland (Norway), F. Hartog (Netherlands), E. Tosco (Italy), and L. Morissens (Belgium). The study is in three volumes: I. *General Theory*; II. *Country Studies: Economic Policy in the United States, United Kingdom, and Norway*; III. *Country Studies: Economic Policy in Belgium, The Netherlands, France, Italy, and Western Germany*. This material is in general paraphrased, and on occasion blended in with additions made for the present paper. In any case, the authors are grateful to the North-Holland Publishing Company for permission for use of the excerpts and tabular material. An extension of this analysis appears in E. S. Kirschen and others, *Economic Policies Compared—West and East* (Amsterdam: North-Holland Publishing Company, 1974).

28

explain which instruments are commonly used for which objectives, and they identify the conflicts which occur and the choices which must be made by government policy makers.

OVERALL TERMINOLOGY

By "policy," we mean action taken by the government in pursuit of certain aims, examples of which are:

raising the population's standard of living;

preserving law and order;

guarding the freedom of expression and choice;

reducing social tensions;

defending the country from outside attack;

making adequate provision for health and education.

It must also be recognized that governments in the eight countries chosen for special study were elected, and that one of their aims was to keep the electorates' support. All these aims have, to a greater or lesser extent, an economic aspect. The standard of living is obviously an economic matter, but the other aims, too, usually require some kind of government intervention in economic affairs. Preparations for defense or expenditure on health, for instance, require that resources are diverted from productive uses.

Economic policy, therefore, is the economic aspect of government policy in general: it is *the deliberate intervention of the government in economic affairs to further its aims.* In pursuit of these aims, governments have tended to set for themselves certain specific *objectives* which can be stated in economic terms, and which (at least in principle) are capable of measurement (either ordinal or cardinal).

To put its economic policies into effect, a government either alters certain economic quantities (such as bank rates or tax rates), or makes changes in the economic structure (such as nationalization). The economic quantities which the government can change, or the types of intervention in the economic structure, we call *instruments*. The government selects, from a wide range of instruments, those that will in its opinion most nearly achieve its objectives. The use of an instrument does not normally bring about changes in objectives directly: it operates on other economic quantities. For instance, a government may have expansion of production as its objective. It may choose to increase private consumption, investment, or exports, and to effect these increases it can select from a large number of possible instruments—such as a guaranteed minimum wage or export subsidies.

Finally, the use of a particular instrument on a particular occasion we call a *measure*. A measure is taken to promote one or more objectives. This means that there is no measure without an objective.

THE OBJECTIVES OF ECONOMIC POLICY

For economic analysis as well as for political decision making, a classification of the objectives is necessary. There are many ways of classifying objectives, but none of them is perfect. The reasons for this deficiency are the following:

1. Economic policy was not devised in one day by a brain trust. Objectives appeared in the course of history, one by one, as new problems arose and as policy makers became more fully conscious of old problems. This process resulted in overlappings and contradictions. Some objectives are complementary—when the achievement of one helps in the achievement of another; other objectives conflict—when the achievement of one is detrimental to the achievement of another.[2]

2. Problems are not considered in the same way by the politician (who makes decisions) and by the economist (who sometimes inspires decisions). The politician may be led to classify objectives according to the preferences expressed by the various policy makers who influence economic policy; from this point of view, he will distinguish objectives which serve the general welfare of the nation from those which serve particular interests, and, among the latter, he will consider separately the objectives aiming at the promotion of various particular interests. The economist, on the other hand, will tend to rationalize economic policy on the basis of his views about the workings of economic mechanisms. In his classifications, he might thus use such criteria as demand, production, or incomes, which will obviously lead to something very different from the list of objectives stated by politicians.

In *Economic Policy in Our Time* objectives were classified according to the following statement of principles:

> In producing our classification of objectives, we tried to find the one which was most useful in showing up the important differences in the policies of our nine countries.[3] The classification has been derived partly from the analysis of actual economic policy in these countries, and it takes into account the objectives which the various governments themselves have stated from time to time. It also uses the various systematizations which have been prepared by other economists.

The criteria applied in our classification are the following:

1. The number of objectives was kept small enough to render the classification easy to handle, but large enough to keep international comparisons meaningful.

---

[2] This point of conflict is discussed in the later section "Conflicts and Choices."

[3] Editor's note: The eight countries listed in footnote 1 plus Luxembourg.

2. The objectives were divided into two groups: mainly short-term and mainly long-term. This is because it is of interest to examine separately the various methods used in the different countries to counteract short-term cyclical fluctuations, and the methods used to pursue longer-term economic policies. However, all the short-term objectives have long-term aspects as well. For instance, the objective of maintaining full employment was most commonly a short-term cyclical problem, but governments have also had long-term full employment objectives, e.g., of reducing structural unemployment.

3. The longer-term objectives were divided into major and minor ones. If, in the years we were surveying, most countries had an objective and most countries considered it important, then we classed it as a major objective—otherwise as minor.

4. When an objective appeared to be the result of a regrouping which is meaningful for the economist but not for the policy maker, we subdivided the objective. This is the case for the improvement in the allocation of factors of production. But when an objective had a composite nature that was not the result of economists' arrangements, the objective was not subdivided. Thus, we kept together the protections given to various industries, the satisfaction of the various collective needs, or the improvement in the pattern (i.e., relative importance of the various items) of private consumption.

5. When an objective could be given two opposite meanings, we did not subdivide it into two objectives. For example, the improvement in the distribution of income can mean a move toward greater or lesser equality; similarly, according to its state, a balance of payments can be improved either by reducing its deficit or by reducing its surplus. Thus, when we use the word "improvement" this implies nothing more than that, in the judgment of the government which took the measures, any change was an improvement.

6. We have not included all the various objectives which may have been in the mind of some particular minister in one or another of the nine countries at some time. At various times, for instance, some people have elevated to the rank of objectives such things as the balanced budget, the reduction of the national debt, or the preservation of a particular exchange rate. We regard these matters as constraints on the use of instruments.

The classification of objectives (as formulated in *Economic Policy in Our Time*) is shown in the left-hand column of Table 1. At the head of the columns are listed the main aims which seem to have been expressed by the various objectives. There are of course many overlappings between the aims, mostly because aims incline to be philosophical notions. (The x's in the columns mean that the aim was expressed by the objective.)

In this section the first four objectives in Table 1 will be considered. For each objective we give a definition and the methods of quantification.

TABLE 1
Classification of the Objectives of Economic Policy and Aims Expressed by These Objectives

Objectives	Internal Aims					
	Material Welfare	Equity	Reduction of Social Tensions	Promotion of Human Values	Ethics and Religion	Protection of Persons and Properties
Mainly Short-Term						
1. Full employment	x	x	x	x		
2. Price stability	x	x	x			
3. Improvement in the balance of payments	x					
Mainly Long-Term (major)						
4. Expansion of production ..	x					
5. Improvement in the allocation of factors of production						
a. Promotion of internal competition	x	x	x			
b. Promotion of coordination	x					
c. Increase in the mobility of labor, within countries	x			x		
d. Increase in the mobility of capital, within countries	x					
e. Promotion of the international division of labor	x					
6. Satisfaction of collective needs:						
a. General administration	x	x	x		x	x
b. Defense						
c. International affairs ..	x					
d. Education	x	x		x	x	
e. Public health	x	x		x		
7. Improvement in the distribution of income and wealth .	x	x	x	x		
8. Protection and priorities of particular regions or industries	x	x	x	x	x	
Mainly Long-Term (minor)						
9. Improvement in the pattern of private consumption ...				x	x	
10. Security of supply	x					
11. Improvement in the size or structure of the population	x		x		x	x
12. Reduction in working hours	x			x		

Note: The x's in the columns mean that the aim was expressed by the objective.

	External Aims		
External Security	Political Power	International Solidarity	Personal Aims
		x	
		x	
	x	x	
	x	x	
x	x	x	
x	x		
x	x	x	
	x		
		x	
		x	
x	x		
x	x		x

Full Employment

1. Definition: Prevention or Reduction of Unemployment. Governments have been mainly concerned with the objective of preventing and
reducing short-term cyclical unemployment, caused, for example, by a
decline in exports or by the ending of an investment boom. But some
have also had long-term policies which were specifically directed to reduce noncyclical unemployment: for instance, frictional unemployment
—unemployment due to the delay in matching vacancies with the unemployed who are capable of filling them; or structural unemployment—
for instance, unemployment due to the decline of a particular industry,
or to the fact that industry is moving away from a particular region.

2. Methods of Quantification. Full employment may be expressed as
a given or a maximum ratio between the number of unemployed and the
working population; or it may be expressed as an equality between the
number of unemployed and the number of unfilled vacancies.

*   *   *   *   *

Price Stability

1. Definition: Maintaining General Stability of Prices. Throughout
most of our period, most governments tended to regard price stability
as a short-term problem: the tendency to rising prices was something
to be corrected by "conjunctural" policies. More recently, an increasing
number of governments began to regard this tendency as a long-term
problem which might require structural changes in the economy.

2. Methods of Quantification. The objective may be expressed as a
maximum annual increase in the retail price index.

*   *   *   *   *

Improvement in the Balance of Payments

*1. Definition: Maintaining a "Satisfactory" Balance of Payments and
a "Satisfactory" Stock of Gold and Foreign Exchange.* Usually, the objective was the short-term one of maintaining or increasing exchange
reserves. Sometimes there was concern about the balance of payments
on current and/or capital accounts (when a rise in the reserves results
only from the inflow of short-term money). Some countries, in addition
to the short-term difficulties with their exchange reserves occasioned by
the trade cycle, also had a long-run need to improve the proportion of
their output which is exported, notably to meet import developments.
A balance of payments surplus was thus needed. Some countries aimed

to reduce the rate at which their reserves were rising—partly because they considered that their export surplus was becoming inflationary, and partly because other countries were protesting that their own reserves were being run down too fast. There were other long-term balance of payments problems as well—such as the problem of changing the regional pattern of exports: for instance, by increasing the proportion going to dollar markets.

2. *Methods of Quantification.* The objective could be expressed in one of the following ways: minimum level of exchange reserves; minimum ratio between the reserves and the value of imports; difference between exports and imports (in current and/or capital accounts).

*   *   *   *   *

Expansion of Production

1. *Definition: "Satisfactory" Rate of Growth in the Real National Product.* Generally, the objective is to increase the rate of growth per head of the population, since this is a measure of the increase in the standard of living. In some cases, however, the overall rate of growth also mattered, when expansion was linked to the political power of the nation.

2. *Methods of Quantification.* This objective could be expressed as a minimum rate of increase of the GNP (total or per head).

*   *   *   *   *

THE INSTRUMENTS OF ECONOMIC POLICY

The instruments are commonly listed in five categories: public finance, money and credit, the exchange rate, direct controls, and changes in the institutional framework. Instruments included in each category are shown in Table 2.

1. The instruments of *Public Finance* cover most income and expenditure items of central governments and local governments, as well as balances between income and expenditure.

2. The instruments of *Money and Credit* include those which serve to make it either more difficult or easier for persons, companies, or governments to borrow money; they include, for instance, measures designed to change the rate of interest or to increase or reduce bank advances.

3. The *Exchange Rate* is the ratio between the national currency and one or more foreign currencies. Changes in the exchange rate include both general revaluations and devaluations, changes for particular transactions, or changes against particular currencies. They also include any change in the type of exchange-rate system.

TABLE 2
Instruments Used for Each Objective: Synthesis for Nine Countries

Objectives	1. Current Balance	2. Overall Balance	3. Government Investment	4. Subsidies and Capital Transfers to Enterprises	5. Transfers to Households	6. Government Stock Changes	7. Current Purchases of Goods and Services	8. Wages and Salaries	9. Transfers to the Rest of the World	10. Direct Taxes on Households' Incomes	11. Direct Taxes on Enterprises' Incomes	12. Indirect Taxes on Internal Transactions	13. Customs Duties	14. Social Security Contributions
	A Balances		B Government Expenditure							C Government Revenue				
1. Full employment	X	X	I	X	X	X	X	X		X	X	X	X	X
2. Price stability	I	I	I	X	X		X	X	X	X	I	I	X	X
3. Improvement in the balance of payments	X	X	X	X			X	X	X	X	X	X	I	X
4. Expansion of production	X		I	I				X		X	I		X	
5a. Promotion of internal competition														
b. Promotion of coordination														
c. Increase in the mobility of labor				X	X			X						
d. Increase in the mobility of capital										X				
e. International division of labor					X				X				I	
6. Satisfaction of collective needs			I		X	X	I	I	X					
7. Improvement in the distribution of income and wealth	X	X	I					X		I		X		X
8. Protection and priorities to regions or industries	X	I			X	X				X	X	X	I	X
9. Improvement in the pattern of private consumption			X									X		
0. Security of supply			X			X						X	X	
1. Improvement in the size or structure of population					X					X				
2. Reduction in working hours														
Number of objectives (x's, I's) served	4	3	7	10	6	4	5	7	3	7	6	7	7	6
Number for which the instrument was important (I)	1	1	4	2	1	0	1	1	0	1	2	1	3	0

Source: E. S. Kirschen and others, *Economic Policy in Our Time* (Amsterdam: North-Holland Publishing Company. 1964), vol. I, table VII–1, facing p. 148.

4. The instruments of *Direct Control* include the powers to fix prices, quantities, or values, generally by fixing maxima or minima.

5. The general categories of *Changes in the Institutional Framework* are identified in Table 2: (1) changes that alter the basic system within which other instruments are used—for instance, a substantial change in the credit system; (2) changes that do not affect the other families of instruments, but have a direct bearing themselves on the process of production—for instance, anticartel legislation; (3) changes that create new international institutions, and which, therefore, limit the freedom of national governments.

The uses of instruments may take various forms. Usually, they are imperative, backed by the force of the law. This is the case for government revenue instruments and, generally, for direct controls.

A government may at times use persuasion (mainly in the field of money and credit and of direct control) with the threat—expressed or implied—of statutory measures if its wishes are not complied with. In some cases, however, persuasion amounts to little more than mild suggestion, or the government refrains from showing the instruments which it will use if need be. For example, it may be arbitrary to say that a general campaign against price rises is a use of price control, when in fact the government may have recourse to an increase in direct taxes. Such a campaign has nevertheless been considered as a use of price control, for there is no dividing line between the strong and the mild varieties of persuasion.

The dividing line between the various categories of instruments is not always clear, and the classification given in Table 2 can thus be criticized. Among the borderline cases of classification are the following:

1. Restrictions exercised in the field of credit were included among the money and credit instruments; this seemed more appropriate than leaving them with price and quantity controls.

2. All government debt operations—both new borrowing or lending and operations in existing debt—have also been considered as money and credit instruments, though there are strong grounds for listing them in public finance.

3. The dividing line between changes sufficiently large to be considered changes in the institutional framework and changes within the existing framework is also necessarily an arbitrary one. For instance, the decision to impose indirect taxes on a new range of goods would not be considered an institutional change big enough to be included here. On the other hand, the creation of a tax on the value added counts as a change in the institutional framework. Similarly, the setting up of any major new machinery or institution for exercising direct control is included among changes in the institutional framework; the operation of the machinery or institution after it is set up is included among direct controls.

Table 2 (drawn from *Economic Policy in Our Time*) shows which instruments were used for each objective and which objectives were served by each instrument in the eight countries (synthesized) during the period of our consideration. When the letter *I* replaces a cross in the table, this indicates that the policy makers considered an instrument to be particularly important for an objective.

Since such tables indicate the relations between instruments and objectives which the governments used in their economic policies, they provide a basis for beginning the construction of economic policy models. The information must, however, be supplemented by:

1. Relations between instruments and noncontrollable variables (such as private investment and foreign trade) and between such variables and objectives, as the instruments often act on the objectives through such variables.

2. Other possible relations between instruments and objectives which were not used by the governments but could have been used if the governments had so desired.

3. Relations indicating unintended effects of instruments on objectives.

4. Relations between objectives (some information on this subject is given in the section that follows).

Conflicts and Choices

So far, objectives have been dealt with independently of each other, and we have only endeavored to find out which instruments were used consciously in order to reach them. In actual fact, of course, matters are much more complicated, since in present-day economies interrelationships are numerous and important. Some of the instruments used for one objective may have effects on other objectives; some instruments interfere with each other; and the total number of available instruments is sometimes smaller than the total number of objectives. The objectives will be found to be independent, or complementary, or conflicting. These various interactions may reinforce the efficiency of instruments, but may also weaken their effects and lead to conflicts that can only be solved by choices.

One could conceivably construct a table that shows, for a given country and at a given time, all the relationships between objectives, but because of the changing effects of instruments on objectives, we have not attempted to do this. Some material, however, can be drawn from the national studies of economic policy, 1949 to 1961. As illustrations of practical cases of interrelations, we present the main conflicts between objectives, . . . and the main cases of complementarity. . . .

Table 3 indicates the main conflicts between objectives, with the x's in the columns indicating the most important conflicts experienced in one

TABLE 3
Main Cases of Conflicts between Objectives in Nine Countries

	Price Stability	Balance of Payments (Reduction of Surplus)	Expansion of Production	Coordination	International Division of Labor	Collective Needs (All)	Redistribution of Incomes	Protection
Full employment	x	x						
Price stability			x			x	x	
Balance of payments (reduction of deficit)			x		x	x	x	
Expansion of production							x	x
Internal competition				x				x
International division of labor								x

Note: The x's indicate the most important conflicts experienced in one or more of the nine countries studied.

or more of the nine countries studied. In most cases the conflict is between an objective served by increased government expenditures and/or reduced taxes (full employment, expansion of production, satisfaction of collective needs, improvement in income distribution) and an objective served by reduced expenditure and/or increased taxes (price stability, reduction of the deficit in the balance of payments). Sometimes, however, the conflict is between an objective which requires trade liberalization (international division of labor, internal competition, price stability) and an objective which requires restrictions (reduction of deficit in the balance of payments, protection).

*   *   *   *   *

The most common cases of intended complementarities found in the . . . countries studied were the following:

full employment and expansion
full employment and protection
price stability and balance of payments
price stability and redistribution of incomes
expansion and collective needs
expansion and protection
redistribution of incomes and protection
redistribution of incomes and pattern of private consumption

The order of priority of the objectives that are in fact selected depends on: the economic structure of the country; the disequilibriums (economic fluctuations as well as social or political events); the preferences of the various policy makers; and the influence of the various policy makers. Only the last two elements (which comprise the role of policy makers) are dealt with here.

In a democracy the powers of the state are exercised by parliament and the administrative government. The latter is, in its turn, the result of coalitions of political parties. However, the party (or parties) in power must come to terms not only with the opposition, but also with other categories of policy makers, notably the administration and interest groups. . . .

Preferences of Political Parties. Table 4 (drawn from *Economic Policy in Our Time*) indicates the *a priori* preferences of three political groupings found in eight of the countries. Three objectives not included in the table, since they were considered negligible by almost all of the political groupings in these countries, are improvement in the pattern of private consumption; security of supply; and improvement in the size or structure of the population.

Preferences of Administrations. Government administrations play a decisive role in the choice of instruments, for this requires the assistance of experts. And although the administration role is less important for the choice of objectives, it is still not negligible. Administrations are obviously preoccupied with objectives within their own fields of reference. Thus, a Ministry of Finance will be particularly concerned with short-term economic objectives (notably, price stability and improvement in the balance of payments), as also will the Central Bank. A planning commission or bureau, the industrial ministries, or the general directorate for industrialization will be preoccupied with the objective of expansion, while ministries for special sectors (agriculture, industry, commerce, transport) will frequently support the claims of corresponding interest groups for protection, priorities, and distribution of income.

The preferences of an administration are a function, on the one hand, of its recruitment system and of its standing and, on the other hand, of studies that it may undertake concerning the social and economic needs of the community. Thus, an administration which goes in and out of office with the political party in power (as in the United States) has few preferences clearly distinct from those of the party, at least for some time after an election; the most important exceptions are those parts of administrations with the most permanent structures, in particular (as in the United States) the armed forces, the public works department, the Federal Reserve System. Similarly, in Norway, where the Socialist party has been in power for twenty-five years, a slow penetration of the administration by the party—or at least its views and preferences—appears to have occurred, and the definitions of the main objectives of economic policy seem to be made in common, notably in the preparation of the four-year program before each electoral campaign for a new parliament.

TABLE 4
Preference of Political Groupings with Regard to Objectives of Economic Policy:
Synthesis for Eight Countries (excluding Luxembourg)

Objectives	Socialists	Center	Conservative
Dominant	Full employment. Improvement in income distribution.	——	Price stability.
Dominant or significant	Collective needs (other than defense). Expansion of production.	Price stability. Expansion of production.	Collective needs (defense).
Significant	Reduction in working hours. Allocation (coordination).	Full employment. Collective needs (all). Allocation (international division of labor). Improvement in income distribution.	Improvement in the balance of payments. Allocation (international division of labor). Protection-priorities.
Significant or minor ..	Protection-priorities. Price stability. Allocation (international division of labor). Allocation (internal competition).	Protection-priorities. Allocation (internal competition). Improvement in the balance of payments.	Expansion of production. Full employment.
Minor	Improvement in the balance of payments. Collective needs (defense).	Allocation (coordination). Allocation (mobility of factors of production). Reduction in working hours.	Allocation (internal competition). Collective needs (other than defense). Allocation (mobility of factors of production). Improvement in income distribution.
Negligible	Allocation (mobility of factors of production).	——	
Negligible or hostile to the objective	——	——	Reduction in working hours. Allocation (coordination).

Source: E. S. Kirschen and others, *Economic Policy in Our Time* (Amsterdam: North-Holland Publishing Company, 1964), vol. 1, table IX-2, p. 227.

But in the countries endowed with very stable administrations (United Kingdom, Netherlands) and very centralized ones (France), the administration plays an active role in the choice of objectives, and divergence of views as between administrations and the politicians in power may very well occur when their standpoints diverge, owing, for instance, to different social backgrounds. Thus to define valid and coherent objectives may become more difficult.

Perhaps as important as an administration's recruitment methods are its rejuvenation and the modernization of its intellectual training. A relatively young administration will be more receptive to objectives for expanding production than to those for price stability or the maintenance, at any cost, of the exchange reserves. Above all, it will be more acutely conscious of interdependence between objectives and instruments, of the essential unity of economic policy, and consequently of the need to test (as far as possible) its internal consistency *ex ante*. On the other hand, there is danger that a young administration will overlook the preoccupations of the people, and steep itself in technocracy.

Finally, it is the job of an administration to undertake studies, as objectively as possible, of existing or potential public needs. In this respect, an administration's tasks have been very greatly enlarged in the last ten years in most of the countries under examination. Admittedly, with the disappearance of the wartime economies, its powers of direct economic management have been reduced, but its responsibilities for study and forecasting have grown. Not only has the apparatus of official statistics been generally extended, but a number of objectives in political economy are no longer decided on without detailed study in advance, conducted by trained administrators. This is the case with housing, town-planning, education, and public health.

Apart from these "public needs," the intellectual activity of administrations has developed differently according to country and subject. In countries politically attached to economic liberalism (Germany, Belgium, and the United States) or principally preoccupied with financial equilibrium (England), the role of the administration is especially important for definition and the measurement of objectives concerned with the trade cycle. In other countries, the role extends more and more to objectives concerned with structure—notably economic expansion, improvement in the allocation of factors of production, and the priorities and forms of protection for industries or regions.

This extension of the field of administration into matters of economic policy is not, however, caused only by the pressure of indisputable necessity. In part it is the effect of "Parkinson's Law," whereby all established administrations tend to develop and perpetuate themselves, whatever their utility at any given moment.

Preferences of Interest Groups. The preferences of interest groups are concerned with partial objectives inspired by the particular interests which they defend. The efforts of these groups are therefore directed fundamentally toward the following objectives: protection and priorities to particular regions or industries; improvement in income distribution; improvement in the allocation of factors of production through internal competition. The criteria for their choices are simple: the defense of acquired positions and the conquest of new positions favorable for the economic or social group which they represent.

*   *   *   *   *

part II

Capitalist Market Economy

The basic characteristics of a capitalist economic system
are (1) private ownership of, and private enterprise
with, the means of production; (2) the predominance
of economic gain as the guiding force in production
decisions; and (3) reliance on markets and prices to
allocate resources and distribute income.

The following selections examine the nature,
strengths, and weaknesses of a capitalist market economy. In the classic article reprinted in Selection 4,
Hayek shows how the decentralized price system would
ideally assemble and coordinate the available knowledge
of the economy in order to allocate resources and distribute income efficiently. In Selection 5, Okun argues
that income differences in a capitalist market economy
can be justified on grounds of personal freedom and
efficiency, but that selective government intervention is
needed to correct some deficiencies of the market.
Selections 6 and 7 then examine, respectively, French
and Japanese attempts to steer the private economy by
aggregative "indicative" planning.

4

THE PRICE SYSTEM AS A MECHANISM FOR USING KNOWLEDGE*

Friedrich A. Hayek

Efficiency in resource allocation requires full use of knowledge of the opportunities of supply and demand in the economy. Hayek argues that decentralized decisions in response to prices determined by market forces can utilize this knowledge much better than central planning, which is unable to assemble all the detailed information needed for sound decisions. Market prices can serve as proper guides to economic decisions because they are "rates of equivalence" which embody the whole end-means structure of the economic system. At the same time, the price system achieves "economy of knowledge" by concentrating in simple and unambiguous signals for action the information relevant for each participant in the economic process. On the basis of these price signals, decentralized decisions can be made that are consistent with the activity of the economic system as a whole.

I

What is the problem we wish to solve when we try to construct a rational economic order?

On certain familiar assumptions the answer is simple enough. *If* we possess all the relevant information, *if* we can start out from a given system of preferences and *if* we command complete knowledge of avail-

* Reprinted with permission from *American Economic Review*, vol. 35, no. 4 (September 1945), pp. 519–30. Originally published under the title, "The Use of Knowledge in Society." Friedrich A. Hayek taught at the University of London, the University of Chicago, and the University of Freiburg, Germany.

able means, the problem which remains is purely one of logic. That is, the answer to the question of what is the best use of the available means is implicit in our assumptions. The conditions which the solution of this optimum problem must satisfy have been fully worked out and can be stated best in mathematical form: put at their briefest, they are that the marginal rates of substitution between any two commodities or factors must be the same in all their different uses.

This, however, is emphatically *not* the economic problem which society faces. And the economic calculus which we have developed to solve this logical problem, though an important step toward the solution of the economic problem of society, does not yet provide an answer to it. The reason for this is that the "data" from which the economic calculus starts are never for the whole society "given" to a single mind which could work out the implications, and can never be so given.

The peculiar character of the problem of a rational economic order is determined precisely by the fact that the knowledge of the circumstances of which we must make use never exists in concentrated or integrated form, but solely as the dispersed bits of incomplete and frequently contradictory knowledge which all the separate individuals possess. The economic problem of society is thus not merely a problem of how to allocate "given" resources—if "given" is taken to mean given to a single mind which deliberately solves the problem set by these "data." It is rather a problem of how to secure the best use of resources known to any of the members of society, for ends whose relative importance only these individuals know. Or, to put it briefly, it is a problem of the utilization of knowledge not given to anyone in its totality.

This character of the fundamental problem has, I am afraid, been obscured rather than illuminated by many of the recent refinements of economic theory, particularly by many of the uses made of mathematics. Though the problem with which I want primarily to deal in this paper is the problem of a rational economic organization, I shall in its course be led again and again to point to its close connections with certain methodological questions. Many of the points I wish to make are indeed conclusions toward which diverse paths of reasoning have unexpectedly converged. But as I now see these problems, this is no accident. It seems to me that many of the current disputes with regard to both economic theory and economic policy have their common origin in a misconception about the nature of the economic problem of society. This misconception in turn is due to an erroneous transfer to social phenomena of the habits of thought we have developed in dealing with the phenomena of nature.

II

In ordinary language we describe by the word "planning" the complex of interrelated decisions about the allocation of our available resources.

All economic activity is in this sense planning; and in any society in which many people collaborate, this planning, whoever does it, will in some measure have to be based on knowledge which, in the first instance, is not given to the planner but to somebody else, which somehow will have to be conveyed to the planner. The various ways in which the knowledge on which people base their plans is communicated to them is the crucial problem for any theory explaining the economic process. And the problem of what is the best way of utilizing knowledge initially dispersed among all the people is at least one of the main problems of economic policy—or of designing an efficient economic system.

The answer to this question is closely connected with that other question which arises here, that of *who* is to do the planning. It is about this question that all the dispute about "economic planning" centers. This is not a dispute about whether planning is to be done or not. It is a dispute as to whether planning is to be done centrally, by one authority for the whole economic system, or is to be divided among many individuals. Planning in the specific sense in which the term is used in contemporary controversy necessarily means central planning—direction of the whole economic system according to one unified plan. Competition, on the other hand, means decentralized planning by many separate persons. The half-way house between the two, about which many people talk but which few like when they see it, is the delegation of planning to organized industries, or, in other words, monopoly.

Which of these systems is likely to be more efficient depends mainly on the question under which of them we can expect that fuller use will be made of the existing knowledge. And this, in turn, depends on whether we are more likely to succeed in putting at the disposal of a single central authority all the knowledge which ought to be used but which is initially dispersed among many different individuals, or in conveying to the individuals such additional knowledge as they need in order to enable them to fit their plans in with those of others.

III

It will at once be evident that on this point the position will be different with respect to different kinds of knowledge; and the answer to our question will therefore largely turn on the relative importance of the different kinds of knowledge: those more likely to be at the disposal of particular individuals and those which we should with greater confidence expect to find in the possession of an authority made up of suitably chosen experts. If it is today so widely assumed that the latter will be in a better position, this is because one kind of knowledge, namely, scientific knowledge, occupies now so prominent a place in public imagination that we tend to forget that it is not the only kind that is relevant. It may be admitted that, so far as scientific knowledge is concerned, a body of suitably chosen experts may be in the best position to command all the best knowledge available—though this is of course merely shifting the difficulty to the problem of selecting the experts. What I wish to point out is that, even assuming that this problem can be readily solved, it is only a small part of the wider problem.

Today it is almost heresy to suggest that scientific knowledge is not the sum of all knowledge. But a little reflection will show that there is beyond question a body of very important but unorganized knowledge which cannot possibly be called scientific in the sense of knowledge of general rules: the knowledge of the particular circumstances of time and place. It is with respect to this that practically every individual has some advantage over all others in that he possesses unique information of which beneficial use might be made, but of which use can be made only if the decisions depending on it are left to him or are made with his active cooperation. We need to remember only how much we have to learn in any occupation after we have completed our theoretical training, how big a part of our working life we spend learning particular jobs, and how valuable an asset in all walks of life is knowledge of people, of local conditions, and special circumstances. To know of and put to use a machine not fully employed, or somebody's skill which could be better utilized, or to be aware of a surplus stock which can be drawn upon during an interruption of supplies, is socially quite as useful as the knowledge of better alternative techniques. And the shipper who earns his living from using otherwise empty or half-filled journeys of tramp-steamers, or the estate agent whose whole knowledge is almost exclusively one of temporary opportunities, or the *arbitrageur* who gains from local differences of commodity prices, are all performing eminently useful functions based on special knowledge of circumstances of the fleeting moment not known to others.

It is a curious fact that this sort of knowledge should today be generally regarded with a kind of contempt, and that anyone who by such knowledge gains an advantage over somebody better equipped with theoretical or technical knowledge is thought to have acted almost disreputably. To gain an advantage from better knowledge of facilities of communication or transport is sometimes regarded as almost dishonest, although it is quite as important that society make use of the best opportunities in this respect as in using the latest scientific discoveries. This prejudice has in a considerable measure affected the attitude toward commerce in general compared with that toward production. Even economists who regard themselves as definitely above the crude materialist fallacies of the past constantly commit the same mistake where activities directed toward the acquisition of such practical knowledge are concerned—apparently because in their scheme of things all such knowledge is supposed to be "given." The common idea now seems to be that all such knowledge should as a matter of course be readily at the command of everybody, and the reproach of irrationality leveled against the existing economic order is frequently based on the fact that it is not so available. This view disregards the fact that the method by which such knowledge can be made as widely available as possible is precisely the problem to which we have to find an answer.

IV

If it is fashionable today to minimize the importance of the knowledge of the particular circumstances of time and place, this is closely connected with the smaller importance which is now attached to change as such. Indeed, there are few points on which the assumptions made (usually only implicitly) by the "planners" differ from those of their opponents as much as with regard to the significance and frequency of changes which will make substantial alterations of production plans necessary. Of course, if detailed economic plans could be laid down for fairly long periods in advance and then closely adhered to, so that no further economic decisions of importance would be required, the task of drawing up a comprehensive plan governing all economic activity would appear much less formidable.

It is, perhaps, worth stressing that economic problems arise always and only in consequence of change. So long as things continue as before, or at least as they were expected to, there arise no new problems requiring a decision, no need to form a new plan. The belief that changes, or at least day-to-day adjustments, have become less important in modern times implies the contention that economic problems also have become less important. This belief in the decreasing importance of change is, for that reason, usually held by the same people who argue that the importance of economic considerations has been driven into the background by the growing importance of technological knowledge.

Is it true that, with the elaborate apparatus of modern production, economic decisions are required only at long intervals, as when a new factory is to be erected or a new process to be introduced? Is it true that, once a plant has been built, the rest is all more or less mechanical, determined by the character of the plant, and leaving little to be changed in adapting to the ever-changing circumstances of the moment?

The fairly widespread belief in the affirmative is not, so far as I can ascertain, borne out by the practical experience of the business man. In a competitive industry at any rate—and such an industry alone can serve as a test—the task of keeping cost from rising requires constant struggle, absorbing a great part of the energy of the manager. How easy it is for an inefficient manager to dissipate the differentials on which profitability rests, and that it is possible, with the same technical facilities, to produce with a great variety of costs, are among the commonplaces of business experience which do not seem to be equally familiar in the study of the economist. The very strength of the desire, constantly voiced by producers and engineers, to be able to proceed untrammeled by considerations of money costs, is eloquent testimony to the extent to which these factors enter into their daily work.

One reason why economists are increasingly apt to forget about the constant small changes which make up the whole economic picture is probably their growing preoccupation with statistical aggregates, which show a very much greater stability than the movements of the detail. The comparative stability of the aggregates cannot, however, be accounted for—as the statisticians seem occasionally to be inclined to do—by the "law of large numbers" or the mutual compensation of random changes. The number of elements with which we have to deal is not large enough for such accidental forces to produce stability. The continuous flow of goods and services is maintained by constant deliberate adjustments, by new dispositions made every day in the light of circumstances not known the day before, by B stepping in at once when A fails to deliver. Even the large and highly mechanized plant keeps going largely because of an environment upon which it can draw for all sorts of unexpected needs; tiles for its roof, stationery for its forms, and all the thousand and one kinds of equipment in which it cannot be self-contained and which the plans for the operation of the plant require to be readily available in the market.

This is, perhaps, also the point where I should briefly mention the fact that the sort of knowledge with which I have been concerned is knowledge of the kind which by its nature cannot enter into statistics and therefore cannot be conveyed to any central authority in statistical form. The statistics which such a central authority would have to use would have to be arrived at precisely by abstracting from minor differences between the things, by lumping together, as resources of one kind, items which differ as regards location, quality, and other particulars, in a way which may be very significant for the specific decision. It follows from this that central planning based on statistical information by its nature cannot take direct account of these circumstances of time and place, and that the central planner will have to find some way or other in which the decisions depending on them can be left to the "man on the spot."

V

If we can agree that the economic problem of society is mainly one of rapid adaptation to changes in the particular circumstances of time and place, it would seem to follow that the ultimate decisions must be left to the people who are familiar with these circumstances, who know directly of the relevant changes and of the resources immediately available to meet them. We cannot expect that this problem will be solved by first communicating all this knowledge to a central board which, after integrating *all* knowledge, issues its orders. We must solve it by some form of decentralization. But this answers only part of our problem. We need decentralization because only thus can we ensure that the knowledge of the particular circumstances of time and place will be promptly used. But the "man on the spot" cannot decide solely on the basis of his limited but intimate knowledge of the facts of his immediate surroundings. There still remains the problem of communicating to him such further information as he needs to fit his decisions into the whole pattern of changes of the larger economic system.

How much knowledge does he need to do so successfully? Which of the events which happen beyond the horizon of his immediate knowledge are of relevance to his immediate decision, and how much of them need he know?

There is hardly anything that happens anywhere in the world that *might* not have an effect on the decision he ought to make. But he need not know of these events as such, nor of *all* their effects. It does not matter for him *why* at the particular moment more screws of one size than of another are wanted, *why* paper bags are more readily available than canvas bags, or *why* skilled labor, or particular machine tools, have for the moment become more difficult to acquire. All that is significant for him is *how much more or less* difficult to procure they have become compared with other things with which he is also concerned, or how much more or less urgently wanted are the alternative things he produces or uses. It is always a question of the relative importance of the particular things with which he is concerned, and the causes which alter their relative importance are of no interest to him beyond the effect on those concrete things of his own environment.

It is in this connection that what I have called the economic calculus proper helps us, at least by analogy, to see how this problem can be solved, and in fact is being solved, by the price system. Even the single controlling mind, in possession of all the data for some small, self-contained economic system, would not—every time some small adjustment in the allocation of resources had to be made—go explicitly through all the relations between ends and means which might possibly be affected. It is indeed the great contribution of the pure logic of choice that it has demonstrated conclusively that even such a single mind could solve this kind of problem only by constructing and constantly using rates of equivalence (or "values," or "marginal rates of substitution"), i.e., by attaching to each kind of scarce resource a numerical index which cannot be derived from any property possessed by that particular thing, but which reflects, or in which is condensed, its significance in view of the whole means-end structure. In any small change he will have to consider only these quantitative indices (or "values") in which all the relevant information is concentrated; and by adjusting the quantities one by one, he can appropriately rearrange his dispositions without having to solve the whole puzzle *ab initio*, or without needing at any stage to survey it at once in all its ramifications.

Fundamentally, in a system where the knowledge of the relevant facts is dispersed among many people, prices can act to coordinate the separate actions of different people in the same way as subjective values help the individual to coordinate the parts of his plan. It is worth contemplating for a moment a very simple and commonplace instance of the action of the price system to see what precisely it accomplishes. Assume that somewhere in the world a new opportunity for the use of some raw material, say tin, has arisen, or that one of the sources of supply of tin has been eliminated. It does not matter for our purpose—and it is very significant that it does not matter—which of these two causes has made tin more scarce. All that the users of tin need to know is that some of the tin they used to consume is now more profitably employed elsewhere, and that in consequence they must economize tin. There is no need for the great majority of them even to know where the more urgent need has arisen, or in favor of what other needs they ought to husband the supply. If only some of them know directly of the new demand, and switch resources over to it, and if the people who are aware of the new gap thus created in turn fill it from still other sources, the effect will rapidly spread throughout the whole economic system and influence not only all the uses of tin, but also those of its substitutes and the substitutes of these substitutes, the supply of all the things made of tin, and their substitutes, and so on; and all this without the great majority of those instrumental in bringing about these substitutions knowing anything at all about the original cause of these changes. The whole acts as one market, not because any of its members survey the whole field, but because their limited individual fields of vision sufficiently overlap so that through many intermediaries the relevant information is communicated to all. The mere fact that there is one price for any commodity—or rather that local prices are connected in a manner determined by the cost of transport, etc.—brings about the solution which (it is just conceptually possible) might have been arrived at by one single mind possessing all the information which is in fact dispersed among all the people involved in the process.

VI

We must look at the price system as such a mechanism for communicating information if we want to understand its real function—a function which, of course, it fulfills less perfectly as prices grow more rigid. (Even when quoted prices have become quite rigid, however, the forces which would operate through changes in price still operate to a considerable extent through changes in the other terms of the contract.) The most significant fact about this system is the economy of knowledge with which it operates, or how little the individual participants need to know in order to be able to take the right action. In abbreviated form, by a kind of symbol, only the most essential information is passed on, and passed on only to those concerned. It is more than a metaphor to describe the price system as a kind of machinery for registering change, or a system of telecommunications which enables individual producers to watch merely the movement of a few pointers, as an engineer might watch the hands of a few dials, in order to adjust their activities to changes of which they may never know more than is reflected in the price movement.

Of course, these adjustments are probably never "perfect" in the sense in which the economist conceives of them in his equilibrium analysis. But I fear that our theoretical habits of approaching the problem with the assumption of more or less perfect knowledge on the part of almost everyone has made us somewhat blind to the true function of the price mechanism and led us to apply rather misleading standards in judging its efficiency. The marvel is that in a case like that of a scarcity of one raw material, without an order being issued, without more than perhaps a handful of people knowing the cause, tens of thousands of people whose identity could not be ascertained by months of investigation, are made to use the material or its products more sparingly; i.e., they move in the right direction. This is enough of a marvel even if, in a constantly changing world, not all will hit it off so perfectly that their profit rates will always be maintained at the same constant or "normal" level.

I have deliberately used the word "marvel" to shock the reader out of the complacency with which we often take the working of this mechanism for granted. I am convinced that if it were the result of deliberate human design, and if the people guided by the price changes understood that their decisions have significance far beyond their immediate aim, this mechanism would have been acclaimed as one of the greatest triumphs of the human mind. Its misfortune is the double one that it is not the product of human design and that the people guided by it usually do not know why they are made to do what they do. But those who clamor for "conscious direction"—and who cannot believe that anything which has evolved without design (and even without our understanding it) should solve problems which we should not be able to solve consciously—should remember this: The problem is precisely how to extend the span of our utilization of resources beyond the span of the control of any one mind; and, therefore, how to dispense with the need of conscious control and how to provide inducements which will make the individuals do the desirable things without anyone having to tell them what to do.

CAMROSE LUTHERAN COLLEGE
LIBRARY

58

The problem which we meet here is by no means peculiar to economics but arises in connection with nearly all truly social phenomena, with language and most of our cultural inheritance, and constitutes really the central theoretical problem of all social science. As Alfred Whitehead has said in another connection, "It is a profoundly erroneous truism, repeated by all copybooks and by eminent people when they are making speeches, that we should cultivate the habit of thinking what we are doing. The precise opposite is the case. Civilization advances by extending the number of important operations which we can perform without thinking about them." This is of profound significance in the social field. We make constant use of formulas, symbols and rules whose meaning we do not understand and through the use of which we avail ourselves of the assistance of knowledge which individually we do not possess. We have developed these practices and institutions by building upon habits and institutions which have proved successful in their own sphere and which have in turn become the foundation of the civilization we have built up.

The price system is just one of those formations which man has learned to use (though he is still very far from having learned to make the best use of it) after he had stumbled upon it without understanding it. Through it not only a division of labor but also a coordinated utilization of resources based on an equally divided knowledge has become possible. The people who like to deride any suggestion that this may be so usually distort the argument by insinuating that it asserts that by some miracle just that sort of system has spontaneously grown up which is best suited to modern civilization. It is the other way round: man has been able to develop that division of labor on which our civilization is based because he happened to stumble upon a method which made it possible. Had he not done so he might still have developed some other, altogether different, type of civilization, something like the "state" of the termite ants, or some other altogether unimaginable type. All that we can say is that nobody has yet succeeded in designing an alternative system in which certain features of the existing one can be preserved which are dear even to those who most violently assail it—such as particularly the extent to which the individual can choose his pursuits and consequently freely use his own knowledge and skill.

VII

It is in many ways fortunate that the dispute about the indispensability of the price system for any rational calculation in a complex society is now no longer conducted entirely between camps holding different political views. The thesis that without the price system we could not preserve a society based on such extensive division of labor as ours was greeted with a howl of derision when it was first advanced by von Mises

CAMROSE LUTHERAN COLLEGE
LIBRARY

twenty-five years ago. Today the difficulties which some still find in accepting it are no longer mainly political, and this makes for an atmosphere much more conducive to reasonable discussion. When we find Leon Trotsky arguing that "economic accounting is unthinkable without market relations"; when Professor Oscar Lange promises Professor von Mises a statue in the marble halls of the future Central Planning Board; and when Professor Abba P. Lerner rediscovers Adam Smith and emphasizes that the essential utility of the price system consists in inducing the individual, while seeking his own interest, to do what is in the general interest, the differences can indeed no longer be ascribed to political prejudice. The remaining dissent seems clearly to be due to purely intellectual, and more particularly methodological, differences.

A recent statement by Professor Joseph Schumpeter in his *Capitalism, Socialism, and Democracy* provides a clear illustration of one of the methodological differences which I have in mind. Its author is preeminent among those economists who approach economic phenomena in the light of a certain branch of positivism. To him these phenomena accordingly appear as objectively given quantities of commodities impinging directly upon each other, almost, it would seem, without any intervention of human minds. Only against this background can I account for the following (to me startling) pronouncement. Professor Schumpeter argues that the possibility of a rational calculation in the absence of markets for the factors of production follows for the theorist "from the elementary proposition that consumers in evaluating ('demanding') consumers' goods *ipso facto* also evaluate the means of production which enter into the production of these goods."[1]

Taken literally, this statement is simply untrue. The consumers do nothing of the kind. What Professor Schumpeter's "*ipso facto*" presumably means is that the valuation of the factors of production is implied in, or follows necessarily from, the valuation of consumers' goods. But this, too, is not correct. Implication is a logical relationship which can be meaningfully asserted only of propositions simultaneously present to one and the same mind. It is evident, however, that the values of the factors of

---

[1] J. Schumpeter, *Capitalism, Socialism, and Democracy* (New York: Harper & Bros., 1942), p. 175. Professor Schumpeter is, I believe, also the original author of the myth that Pareto and Barone have "solved" the problem of socialist calculation. What they, and many others, did was merely to state the conditions which a rational allocation of resources would have to satisfy, and to point out that these were essentially the same as the conditions of equilibrium of a competitive market. This is something altogether different from showing how the allocation of resources satisfying these conditions can be found in practice. Pareto himself (from whom Barone has taken practically everything he has to say), far from claiming to have solved the practical problem, in fact explicitly denies that it can be solved without the help of the market. See his *Manuel d'économie pure* (2 ed., 1927), pp. 233–34. The relevant passage is quoted in an English translation at the beginning of my article on "Socialist Calculation: The Competitive 'Solution,'" in *Economica*, New Series, vol. 7, no. 26 (May 1940), pp. 125–49.

production do not depend solely on the valuation of the consumers' goods but also on the conditions of supply of the various factors of production. Only to a mind to which all these facts were simultaneously known would the answer necessarily follow from the facts given to it. The practical problem, however, arises precisely because these facts are never so given to a single mind, and because, in consequence, it is necessary that in the solution of the problem knowledge should be used that is dispersed among many people.

The problem is thus in no way solved if we can show that all the facts, *if* they were known to a single mind (as we hypothetically assume them to be given to the observing economist), would uniquely determine the solution; instead we must show how a solution is produced by the interactions of people each of whom possesses only partial knowledge. To assume all the knowledge to be given to a single mind in the same manner in which we assume it to be given to us as the explaining economists is to assume the problem away and to disregard everything that is important and significant in the real world.

That an economist of Professor Schumpeter's standing should thus have fallen into a trap which the ambiguity of the term "datum" sets to the unwary can hardly be explained as a simple error. It suggests rather that there is something fundamentally wrong with an approach which habitually disregards an essential part of the phenomena with which we have to deal: the unavoidable imperfection of man's knowledge and the consequent need for a process by which knowledge is constantly communicated and acquired. Any approach, such as that of much of mathematical economics with its simultaneous equations, which in effect starts from the assumption that people's *knowledge* corresponds with the objective *facts* of the situation, systematically leaves out what is our main task to explain. I am far from denying that in our system equilibrium analysis has a useful function to perform. But when it comes to the point where it misleads some of our leading thinkers into believing that the situation which it describes has direct relevance to the solution of practical problems, it is time that we remember that it does not deal with the social process at all and that it is no more than a useful preliminary to the study of the main problem.

5

REWARDS IN A MARKET ECONOMY*

Arthur M. Okun

According to Okun, the case for a capitalist market economy rests on three pillars: the link to personal freedoms, the extent to which rewards are related to contributions to production, and the way differential incomes can enhance efficiency. In this selection he explains the types of contributions earning differential rewards, and evaluates the fairness of the resulting unequal distribution of income.

Some conservatives would argue that, if a market economy is functioning properly, people simply get out of it what they put into it. And the resulting differences in income are acceptable and fair—perhaps even ideal. Fair games have losers as well as winners. Rights in the marketplace do not guarantee anyone an income, but then freedom of speech does not guarantee anyone an audience. By this reasoning, fair and equal treatment is provided by the opportunity to induce people to pay for services—just as it is by the opportunity to induce people to listen.

REWARD FOR CONTRIBUTION

With a sprinkling of appropriate assumptions, it can be demonstrated that a competitive market will pay workers and investors the value of their contributions to output. This so-called marginal productivity theory of distribution is the economist's formal way of saying that you take out

---

* Reprinted by permission from his *Equality and Efficiency: The Big Tradeoff* (Washington, D.C.: The Brookings Institution, 1975), pp. 40–50. Copyright © 1975 by The Brookings Institution. Arthur M. Okun is a Senior Fellow at the Brookings Institution.

what you put in. The fruits of labor and capital are converted into dollars and given back to the suppliers. At the turn of this century, that theory of distribution was greeted by some social thinkers as divine revelation of the justice of a competitive economy.[1] Today, however, economists do not invoke the name of the Lord in support of the market. In fact, most of the ardent supporters of the market explicitly reject the claim that distribution in accordance with marginal productivity is necessarily just distribution.[2]

Nonetheless, the ethical appeal of reward for contribution remains very much alive and shows up in subtle ways. When authors distinguish between the deserving and undeserving poor, or the deserving and undeserving rich; when Marxists challenge marginal productivity with a theory that attributes all value to labor input, directly or indirectly; or when egalitarian economists rest their case for altering the verdict of the market on allegedly scientific comparisons of the "utility" of income to different people, they are all paying homage—as supporters or detractors—to the initial presumption that income *ought* to be based on contribution to output.

Therefore, it is worth exploring the ways contributions are rewarded in the marketplace and evaluating the system of rewards in terms of ethical standards. To begin with, the actual pricing of productive services differs from the textbook results of a competitive model in a dozen ways. I will mention only a few. When there is "monopsony"—monopoly power on the buyer's side—in the labor market, the employer may be able to pay workers less than they contribute. Even without monopsony, most markets for labor and capital lack the auction system needed to ensure an equilibrium wage or price that avoids shortages and excess supplies. Moreover, the contributions of two factors that must operate together—like two men on a two-handled saw—cannot always be assessed separately. Finally, as John Kenneth Galbraith has emphasized, the contribution of workers is often judged and their pay set by managers who have interests and objectives of their own, quite distinct from the profitability of their firm.[3]

---

[1] For a discussion of this view as set forth by John Bates Clark, see Mark Blaug, *Economic Theory in Retrospect* (Homewood, Ill.: Richard D. Irwin, Inc., 1962), pp. 403–8; also John Rawls, *A Theory of Justice* (Cambridge, Mass.: Harvard University Press, 1971), pp. 308–9.

[2] See, for example, Frank H. Knight, *The Ethics of Competition and Other Essays* (New York: Harper & Bros., 1935), pp. 54–58; and Friedrich A. Hayek, *The Constitution of Liberty* (Chicago: University of Chicago Press, 1960), pp. 93–100. Friedman is the exception: he does not reject (nor does he embrace) the ethics of reward for contribution; see Milton Friedman, *Capitalism and Freedom* (Chicago: University of Chicago Press, 1962), pp. 161–65. For a contrasting position, see Lester Thurow, "Toward a Definition of Economic Justice," *Public Interest*, no. 31 (Spring 1973), p. 72.

[3] *The New Industrial State* (Boston: Houghton Mifflin, 1967), pp. 124–35.

SOURCES OF PRODUCTIVE CONTRIBUTION

The deviations from the competitive model are serious and significant; yet, I believe, still more fundamental issues about income rewards arise even in the unreal and ideal world of that model. What determines the competitive market value of the services of any citizen? Are the resulting rewards really fair?

The productive contribution of the services I could sell in a hypothetical competitive market depends on four sets of elements: (1) the skills and assets that I have acquired through my lifetime; (2) the abilities and talents with which I was born; (3) the effort I am willing to expend; and (4) the supply and demand situations for other services related to the ones I can offer.

Acquired Assets

What I have to sell today reflects my entire life history, including the nutrition and health care I have received, my education, my previous job experience, and any physical property I have acquired by previous saving or inheritance. To the extent that my current supply of marketable services is augmented by effort (or thrift) that I have exercised previously, I am reaping the harvest from the seeds I planted in the past. But to the extent that my present position reflects heavily the advantages of family background, or privilege, or status, I am reaping what others have sown.

To switch metaphors, some of the contestants get a head start while others have handicaps. Social and economic disparities among families make the race unfair. The importance of the uneven positions at the starting line and the possibilities of making the race fairer are complex and controversial issues. But it seems undeniable in principle that the prizes for the performance would be more defensible ethically if everyone had an even start.

Natural Abilities

Those who shrug their shoulders at the social and economic differences in starting positions emphasize the differences in natural abilities. They argue that these biological differences are even more important. It isn't capitalism's fault that infants differ in endowments at the starting line of birth and even of conception. Such differential talents are, by definition, hereditary rather than environmental; they are given to the individual by his parents rather than developed or earned by him. Thus they preclude truly fair starts.[4] Should everyone therefore stop running races? Obviously

---

[4] Frank H. Knight, *Risk, Uncertainty and Profit* (Boston: Houghton Mifflin, 1921), pp. 374–75; see also Friedman, *Capitalism and Freedom*, p. 164.

not. In real track meets, no official has ever disqualified a runner for having "fast genes."

The non-shoulder-shrugger retorts that society should aim to ameliorate, and certainly not to compound, the flaws of the universe. It cannot stop rain, but it does manufacture umbrellas. Similarly, it can decide to restrict prizes that bestow vastly higher standards of living on people with greater acquired assets or greater innate abilities. With tongue in cheek, Henry Simons of the University of Chicago once developed a tantalizing case for reversing the income distribution: the talented are unavoidably favored by being more talented; giving them higher incomes compounds their accidental and unmerited advantages.[5] John Rawls' tongue was not in his cheek when he stated his "principle of redress": "to provide genuine equality of opportunity, society must give more attention to those with fewer native assets and to those born into the less favorable social positions."[6] Indeed, the principle of redress is a common feature of family life, where extraordinary efforts are often devoted to the education and happiness of handicapped children. Fairness is clearly not interpreted as reward for contribution in such cases.

Effort

Differences in incomes that are associated with differences in effort are generally regarded as fair. If everyone were offered the same hourly wage rate and the opportunity to work as many hours as he or she chose, the resulting discrepancies on payday would be understandable. In fact, it would seem unfair for the person who takes more leisure to get just as much income. Leisure is a form of income and an element in one's standard of living; thus, a sacrifice of leisure must be compensated in other ways if fairness is to be achieved.[7]

Extra income for extra effort is unquestionably useful in providing incentives as well as fair compensation for parting with leisure. The two roles are hard to disentangle. When the fairness issue is viewed in a broad and searching context, some difficult questions arise. Shouldn't society be capable of tolerating diverse individual attitudes toward work and leisure? Would society really want to starve those who might conceivably have lazy genes? Suppose for a moment that incentives are not relevant. If the total input of effort were completely unaffected, would society want the beachcomber to eat less well than his fellow citizens, including others who

---

[5] Henry C. Simons, *Personal Income Taxation* (Chicago: University of Chicago Press, 1938), pp. 12–13.

[6] Rawls, *Theory of Justice*, p. 100.

[7] The same is true about risky, unpleasant, or exhausting work.

do not work, such as children, the elderly, and students on fellowships?

Nor is it obvious, in that broader perspective, that incentives for effort to produce marketable output should take the form principally of purchasing power over marketable output. In a Robinson Crusoe economy, the individual putting forth the effort must get the resulting output. But other societies can provide different kinds of incentives. Many primitive societies allowed those who shirked work to eat just as well as workers,[8] but some insisted that the nonworker eat apart from the rest of the community and others had ceremonies in which the well-fed slacker was publicly scorned by his brother-in-law. When the advanced capitalist economy provides its incentives for productive effort primarily in dollars, that revives the Robinson Crusoe arrangement with the innovation of a monetary system. Should that be viewed as progress or retrogression?

Related Supplies and Demands

The value of my marginal product does not depend solely on my skills and effort. It can be altered greatly by changes in the behavior of other people, even though I keep doing the same old thing no better and no worse than ever. If more economists emerge who are willing to make speeches, or if audiences lose interest in talks given by economists, that would be bad news for my income. But would I then really be less productive? Would I *deserve* a drop in income? Is it ethically (as distinct from pragmatically) desirable for incomes to rest on the shifting sands of technology and tastes?

In view of those dependencies on other people, the concept of *my* contribution to output becomes hazy. Production comes out of a complex, interdependent system and may not be neatly attributable to individual contributors. Henry Ford's mass-produced automobile was a great success in a country with a high average income, three thousand miles for unimpeded driving, an alert and ambitious work force, and a government that could protect travelers and enforce rules of the road. It would have been a loser in Libya. In that sense, most production processes involve "joint inputs," like the two-handled saw.[9] That aspect is recognized in a few private arrangements, which reward teams rather than individuals. The same World Series shares are given to Johnny Bench and the bench-warming third-string catcher, even though their salaries during the regular season are vastly different. Would it be a desirable innovation for some

---

[8] Karl Polanyi, "Our Obsolete Market Mentality," in *Primitive, Archaic, and Modern Economies,* ed. George Dalton (Boston: Beacon Press, 1971), pp. 65–67.

[9] In viewing the whole social and political system as an "input," I am using an unconventional—but nonetheless relevant—concept of joint inputs.

portion of the social output to be shared equally by all the players, like a World Series kitty?

In fact, if everyone received the full measure of *his* marginal product and no joint inputs existed, the economic benefits generated by great entrepreneurs and inventors would accrue entirely to them. There would then be no "trickle-down" of progress to the masses.[10] Benefits do actually trickle down precisely because the big winners do not obtain—or at least do not maintain—the full rewards for their contribution to improved technology, increased knowledge, and accumulated capital. The trickle-down of benefits is a merit of capitalism in the real world, and it works insofar as the distribution of income departs from the strict standard of reward for personal contribution to production.

VARYING VERDICTS

I have dozens of good questions about the fairness of market-determined incomes. But I don't claim to have any good answers. The appraisal is obviously a matter of personal judgment. In mine, incomes that match productivity have no ethical appeal. Equality in the distribution of incomes (allowing for voluntary leisure as a form of income) as well as in the distribution of rights would be my *ethical* preference. Abstracting from the costs and the consequences, I would prefer more equality of income to less and would like complete equality best of all. This preference is a simple extension of the humanistic basis for equal rights. To extend the domain of rights and give every citizen an equal share of the national income would give added recognition to the moral worth of every citizen, to the mutual respect of citizens for one another, and to the equivalent value of membership in the society for all.[11]

Nonetheless, my preference for one person, one income, is not nearly so strong as that for one person, one vote. Equality in material welfare has much lower benefits and far higher costs than equality of political and civil entitlements. Perhaps because material objects do not seem all-important, it is far less invidious to deprive some citizens of automobiles than to deprive them of the right to vote or freedom of religion. Second, while the provision of equal political and civil rights often imposes costs

---

[10] The formal analysis of trickle-down may be viewed along the following lines: Consider capital-deepening without technical change. The profit rate is driven down over time; and rent on previously invested capital is lowered to match the marginal product of new capital. Then benefits trickle down from the "old" capitalists. The marginal product of labor is raised by capital-deepening, so workers get the benefits of the trickle.

[11] I regard this Rawlsian basis for egalitarianism as far sounder than a foundation based on interdependent utilities or interpersonal comparisons of utility. R. H. Tawney had the same idea: ". . . because men are men, social institutions . . . should . . . emphasize and strengthen . . . the common humanity which unites them. . . ." See *Equality*, 5th ed. (London: Allen & Unwin, 1964), p. 49.

on society, the attempt to enforce equality of income would entail a much larger sacrifice. In pursuing such a goal, society would forgo any opportunity to use material rewards as incentives to production. And that would lead to inefficiencies that would be harmful to the welfare of the majority. Any insistence on carving the pie into equal slices would shrink the size of the pie. That fact poses the tradeoff between economic equality and economic efficiency. Insofar as inequality does serve to promote efficiency, I can accept some measure of it as a practicality. I can live with rules of the game that make it fair not to share—just as that lady from Boston insisted. But that is a feature of the universe that I regret rather than enjoy.

Many in our society, including some losers as well as most winners, seem to enjoy the rules of the game and the contest. They cheer loudly for success in the marketplace, and reinforce income incentives by vesting those who succeed with social status. The marketplace becomes a great American game; the winners are made proud and the losers embarrassed. The widespread mental depression that accompanied economic depression among the chronically unemployed of the thirties, the satisfaction derived by those who "make it" into the economic mainstream, and the bourgeois aspirations of the poor all reveal the deeply ingrained market ethic of American society.[12] In a sense, these attitudes preserve some of the features of the primitive societies that invoke ceremonies to penalize the lazy and reward the energetic.

Those who enjoy the game seem particularly fascinated by jackpot prizes. The possibility of "making it big" seems to motivate many Americans, including some who have not made it at all. They dream of rags-to-riches and project that dream from generation to generation. There are enough examples of winners to keep it alive and to encourage education, saving, and bourgeois values. In 1972, a storm of protest from blue-collar workers greeted Senator McGovern's proposal for confiscatory estate taxes. They apparently wanted some big prizes maintained in the game. The silent majority did not want the yacht clubs closed forever to their children and grandchildren while those who had already become members kept sailing along.

On the other hand, those who reject the rules of the game on ethical grounds seem most offended by the reliance on "greed" as a key motivating force in economic life. Greed is deplored because it is an expression purely of self-interest, and because it aims at the acquisition of material things.

---

12 For a discussion of the mental attitude of the unemployed during the thirties, see E. Wight Bakke, *Citizens Without Work* (New Haven, Conn.: Yale University Press, 1940), especially pp. 201–2. For a current treatment of the aspirations of the poor, see Leonard Goodwin, *Do the Poor Want to Work?* (Washington, D.C.: Brookings Institution, 1972), p. 112.

With proper awe for the fundamental philosophical issues concerning the virtues and practicalities of altruism as opposed to self-interest, I will still venture a few personal views. I do not find a reliance on self-interest offensive as an organizing principle for the economy. First, selfishness is a safeguard against the much greater danger of blind allegiance to a leader or to the state. Second, self-interest is consistent with an enlightened selfishness that creates loyalties to family, community, and country, as institutions that benefit the individual and extend his range of interests. Third, I read the lesson of history as teaching that efforts to suppress the tendencies toward self-interest by the individual—in societies as noble as monasteries or as base as Fascist dictatorships—have also severely restricted the rights of the individual.

Nor am I offended by a competition that seeks prizes in the form of material possessions. Surely, some kinds of alternative rewards would be far more oppressive and more invidious—like feudal privileges and membership in the elite party. Indeed, if the losers can still lead a decent life, prizes for the winners in the form of swimming pools and bigger houses seem especially innocuous in terms of their social impact. In short, while I do not find reward for contribution ethically appealing, neither do I find it ethically intolerable—within pragmatic limits.

6

PLANNING IN FRANCE*

Claude Seibel

In France, in addition to indirect guidance of the economy through
monetary and fiscal measures and various kinds of specific intervention, the government has attempted to steer the private economy by
aggregative "indicative" planning. In collaboration with representatives of business, agriculture, and trade unions, the government has attempted to draw up an agreed medium-term plan for the development of the economy. This plan, however, is only "indicative," not
"imperative"—essentially a forecast, not a directive—and it is prepared
only at the branch level, not covering individual private firms. By
coordinating the production and investment programs of the different
branches of the economy, the plan seeks to reduce uncertainty and
risk for individual firms and to promise them a "balanced" market in
which to acquire factors of production and to sell output. Although
firms still make their own decisions freely in the market, they do so
with the benefit of knowledge about the intentions of the rest of the
economy and the government's credit, tax, and price policies.

This selection analyzes French planning from various standpoints.
First, it traces changes in the objectives emphasized in successive
plans. Second, it describes the development of planning techniques.
Third, it discusses the extent of the government's commitment to implementing the plan. Fourth, it examines the attitudes of different
economic interest groups toward planning. It concludes with an evaluation of the influence of planning on the French economy.

* Translated from the French by Elizabeth Henderson. Excerpted by permission from
Economic Planning, East and West, ed. Morris Bornstein (Cambridge, Mass.: Ballinger
Publishing Company, 1975), pp. 153–84, with the omission of tables and references to
foreign-language sources. Copyright © 1975 by Ballinger Publishing Company. Claude
Seibel, now Chief of the Economic and Statistical Information Service of the French
National Ministry of Education, was Chief of the Programming Division of the French
National Institute of Statistics and Economic Studies when he prepared this study.

A system of public planning was inaugurated in France after World War II. A decree dated January 3, 1946 provided for the establishment, within six months, of "a first overall economic modernization and investment plan for metropolitan France and the overseas territories." At the same time, planning machinery was set up in the form of a Conseil du Plan and a Commissariat Général, the latter headed by Jean Monnet as Commissaire Général du Plan. It certainly was Jean Monnet's influence which led the French government to plan at that time not only in terms of making good the war damage, but of modernizing production methods. The major innovation was a break with traditional bureaucratic methods by the creation of Modernization Commissions, in which experts chosen by the Commissariat du Plan from among employers' and trade union groups joined government officials on a footing of equality. But this decree must be seen in the much broader context of a whole set of measures which profoundly altered and strengthened the role of the state in the control and direction of economic development (e.g., the nationalization of key sectors of the economy). More than 25 years have gone by since then, and the initial approach has gradually changed in the light of experience. Forecasting methods have improved, the scope of planning has widened, and planning machinery has become more prominent in government departments—but the plan itself has become less and less imperative, and also more difficult to formulate. With France open toward Europe and markets more and more international, uncertainties increased, while the debate was shifting from "means" to "choices" within society. All this challenged the very nature and the philosophy of planning.

What started out as the "Nation's Plan" became a "medium-term government program," but in fact it appears that the plan is a very weak reference point for short-term economic policy, even if it tries to describe theoretically a set of alternative strategies. The major themes outlined in the First Plan are still there, themes such as modernization, productivity, productive and social investment, regionalization; but the approach has become more qualitative. Concern has shifted to the aims of growth and to its social consequences, and gradually a balance is being struck between economic development and social planning.

As a means of state intervention in the mechanism of a market economy, French planning appears to outside observers to be at the same time innovatory and ambiguous in its relevance to the realities of development. Strictly speaking, it should be discussed in the wider context of the relations between state and society. French planning is one form of these relations, a form peculiar to our country.

It is from this point of view that French planning will here be discussed. The observer of this planning system is struck by the highly pragmatic processes by which it is established and adjusted. It is perhaps its flexible adjustment to the political and social debate which lends public planning in France its essential strength. Pragmatic adaptation has for 25 years governed planning methods and targets as much as prior discussion of the plan and its implementation.

* * * * *

The aims and methods of French planning have changed profoundly since World War II, but no body of theories can be identified by which to explain these gradual changes. As time went on, planning covered wider fields; new and more efficient planning methods made it possible to tackle new problems; a change took place in the significance and purposes of prior consultation, or, as it is called in France, *concertation*; and in spite of the government's stated intention to turn the Plan into a medium-term program of action, official action in fact makes only partial use of planning studies.

All these changes gradually came about in the course of 25 years of planning and five successive Plans; no revision of them is called for by the current implementation of the Sixth Plan.[1]

THE MAIN THEMES OF SUCCESSIVE PLANS

The First Plan: "Modernization or Decline"

By the end of World War II, the French economy was shaken to its roots. Fifteen years of stagnation, with the Great Depression of the thirties and then the destruction wrought by the war, had left their mark. But the French people emerged from the sufferings of the war and the struggles of the Resistance movement with a passion for renewal, manifest in the wave of enthusiasm which followed the liberation. The idea of planning, which had taken shape in the National Resistance Committee, linked up with certain prewar concepts, such as those developed by the group

---

[1] There are a number of good studies on the earlier experience of French planning, including Claude Gruson, *Origine et espoirs de la planification française* [Origin and Hopes of French Planning] (Paris: Dunod, 1968); Pierre Bauchet, *La planification française: du premier au sixième Plan* [French Planning: From the First to the Sixth Plan] (Paris: Editions du Seuil, 1970); and John and Anne-Marie Hackett, *Economic Planning in France* (London: Allen and Unwin; Cambridge, Mass.: Harvard University Press, 1963). Therefore, this paper will concentrate on the current Sixth Plan and beyond.

For this first section, I have drawn on the three following recent studies of French planning: (*a*) Atreize (collective work organized by Paul Dubois), *La planification française en pratique* [French Planning in Practice] (Paris: Collection "Economie et Humanisme," Les éditions ouvrières, 1971); (*b*) Yves Ullmo, "France," in *Planning, Politics and Public Policy: The British, French, and Italian Experience,* ed. Jack Hayward and Michael Watson (New York and London: Cambridge University Press, 1975), pp. 22–51; and (*c*) Gabriel Mignot, *La planification française aujourd'hui* [French Planning Today], internal memorandum (Paris: Commissariat Général du Plan, 1971, duplicated).

X-Crise,[2] or by the *planistes*, and did not conflict with the setting up of the Resistance's "organization committees" during the war. It was no doubt Jean Monnet's personal influence which persuaded General de Gaulle to introduce a system of planning. This first Plan was supported by all social groups, including especially the trade unions. Given the presence of Communist ministers in the government, the nationalization of key sectors of the economy (electricity, transport, etc.), the wider coverage of the social security system and the establishment of joint management committees with worker participation, the Plan indeed appeared to some as the harbinger of a socialist economy.

With *dirigisme* in full swing, Jean Monnet set up the so-called Modernization Commissions as a forum of discussions between government, employers, and trade unions, and launched the idea of a "concerted economy."

The central theme of the First Plan (1947–50, later extended to 1953) was reconstruction. The planners' choices were highly selective, since the main emphasis was on raising production in major basic sectors, whose growth conditions expansion in all other economic activities. The chosen sectors were coal, electricity, steel, cement, farm machinery, and transport. While protectionism ruled supreme, the Plan spoke of the need to move towards an opening up of frontiers.

The Second and Third Plans: "From Growth to International Competition"

The Second Plan (1954–57) and later the Third Plan (1958–61) were of less consequence than the First and commanded less support; but they served to put across the idea that economic growth can and must be pursued after the completion of postwar reconstruction. The result was a fundamental change in the attitude of the French people, and more especially of its ruling classes.

Modernization of the economy and expansion remained the major aims. Both Plans tried to promote certain reforms, called "basic actions" in the Second Plan, and "imperative tasks" in the Third. There were no decisions, strictly speaking, but rather general guidelines and recommendations regarding such things as vocational training, research, the organization of agricultural markets, investment, the sources of investment finance, etc.

One of the dominant ideas was the reintroduction of competition, followed by the opening up of the economy to the outside world in connection with the beginnings of the new Europe. As the Third Plan proclaims

---

[2] A group organized at the time of the 1929–30 crisis by former students of the Ecole Polytechnique, including Alfred Sauvy, Jean Ullmo, Pierre Massé, and Louis Wallon. The group advocated active state intervention and planning.

(para. 20): "Our country cannot choose a policy of protectionism and reliance on its own resources without at the same time incurring the danger of finding itself in a few years' time impoverished, isolated and, as it were, left behind by history." The preparation of the Plans thus helped to replace the image of a stagnating or crisis-prone economy by one of a growing economy.

The Fourth Plan: "A Less Incomplete Concept of Man"

The recovery of the French economy after the 1957–58 recession, the entry of France into the European Economic Community (EEC), the rejuvenation of the labor force predictable from the postwar baby boom, the political stability of the early years of the Fifth Republic, and General de Gaulle's predilection for the idea of economic planning all combined to create a favorable climate for the Fourth Plan. It became an act of political faith sanctioned by a vote of Parliament and described by General de Gaulle as a "passionate commitment." Consultation between government, employers, and trade unions in the Modernization Commissions gained new vigor.

The Fourth Plan (1962–65) stressed the social aspects of planning. The "modernization and investment plan" turned into an "economic and social development plan." Beyond expansion, modernization, and priority for investment, two new themes appear for the first time; concern with the distribution of the fruits of expansion, and regional development. Alongside a high overall rate of growth (5.5 percent annually), we find a target rate of 10 percent annually for social investment (housing, education, health)—a target which, incidentally, was met by and large.

But the implementation of the Fourth Plan got into serious trouble as early as 1963, when prices soared and the balance of payments got into deficit. A policy of stabilization by demand containment became necessary, and preparations for the Fifth Plan began in the inauspicious atmosphere of the stabilization program introduced by the Finance Minister, Valéry Giscard d'Estaing. Both partners in industy—labor and management—disliked the idea of an incomes policy and were in no mood to discuss, let alone "concert," anything with the planners.

The Fifth Plan: "This Competitive World . . ."

At the Incomes Conference late in 1963 the Planning Commissioner, then Pierre Massé, tried to reconcile expansion and price stability by an incomes policy. But nobody seemed ready to take this road—not the trade unions, nor the employers, nor even the government.

By that time, the French economy began to open its borders, and the maintenance of its competitiveness by strict control of domestic price rises was given top priority, the more so since France's membership in the EEC greatly restricted the use of other, traditional means of reducing the external deficit, such as import quotas, custom duties and, as a last resort, devaluation. If domestic prices are to be prevented from rising too fast, the growth of money wages has to slow down, and this might have been achieved by an active policy of structural reform (through employment policy or the reorganization of firms). But knowing that this would take a long time to put into effect, and doubtful about the scale of the results, the authors of the Fifth Plan proposed another way, namely, "a certain amount of slack on the labor market." It was hoped that this, without involving too much unemployment, would keep down wage increases sufficiently to slow down the price rise.

This was the reasoning behind the Fifth Plan (1966–70). In practice, it led to the choice of an annual growth rate of 5 percent[3] between 1965 and 1970, "slightly below the physical limit of our capacity."

In the absence of agreement on an incomes policy, the Fifth Plan set out "indicative norms" regarding the desired pace of income growth, together with a consistent set of targets for the real distribution of the fruits of expansion among consumption, productive and social investment, and the external balance on goods and services account.

Anxious to submit the Plan to a more democratic discussion, the government arranged, a year ahead of its adoption, for a parliamentary debate on its options, that is to say on the major policy lines underlying the preparation of any plan as such.

The implementation of the Fifth Plan was proceeding more or less on course, when the social upheavals of May and June 1968 disrupted every economic balance as well as the implementation of the Plan. It is true that expansion of gross domestic product slightly exceeded the target and productive investment got even more priority over consumption than had been planned; but social investment fell badly behind, as the chief victim of the budget cuts of November 1968 and the 1969 devaluation. Price and income movements diverged widely from the indicative norms. The guidelines for prices, somewhat unrealistic to begin with, were completely disregarded, and so were those concerning wage restraint and the upgrading of farm incomes; only social benefits followed the course laid out by the Plan.

But it was not merely the consequences of May 1968 that called the Fifth Plan in question. It would be more correct to say that the origins of the social crisis called in question the logic of the Fifth Plan. In a society undergoing such profound changes as the French, mainly under the impact of international competition, strains like unemployment and restrictions on purchasing power gains enabled an explosive situation to develop.

---

[3] The growth rate of 5 percent by the 1959 system of national accounts corresponds to 5.7 percent annually if recalculated by the 1962 system.

The Sixth Plan: "The Industrial Imperative"

In spite of the shock generated by the social crisis, a start was made in October 1969 with the preparation of the Sixth Plan (1971–75). At once the employers made it clear that they wanted strong expansion and priority for industrial development. "The industrial imperative" for the progressive group of employers, "the imperative of the industrialists" for the trade unions—these were the slogans to which the contents of the Sixth Plan had to be fitted. Balanced growth was no longer expected from containment of domestic demand, as in the Fifth Plan, but rather from an "active policy of stimulating supply." Social policy remained timid, placing the stress mainly on help to the most underprivileged groups (increase in the lowest wages and in old-age pensions, care for the handicapped).

Prospects for the Seventh Plan: "Growth—To What End?"

At a time when international monetary difficulties and inflationary pressures throughout the Western world are surrounding the outcome of the Sixth Plan with mounting uncertainties, society is beginning to ask itself what is the point of all this economic growth so dear to the planners (the British economist Andrew Shonfield speaks of French planners as an "expansion lobby"). And so French planners, as they get ready to prepare the Seventh Plan (1976–80), are faced with a challenge. They must allow not only for the necessary economic consistency, but for new social and ecological aims dictated by the present stage of development.

CHANGING METHODS FOR A WIDER RANGE OF PROBLEMS

The preparation of French Plans has always been accompanied by a host of planning studies and economic projections. As the range of issues treated by the planners widened and became more diversified, better tools of analysis and forecasting became available to them thanks to improvements in economic information (statistics and national accounts). Actually, progress in information and in planning systems is closely connected for, to a large extent, it was the questions the planners asked which called forth—not always very quickly—more detailed information.

Input-output tables have been used since the Second Plan, and even more so the Third, as the primary means of presenting a synthetic picture of the quantitative aspects of the economy. The First Plan made do with such fragmentary data as were needed for forecasting output in the priority sectors, but subsequently the planners wanted full coverage and were thus led to work out detailed projections of the volume of output and its uses.

The required input-output table was drawn from the national accounts. This technique had its heyday at the time of the Fourth Plan, when it was used as a basis for a "general market study." This, in the view of Pierre Massé, then Planning Commissioner, was to provide economic agents with all the information, in global and in detailed terms, they might need on the growth prospects of private and public demand and of production.

The problems of income distribution and price formation in time focused attention on the need to work out an overall economic table (*tableau économique d'ensemble*—TEE). This had to do with the transition from a protected to an open economy. Once France's membership in the Common Market began to show its effects, it intensified the pressure of international competition on the French economy. It was no longer enough to produce in order to sell; one must produce at competitive prices.

State intervention, too, gradually underwent a change in the direction of *indirect* influences on the market mechanism (e.g., by fiscal and budget policy). The detailed effects of such state intervention do not show up at the stage of equilibrium in volume terms (output and its uses), but at that of the formation of incomes, expenditure and prices on different markets.

Beginning with the Third Plan, but mainly on the occasion of the Fourth, the construction of an overall economic table made it possible to study the saving-investment equilibrium as well as problems of income distribution.

The study of financial consistency requires projections in a table of financial operations (*Tableau d'opérations financières*—TOF). Taking overall real and financial equilibrium for granted, a consistency test account is constructed to check whether planned investment can be financed within the framework of existing (or proposed) financial institutions, due allowance being made for the rigidity and separation of financial circuits, which are rather pronounced in France. Such a table was prepared experimentally for the Fourth Plan and came into effective use in the Fifth, when the government was proposing to channel its intervention in the financing of productive investment through the private banking sector. There was much talk at the time about the "disengagement of the Treasury," and it became clear that this meant that the private banks would have to "transform" a major part of the short-term funds accruing to them into medium- and long-term loans to enterprises for the purpose of financing productive investment.

Alongside these studies designed to test the consistency of the norms set by the government for its own action, experimental work was started on the financial analysis of enterprises by sectors, with a view to improving sectoral price projections. Each sector was examined to see if the price forecasting was consistent with the financial assets and the possibilities for self-financed investments required by growth. This work brought to light inconsistencies in the financial flows of certain sectors which might have compromised these sectors' investments.

Formal Model-Building: The Physical-Financial Model FIFI

Without a formal exposition of the behavior of economic agents, the macroeconomic projections were unable to play their part of verifying the consistency between the government's chosen norms and the behavior of agents. In any case, it was a slow and clumsy business to calculate all these projections by hand, and it was impossible to show more than a very few volume-value interdependences. Taking advantage of the new, more sophisticated econometric models and of computer calculation, French planners, when preparing the Sixth Plan, worked out a semiglobal (seven enterprise sectors) medium-term simulation model for the whole of the French economy. The model is built so as to show the impact of international competition on the French economy. Assuming that in industry, the sector fully exposed to such competition, there is a constraint on domestic price formation, the model shares out the market for industrial products between financially possible domestic production and substitutable imports. That is, the model determines domestic production and demand, and imports are obtained as the difference. This is in effect a transposition of the neoclassical theory of the firm to the scale of an entire sector, because the sector faces given prices and its production is determined by its financial possibilities. In the other sectors price is a variable which can be influenced at will either by government (administered prices) or by firms (sectors sheltered from international competition). For the latter case it is assumed that cost and profit changes are passed on to the medium-term supply price of firms according to a Keynesian-type mechanism of inflationary gap. By stressing the medium-term importance of the French economy's price competitiveness, the FIFI model suggested that priority should be given to policies susceptible of increasing price competitiveness, that is, of stimulating the supply of marketable output, especially in industry.

Toward a System of Medium-Term Models

The synthetic macroeconomic model was not the only one prepared for the Sixth Plan. Around the central model are grouped a number of peripheral ones, which can provide detailed information in response to questions asked by certain working parties and commissions. There exists, for example, a set of models for the national and local governments and the social security system; these are compatible with the central model but much more detailed. They are used to study fiscal and financial policies, for example, how to obtain equilibrium in the social security system. Similarly, the output projections of the FIFI model's seven enterprise sectors did not tell the production commissions all they needed to know, and so detailed projections were worked out for 29 branches, subject, of course, to consistency with the semiglobal equilibrium of the overall model. It may well be that in the future we shall build more such articulated systems of models, which together will furnish detailed medium-term projections whose consistency will be safeguarded by their being fitted into one global model.

Present Trends in Macroeconomic Model-Building

Three further developments are afoot in France at present. (1) Simultaneous description of economic equilibrium and financial circuits in the model FIFI-TOF. This is the central tool in the preparation of the Seventh Plan, and it is hoped to subsequently integrate in its structure the effects of the money-creating mechanisms and the financial repercussions on the physical and economic elements of equilibrium (productive investment, housing investment, price formation, etc.). (2) Combination of regional and spatial development aspects in the model REGINA (REGIonal-NAtional) should make it possible to test the effects of regional development policy on national equilibria, by distinguishing five major regions of France and three urbanization zones in each of them. (3) Clarification of the relations between medium-term projections and short-term forecasts in a short-term/medium-term model called STAR, on which research is now in hand in the Forecasting Division of the Ministry of Finance; the idea is to lengthen the forecasting horizon of the "economic budgets" (forecasts of economic accounts for the next one or two years) and, in the course of Plan implementation, to analyze the reasons of any divergences from medium-term projections.

Microeconomic tools occupy a less important place in French planning. However, the sort of economic calculation which public enterprises have long used in investment choices is increasingly finding its way into government departments under the influence of what the Americans call Planning, Programming, Budgeting System (PPBS) and the French call *Rationalisation des choix budgétaires* (RCB). These techniques are used in an attempt to introduce economic calculation into more detailed official programming. Decentralized short- and medium-term "program budgets" should add realism to the national plan, but would certainly involve problems of synthesis when it comes to choices among different fields of public activity.

FROM DIRIGISME TO INDICATIVE PLANNING

French planning very quickly broke away from the postwar *dirigisme* of economic policy. The latter was still much in evidence in the methods by which the First Plan was implemented, e.g., the use of Marshall Aid counterpart funds for investment, import licenses, etc., but this was no longer true of the Second Plan, when the Commissariat Général du Plan was able to exert only an indirect influence on the chief instruments of *dirigiste* policy applied by other divisions of the Ministry of Finance (to which the

Planning Commission belonged until 1962, when it became attached directly to the Prime Minister's office). Short-term difficulties in plan implementation as well as political vicissitudes explain why, as the years went on, planning became more and more "indicative" with respect to short-term policy, for which the Ministry of Finance retained responsibility. During the period of the Third Plan, the advent of the Fifth Republic and France's entry into the Common Market made it neccesary to resort to an interim plan for the years 1960 and 1961. No sooner had the Fourth Plan (1962–65) got under way, than it was seriously upset by the introduction of a stabilization program. And as regards the Fifth Plan (1966–70), finally, the upheavals of May and June 1968 produced a shock so strong that the initial design had in effect to be abandoned.

From Warning Signals to Review Procedures

Faced with these repeated vagaries of economic reality, the planners tried to do two things. They chose a few of the more important plan targets and then tried to obtain firmer commitments from the government with respect to this hard core of targets. These preoccupations are the origin of the system of warning signals, which give notice of any significant departure from the planned targets in matters of expansion and equilibrium. In the intention of its authors, this system was to be an element of economic strategy in plan implementation; any significant overshooting of the point where the warning signal flashed would *automatically* lead to a decision either to abandon the target or else to apply corrective policy. The warning signals of the Fifth Plan were indeed able to indicate divergences in plan implementation, but official reactions were apparent only in ministerial communiqués. The bodies responsible for short-term economic policy —the Ministry of Finance and its main Services—refused to take the Plan as a point of reference for their actions, and the original Plan figures were neither defended nor revised. In addition, the practice of monthly checks was clumsy and eventually became almost meaningless because it was done too frequently.

In spite of difficulties in Plan implementation, the monthly warning signals flashed rarely, and the annual ones (gross domestic product and productive investment) never, though admittedly the danger point at which the latter were to be activated was set very low (GDP, 2 percent; investment, 2.5 percent).

The relative price increase in France compared with prices abroad exceeded the 1 percent limit for three consecutive months in January 1968, as a result of the extension of the value-added tax to retail trade. It did not drop back below this limit until February 1970, but this may be explained by the high rate of word inflation (6 percent annually).

The other signals were less restrictive and flashed after a time lag of six to twelve months.

In view of these difficulties, the system of warning signals was replaced by a mid-course "Plan Review," to which the government committed itself in advance and which was to be the subject of a Parliamentary debate. In addition, a new set of quarterly indicators is published and widely distributed by the National Institute of Statistics and Economic Studies (Institut National de la Statistique et des Etudes Economiques—INSEE) and the Commissariat Général du Plan.

Hard-Core Targets in Plan Implementation

In their formulation, French Plans have been, and are tending to become, more and more *comprehensive* as regards both the range of problems and the detail in which they are treated. But at the same time the Planning Commission has, among other things, been anxious to place stress on *selectivity* with respect to measures to be introduced or applied in the course of plan implementation. Accordingly, a distinction is made, in the figures of macroeconomic projections, between mere forecasts and targets to which the government commits itself. The clearest example is the introduction to the report on the Sixth Plan, which summarizes only those of the planned targets to which the government has committed itself. Similarly, an attempt was made in the Sixth Plan to concentrate intervention in the field of public finance, while encouraging regional and local decentralization in Plan implementation.

The most sensitive area is that of public investment, which can fall victim to short-term policy more easily than current operating expenses, such as wages and salaries and other current expenditure. The device adopted for the Sixth Plan in this respect was to set an overall figure for public investment as a Plan target without specifying completely the share for each function (health, education, transport, etc.). Part of the investments for each function, ranging from 15 to 40 percent, is considered variable, and the list of projects included is subject to a "priority declaration." On the other hand, a number of programs (with all their expenditure on investment, staff, and operation) were completely planned because of their strategic character; examples are the activities of the National Employment Agency, of the road safety squad, etc. Decentralization in Plan implementation was to be encouraged by recent "Plan contracts" signed by the government and a small number of local authorities grouped in urban communities. The national government grants subsidies to these communities to carry out a public investment program over a three or five year period.

Planning and Decision Making

In spite of all precautions, it seems certain that the implementation of an indicative Plan in a market economy will always involve the planners in some tricky problems. The Plan is part of the varied means of government intervention in development. Yet it has no direct control over any of the other means employed. Nor is planning a continuous process, and hence it is a decision-making one only to a very limited extent. Planning can probably more aptly be described as the opening move in a process of discussion and consultation among government departments and between them and spokesmen of social groups. This process serves to test the approximate consistency of the policies of various government departments, and at the same time to lay down an overall set of general guidelines binding upon government and strengthening its ability to resist the demands of interest groups during a certain period, at most throughout Plan implementation. A case in point may be recalled in connection with the preparation of the Sixth Plan. At that time, the idea gradually gained ground that "tax pressure"—that is, the incidence of taxes, social insurance contributions, and the like—on production, should not increase during the period of the Plan. This rule was put into practice, step-by-step, through a series of tax decisions and has become a benchmark of the implementation of the current Plan.

THE SHIFT FROM THE "CONCERTED ECONOMY" TO A GOVERNMENT PROGRAM

Participation of spokesmen of social groups in Plan preparation was an ingredient of the philosophy of French planning from the outset. In the First Plan this was spelled out quite clearly:

> Since the implementation of the Plan will require the collaboration of all, it is indispensable that all the nation's vital elements take part in its formulation. This is why a working method is proposed which, for each sector, involves joint discussions by officials of the government department concerned, prominent experts and representatives of professional groups (workers, managerial staff, employers). . . .

This is what was meant by a "concerted economy" in contrast to a *dirigiste* one run on bureaucratic or corporative lines. To give effect to this conception, the Commissariat Général du Plan set up and kept at work a large number of commissions and working parties, some of them within the Civil Service.

Planning Machinery

As the range of issues brought within the purview of planning in successive French Plans increased, so did the number of Commissions and Working Parties involved.

Eventually, by the time of the Sixth Plan, the system was reformed in an attempt to enhance the unity and efficiency of the whole body of Commissions. These are now of three kinds: the "horizontal" Commissions, which are responsible for problems common to all activities (e.g., employment, research, etc.), and among which the Commission for the General Economy and Financing takes care of synthesis on the basis of the relevant overall planning studies; the "vertical" Production Commissions, much reduced in number but now including a new single Industry Commission concerned with synthesis and with industrial policy; and the Budgetary Commissions, also called "Commissions of Collective Functions," which deal with major fields of public services (e.g., education, health, etc.). Within separate Commissions, the study of specific problems or those concerned with sectoral activities is delegated to specialized Committees (e.g., a Foreign Trade Committee, twenty-two sectoral Production Committees under the umbrella of the Industry Commission) or to Joint Working Parties in the case of problems common to two or more Commissions (e.g., the Joint Working Party on Vocational Training of the Employment and the Education Commissions). Finally, some of the major Commissions have arranged for technical and production studies to be discussed by Technical Working Parties made up of experts from government departments, employers' associations, and trade unions.

Two new features in the preparation of the Sixth Plan were the development of *long-term study groups*, whose discussions generally preceded those of the Plan Commissions, and the establishment of *administrative groups*, which met before the Commissions, prepared the latter's work and coordinated the position of government departments. The most important among these administrative groups are the Finance-Plan Groups, which have done much to give more prominence to the medium-term view in the work of the Ministry of Finance, to increase the exchange of information between its divisions and the Commissariat Général du Plan, and to define its position in relation to the Sixth Plan.

The Extent of Participation in Plan Preparation

The social groups which were to take part in the preparation of Plans actually do so in varying degree, according to the view they take of the functions of planning and to the position they occupy in French society. Most participants agree that planning is useful as a means of economic and social information,[4] but opinions differ as to what commitments are to result from the planning process. *Farmers* regard planning as an important stage in the traditional discussions with government. Farmers' associations, for example, warmly supported an incomes policy during the Sixth Plan, even though the Fifth Plan had failed in this respect. The

---

[4] The whole set of Commission, Committee, and Working Party reports published by the Commissariat Général du Plan in 1971 constitutes a valuable source of recent studies and information on most aspects of the French economy.

attitude of *employers* changed in the course of time. At first they were rather hostile because of the seemingly *dirigiste* complexion of the whole venture of planning, but later their associations took an active part in the preparation of the Third and Fourth Plans, when the "general market study" was a valuable source of information for them. However, the Conseil National du Patronat Français (CNPF), which in principle represents all private enterprises but in actual fact only the biggest ones, did not abandon its reserved attitude until the Sixth Plan. At that time it publicly took a strong stand in favor of vigorous growth based on industry, because it was anxious to have the Sixth Plan give priority to industrialization; yet its position remained ambiguous owing to an internal conflict of interests between a forward-looking group of large industrialists and the bulk of the owners of small- and medium-sized firms who looked with misgivings at the far-reaching structural changes in French industry.

Trade unions likewise changed their attitude, but in the opposite direction from employers. At first, they liked the apparently socialist implications of planning, but later they increasingly contested the use made of it by government, so much so that sometimes they withheld all participation. The Confédération Générale du Travail (CGT)—which, despite its importance among the unions, was excluded by the government from the planning process until the Third Plan—and its breakaway group Force Ouvière (FO) adopted the same attitude towards planning, in spite of their divergent ideologies (Communist in the first case and reformist-socialist in the second). Both take part actively in meetings, and both withhold collaboration—the one by refusing to agree to anything in the first place and opposing final decisions, the other by paying lip service to agreement but refusing to be committed by it. The Confédération Française Démocratique du Travail (CFDT, the socialist-inspired successor of the Confédération Française des Travailleurs Chrétiens, CFTC) changed course more radically. While it played an active part in economic management in 1962 and raised a claim for "democratic planning," it held aloof from the Sixth Plan when its socialist orientation became stronger. It was so critical of the whole approach of the Sixth Plan that in September 1970 it refused to take any part in the second stage of its preparation.

As regards the *government* and the *planners* themselves, the discussions of the Plans fulfill a certain number of functions, though these, too, have gradually changed in time. The collection of information has lost much of its importance as a result of the general improvement of the whole system of economic and statistical information. The Planning Commission relies more and more heavily on the macroeconomic studies of the National Institute of Statistics and Economic Studies and of the Forecasting Division of the Ministry of Finance. And most government departments have developed their own information programs in connection with PPBS, research and programming units, etc.

Conciliation in the Interests of Compliance

The efforts to conciliate the differing points of view of social groups at the stage of Plan preparation aim at increasing compliance with the Plan. For a long time the planners tried to achieve a *social consensus* regarding the general lines of the Plan, witness Pierre Massé's ambition of a "Nation's Plan." But now it has become clear that the rules of the game of our society are contested at the root by some of the social groups which are part of the planning machinery. Inevitably, this altered the significance of the Plan itself, for its choices and targets increasingly became those of government. The Plan now is to all intents and purposes a medium-term action program for government. Plan discussions still have their function, but it is a function of *social simulation* by which the government's choices are confronted with the preferences (or objections) of social groups in order to test the impact of reform projects and to amend them prior to final decision. This is necessarily a partial process, because five-year planning for fixed dates can take account of only a part of government policies, and because many important decisions are taken outside the procedures of Plan preparation and hence are a datum for them rather than a variable to be influenced. But all in all this seems the lesser evil in comparison with a sort of "rolling" planning in which basic choices would be in danger of being watered down in day-to-day action.

*   *   *   *   *

CONCLUSION

French planning is one particular form of the practices of overall economic management current in developed countries. In the case of France, the most striking feature is the public discussion associated with this system of planning, compared with the informal and unpublicized relations maintained in other countries between the managers of large concerns and government departments. Actually, this public discussion which is known as *concertation* in France does not lead to consensus among the social groups. Furthermore, planning remains partial in that a good many decisions are taken outside its purview, which means that the planners must take account of them rather than influence them. It seems difficult to determine the impact of French planning either on government economic policy or on the decisions of firms about output and investment.

Because planning deals with medium-term trends, its influence on economic policy is seldom direct. However, the pursuit of rapid growth and the curtailment of unemployment, stemming from the Plans, has certainly played an important role in French economic policy since World War II. In the same way, the "Industrial Imperative," the main theme of the Sixth

Plan, inspired the decisions to restructure industrial branches which the industrialists concerned have gradually been carrying out with the assistance of the Ministry of Finance and the Ministry of Industry. Finally, the public investment programs included in the Plan serve as a point of reference for the ministries concerned during annual budget discussions with the Ministry of Finance.

Firms are less influenced by planning, first because only a small number of French enterprises prepare medium-term plans, and second because it is chiefly the big firms that are acquainted with and use the national plan. A study in 1967 of 2,000 firms showed that about 40 percent of the firms used medium-term forecasts (for four years or more), especially for investment, finance, and production; but the influence of the forecasts in the Plan was perceptible only in the big firms, most of which have planning departments and economic research departments.[5] Indirect influences also operate here because the business press and trade associations in each sector perform an intermediary role in transmitting the forecasts of the Plan. The situation is obviously different when a very oligopolistic sector elaborates a rather precise plan for the development of the market, which often is directly taken into account in the national plan (for example, energy, ferrous metallurgy, automobiles). In the competitive sectors with small firms, the impact of national planning is much weaker because the factors of poor plan implementation discussed above operate fully in these sectors.

In short, the effect of indicative planning on the decisions of economic agents appears particularly weak in the French case, and it is difficult to speak of a "self-validating" forecast.[6] At the most, one can assert that indicative planning is a way of giving directions and guidelines for economic and social development.

The political force of French Plans, therefore, is weak, but they do play an essential part in the formulation of "social norms" which, for a limited period and in any given phase of development, rule the behavior of social groups and establish a frame of reference for government action.

In preparing the Seventh Plan, French planners will have to define more precisely just where national planning finds its place between the international level, where production is in the course of powerful transformation, and the decentralized level to be expected as the result of the proposed regional reforms. The extent of social change and the current doubts about

---

[5] Cf. Jean-Jacques Carré, Paul Dubois, and Edmond Malinvaud, *La croissance française* (Paris: Editions du Seuil, 1972), translated by J. P. Hatfield into English as *French Economic Growth* (Stanford, Calif.: Stanford University Press, 1975), chap. 14 on the role of economic planning and information.

[6] Cf. Fernand Martin, "The Information Effect of Economic Planning," *Canadian Journal of Economics and Political Science*, vol. 30, no. 3 (August 1964), p. 339; and Richard P. Du Boff, "The Decline of Economic Planning in France," *Western Political Quarterly*, vol. 21, no. 1 (March 1968), p. 99.

economic growth will perhaps widen the field of planning to take in the social aspects of development. Nevertheless, the difficulties of forecasting and the reserved attitude of both sides of industry work in the direction of reducing the scope of planning, and of formulating the Plan as a set of general guidelines rather than as a detailed program of economic and social policy.

7

PLANNING IN JAPAN*

Ryutaro Komiya[1]

Japan's economic performance—in growth, technological progress, and competitiveness in world markets—in the last 20 years has been remarkable. Foreigners often consider national economic plans a major cause. However, this selection by a leading Japanese economist shows that the medium-term national economic plan in Japan should be regarded only as "a long-term forecast with some flavor of wishful thinking of plan makers as far as its quantitative aspects are concerned." In fact, Japanese indicative plans are largely disregarded not only by the private sector but also by government agencies.

Instead, the economic planning which is significant in Japan operates through the elaborate system of specific "industrial policies." Through tax incentives, credit, and regulation of foreign trade, these policies encourage production, investment, research and development, and exports by particular industries.

When people speak of "economic planning" in Japan they usually have in mind the national economic plan prepared by the Economic Planning Agency once every two or three years. Yet in my view these national plans are not so much a "plan" in the usual sense of the term, and are not as important as they appear at first. Those who are not well informed about economic policy making in Japan might think that the Japanese government largely follows its medium-term (usually five years) national eco-

* Excerpted by permission from *Economic Planning, East and West*, ed. Morris Bornstein (Cambridge, Mass.: Ballinger Publishing Company, 1975), pp. 189–227, with the omission of tables and references to foreign-language sources. Copyright © 1975 by Ballinger Publishing Company. Ryutaro Komiya is Professor of Economics at the University of Tokyo.

[1] Financial support for this study from the Research Fund of the Faculty of Economics, the University of Tokyo, is gratefully acknowledged.

nomic plan when making annual or day-to-day economic policy decisions. In fact, this is not the case. In recent years especially, the national economic plan is becoming less and less relevant to actual economic policy, at least so far as macroeconomic and sectoral quantitative indices are concerned.

This does not mean, however, the Japanese economy is run without much governmental planning. The Japanese government intervenes widely in individual sectors, industries, or regions, and there is much planning on industry as well as regional bases. Many of the plans in individual fields appear to be quite effective in channeling resources into particular industries or regions.

In the following two sections, Japan's national economic planning and planning for individual industries will be discussed respectively. In the last section a few concluding remarks will be made.

NATIONAL ECONOMIC PLANS

The Multiplicity of Plans and the Reasons for Underestimation

The multiplicity of Japan's economic plans is perhaps well known. During the 18 years from 1955 to 1973, the Japanese government announced seven medium- or long-term national economic plans.[2]

Some of the Japanese words appearing in these plans are rhetoric without much substantive meaning and are difficult to translate into English. Even so, these words still indicate what Japanese plan-makers considered the most important policy goals at the time of preparing each plan, and reflect the changing atmosphere of economic policy making in postwar Japan. In the early postwar years, the emphasis was on industrial growth, saving, investment, and export. Later the priority shifted to "balanced growth" (whatever that means), price stability, and international cooperation, and more recently, welfare, quality of life, and environment have been included among most important policy goals.

The natural question will be raised why there are so many national economic plans. An immediate answer is that although each of the plans (except the ten-year National Income Doubling Plan) covered about five years, after its introduction the actual rate of growth surpassed the planned rate substantially, especially in the case of earlier plans, and planning indices became obsolete within a year or two after implementation.[3] Espe-

---

[2] There were national plans drafted before 1955, but they were not officially adopted. For a brief history of Japanese national economic planning in English, see Tsunehiko Watanabe, "National Planning and Economic Development: A Critical Review of the Japanese Experience," *Economics of Planning*, vol. 10 (1970), nos. 1–2, pp. 23–30.

[3] How the plan underestimated the growth rate may be illustrated by the fact that if the "ambitious" (according to the criticisms at the time of its announcement) National Income Doubling Plan had been carried out as planned, the real GNP in 1970, the terminal year of the Plan, would have been only about 70 percent of its actual level.

cially in the case of plans II, IV, and V, the actual level of private investment in plant and equipment by far surpassed the planned targets. Later an
unexpected rapid increase in exports and huge balance-of-payments surpluses were the main factors which made the plans obsolete very quickly.
Also, rapid and unexpected changes in the socioeconomic as well as external conditions made it necessary to change the policy goals declared in the
national economic plan.

Why then have Japan's national economic plans persistently underestimated the rate of growth, at least until around 1970? First, in the period
immediately after the war, most Japanese were not confident either of the
future of the economy or of the nation and themselves. The prewar level
of per capita real income was regained only around 1955: of the nations
which fought World War II, severely defeated Japan took the longest time
to recover from war destruction. The target rate of growth of 5 percent
given in the Five-Year Plan for Economic Self-Support, the first official
economic plan, was severely criticized as too optimistic and as unrealistic
by intellectuals, journalists, and leaders of nongovernment parties. Such a
criticism was not unrelated to a Marxian view of "monopoly capitalism,"
according to which the world capitalist system, which entered the period of
"a general crisis of capitalism" in 1930, was bound to fall into stagnation
and could not continue to grow without undergoing a proletarian revolution or at least a drastic social reform.

Second, having experienced unusually high rates of growth for some time
immediately after the war, still an overwhelming majority of knowledgeable
Japanese did not believe that such high rates would continue to prevail.
Especially those who belonged to the older generations (those who finished
university education before the war) continued to criticize the target rates
of growth in national economic plans as overly optimistic well into the mid-
1960s.[4] It was argued that a high rate of growth was possible in the reconstruction period because capital expenditures to repair war-damaged plant,
equipment, and social overhead capital could raise GNP very quickly,
whereas after the reconstruction period the increase in GNP could be
achieved only by substantial new net investment and/or technological
progress.

Another argument was that the Japanese economy was in a catching-up
process immediately after the war, making use of a large backlog of new
technologies developed in the United States and Europe during the war.
Once such a backlog was exhausted, technological progress in Japan would
be slowed down.

Pessimists also emphasized the balance-of-payments constraint. They
thought that Japan's exports could not continue to grow indefinitely at a
much faster rate than the total volume of world trade, and therefore the

---

[4] Osamu Shimomura, Tadao Uchida, Hisao Kanamori, and I were among the minority optimists.

rate of growth of Japan's raw material and fuel imports, vital for Japan's industrial growth, would be restricted.

Looking back with the hindsight of today, it is obvious that the majority, including the plan makers, underestimated not only the growth potential of the Japanese economy, but also the adaptability of the economy to changing circumstances and the resultant structural changes. The national economic plans predicted more or less correctly the directions of the changes in the industrial structure, the industrial distribution of the labor force, and the composition of exports, but almost always underestimated the extent of such changes.[5]

Contents of a National Economic Plan

To facilitate the understanding of the nature of national economic planning in Japan, I will briefly describe the contents of the latest *Basic Economic and Social Plan*. The Plan is published as a government document of about 170 pages, and consists primarily of two components. [The first is] the plan targets for various items in each of the four major planning areas. For example, under the heading of "creation of a rich environment" the target levels for improvement in air pollution, water pollution, city parks, etc., are stipulated. Similarly target levels are given under the other three broad planning objectives, "ensuring a comfortable and stable civil life," "price stability," and "international cooperation."

Later in the Plan, the policy measures required for achieving each target are explained. But the explanation given in the Plan is largely qualitative rather than quantitative, and sometimes quite vague. Rhetorical and euphemistic words difficult to translate, or almost meaningless words such as "take necessary measures," "promote coordination," "consider improving such and such," appear repeatedly. Moreover, on important policy issues hotly debated currently, the Plan often avoids indicating the future directions of government policy. For example, on the problem of the price of land, which has been rising very rapidly recently and causing social unrest among the urban population, the Plan says little beyond what has already been said. On the price policies of public corporations such as national railways and on the problems of cartels and resale price maintenance, all of which are considered by many Japanese as the crucial areas for policies to curb inflation, the Plan spends several paragraphs, but says almost nothing meaningful. Or, while emphasizing very strongly international cooperation and avoidance of protectionism, the Plan says nothing about Japan's own agricultural protection. But, as explained later, the national economic plan

---

[5] Hence it is a mistake to think that the Japanese government intentionally underestimated the growth rate in order to boast about the overfulfillment afterwards. Not only the government but also the majority of Japanese underestimated the growth and structural changes, and those critical of the government often did so more than the plan makers.

under Japan's present institutional setting is bound to be elusive on such specific policy issues. . . .

The appendix of the Plan gives detailed national income accounts and an industry breakdown of output and employment in 1977. It is the failure of this part of the earlier national plans to predict the future course of the economy accurately enough that caused the large discrepancies between actual and planned figures within a few years after the introduction of the Plan, and quickly made the Plan obsolete. Earlier plans gave these figures as "planned" or "targets," but in recent plans these figures for the terminal year of the planning period are called "predicted" or "estimates."

Apart from the large discrepancies in the past, some academic economists are critical of the procedure by which the estimates in recent national economic plans were derived. Although the general framework of the macroeconometric model used in the projection was made public, the procedure in deriving the predicted figures for 1977 was not. Only a few of the values for exogenous parameters and policy variables used in the predictions are explicitly given in the Plan. It is difficult, therefore, for outsiders to evaluate the overall validity of the predictions. The premises under which the predictions are made should be made public, according to the criticism. Especially in the case of the estimates for price deflators, some doubts have been entertained as to compatibility with other estimates: it is generally thought that for an obvious political reason the government chose artificially low figures for the rate of price increase.

Process of Plan Making

To clarify the nature of Japan's national economic plans, it is necessary to describe the process by which the plan is prepared and announced.

The formal process is that first the prime minister requests the Economic Council to prepare a national plan, and then the Council presents its report to the prime minister. In the case of the latest plan, Prime Minister Kakuei Tanaka requested the Council in August 1972 to prepare "a new long-term economic plan which aimed at enhancement of civil welfare and promotion of international cooperation, in view of rapid changes in the domestic and external circumstances."

The Economic Council is an advisory committee reporting to the prime minister, and consisted in 1972 of about thirty members outside of the government. Its overwhelming majority were presidents and chairmen of big corporations and ex-government officials.[6] Its *Basic Economic and So-*

---

[6] Eighteen members were from big business (most of them presidents or chairmen of firms); four, previously high-ranking government officials; five, academics (four of them professors emeriti, that is, retired from universities); and two, labor union representatives. Even this distribution is more diversified than the situation before; at the time of the Medium-Term Economic Plan (1965), of thirty members of the Council all were executives of big business or ex-government officials, except two professors emeriti.

cial Plan was reported to the prime minister in February 1973, and at the Cabinet meeting a few days later the Plan was formally adopted without any modification "as the guiding principle for managing the national economy during fiscal years 1973 through 1977."

The above might give an impression that the Economic Council or its members are responsible for preparing the plan. In reality, it may be said without much exaggeration that the Council members' involvement in plan making is minimal. In the first place, the Council has many subcommittees. The total number of members of these subcommittees amounted almost to two hundred in the case of the latest plan. They are again dominated by men from big business and ex-government officials. Preparation and deliberation of the plan were done mainly at meetings of these subcommittees. The Council itself met only a few times: usually it simply approves whatever is prepared by subcommittees or by the secretariat. Membership on the Council is largely honorary. After all, most members are very busy men with their own business or profession and can afford little time to study national economic problems carefully. The last point also applies to the members of the subcommittees.

Hence, second, it is only natural that the secretariat for the Council, the Economic Planning Agency (EPA)—or more precisely its Bureau of Comprehensive Planning—dominates the process of plan making. In addition to the officials of EPA, officials of various ministries and agencies attend the meetings whenever matters on which they have jurisdiction are discussed. Together with officials of EPA, they act as the secretariat of subcommittees: they collect necessary materials, prepare documents, and draft plans. Indeed, the ministries and agencies have a very strong voice on subjects relevant to them.

It might be asked what happens if the opinions of the members of the Council or its subcommittees are opposed to those of government officials. Such a conflict rarely happens. All members know that the officials of ministries and agencies have virtual vetos, and do not waste time fighting against them. To begin with, EPA selects as members of the Council or its subcommittees only those who will behave well, that is, those who cooperate with government officials. It is easy to recruit cooperative and more or less capable members, since being a member of the Council, one of its subcommittees, or any other governmental committee carries some public (rather than professional) prestige, although pecuniary remuneration is negligible. Also, for those outside of the government, the access to information is often an important advantage drawn from being a member of a government committee.

The Nature of the National Economic Plan

The two components of Japan's national economic plan mentioned above must be distinguished in discussing the nature of the national plan.

On the one hand, the national plan is a compilation of current opinions on economic policy issues, and to the extent that the planning targets for specific policy aims reflect the conclusions which have been reached by the various councils and ministries having jurisdiction over them, such targets in the plan are more or less thought of as something to be achieved through governmental efforts during the planning period. But since such planning targets are discussed and set by the respective councils and ministries first, and since the national plan is simply a collection of such planning targets in individual fields already at hand, with little attempt at coordination and elimination of inconsistencies among targets, it is misleading to consider the national plan as setting binding policy targets in individual policy areas.

On the other hand, the national economic plan gives "estimates" for macroeconomic variables such as the rate of growth of real GNP, its components, the balance of payments, the price indices, and so on during the planning period. This part of the plan is a prediction or a long-term forecast, as reliable or unreliable as a long-term weather forecast, of the future state of the economy, with some flavor of wishful thinking added.

The national economic plan is not binding: nobody feels much obliged to observe, or be responsible for, the figures given in the plan. This is especially true of estimates for macroeconomic variables, but is true also of planning targets for specific policy aims. The Ministry of Finance, the most powerful government ministry in economic policy matters, has not been enthusiastic about rigid economic planning, and for understandable reasons. Other government offices too have considered the national economic plan as primarily a forecast rather than a rigid plan which must be followed faithfully. I will explain the reasons why the national plan has been considered as nonbinding, first in regard to the private sector, and then in regard to the public sector.

Private Sector. Past macroeconometric experience shows that it is difficult to predict variables pertaining primarily to the private sector more or less accurately for planning purposes beyond the time span of six months, or at most, one year. Two major sources of errors in macroeconometric prediction are (1) changes in the economic structure over time, or the failure of behavioral equations in the macroeconometric model used to give good estimates for the future, even when exogenous variables to be given from outside the model are correctly predicted; and (2) errors in predicting exogenous variables. My general impression is that for private investment in plant and equipment, certain categories of inventory investment, and price deflators, errors due to (1) are substantial; whereas for exports and the balance of payments, the main source of errors is (2).

The fact that errors of type (1) have been substantial, indicates that we do not yet know the mechanism of the economy accurately enough for the purpose of planning. Private firms in contemporary Japan are still a fertile source of energy and creative initiatives, and their activities can often be unpredictable.

Suppose, for example, that in one year private investment in plant and equipment in a certain sector rises sharply beyond the "planned" level. Should private investment then be restrained, and if the answer is yes, by what means? At least in Japan, in most cases the government does not know whether it is desirable from a national economic point of view to restrain such an unexpected rise in private investment beyond the "planned" level. The government may tighten the money supply if it expects overall inflationary pressure to develop as a result of a general rise in private investment. Or it may intervene in a particular sector if an obvious excess capacity situation is foreseen as a result of too high a rate of investment there. Generally speaking, however, the "planned" figures in the medium-term national economic plan have never been considered as binding targets according to which the government should regulate the variables pertaining to the private sector.

In addition to unexpected developments from within the Japanese economy, there are errors of type (2), that is errors in predicting exogenous variables. From a planning point of view, the international economic conditions surrounding Japan several years ahead are especially difficult to predict. Unpredictable changes in world economic conditions can affect substantially the course of an economy, such as the Japanese, heavily dependent on international economic relations.

For these reasons the Japanese government has not paid much attention to the national economic plan when making short-run policy decisions affecting the private sector. Its macroeconomic policies, fiscal and monetary policies in particular, are determined primarily by considering the levels of domestic effective demand and employment, the balance of payments and movements of price indices. When the government steers fiscal and monetary policies watching these macroeconomic indicators, it can naturally end up with overall and sectoral growth rates which are quite different from those given in the medium-term plan, and discrepancies accumulate as time goes by.

It must also be noted that for many variables pertaining to the private sector, the government may not really have at hand policy instruments which can be used to correct effectively the actual course of these variables when they deviate from their "planned" course. Just consider, for example, Japan's huge balance-of-payments surpluses in the last few years, and how difficult and painful it has been to reduce them. Another example is price inflation: not only in Japan but in many countries of the world governments are having great difficulties in restraining the rise in prices.

Public Sector. It might be asked whether the government follows the plan at least as far as variables pertaining to the public sector. What is the use of the plan if the government itself does not feel obliged to observe, for example, the planned level of its own public investment in individual fields?

There are several reasons why even the planned levels of variables pertaining to the public sector are not closely followed by government ministries and agencies, except possibly at the very beginning of the planning period. First, when the actual GNP, the level of private investment, the balance of payments, and so on differ substantially from their predicted levels, it is meaningless or even harmful to stick to the plan only so far as the public sector is concerned. To do so will destroy the balance between the public and private sectors.[7]

Second, the government budget and "investment and financing plan" are voted upon by the National Diet on a rigid annual basis. Only in very special cases does the Diet allow the government to make commitments on capital expenditures beyond the fiscal year. In a democratic society, the Diet and the government budget should respond to the changing needs of its citizens, and the principle of annual deliberation of the government budget has never been challenged. In particular, the parties opposing the government party are against long-run commitments and planning, in the hope that they will win power in the next election and will change economic policies drastically.[8]

Third, the Ministry of Finance, and especially its Bureau of Budget, the most influential government office on the matter of economic policy, has a tradition of economy in, and noncommitment to, public expenditures. Officials of the Bureau of Budget always try to economize and curtail public expenditures in the face of other ministries' and agencies' requests for appropriations. Budget officials think that if the Ministry of Finance once in some way commits itself to a long-term expenditure plan, it would be difficult to cancel or reduce the expenditures for a certain item previously agreed upon in the plan, whereas there will always be requests for new or additional appropriations when circumstances change. Thus according to their view a long-run plan for government expenditure or public investment will give rise to an expansionary bias or a tendency for "increasing fiscal rigidity" which they want to avoid.[9]

---

[7] This is what actually happened to some degree. As a result of an unexpectedly high rate of growth of the private sector, the public sector in general has been lagging behind, and especially public investment in social overhead capital and public policies against environmental pollution have so far been very inadequate.

[8] J. E. Meade asks but does not answer the following question. "Moreover, what is the legitimate use which, in a democratic society, one government may make of its own social welfare function? Should it rigidly commit resources to uses which will satisfy its own ideas about future social welfare without leaving any flexibility for them to be turned to the satisfaction of alternative objectives favored by the opposition party which may well in turn become the government—presumably because of some change in social values among the electorate itself?" Meade, *The Theory of Indicative Planning* (Manchester, Eng.: Manchester University Press, 1970), p. 72.

[9] This is also the reason why Ministry of Finance officials purposely try to underestimate the rate of economic growth in the government's annual economic outlook, which is the basis for the government budget. If a high rate of growth is expected, tax revenue

Also, not only do officials of the Ministry of Finance have an inclination to dislike long-term fiscal planning, but long-run planning is really difficult in regard to certain fiscal expenditures. Certain items in the budget, such as rice price supports, national medical insurance, price and investment policies of national railways, social security and welfare programs, and national defense plans, have long been difficult political issues, and very hotly debated during the process of budget compilation every year. Anyone who knows the political conflicts of these issues can understand that it is really difficult to make a long-run quantitative plan for these expenditure items.

Forecast Rather than Planning

Thus nobody considers the national economic plan as a rigid, binding plan which must be followed by the government. When the Ministry of Finance makes decisions on the annual budget, the Bank of Japan on money supply, and the Ministry of International Trade and Industry (MITI) on industrial policies, they pay little attention to the national economic plan. There is not much substance in the national plan which can be usefully referred to when government ministries and agencies make important policy decisions in their respective fields. Or putting it differently, it appears that government ministries and agencies other than the Economic Planning Agency tend to try to incorporate in the national economic plan as little as possible of those elements which they consider may bind them rigidly and undesirably in the future.

Therefore, Japan's national economic plan should be interpreted as a long-term forecast, with some flavor of wishful thinking of plan makers, as far as its quantitative aspects are concerned. Interpreted in this way, it is not surprising that the government publishes a five-year national plan as often as once every two or three years. This is similar to a long-run (one to three months) weather forecast announced once or twice a month.

The Reason for the National Plans and Their Effects on Growth

If the national economic plans have not been intended to regulate the variables pertaining to either the private or the public sector, one might

---

will also be expected to increase substantially, the income-elasticity of tax revenues being greater than unity. This will invite bolder requests for appropriations as well as for tax relief. Obviously such purposeful underestimation is not a rational step in planning if a single optimizing body is going to make a plan. But since the budgetary process is essentially a political game, the attempt to underestimate tax revenues may well be rational from the viewpoint of Ministry of Finance officials, who want to leave something in reserve in order to avoid inflationary developments in the face of irresponsible pressure groups demanding big public expenditures and tax relief.

Incidentally, in recent years the government's budget bill has never been modified by the Diet. What is submitted by the cabinet is always passed by the Diet, so that the real budgetary process is in preparing the government's budget bill.

ask, first, what is the reason for or the use of such plans—what functions are they supposed to perform—and second, what is their effect upon Japan's economic growth.

My immediate reaction to the first question is that in a democratic society in which various political forces of different strength are at work, the existing institutions such as economic plans, the tariff system, and price controls—or the government agencies responsible for them—are not always performing useful functions from the viewpoint of the economy or the society as a whole. Quite often they are established, or continue to exist, as a result of politically influential groups acting in their own interests, or simply as a political compromise between powerful pressure groups. This is a great difference from the situation in which a single optimizing entity makes consistent, rational decisions. A democratic society cannot be supposed to behave always consistently and rationally, as an individual or as an enterprise might be.

Moreover, illusions, misunderstandings, and wrong theories, sometimes willfully cultivated and exploited by certain groups to their advantage, often play an important role. Therefore, one must not suppose that there is always a good "reason" for the existing economic plans or that they always perform some useful functions for the society.

In the period immediately after the war, the Japanese majority's confidence in the functioning of price mechanisms was at a low point, and great hopes were entertained for national economic planning. Once the Economic Planning Agency was established, it became very difficult to curtail its personnel or to change its name to "forecasting" or "research," instead of "planning"—not to speak of abolishing it. EPA and plan making became a convenient platform for information exchanges among government ministries and between the government and the private sector, although national economic planning has turned out to amount to little more than forecasting.

From the private sector's point of view, there is little reason to object to the present setup. The big businesses obtain information through their representatives participating in the plan-making process. Nongovernment political parties are strongly against the national economic plans published by the Conservative government, because of the growth-oriented, probusiness bias of the plans, but they are not against economic planning as such, for obvious ideological reasons.

Turning now to the second question of the effects of the national plans on economic growth, it seems to me that what is called the "announcement effect" of the national economic plans might have been quite substantial, especially in the case of the "Income Doubling" ten-year plan in 1960. However, the announcement effect would have depended not so much on the contents of the plans as on the government's political will, expressed in the plan, to give a top priority to industrial growth. It is sometimes argued that indicative planning would promote growth by reducing uncertainty and business risks through information exchanges. But apparently this has not been the case in Japan, as earlier national economic plans persistently underestimated both the growth rate and structural changes substantially, and therefore one cannot say that uncertainty was reduced much by economic planning.

The Income Doubling Plan was much publicized by the then Prime Minister Ikeda, and probably carried a considerable propaganda effect. It looked more or less plausible and prompted private firms to invest more boldly than before. For some time after its publication, it became fashionable among larger companies to publish their own overall long-term management plan for a five- or ten-year period. When making companies' plans, the national or sectoral rate of growth was taken for granted, so to speak, and each company added a plus factor to the industry average rate of growth, hoping for an increasing market share for itself. But here again in practice few companies paid much attention to their long-term plan in making actual investment decisions, since most such plans turned out to underestimate growth potentials. Shortly afterwards, long-term management planning went out of fashion.

Thus the Income Doubling Plan may be said to have had a considerable impact on Japan's growth in the early 1960s. However, what was important was not so much the contents of the national plans as the political will to promote industrial growth. Even without national plans, if the government would have made clear its willingness to promote growth, and fiscal, monetary, and industrial policy measures for that purpose, almost the same effect would have been obtained. The situation would then have been similar to West Germany in postwar years.

Japan's national economic plan thus amounts to little more than a long-run forecast. Yet this does not mean that the Japanese economy is an overwhelmingly free market economy run without much governmental planning. In fact, the government intervenes extensively in particular industries and markets, but governmental planning or policy is primarily organized on an industry or sectoral basis.

*   *   *   *   *

INDUSTRIAL POLICIES[10]

It is perhaps well known that the Japanese government has developed an elaborate system of industrial policies to promote industrial development, intervenes in industries and markets extensively, and cooperates closely with private firms. But how decisionmaking on industrial policies is or-

---

[10] This section is an elaboration of a section in the author's earlier study, "Japan and the World Economy," in *Toward a New World Trade Policy: The Maidenhead Papers*, ed. C. Fred Bergsten (Lexington, Mass.: D. C. Heath and Co., 1975).

ganized, what kinds of policy measures are used, and what the real contents of industrial policies are, seem to be little known outside of Japan. Even in Japan the overall system of industrial policies has rarely been explicitly explained, and matters which are common sense for insiders are often little known to the general public (including academics), although fragmentary information is abundantly reported in newspapers from time to time. It is therefore quite difficult to describe the system. This section attempts to give a general idea of the system of industrial policies in postwar Japan.

The term "industrial policy" as used here refers to government policy undertaken to change the allocation of resources among industries, or the levels of certain productive activities of private enterprises in individual industries, from what they would be in the absence of such a policy. An industrial policy is concerned with encouraging production, investment, research and development, modernization and reorganization in certain industries, and discouraging such activities in others. Protective tariffs and excise taxes on luxuries are "classic" examples of the measures of industrial policies so defined.

The system of industrial policies has been steadily changing in postwar Japan. Especially in the last few years it has been undergoing a rapid change. The following describes the state of affairs predominant in the 1960s.

The Process of Policymaking

Generally speaking the National Diet does not fulfill its formal function in formulating industrial policies. The parties in opposition to the government are not much interested in industrial policies, apart from their overall accusation about the government's "preoccupation with production to the neglect of civil welfare," or the government's collaboration with "monopoly capitalists." Almost any bill prepared and presented by the government (administration) is approved by the Diet, so that the real policy decision is made within the government, or jointly by the government and the industry.

The principal entities which exert important influence in the process of industrial policy making are: (a) the government's *genkyoku* offices and (b) its coordinating offices and, on the side of the private sector, (c) industry associations and (d) councils. Also, (e) the *Zaikai* (the central businessmen's circle)[11] and (f) banks supplying funds to the industry may have some influence on industrial policies. Usually no one entity has an overwhelming influence, and the game of industrial policy making is played

---

[11] An informal, not too well-defined group of top-ranking, well-informed businessmen, who meet and consult with each other quite often and act as the spokesmen of the big business community. Most of them occupy prominent positions in formal business organizations.

primarily through mutual persuasion, coordination, and sometimes threats. If one group can persuade others concerned that a certain policy is desirable for the national economy or for the industry—very often these two are intentionally mixed—it will succeed in putting the policy into effect.

The Genkyoku *and Coordinating Offices.* One of the notable characteristics of industrial policy making in Japan is an important role played by the government offices generally called *genkyoku*. The word *genkyoku* may be literally translated as an "original bureau" or an "original government office," meaning the government office having the primary responsibility for the industry in question.

To each industry there corresponds a *genkyoku*, which supervises the industry, and is responsible for policies toward the industry. Quite a few capable and dedicated government officials in the *genkyoku* work on the policy problems of that particular industry.

MITI is the largest *genkyoku* ministry and is subdivided into smaller *genkyoku* offices. As of 1970, five of MITI's nine "bureaus" were *genkyoku* bureaus: namely, the Bureau of Heavy Industries, Bureau of Chemical Industries, Bureau of Textiles and Sundries,[12] Bureau of Coal and Other Mining, and Bureau of Public Utilities. These bureaus are further divided into divisions, most of which are *genkyoku* divisions in charge of particular subdivisions of industries. For example, the Bureau of Heavy Industries has divisions of iron and steel, industrial machinery, electronics, automobiles, aircraft, rolling stock, and several others.

Not all bureaus of MITI are *genkyoku* bureaus, which are sometimes called "vertical divisions." Again as of 1970, MITI's "horizontal division" bureaus were: the Bureau of International Trade, Bureau of Trade Development, Bureau of Enterprises, and Bureau of Pollution and Safety. These "horizontal division" bureaus and the Minister's Secretariat (*Kambō*) often have their own policy ideas and take leadership. They also act as coordinators and mediators within MITI.[13]

MITI is not the only *genkyoku* ministry supervising manufacturing industries. Besides agriculture, the Ministry of Agriculture supervises the forestry, fishing, food processing, and nonalcoholic beverage industries. The pharmaceutical industry is under the Ministry of Welfare, and shipbuilding (not only shipping) is under the Ministry of Transportation. The Ministry of Finance is naturally the *genkyoku* for banking, security dealers, and insurance, but it also supervises the alcoholic beverage industry.

A *genkyoku* office is responsible for policy planning related to the industries which it supervises. First, special laws concerning particular industries

---

[12] "Sundries" refers to household goods produced by more or less labor-intensive, small-business light manufacturing industries, such as footwear, leather goods, stationery, and most items sold in variety stores.

[13] MITI underwent an extensive reorganization in 1973. See fn. 14 below.

—such as the "Petroleum Industry Act" (1962), the "Law on Temporary Measures for Promoting Machinery Industries" (1956), a similar law for electronics industries (1957), and another for textile industries (1967)— are prepared and administered primarily by the *genkyoku* offices. Second, the plans for (1) special tax incentives given to particular industries, (2) changes in tariff rates, (3) policy on import liberalization, and (4) policy on liberalization of foreign (inward) direct investment are first prepared by the *genkyoku* offices. Third, authorization of (5) individual patent and know-how contracts, (6) joint ventures between foreign and Japanese companies—most of which have been subject to screening and authorization case by case until recently—and (7) new productive facilities—where such authorization is mandatory as in petroleum refining, shipbuilding or electric power supply—rests primarily with the *genkyoku* office. Fourth, on the allocation of low-interest funds from government financial institutions, especially the Japan Development Bank, the *genkyoku* office and the Ministry concerned have an almost decisive voice.

The policy on (1) through (6) above prepared by the specific *genkyoku* office is discussed and coordinated first at the ministry level, and then goes to the Ministry of Finance. On (1), the Bureau of Tax; on (2) and (3) the Bureau of Tariffs; and on (4), (5) and (6) the Bureau of International Finance—all of the Ministry of Finance—have final responsibility within the government, and exercise some coordinating function. But it is often difficult for Ministry of Finance officials to change what has been decided and requested by the respective ministries.

The Fair Trade Commission is in charge of antitrust policy, and is another important government agency in the process of industrial policy making. In the 1950s it was largely neglected, but during the 1960s its relative strength within the government rose substantially.

Industry Associations. The industry associations such as the Japan Iron and Steel Federation, Japan Automobile Industry Association, Japan Shipbuilding Industry Association, and hundreds of similar and often subdivided associations are counterparts of the respective *genkyoku* offices. Usually the industry association collaborates closely with the *genkyoku* in charge of the industry, but the relation between them varies from one industry to another. From the industry's point of view, or from the point of view of its leading firms, whose presidents or chairmen alternate as the president of the association, the chief function of the industry association is to persuade the *genkyoku* to take measures favorable to the industry. From the *genkyoku's* point of view, the industry association and its members should cooperate with the *genkyoku* in the latter's execution of industrial policies, and persuade disobedient or dissident members. Sometimes, however, an industry association has diversified opinions, or the *genkyoku* office and the industry may be opposed to each other. In industries dominated by small business, firms in the industry may not be able to organize an association by themselves and may ask the help of the *genkyoku* office to organize one. Typically the industry association and the *genkyoku* spend much time negotiating with, and trying to persuade, each other to reach a satisfactory solution to the industry's problem.

Councils. Just as the Economic Council reports to the prime minister on national economic planning, there are many councils which report to each minister on specific problems. In the case of MITI, as of 1970 there were 27 councils and investigation committees composed of members from outside the government which advised the minister on specific issues. Fifteen of them were to report on problems of industrial policies: Council on Industrial Structure, on industrial policies in general; and Councils on Machinery Industries, Petroleum, Mining, Coal Mining, Promotion of Electronic Data Processing, Technologies in Light Industries, Industrial Location and Water Supply, and various others, on policies in their respective fields.

The nature and role of these councils, the composition of their membership, their deliberation procedures, and the role of the secretariat are more or less similar to those of the Economic Council, and therefore need not be discussed here.

Industrial Policies and the National Economic Plan

Not only on industrial policies but also on other important policy issues there are councils reporting to the minister in charge, and the national economic plan reflects the opinions of these councils to the extent that they have already reached conclusions acceptable to government officials. The national economic plan is, for one thing, a compilation of such opinions, as noted in the first section above. But it often happens that councils reporting to various ministers are still discussing their assigned problems when the national economic plan is drafted. Then the statement in the national plan on such problems can hardly be anything but obscure and elusive.

Thus to some extent the national economic plan reflects industrial policies in individual fields. On the other hand, when making decisions on industrial policies, ministries and councils take into account the growth rate and other macroeconomic and sectoral planning indices, as well as the order of policy priority expressed in the plan. Especially in the year in which a new national economic plan is published, the national plan is referred to when *genkyoku* ministries negotiate with the Ministry of Finance on budgetary appropriations. However, the national plan is in no way binding on the government, as explained in the first section, and is referred to primarily as a sort of official forecast. Since the plan has tended to underestimate the growth rate as well as structural changes, if ministries stuck too much to macroeconomic and sectoral indices in the national plans, they would have ended up with insufficient appropriations. The national economic plan has been considered, therefore, as no more than a long- or medium-term forecast when ministries make annual decisions on and execute industrial policies.

*   *   *   *   *

CONCLUDING REMARKS

Japan's medium- or long-term national economic plans prepared and published by the Economic Planning Agency should be viewed primarily as a sort of official forecast, accompanied by a collection of current opinions on certain policy issues. They have not been intended as a plan to be followed more or less faithfully by the government in making annual or day-to-day decisions on matters of fiscal, monetary, industrial, or other economic policies.

The nationwide "Comprehensive" regional plans of 1962 and 1969 are also more a forecast than a plan in the usual sense of the term. The 1969 Comprehensive Development Plan gives estimates for regional distribution of population and income in 1985, and lists all kinds of measures considered desirable from the viewpoint of each region's development, but it includes little if any attempt at implementation, and the quantitative estimates and policy measures in the Plan remain unrelated to each other. Also, the contents and planning process of the "Comprehensive" regional plans are largely unrelated to those of the national economic plans, although they are published by the same government agency—the Economic Planning Agency (but by different bureaus in it).

Both national economic plans and the "Comprehensive" regional plans are referred to and taken into consideration by government ministries, agencies, and local governments, as well as by private firms and industry associations, when they make their own plans and decisions. But nobody feels obligated to observe these plans. They consider these plans primarily forecasts as reliable or unreliable as a long-term weather forecast. The fact that national plans underestimated substantially both growth rates and structural changes in the past and had to be replaced within two or three years after their announcement, in spite of their official coverage of five to ten years, limited the usefulness and the prestige of these plans as long-term forecasts. But, in an economy like postwar Japan's, which has been undergoing rapid growth and structural change, on the one hand, and is heavily dependent upon international economic relations and therefore subject to external disturbances, on the other, the task of economic forecasting is admittedly a very difficult one.

Since Japan's national economic plan is primarily a forecast, asking about its effects upon economic growth is like asking about the effects of weather forecasting upon agricultural production. A forecast, whether economic or meteorological, must be useful to the extent that it predicts the future accurately. In the case of Japan, however, the additional advantage of having a central economic plan—beyond what is done by research organizations, individual government ministries, and private firms—seems to have been relatively small, since the forecasts given in national economic plans cannot be said to have been much superior to those by others, especially in earlier years.

It must not be thought from the above, however, that the postwar Japanese economy is predominantly a free enterprise, market economy run without much governmental planning or intervention. Much planning and intervention are conducted at sectoral levels. The Ministry of International Trade and Industry, other ministries, and their subdivisions, acting as *genkyoku* offices having supervisory and planning responsibilities over individual industries, intervene extensively in their respective areas of administrative jurisdiction. Industrial policies planned and administered by them appear to have been quite effective in channeling resources into particular industries or sectors. Also, some of the central government's regional programs—which give grants-in-aid, low-interest loans, tax-incentives, and priority for social overhead investment to local governments and certain private firms in particular regions—must have been effective at least to some extent in reallocating population and industries among regions.

*　*　*　*　*

Although the interest of the general public in the Japanese government's national economic plan has been declining gradually, the government is likely to continue to prepare and publish a medium-term national economic plan once every two or three years. In fact, it was reported in the press that in view of the impact of the recent oil crisis on the Japanese economy the Economic Planning Agency is now contemplating the revision of the Basic Economic and Social Plan, and has made a "trial" calculation of the likely effects of the oil crisis on Japan's rate of economic growth and other macroeconomic indices. Since the national economic plan appears to many people to be helpful as a sort of official forecast, and since the plan-making process is a useful ground for information exchange and communication, there is no prospect of a substantial change in the present institutional set-up of plan making in the near future.

The medium-term national economic plan will be viewed more and more as a forecast rather than a plan in the usual sense of the term. But any attempt to change the name from the "national economic plan" to, say, the "national economic projection" or "forecast" will be strongly resisted by "plan" makers in EPA. Such a change would be considered by the "plan"-making officials as degrading the importance of their work.

The public interest in regional planning is increasing in Japan. This is

because of excessive congestion and pollution problems in heavily industrialized and overpopulated areas, the increasing disparity in income levels
between the industrialized center and the predominantly agricultural
periphery, and the resulting large outflow of population from peripheral
regions. Whether or not Prime Minister Tanaka's ambitious "Remodeling
the Japanese Islands" program is successfully enacted into new legislation,
the government's already extensive intervention and planning in the process
of regional allocation of industries and population will be intensified in the
future.

On the other hand, in the last few years the Japanese government has
been dismantling and reorganizing its elaborate system of industrial policies. It has been in the process of disengagement from excessively protective and overly paternalistic policies. At the request of foreign governments, especially the United States, to liberalize tight controls in various
spheres of the economy, since around 1969 the Japanese government has
moved to abolish or reduce considerably quantitative import restrictions
and direct controls on patent and know-how contracts and foreign direct
investment in Japan. Toward the end of the 1960s Japan's trade balance
showed large surpluses. Many Japanese industries, well protected and given
various forms of assistance under the elaborate system of industrial policies,
have already become full-fledged export industries acquiring increasingly
larger shares in the markets of industrialized countries. Environmental pollution and disruption caused by industry became very serious in many regions of Japan. All this led to a sudden but belated change in the order of
priority among policy objectives. Industrial development can no longer be
the primary objective of industrial policies. Prevention of pollution and
disruption of human life, consumer's interests, harmonious international
economic relations, and price stability are now considered as important
policy objectives in preference to industrial development and technological
progress.[14]

---

[14] An extensive reorganization of MITI in April 1973, symbolizes the changing objectives of industrial policies. The number and the relative importance of vertical *genkyoku*
bureaus and divisions were substantially diminished and those of horizontal ones were
increased. Now only three out of eight bureaus of MITI are vertical *genkyoku* bureaus,
as compared with six out of ten in 1965.

part III

Socialist Market Economy

Market socialism seeks to combine the socialist principles of (1) collective ownership and (2) limited inequality in income distribution with (3) the use of markets and prices to allocate resources and goods. However, around this central core there are various possible schemes of economic organization, differing in the combination of planners' and consumers' sovereignty, the method of price formation, the nature of enterprise management, and so forth.

The first blueprints for market socialism originated in response to the argument of some prominent economists in the 1920s that rational economic calculation and thus efficient allocation of resources were in principle impossible in a socialist economy. The most famous member of this school was Ludwig von Mises, whose views are summarized in Selection 8.

To refute this conclusion, Oskar Lange developed the model of market socialism presented in Selection 9, and later modified somewhat in Selection 10. In his model, the prices of consumer goods and labor services are determined by market forces, while a Central Planning Board attempts by trial and error to fix prices for producer goods which equate supply and demand. (In another variant, proposed by Abba Lerner and others, the prices of producer goods are determined directly by the interplay of the supply and demand of socialist firms in a market for capital goods.) Given these "parametric" prices and some very broad rules, state-appointed enterprise managers decide the outputs and inputs of their firms.

In contrast, in the "participatory" version of market

socialism, each firm is managed by its workers. Selection 11 sketches a model of such an economy, which is then evaluated from various standpoints in Selection 12. Selection 13 examines the operation of such a socialist market economy, with worker management of firms, in Yugoslavia.

8

ECONOMIC CALCULATION IN SOCIALISM*

Ludwig von Mises

Mises denies the possibility of economic calculation and rational resource allocation in socialism. He argues that economic calculation can take place only by means of money prices established in a market for producer goods resting on private ownership of the means of production. Because such markets cannot, by definition, exist in socialism, he concludes that a socialist economy cannot achieve efficient allocation of resources. "Artificial" markets in socialism cannot successfully replace the true markets of capitalism in pricing producer goods so as to use them most effectively.

Without calculation, economic activity is impossible. Since under Socialism economic calculation is impossible, under Socialism there can be no economic activity in our sense of the word. In small and insignificant things rational action might still persist. But, for the most part, it would no longer be possible to speak of rational production. In the absence of criteria of rationality, production could not be consciously economical.

For some time possibly the accumulated tradition of thousands of years of economic freedom would preserve the art of economic administration from complete disintegration. Men would preserve the old processes not because they were rational, but because they were sanctified by tradition.

---
* Reprinted from *Socialism: An Economic and Sociological Analysis,* translated from the German by Jacques Kahane (London: Jonathan Cape Limited, 1936; 2d ed.: New Haven, Conn.: Yale University Press, 1951), pp. 119–22, 137–42, by permission of Jonathan Cape Limited and the Executors of the Ludwig von Mises Estate. This volume is an expanded translation of *Die Gemeinwirtschaft,* originally published in 1922. Ludwig von Mises was Professor of Economics at the University of Vienna and New York University.

In the meantime, however, changing conditions would make them irrational. They would become uneconomical as the result of changes brought about by the general decline of economic thought. It is true that production would no longer be "anarchical." The command of a supreme authority would govern the business of supply. Instead of the economy of "anarchical" production the senseless order of an irrational machine would be supreme. The wheels would go round, but to no effect.

Let us try to imagine the position of a socialist community. There will be hundreds and thousands of establishments in which work is going on. A minority of these will produce goods ready for use. The majority will produce capital goods and semimanufactures. All these establishments will be closely connected. Each commodity produced will pass through a whole series of such establishments before it is ready for consumption. Yet in the incessant press of all these processes the economic administration will have no real sense of direction. It will have no means of ascertaining whether a given piece of work is really necessary, whether labor and material are not being wasted in completing it. How would it discover which of two processes was the more satisfactory? At best, it could compare the quantity of ultimate products. But only rarely could it compare the expenditure incurred in their production. It would know exactly—or it would imagine it knew—what it wanted to produce. It ought therefore to set about obtaining the desired results with the smallest possible expenditure. But to do this it would have to be able to make calculations. And such calculations must be calculations of value. They could not be merely "technical"; they could not be calculations of the objective use-value of goods and services. This is so obvious that it needs no further demonstration.

Under a system based upon private ownership in the means of production, the scale of values is the outcome of the actions of every independent member of society. Everyone plays a two-fold part in its establishment, first as a consumer, secondly as producer. As consumer, he establishes the valuation of goods ready for consumption. As producer, he guides production-goods into those uses in which they yield the highest product. In this way all goods of higher orders[1] also are graded in the way appropriate to them under the existing conditions of production and the demands of society. The interplay of these two processes ensures that the economic principle is observed in both consumption and production. And, in this way, arises the exactly graded system of prices which enables everyone to frame his demand on economic lines.

Under Socialism, all this must necessarily be lacking. The economic administration may indeed know exactly what commodities are needed most urgently. But this is only half the problem. The other half, the

---

[1] Editor's note: Producer goods.

valuation of the means of production, it cannot solve. It can ascertain the value of the totality of such instruments. That is obviously equal to the value of the satisfactions they afford. If it calculates the loss that would be incurred by withdrawing them, it can also ascertain the value of single instruments of production. But it cannot assimilate them to a common price denominator, as can be done under a system of economic freedom and money prices.

It is not necessary that Socialism should dispense altogether with money. It is possible to conceive arrangements permitting the use of money for the exchange of consumers goods. But since the prices of the various factors of production (including labor) could not be expressed in money, money could play no part in economic calculations.

Suppose, for instance, that the socialist commonwealth was contemplating a new railway line. Would a new railway line be a good thing? If so, which of many possible routes should it cover? Under a system of private ownership we could use money calculations to decide these questions. The new line would cheapen the transportation of certain articles, and, on this basis, we could estimate whether the reduction in transport charges would be great enough to counterweigh the expenditure which the building and running of the line would involve. Such a calculation could be made only in money. We could not do it by comparing various classes of expenditure and savings in kind. If it is out of the question to reduce to a common unit the quantities of various kinds of skilled and unskilled labor, iron, coal, building materials of different kinds, machinery and the other things which the building and upkeep of railways necessitate, then it is impossible to make them the subject of economic calculation. We can make systematic economic plans only when all the commodities which we have to take into account can be assimilated to money. True, money calculations are incomplete. True, they have profound deficiencies. But we have nothing better to put in their place. And under sound monetary conditions they suffice for practical purposes. If we abandon them, economic calculation becomes absolutely impossible.

This is not to say that the socialist community would be entirely at a loss. It would decide for or against the proposed undertaking and issue an edict. But, at best, such a decision would be based on vague valuations. It could not be based on exact calculations of value.

A stationary society could, indeed, dispense with these calculations. For there, economic operations merely repeat themselves. So that, if we assume that the socialist system of production were based upon the last state of the system of economic freedom which it superseded, and that no changes were to take place in the future, we could indeed conceive a rational and economic Socialism. But only in theory. A stationary economic system can never exist. Things are continually changing, and the stationary state, although necessary as an aid to speculation, is a theoretical assumption to which there is no counterpart in reality. And, quite apart from this, the maintenance of such a connection with the last state of the exchange economy would be out of the question, since the transition to Socialism with its equalization of incomes would necessarily transform the whole "set" of consumption and production. And then we have a socialist community which must cross the whole ocean of possible and imaginable economic permutations without the compass of economic calculation.

All economic change, therefore, would involve operations the value of which could neither be predicted beforehand nor ascertained after they had taken place. Everything would be a leap in the dark. Socialism is the renunciation of rational economy.

*　　*　　*　　*　　*

Some of the younger socialists believe that the socialist community could solve the problem of economic calculation by the creation of an artificial market for the means of production. They admit that it was an error on the part of the older socialists to have sought to realize Socialism through the suspension of the market and the abolition of pricing for goods of higher orders; they hold that it was an error to have seen in the suppression of the market and of the price system the essence of the socialistic ideal. And they contend that if it is not to degenerate into a meaningless chaos in which the whole of our civilization would disappear, the socialist community, equally with the capitalistic community, must create a market in which all goods and services may be priced. On the basis of such arrangements, they think, the socialist community will be able to make its calculations as easily as the capitalist entrepreneurs.

Unfortunately the supporters of such proposals do not see (or perhaps *will* not see) that it is not possible to divorce the market and its functions in regard to the formation of prices from the working of a society which is based on private property in the means of production and in which, subject to the rules of such a society, the landlords, capitalists, and entrepreneurs can dispose of their property as they think fit. For the motive force of the whole process which gives rise to market prices for the factors of production is the ceaseless search on the part of the capitalists and the entrepreneurs to maximize their profits by serving the consumers' wishes. Without the striving of the entrepreneurs (including the shareholders) for profit, of the landlords for rent, of the capitalists for interest and the laborers for wages, the successful functioning of the whole mechanism is not to be thought of. It is only the prospect of profit which directs production into those channels in which the demands of the consumer are best satisfied at least cost. If the prospect of profit disappears the mechanism of the market loses its mainspring, for it is only this prospect which sets it in motion and maintains it in operation. The market is thus the focal point of the capitalist order of society; it is the essence of Capitalism. Only under Capitalism, therefore, is it possible; it cannot be "artificially" imitated under Socialism.

The advocates of the artificial market, however, are of the opinion that an artificial market can be created by instructing the controllers of the different industrial units to act *as if* they were entrepreneurs in a capitalistic state. They argue that even under Capitalism the managers of joint stock companies work not for themselves but for the companies, that is to say, for the shareholders. Under Socialism, therefore, it would be possible for them to act in exactly the same way as before, with the same circumspection and devotion to duty. The only difference would be that under Socialism the product of the manager's labors would go to the community rather than to the shareholders. In such a way, in contrast to all socialists who have written on the subject hitherto, especially the Marxians, they think it would be possible to construct a decentralized, as opposed to a centralized, Socialism.

In order to judge properly such proposals, it is necessary in the first place to realize that these controllers of individual industrial units would have to be appointed. Under Capitalism the managers of the joint stock companies are appointed either directly or indirectly by the shareholders. In so far as the shareholders give to the managers power to produce by the means of the company's (i.e., the stockholders') stock they are risking their own property or a part of their own property. The speculation (for it is necessarily a speculation) may succeed and bring profit; it may, however, misfire and bring about the loss of the whole or a part of the capital concerned. This committing of one's own capital to a business whose outcome is uncertain and to men whose future ability is still a matter of conjecture whatever one may know of their past, is the essence of joint stock company enterprise.

Now it is a complete fallacy to suppose that the problem of economic calculation in a socialist community relates solely to matters which fall into the sphere of the daily business routine of managers of joint stock companies. It is clear that such a belief can only arise from exclusive concentration on the idea of a stationary economic system—a conception which no doubt is useful for the solution of many theoretical problems but which has no counterpart in fact and which, if exclusively regarded, can even be positively misleading. It is clear that under stationary conditions the problem of economic calculation does not really arise. When we think of the stationary society, we think of an economy in which all the factors of production are already used in such a way as, under the given conditions, to provide the maximum of the things which are demanded by consumers. That is to say, under stationary conditions there no longer exists a problem for economic calculation to solve. The essential function of economic calculation has *by hypothesis* already been performed. There is no need for an apparatus of calculation. To use a popular but not altogether satisfactory terminology we can say that the problem of economic calculation is of economic dynamics: it is no problem of economic statics.

The problem of economic calculation is a problem which arises in an economy which is perpetually subject to change, an economy which every day is confronted with new problems which have to be solved. Now in order to solve such problems it is above all necessary that capital should be withdrawn from particular lines of production, from particular undertakings and concerns and should be applied in other lines of production, in other undertakings and concerns. This is not a matter for the managers of joint stock companies; it is essentially a matter for the capitalists—the capitalists who buy and sell stocks and shares, who make loans and recover them, who make deposits in the banks and draw them out of the banks again, who speculate in all kinds of commodities. It is these operations of speculative capitalists which create those conditions of the money market, the stock exchanges and the wholesale markets which have to be taken for granted by the manager of the joint stock company, who, according to the socialist writers we are considering, is to be conceived as nothing but the reliable and conscientious servant of the company. It is the speculative capitalists who create the data to which he has to adjust his business and which therefore give direction to his trading operations.

It follows therefore that it is a fundamental deficiency of all these socialistic constructions which invoke the "artificial market" and artificial competition as a way out of the problem of economic calculation, that they rest on the belief that the market for factors of production is affected only by producers buying and selling commodities. It is not possible to eliminate from such markets the influence of the supply of capital from the capitalists and the demand for capital by the entrepreneurs, without destroying the mechanism itself.

Faced with this difficulty, the socialist is likely to propose that the socialist state as owner of all capital and all means of production should simply direct capital to those undertakings which promise the highest return. The available capital, he will contend, should go to those undertakings which offer the highest rate of profit. But such a state of affairs would simply mean that those managers who were less cautious and more optimistic would receive capital to enlarge their undertakings while more cautious and more sceptical managers would go away empty-handed. Under Capitalism, the capitalist decides to whom he will entrust *his own* capital. The beliefs of the managers of joint stock companies regarding the future prospects of their undertakings and the hopes of project makers regarding the profitability of their plans are not in any way decisive. The mechanism of the money market and the capital market decides. This indeed is its main task: to serve the economic system as a whole, to judge the profitability of alternative openings and not blindly to follow what the managers of particular concerns, limited by the narrow horizon of their own undertakings, are tempted to propose.

To understand this completely, it is essential to realize that the capitalist does not just invest his capital in those undertakings which offer high interest or high profit; he attempts rather to strike a balance between his desire for profit and his estimate of the risk of loss. He must exercise foresight. If he does not do so then he suffers losses—losses that bring it about that his disposition over the factors of production is transferred to the hands of others who know better how to weigh the risks and the prospects of business speculation.

Now if it is to remain socialistic, the socialist State cannot leave to other hands that disposition over capital which permits the enlargement of existing undertakings, the contraction of others and the bringing into being of undertakings that are completely new. And it is scarcely to be assumed that socialists of whatever persuasion would seriously propose that this function should be made over to some group of people who would "simply" have the business of doing what capitalists and speculators do under capitalistic conditions, the only difference being that the product of their foresight should not belong to them but to the community. Proposals of this sort may well be made concerning the managers of joint stock companies. They can never be extended to capitalists and speculators, for no socialist would dispute that the function which capitalists and speculators perform under Capitalism, namely directing the use of capital goods into that direction in which they best serve the demands of the consumer, is only performed because they are under the incentive to preserve their property and to make profits which increase it or at least allow them to live without diminishing their capital.

It follows therefore that the socialist community can do nothing but place the disposition over capital in the hands of the State or to be exact in the hands of the men who, as the governing authority, carry out the business of the State. And that signifies elimination of the market, which indeed is the fundamental aim of Socialism, for the guidance of economic activity by the market implies organization of production and a distribution of the product according to that disposition of the spending power of individual members of society which makes itself felt on the market; that is to say, it implies precisely that which it is the goal of socialism to eliminate.

If the socialists attempt to belittle the significance of the problem of economic calculation in the Socialist community, on the ground that the forces of the market do not lead to ethically justifiable arrangements, they simply show that they do not understand the real nature of the problem. It is not a question of whether there shall be produced cannons or clothes, dwelling houses or churches, luxuries or subsistence. In any social order, even under Socialism, it can very easily be decided which kind and what number of consumption goods should be produced. No one has ever denied that. But once this decision has been made, there still remains the problem of ascertaining how the existing means of production can be used most effectively to produce these goods in question. In order to solve this problem it is necessary that there should be economic calculation. And economic calculation can only take place by means of money prices established in the market for production goods in a society resting on private property in the means of production. That is to say, there must exist money prices of land, raw materials, semimanufactures; that is to say, there must be money wages and interest rates.

Thus the alternative is still *either* Socialism or a market economy.

9

ON THE ECONOMIC THEORY
OF SOCIALISM*

Oskar Lange

In Lange's model of market socialism, households, the Central
Planning Board (CPB), and socialist managers share in the decisions
which guide the economy. Consumer preferences, expressed in a
market for consumer goods, decide the goods to be produced. Prices
of consumer goods and labor services are determined by the interplay in the market of the supply and demand of households and
socialist firms. The CPB, by trial and error, sets the prices of producer goods so as to equate the supply and demand for each good.
Given these "parametric" prices, the managers of socialist enterprises
and industries determine their inputs and outputs according to two
broad rules. First, they must combine factors of production so as to
minimize the average cost of production for any output. Second,
they must fix output at the level where marginal cost equals the
price. In combination, these two rules secure the most economical
production of the optimum output.

The CPB distributes a social dividend to households which reduces the inequality of income resulting from market-determined
wages. It also decides the rate of investment and then sets an interest
rate on capital which equates the demand for capital, on the part of
socialist managers, to the amount available.

* From Oskar Lange and Fred M. Taylor, *On the Economic Theory of Socialism*,
ed. Benjamin E. Lippincott (Minneapolis: University of Minnesota Press, 1938), pp.
72–86. © 1938 University of Minnesota, 1966 B. E. Lippincott. Originally published
in *Review of Economic Studies*, vol. 4, no. 1 (October 1936), pp. 60–66. Reprinted
with the permission of the *Review of Economic Studies* and the University of Minnesota Press. Oskar Lange was Professor of Economics at the University of Chicago and
Professor of Political Economy at Warsaw University.

In order to discuss the method of allocating resources in a socialist economy we have to state what kind of socialist society we have in mind. The fact of public ownership of the means of production does not in itself determine the system of distributing consumers' goods and of allocating people to various occupations, nor the principles guiding the production of commodities. Let us now assume that freedom of choice in consumption and freedom of choice of occupation are maintained and that the preferences of consumers, as expressed by their demand prices, are the guiding criteria in production and in the allocation of resources. . . .

In the socialist system as described we have a genuine market (in the institutional sense of the word) for consumers' goods and for the services of labor. But there is no market for capital goods and productive resources outside of labor.[1] The prices of capital goods and productive resources outside of labor are thus prices in the generalized sense, i.e., mere indices of alternatives available, fixed for accounting purposes. Let us see how economic equilibrium is determined in such a system. Just as in a competitive individualist regime, the determination of equilibrium consists of two parts. (A) On the basis of *given* indices of alternatives (which are market prices in the case of consumers' goods and the services of labor and accounting prices in all other cases) both the individuals participating in the economic system as consumers and as owners of the services of labor and the managers of production and of the ultimate resources outside of labor (i.e., of capital and of natural resources) make decisions according to certain principles. These managers are assumed to be public officials. (B) The prices (whether market or accounting) are determined by the condition that the quantity of each commodity demanded is equal to the quantity supplied. The conditions determining the decisions under A form the *subjective*, while that under B is the *objective*, equilibrium condition. Finally, we have also a condition C, expressing the social organization of the economic system. As the productive resources outside of labor are public property, the incomes of the consumers are divorced from the ownership of those resources and the form of condition C (social organization) is determined by the *principles of income formation adopted.*

The possibility of determining condition C in different ways gives to a socialist society considerable freedom in matters of distribution of income. But the necessity of maintaining freedom in the choice of occupation limits the arbitrary use of this freedom, for there must be some connection between the income of a consumer and the services of labor performed by him. It seems, therefore, convenient to regard the income of consumers as composed of two parts: one part being the receipts for the labor services

---

[1] To simplify the problem we assume that all means of production are public property. Needless to say, in any actual socialist community there must be a large number of means of production privately owned (e.g., by farmers, artisans, and small-scale entrepreneurs). But this does not introduce any new theoretical problem.

performed and the other part being a social dividend constituting the individual's share in the income derived from the capital and the natural resources owned by society. We assume that the distribution of the social dividend is based on certain principles, reserving the content of those principles for later discussion. Thus condition C is determinate and determines the incomes of the consumers in terms of prices of the services of labor and social dividend, which, in turn, may be regarded as determined by the total yield of capital and of the natural resources and by the principles adopted in distributing this yield.[2]

A. Let us consider the subjective equilibrium condition in a socialist economy:

1. Freedom of choice in consumption being assumed,[3] this part of the subjective equilibrium condition of a competitive market applies also to the market for consumers' goods in a socialist economy. The incomes of the consumers and the prices of consumers' goods being given, the demand for consumers' goods is determined.

2. The decisions of the managers of production are no longer guided by the aim of maximizing profit. Instead, certain rules are imposed on them by the Central Planning Board which aim at satisfying consumers' preferences in the best way possible. These rules determine the combination of factors of production and the scale of output.

One rule must impose the choice of the combination of factors which minimizes the average cost of production. This rule leads to the factors being combined in such proportion that the marginal productivity of that amount of each factor which is worth a unit of money is the same for all factors. This rule is addressed to whoever makes decisions involving the problem of the optimum combination of factors, i.e., to managers responsible for running existing plants and to those engaged in building new plants. A second rule determines the scale of output by stating that output has to be fixed so that marginal cost is equal to the price of the product. This rule is addressed to two kinds of persons. First of all, it is addressed to the managers of plants and thus determines the scale of output of each plant and, together with the first rule, its demand for factors of produc-

---

[2] In formulating condition C capital accumulation has to be taken into account. Capital accumulation may be done either "corporately" by deducting a certain part of the national income before the social dividend is distributed, or it may be left to the savings of individuals, or both methods may be combined. But "corporate" accumulation must certainly be the dominant form of capital formation in a socialist economy.

[3] Of course there may be also a sector of socialized consumption the cost of which is met by taxation. Such a sector exists also in capitalist society and comprises the provision not only of collective wants, in Cassel's sense, but also of other wants whose social importance is too great to be left to the free choice of individuals (for instance, free hospital service and free education). But this problem does not represent any theoretical difficulty and we may disregard it. [Editor's note: Gustav Cassel, 1866–1945, was a Swedish economic theorist whose writings included *The Theory of Social Economy* (1st German ed., 1918; English trans. 1923).]

tion. The first rule, to whomever addressed, and the second rule when addressed to the managers of plants perform the same function that in a competitive system is carried out by the private producer's aiming to maximize his profit, when the prices of factors and of the product are independent of the amount of each factor used by him and of his scale of output.

The total output of an industry has yet to be determined. This is done by addressing the second rule also to the managers of a whole industry (e.g., to the directors of the National Coal Trust) as a principle to guide them in deciding whether an industry ought to be expanded (by building new plants or enlarging old ones) or contracted (by not replacing plants which are wearing out). Thus each industry has to produce exactly as much of a commodity as can be sold or "accounted for" to other industries at a price which equals the marginal cost incurred *by the industry* in producing this amount. The marginal cost incurred by an industry is the cost to that industry (not to a particular plant) of doing whatever is necessary to produce an additional unit of output, the optimum combination of factors being used. This may include the cost of building new plants or enlarging old ones.[4]

Addressed to the managers of an industry, the second rule performs the function which under free competition is carried out by the free entry of firms into an industry or their exodus from it: i.e., it determines the output of an industry.[5] The second rule, however, has to be carried out irrespective of whether average cost is covered or not, even if it should involve plants or whole industries in losses.

Both rules can be put in the form of the simple request to use always the method of production (i.e., combination of factors) which minimizes

---

[4] Since in practice such marginal cost is not a continuous function of output we have to compare the cost of each additional *indivisible input* with the receipts expected from the additional output thus secured. For instance, in a railway system as long as there are unused carriages the cost of putting them into use has to be compared with the additional receipts which may be obtained by doing so. When all the carriages available are used up to capacity, the cost of building and running additional carriages (and locomotives) has to be compared with the additional receipts expected to arise from such action. Finally, the question of building new tracks is decided upon the same principle. Cf. A. P. Lerner, "Statics and Dynamics in Socialist Economics," *Economic Journal*, vol. 47, no. 186 (June 1937), pp. 263–67.

[5] The result, however, of following this rule coincides with the result obtained under free competition only in the case of constant returns to the industry (i.e., a homogeneous production function of the first degree). In this case marginal cost incurred by the industry equals average cost. In all other cases the results diverge, for under free competition the output of an industry is such that average cost equals the price of the product, while according to our rule it is marginal cost (incurred by the industry) that ought to be equal to the price. This difference results in profits being made by the industries whose marginal cost exceeds average cost, whereas the industries in which the opposite is the case incur losses. These profits and losses correspond to the taxes and bounties proposed by Professor Pigou in order to bring about under free competition the equality of private and social marginal net product. See A. C. Pigou, *The Economics of Welfare*, 3d ed. (London: The Macmillan Company, 1929), pp. 223–27.

average cost and to produce as much of each service or commodity as will equalize marginal cost and the price of the product, this request being addressed to whoever is responsible for the particular decision to be taken. Thus the output of each plant and industry and the total demand for factors of production by each industry are determined. To enable the managers of production to follow these rules the prices of the factors and of the products must, of course, be given. In the case of consumers' goods and services of labor, they are determined on a market; in all other cases they are fixed by the Central Planning Board. Those prices being given, the supply of products and the demand for factors are determined.

The reasons for adopting the two rules mentioned are obvious. Since prices are indices of terms on which alternatives are offered, that method of production which will minimize average cost will also minimize the alternatives sacrificed. Thus the first rule means simply that each commodity must be produced with a minimum sacrifice of alternatives. The second rule is a necessary consequence of following consumers' preferences. It means that the marginal significance of each preference which is satisfied has to be equal to the marginal significance of the alternative preferences the satisfaction of which is sacrificed. If the second rule was not observed certain lower preferences would be satisfied while preferences higher up on the scale would be left unsatisfied.

3. Freedom of choice of occupation being assumed, laborers offer their services to the industry or occupation paying the highest wages. For the publicly owned capital and natural resources a price has to be fixed by the Central Planning Board with the provision that these resources can be directed only to industries which are able to "pay," or rather to "account for," this price. This is a consequence of following the consumers' preferences. The prices of the services of the ultimate productive resources being given, their distribution between the different industries is also determined.

B. The subjective equilibrium condition can be carried out only when prices are *given*. This is also true of the decisions of the managers of production and of the productive resources in public ownership. Only when prices are given can the combination of factors which minimizes average cost, the output which equalizes marginal cost and the price of the product, and the best allocation of the ultimate productive resources be determined. But if there is no market (in the institutional sense of the word) for capital goods or for the ultimate productive resources outside of labor, can their prices be determined objectively? Must not the prices fixed by the Central Planning Board necessarily be quite arbitrary? If so, their arbitrary character would deprive them of any economic significance as indices of the terms on which alternatives are offered. This is, indeed, the opinion of Professor Mises.[6] And the view is shared by Mr.

---

6 "Economic Calculation in the Socialist Commonwealth," reprinted in *Collectivist Economic Planning*, ed. F. A. Hayek (London: Routledge and Kegan Paul, 1935), p. 112.

Cole, who says: "A planless economy, in which each entrepreneur takes his decisions apart from the rest, obviously confronts each entrepreneur with a broadly given structure of costs, represented by the current level of wages, rent, and interest. . . . In a planned socialist economy there can be no objective structure of costs. Costs can be imputed to any desired extent. . . . But these imputed costs are not objective, but *fiat* costs determined by the public policy of the State."[7] This view, however, is easily refuted by recalling the very elements of price theory.

Why is there an objective price structure in a competitive market? Because, as a result of the parametric function of prices, there is generally only *one* set of prices which satisfies the objective equilibrium condition, i.e., equalizes demand and supply of each commodity. The same objective price structure can be obtained in a socialist economy if the *parametric function of prices* is retained. On a competitive market the parametric function of prices results from the number of competing individuals being too large to enable any one to influence prices by his own action. In a socialist economy, production and ownership of the productive resources outside of labor being centralized, the managers certainly can and do influence prices by their decisions. Therefore, the parametric function of prices must be imposed on them by the Central Planning Board as an *accounting rule*. All accounting has to be done *as if* prices were independent of the decisions taken. For purposes of accounting, prices must be treated as constant, as they are treated by entrepreneurs on a competitive market.

The technique of attaining this end is very simple: the Central Planning Board has to fix prices and see to it that all managers of plants, industries, and resources do their accounting on the basis of the prices fixed by the Central Planning Board, and not tolerate any use of other accounting. Once the parametric function of prices is adopted as an accounting rule, the price structure is established by the objective equilibrium condition. For each set of prices and consumers' incomes a definite amount of each commodity is supplied and demanded. Condition C determines the incomes of the consumers by the prices of the services of ultimate productive resources and the principles adopted for the distribution of the social dividend. With those principles given, prices alone are the variables determining the demand and supply of commodities.

The condition that the quantity demanded and supplied has to be equal for each commodity serves to select the equilibrium prices which alone assure the compatibility of all decisions taken. *Any price different from the equilibrium price would show at the end of the accounting period a surplus or a shortage of the commodity in question.* Thus the accounting prices in a socialist economy, far from being arbitrary, have quite the same

---

[7] G. D. H. Cole, *Economic Planning* (New York: Alfred A. Knopf, Inc., 1935), pp. 183–84.

objective character as the market prices in a regime of competition. Any mistake made by the Central Planning Board in fixing prices would announce itself in a very objective way—by a physical shortage or surplus of the quantity of the commodity or resources in question—and would have to be corrected in order to keep production running smoothly. As there is generally only one set of prices which satisfies the objective equilibrium condition, both the prices of products and costs[8] are uniquely determined.[9]

Our study of the determination of equilibrium prices in a socialist economy has shown that the process of price determination is quite analogous to that in a competitive market. The Central Planning Board performs the functions of the market. It establishes the rules for combining factors of production and choosing the scale of output of a plant, for determining the output of an industry, for the allocation of resources, and for the parametric use of prices in accounting. Finally, it fixes the prices so as to balance the quantity supplied and demanded of each commodity. It follows that a substitution of planning for the functions of the market is quite possible and workable.

Two problems deserve some special attention. The first relates to the determination of the best distribution of the social dividend. Freedom of choice of occupation assumed, the distribution of the social dividend may affect the amount of services of labor offered to different industries. If certain occupations received a larger social dividend than others, labor would be diverted into the occupations receiving a larger dividend. Therefore, the distribution of the social dividend must be such as not to interfere with the optimum distribution of labor services between the different industries and occupations. The optimum distribution is that which makes the differences of the value of the marginal product of the services of labor in different industries and occupations equal to the differences in the marginal disutility[10] of working in those industries or

---

[8] Hayek maintains that it would be impossible to determine the value of durable instruments of production because, in consequence of changes, "the value of most of the more durable instruments of production has little or no connection with the costs which have been incurred in their production" (*Collectivist Economic Planning*, p. 227). It is quite true that the value of such durable instruments is essentially a capitalized quasi-rent and therefore can be determined only after the price which will be obtained for the product is known (cf. ibid., p. 228). But there is no reason why the price of the product should be any less determinate in a socialist economy than in a competitive market. The managers of the industrial plant in question have simply to take the price fixed by the Central Planning Board as the basis of their calculation. The Central Planning Board would fix this price so as to satisfy the objective equilibrium condition, just as a competitive market does.

[9] However, in certain cases there may be a multiple solution.

[10] It is only the *relative* disutility of different occupations that counts. The absolute disutility may be zero or even negative. By putting leisure, safety, agreeableness of work, etc., into the preference scales, all labor costs may be expressed as opportunity costs. If such a device is adopted, each industry or occupation may be regarded as producing a joint product: the commodity or service in question *and* leisure, safety, agreeableness of work, etc. The services of labor have to be allocated so that the value of this marginal *joint* product is the same in all industries and occupations.

occupations.[11] This distribution of the services of labor arises automatically whenever wages are the only source of income. *Therefore, the social dividend must be distributed so as to have no influence whatever on the choice of occupation.* The social dividend paid to an individual must be entirely independent of his choice of occupation. For instance, it can be divided equally per head of population, or distributed according to age or size of family or any other principle which does not affect the choice of occupation.

The other problem is the determination of the rate of interest. We have to distinguish between a short-period and a long-period solution of the problem. For the former the amount of capital is regarded as constant, and the rate of interest is simply determined by the condition that the demand for capital is equal to the amount available. When the rate of interest is set too low the socialized banking system would be unable to meet the demand of industries for capital; when the interest rate is set too high there would be a surplus of capital available for investment. However, in the long period the amount of capital can be increased by accumulation. If the accumulation of capital is performed "corporately" before distributing the social dividend to the individuals, the rate of accumulation can be determined by the Central Planning Board *arbitrarily.* The Central Planning Board will probably aim at accumulating enough to make the marginal *net* productivity of capital zero,[12] this aim being never attained because of technical progress (new labor-saving devices), increase of population, the discovery of new natural resources, and, possibly, because of the shift of demand toward commodities produced by more capital-intensive methods.[13] But the rate, i.e., the *speed,* at which accumulation progresses is arbitrary.

The arbitrariness of the rate of capital accumulation "corporately" performed means simply that the decision regarding the rate of accumulation reflects how the Central Planning Board, and not the consumers, evaluate the optimum time-shape of the income stream. One may argue, of course, that this involves a diminution of consumers' welfare. This diffi-

---

[11] If the total amount of labor performed is not limited by legislation or custom regulating the hours of work, etc., the value of the marginal product of the services of labor in each occupation has to be *equal* to the marginal disutility. If any limitational factors are used, it is the marginal *net* product of the services of labor (obtained by deducting from the marginal product the marginal expenditure for the limitational factors) which has to satisfy the condition in the text.

[12] Cf. Knut Wicksell, "Professor Cassel's System of Economics," reprinted in his *Lectures on Political Economy,* ed. L. Robbins (2 vols.; London: Routledge and Kegan Paul, 1934), vol. I, p. 241.

[13] These changes, however, if very frequent, may act also in the opposite direction and diminish the marginal *net* productivity of capital because of the risk of obsolescence due to them. This is pointed out by A. P. Lerner in "A Note on Socialist Economics," *Review of Economic Studies,* vol. 4, no. 1 (October 1936), p. 72.

culty could be overcome only by leaving all accumulation to the saving of individuals.[14] But this is scarcely compatible with the organization of a socialist society.[15] . . .

Having treated the theoretical determination of economic equilibrium in a socialist society, let us see how equilibrium can be determined by a method of *trial and error* similar to that in a competitive market. This method of trial and error is based on the *parametric function of prices*. Let the Central Planning Board start with a given set of prices chosen *at random*. All decisions of the managers of production and of the productive resources in public ownership and also all decisions of individuals as consumers and as suppliers of labor are made on the basis of these prices. As a result of these decisions the quantity demanded and supplied of each commodity is determined. If the quantity demanded of a commodity is not equal to the quantity supplied, the price of that commodity has to be changed. It has to be raised if demand exceeds supply and lowered if the reverse is the case. Thus the Central Planning Board fixes a new set of prices which serves as a basis for new decisions, and which results in a new set of quantities demanded and supplied. Through this process of trial and error equilibrium prices are finally determined. Actually the process of trial and error would, of course, proceed on the basis of the prices *historically given*. Relatively small adjustments of those prices would constantly be made, and there would be no necessity of building up an entirely new price system.

---

[14] This method has been advocated by Barone in "The Ministry of Production in the Collectivist State," in *Collectivist Economic Planning*, ed. F. A. Hayek (London: Routledge and Kegan Paul, 1935), pp. 278–79.

[15] Of course, the consumers remain free to save as much as they want out of the income which is actually paid out to them, and the socialized banks could pay interest on savings. As a matter of fact, in order to prevent hoarding they would have to do so. But *this* rate of interest would not have any necessary connection with the marginal *net* productivity of capital. It would be quite arbitrary.

10

THE COMPUTER AND
THE MARKET*

Oskar Lange

In the preceding selection, written in the 1930s before the development of electronic computers, Lange presented a model intended to minimize centralized calculation by relying on market forces to "solve the millions of equations" involved in resource allocation and income distribution in a modern economy. In this article, written 30 years later, after the development of computers, Lange argues that centralized calculation, involving mathematical programming with computers, is both feasible and necessary for various purposes, especially long-term planning. But it still must be used in combination with, rather than in place of, the market in a socialist economy.

I

Not quite 30 years ago I published an essay *On the Economic Theory of Socialism*.[1] Pareto and Barone had shown that the conditions of economic equilibrium in a socialist economy could be expressed by a system of simultaneous equations. The prices resulting from these equations furnish a basis for rational economic accounting under socialism (only the static equilibrium aspect of the accounting problem was under consideration at that time). At a later date Hayek and Robbins maintained that the Pareto-Barone equations were of no practical consequence. The

* Reprinted by permission from *Socialism, Capitalism and Economic Growth: Essays Presented to Maurice Dobb*, ed. C. H. Feinstein (Cambridge: Cambridge University Press, 1967), pp. 158–61.

[1] *Review of Economic Studies*, vol. 4, no. 1 (October 1936), pp. 53–71, and no. 2 (February 1937), pp. 123–42; reprinted in Oskar Lange and Fred M. Taylor, *On the Economic Theory of Socialism*, ed. Benjamin E. Lippincott (Minneapolis: University of Minnesota Press, 1938).

solution of a system of thousands or more simultaneous equations was in practice impossible and, consequently, the practical problem of economic accounting under socialism remained unsolvable.

In my essay I refuted the Hayek–Robbins argument by showing how a market mechanism could be established in a socialist economy which would lead to the solution of the simultaneous equations by means of an empirical procedure of trial and error. Starting with an arbitrary set of prices, the price is raised whenever demand exceeds supply and lowered whenever the opposite is the case. Through such a process of *tâtonnements*, first described by Walras, the final equilibrium prices are gradually reached. These are the prices satisfying the system of simultaneous equations. It was assumed without question that the *tâtonnement* process in fact converges to the system of equilibrium prices.

Were I to rewrite my essay today my task would be much simpler. My answer to Hayek and Robbins would be: so what's the trouble? Let us put the simultaneous equations on an electronic computer and we shall obtain the solution in less than a second. The market process with its cumbersome *tâtonnements* appears old-fashioned. Indeed, it may be considered as a computing device of the pre-electronic age.

II

The market mechanism and trial and error procedure proposed in my essay really played the role of a computing device for solving a system of simultaneous equations. The solution was found by a process of iteration which was assumed to be convergent. The iterations were based on a feed-back principle operating so as to gradually eliminate deviations from equilibrium. It was envisaged that the process would operate like a servo-mechanism, which, through feedback action, automatically eliminates disturbances.[2]

The same process can be implemented by an electronic analogue machine which simulates the iteration process implied in the *tâtonnements* of the market mechanism. Such an electronic analogue (servo-mechanism) simulates the working of the market. This statement, however, may be reversed: the market simulates the electronic analogue computer. In other words, the market may be considered as a computer *sui generis* which serves to solve a system of simultaneous equations. It operates like an analogue machine: a servo-mechanism based on the feedback principle. The market may be considered as one of the oldest historical devices for solving simultaneous equations. The interesting thing is that the solving mechanism operates not via a physical but via a social process. It turns

---

[2] Cf. Josef Steindl, "Servo-mechanisms and Controllers in Economic Theory and Policy," in *On Political Economy and Econometrics: Essays in Honour of Oskar Lange* (Elmsford, N.Y.: Pergamon Press, 1965), pp. 552–54 in particular.

out that the social processes as well may serve as a basis for the operation of feedback devices leading to the solution of equations by iteration.

III

Managers of socialist economies today have two instruments of economic accounting. One is the electronic computer (digital or analogue); the other is the market. In capitalist countries too, the electronic computer is to a certain extent used as an instrument of economic accounting. Experience shows that for a very large number of problems linear approximation suffices; hence the wide-spread use of linear programming techniques. In a socialist economy such techniques have an even wider scope for application: they can be applied to the national economy as a whole.

It may be interesting to compare the relative merits of the market and of the computer in a socialist economy. The computer has the undoubted advantage of much greater speed. The market is a cumbersome and slow-working servo-mechanism. Its iteration process operates with considerable time-lags and oscillations and may not be convergent at all. This is shown by cobweb cycles, inventory and other reinvestment cycles as well as by the general business cycle. Thus the Walrasian *tâtonnements* are full of unpleasant fluctuations and may also prove to be divergent. In this respect the electronic computer shows an unchallenged superiority. It works with enormous speed, does not produce fluctuations in real economic processes and the convergence of its iterations is assured by its very construction.

Another disadvantage of the market as a servo-mechanism is that its iterations cause income effects. Any change in prices causes gains and losses to various groups of people. To the management of a socialist economy this creates various social problems connected with these gains and losses. Furthermore, it may mobilize conservative resistance to the iteration process involved in the use of the market as a servo-mechanism.

IV

All this, however, does not mean that the market has not its relative merits. First of all, even the most powerful electronic computers have a limited capacity. There may be (and there are) economic processes so complex in terms of the number of commodities and the type of equations involved that no computer can tackle them. Or it may be too costly to construct computers of such large capacity. In such cases nothing remains but to use the old-fashioned market servo-mechanism which has a much broader working capacity.

Secondly, the market is institutionally embodied in the present socialist economy. In all socialist countries (with the exception of certain periods when rationing was used) consumers' goods are distributed to the population by means of the market. Here, the market is an existing social institution and it is useless to apply an alternative accounting device. The electronic computer can be applied for purposes of prognostication but the computed forecasts have later to be confirmed by the actual working of the market.

An important limitation of the market is that it treats the accounting problem only in static terms, i.e. as an equilibrium problem. It does not provide a sufficient foundation for the solution of growth and development problems. In particular, it does not provide an adequate basis for long-term economic planning. For planning economic development long-term investments have to be taken out of the market mechanism and based on judgement of developmental economic policy. This is because present prices reflect present data, whereas investment changes data by creating new incomes, new technical conditions of production and frequently also by creating new wants (the creation of a television industry creates the demand for television sets, not the other way round). In other words, investment changes the conditions of supply and demand which determine equilibrium prices. This holds for capitalism as well as for socialism.

For the reasons indicated, planning of long-term economic development as a rule is based on overall considerations of economic policy rather than upon calculations based on current prices. However, the theory and practice of mathematical (linear and non-linear) programming makes it possible to introduce strict economic accounting into this process. After setting up an objective function (for instance, maximizing the increase of national income over a certain period) and certain constraints, future shadow prices can be calculated. These shadow prices serve as an instrument of economic accounting in long-term development plans. Actual market equilibrium prices do not suffice here; knowledge of the programmed future shadow prices is needed.

Mathematical programming turns out to be an essential instrument of *optimal* long-term economic planning. In so far as this involves the solution of large numbers of equations and inequalities the electronic computer is indispensable. Mathematical programming assisted by electronic computers becomes the fundamental instrument of long-term economic planning, as well as of solving dynamic economic problems of a more limited scope. Here, the electronic computer does not replace the market. It fulfills a function which the market never was able to perform.

11

THE PARTICIPATORY ECONOMY*

Jaroslav Vanek

This selection sketches some of the key features of Vanek's model of an economy composed of firms managed by their workers—in contrast to the firms run by state-appointed officials discussed by Lange. First Vanek explains the five characteristics which define the labor-managed or participatory economy. Then he examines various aspects of its operation, including competition, labor relations, stability of employment and prices, income distribution, externalities, and innovation. Vanek concludes that the participatory economy is superior to other systems on both economic and noneconomic grounds.

CHARACTERISTICS OF THE PARTICIPATORY ECONOMY

*   *   *   *   *

To use an analogy, we may liken the labor-managed economy—or for that matter, any economy—to a motor vehicle. If we want to become acquainted with the vehicle, we should learn principally about two things: one, what are the vehicle's main component parts, and two, what is its moving force? Accordingly, we will first introduce a set of defining characteristics of the labor-managed economy, and then explain what its principal moving force is—that is, the motivation on which economic actions within it are actually taken. Pushing the analogy a step further, we may

---

* Reprinted from Jaroslav Vanek, *The Participatory Economy: An Evolutionary Hypothesis and a Strategy for Development* (Ithaca, N.Y.: Cornell University Press, 1971), pp. 8–14, 21–22, 25–30, 34–38. Copyright © 1971 by Cornell University. Used by permission of Cornell University Press. A more detailed and technically rigorous exposition appears in his *The General Theory of Labor-Managed Market Economies* (Ithaca, N.Y.: Cornell University Press, 1970). Jaroslav Vanek is Professor of Economics at Cornell University.

also ask how the vehicle compares with other vehicles in respect to the main component parts. And going still another step, we may want to learn how the moving force—that is, the motor—compares with that of other vehicles. These other aspects of characterization by comparison will also concern us. . . .

The first of our five defining characteristics is quite obvious. The labor-managed or participatory economy is one based on, or composed of, firms controlled and managed by those working in them. This *participation in management* is by *all* and on the basis of equality, that is, on the principle of one-man one-vote.[1] It is to be carried out in the most efficient manner—in the majority of cases through elected representative bodies and officers: a workers' council, an executive board, and the director of the firm.

Clearly, the exact form of labor management that is most efficient can vary from enterprise to enterprise and from one labor-managed economy to another, and as such need not concern us here. It could not be over-emphasized that the participation in control and management derives uniquely and unalterably from *active* participation in the enterprise. Participation in ownership in no way and under no circumstances entails the right to control and manage; whether active participants are also owners of the assets of the firm or whether they contribute to the formation of such assets through undistributed earnings, it is not these contributions but their active participation that entitles them to control and manage.

The second general characteristic is related to and, in a sense, derives from the first. It is *income sharing*. The participants of the labor-managed firm, after they have paid for all material and other costs of operation, share in the income of the enterprise. This sharing is to be equitable, equal for labor of equal intensity and quality, and governed by a democratically agreed-on income-distribution schedule assigning to each job its relative claim on total net income. Of course, not all of net income needs to be distributed to individual participants; a collectively agreed-on share can be used for reserve funds, various types of collective consumption, or investment. In the last-mentioned instance, however, for reasons which will become apparent . . . , it may be preferable to recognize the contributions of savings to the firm's capital formation as individual claims of each participant, and express them in the form of fixed-interest-bearing financial obligations of the firm. Of course, recalling our first defining characteristic, such financial claims cannot under any circumstances carry a right to control or management of the firm.

---

1 Alternatively, in a more sophisticated and generally superior voting scheme where the voters are allowed to assign different weights to alternative issues simultaneously to be decided on, each voter is given the same number of points. This reflects the principle of equality of importance among members engaging in the democratic process of decision making.

These considerations of financing bring us to the third basic characteristic of participatory economies. The working community which has the exclusive right to control and manage the activities of the firm does not, as such, have the full ownership—in the traditional sense of the word "ownership"—of the capital assets which it uses. Perhaps the term *usufructus*, the right of enjoying the fruits of material goods, is a more appropriate one. The working community can enjoy the fruits of production in which the plant and equipment were used, but it must pay for this a contractual fee—or rental, or interest on the financial liability brought about by the purchases of such real assets. The community cannot destroy the real assets or sell them and distribute the proceeds as current income. In turn, the lenders of financial capital have no right of control whatsoever over the physical assets of the firm as long as the working community meets its debt-servicing obligations; the same holds for those who may lease physical assets to the firm, as long as the corresponding obligations of the labor-managed firm are met.

Whereas the first three defining characteristics pertain to individual firms, the remaining two bear on the relations among firms and, more generally, among all decision-making units of the participatory economy. The fourth characteristic is that the labor-managed economy must always be a *market economy*. This implies, among other things, that the economy is fully decentralized. All decision-making units, firms, households, associations, and the public sector decide freely and to their best advantage on actions they take, without direct interference from the outside. Economic planning and policy may be implemented through use of indirect policy instruments, discussion, improved information, or moral suasion, but never through a direct order to a firm or a group of firms. The economic relations among the above-mentioned decision-making units are settled through the conventional operation of markets, which is perfectly free whenever there are a sufficiently large number of buyers or sellers. Only in situations of monopolistic or monopsonistic tendencies can the public authorities interfere—and then only by fixing of maximum or minimum prices, or, preferably, by rendering the market structure more competitive, either through stimulation of entry or through opening up of the market to international competition. This ought not to be interpreted to mean that values determined by free market operation are desirable in any normative sense; a given society may prefer values different from those established by free competition (e.g., it may desire to make cigarettes prohibitively expensive) but if it does, it must reach its aims through legitimate tools of policy (a high tax on cigarettes or an import duty on imports of tobacco).

We come finally to the fifth basic characteristic. It bears on the human factor which in the participatory economy no longer is a mere factor of production but also—and perhaps primarily—the decision-making and thus creative and entrepreneurial factor. We may refer to the fifth characteristic as *freedom of employment*. It simply indicates that the individual is free to take, not to take, or to leave a particular job. At the same time, the labor-managed firms are free to hire or not to hire a particular man. However, the firms can, as a matter of their collective and democratic decision, limit in various ways their own capacity to expel a member of the community even where strictly economic considerations might call for doing so.

These considerations of freedom of employment—especially the one regarding the right to dismiss—lead us to the second part of identification of the participatory economy. What is the basic motivational force—or in the transposed sense suggested earlier, what is the motor—of the participatory firm and thus of the labor-managed economy as a whole?

In classical capitalism the moving force was the maximization of profit. In the Galbraithian new industrial state it is the self-interest of the upper management stratum of the large corporation, and in Soviet-type systems it is a combination of the fear of penalties attached to plan nonfulfillment and various types of bonuses extended to the plant manager.

In the participatory economy it is a combination of the interests of the members of the labor-managed firms as individuals on the one hand, and as a collective on the other. More specifically, and thinking first of the problem in pecuniary terms, the labor-managed firm's aim is the *maximization of income* for each of its members. Of course, this must be done in conformity with an income-distribution schedule reflecting the comparative shares belonging to each job agreed on democratically in advance; once the schedule is given, the highest income is attained for all participants at each level as soon as it is attained by any single participant.

This pecuniary objective of income maximization can be thought of as the crude form of the moving force of the labor-managed systems. It reflects an important part of the true motivation, and it lends itself to a simple formal analysis of the behavior of the labor-managed firms and of the labor-managed systems as a whole. It does not by any means contain the whole truth, however, and in many concrete situations will not even be seen as the principal objective by the participants of actual labor-managed firms.[2]

The true objective of the participatory firm is complex and multidimensional. If we insisted on reducing it to a single variable, we could not do otherwise than to say that the single variable is the degree of sat-

---

[2] In discussion with practical economists, enterprise directors, or workers in Yugoslavia, the income-maximizing motive will often not be recognized—or will be recognized only after some reflection—and other objectives, such as maximum growth, maximum surplus value, and maximum employment will be given. As an even more extreme point of view—one that certainly cannot be dismissed on a priori grounds—some will say that the objective of the participatory firm is simply what the majority of participants wants, there being no single identifiable motive.

isfaction of the individuals within the collective. Of course, monetary income may be an important ingredient of the satisfaction, especially in very poor environments, but it is definitely not the only one. The working collective can, for example, sacrifice some money income in exchange for additional leisure time, lesser intensity of work, better human relations—or even a kinder managing director. If this is so, all the alternatives mentioned must be considered as a part of the participatory firm's objective and thus as a component of the moving force of the labor-managed economy. In fact, the broader interpretation of the motivation base can include even objectives which normally would not be included under the heading of "self-interest," such as giving employment to others in the community, preventing unfavorable external effects of production such as air or water pollution, and many others.

For purposes of the evaluation of the functioning and performance of the participatory economy which we want to carry out in the next section, it will be useful to retain the distinction between the two levels of understanding of motivation in the participatory economy. We may refer to the crudely functioning income-maximizing objective as the *narrow motivation principle* and to the other, truer objective—which embraces a multiplicity of particular objectives—as the *broad motivation principle*.

* * * * *

OPERATION OF THE PARTICIPATORY ECONOMY

Using the image of a vehicle as we did in the preceding section—or to be more specific, a bus—it is possible to ask a number of questions about the efficiency or degree of perfection of its operation. For example, how much transportation service does the bus provide per unit of fuel, labor, or capital invested? What is its maximum speed? Are seats in the front of the bus as comfortable as those in the back? Similarly, economists attempting to evaluate the performance of a given economic system will try to answer comparable questions: How close does the system come to the producible maximum consistent with resources? How fast can it grow— that is, expand its productive resources? How desirable is the income distribution to which it leads?

In this section we will ask about a dozen fundamental questions of this type about the participatory economy and attempt to answer them in a manner intelligible to the general reader. (At times, this will mean simply stating the conclusions of arguments presented in full in my earlier, more technical work on the participatory economy,[3] or providing only partial

---

[3] *The General Theory of Labor-Managed Market Economies* (Ithaca, N.Y.: Cornell University Press, 1970).

evidence.) Our answers will allow us to make a summary evaluation of the participatory system. . . . Both in the individual arguments and in the overall conclusion, we will try to evaluate the participatory economy in two ways—on its own, that is, against an absolute standard of perfection, and in comparison with other economies, especially those found in the majority of countries in the western world.

*   *   *   *   *

Turning now to the question of market concentration and monopolistic tendencies, we may say that in this context the deviation from the optimum in the participatory economy will generally not be considerable. It will certainly be less than in western capitalist market structures. Several arguments can be offered to substantiate this proposition. First, on strictly psychological and sociological grounds, in self-governing bodies which participate in collective income, there will be a natural tendency to break into the smallest possible operational units (collectives) consistent with economic efficiency. The simple reason for this is the natural desire not to have men functionally remote from one's position participate in decisions and income. Traditional and modern capitalist firms have, by contrast, the well-known tendency to grow without bounds, the interests of the majority of employees being neglected. Very often the capitalist firms will tend to grow even well beyond a size that would be warranted on grounds of efficient operation.

Another argument is more economic and its full development would call for an undue amount of technical analysis; its common sense can be explained, however, without much difficulty. Suppose that a labor-managed firm operates at a level or scale of operation which permits it to be efficient and competitive with other firms in its industry. At that level of operation each worker makes a given income. If now the firm were to double its output—without affecting price significantly—the income per laborer would by and large remain unchanged assuming that the internal efficiency of the firm were not affected. The conclusion is that under the assumed conditions (which, incidentally, are often encountered in reality) there would be no special desire on the part of the firm to grow because such growth would not improve the income of each worker. And consequently, from this point of view at least, there would be only a slight tendency within the industry to reduce competition—that is, lower the number of firms—once each firm attained its efficient scale of operation. By contrast, under capitalist conditions, doubling of output in our above example would have doubled profits, and this indeed would have served as a powerful incentive to growth and, in many cases, to an eventual complete elimination of competition.

Still another among the several arguments regarding the degree of competition is related to questions of product differentiation, sales promotion, and advertising. Because it concerns such a large number of markets in the real world and also for other reasons, to which we will turn presently, it is probably the most important argument in this general case. The participatory firm differentiating and promoting its product will, as can be shown,[4] in the overwhelming majority of cases engage in less promotional activity and operate at a lower level of output than a comparable capitalist firm. This leads to the conclusion that other things being equal, differentiated oligopolies (e.g., soft drinks, tooth paste, cigarettes, automobiles, and just about all modern final manufactured goods) under labor management will be much more competitive than capitalist oligopolies as we know them in the western world. Moreover, and perhaps more important, the participatory alternative will advertise and promote less and thus utilize national resources more efficiently. Especially if we realize that the participatory firm will tend to omit some of the most aggressive forms of promotional activity, and if we recall of what low taste and quality such activity often is and what effects it may have on the minds, outlooks, and values of the public, the comparative advantages of labor management, on this account only, emerge as quite considerable.[5]

To sum up the arguments on competitiveness and market structure: we can say, without exaggeration, that the participatory economy naturally tends to embody the principal of "live and let live" much more than other market economies known to us today. There is far less urge to eliminate one's rival from the market. And this, let it be noted, carries within itself no implication of lesser efficiency. On the contrary, there is every reason to believe that oligopolies will on the whole be more efficient under labor management than under capitalism.

Even more obvious—not calling for any refined economics—is the related fact that in the participatory regime, by and large, there is no place for the labor-versus-management conflict. In consequence, the costs to society and to individual firms of strikes and other types of overt economic warfare are eliminated and the moral and mental costs of animosity, anger, and hatred are reduced.

Although this goes beyond the confines of economics, . . . it may be pointed out here that both of the arguments just made are bound to have far-reaching salutary effects on individuals and society. Both the "live and let live" forces of participation and the elimination of the major source of conflict in enterprises will necessarily be reflected in human attitudes and human relations throughout and even outside of the eco-

---

[4] This slightly involved technical argument is developed in *The General Theory of Labor-Managed Market Economies*, chap. 6, section 7.

[5] Cf. Lewis Mumford, *The Myth of the Machine* (New York: Harcourt, Brace & World, 1970).

nomic world, because the men acting in the economic, social, intellectual, family, or religious worlds will by and large carry the same habits, prejudices, experiences, and attitudes from one world to another.

We may now return to less abstract considerations, and examine the participatory economy from the point of view of what is usually referred to as macroeconomics. In this field we ask questions about the overall —or global—performance of an economic system. For example, does it guarantee full employment, or is it likely to lead to significant fluctuations in income or prices, or is it likely to generate inflationary forces?

Regarding the first question, the answer is that the participatory economy effectively does guarantee full employment. It does so in the sense that the economy normally will operate at, or very near, full employment, and if, as a result of some drastic disturbance, unemployment were to arise, there are forces inherent in the system that will tend to restore full employment. In this respect, the participatory economy has a definite edge over capitalist economies as we know them in the western world.

A similar advantage, absolute with respect to an absolute standard and relative with respect to other market systems, is that the participatory economy is far less likely to undergo cyclical depressions than are western market economies, and if such cycles were to occur they would be much less important.

By contrast, and deriving from the same forces, there is more likelihood in the participatory economy to encounter variations, both up and down, in the general price level. But by no means can this disadvantage be so serious as to offset the advantages of lesser or no fluctuations in real income, national product, and employment. No one will doubt that five percent of the labor force thrown out of work is incommensurably worse than a five percent change in prices.

When it comes to long-range stability of prices, that is, the likelihood of secular inflationary pressures, the labor-managed economy again promises to lead to satisfactory solutions. With no union power to fix wage rates, and a natural tendency of participatory firms to hold employment, prices can move down as easily as they can move up.

This, over long periods, can add up to overall secular price stability if monetary policy is not inflationary. By contrast, in the capitalist economy, where wages and prices are reduced far less willingly than they are increased, secular inflation is a virtual necessity in any economy committed to a full employment policy.

Thus far we have considered the principal aspects of the performance of the labor-managed economy in what we may refer to as its simplified or dehumanized form. Perhaps the second adjective is more descriptive of what we mean. All the results obtained up to this point are inherent in the participatory market economy merely on the assumption that the enterprises maximize income per man, each worker supplying work of equal and constant quality. This assumption is incomplete, and may be termed "dehumanized" because it neglects several key facts about the nature of the participatory economy. The most important among these are: (1) in each firm men of many different skills are brought together to cooperate, and this raises, among others, problems of income distribution; (2) besides being workers in their firms, the participants also share in the responsibility of management, which involves a good deal more than decisions to maximize income per man; (3) the quality of work is not, in fact, a constant for each man, and the process of participation in decision making coupled with income sharing tends to influence the quality, intensity and duration of work of each member of the enterprise.

Without going into the technical aspects of the question, it can be said that remuneration and income distribution among different job categories in the labor-managed firm will be influenced by two major sets of forces: (1) market forces and (2) the collective expression of the will and distributional attitudes of the working community. Market forces, and, more specifically, competition among firms (both existing and potential entrants into an industry) and individuals will guarantee that there would not be in the economy major differences in remuneration for identical jobs performed with comparable intensity of work. On the other hand, the participatory decision-making process is bound to lead to income-distribution patterns within the enterprise reflecting the will of the collective; and this can be expected to lead to income-distribution patterns somewhat more equal than would result from market forces only.

* * * * *

It would be impossible to list all the special effects—or what we may refer to as the special dimensions—of labor management, nor can we present a complete discussion of any single one of them. Nonetheless, we may attempt a brief account of some of the more important of these effects.[6]

We may start at random, selecting an argument of direct relevance to western industrial societies. It has to do with so-called external diseconomies, such as air or water pollution. The managers of labor-managed firms —that is, workers and employees—who live in the vicinity of their air- or water-polluting plants, are more likely to take care of, or reduce, the undesirable external effects, even at a cost, than capitalist owners who may live thousands of miles away or may never have seen the businesses they own.

Another favorable point is that some laborer-managers may decide to take out some of their incomes in kind, say, in the form of a less strenu-

---

[6] See also *The General Theory of Labor-Managed Market Economies*, chaps. 13 and 14.

ous or more hygienic job, where the principle of pecuniary profit maximization in the capitalist firm would not permit such a job improvement. A naïve person may object that this will make the participatory economy produce less real output than the capitalist; but it must be remembered that the building of the pyramids did not maximize social welfare, even if it may have maximized physical output.

For similar reasons, the participatory firm will be more likely to support education, training, and retraining of its members, when a strict profit motive might not suffice to do so. This phenomenon, actually verifiable in Yugoslavia, is of considerable importance for labor force development in the less-advanced countries.

Being much more closely related and exposed to local living conditions in the village, town, or borough, the worker-managers of the participatory firms are in a much better position to cope with social ills than are capitalist managers. The latter, who either have no direct exposure to such ills or are expected to maximize returns for the owners, cannot use the weight and resources of their positions.

Still another argument bears on collective consumption of various kinds by the membership of the participatory firm. In many instances, again most frequently in poorer countries, the community of the labor-managed firm may be the only group powerful enough, financially and organizationally, to initiate and carry out projects for collective consumption, such as housing projects, recreation facilities, and even school facilities. While it is true that other—that is, nonparticipatory—firms can do likewise, a strong case can be made to the effect that the participatory ones will be more apt and willing to assume such functions.

This sketch of some of the more important positive factors ought to be complemented by arguments of comparable weight that are negative or unfavorable to labor management. In my opinion, there are only two such arguments—and it is disputable whether even these are actually unfavorable. First, it can be argued that democratic processes of decision making are often slower, more roundabout, and more friction-generating than dictatorial or administrative fiat decisions, and this may have unsalutary effects on the economic performance of the enterprise. While there is a good deal of truth in this notion, it also must be recognized that as in political democracy, all is a matter of degree of participation, and the proper degree can itself be sought through democratic procedures. Just as in the political sphere it would be highly inefficient to have a full participation on every small decision, it would be equally inefficient—or at least extremely risky—democratically to delegate full powers in all matters to a director of the firm (or, for that matter, to the president of a country) for twenty years. But the democratic process itself is in a position to strike the proper balance between such extremes. And the balance it strikes, after all, should be efficient in the sense that it is favored by the majority, even if it may imply a slightly lower output and income than might be reached otherwise. The well-being, collective and individual, of the working community is at least as much a positive good as the last five dollars earned or unearned. Also, it may be expected that the democratic decision-making process can be made both more speedy and more efficient, in the sense of leading to results superior to those obtainable by simple majority rule.

The second argument, only a part of which is unfavorable to the participatory solution, is related to the question of inventive and innovative activity. It cannot be denied that with smaller size and a lesser push toward growth in the participatory firm, there will be less possibility to finance *major* invention, innovation, and product development by such firms, as compared to their capitalist counterparts. Of course, a counter-argument could be given to the effect that innovation and invention can be assumed by independent labor-managed research firms fully devoted to such activity. But the real counterbalancing argument is that in the context of *minor* inventive and innovative activity, the participatory firm has a distinct advantage. Not only are the workers directly concerned to put into practice improvements they have thought of because they realize the direct benefits that this offers them, but the participatory regime also provides them with appropriate channels of communication, through their elected representatives or otherwise, to have their ideas studied and adopted.

*   *   *   *   *

12

IS WORKERS' SELF-MANAGEMENT
THE ANSWER?*

J. R. Shackleton[1]

This selection first explains where workers' self-management lies in a spectrum of possible arrangements for the distribution of powers and functions between workers and managers. Next, the author examines the main assumptions and results of economic models of self-management. He then considers some possible problems in an economy composed of self-managed firms, including unemployment, market structure, externalities, growth, and public goods.

THE BACKGROUND

In the last ten years there has been in many Western societies a revulsion against large-scale organizations and institutions. The assumption that bigger means better has increasingly been challenged, and calls have been made for decentralization and "participation" in all areas of life. In the industrial sphere in particular such changes have often been presented as a virtual panacea for the problems we face. Their advocates have stressed the way in which alienation, worker discontent, and inequality might be alleviated, but they have also often argued that productivity, efficiency, and responsiveness to change would be greater than they are at present.

The most systematic articulation of such arguments has been the one offered by those socialists whose critique of contemporary capitalism has

* Reprinted by permission from *National Westminster Bank Quarterly Review*, February 1976, pp. 45–57, with the omission of some references. J. R. Shackleton is Lecturer in Economics at the Polytechnic of Central London.

[1] The author is grateful to F. J. Pierce, M. J. Ashcroft, and D. Marsh for helpful detailed comment on an earlier draft. Belated thanks are also due to Professor M. H. Peston for suggesting that the author take an interest in the subject.

been extended to cover the bureaucratized state planning which functions in the Soviet Union and its dependencies. Interest has been revived in alternative organizational forms based on developments of an older tradition embodied in 19th-century producer cooperatives, the Paris commune, guild socialism, syndicalism, and the spontaneous soviets of the early days of the Russian Revolution.

To be more precise, many socialists, including even some "mainstream" politicians, have been arguing for increasing worker involvement in the management of industrial enterprises, leading perhaps to eventual workers' self-management of the kind pioneered in Yugoslavia since the break with Stalinism. In Great Britain, the Institute for Workers' Control has been a powerful voice for this movement—a movement which was given added impetus by the establishment with government financial support of a number of experimental workers' cooperatives such as the Meriden motorcycle factory and the Scottish Daily News.

Simultaneously, though independently, something has been stirring in the academic undergrowth. Several eminent economists have produced books or papers subjecting an economy based on workers' self-management to the same kind of theoretical analysis, employing the same technical apparatus, that economists have long devoted to the workings of capitalist economies. This article does not refer to this literature in detail, but rather discusses some of the implications which seem to follow from it. The aim is to apply the economist's perspective to a debate which is currently couched overwhelmingly in political and ideological terms.

FORMAL RELATIONSHIPS CLASSIFIED

First, we need to define precisely what we are considering. In discussing workplace organization it is possible to conceptualize a number of "ideal types" of relationship between management and workers which can be arranged in a crude typology as in Table 1. This table distinguishes between different formal distributions of power and functions. It can, of course, be argued that the informal practices are similar in very different formal situations. For this article, however, this is not a crucial point.

"Managerial autonomy" epitomizes the situation of worker powerlessness which has been held by writers since Marx to be the root of discontent with industrial society. It is the *locus classicus* of alienation and as such has usually been associated with the early days of the industrial revolution and the unfettered operation of the market for labour. We might, however, postulate that such a situation could recur in different contexts—for instance in a totalitarian society where all formal decision-making power rests in the higher echelons of a bureaucratic state.

"Industrial democracy" represents the kind of formal situation which has developed in many Western countries in the last hundred years—

TABLE 1
Relationship between Workers and Management

Type of Relationship	Some Characteristics
Managerial autonomy	Ordinary worker treated solely as factor of production. No collective bargaining rights. Rigorous factory discipline.
Industrial democracy	Existence of independent trade unions in "oppositional" role. Collective bargaining permitted.
Participation/consultation	Worker representation on executive or pseudo-executive bodies. Major management initiatives discussed with workers before implementation.
Workers' control	Workers have effective veto on management decisions; exercise pressure on management to take decisions favourable to workers.
Workers' self-management	Executive powers ultimately rely on workers for their legitimacy. Elected top managers subject to recall by workers. Shop-floor control of immediate working environment.

management's power circumscribed by the existence of unions which bargain on behalf of workers over a strictly limited range of issues, mainly pay and conditions of service. The term "industrial democracy" is used in a neutral sense as far as possible; it simply echoes the influential terminology of Hugh Clegg.[2] In his work an analogy is drawn between the role of trade unions and the role of a "loyal opposition" in a parliamentary democracy. In this view the role of workers' organizations is essentially defensive; apart from pay and service conditions, all productive and organizational initiative remains with the management.

"Participation/consultation" encompasses German-style "codetermination": Workers are represented on boards of directors or other executive bodies but their power is strictly limited and they are not directly responsible to shop-floor workers. That is to say, when elected they are not easily removed and they are not mandated to follow policy determined by workers. Although some movements towards the extension of such a system have been made in the British context, many unionists remain highly sceptical of these schemes, suspecting that they are devices to head off or contain shop-floor militancy by producing a situation of role conflict for worker representatives. The interest occasionally shown in such schemes by employers' organizations and members of the Conservative and Liberal Parties adds to such suspicions.

---

[2] Hugh Clegg, A New Approach to Industrial Democracy (Oxford: Blackwell, 1960).

"Workers' control" is rather different. It is much more obviously a transitional stage—a political strategy rather than a settled and enduring industrial relations system. As it appears in the literature of the Institute for Workers' Control,[3] for instance, it is a strategy for increasing steadily the influence of shop-floor workers on the operation of firms. Building on existing workshop practices such as controls on speeds of operation and other so-called "restrictive practices," the aim is to use all means possible to extend workpeoples' control over their working environment, gradually widening the scope of collective bargaining far beyond the limits envisaged by the advocates of "industrial democracy." This programme is coupled with a more orthodox political campaign to extend nationalization—though not Morrison-style nationalization.[4] The emphasis is on a structure of operation which would be much more responsible to worker and community interests.

As indicated, workers' control is seen as a process of gradually extending checks on management prerogatives until eventually the workers are virtually in control as they have an effective veto on their firms' operations. It is argued that the experience gained in this process will prepare workers eventually to take over the running of enterprises themselves, on the basis of elected "worker-managers" whose powers derive directly from the workers and who are subject to their direction over broad issues of policy.

This, then, would be our "workers' self-management"—a system where the conventional distinction between management and workers disappears and labour is no longer treated purely as a factor of production. It is on this type of system that we concentrate in the rest of the article. As there is only one functioning economic system, the Yugoslav, which even approximates to this, we shall adopt a largely speculative and theoretical approach. We want to see how such a system is likely to function and what problems are likely to be involved in its operations.

SOME ASSUMPTIONS

Economists typically set up theoretical models of situations they wish to examine by stating certain assumptions about technology and behaviour and seeing what consequences follow from such assumptions. Sometimes it is argued that such models can be "tested" by comparing predicted consequences with observed events. In this particular case we have little or no empirical data to "test" our models with (even if this is methodologically correct). So we have to pay close attention to the assumptions that are being made.

---

[3] See, for instance, K. Coates and T. Topham, *The New Unionism: The Case for Workers' Control* (London: Owen, 1972; Harmondsworth, Eng.: Penguin, 1974).

[4] Editor's note: Herbert Morrison (1888–1965) was a leader of the British Labor Party and advocate of nationalization of industry.

Many of the assumptions being made by those economists who have written on this subject, for instance those about technology, are common to virtually all economic models currently discussed. We need not be concerned too closely with these. But it is worth spelling out the particular assumptions made in the literature about theoretical systems of workers' self-management:

1. Ownership of the capital embodied in a particular enterprise does not lie with the workers. It remains the property of the state, and usually the workers who operate with this capital have to pay interest or taxes on the capital out of the enterprise's income. This can be treated formally as analogous to a situation where workers hire capital, in the same way as in a capitalist economy capitalists hire workers. Additional capital can be obtained from the state by paying the going interest rate (assumed to be such that the market is cleared and there is no excess demand for funds) or from retained earnings.

2. This capital, the labour of the workers and other inputs (such as raw materials and semimanufactures) purchased from outside are combined to produce goods which are sold either in a free market or at state-determined prices. (Under "ideal" conditions these prices would be equivalent, reflecting the marginal social cost of production.)

3. The difference between sales revenue and costs of inputs (plus taxes and other obligatory payments where appropriate) constitutes the workers' income. This income, then, emerges as a residual rather than a fixed wage payment as under capitalism or a planned economy. The workers bear the risk that revenues may not exceed costs, just as entrepreneurs bear this risk in theoretical models of capitalism, and as the whole community does under what we might call "traditional" socialism, or "state capitalism." It is assumed that the worker-managers will attempt to maximize the size of the surplus over costs per worker, though of course the actual distribution of this surplus amongst the different grades of workers is a matter for separate consideration. Presumably this too is decided on the basis of democratic discussion.

These assumptions may be queried for a number of reasons. It may be argued that in reality no entrenched central authority would be willing to devolve economic power in the way suggested and that the concentration of industrial and political power over the last century is irreversible. This may be so, but our purpose here is to consider the implications of an "ideal type" and this objection is not strictly relevant. Similarly it has been argued that in practice nominally worker-controlled enterprises would in effect be controlled by a managerial elite who would run them in their own interests rather than those of the workers. Reference is made to studies which suggest that workers' self-management in Yugoslavia operates in this way. Again, however, this is irrelevant where we are considering what would happen were a system on these lines to function as specified.

Perhaps more importantly, it has been argued that a changeover to a system of workers' self-management would produce fundamental changes in people's behaviour so that workers, rather than simply attempting to maximize their incomes as the model assumes, would take into account wider social implications. This is possible, but self-interest appears to be an extremely tenacious and not wholly malign phenomenon. Radical behavioural changes seem likely to require massive "re-education" programmes which, however, are probably ruled out by the desire of most advocates of decentralization to minimize the power of the postcapitalist state.

It is also important to bear in mind that "workers' self-management" is a term which can describe several different kinds of organizational structure, each of which may lead to different patterns of behaviour. The policies adopted towards retaining or paying out earnings—whether workers on leaving a "firm" have a right to take with them any share of the retained earnings, whether workers can demand a fee from new workers entering the self-management organization, and many other specific issues —have a great bearing on the social implications of self-management and on economic behaviour.

ANALYTICAL RESULTS

The recent flurry of academic writings by economists has produced a number of interesting results. One of these is that an economy of labour-managed firms operating under the same technical conditions and same conditions of free exit and entry as the traditional text-book entrepreneurial economy would be equally capable of reaching what economists call "Pareto-optimal" equilibrium. That is to say that in the long run the self-managed economy would, given the specified conditions, settle down to a position where the marginal cost of producing a particular output is just equal to the price that consumers are prepared to pay for that output. At this equilibrium position any conceivable reallocation of existing resources could only make one individual or group of individuals better off by making at least one other individual worse off. This has long been held by economists to be the only meaningful definition of efficiency in an economic system, and the discovery that such reasoning lends support to the idea of workers' self-management has been welcomed by its academic advocates such as Vanek.[5]

However, if conditions of imperfect competition prevail, workers may feel that it is preferable to maximize the earnings per existing worker rather than the total earnings of the group. This implies keeping production

[5] Jaroslav Vanek, "Decentralization under Workers' Management: A Theoretical Appraisal," *American Economic Review*, vol. 59, no. 5 (December 1969), pp. 1006–14. [The preceding selection presents Vanek's views.—Editor]

down. If production were to increase, total earnings may be much higher, but earnings per worker would be lower, because of the extra staff needed. Thus a system with worker-management could be more restrictive than a monopoly in the capitalist world, and much more restrictive than a competitive system would permit.

In other ways the short-term responses of the two systems differ significantly. Consider a change in one of the parameters facing the individual enterprise in the two systems. Suppose the market price (which may be a centrally determined, though optimal, price in a socialist economy) of a good rises. Other things being equal, this means that demand for the good has risen relative to its supply, and in normal circumstances the optimal response of an economic system is to increase output. In theoretical models of capitalist market economies there are two mechanisms by which the desired increase in output is brought about. First, in the short run, existing firms with the usual upward-sloping marginal cost curves find that their marginal revenue now exceeds their marginal cost and, following the profit-maximizing rule, they expand their output accordingly. Second, in the long run, higher profits as a result of the price change encourage existing firms to invest in expanded capacity and, perhaps more in the theoretical world of the textbooks, new firms will be attracted into the industry by the lure of higher-than-normal rates of profit.

In an economy of labour-managed firms, by contrast, the short-run response of an enterprise to a rise in price may be decidedly perverse. It has been shown, for instance by Meade,[6] that a labour-managed enterprise of the kind specified here might actually have to *reduce* output and employment in these circumstances if average earnings are to be maximized. There are two major determinants of the optimum (or average-earning-maximizing) level of output for the worker-managed enterprise. On the one hand, in the short run the capital stock and associated interest charges are fixed, and so it is in the workers' interest to maximize output to spread the burden of these costs as much as possible. On the other hand, with a fixed capital stock the marginal productivity and the average ouput per head will decline, at least at some stage; consequently there will be an incentive to keep employment fairly low so that the value of output per head will remain high.

These two influences on the optimal level of output and employment pull in opposite directions. Consequently, when the selling price per unit of output rises, it increases the value of output per man and increases the importance of the second influence at the expense of the first. As a result the level of output and employment which maximizes average earnings may fall. In practice it seems doubtful that workers would agree to reduce employment, even though it might be possible to compensate the re-

---

6 J. E. Meade, "The Theory of Labour-Managed Firms and of Profit-sharing," *Economic Journal*, vol. 82, no. 325 (March 1972), Supplement, pp. 402–28.

dundant and still increase earnings for the remaining "partners." It would be safer simply to say that employment and supply would be price-inelastic.

This short-term tendency to curtail production, coupled with the fact that a "normal" reaction by the individual enterprise in the long run seems to require significant economies of scale, points to the importance of "free entry" into industries if the labour-managed system is to function appropriately. If existing enterprises reduce or hold constant the level of output of a product when the demand for it, expressed as a price rise, increases, it is clear that increased supply depends heavily on new enterprises entering the industry, attracted by the higher earnings now seen to be available. In a capitalist model the existence of higher profits in the industry induces entrepreneurs to invest capital. In the labour-managed situation things are rather different. What is required is for unemployed workers or workers in lower-paid work to get together to form new cooperatives to compete with existing firms. As workers in this kind of society will possess few assets, their plans will be heavily dependent on loans from the state. Indeed the state will in all probability have to take the initiative to set up such enterprises, and then hand them over to the workers.

Alternatively, of course, the state could manipulate taxes and interest rates to encourage existing firms to take on more labour and to increase output more than they otherwise would have done. But either way it would appear that this perverse adjustment mechanism implies a considerable continuing role for the state if a labour-managed system of this kind is to be "efficient" in responding to change.

SOME POLICY PROBLEMS

This belief is strengthened when we look in more detail at the problems involved in the operation of a labour-managed economy.

Unemployment

For instance where foresight is less than perfect and where enterprises possess autonomy in determining the size of their partnerships, unemployment remains a distinct possibility. Where resources are unemployed in a (post-Keynesian) capitalist economy, the central government usually intervenes to raise the level of aggregate demand, using either fiscal or monetary means. However, in a labour-managed economy such measures would tend to raise prices but leave output and employment unchanged (if not actually *reduced*) because of the short-run adjustment process described. Is the answer then, paradoxically, to reduce aggregate demand so as to depress prices and thus encourage employment expansion? In a formal sense, our model suggests yes: but in practice the relative inelasticity of short-run supply probably cuts both ways and the uncertainty induced by falling demand will probably deter the expansion of output and employment which our simple model would predict. The appropriate prescription for unemployment is likely to involve longer-run measures such as policies to promote new enterprises and encourage structural change.

This short-run unresponsiveness of a labour-managed system to conventional macroeconomic policy instruments might seem to be a strong argument against its institution; but against this there are compensations. Short-run employment inelasticity implies that once the system is at a high level of output and employment it will tend to remain there; the fluctuations intrinsic to capitalist economies will not be present. A labour-managed economy ought to require less short-term government intervention than a capitalist economy, and this can be argued to be a strong point in its favour.

Market Structure

Related to this is the question of market structures and monopolies policy. Ward[7] showed that in conditions of imperfect competition the labour-managed enterprise would be more restrictive in its output policy than the capitalist firm in equivalent market and technological conditions. This result follows from the kind of reasoning we have been discussing: the level of output which maximizes average earnings (or surplus per man) in the labour-managed enterprise faced with a downward-sloping demand curve is lower than that which maximizes profits for the entrepreneurial firm.

On the other hand, another result implied by the same analysis is that the typical labour-managed enterprise will be smaller than the typical capitalist firm in these similar circumstances, so that, in a sense, there will be room for more enterprises in a particular industry. This should tend to make the economy more competitive. The consensus of opinion among writers who have covered this issue seems to be that labour-managed economies will tend to be more competitive, but only if the government takes action where necessary to set up new enterprises as required.

Inflation

In relation to our current macroeconomic preoccupation, inflation, Vanek has argued that a labour-managed system possesses a comparative advantage over an entrepreneurial system in that "wages" are no longer a prime cost of production; rather, "earnings" are a residual. Hence, it is argued, "wage-push" cannot be an independent cause of inflation. Workers

---

[7] Benjamin Ward, "The Firm in Illyria: Market Syndicalism," *American Economic Review*, vol. 48, no. 4 (September 1958), pp. 566–89.

will see that, all other things being equal, an increase in their remuneration will directly involve a price increase. They will be much more aware of the market conditions facing them, and the consequences for jobs of attempts to raise prices in unfavourable market conditions will be immediately apparent. Hence there will be less inflation.

However, Vanek's model of inflationary processes seems naive in view of the current debate on inflation and the role of monetary factors. As Meade[8] has stressed, the labour-managed economy's equivalent of wage-push—increasing earnings by raising prices—can persist without causing sales to fall if central monetary authorities can be cajoled into a *pari passu* expansion of the money supply. Certainly the Yugoslav version of self-management has not been notably successful in eradicating inflation.[9]

Externalities

Looking now more generally at the problems thrown up by a decentralized industrial economy, we may note that in a capitalist economy central government interventions characteristically attempt to ameliorate situations where there is a divergence between social and private costs and benefits. In other words, although orthodox economic analysis may approve in principle of the Pareto-optimal equilibrium theoretically brought about by the workings of competitive capitalism, it has been recognized for a long time that in practice there may be so-called externalities in production and consumption. A smoky factory chimney causes costs to people who hang out their washing; a noisy party makes life difficult for the neighbours. On the positive side, your vaccination against smallpox lessens my chances of contracting the disease; your compulsory education makes it easier for me to communicate with you. A. C. Pigou[10] was one of the first academic economists to formalize this in his distinction between what he called the "marginal social net product" or net gain to society as a result of an economic activity and the "marginal trade net product" or net gains to the economic actor or actors directly involved—a distinction which, somewhat refined, is at the center of modern techniques of cost-benefit analysis.

In so far as these divergences arise for technical reasons, and not simply because of the property relations under capitalism, we might expect them to recur in the different institutional context of workers' self-management. Such problems as pollution are clearly not confined to capitalism, nor is their persistence attributable to the level of political consciousness of the

---

[8] Meade, "The Theory of Labour-Managed Firms . . ."

[9] Editor's note: See Selection 25 by Portes.

[10] A. C. Pigou, *The Economics of Welfare* (London: Macmillan, 1920).

members of a cooperative enterprise. It may simply be that decision making in these areas should not be left to the individual enterprise.

Investment and Growth

Difficulties may arise from workers' attitudes towards investment and growth. From the point of view of an individual enterprise, workers have to decide how much of current earnings to disburse in the form of pay and how much to reinvest. They have also to determine how much to borrow for further investment, and consequently the level of external debt to saddle themselves with. If we consider solely workers in the one firm, it is not at all clear that any one choice is intrinsically preferable to any other. Workers may decide collectively to go flat out for high levels of investment and growth, or they may decide to take things easy, enjoying a higher standard of living now but a relatively lower one in the future. But if their "rates of time preference" differ significantly from that of society as a whole, the interests of the workers in a particular enterprise may conflict with those of other members of the society. And it is quite reasonable to suppose that such differences occur. A low growth rate for some enterprises will restrict the choices available to workers in other enterprises. It also means a slow rate of growth of the surplus available to support the old and the young and other nonproductive citizens, and this may be of considerable significance where the structure of the population is changing rapidly. Even if workers in individual firms are willing to subordinate their own interests to those of society as a whole, they may not be in possession of the facts needed to make such a choice.

Such considerations spotlight the naivete of the arguments of many advocates of workers' self-management. Potential conflicts between the perspectives of different groups in society emerge as intrinsic to decentralized economic systems of any complexity. They are not dependent on the malevolence of individuals or groups but are rather a symptom of an information problem. A role for a centralized coordinating agency again seems implied.

Public Goods

Another area of government intervention, historically the most important, is in the provision of what economists call "public goods." Strictly speaking this description applies to goods which would not be provided under decentralized capitalism because nonpurchasers cannot be excluded from the benefits resulting from their provision and will thus try to get a "free ride." As a result no individual will be willing to buy such goods even though he may get positive utility from consuming them. More generally the term has come to mean those goods which are provided by public authorities—from revenue raised by taxation—because their provision would be inadequate under free enterprise. It is clear that such goods would continue to exist under a system of labour-managed enterprises. There would continue to be substantial numbers of workers who were producing services such as education and medical care, services where the level of provision would be a political rather than a market decision. In these fields workers would inevitably remain employees in a formal sense, though this is not of course to say that public services could not be much more democratically run, and decentralized, than they are today.

SOME CONCLUSIONS

This catalogue of the policy problems of a decentralized labour-managed economy could be extended. But enough has been said to substantiate the essential thesis of this article—that a system of workers' self-management does not abolish the complex of problems faced by modern industrial economies. It is possible to argue that some of these problems could be relieved by a reversion to self-sufficient communities (where, for instance, all the relevant "externalities" would be "internalized"). Certainly agricultural communes on the Chinese model, say, would minimize some of the effects of the conflicts touched upon here. However, the interest in workers' self-management discussed earlier in the article cannot in the main be interpreted as a back-to-the-land movement (if such a programme were, indeed, feasible). And if we assume a continued adherence to a complex industrial economy with a high degree of specialization and division of labour, the problems remain—and with them the need for some central coordination.

It is more usual in discussions of self-management to stress the benefits of such a system in terms of a reduction in the discontent of the working situation and the enhancement of the dignity of the worker. If these intangible benefits have been underplayed here, it is not because the author considers them insignificant. On the contrary, they are recognized as extremely powerful arguments in favour of self-management as a principle. But as we have very little empirical evidence of such benefits, we have largely to take them on trust and it seems sensible to pay some attention to the probable economic implications of such a system.

Whether or not one is an advocate of self-management, it needs to be recognized that this principle in itself cannot provide all the answers. Certainly it seems odd that many socialists who recognize the problems arising from decentralized capitalism with some acuity have not considered how far such problems may be endemic to all decentralized economic systems. In any currently conceivable economic system a central government is likely to continue to play a major role. Emphasis on the need for decentralization should not detract from the need to devise some more effective democratic control over the large government bureaucracies which will continue to exercise considerable power. This appears to be a point worth emphasizing, too, when considering affairs outside the economic system as narrowly defined. The current preoccupation with neighbourhood councils, community action groups, and so forth is probably correctly interpreted as disillusion with mass politics; but there are very real limits to the extent to which they can be substitutes for it. No man is an island, nor is any single community or collective—not in the late 20th century.

13

THE DECENTRALIZED
SELF-MANAGED
ECONOMIC SYSTEM
OF YUGOSLAVIA*

The World Bank

This selection explains the organization and operation of the Yugoslav socialist market economy, in which the responsibility for the management of a firm is entrusted to its workers. The first part traces the progressive decentralization of decision making over production, investment, public finance, and other aspects of economic activity. The second part discusses the current economic system—particularly the operation of the self-managed enterprise, including management arrangements, the distribution of enterprise income, and some of the implications for production and investment decisions.

THE EVOLUTION OF THE DECENTRALIZED
SELF-MANAGED SYSTEM, 1950–1971

Basic Ideas and Characteristics

The Yugoslavs began to evolve a new economic system in 1950. This system represents more than simply a reaction to the experiences with the centrally administered economy of the early postwar years triggered by the disagreements with the Soviet Union. It marks a search for a new kind of socialist society. The system may be termed a "socialist market economy"

* Reprinted by permission from *Yugoslavia: Development with Decentralization* (Baltimore, Md.: Johns Hopkins University Press for the World Bank, 1975), pp. 29–52, with the omission of some tables and footnotes. Copyright 1975 by the International Bank for Reconstruction and Development.

154

or a "socialist democracy" depending on whether the economic or political content of the evolution is stressed.

There are a number of interconnected elements that underlie the system. First, a basic tenet of the Yugoslav system is that a state is not socialist "until it begins to wither away."[1] Nationalization of resources and their management by the state are regarded only as "the first, and the lowest, form of socialism" (Kardelj) which, if there is a strong bureaucracy exploiting power for its own ends, degenerates into "state capitalism." Second, and connected to this, instead of state ownership and control there are social ownership and control of the means of production. The concept is a philosophical one. Social ownership as an economic category is not vested in any holder. No one holds the right of social ownership, not even the federation. . . . But, the law recognizes a special property right which it calls the "right to use."[2] Under social ownership, the worker is vested with the management of the means of production and the right to dispose of the product. Workers' self-management is seen as the fundamental principle of social organization, without which socialism is not possible, because without workers' self-management they would not have the disposition of the "surplus value" created in production. Third, the decentralization of political and economic decisions from the federal government to republics, communes, and enterprises is necessary because workers' management cannot be meaningful without it. Fourth, as a corollary of decentralized decision making there has to be a greater reliance on markets as a guide to the allocation of resources. This means the reduction of centralized planning and control. There has to be a decentralization of the planning function to the enterprises, the communes, and the republics. The plan for the economy as a whole is "only aimed at channelling and coordinating the trends of general development."

The evolution of the system designed to incorporate these basic principles has been characterized, first, by a pragmatic experimental, and relatively nondogmatic approach. For example, despite the basic idea of social ownership of property, peasant ownership of land is accepted subject to prescribed limits as to size of holding. The experimentation stems at least partly from the unique nature of the system. The Yugoslavs have no model

---

[1] E. Kardelj, Address to Federal Assembly, April 2, 1952. President Tito, in a speech to the Federal Assembly, July 26, 1950, also expressed the same idea when he said that: "Marx, Engels, and Lenin teach us that the state begins to wither away from the moment when the proletariat comes to power."

[2] "Development of Forms of Ownership in Yugoslavia," *Yugoslav Survey*, vol. 4, no. 1 (January–March 1963), p. 686. Also see Branko Horvat, "Yugoslav Economic Policy in the Post War Period: Problems, Ideas, Institutional Developments," *American Economic Review*, vol. 61, no. 3 (June 1971), part 2, pp. 106–8; and V. Račić, "Fundamental Characteristics of the Yugoslav Economic System," in *Yugoslav Economists on Problems of a Socialist Economy*, ed. Radmila Stojanović (White Plains, N.Y.: International Arts and Sciences Press, 1964).

to follow and the workability of ideas and institutions has to be judged by practice, and changes made on the basis of experience. Second, at no stage during the development of the system has the process of reform and rethinking been brought to a halt. The laws of the new system have been changed frequently. Often the existing system did not correspond to the legal framework because the realities of its functioning sometimes led to a tacit abandonment of statutes inconsistent with its further development. Sometimes practice preceded the legal enactment, and sometimes laws that were enacted were never put fully into practice. Progress was not easy; finding an appropriate balance between the objective of decentralization and self-management on the one hand, and the need for coordination of decisions, economic stability, and management at the macroeconomic level, and other problems, had to be faced from the start. Finally the whole process had occurred in an environment of relatively free and open discussion at all levels and has been marked by a deep involvement of all elements in Yugoslav society.

It would not be correct to view the Yugoslav system as a halfway house between a socialist system of the Soviet type and a capitalist system. It is basically a socialist system based on Marxist doctrines, which reflects the view that the Soviet model does not solve the problem of the "alienation" of the worker from capital and from the product of his work (characteristic of capitalist society). The evolution of the system has been marked by discontinuities—periods of rapid changes (e.g., 1953, 1961, 1965 and 1971) have been followed by periods of consolidation, marked by attempts to organize. This is in line with Yugoslav political theory. The Program of the League of Yugoslav Communists adopted at the Seventh Congress (1958) considered "impetuosity to accept artificially created forms" to be "just as harmful as the conservative retention of obsolete forms." More concretely it warned against two "equally dangerous and harmful tendencies . . . first, against the tendency toward an anarchist underestimation of the role of the state . . . and secondly, against the tendency to transform the state into an all embracing force."[3] During the whole period of evolution of the new system there have been stages when reaction against protagonists of one of the other ideologies was dominant.

The Period of Transition, 1950–1953

Although, as noted, the principle of self-management was introduced in 1950, its practice was redefined and extended during the next few years. In 1952 the control of all state enterprises was formally vested in the workers' councils, who were regarded as the trustees for the fixed capital which was provided to them by the Yugoslav state. At the same time all produc-

---

[3] *The Program of the League of Yugoslav Communists* (Belgrade: Edition Jugoslavije, 1958), p. 125.

tion decisions became the responsibility of the enterprises. Machinery and procedures were defined for consulting workers' councils and providing for the executive direction of enterprises. Initially the director of each enterprise was still appointed centrally, but late in 1952 the appointment was vested in the local authority (the commune), and in the following year this was replaced by a system of appointment after public advertisement by a committee representing the commune and workers' council concerned.

The move towards greater reliance on the market was not the result of a conversion to forms of economic reasoning then almost unknown in Yugoslavia, but was adopted because it seemed a necessary consequence of the principle of self-management. The process of decentralizing decisions to enterprises began in 1950, but gathered momentum in the following year. The federal ministries which had devised and administered the plan were abolished, to be replaced by secretariats with much smaller staff and greatly restricted functions. In December 1951 a law on "Planned Management of the National Economy" established from 1952 a system of annual plans (a second five-year plan was not embarked on until 1956), and introduced the practice of what was known as planning of "basic proportions," in which the amount and broad allocation of investment were determined, while the decisions regarding quantity and quality of output and its price were left to enterprises. Before 1952 the investment allocations of the plan were implemented through the budget. This arrangement was abolished with the Law on Planned Management. Initially, the National Bank of Yugoslavia was responsible for actually channelling funds into projects. However, in December 1953 a system of auctions for investment loans was instituted as the device for allocating investment funds to individual enterprises, along the basic proportions laid down by the plan. Bids received from enterprises were evaluated and those offering the most competitive terms were accepted.

At the same time the wide variety of prices and markets was replaced by a single price structure, while rationing was abolished and the scope of price control reduced. Centralized distribution of materials and finished products was abolished with the ministries which had operated it. According to a law of January 1951, prices of products that were not regulated were to be equated to average cost of production (determined by the price commission on the basis of reports of producing enterprises) plus a margin specified for each industry by the government. For consumer goods and for enterprises producing for a local market, the price so determined was to be a minimum. Obviously the method for setting prices did not provide any incentive to reduce average costs and protected existing enterprises against competition from new, more efficient producers. However, it did signify the acceptance of profit as an economic incentive and criterion. The relative freedom of enterprises to fix prices led to price and market agreements among enterprises which were made illegal in 1955. Some relaxation of controls was also attempted in foreign trade, where restrictions were greatly reduced following a revaluation in 1952 of the dinar to one sixth of its former official rate.

In agriculture, there was an almost complete reversal of the objectives and policies which had been adopted in the early postwar years. The idea that the socialization of the peasant is necessary for the socialization of the country was replaced by the belief that the development of the socialist nonagricultural sector would eventually lead to the socialization of the peasant. Consequently the Yugoslav economy emerged divided into a socialist sector and private sector, with the former identified as the modern sector. The process of socialization was viewed as one of rapid expansion of the social sector, so that the weight of the private sector in the economy diminished over time. After 1951 the practice of imposing crop patterns was discontinued, and in the following year the extremely unpopular system of compulsory deliveries came to an end. In March 1953, a law was passed, by which production cooperatives could be dissolved and their land returned to the peasants who had contributed it. This resulted in a very sharp reduction in the number of these cooperatives, particularly in the Vojvodina. Also in 1953 a further instalment of land reform was introduced, by which the 35 hectare limit on private holdings was brought down to 10 hectares, with the stipulation that the excess was to be made available only for state farms or cooperatives. In addition a new system of taxation was introduced according to which farmers were to be taxed according to the market value of their production.

The changes concerning economic policy were accompanied by a series of complementary political and constitutional changes. In 1952 the Communist Party of Yugoslavia changed its name and formal status, and was reborn as the League of Communists. In 1953 the principal changes of the recent period were brought together and codified in a new Constitutional Act. Article 4 of the new constitution provided that:

> Social ownership of means of production, the self-government of producers in the economy, and the self-government of working people in the commune, city and district represent the basis for the social and political system of the country.

Besides providing a new basis for the federal parliament and executive, the Constitution of 1953 gave greater powers to the local authorities below the level of the republics. The districts, the next tier under the republics, acquired a share in local enterprise revenues, together with some independent rights of taxation, while the size and responsibilities of the communes were increased. Nevertheless the Federal Government remained the dominant authority with respect to both taxation rights and the financing of investment.

The Period of Elaboration and Consolidation, 1954–1964

The development of the system after 1953 followed the general principles and the lines of development already mentioned—self-management, decentralization, liberalization, and increased reliance on the market—as the Yugoslavs tried to work out the practical implications of the approach that they had adopted, and discover how best to implement the basic principles. In the event, decentralization and self-management proceeded at two levels. First, decentralization at the political level increased autonomy for republics and local governments and reduced the role for the federal government. Secondly, there was a reduction of state regulation and control over enterprise decisions at all levels; federal, republic, and communal.

Self-Management in Enterprises. The development of enterprise self-management is illustrated by the evolution of the system of distribution of enterprise income.[4] Up to 1954 the enterprises had little control over their resources. The wage and salary system was fixed by the state, which also determined the use of other funds. In 1954 a new system of determining net profits was introduced, under which the total wage bill was still determined on the basis of average salaries for specified categories of workers fixed in the social plan. However, the enterprise could distribute the total amount thus determined among the workers, in accordance with pay scales determined by the workers' councils. A proportion of the net profit could also be paid out to workers, but this proportion was determined by the state. The authority of workers' councils in this field was increased significantly in 1958, when a new scheme of income distribution within enterprises was adopted and implemented, particularly after some revisions in 1961.

The revised system dropped the idea of net profit and replaced it with that of net income. Net income was defined as gross revenue *minus* material costs, depreciation and taxes. It, therefore, was not net of the wage bill. The allocation of the net income between personal income payments to workers and other uses was now entrusted to the workers' councils. This meant that workers' councils were now accepted as responsible bodies, which would not pay out the whole net income in income to workers at the expense of "accumulation" and other enterprise funds. However, there was a tendency for a sharp increase in wages after the system was adopted. Enterprises found themselves in liquidity difficulties too, because insufficient attention had been given to financial conditions of the enterprise when

---

[4] There were other developments indicating increasing self-management. For example until 1958 the directors of enterprises were appointed by a committee on which the enterprise had one-third representation. After 1958, half the members of the committee were from the enterprise. At present the workers' council appoints the director from a list approved by the selection committee.

determining the proportion of net income to be paid out in wages. Consequently guidelines for the allocation of net income between personal income payments and other uses were imposed again in 1962.

The guidelines aimed to discourage personal income payments above a prescribed minimum level, by imposing large obligatory payments from the net income. The payments were calculated as follows: from the net income, socially prescribed minimum personal incomes were deducted and the contributions progressively related to the remainder. After these obligatory payments were made, the little there was left for the enterprise to play with could be added to the socially prescribed minimum wage bill or used for other purposes. The major difficulty with the system was that there was no incentive for the enterprise to reduce costs, because the resultant increase in net income only increased the base on which the obligations were calculated. The contributions were abolished in 1964 when the enterprises finally secured a greater control over the distribution of their net income.

The increasing control of the enterprises over the distribution of their income is illustrated by the increase in the proportion of enterprise income at their disposal in the form of net personal incomes, depreciation, and enterprise funds. This proportion increased from 43 percent in 1959 to 55 percent in 1964 and 62 percent in 1966.

The Finance of Investment. The development of the system of investment allocation was a second area in which decentralization and self-management gradually increased. The Law on Banks passed in 1954 permitted communal banks to be established by local governments to supplement the role of the National Bank, and to be subject to its control. The banks were expected to collect savings and other funds from enterprises in their areas and control and execute the local government budget. In addition, three specialized banks were established for implementing the credit and investment policy of the government. The Bank for Foreign Trade was established in 1955, followed by the Investment Bank in 1956 and the Agricultural Bank in 1958. Funds were allocated to these banks from the government's General Investment Fund and they were responsible for financing the most efficient projects within the framework of the social plan. The increasing role of the banks in allocation of finance was expected to improve efficiency and economy in the use of funds, without eliminating the influence of government on the volume and pattern of investment. In 1956 it was enacted that investment policy would be implemented by the Yugoslav Investment Bank, which would consider a number of criteria in allocating credit, including the proportion of internal financing of the project, the term involved in construction, the profitability of the project, and its foreign exchange effect. It is not clear how these criteria were interpreted and what was the weight given to them. The banks acted primarily as agents for the distribution of state investment credits until 1963. Since almost all the resources of the banks came from the government, its influence on credit allocation continued to be dominant.

The decentralization of investment decisions in Yugoslavia did not take place until the mid-1960s.

Decentralization and Self-Government.   Parallel with the development of enterprise autonomy, there was progressive decentralization of the powers of the federation to republics and local governments. The basic idea was that self-management at the territorial level meant increasing self-government by communities.[5] At the same time republic and local governments were given an expanding role in the "supervision" of enterprises in their territory, at least in the initial stages. Instead of centralized state control at the federal level, enterprises faced decentralized state regulation at the commune level.

One aspect of this development was an attempt to make republic and local governments financially independent of the federation by developing their own revenue resources. As a result, while in 1948 about 54 percent of the total revenue of local and republic governments was derived from their own sources, in 1954 the proportion had increased to about 73 percent. In general, however, the local governments were not financially independent and continued to depend on sharing in federal revenues and on subsidies from the federal budget for a significant proportion of their finances. The principle of separate revenue sources for each level of government was abandoned during 1960–64 but reintroduced in 1965.

The attempt to increase financial independence and resources was accompanied by a significant increase in the role of nonfederal governments in investment financing. In particular, the importance of local governments continued to grow until 1964, when they accounted for one fifth of total investment expenditure in the social sector and three fifths of the investment expenditure financed by the state.

The law on local self-government adopted in 1955 stated that the commune was "the basic political-territorial organization of self-government," and gave it a variety of functions and responsibilities, both legislative and administrative. Its functions included the preparation of a social development plan for the area, the supervision of economic enterprises and the provision of municipal services and infrastructure, including not only public utilities but also services like education, roads, and hospitals. Communes were also responsible for the social property on their territory, as well as that under the control of enterprises in their area. The communal government had an important (initially a decisive) voice in the appointment of directors of enterprises. It also approved the wage schedules of individual enterprises since 1954 and continued to do so, even after the system of "net income" was adopted in 1958. The communes were also the founding members of the communal banks, of which there were 206 in

---

[5] "In daily life every man appears in a double capacity: as a producer and as a citizen. Thus direct democracy will also have two aspects: one relating to the work place, the other to the territory where citizens live." Horvat, "Yugoslav Economic Policy," p. 153.

1964.[6] Hence the communes were, and are, an important factor in financing enterprise investment.

The growth in the importance of local self-government was accompanied by a reduction in the number of communes, and an increase in their average size. The total number of communes declined from 4,156 in 1953 to 500 in 1970, and the average population per commune increased from 4,000 to about 40,000. The main reason for this tendency was that large communes could benefit from economies of scale in various commune activities. There also developed a large degree of intercommune cooperation for the pursuit of joint interests, for example, in infrastructure. Since the larger average size of the communes implies less direct self-government, local communities have been created for specific localities within the commune since 1963, with their own system of self-government. One factor affecting the real degree of self-government in the commune is the question of resources. In 1960 only 9 percent of the communes were able to cover their needs. All others had to rely on higher levels of government for subsidies and other financial help.

The Five-Year Plan, 1957–1961. The Second Five-Year Plan (1957–61) marked a return to medium-term planning after some years of annual plans. The period of annual plans had been used to a large extent to complete projects initiated during the period of centralized planning and, therefore, was characterized by the development strategy of the earlier period. During the second plan there was a reorientation of the pattern of development from one emphasizing heavy industries and producer goods, to one encouraging the production of consumer goods and finished products with the object of improving standards of living. The shift is termed in Yugoslavia as one from an "intensive" to an "extensive" pattern of development. The plan aimed at a growth in living standards of nearly 8 percent per year, and at the elimination of shortages and bottlenecks arising from the earlier pattern of development, through a faster development of agriculture and industries producing final goods. The plan was very successful and was declared completed in 1960 when most of its targets were fulfilled.

The emphasis on agriculture marked a significant change. The objective was to increase production so that food imports would not be a burden on the balance of payments. The role of the peasant in attaining this objective was recognized, and cooperation between peasant farmers and the social sector in agriculture was encouraged both as a method for getting higher production, as well as for demonstrating to the peasants the advantages of socialized agriculture.[7] Investment in agriculture was increased both

---

[6] Communal banks disappeared subsequently as an attempt was made to reduce their narrow territorial approach. As founder members, commune governments continue to have influence on lending policies of the commercial banks that replaced the communal banks.

[7] See *The Program of the League of Yugoslav Communists* (Belgrade: Edition Jugoslavije, 1958), pp. 149–50.

through the newly-founded Agricultural Bank and through investment funds. The increase of relative prices of agricultural commodities improved the terms of trade for agriculture and was an important incentive for growth of output.[8]

While significant progress towards decentralization and self-management had been made by 1964, it was much less than would appear at first sight. There continued to be a large degree of central control of the economy, and particularly of investment, in the interests of coordination and stabilization or ensuring what were termed the "basic proportions" of development. The emphasis placed on achieving greater regional equality was another reason for central intervention in investment allocation. There was also a large degree of control of prices and wages. The state continued to control the prices of 70 percent of the products, and thus exercised a strong influence on the pattern of decentralized resource use. In the field of foreign trade as well, the failure of the attempts to reduce controls in 1952 had been followed by an increase in restrictions, nor was a second major reform of the foreign exchange system in 1962 very successful. The relatively slow progress was partly the normal concomitant of the problems of developing a new and, in many ways, unique economic system. The process of "learning by going" was a difficult one. In addition, there was also some resistance to the ideas of the new economic system and its implications, which slowed the process of decentralization and self-management. Such views were increasingly voiced in 1961 and 1962 when there was a reduction in the rate of growth. This was attributed to the significant increase in enterprise autonomy that occurred in 1961, and a return to the old system of income distribution in enterprises and greater state influence in investment allocation was demanded. The ideological opposition was defeated. The Constitution of 1963 and the Eighth Congress of the League of Communists of Yugoslavia in 1964 reaffirmed the basic principles of Yugoslav development.

The New Constitution, 1963.   The new constitution, which is still in effect though with major amendments, summed up the progress of the preceding decade and set the stage for the next steps in the evolution of the system. It was presented by Kardelj as: "not only the constitution of the state but also a specific social charter which will provide the material basis for the faster internal development of the system of social self-government," and stated that: "the basis of the social economic system of Yugoslavia is free, associated work with socially-owned means of labor and self-management of the working people in production and in distribution of the social product in the working organization and social community." The citizens' right to "social self-management" was stated to be "inviola-

---

[8] Between 1956 and 1962, the index of producers' prices in agriculture increased by 64 percent, compared to an increase of 14 percent in industrial producer prices.

ble" and was to be applied in all spheres of economic, social and political life.[9] The constitution defined in greater detail than before the institutions for local government, and gave greater importance to the commune. It also incorporated the progress made in the development of workers' self-management. The Federal Assembly was reorganized with five chambers— the Federal Chamber (incorporating the Chamber of Nationalities), the Chambers of Economic Affairs, Education and Culture, Social Welfare and Health, and Political Organization.[10] Representation in all the chambers was on the basis of population, except in the Chamber of Nationalities in which each republic had equal representation, and the two autonomous provinces had half of that of a single republic. Election to all the chambers except the Federal Chamber was indirect, through communal assemblies. Representatives to the Federal Chamber were to be elected from candidates nominated by the communal assemblies through direct election in each constituency. There was an attempt to enforce wide participation of the people in the process of government by providing that no one could be elected to the same chamber more than twice consecutively.

The Economic Reform, 1965

By the mid-60s there was increasing dissatisfaction with the progress made in establishing a decentralized market-oriented, self-managed economic system. As already mentioned, a large degree of government control on prices continued. There were several reasons for this. First, the price system was used as an indirect way of regulating the allocation of resources and influencing the investment and production decisions of enterprises. It was one way of achieving the "basic proportions" of development. Second, to prevent high costs and the price escalation of finished goods, prices of power, raw materials, and intermediate goods were kept low and a complex system of subsidies and compensation was maintained to keep enterprises in these areas solvent. Third, given the high rate of investment, restrictions on imports, and the tendency for wages to rise and large fluctuations in agricultural production to emerge, there were, in general, strong inflationary pressures as well as a tendency for monopolistic price increases, and price control was an important weapon for suppressing inflation. "Consequently, the practice of administrative interference in the economy was longest and most extensively retained in the price sector."[11] The system of prices was

---

[9] The quotations are from Article 6 and Article 34.

[10] The assembly system was modified by a Constitutional Amendment in 1968. The Chamber of Nationalities became an independent unit at that time. It represented the continued importance of the complex nationalities problem in Yugoslavia. It was to meet occasionally when questions relating to the equality of rights of republics and nationalities arose, or when demanded by the majority of delegates of any republic.

[11] "Price Formation and Social Price Control," *Yugoslav Survey*, vol. 9 no. 1 (February 1968), p. 51.

the major object of attack. It was argued that administrative control of prices may have been acceptable in an underdeveloped agrarian economy, but Yugoslavia had passed beyond that stage. The complex production structure that had been created was being inhibited and distorted because of price controls. The recession in the rate of economic growth in 1961 and 1962 led to serious questioning. This was intensified during the immediately following years when there were severe balance of payments difficulties. Exports of goods averaged two thirds of imports during 1962–64, and for the convertible area only three fifths. The balance of payments question was crucial for the future with the expected decline in external assistance on soft terms. The problem was attributed to rapid increase of imports. (Imports of goods increased at about 27 percent per year during 1960–64.) One reason for this, it was claimed, was domestic price policies, which, by depressing raw material prices, led to a relatively slow development of the domestic resource base, at a time when final goods production, and, therefore, industrial raw material needs were expanding. The domestic price system, which sheltered domestic industry from international competition through restrictions in foreign trade, was also blamed for the relatively poor export growth. Producers of final products preferred to sell on the domestic market and exports had to be subsidized. In 1964 export subsidies totalled 2.7 billion dinars, or 20 percent of the value of exports.[12]

Other aspects of the inefficiency of past development also caused discontent. Despite the rapid growth and the institutional development of the 1950s there continued to be a great emphasis on high rates of investment. These were secured at the expense of a slower growth in private consumption. The share of the latter in GNP declined from 56 percent in 1957 to 51 percent in 1964. Over the same period, private consumption per capita increased at 4.4 percent per year, while per capita investment increased at 8 percent per year. It was believed that the time had arrived for modifying priorities between investment and consumption. It was also believed that the slow growth in per capita consumption was largely a result of the "extensive" pattern of development in Yugoslavia, in which increases in employment rather than of productivity per worker were emphasized. It was argued that for greater efficiency, competitiveness, and higher living standards for the workers (in the social sector), a shift to an "intensive" pattern of development was needed.

A third aspect of development during the past decade which had become increasingly suspect was the system of investment allocation. Though there had been significant progress in the diversion of resources from the federal level to republics, local governments, and the enterprises, the Federal Government was the largest single source for investment funds. Since the Federal General Investment Fund was allocated

12 Dusan Bilandžić, *Management of Yugoslav Economy, 1954–66* (Belgrade: Yugoslav Trade Unions, 1967), p. 109.

among enterprises, republics, and communes either directly, or through the banking system, the federation had almost full control of investment allocation through a process of leverage. The banks, since they operated with state funds, were, therefore, subject to its influence. A second aspect of investment allocation in the late 1950s, which was also questioned, was related to the regional development question. In the system of investment financing, the designated underdeveloped regions received special privileges. It was widely argued, particularly by the representatives of the developed regions, that this policy led to significant distortions in resource allocation and had encouraged waste.

As a result of all these factors, the economic reform of 1965 was carried out and the Yugoslav economic system was given, more or less, its present shape. The period 1950–65 has been called that of the birth of the self-management system. The reform consisted of a number of measures adopted during 1964–67 which were designed to achieve three major objectives: (1) to give greater autonomy to enterprises and limit the role of state in the economy by reducing taxation on enterprises and leaving investment decisions to them; (2) to correct by major price adjustments the long-standing distortions in relative prices, and thus improve the pattern of output and investment; (3) by devaluing the dinar, approximately halving customs tariff rates, and liberalizing imports and the foreign exchange regime, to integrate the economy more closely with the world economy and exert pressure on Yugoslav enterprises to increase efficiency. The measures were adopted over a number of years with the reduction in taxation of enterprises occurring in 1964, the devaluation and the principal price adjustments in July 1965 and the liberalization of the foreign exchange regime in January 1967.

The economic reform involved a major reorientation of economic policy and strategy which has dominated the pattern of development in subsequent years. This reorientation is clearly defined in the Social Development Plan 1966–70, which was adopted in July 1966. The first "basic intention" of the plan was "to ensure a gradual redistribution of national income in favor of personal incomes, so that they may not only bring about an improvement in the standard of living but also become a factor conducive to rational production and spending."[13] Increase in personal incomes would be an incentive for increasing productivity and efficiency of resource use. Secondly, the plan emphasized the "intensification of socioeconomic activity." It was stated that while in the 1950s labor productivity accounted for only 10 percent of production and income gains, the proportion would be 70 percent during the plan period. Thirdly, to allow "integration of the Yugoslav economy in the international division of labor," it

---

[13] Rikard Stajner, "The Fundamentals of Yugoslavia's 1966–70 Social Development Plan," Yugoslav Survey, vol. 7, no. 27 (October–December 1966), pp. 3863–68, from which the other quotations in this paragraph are also taken.

was necessary to achieve rapid export growth, which itself depended on the rapid adoption of modern technology in production. Production itself would be reoriented away from the domestic market "to what is profitable to produce in world proportions." Fourthly, to attract modern technology and to improve efficiency, foreign investment was to be encouraged. Fifthly, the role of the state in investment decisions was to be reduced significantly, partly by reducing its role in investment finance. In 1963 the various state investment funds were abolished, and the resources transferred to the banks. It was envisaged that: "in the future, the Federation will no longer dispose of the present amount of investment funds . . . but will only accumulate and build up funds indispensable for the development of underdeveloped regions."

The economic reforms were successful in bringing about a large degree of decentralization of decision making and in reorienting the pattern of economic development in Yugoslavia in the stated directions. However, the reform required radical readjustment within the economy. Also, in order to stabilize prices, it was accompanied by a tight monetary policy. Consequently the period 1966–68 was marked by unemployment and stagnation while the reform was implemented. The resumption of rapid economic growth in the middle of 1968, and the boom of 1969 and 1970, brought to the forefront issues of economic stabilization, of coordination of economic policies and investment decisions, and of balance of payments deficits.

Nationalism and Constitutional Change

The growth of decentralization was accompanied by a surfacing of the nationality question. To ignore it has not been a part of Communist party thinking. The program adopted by the Seventh Congress of the League of Yugoslav Communists in 1958 emphasized that the creation of a "new Yugoslav consciousness" did not mean the renunciation of national identity by people of different nationalities. At the Sixth Congress (1964) Kardelj stated that: "The point of departure in economic relations between the nationalities is economic independence for the people of each nationality."[14] The Amendments to the Constitution of 1963 adopted in 1968 gave increased rights and responsibilities to the republics. The structure of the Federal Assembly was modified and the Chamber of Nationalities was given much greater importance. There was a concomitant improvement in the position of ethnic minorities. The 1963 Constitution provided that in areas with mixed populations all nationalities would be represented in

---

[14] *Practice and Theory of Socialist Development in Yugoslavia*, the basic document of the Eighth Congress of the League of Yugoslav Communists (Belgrade: Medžunarodna Politika, 1965), p. 100. Kardelj went on to point out that: "there can obviously be no question only of independence but interdependence as well."

government and in workers' councils in proportion to their population. The Constitutional Amendment of 1968 gave a "fuller, more independent constitutional and legal status" to the autonomous provinces of Kosovo and Vojvodina.

The Constitutional Amendments adopted in July 1971 were the most significant steps in the development of the economic system since the reform. First they carried the trend towards greater self-management in the republics much further. Secondly, they marked a major step in the development of the system of self-management in enterprises. They established, thirdly, a collective presidency at the federal level in preparation for President Tito's eventual retirement from the active political scene. Finally, they provided a new institutional framework for coordinating economic policy and decisions. The changes in the legal framework required to implement these changes have not yet been completed. However, after an initial period of adjustment and dislocation, the new system has begun to work.

The republics and autonomous provinces now have more economic responsibilities, while the authority of the Federal Government has been narrowed and redefined. Major economic (particularly fiscal) responsibilities were transferred to the republics and autonomous provinces. National defense, internal security, and foreign policy as well as the FAD[15] continue to be federal responsibilities. The Federal Government also retains executive and coordinating functions for monetary policy; foreign exchange policies; the control of prices of basic commodities and services; and certain tax and expenditure policies. The extent of federal competence in these fields is, however, normally limited by the necessity to secure agreement of the republics and autonomous provinces before new measures can be undertaken by the federation. The Federal Government, however, retains sufficient initiative and control in the form of its responsibility for maintaining the unity of the Yugoslav market as well as emergency powers.

Since important matters cannot be decided without the approval of all republics and provinces, five Interrepublican Committees were established to deal with (1) development policy, (2) foreign trade and the foreign currency system, (3) the monetary system, (4) internal market matters and (5) financial matters. Each committee is chaired by a member of the Federal Government. There is also a Federal Coordination Committee consisting of the President of the Federal Government, the presidents of the governments of the republics and autonomous provinces, and five members of the Federal Government. There are intricate rules for approval of legislation where there is disagreement among the republics and to allow

---

15 Editor's note: Fund for Financing the Accelerated Development of the Underdeveloped Regions.

for the continuity of government while discussion continues. The Social Development Plan is also an important instrument for coordinating economic policies at different levels.

A system of "social agreements" and "self-management agreements" was created as a major new technique for coordinating the economic behavior of enterprises. The system—which involves tripartite "social agreements" between the state, the trade union and the enterprises, and subsequent "self-management" agreements among enterprises in the same branch of activity—has been used, at first, mainly to develop and implement an incomes policy. The agreements are binding on the enterprises that enter into them. While enterprises are not forced to enter these agreements, the federal, republic, or local government can proclaim a "social agreement" as generally binding, if the enterprises are unable to negotiate a "self-management" agreement.

The Constitutional Amendments and the proposed implementing legislation included basic changes affecting enterprises that are likely to have significant effects in the long run. An enterprise was given the right to invest funds in another enterprise and claim in return a part of the surplus. This could eventually have far-reaching implications for the mobility of capital, mergers, and the emergence of conglomerates. Joint ventures among domestic enterprises may become more frequent in the future. On the other hand, a subunit of an enterprise may invoke the right of self-management and constitute a separate organization provided it does not violate contractual obligations. In a further effort to attract foreign firms into joint ventures with Yugoslav firms, it was stated that the rights of foreign partners cannot be diminished by changes in legislation enacted after a joint venture contract has been finalized. To the extent that foreign firms have been inhibited during the past by uncertainties about their legal status this may help to increase joint ventures.

Since the new system relies on consensus, every republic has, in effect, the power of veto. The process of reaching agreement on policies and solutions is sometimes cumbersome and slow and there may be a tendency for recourse to ad hoc and temporary measures on difficult issues while consensus is being hammered out. It must also be remembered, in this context, however, that, to a certain extent, the Constitutional Amendments only formalized a situation that had already emerged. Reconciliation of republic interests and aspirations had already become a major factor influencing and sometimes delaying federal action, even before 1971.

The Yugoslavs point out that one of the advantages of the recent changes explicitly recognizing the views of the republics, is that policy decisions, once made, reflect an agreement and are therefore more likely to be implemented than in the past. The delay in arriving at policy understandings is, in their view, more than compensated by the greater certainty of the eventual outcome. It is also argued that as the republics are now responsible for many facets of development they can more rapidly take decisive steps to resolve their own specific problems.

THE PRESENT INSTITUTIONAL FRAMEWORK

The Federal, Republic, and Local Governments

The structure of the government gives explicit recognition to the different nationalities and republics. The political structure of the Federal Government is shown in Figure 1. It is guided by a Presidency consisting at present of 23 members, which will be reduced to 22 members on the retirement of President Tito. The Presidency will then consist of three members from each republic and two members from each autonomous province. Members are nominated by their respective republics and approved by the Federal Assembly for a term of five years. The executive branch of the federation is the Federal Executive Council (FEC) which consists of 28 members, chosen from among the republics for a term of four years on the same representative basis as the Presidency. The Federal Assembly is a five-chamber body. All legislation has to be approved by the Chamber of Nationalities and by one of the other four chambers depending on its competency. For economic matters, the Economic Chamber has to give its approval.

The governments of republics and autonomous provinces are organized on the basis of their own constitutions along similar lines as the Federal Government, except that there are no equivalent for the Presidency and no constitutionally established committees for coordination. The Republican Assembly also has five chambers in line with the Federal Assembly, and the Executive Council of the republic is responsible for the implementation of policies adopted by the assembly.

Local government at the commune level, and even below, at the level of local communities, is a most important element in self-government. The Communal Assembly consists of two chambers, one elected by all citizens and the other by employed personnel. In addition to the elected chambers there are commissions, councils, and committees established for specific purposes.

Enterprises and Workers' Self-Management

The basis of the Yugoslav economic system is the worker-managed enterprise or "work organization."[16] The enterprise is an autonomous body with the status of a legal person, with freedom to contract for capital

---

16 The term "work organization" includes not only business enterprises but all organizations in the field of public services, research, and education, etc.

FIGURE 1
Political Structure of the Federation

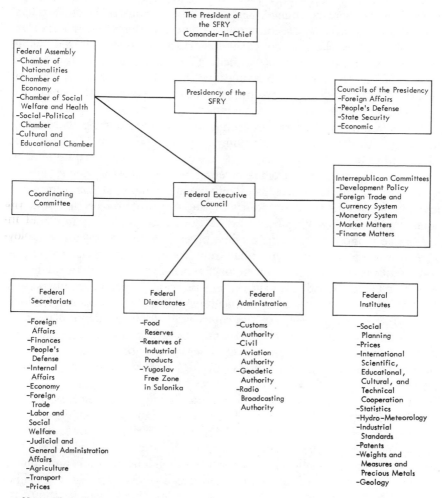

Note: The official name of Yugoslavia is the Socialist Federal Republic of Yugoslavia (SFRY).

goods, raw materials, and workers. The assets of the enterprises are social property but it can mortgage or dispose of them. The enterprise is free to determine what to produce, how to produce it, how much of it to produce and, in principle, the price of its product.

An enterprise can be established by any group of persons, but is usually set up together by communes and other working organizations, which are termed its founder members. Although the founder members have influence in the early stages of the enterprise, once it is operating fully, it comes under the control of the workers.

The management of an enterprise is carried out by a workers' council elected by all the employees (the work collective); a managing board elected by the workers' council; and a director, appointed by the workers' council and approved by the commune. Where an enterprise consists of less than 30 persons, there is no elected workers' council, and the whole working community acts as a council. This arrangement is also legally permissible in any working community with up to 70 persons. Where the enterprise is larger than 70 persons, the workers' council must consist of a minimum of 15 persons, with no maximum.

When an enterprise has less than ten working members, there is no managing board, but above that number, a managing board must consist of a minimum of five persons, once again without any maximum. The director of the enterprise attends meetings of the workers' council and is a member of the managing board. The management of the enterprise, including decisions on basic policy, is the responsibility of the workers' council and the managing board, while the responsibility for implementing decisions and for organizing production is given to the director alone.

The workers' council meets collectively. Its members are elected by the vote of all the workers and each member serves for two years, with half the members being elected annually. To ensure wide participation, no person can serve more than two terms consecutively. The workers' council decides on the internal relationships in the enterprise, adopts economic plans and annual financial reports, and decides on the utilization of funds and the distribution of the enterprise earnings between personal income and investment. The workers' council also decides matters concerning employment and dismissal of personnel.

In all large enterprises there have been distinguished, since 1959, economic units termed "basic units of associated labor" with important self-management rights. The units are distinguished on the basis of technological, economic, or other characteristics. Each unit is entitled to elect a workers' council. Usually there are workers' councils for each unit and a separate workers' council for the enterprise as a whole (see Figure 2). The workers' council of each unit is permitted to take individual decisions applicable within the unit as long as their decisions do not harm other units of their enterprise.

When an enterprise has not been operating successfully and has been unable to meet the income payment of its members, it is usual to appoint assignee management, normally chosen by the commune. Such assignee management is limited in the first instance to one year, though this can be continued where necessary. In earlier times the choice of the director was made jointly by the commune and the workers' council, but in 1968 the responsibility of the choice of the director was given to the workers' council alone, although the short list of names from which the appointment is made was to be drawn up in consultation with the commune.

FIGURE 2
Self-Management at Different Levels of a Large Enterprise

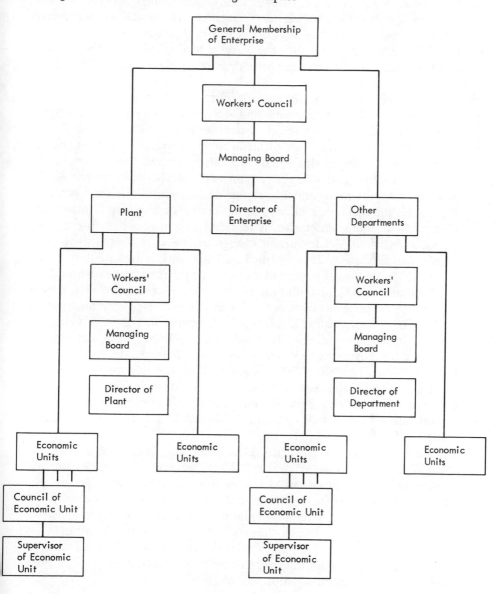

The role of the director in the enterprise has come in for much discussion and criticism. A proper balance (and coordination) between management by the director and self-management by the workers is not always found in practice though it can exist in theory. The workers' council is supposed to formulate policy, and the director to implement it; the workers' council is supposed to make the basic decisions and the director the day-to-day ones.

The director is given the responsibility of ensuring that the enterprise fulfills its legal obligations and does not ignore its social responsibilities. In addition, the social responsibility of the enterprise is also ensured through a wide range of financial and accounting regulations, inspection and control of the Social Accounting Service, tax and credit and price policies, the economic associations and chambers of economy, social and self-management agreements, as well as the influence of the commune, the Association of Trade Unions, and the League of Yugoslav Communists. Competition among enterprises is regarded as a strong influence against nonsocial behavior. An important change in the legal framework is presently under discussion. It would make all the workers in an enterprise responsible for any illegal actions of an enterprise that they are cognizant of.

As pointed out, the evolution of the system of income distribution within an enterprise has been one index of the growth of enterprise autonomy.[17] The system existing at present is illustrated in Figure 3. The gross income of the enterprise is the total receipts, from which the cost of materials, tax payments and depreciation are deducted to yield the net income of the enterprise. The allocation of the net income between personal income payments and accumulation of funds is decided by the workers' council of the enterprise within general regulations of allocation to certain funds, to the Housing Fund, for instance. The personal income is distributed by economic units which usually have their own reserve funds and funds for incentive payments. Only after these have been deducted is the individual's income determined. Thus the worker's personal income consists of various components: (1) basic salary established for the job, (2) bonuses paid by the economic unit for exceptional performance, (3) share in the "profits" of the economic unit because of *its* superior performance, and (4) share in the "profits" of the enterprise determined by market conditions, etc. Thus the worker does not know his actual receipts during (say) the year in advance, but only his basic salary and, to some extent, the incentives for superior performance.

---

17 See Jiri Kolaja, *Workers' Councils: The Yugoslav Experience* (London: Tavistock Publications, 1965); Benjamin Ward, "The Nationalized Firm in Yugoslavia," *American Economic Review*, vol. 55, no. 2 (May 1965), pp. 65–74; Branko Horvat and Vlado Rašković, "Workers' Management in Yugoslavia: A Comment," *Journal of Political Economy*, vol. 67, no. 2 (April 1959), pp. 194–98; and "Workers' Self-Management in Economic (Working) Units," *Yugoslav Survey*, vol. 4, no. 12 (January–March 1963), pp. 1690–1704.

FIGURE 3
Distribution of Income within an Enterprise

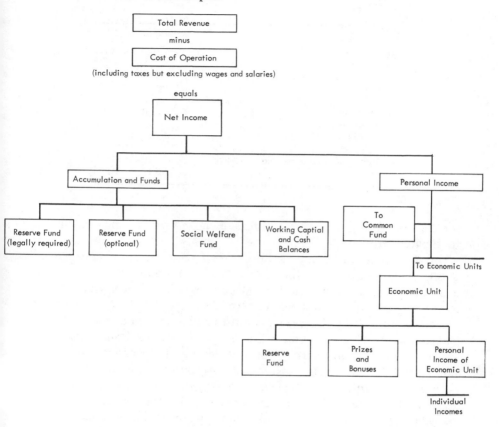

The role of the workers' councils and the autonomy of Yugoslav enterprises have been the subject of much study and debate.[18] One view is that the director is actually in control of the management of the enterprise because he is better informed and can "manage" the decisions of the workers' council. Another theory is that the councils themselves are controlled by the better educated, highly skilled workers, so that the system represents management by an elite group in the enterprise. There is some evidence that the proportion of representation of the "middle class"—skilled and highly skilled manual workers and employees with secondary and lower school education—has increased in workers' councils (Table 1). The total of the

---

[18] Veljko Rus, "Influence Structure in Yugoslav Enterprise," *Industrial Relations,* vol. 9, no. 2 (February 1970), pp. 148–60; Emerik Blum, "The Director and Workers' Management," in *Yugoslav Workers' Selfmanagement,* ed. M. J. Broekmeyer (Dordrecht, Holland: D. Reidel Publishing Co., 1970), pp. 172–92; and Ichak Adizes, *Industrial Democracy: The Yugoslav Style* (New York: Free Press, 1971).

TABLE 1
Membership of Workers' Councils and Managing Boards,
1960 and 1970 (percent)

	1960	1970
Manual workers	76.9	67.5
Unskilled	7.3	7.6
Semiskilled	13.6	9.0
Skilled	40.9	33.7
Highly skilled	15.1	17.2
Other employees	23.1	32.5
Lower education	0.6	6.5
Secondary education	6.7	15.9
Professional education	11.7	4.1
High level of professional education	4.1	6.0
Total	100.0	100.0

middle four groups in workers' councils increased from 63 percent in 1960 to 73 percent in 1970.

In any discussion of the question, three factors must be kept in mind. Firstly, who *really* controls the working of the enterprise is to some extent a metaphysical question which could be answered differently at different levels of philosophical abstraction. Secondly, it is clear that the degree of workers' control varies between enterprises and sectors of activity. Nor is it static, but changes over time with directors and the leadership in the workers' councils and managing boards. Thirdly, the workers' councils do not control the day-to-day working of enterprises and are not meant to do so.[19] They lay down general policies and have to make important decisions, though they do not always do so. The fact that the director has to be reelected every four years is an important safeguard. Further, self-management rights are constitutionally guaranteed and their violation by an autocratic director may, and sometimes does, lead to criminal prosecution. It is our judgement that the system does, in practice, incorporate a large degree of workers' participation and involvement in enterprise decision making, and marks significant progress towards the workers' self-management ideal.

More significant economic issues are related to the efficiency of the system of workers' management in the allocation and mobilization of resources. Economic analysis as well as experience have pointed out several problems that could face an economy based on workers' self-management.

1. The workers may pay out an excessive proporton of enterprise income in personal income payments and leave relatively inadequate amounts for reinvestment. This danger has always been recognized. In the early years, attempts were made to limit enterprise autonomy in the allocation of its income to ensure a sufficient level of enterprise savings. A recent in-

---

[19] In Energoinvest, the workers' council of 100 members (representing a total of 13,500 workers in 1970) met once every three months, according to Blum, "The Director and Workers' Management."

novation has been to introduce a system of social agreements between involved parties (governments, trade unions, enterprises) to regulate the proportion the enterprise pays out in personal incomes.

2. It has been argued that an enterprise's incentive to invest would be relatively weak under self-management, since savings out of the workers' personal income would belong to them, while amounts reinvested in the enterprise are under social ownership. In fact, reinvestment rates by enterprises have been fairly high, partly because the low real cost of borrowed funds in an inflationary environment encourages borrowing for investment purposes, and banks making loans require a certain proportion of an enterprise's own funds in an investment being financed. Also, given the relatively low mobility of labor, the workers do gain in the shape of higher personal incomes in the future if the enterprise maintains a high rate of investment. In addition if the enterprise expands, job opportunities are created for members of the worker's family. Another reason for high investment rates by Yugoslav enterprises has been the low degree of risk that investment involves for workers. The decentralization of the investment decisions has not been accompanied by a significant decentralization of the risks. Enterprises and workers making poor investment decisions do not have to pay commensurate financial penalties, because the state guarantees minimum levels of personal income.

3. There is a bias towards capital-intensive techniques of production which may imply misallocation of resources in worker-managed enterprises. If the enterprise aims to maximize net income per worker, it would tend to maximize the product per worker, and this would give a bias towards capital-intensive techniques which add to enterprise income without adding to those who share in it.

4. There may be allocative inefficiency resulting from the lack of mobility to capital. The savings generated in an enterprise tend to be invested in it, rather than moving to possibly more productive uses through the channel of a capital market. The Yugoslavs have not yet come up with an institutional substitute, though a number of developments have occurred. Constitutionally, enterprises are allowed to invest funds in other enterprises and receive payment. Cooperation in production and trade between enterprises with contractual inter-enterprise transfer of funds has also emerged. However, much progress has yet to be made for efficient intermediation of investment funds.

The Banking System

Since the mid-1960s the role of the banks in financing investment has increased sharply. Following the Banking and Credit Law of 1965 any group of economic or political organizations could set up a bank by subscribing the legally determined minimum of the initial "credit fund" (equity capital). Each participant (founder member) is represented in the bank's assembly (the highest managing authority) in proportion to its subscription, subject to an upper limit of 10 percent of the voting power. The limit is mainly designed to prevent bank policy being dominated by a state unit or one or two large enterprises. All banks are permitted to operate throughout Yugoslavia, and their activities cannot be limited by the local governments of territories in which they operate. A bank assembly decides on business policy and conditions for granting credits, agrees on the division of income, elects the Executive Committee, and appoints members of the Credit Committee and the Manager of the bank. The Executive Committee carries out the business policy laid down by the Assembly, while the Manager, appointed by the Executive Committee after a commission has held a public competition, is responsible for the day-to-day activities of the bank and is an ex officio member of the Executive Committee. Under the new law passed in 1971 the income earned by the bank is divided among its founders, but sociopolitical communities do not share in this division. Also conditions are laid down preventing a bank from granting credits to one client exceeding 30 percent of the total investment of the bank.

The banking system is regarded as playing a crucial role in the mobilization of savings and their allocation to the most efficient use. In fact the allocation of funds has tended to be influenced by many other considerations apart from "profitability" of projects, including government policies and the founder members, who are also the chief borrowers. The power of founder members is seen in the relatively low interest rates that have persisted despite the removal of ceilings on interest rates in 1971. The banks have, however, also come in for criticism as being too powerful in determining the allocation of funds, and being a serious hurdle to greater autonomy of workers' self-managed enterprises. The legal provision in the banking law of 1971, which vested the control of the funds generated through the bank operations in the founder members, was, at least in part, a reaction to what was regarded as arbitrary misuse of these funds by the bank managers.

The feeling that banks are too powerful has been encouraged by the merger movement among the commercial banks. In 1966 there were 111 banks. In 1970 their number was reduced to 64. These mergers have resulted in the emergence of some very large banks with practically a national field of operation. However, the mergers may permit an increase in the regional mobility of funds which may be desirable, if it results in improved regional allocation.

Chambers of Economy

With the growth of decentralization, self-governing associations of enterprises (komoras) were established in each branch of industry as early as 1954. Membership in these was made compulsory in 1958. Every enterprise is required to belong to the Chamber of Economy of the republic or autonomous province in which it is situated. In addition there is a federal chamber of economy to which each republic chamber must belong. A chamber of economy has a number of important responsibilities, which include examining all types of economic legislation before it is sent to the federal and republic assemblies; collecting and analyzing plans of enterprises; preparing estimates of markets, particularly foreign markets; undertaking research into new products; and providing a general economic service for its members. Each chamber is divided into a number of industrial groups which work together on common problems assisted by professional staff, including economists and engineers.

The chambers of economy play a major role not only in the formulation but also in the implementation of economic policies. For example, in the foreign exchange system the global exchange quota for importers is allocated among sectors of industry and enterprises on the basis of recommendations of the Chamber of Economy of Yugoslavia. These recommendations themselves are arrived at on the basis of discussions with the republican chambers of economy.

In addition to chambers there are associations of producers of similar commodities, which also play a role in coordinating the decisions of enterprises, and giving technical and marketing assistance to members.

The Trade Unions

The trade unions are relatively less important in the Yugoslav economic system, their major task being viewed as increasing the effectiveness of workers' self-management. Each enterprise has its own trade union branch and these are organized along industrial lines. Associations of trade unions of different branches exist at the commune and the republic level. The Confederation of Trade Unions (sindikat) of Yugoslavia is concerned with the broad lines of development of self-management and plays a role in initiating and commenting on draft legislation.[20] An important part of the function of trade unions is to combat tendencies "towards localism and chauvinism" on the part of enterprises and workers' councils. They also fulfill the normal trade union role of "protecting" individual workers from arbitrary decisions of directors and workers' councils. In 1971, the total membership of trade unions was 3.5 million, 91 percent of the total social sector employment. However, not all members are employed in the social sector.

The League of Communists (LCY)

With the development of the new economic system the role of the LCY has also changed. The renaming of the party in 1952 was indicative of this

[20] "The Confederation of Trade Unions of Yugoslavia," *Yugoslav Survey*, vol. 11, no. 3 (August 1970), pp. 34–64.

change. The role of the party was considered to be not to direct and command through control of the machinery of the state, but to play the leading role through discussion, education and propaganda, in the development of the new economic system.[21] However, this was not meant to imply that the importance of the LCY should decline. As its Program stated in 1958, because of the existence of "antagonistic forces" which endanger the existence of socialism: "the working class cannot give up the weapon of its class struggle, the dictatorship of the proletariat and the leading role of the League of Yugoslav Communists."[22] The process of decentralization, however, was implemented also within the party organization and the report on the Eighth Congress of the LCY (1964) commented that the independence and initiative of the organizations within the LCY had increased, so that instead of being "agents for passing on views and executors of tasks assigned" they were becoming participants in "the adoption of conclusions and decisions."[23] The process of decentralization had its own see-saw evolution. There was a noticeable tightening of party discipline in 1958. A struggle within the party in the early 1960s between those in favor of greater self-management and those for greater centralization resulted in the success of the former. A major reorganization giving greater independence to republican communist parties followed the Ninth Congress (1970). This was a period of resurgence of nationalist ideas and to some extent these ideas also gained influence in the party. At the Second Conference of the LCY in January 1972, the party challenged the more extreme symptoms of nationalist thinking. Since then there has been an increase in the influence on republic parties of the LCY and its Presidium.

The LCY is a key influence on all facets of Yugoslav life, and basically determines the direction and pace of development of the system. The total membership of the party was just over a million in 1971, only about 5 percent of the population, and the membership has not increased very rapidly. In fact in the recent measures for revitalizing the party it is stressed that a smaller, more highly disciplined and organized LCY would make a better "vanguard" of the country's social development. There is a branch of the party in every enterprise, and members are expected to be active in influencing decisions and ensuring that they are in line with national policy. The proportion of party members in workers' councils, management boards and other organizations and institutions of self-management is much

---

21 "The basic principle governing the work of the LCY . . . is not one of domination, but of stimulation of activities and initiative among the public . . . in the development of new-type socialist relationships." *Program of the League of Yugoslav Communists*, p. 245.

22 *Program of the League of Yugoslav Communists*, p. 244.

23 *Practice and Theory of Socialist Development in Yugoslavia*, p. 312.

larger than their share in the population. The influence of the party is seldom exercised directly, and tends to be underestimated.[24]

The Socialist Alliance of Working People of Yugoslavia (SAWPY)

The SAWPY was, in the period of centralized planning, known as the People's Front, and was viewed as a forum through which all citizens accepting generally socialist aims can participate in the building up of the new system. The SAWPY, with a membership of about eight million, includes individuals as well as organizations, and is organized at the level of the commune, the republic and the federation. The role of the SAWPY in economic decisions is not very large. It is more concerned with the political aspects of "socialist democracy" and plays an important role in the election system, determining election programs, and nominating candidates, etc.

The Instruments of Economic Policy and Coordination

The Yugoslav economic system possesses a number of institutions and instruments for formulating, interpreting and implementing economic policies. Some of these are familiar tools of economic policy, for example, monetary and fiscal management, social development plans, price and income policies, etc. There are others whch are uniquely Yugoslav, such as social agreements and self-management agreements which are a constitutionally enshrined method for substituting coordination on a self-management basis for the role of the state. These instruments and institutions have had a mixed success in ensuring rapid social and economic development and stability and in improving economic efficiency. However, in any evaluation of the Yugoslav institutional and policy framework, the success achieved in combining rapid growth and institutional change should not be overlooked. If to this is added the significant progress in democratizing the socioeconomic framework and giving the ordinary worker a high degree of freedom and influence in decision making, the Yugoslav economic system has to be judged a success.

---

[24] In a study of self-management in two factories Kolaja asked 78 workers about the most important influence in the enterprises. Forty-five thought that it was the workers' council, 27 that it was the director, four that it was the LCY, and only two that it was the trade union (Kolaja, *Workers' Councils,* p. 38). Studies by Rus and Kavić also came to similar conclusions (Rus, "Influence Structure," p. 149).

part IV

Centrally Planned Economy

Central planning may take place in a capitalist or a socialist institutional framework. In a capitalist economy in wartime, there is likely to be a large amount of central planning, as the government mobilizes and deploys the nation's resources for the war effort. Even in peacetime, some central planning of a more limited kind occurs in some sectors, such as military production, transportation, and fuel and power. A fascist economy, such as that of Nazi Germany, preserves the outward forms of the capitalist institutions of private property and enterprise, but it subjects them to comprehensive regulation in the interests of the state as defined by the supreme leader at the head of the totalitarian government.

Contemporary centrally planned economies are socialist, combining public ownership with two other features. (1) There is comprehensive and detailed planning and control of almost all phases of economic life, in response to planners', rather than consumers', sovereignty. (2) Resources are allocated primarily by administrative "commands" in real (physical) terms—such as production targets, allocation orders, and rationing—rather than chiefly by markets and prices. The selections which follow explain and evaluate both the theoretical basis of central planning and its practice in the Soviet Union, Eastern Europe, and China.

In Selection 14, Brown and Neuberger analyze the goals of centrally planned economies, how they try to achieve them, and the intended and unintended results. The many points made succinctly in this chapter are illustrated in detail in the subsequent case studies. In

Selection 15, Drewnowski discusses a specific issue facing centrally planned economies—the various possible combinations of planners' and consumers' sovereignty.

Selection 16 analyzes and evaluates the Soviet experience in central planning, which has served as the prototype for other Communist countries. This article emphasizes the Soviet approach to the planning of industry. Selection 17 examines closely the effort, in the Soviet Union and Eastern Europe, to apply central planning to agriculture, the sector of the economy commonly deemed least appropriate for centralized administration. Selection 18 considers the operation and problems of the foreign-trade sector of these economies. Selection 19 discusses recent efforts to "reform" the centralized economic systems in Eastern Europe.

Although China adopted the Soviet "model" of socialist central planning, it was modified for both pragmatic and ideological reasons. The administration of Chinese industry is explained in Selection 20, and the agricultural communes are discussed in Selection 21.

14

BASIC FEATURES OF A CENTRALLY PLANNED ECONOMY*

Alan A. Brown
and
Egon Neuberger

    The authors provide a concise systematic summary of the key features of a centrally planned economy. They discuss in turn its objectives, the planning mechanisms to achieve these objectives, desired effects from the operation of these mechanisms, undesired consequences, and adjustment mechanisms to deal with undesired consequences. The article thus constitutes a brief but comprehensive sketch of a centrally planned economy in operation.

We may identify the basic features of a centrally planned economy (CPE) in terms of its objectives and modi operandi.[1] Let us consider these in sequence under five major headings: objectives and key elements, planning mechanisms, desired effects, undesired consequences, and adjustment mechanisms.[2]

---

* From *International Trade and Central Planning: An Analysis of Economic Interaction,* ed. Alan A. Brown and Egon Neuberger (Berkeley and Los Angeles: University of California Press, 1968), pp. 405–14, with the omission of some footnotes and source references. Copyright © 1968 by The Regents of the University of California; reprinted by permission of the University of California Press. Alan A. Brown and Egon Neuberger are Professors of Economics at the University of Windsor and the State University of New York (Stony Brook), respectively.

[1] As a cautionary note, we may add that this conceptual model attempts to illuminate only the traditional CPE; it does not deal with recent changes resulting from economic reforms.

[2] The sketch of the closed CPE which follows was inspired by Professor David Granick's imaginative organizational model of Soviet planning (David Granick, "An Organizational Model of Soviet Industrial Planning," *Journal of Political Economy,* vol.

OBJECTIVES AND KEY ELEMENTS

Objectives[3]

Rapid Growth and Industrialization. Planners in traditional CPEs aim at a very high rate of economic growth, as a rule much higher than the rate maintained in market-type economies (MTEs). Not all economic sectors, however, are promoted equally; the result is unbalanced growth. Expansion of industrial sectors is stressed—more specifically, producers' goods and particularly certain heavy industries, such as mining, metallurgy, and machinery production. Attempts to satisfy an ever-increasing demand for industrial inputs lead to a chronic neglect of agriculture, a trend enhanced by the planners' ideological orientation (i.e., their mistrust and fear of the peasantry). Unbalanced industrial growth is generally pursued without regard for the relative resource endowment of individual CPEs.

Centralization. This term is a shorthand expression that includes both *centralized planning* and *centralized control* of economic activities. Thus, centralization means, on the one hand, that important planning decisions are reserved to the system's directors (to use Professor Bergson's expres-

---

67, no. 2 [April 1959], pp. 109–30). An increasing number of Western economists have also constructed models of CPEs, and only a few of these can be listed here. Professor Bergson, in one of his recent works, presents an analytical framework of the Soviet economy within which he interprets Soviet behavior patterns and assesses economic efficiency (Abram Bergson, *The Economics of Soviet Planning* [New Haven, Conn.: Yale University Press, 1964]). Professor Montias, in his appraisal of the Polish experience, provides a thorough introduction to the theory of central planning (John Michael Montias, *Central Planning in Poland* [New Haven, Conn.: Yale University Press, 1962]). Professors Balassa (Bela A. Belassa, *The Hungarian Experience in Economic Planning* [New Haven, Conn.: Yale University Press, 1959]) and Kornai (János Kornai, *Overcentralization in Economic Administration: A Critical Analysis Based on Experience in Hungarian Light Industry*, trans. by John Knapp [London: Oxford University Press, 1959]) both use theoretical models of central planning to analyze economic planning in Hungary. A very comprehensive treatment of different models of CPEs and of some alternative Communist economic systems appears in a book by Professor Wiles (*The Political Economy of Communism* [Cambridge, Mass.: Harvard University Press, 1962]). The fruits of a collective undertaking on various aspects of planning in the Soviet Union and in East Europe have been published in a volume edited by Professor Grossman; the editor's Introduction contains not only a summary of the other contributions but also a succinct model of CPEs (*Value and Plan: Economic Calculation and Organization in Eastern Europe*, ed. Gregory Grossman [Berkeley: University of California Press, 1960]). Also, an article by Professor Grossman serves as a useful theoretical frame of reference for Soviet-type systems ("Notes for a Theory of the Command Economy," *Soviet Studies*, vol. 15, no. 2 [October 1963], pp. 101–23). In a *Festschrift* honoring Professor Gerschenkron, there are several models of Soviet planning (*Industrialization in Two Systems: Essays in Honor of Alexander Gerschenkron*, ed. Henry Rosovsky [New York: John Wiley & Sons, Inc., 1966]). Attention will be called, as we proceed, to other contributions relating to specific features of CPEs.

[3] Although preference functions are obviously multidimensional, we attempt to call attention here only to those goals that have been explicitly and strongly stressed by the planners.

sion), and, on the other, that decisions are communicated to operational units by direct commands or directives. This implies a set of institutional mechanisms whose function is to assure the fulfillment of commands. Centralization, it may be added, is at once an important policy objective and a modus operandi of the system (via certain mechanisms to be discussed below). The planners have a revealed preference for centralization per se, pursuing it even at the expense of growth.

Key Elements

The basic goals of rapid growth and centralization give direction and shape to the system. The following six key elements represent a relatively complete shorthand description of the CPE.

Socialist Economy (or *Social Ownership*). According to Western economic terminology, public ownership of the means of production. (While this is one of the independent goals, it is also a means of achieving the goal of centralization, and to some extent the goal of rapid growth.)

Command Economy. Centralized bureaucratic management of the economy, with detailed physical planning and supply.

Pressure Economy. Emphasis on a high rate of forced savings at the macro-level; and on taut planning of outputs, inputs, and inventories at the micro-level.

Priority Economy. Planning based on priorities, reflecting the dominance of political and ideological criteria over economic considerations in the overall formulation of economic policy; e.g., primacy of industry over agriculture, or producers' goods over consumers' goods, and of material goods over services—except for high priority of education, especially technical education of the labor force.

Extensive Development.[4] Output-oriented planning, with stress on ever-increasing quantities of output, achieved with massive infusions of labor and capital inputs.

Closed Economy. Primacy of domestic economic considerations over the exigencies of foreign trade, foreign trade plans being merely addenda to domestic plans. (This is again an independent goal, as well as a means of achieving the goal of centralization.)

PLANNING MECHANISMS

Every economic system requires certain mechanisms, or institutional devices, to achieve its basic goals. In a CPE the planning mechanisms are de-

---

[4] This term has gained wide acceptance in Eastern Europe as a descriptive reference to the policies followed under the Stalinist system; we are adapting it to describe the specific feature described below.

signed to foster rapid economic growth (particularly in the high-priority sectors) and to safeguard centralization. We may identify three primary mechanisms (vertical coordination and control, system of material balances, and taut planning) and three secondary mechanisms (discontinuous planning, discontinuous incentives, and multiple criteria).

Primary Planning Mechanisms

Vertical coordination and control[5] means a predominant reliance on vertical channels of coordination and control as a basic method of centralization. This emphasis on the "vertical connections" in the economy (i.e., direct orders from above) reflects an effort by the planners to reduce their dependence on the "horizontal connections" (i.e., spontaneous, immediate contacts among operational units).[6] This mechanism manifests itself in a threefold separation of economic activities: (*a*) among different sectors of the economy (*intersectoral separation*), (*b*) among the enterprises in given sectors (*interfirm separation*), and (*c*) among departments within given administrative or producing units, as within a ministry or firm (*interdepartmental separation*).

System of material balances is a technique to achieve consistency among the various plans. It has two important aspects (*a*) *physical planning*, the balancing of equations in physical units to assure a flow of supplies mainly to high-priority sectors, and (*b*) *sequential planning*, the use of successive approximations rather than simultaneous equations to facilitate the planning process.

Taut planning aims at the swiftest possible central mobilization of all available resources—by means of continual sellers' markets—to facilitate rapid growth. It also serves as a technique to motivate operational units. We may distinguish three aspects of taut planning: (*a*) *output* (*target*) *maximization*, (*b*) *input* (*or input coefficient*) *minimization*, and (*c*) *inventory minimization*.

Secondary Planning Mechanisms

Discontinuous planning may be viewed as an elongation of the Robertsonian "planning day" (or Hicksian "week"), i.e., the period during which

---

5 János Kornai in his "Model of Economic Mechanisms" distinguishes between vertical connections ("a matter of authority and subordination") and horizontal connections (which "involve contacts [of an enterprise] with other enterprises . . . [all] having equal legal rights and standing") (*Overcentralization in Economic Administration*, pp. 191 ff.).

6 Kornai says, ". . . these vertical connexions are the dominant ones. . . . The influences which result from direct contacts between enterprises are dwarfed by those which reach them from the centre" (*Overcentralization in Economic Administration*, p. 194).

plans are supposed to remain unchanged.[7] This is also a device to facilitate central planning, since the planners attempt to keep relatively long "planning days" (they sanction interrelated plan revisions only infrequently or discontinuously) so as to minimize the burden of planning.

Discontinuous incentives imply a sharp line of demarcation in the incentive system between success and failure. The purpose is to encourage fulfillment of a centrally specified output pattern. To achieve this purpose, the incentive system is designed to offer rewards if the plans are fulfilled 100 percent (particularly, the physical output plan); failure is defined as falling short of the established quotas. Consequently, little attention is paid to differences of degree.[8]

Multiple criteria mean the absence of a single common standard of value, whether in the planning process (e.g., prices) or in the control mechanism (e.g., profits). The tendency to postulate output targets and input norms in nonadditive, heterogeneous units is functionally related to the system of material balances (i.e., to physical planning). Multiple criteria are also used in assessing the fulfillment of plans, i.e., in measuring the performance of operational units. Thus, multiple criteria and the corresponding proliferation of instructions are means of safeguarding central control, although they often do not accomplish this purpose satisfactorily.[9]

DESIRED EFFECTS[10]

The CPE is able, at least theoretically, to produce certain effects that, given the preferences of the system's directors, are considered desirable. It should be noted that, in practice, some of these effects are attenuated or altogether negated for reasons to be discussed as we proceed.

Socioeconomic Reorganization

Formation of a New Elite. The system is able to orient the whole country toward the goal of economic development, replacing those unin-

---

[7] J. R. Hicks says, "I shall define a week as that period of time during which variations in prices can be neglected. For theoretical purposes this means that prices will be supposed to change, not continuously, but at short intervals" (*Value and Capital*, 2d ed. [Oxford: Clarendon Press, 1946], pp. 122–23).

[8] Castigating the practice of "turning '100 percent' into a fetish," Kornai says, "premiums are not paid until the degree of fulfillment of the relevant plan index reaches 100 percent" (*Overcentralization in Economic Administration*, p. 128).

[9] Kornai writes that "excessive centralization inevitably leads to an undue proliferation of instructions" (*Overcentralization in Economic Administration*, p. 204). "The more instructions are given, the greater the tendency of ministries and other highly placed authorities to 'dictate' and to rely on ordering people about" (*Overcentralization in Economic Administration*, p. 203).

[10] The most comprehensive treatment may be found in Wiles, *The Political Economy of Communism*, pp. 253–63, where many of the points listed below are discussed at length.

terested in or hostile to rapid growth and centralization with a new elite of greater reliability. The new cadres are fully committed to the fundamental objectives of the system. This is accomplished by substituting a new ruling ideology for the old, and shifting power to adherents of the new ideology. The change is aided by the key elements cited above, especially social ownership, the pressure economy, and the command economy.

Income Distribution. Social ownership makes economic development possible without resort to a highly unequal income distribution, a precondition usually considered necessary to attain a sufficiently high level of investment from private voluntary saving. In practice, however, the wage differentials needed for incentive purposes and the lack of progressive taxes combine to widen the dispersion of disposable incomes in CPEs.

Population Policy. The CPE, by focusing on economic development and giving power to a new elite imbued with a development ideology, should be in a strong position to deal with one of the most crucial issues facing underdeveloped countries—the problem of population growth. But none of the key elements of the system deals directly with this question, and none of the countries that have adopted such a system has developed a consistent long-term population policy.[11]

Mobilization of Inputs

Capital Formation. The elements of social ownership, the pressure economy, and the command economy are used to impose very high rates of forced saving and investment, with the corollary effect of greater capital formation than under alternative economic systems.

Labor Recruitment. Extensive development, the priority economy, and the socialist economy facilitate the utilization of relatively abundant agricultural labor and unemployed urban labor, as well as the recruitment of women into the labor force.

Labor Training. Another desirable effect is the improvement of the educational levels and vocational skills of the population, a goal promoted by both the priority economy and social ownership (since education becomes a more important avenue of social mobility).

Acceleration and Channeling of Economic Development

Growth of GNP. The pressure economy, the priority economy, and extensive development are jointly utilized to achieve a rapid increase of the gross national product, although not necessarily of the standard of living.

Direction of Development. An important function of the priority

---

[11] An excellent discussion of the ramifications of this omission may be found in Oleg Hoeffding, "State Planning and Forced Industrialization," *Problems of Communism*, vol. 8, no. 6 (November–December 1959), pp. 38–46.

economy, the command economy, and social ownership is the ability to concentrate on high-priority objectives (e.g., giving the lion's share of investment funds to industry, especially to its favored branches) and to bring about a rapid structural transformation of the economy.

Regional Development. Attempts to bring the less-developed regions of the country to the more-developed level—together with a corollary tendency toward greater sociopolitical cohesiveness—are also promoted by the priority economy, the command economy, and social ownership.

Alleviation of Market Imperfections

Externalities. The ability to internalize external economies and diseconomies, while clearly a theoretical effect of the CPE—particularly of the command economy, the priority economy, and social ownership—is not easily realized in practice, since central planning organs are not monolithic units and do not have the necessary data and tools to assess externalities accurately.

Restrictive Influences. Social ownership, the pressure economy, and the command economy can be used, with at least partial success, to reduce monopolistic misallocation of resources and organizational slacks by tightly controlling managerial power and severely limiting trade-union interference.

Technological Progress. Control over management and labor and the absence of artificial monopolies based on patents foster a more rapid diffusion of existing technological knowledge. This desirable effect is related to social ownership and certain features of the command economy. Other elements of the system, however—such as the pressure economy, the closed economy, and extensive development—tend to work in the opposite direction.

Promotion of Economic Stability

Price-Wage Stabilization. Elements of the CPE (the command economy and the closed economy) enable the system's directors to control undesirable price and wage fluctuations. If severe inflationary pressures do build up periodically, as has happened in the past, they can be prevented from affecting resource allocation in part by controlling the wage-price spiral.

Insulation from International Business Cycles. CPEs also have more power than MTEs to prevent, at least for a time, external cyclical pressures and disturbances in the balance of payments from dominating domestic economic policies; this is a primary effect not only of the closed economy but also of the command economy. The system's directors do not feel the need to engage in a stop-go policy of investment and growth, nor have the banks the authority to insist on it.

UNDESIRED CONSEQUENCES

We turn now to various undesired consequences of CPEs, rooted in the objectives, key elements, and specific features of the planning system.[12] Although these undesired consequences are interrelated, we may separate them for analytical purposes into four major categories: administrative inefficiencies, unreliable valuation criteria, microeconomic inefficiencies, and macroeconomic problems.

Administrative Inefficiencies

Formal Organization. In its traditional form, the CPE is hypercentralized (i.e., its centralization interferes with economic efficiency) and rigidly organized. Its features, which are embedded in the bureaucratic framework of the command economy, lead to various macroeconomic maladjustments. The absence of flexibility pervades all sectors of the economy, from the Central Planning Board to every subordinate level. It presents serious problems, periodically, in the supply system (where cumulative shortages can arise because of the unavailability of crucial inputs through legal channels, regardless of prices that firms may be willing to pay) and particularly in foreign trade (where potential gains depend on flexible responses to ephemeral changes). First among the specific problems is an overemphasis on vertical coordination and control channels (and a corresponding neglect of horizontal links among the enterprises), which increases the need for more information in the formulation and implementation of plans. This, along with discontinuities in planning, leads to (a) lags in administrative response, (b) the neglect of special requirements or atypical conditions, and (c) cumulative shortages, which are rendered particularly acute by taut planning (e.g., efforts to keep reserves as low as possible). Thus, the planning mechanisms not only create initial bottlenecks but also generate further repercussions.

Informal Bargaining. On close inspection, it appears that the CPE, in spite of its highly centralized formal organization, is not a system of rational decision making by an omniscient and monolithic unit. Although vertical command channels are overemphasized officially, the formulation and implementation of plans are pervaded at all levels by bargaining. Results more often reflect the power of individuals than the intrinsic strength of their case, and our attempts to explain or predict the behavior of CPEs may be better served at times by tools of game theory than by traditional economic theories of rational resource allocation.

---

[12] Operationally, it would be difficult to determine whether the emphasis on growth or that on centralization was fundamentally more responsible for the undesired consequences. Although in practice they are joint products, Professor Levine has recently tried to separate the causes analytically, assigning most of the blame to pressure in the system (*Industrialization in Two Systems*, especially pp. 269 ff.).

Unreliable Valuation Criteria

Domestic Prices. There are nonsystematic aberrations of domestic prices both from prevailing scarcity ratios and from planners' preferences, primarily because several features of the system tend to immobilize the market mechanism.[13] Without a trial-and-error method, it would be difficult to establish a set of economically meaningful prices for even a handful of basic commodities (e.g., to derive synthetic or shadow prices by means of mathematical programming); and, in any case, the problem of the lack of price flexibility would remain. In a centralized economic system, interrelated price adjustments or general price reforms are too costly and can be undertaken only at infrequent intervals. Several key elements of the system —the command economy, the priority economy, and the closed economy— militate against rational pricing in a CPE. The inability of the planners to formulate economically meaningful and sufficiently flexible prices may also be directly attributed to certain specific planning mechanisms. First, the emphasis on vertical channels and the corresponding neglect of horizontal connections among operational units slow the transmission and reduce the reliability of information. Second, material balancing, with its stress on quota fulfillment in physical terms, delegates financial accounting to a subsidiary role in the planning process. Third, taut planning and its corollary, periodic supply shortages, inhibit equilibrium pricing.

Exchange Rates. Closely connected with irrational domestic prices is the system of generally arbitrary exchange rates. Both the command economy and the priority economy are to blame, although the closed-economy element is chiefly responsible. While foreign trade decisions are not made primarily on the basis of official exchange rates, the lack of reliable and explicit comparisons between external prices and internal costs tends to interfere with planning as well as with control. Arbitrary exchange rates, like irrational domestic prices, are a contributory cause of macro- and microeconomic inefficiencies.

Microeconomic Inefficiencies

Incentive System. Within the pressure economy and the command economy, multiple criteria and discontinuous incentives give rise to a series of problems at the microeconomic level. Both of these aspects of the planning system tend to make incentives dysfunctional: (*a*) multiple criteria

---

[13] Other fundamental problems include ideological mistrust and a lack of intellectual appreciation of the market mechanism, but the desire for centralization and the use of centralized devices of the system are probably the most important reasons for the irrationality of the prices. As Professor Grossman has expressed it: "But most important, to be workable, a market mechanism would require a dispersion of power and a degree of slack in the economy that the regime may be unwilling to grant" (*Value and Plan*, pp. 9–10).

lead to uncertainties, or *ambiguous motivation*; and (*b*) discontinuous in-centives lead to an exaggerated schism between success and failure, or *dichotomous motivation*. The final consequence is an all-or-nothing philosophy. First, up to a point, there are strong incentives for *simulation* (a familiar manifestation of this is the "assortment problem," the willful mis-classification of commodities to show favorable results) and *storming* (regular seasonal spurts in production to fulfill the quota). Second, when simulation is not likely to help, the performance of enterprises tends to suffer more than necessary because of temporary lethargy and (especially) illicit *hoarding*, which occurs to facilitate plan fulfillment in subsequent periods.

Productivity. Extensive development, the pressure economy, the closed economy, and the command economy are jointly responsible for various microeconomic inefficiencies: slow rate of technological and product in-novation, poor quality of output, and low productivity of labor and capital (long gestation period, inefficient choice of investment or its location, low-capacity utilization because of supply bottlenecks, and inadequate charges for capital use). At the same time, excessive inventories of unneeded inputs and unsold outputs accumulate.

Firm Size and Specialization. Elements of the command economy, the pressure economy, the priority economy, and the closed economy lead to a pattern of interfirm relationships with: (*a*) a bias toward giant plants with high transport costs and unused capacity, as well as an absence of smaller enterprises needed to provide forward and backward linkages; and (*b*) the presence of nonspecialized enterprises, aiming at narrow self-suf-ficiency, producing many commodities in small series, and engaging in subcontracting as little as possible.

Microeconomic Problems

Consumer Satisfaction. The priority economy, the command economy, and social ownership tend to keep consumer satisfactions at relatively low levels because of the high rates of forced saving, the low priority of agri-culture and consumer goods industries, and the neglect of service industries (which in turn lead to such corollary problems as the wrong assortment of products in terms of type, size, and style, and the unavailability of products in certain localities).

Agriculture. The past collectivization of agriculture and the low priority assigned to it subsequently (keeping agricultural incomes low and making life miserable for peasants)—the consequences of social ownership and the priority economy—have caused an exodus of the best workers from agriculture. While this neglect of agriculture makes extensive develop-ment possible and allows increases in industrial output, it nonetheless debilitates long-term agricultural performance, increases social problems in overcrowded cities, reduces—as mentioned above—the level of consumer satisfaction, and contributes to balance-of-payments problems.

International Specialization. The closed economy, the command economy, and the priority economy are responsible for the relative neglect of traditional export industries and the failure to develop new specialized export industries based on present or prospective comparative advantage. As a result, CPEs become dependent on the exportation of commodities that happen to be in temporary excess of domestic needs. Similarly, the lack of an optimal long-term import policy leads to the importation of commodities in temporary short supply, rather than those in which the country has a comparative disadvantage.

ADJUSTMENT MECHANISMS

CPEs employ certain adjustment mechanisms in an attempt to deal with the undesirable consequences discussed above. These mechanisms may be divided into external and internal safety valves. The *external safety valves,* or *ad hoc* imports, . . . are often used to alleviate planning errors or unforeseen disturbances. . . .[14] By *domestic safety valves* is meant the semi-legal mechanisms whose function is to introduce a measure of flexibility— by means of informal decentralization—into the rigidly centralized system. Two allied devices, selective violation of instructions and priority planning, are also used to cope with some of the undesired consequences.

Selective Violation of Instructions. Informally, planning authorities are inclined to overlook a case of the neglect of certain instructions by enterprises so long as the more important instructions are observed (chiefly, the fulfillment of physical output plans). There is, as it were, a hierarchy among instructions, the more important ones being safeguarded at the expense of the less important.[15]

Priority Planning. There is a similar hierarchy among various branches of production, i.e., among products of different industries. Thus, priority planning is a means of assuring fulfillments, or overfulfillments, of high-priority output targets—ranking high in the preferences of the system's directors. This occurs at the expense of low-priority goods—commodities that the directors consider to be more expendable, at least in the short run (traditionally, agricultural products and consumer goods).

---

[14] See Alan A. Brown, "Towards a Theory of Centrally Planned Foreign Trade," in *International Trade and Central Planning: An Analysis of Economic Interactions,* ed. Alan A. Brown and Egon Neuberger (Berkeley: University of California Press, 1968), pp. 57–93.

[15] Let us once again cite Kornai: "According to what their consequences are, some instructions have much 'authority' and 'weight,' and are very effective, while others are of more or less formal importance only, having their existence only on paper. Thus, a definite order of the importance of the tasks which arise in the course of the economic process is formed" (*Overcentralization in Economic Administration,* p. 122).

15

DUAL PREFERENCE SYSTEMS IN SOCIALISM*

Jan Drewnowski[1]

In socialism (and also in capitalism), two systems of preferences must be distinguished: the multiple system of individual preference functions of consumers, and the single state preference function. The latter embodies the state's economic policy, as formulated by the government and as revealed by its economic activities. In contemporary socialist centrally planned economies, state preferences determine the distribution of resources among consumption, military programs, and investment, as well as the composition of military and investment output. However, a dual preference system exists in the sphere of consumer goods production, where state and individual preferences jointly decide the allocation of resources and distribution of goods.

Drewnowski distinguishes three possible combinations of state (planners') and individual (consumers') preferences, with increasing degrees of influence for the latter. In the "first-degree market economy," households possess only consumer choice in the purchase of consumer goods, the quantities of which are fixed by the planners. In

* Excerpted from Jan Drewnowski, "The Economic Theory of Socialism: A Suggestion for Reconsideration," *Journal of Political Economy*, vol. 69, no. 4 (August 1961), pp. 341–54, by permission of The University of Chicago Press. Copyright 1961 by The University of Chicago Press. Jan Drewnowski is Professor of Economic and Social Planning at the Institute of Social Studies (The Hague).

1 When this was written I was a guest of the Center for International Studies, Massachusetts Institute of Technology, as a Ford Foundation exchange professor. I wish, therefore, to express my thanks to the Foundation, which made my work possible, and to all those economists in Cambridge, Massachusetts, with whom I had the opportunity to discuss many problems relevant to the subject of this paper. As it is impossible to give all their names here, I shall only say that my greatest debt is to Professor Paul N. Rosenstein-Rodan, from whom I received constant help and encouragement during my stay at M.I.T.

the "second-degree market economy," consumer preferences also influence which goods are to be produced, with the resources allocated by the planners, by the existing plants producing consumer goods. In the "third-degree market economy," the pattern of new investments in plants producing consumer goods also responds to consumer demand. Even in the last case, however, planners' preferences determine the overall magnitude of consumption (its share in national product) and the amount of investment devoted to consumer goods industries. As Drewnowski notes, most of the Communist economies are now in transition from a "first-degree market economy" to a "second-degree market economy," extending the sphere of influence of individual preferences somewhat.

THE STATE PREFERENCE FUNCTION

A satisfactory theory of the socialist economy must be able to explain how a socialist economy actually works. Such a theory is, of course, the ultimate aim, but what is attempted in this paper is the much more limited objective of making the main elements of the socialist economy subject to the tools of economic analysis. I shall, therefore, state the problems rather than solve them; I shall remain on a high level of abstraction and be concerned only with the most crucial problems. The first concept we must tackle is that of the state preference function. This concept is significant in either system but is fundamental to the theory of socialism; and it ought to be expressed in such a way as to make possible the substitution of numerical data for its variables. Second, a framework must be provided for analyzing the interrelation between the state and individual preference functions. All the more detailed analysis (for which, it is hoped, the approach presented here will provide a basis) is left to some future studies.

The preference function of the state has the same formal features as does the individual preference function. Its independent variables represent the means by which the state achieves its aims. They must be expressed in some measurable way.[2] The simplest solution would be to express those variables in quantities of final goods or services available in the national economy for consumption, investment, or export. The variables so expressed we may call the "goods" of the state preference function. These "goods" will usually be aggregates, such as food, clothing, rolling stock, etc. This implies a further problem of disaggregating the totals into particular goods, which may be a rather intricate process but which for the time being we shall ignore.

---

[2] If, therefore, we consider such a state aim as "education," we have to make it measurable by expressing it by the number of classrooms in use or, better still, by the number of classroom-hours per month or year.

The value of the function which the state maximizes may be taken to represent some sort of "state utility"; but it may also have another significance which I shall explain later.

The function may be represented by an indifference map, the curves of which will be convex to the origin (decreasing marginal rate of substitution). This is a familiar property of a preference function, which can be accepted as a property of the state function without raising any serious problems; but it is not a very illuminating property. The important problem is the shape of the function. Even a fragment of it would suffice, but no state so far has published a white or blue book containing its preference function. The preference function is implicit in the state's activities, but it is never stated explicitly. However, neither is the consumer's preference function, and that has not prevented economists from making it the basic concept of economic theory.

The consumer's preference function has to be revealed,[3] and so has the state preference function. The consumer's preference function is revealed through the consumer's market behavior. This is not an ideal way of discovering the preference function, but we have no better device. Its main defect is that the consumer's preference function is revealed only after he has acted on the market. The manifestation of the consumer's preferences in the form of demand is an "ex post" phenomenon.

With the state preference function we are in a better position. We have not only ex post facto manifestations of the function in the form of actually executed policies of the state but also what we may call "declared targets of policy," which are "ex ante." In a socialist state these targets are officially determined and published as a national economic plan.

A published plan is, of course, a "coordinated" one (a term from the parlance of planning commissions), and that means not only that the plan is feasible in terms of resources and techniques but also that all the resources and technical possibilities are to be used fully. A plan determines the "ex ante" equilibrium of the system.

If this is the case, the point of equilibrium must be on the production-possibility curve. The shape of the production-possibility curve, at least in the range where production is practical, must be assumed to be known. Consequently, if we have a point on the production-possibility curve, we have also the transformation rate at this point and in its immediate vicinity.

But a "coordinated" and approved plan implies also that the targets of the plan correspond to what the state considers most desirable. Therefore, the coordinates representing the targets determine a point which is not only on the production-possibility curve but also at the point on the curve that the state considers best. In other words, that point is a point of equi-

---

[3] P. A. Samuelson, "Consumption Theory in Terms of Revealed Preference," *Economica*, New Series, vol. 15, no. 60 (November 1948), pp. 243–51.

librium determined by the production possibilities and the preferences of the state. A state indifference curve can be drawn through that point. Its slope would, of course, be equal to the slope of the production-possibility curve.

The segment of the state preference function directly adjoining the equilibrium point would therefore be revealed. It is, of course, only a small segment of the function, but it gives us important information: the rate of substitution between or relative valuation of the two state "goods" in the neighborhood of the equilibrium point.

The procedure may be generalized and applied to many goods, in which case a whole system of rates of substitution will be revealed. These rates will be equal to the slopes of the indifference curves of the state preference function near the equilibrium points. They may also be looked upon as relative shadow prices implicit in the state's decisions about quantities. We may call these prices "state preference prices." They constitute a price system connected to and consistent with the plan targets expressed in physical quantities. In its policies the state should maintain this link between quantities and prices as a condition of consistency. In other words, state preference prices ought to be included in the state plan as an important supplementary chapter to the chapter containing quantities.[4]

The state preference prices are relative prices, but there is nothing to prevent us from making them absolute by expressing them in any arbitrary unit we may choose. Once we do that, the sum total of values of all products (which is being maximized by the state) ceases to be some "state utility"—an ordinal concept—and becomes a value of national product expressed in whatever units we choose—a quantity measurable in cardinal numerals. To distinguish it from the national product as understood in the ordinary way, we may call it the "state-preference national product."

There is really nothing new or surprising in this. The state-preference national product is a purely conventional concept, and a similar measure could be constructed for any preference function. It is only when there are numerous individual preference functions with utilities having no common measure that this concept cannot be applied. With a single state preference function the state preference national product is merely one way of evaluating the real national income. A problem that is insoluble if we look at it form the point of view of many individual preference functions is, of course, simple if we start from one function only.[5] And again

---

[4] As things happen now in socialist states, the prices are not part of the national plans. And it may be taken for granted that, if the state-preference-price criteria were applied, some inconsistencies in the plans would be discovered. This is exactly one of the points at which we have to introduce some normative element into our analysis.

[5] P. A. Samuelson, "Evaluation of Real National Income," *Oxford Economic Papers*, vol. 2, no. 1 (January 1950), pp. 1–21.

this simplified approach, which is of no use under individualistic assumptions, may be useful for our analysis of a socialist society.

What we have done is to show how the state preference function is revealed by the data that are declared by the state. This is a realistic approach, because in practice the socialist state determines plan targets in physical quantities, and the rates of substitution which indicate the shape of its preference function are implicit and have to be revealed. But this is not the only procedure that could be used. Contrary to what is possible with consumers' preferences, the state might very well declare not the production targets but the shape of the function itself. By confronting the preference function with production possibilities, the planners might then determine the production targets. To a theoretical economist, such a procedure presumably is simpler and states the issues more clearly. But what the opinion of the practical planner would be is an open question. What is really important is to have target quantities of "goods" consistent with transformation rates and state preference prices, both elements being equally valid parts of the national plan. This alone would be a great improvement on the present system because it would require an internally consistent model of the whole interdependent national economy and, consequently, would necessitate concentration on the determinateness of the system. This is important because overdeterminateness is the curse of socialist economies. And note that it is not an overdeterminateness of the theoretical model, which can trouble only the armchair economist counting his equations, but an overdeterminateness in practice which leads to uninvited and mostly unpredictable consequences.[6]

This has been, of course, a very simplified presentation of the problem. For practical planning purposes we must make much more elaborate assumptions. What is intended here is only to show the lines along which this sort of problem can be attacked.

THE ZONES OF INFLUENCE IN A SOCIALIST ECONOMY

So for I have concentrated on the state preference function. But the crucial problem of an economic theory of socialism is the interaction of the state and individual preferences.

If we take a short-term view, we may abstract from the influence the individual has on the state preference function through political channels and consider the state and individual preference functions to be independent of each other.

---

[6] By "overdeterminateness in practice" I mean the overdeterminateness of the system of decisions taken by the state. These decisions determine the "ex ante" equilibrium which, in socialism, is an emphatically practical phenomenon, since the state's decisions lead to real actions. The socialist system, like any system, cannot be either overdetermined or underdetermined "ex post," but, if it is overdetermined "ex ante," it determines itself "ex post" in a way not desired or expected by the planners.

There may be areas in which state and individual preferences do not meet, that is, areas in which each unit is confronted with possibilities depending only on natural or technical conditions. But where they meet they constitute restraints for each other. Each of them (or, rather, the activities resulting from each of them) becomes a part of the environment restraining the actions resulting from the other's preferences. We must try, therefore, to determine the zone in which state preferences are supreme (the zone of state influence), the zone in which individual preferences are supreme (the zone of individual influence), and the zone in which state and individual preferences meet (the zone of dual influence). To determine which part of the national economy belongs to which zone means to define the nature of the economic system in question.

Capitalism once was, or was, at least, considered, a system in which the whole national economy belonged to the individual zone. But in present-day capitalism there is usually some state zone and a quite significant dual-influence zone.

At this point one more important difference between the two systems must be stated: Capitalism is a system in which the boundary lines between the zones as defined above are fairly stable. The reason is, of course, the greater rigidity of economic institutions under capitalism. The most important single cause of this rigidity is the link that exists in capitalism between private property and production. This link is in fact a basic feature of capitalism. When there is private property in production, the organization of the system cannot easily be changed without affecting private property rights. Indeed, any encroachments by the state on the economic life of the country are difficult. Capitalism has certainly changed in the last hundred years—the state- and dual-influence zones have expanded, and the individual zone has contracted. But the change has been slow and painful; the economic theory of capitalism tacitly recognizes this fact by taking the institutional framework of capitalism for granted and not bothering much about examining the consequences of its changes.

Socialism may be defined as a system in which the national economy is divided between the state- and the dual-influence zones. No individual zone exists under full socialism. The boundary between the state- and the dual-influence zone, however, may be anywhere in the range between the limiting case in which the whole national economy is in the state zone and that in which the state zone is not much more extensive than in capitalism. This makes socialism a system of which many different variants may exist and in which the change from one variant to the other can be made fairly easily and promptly by nothing more than a governmental decision, since many institutional rigidities characteristic of capitalism do not exist under socialism.

In socialism institutional changes are a part of the operation of the system. Changes in the position of the boundary between state- and dual-influence zones may occur at any time and may sometimes be instantaneous. Institutional changes inside each zone are even easier,[7] institutional change may often take less time than changes in capital equipment. The theory must take account of this and look upon institutional changes as a particular class of available alternatives.

This sort of approach would permit an economic theory more general in nature than the traditional theory of capitalism. In such a theory capitalism would be considered as a small range of special cases in which the zone of state influence is fairly limited and the institutional setting is fairly rigid. Socialism would be represented by a much wider range of special cases at the opposite end of the scale where no zone of individual influence is allowed but where one case can easily be transformed into another. Intermediate systems, such as "the welfare state," or "people's democracies on the way to socialism," can be defined in a similar way.

I must now attempt a more detailed analysis of the zones of state, dual, and individual influence, and try to determine the nature of the boundary line between those zones. This will require a theoretical model, which must be a simplification of reality, but I shall try to keep it as close as possible to what happens in socialist economies.

The state zone is the part of the national economy in which the scales of values are the preferences of the state. No consumers' preferences enter into the picture. In socialism this situation exists as a rule in the investment-goods industries, where resources, capital equipment, and products are all owned by the state.

In all branches producing consumer goods there is the possibility of a dual-influence zone, with the boundary of the state zone being drawn differently in different cases.

Let us start with the limiting case and assume that all the national economy belongs to the state zone; consumers' preferences have no significance. The only restraints are then natural resources and techniques. This is the familiar theoretical dictatorship model. It corresponds roughly to "war communism," a system that existed in Soviet Russia for a short time during the civil war, 1918–20.

The quantities of all goods produced and the distribution of them among the members of the population are determined by the state. In other words, there is a full rationing system. This sort of model is not realistic in present circumstances and of little use except as a limiting theoretical case of the institutional alternatives. We may describe this case as a case of "no market economy."

The next alternative would be a system in which consumer goods are sold in the market. In this market the state is the only supplier and determines all the quantities brought for sale. The consumers (as buyers) are

---

[7] For example, changes in the sizes of enterprises, which are of considerable importance but cannot be discussed here because of limited space.

free to buy as much or as little as they want. The state, being anxious to sell what is produced, will adjust the prices to consumer demand so as to have no unsold stocks. It may, therefore, be said that quantities are fixed by the state, but prices are determined by the consumer demand according to consumers' tastes.

The difference between this case and the previous one is that the distribution of consumer goods has been transferred from the state zone to the dual-influence zone or, preferably, that the boundary between the zones has been moved so as to leave the distribution of consumer goods in the dual-influence zone and permit a market for consumer goods to be established.

On that market, it must be noted, consumers' preferences (strictly, consumers' demands) influence prices and the distribution of goods only. The quantities of particular goods are *not* affected, nor are the resources used in their production, nor the distribution of resources among particular producing plants.

This is a very typical situation in present-day socialist economies—an equilibrium between supply and demand on the market for consumer goods is maintained by adjusting prices, whereas quantities produced are not affected by demand at all and are governed by the central plan. We may call this case a "first-degree market economy."[8]

The "second-degree market economy" exists when the next adjoining range of economic variables is transferred from the state- to the dual-influence zone. In other words, these variables are made to depend not only on state but also on consumers' preferences. This "adjoining range" includes the quantities produced of particular consumer goods, the quantities of resources (excluding new investments) used in their production, and the distribution of resources among particular plants.

This would leave unaffected by the change the aggregate quantity of consumer goods, the aggregate quantity of resources used in producing consumer goods, and the capital equipment employed in industries producing consumer goods. The second (unaffected) set of quantities being kept constant, the first set of quantities will be determined by adjusting production to consumers' demands and maximizing profits in the whole consumer-goods sector. The principle of maximization of profits would assure rational distribution of resources and the production of rational quantities of particular goods.

The second-degree market economy corresponds roughly to the system

---

[8] It might be possible to conceive a *first-degree market economy* in which prices are fixed by the state and quantities determined by consumers' preferences. This possibility of applying alternative instruments of economic policy seems to be of considerable theoretical interest. It is probable that it could be applied to higher degree market economies. In the present article only the simplest case is presented.

aimed at by the "decentralization reforms" and "model reconsiderations" which are at present taking place in the people's democracies.

The "third-degree market economy" exists when the determination of the pattern of new investments in plants producing consumer goods depends on the consumers' demands for finished products. This means that decisions concerning what sorts of investment are to be made and to which plants they should be assigned are transferred from the state- to the dual-influence zone. The aggregate quantities of produced consumer goods, of resources used, and of new investments remain in the state zone.

This simple classificatory system may be made more complicated in many ways; for example, the consumer-goods sector may be divided into a number of subsectors. But our aim here is simply to demonstrate how the interaction of state and consumers' preferences and their differing spheres of influence can be taken into account.

One more important observation might be added: As a result of the dual influence of the state and the consumers, the socialist economy will have two independent sets of prices, one coming from the state preference function and one from the consumers' preference functions. Both systems of prices are rational and "correct" in their particular way. The "state" prices will be applied to all dealings between state enterprises and will be used in all national accounting calculations. The "consumers'" prices will apply to sales by state enterprises to consumers. The coexistence of these two sets of prices must be a characteristic of a rationally managed socialist economy.[9]

CONCLUSIONS

The aim of this article has been to lay a basis for a realistic theory of a socialist economy. It started from the fact that there are two sets of preference functions that are effective in a national economy: the preference functions of the population, which manifest themselves in purchases and sales in the market, and the state preference function, which is expressed by the economic plans and policies of the state. Both are necessary to express the economic interests and aspirations of the population. The population influences the state preference function through political channels. A perfect democracy might be defined as a system in which the state's preferences represent people's interests in an accurate way. The examination of the working of these political channels is, however, outside the scope of economics and must be left to political science. What the economist has to do is to take account of the observable fact that two systems of prefer-

---

[9] This opinion has a normative element in it. The necessity of two simultaneous systems of prices is not generally recognized. No clear, uniform principle for determining prices has so far been accepted in socialist countries.

ence exist and are sources of decisions in every economy and to try to understand the results of their interaction. The existence of dual preference systems ought to be comprised in the economic theory of any system, but it is basic to the development of a theory of the socialist system. From these assumptions some fundamental propositions for the economic theory of socialism were derived.

The preferences of the state were examined in some detail. It was found that in a contemporary socialist state they exist in an implicit form but may be "revealed" by the declarations and activities of the state.

A method was suggested for attaching numerical values to the state preference system. It could be used to make the socialist system internally consistent and not overdetermined.

Once the concept of the state preference function was defined, its interaction with individual preference functions had to be explained. The possibility of various institutional arrangements was discussed and the principles of interaction stated. It was suggested that this might lead to a more general theory that would embrace both the theory of capitalism and the theory of socialism as special cases. To explain the interaction of state and individual preferences, the device of zoning the national economy was introduced, the zone of dual influence being the crucial one. It was noted that some sorts of market exist in that zone. Their properties differ considerably from those of capitalist markets.

All this has been a suggestion for a new approach to the economic theory of socialism. The theory itself still remains to be worked out.

It is possible to list some fundamental problems that ought to be examined first. The working of the markets under "zoning" conditions is, perhaps, the most important problem. Particular attention should be paid to the labor market, which also falls under the "zoning" system but was not discussed here. Then comes the problem of the socialist state enterprise, which has to take decentralized decisions consistent with the preferences of the state. Collective consumption, a feature of socialism, should be examined along with the problem of the markets. Then, of course, an analysis of growth must be initiated, since growth problems are crucial in every socialist system. The investigation of monetary problems may be considered less urgent, but would present ample scope for concepts differing widely from those used in capitalism.

Very much remains to be done. It is hoped that the approach suggested in this article will be of use in that work.

16

ECONOMIC PLANNING
IN THE USSR*

R. W. Davies

The Soviet economic system has served as a prototype for other Communist countries, giving rise to the term "Soviet-type economy" in the literature of comparative economic systems. In this selection, Davies tells how a comprehensive scheme of central planning and administrative control was adopted, beginning in the late 1920s, to mobilize resources for rapid industrialization. He examines physical planning, financial planning, and the direction of the labor force, noting the advantages and disadvantages of the methods employed. The author shows why this "mobilization" model is less suitable for the more "mature" contemporary Soviet economy and explains the resulting changes in resource allocation, economic organization, and planning techniques. He then evaluates possibilities for further improvements in Soviet economic planning and management.

THE SOVIET PLANNING PROCESS FOR
RAPID INDUSTRIALIZATION

An Outline of the System

The Soviet government set itself the objective of a more rapid rate of industrialization, with a greater investment in capital-consuming indus-

* Revised from "The Soviet Planning Process of Rapid Industrialization," *Economics of Planning*, vol. 6 (1966), no. 1, pp. 53–67, and "Planning a Mature Economy in the USSR," *Economics of Planning*, vol. 6 (1966), no. 2, pp. 138–52. Copyright 1978 by R. W. Davies. Reprinted by permission. R. W. Davies is Professor and Director of the Centre for Russian and East European Studies at the University of Birmingham, England.

tries and processes, than could be achieved within the framework of the market economy of the 1920s. The main objective was achieved, but with a much slower increase in living standards (consumer goods, agricultural output) than had been intended. To enforce its priorities, the Soviet government abandoned the major assumptions of its earlier policy:

1. A market relationship with the peasant was replaced by administrative or coercive control over his output. The centers of economic and political resistance in the rural commune were destroyed, and hundreds of thousands of *kulak* families were expelled from their home villages. Twenty-five million individual peasant farms were combined into 250,000 collective farms (*kolkhozy*), one or several to each village. The old boundaries and strips were destroyed, and most land and cattle were pooled and worked in common. Agricultural machinery was gradually made available from several thousand state-owned Machine and Tractor Stations (MTS). The *kolkhoz* was required to supply a substantial part of its output to the state collection agencies at low fixed prices in the form of compulsory deliveries. These supplies were then used by the state (*a*) to make available a minimum amount of foodstuffs to the growing urban population, and (*b*) for export. Exports of grain fell from 9 million tons in 1913 to 2 million tons in 1926–27 and 178 thousand tons in 1929. They rose (temporarily) to 4.8 million tons in 1930 and 5.1 million tons in 1931, and this increase was used to pay for imports of equipment and industrial materials.

2. Inflation was permitted to develop: The wages of the expanding industrial and building labor force were partly met by increasing the flow of paper money. Prices began to rise, but the inflation was partly repressed through price control in both the producer goods market and the retail market. (Private shops and trading agencies were taken over by the state to facilitate this.) For several years (1929–35) a rationing system was introduced in the towns, supplemented by state sales of goods above the ration at high prices. Foodstuffs were also sold extensively by the peasants at high prices on the free market. In this way, the available supply of consumer goods and foodstuffs was distributed over the old and the new urban population, and consumption per head in the towns was forced down.

3. Within industry, the system of physical controls which had already existed during the 1920s was greatly extended. Prices were fixed, and there was no market for producer goods. Instead, materials and equipment were distributed to existing factories and new building sites through a system of priorities, which enabled new key factories to be built and bottlenecks in existing industries to be widened. The plan set targets for the output of major intermediate and final products, and the physical allocation system was designed to see these were reached.

To sum up these first three points: the policies of 1928–32 enabled a new allocation of GNP to be imposed on the economy. The discussions of the 1920s had assumed that savings would be made by the state within the framework of a dynamic equilibrium on the market between agriculture and industry. This placed a constraint on the proportion of GNP which could be invested, and on the allocation of that investment (investment in consumer goods industries would need to be sufficient to enable the output of consumer goods to increase at the rate required for equilibrium). Now this constraint was removed. Urban and rural living standards were temporarily depressed, and physical controls were used to divert resources to the establishment of new capital-intensive industries and techniques which gave no return during the construction period, and were relatively costly in the medium-term. This method of obtaining forced savings through physical controls resembled the wartime planning controls used in capitalist economies to shift resources towards the end product of the armament and maintenance of the large armed forces. In the Soviet case, the end product was the capital goods industries and the maintenance of the workers employed in building and operating them. But in both cases a shift in the allocation of resources which could not easily be achieved through manipulating the market mechanism was achieved through direct controls.

4. However, the system was not one simply of physical controls. Within a few years, the following features, stable over a long period, supplemented the system so far described:

a. Each peasant household was permitted to work a private plot, and to own its own cow and poultry. After obligations to the state had been met, the separate households and the *kolkhoz* as a unit were permitted to sell their produce on the free market ("collective farm market"), on which prices were reached by supply and demand. Here an important part of all marketed foodstuffs was bought and sold. The large flow of money to the peasants through these sales compensated them for the low prices they received for their compulsory deliveries to the state.

b. With some important exceptions, the employee was free to change his job. A market for labor existed, if a very imperfect one, and wage levels were formed partly in response to supply and demand. A corollary of this was that cost controls and profit-and-loss accounting were introduced in industry, to supplement the physical controls.

c. Rationing of consumer goods was abolished, and an attempt was made to balance supply and demand on the consumer market, as a whole and for individual goods, through fiscal measures, notably a purchase tax (the "turnover tax") differentiated according to commodity.

5. A large variety of unplanned and even illegal activities between firms supplemented and made feasible the rather crude controls of the central plan and must be considered as part of the logic of the system. Black and "gray" markets for consumer goods emerged as a result of the shortages which, as we shall see, were endemic in the system.

The Planning Process

In this section, the planning process is described as it operated in 1935–41 after the abolition of the rationing of consumer goods, and again in the post-war years from 1947 onwards. It should be borne in mind, however, that many of its features continue without basic alteration even now. The modifications introduced after Stalin's death in 1953 are discussed below.

We have so far established that Soviet plan controls during rapid industrialization may be divided schematically as in Figure 1. Each enterprise received a set of output targets and input allocations with which to fulfil them. At the same time its monetary expenditures were controlled by financial or cost plans, which were less important to it than its output plan, but which came into operation if the pressure from above for higher output led the enterprise to increase its money expenditures excessively.

Disaggregation. A key problem for the central planners was to disaggregate their major decisions so that they would be enforced at the plant level, and to aggregate information and proposals so as to be able satisfactorily to take into account the effect of their past and present decisions on different parts of the economy. In Soviet planning, this was normally dealt with in the following ways:

1. Economic organization was adapted to handle this problem.

    a. Factories were placed under the control of ministries or their production departments (*glavki*), each of which was responsible for a particular group of products (e.g., iron and steel, motor

FIGURE 1
Principal Planning Controls over Industrial Activity

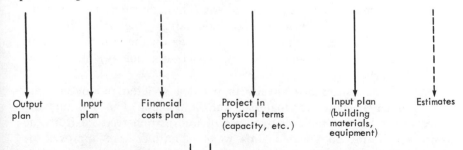

| Output plan | Input plan | Financial costs plan | Project in physical terms (capacity, etc.) | Input plan (building materials, equipment) | Estimates |

For existing enterprises   For capital construction

vehicles). Each ministry was given very considerable powers over its constituent firms, each of which usually consisted of a single factory. The government was therefore to a considerable extent concerned only with handling transfers *between* industries.

b. Smaller factories producing low-priority items were placed under the control of the government of one of the constituent republics, or under local authorities. In the past, the government tended not to bother with them, and to treat allocations to them as a residual.

c. Within the State Planning Committee (Gosplan), which was an advisory body to the government, and within each ministry or subministry, departmental organization mirrored the planning arrangements. In the iron and steel industry, for example, there were separate departments of the ministry responsible for sales of the industry's product, for supplies to the industry, for production plans of iron and steel works, and for capital construction. Within Gosplan, there were separate departments concerned with production, allocation, and construction. This is illustrated schematically in Figure 2.

2. The time-horizon was divided so as to disaggregate. Five-year plans set broad rates of growth for GNP by sector of origin and end use, and listed the output targets for important intermediate and final products, and the location and intended capacity of all major construction projects. Annual plans (known as "operational" plans) handled the detailed application of these longer term plans in a particular year. Quarterly and even monthly partial plans handled particular industries or aspects of planning.

3. Planning procedures are designed so as to enable more or less systematic aggregation and disaggregation. We give the procedure for the annual plan as an example in Figure 3:

Stage I. Gosplan possessed a mass of data on past performance, and it or the government issued a statement about the principal economic magnitudes to be aimed at for the following year. These directives indicated the main proportions and principal production targets, the proposed investment allocation for each ministry, and proposals for the growth of output per man-year ("labor productivity," in Soviet terminology) and the reduction of costs.

Stage II. Ministries had already prepared a skeleton production program and set of claims for materials and equipment. This was now adjusted in the light of the directives and of information received from the firms. The forms on which claims were submitted were approved by Gosplan. The products itemized generally correspond to the nomenclature of the national production and supply plans, which included up to 5,000

FIGURE 2
Central Economic Administration

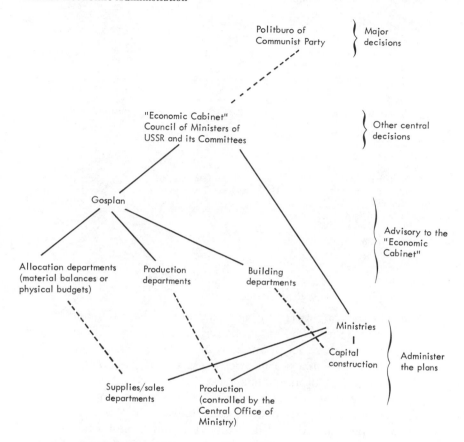

product groups. There were usually substantial differences between (a) the ministries' output proposals and supply claims and (b) the original directives.

Stage III. Gosplan now had the job of fitting together the ministry plans and its own draft plans. In this "period of coordination and reconciliation" the heads of firms and ministries negotiated with the government in Moscow. From this there emerged the national economic plan, with its constituent production, supplies (allocation), and investment plans. This whole negotiation was conducted in terms of, say, 30 times as many major indicators as were set out in the original directives.

Stage IV. The ministries now disaggregated the national economic plan to the level of the firm.

4.   These aggregation and disaggregation procedures were assisted by two important sets of what might be termed "control coefficients":

FIGURE 3
Procedure for Annual Planning

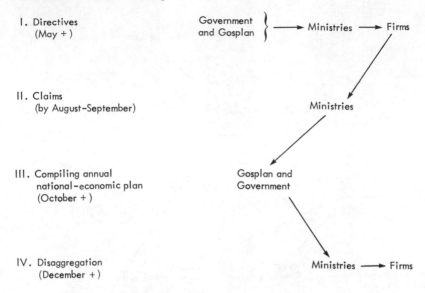

I. Directives
(May +)

II. Claims
(by August–September)

III. Compiling annual
national-economic plan
(October +)

IV. Disaggregation
(December +)

    a. Output targets (or success indicators). The fulfillment of these was the main driving motive of the Soviet firm and even ministry. (Managerial promotions and salaries tended until 1959 to be related almost exclusively to success in fulfillment of output targets.) Output targets were given for very broad groups of products at the national level, and they were supplemented by the sales departments of each ministry, whose disaggregation of the planned output target for a product group was supposed in theory to be binding on the firm. We return to the difficulties involved here later.

    b. Norms or consumption standards. At the shop-floor level, hundreds of thousands of specific consumption standards were used to control the production process and to cut down waste. But even at the plant level, discussion proceeded on the basis of aggregated standards, and a further aggregation took place between plant and ministry. Gosplan used overall input coefficients to check the claims of ministries, and many of these were incorporated in the plan. These could be of the form

x physical units of input of A for *y* physical units of output of B; e.g., tons of crude steel per ton of rolled steel.

or

x physical units of input of A for *y* value-units of ouput of B; e.g., tons of cement per 1 million rubles' building and assembly work.

Different consumption standards were applied to different processes and even to different plants. These were probably quite reliable as a rough measure of efficiency and of reliability of claims, and a useful device for handling complex production activities centrally.

Coordination. The outline so far given of the planning process during rapid industrialization is unrealistic, for it assumes much smoother control than was possible in practice. Smooth planning was vitiated by:

1. Uncertainty. Innovations, mistakes, and bottlenecks were not predicted with any accuracy. Future proportions of coal and oil output, for example, were quite wrongly predicted even after World War II.

2. "Tight" planning. The plan was used as an instrument for forcing up production, and all targets were deliberately strained, all stocks minimized. This reinforced uncertainty and encouraged the emergence of unexpected bottlenecks. (In the early 1930s annual as well as five-year plan targets were sometimes wildly exaggerated.)

Moreover, we have so far been writing as if planning started from a clean sheet with each planning period. In fact, of course, planners work *at the margin.* Of a steel output of 12 million tons, as much as 10 million tons in an annual plan may be irrevocably committed to existing activities. Even in a five-year plan, possible shifts may be small: during the second five-year plan (1933–37), for example, most capital investment was devoted to completing projects already started during the first plan (1928–32) or earlier.

The "coordination and reconciliation" activities undertaken by Gosplan in drawing up the annual plan were therefore limited by uncertainty, by the consequences of tight planning, and by existing commitments. Gosplan had two functions here. First, it sought to balance programs by eliminating existing or potential bottlenecks due to the excess of demand over supply. To do this it followed a regular procedure and used a list of priorities. Thus it might cut cement supplies to housing in order to have enough to push through a crash program to complete a steel foundry needed to produce certain types of steel required by priority industries. Second, it tried to inject into departmental programs the priorities and investment programs favored by the government. Thus it might increase cement supplies to the constructors of new chemical factories which are regarded as urgent.

In the coordination procedure, a great deal of use was made by Gosplan of "material balances" or physical budgets, showing supplies and requirements for different product groups or types of equipment. These physical budgets were adjusted by the appropriate Gosplan department through a fairly crude procedure of rule-of-thumb iteration. These were not input-output tables, for no technical coefficients had been calculated; sometimes a rough allowance was made for indirect outlays (e.g., of steel needed to make more machinery for motorcar factories if the output of motorcars was increased, as well as direct outlays of steel on the motorcars themselves). The procedure was therefore slow and inexact.

Financial Planning

1. Our account so far has been primarily concerned with physical planning. But as we have seen, a money flow corresponded to all the physical flows, and some of the money transactions in the system (e.g., wage payments, sales on the collective-farm market, sales on the retail market generally) were not accomplished by physical controls. Once the inflationary process had led to the initial reallocation of GNP in 1928–30, financial equilibrium was a subsidiary goal of the government. What was required was that money payments to the population (wage payments by the state, payments by the state to *kolkhozy* which were then distributed to their members, etc.) should not exceed the value of the supply of commodities available on the state-controlled market at fixed prices and on the collective-farm market at market prices. As payments by the state included the earnings of persons employed in the investment goods industries, in the social services, and in the armed forces, a gap existed between the cost-price of consumer goods (equal to the cost of wages in that sector and the materials, etc., it employed) and the total monetary demand.

This gap needed to be covered by taxation, and could be met in principle in one or all of three ways: (*a*) by direct taxation; (*b*) by allowing the profits of enterprises to rise and then taxing them; or (*c*) by an indirect tax, which could be an equiproportional markup on all goods, or imposed only on consumer goods.

    a.   Direct taxation was of minor importance. There were no legal incomes uncontrolled by the state (except for peasant earnings on the free market) available to tax, and high income tax on state employees was regarded as undesirable.

    b.   In the early stages, the authorities were unwilling to allow profits to rise, because they feared that monetary pressure on the retail market would lead to very high profits in the consumer goods industries.

    c.   The misnamed "turnover tax" therefore became the main source of tax. It was a markup on the wholesale price of consumer goods and the low delivery price of foodstuffs. The markup was differentiated by product for social reasons and to bring about a rough equality between the supply and the demand for each product. It was argued that a high level of tax on producer goods, which were mainly sold to the state, would merely mean that the state would have to reimburse itself from a still higher tax rate on consumer goods.

Figure 4 illustrates the principal money flows in the system.

FIGURE 4

Soviet Financial Planning: A Simplified Picture (not to scale)

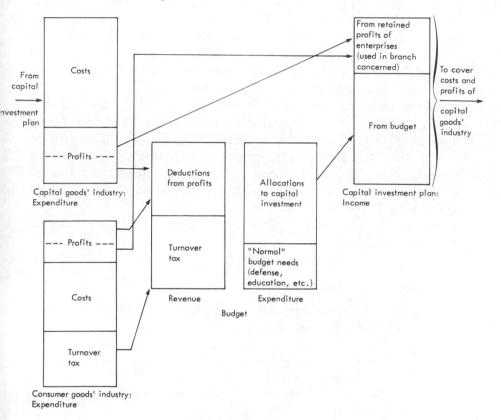

2. Prices in the producer and the consumer goods industries therefore had a common base. They were reached as follows:

    a.   costs of production, including wages, the cost of materials, overheads, a small allowance for depreciation, but no interest charge on capital;

    b.   a small markup for profits;

    c.   trade and transport costs.

To these was added in the case of consumer goods

    d.   turnover tax (differentiated by product) to reach the retail price.

Profits were partly taxed, partly retained by the firm or industry; a high proportion of profits in excess of the plan was placed at the disposal of the firm in the "Director's Fund," later known as the "Fund of the Firm."

It will be noted that the prices of producer goods were unresponsive to supply and demand, and could remain stable for many years. Each industry received a price for its product equal to average costs for the industry plus a small margin for profit. But the industry itself could pay differential prices, offering high prices to high-cost firms and low prices to low-cost firms. However, prices included no systematic allowance for the varying richness of the capital stock of firms producing similar products. In practice, the rate of profit earned on different products varied enormously, owing to the hit-and-miss way in which prices were fixed.

3. Elaborate arrangements were made to control the flows of (a) short-term loans (for seasonal stocks, goods in transit, etc.), (b) wages, (c) allocations to investment (mainly financed by the budget), and (d) cash through the State Bank (responsible for working capital) and specialized investment banks (responsible for allocations to fixed capital). All these devices aimed at maintaining the financial equilibrium, which was secured through balancing money incomes against money expenditures through the fiscal system. In the end, inflation was brought under control over a short period before World War II (1935–37) and in a more systematic way after the war (1948–   ). Between 1948 and 1953, retail prices were even substantially reduced.

Labor and Labor Controls

1. The following were the principal devices used by the government to control the urban labor force:
   a. When unemployment had been absorbed, recruitment of labor from the villages to the towns was organized systematically on contract with the collective farms (by about 1932).
   b. Training and education of semiskilled, skilled, and technical manpower were systematically planned.
   c. At various stages (particularly in the war and postwar years from 1940 to 1951), scarce grades or types of manpower were restricted in their movement or even subject to allocation.
   d. Prisoners in labor camps were used extensively in the mining, timber, and building industries in remote regions and even at times in advanced activities such as aircraft and rocket design.
2. In spite of these measures, labor was highly mobile, particularly in the early 1930s, and both central planners and factory managements utilized money wages to influence the allocation of labor—hence a form of labor market emerged, though studies of Soviet production functions have confirmed that it was highly imperfect:
   a. The government approved national scales for different grades and types of labor in different areas, and adjusted the scales

from time to time to take account of demand and supply. There was a high differential for skill.

b. There was an elaborate piece-rate and bonus system to encourage higher productivity.

c. Management could in practice manipulate bonuses and classifications to attract scarce kinds of labor.

3. Unskilled and even semiskilled labor were not basically a scarce factor of production (owing to the existence of a large stock of labor in the countryside). There was therefore a recurrent tendency to substitute labor for capital. This has been well described as a "labor-intensive variant of capital-intensive industrialization."

4. The need for labor coupled with the pressure to fulfill the output plan encouraged management to overspend its allocation for wages, and made for an inflationary situation. Control by the State Bank over wage payments was the most important single device for maintaining wage stability.

5. Government control over trade unions has assisted wage policy. The central wage bargaining process was eliminated in 1929. At the same time, a policy of cutting the rate for the job as techniques and organization improved was systematically enforced, so that money wages rose *less* than output per man.

6. But the government, as well as firmly controlling wage rates, also took responsibility for social conditions. While working and housing conditions in the early years were very poor, hours of work were restricted to seven to eight hours daily. Pensions, sickness and maternity benefits, vacations with pay, and welfare services (crèches, factory clubs, canteens), largely administered through the trade unions, were more generous than was the case in many Western countries at a similar stage of industrialization. Some social benefits (particularly housing tied to the factory) were used to influence the movement of labor (high priority factories tended to have better facilities and housing; benefits were partly dependent on the length of service at the particular factory).

Strengths and Weaknesses of the Soviet Planning System

No adequate "cost-benefit analysis" of the Soviet system or its constituent parts has yet been attempted. Here we simply list some of its principal achievements and disadvantages:

Advantages

1. The system succeeded in enforcing allocation of a very high proportion of GNP to investment over a long period. Within this allocation, resources were concentrated on the growth-inducing producer goods industries, which were transformed from high-cost to low-cost industries. In

general, it is possible with this kind of mechanism to enforce successfully high-priority crash programs (e.g., the sputniks).

2. A high degree of centralization enabled the planners to inculcate the latest technology, imported from more advanced economies, into the whole economy at a rapid rate. Project institutes, such as *Gipromez* (the State Institute for Projects of Iron and Steel Works), were able to plan large-scale technological advances for a whole industry on a national scale. For many major technological problems, the Soviet system of centralized research also proved effective at a more advanced stage of development (e.g., nuclear research).

3. Considerable economies of scale (including economies from standardization) and economies of effort were possible in nationally planned industries.

4. The output drive from above, characteristic of Soviet planning throughout rapid industrialization provides a powerful instrument for enforcing high capacity utilization, and for keeping management and men working at a high pace.

Disadvantages

1. The cost of concentrating resources on producer goods industries was very high. Thus the policy adopted towards the peasantry led to a drastic decline in agricultural production. Hunger and famine resulted. The slaughter and death from undernourishment of large numbers of draft animals also undermined the state plans for industry. It forced the state to reallocate unexpected resources to the agricultural equipment industry and hence to the high-grade steel industry. It also had a drastic long-term effect on peasant morale.

2. When the central planners made a *wrong* technological choice, the cost (because the policy was carried out on a national scale) was proportionately heavy. For example, there was overinvestment in the coal industry and underinvestment in oil and chemicals.

3. Centralized administrative planning is inherently clumsy in its effects at the point of production. If the success indicators are very detailed, initiative and innovation at the factory level are prevented. But if they are not very detailed, factories produce what is easier to produce, rather than what is wanted. Control of quality through success indicators is also very difficult. The sellers' market which was coupled with Soviet administrative planning reinforced these difficulties. At the same time it led to the tendency for each industrial ministry to become a self-contained "empire," carrying out wasteful backward integration in order to control its supplies. If advertising and inflated sales organizations are a high cost of modern capitalism, inflated supplies organizations were (and are) a high cost of Soviet central planning.

To sum up with an example: Central planning enabled the construction of iron and steel works, using home-manufactured equipment, which in their main technologies were as good as those in the United States, and were utilized at a higher capacity. It also produced a situation where Soviet bedsteads were the heaviest in the world (because planned in tons), were produced on too small a scale (because made under several ministries) and therefore costly, and owing to the sellers' market could be made of iron, when the consumer would have preferred something more modern.

This is a mere list of factors. Economists need to ask themselves: *how* costly and beneficial were these various factors? How far were the advantages and disadvantages of the system inextricably tied together? Could the Soviet strategy for rapid growth, or some features of it, be employed without the disadvantages? How many of the unsuccessful features were due to the special conditions of Russia (including the difficult external and internal position of the government) and to the inexperience and imperfect knowledge of the people who made the system?

PLANNING A MATURE ECONOMY IN THE USSR

Economic Theory and the Soviet Economy

1. Traditional economic theory contrasts two types of system: the competitive or market system, with its "ideal type" of perfect competition, and the "command economy," or "planning under a dictator." These are treated as two possible alternative methods of allocating resources.

    a. The *market economy* is divided into competing units: a large number of individual consumers bargain with a large number of producers on the market. The goal of the producer is to maximize his profit; the goal of the consumer is to maximize his satisfaction. The resulting demand and supply are equated through price.

    The decisions on the consumer market are reflected back into the factor market, where a similar bargaining process settles the distribution of incomes between factors, and the distribution of the factors.

    As a result, resources in such an economy are allocated "rationally," by which the economist means "in accordance with the desires of the consumers."

    b. In the *command economy* (often referred to as *planning under a dictator*), final demand is determined not by individual consumers but by the decision of the central authority, as "whims of the dictator," or "planners' preferences" replace "consumers' preferences." The central authority also controls the allocation of all factors of production and the distribution of income. The system is completely centralized: its difficulty lies in the ability of the "dictator" to work out the "thousands of equations" involved in transforming his preferences into practical economic decisions.

2. How far does this theory provide an effective framework of analysis for contemporary capitalism and for Soviet planning?

   a. The development of economic analysis in the past 40 years has involved a number of realistic modifications of the original theory as applied to modern capitalism:

   (1) In many cases free entry into industries will be restricted and a state of imperfect competition will exist; at equilibrium, output may be lower and price higher than under perfect competition. However, economies of scale may make for lower costs in a highly organized oligopolistic industry. Advantage and disadvantage must be carefully examined.

   (2) While consumer *choice* exists, advertising, imperfect knowledge, and the power of initiative of the large firm mean that consumer *sovereignty* is quite restricted.

   (3) The assumption of permanent equilibrium in the system is a microeconomic one. At the level of macroeconomics, supply does not create its own demand and hence the possibility of underemployment of factors exists. Macroeconomic equilibrium requires government intervention.

   (4) The large government sector requires separate analysis. Nationalized industries produce as monopolies, but often with their "maximum profit" goal constrained; and as consumers they control a large part of the market for certain intermediate goods (e.g., an electricity board purchasing power-station equipment). The defense, education, and health departments of central and local governments are also large buyers and often act as oligopsonies. State fiscal, monetary, and tariff policies regulate the market.

   (5) The view that firm's economic behavior can be understood solely in terms of aiming at maximum profit in response to market price is an insufficient one. Within the large firm, decisions will be taken administratively (through the hierarchy) or by a cooperative or bargaining process; and much interfirm behavior may also be explained in this way. Industry is not an infinite number of atoms responding to price, but a finite number of blocs. The bloc as a whole reacts to price, but also has

dealings with other blocs which are to be explained in terms of organization theory rather than of the price mechanism; and bargaining and administrative processes help to explain economic behavior within each bloc.

b. Even with these modifications the original theory retains much validity:

(1) If firms do not always aim at maximizing their profits, they are concerned with making a satisfactory level of profits ("satisficing").

(2) There is consumer choice, and a market process also operates for intermediate goods and (partly) on the factor market.

(3) In spite of the considerable role of the government, a large segment of investment is still determined by the decisions of individual entrepreneurs (or entrepreneurial firms).

c. These developments of Western economic theory are of direct relevance to our understanding of the Soviet system:

(1) Physical planning is not something unknown in capitalist economies. In the Soviet economy, relationships between firms are regulated by administrative and bargaining processes; in a competitive system they are largely regulated by the market. But analogies to all the administrative and bargaining processes described in the section on "the planning process" above may be found within the capitalist firm, and within the government sector (compare the process for making fiscal estimates in a market economy with the procedures for plan compilation in Soviet industry). The "thousands of equations" predicted by Western economic theory are simplified by the existence of "administrative decentralization." Subsystems of economic administrators share decision making with the Council of Ministers; and bargaining and pressure from lower units assist the decision-making process. Moreover, like decisions by private entrepreneurs, planners' decisions are made only "at the margin."

(2) Some important economic activity in the USSR is to be explained in terms of a market mechanism, though most Soviet markets are highly imperfect. As we have seen, there is a partial market for labor, a fixed-price market for retail consumer goods, a free market for part of retail food sales; and various unofficial or illegal markets operate in practice.

Modern capitalist economies are imperfectly competitive and have important elements of administrative control. The Soviet economy is not entirely "planned from the center," and imperfect markets exist for certain purposes.

The Soviet Economy as a Special Case of Planned Economy

The Soviet planning system of the 1930s–1950s is not the only possible form of planned economy. In Soviet experience alone, at least two other forms of planning system have existed. In the period of *War Communism* (1918–20), industry was nationalized and industrial output was allocated physically. Owing to inflation the economy was virtually moneyless: labor was directly controlled, consumer goods were rationed, and agricultural output subject to requisition. However, peasants continued to work their own land, and no serious attempt was made to socialize agriculture. This system was the closest approach in principle to the "ideal form" of the command economy in the history of the Soviet system, though it existed side-by-side with illegal market activities on a very large scale. In the period of the *New Economic Policy* (1921–29), as in present-day Poland, state ownership of industry was combined with private agriculture through a regulated market. The effectiveness of planning was constrained by the existence of the market, but central goals were to some extent enforced.

A considerable variety of forms of central planning is to be found in Eastern Europe.

The systematic study of forms of economic organization has so far been little developed. One may distinguish two basic ways of classification.

Ownership. A planned economy is unlikely to be one in which all economic activity is nationalized. It will be a "mixed economy," combining private ownership with state ownership and possibly embracing different forms of state ownership (very varied forms of public ownership have been experienced, incorporating different degrees of state, consumer, and workers' control). In this spectrum, the Soviet economy lies considerably toward the "state" end, particularly as far as industry is concerned. Nearly all industrial activity is nationalized, and since 1918 forms of syndicalism or "guild socialism" have been firmly rejected in favor of "one-man management" by administrators appointed by the state and liable to instant dismissal. The argument for this has always been in terms of economic efficiency and of the need to enforce a central state policy.

Allocation of Resources. Various forms of "market socialism" are in principle conceivable, and have been much discussed among economists (especially in Poland and Yugoslavia). To what extent can a scale of preferences (of planners or individual consumers or a combination of both) be put into effect through a market, on which state firms aim to maximize their profits in simulation of private enterprises? Prices in "market socialism" might be formed freely, or might be fixed by the planners, but would, of course, need to reflect the chosen preference-scale more or less exactly, as they would indicate to the producer what he should produce, and how he should allocate resources (including investment).

The alternative approach is the one followed by the Soviet government: to allocate resources by direct physical controls, and to allow some degree of decentralization in decision making to other controllers at industry, region, or plant level.

In terms of the methods used for allocating resources, planning systems might be classified (a) by the relative strengths in them of the "market principle" and the "physical planning principle," (b) by the degree to which, within the market sector, the government regulates the market (imposes its preferences), and (c) by the degree to which decision making is decentralized within the physical planning sector.

We have not made any allowance for the *effectiveness* of controls. Should the degree of planning be measured not only by the all-embracingness of the planners' goals and the detailedness of their controls, but also by the extent to which the planners succeed in fulfilling their goals in the actual allocation of resources? For instance, War Communism was in principle a highly centralized system. But in practice central decisions were usually ineffective; illegal barter and local quasi-markets tended to dominate economic life. What was the "real" economic system? Again, where was there more planning—in industry under War Communism, where detailed orders were not enforced, or in agriculture under the New Economic Policy, where indirect controls succeeded to some extent in moving agriculture in the direction desired by the central government? Further, good planners of course incorporate the knowledge of their objective possibilities into their goals. But is a planner whose goals are very limited, but successfully achieved, as "effective" as, say, the Soviet planners in 1929–31, who set quite impossible goals but did succeed in reallocating resources very drastically in the desired direction?

Planning a More Mature Economy

The basic allocation decisions and the planning process in the USSR in 1928–53 probably had stronger "functional" elements than "dysfunctional" elements in the stage of moving the Soviet economy from a semiagrarian economy to an industrialized economy. But as the economy matured, the "dysfunctional" elements certainly became more prominent. The changed context may be summarized as follows:

1. Soviet industrial output per head is now above the British level for industry as a whole, and it is already above the U.S. level for some im-

portant producer goods, including steel. The economy is vastly more complex than it was in the 1930s.

2. The Industrial Revolution has been accompanied by major social changes:

   a. In 1928, two thirds of the population were illiterate; now, nearly everyone can read and write.

   b. In 1928, some 3 million persons were employed in industry; in 1975, over 34 millions.

   c. In 1928, some 5 percent of the state-employed labor force (i.e., excluding peasants and collective farmers) had received professional or semiprofessional education; the figure for 1975 was about 22 percent.

3. There is a long-term trend for labor to become scarcer. Annual additions to the industrial labor force (in terms of man-hours) amounted to 4.2 percent in 1951–55 and only 1.5 percent in 1971–75 and the planned annual increase in 1976–80 is only 0.7 percent. Increased production is already now obtained mainly from increased labor productivity. In the future, it will be obtained almost exclusively from this source. But (for reasons that will be indicated below) it is also difficult to increase capital investment substantially. Increases in production therefore depend to a much larger extent than in the past on increased efficiency in the use of resources.

4. Since World War II vast technological advances have occurred in the industrialized capitalist countries, especially in science-based industries (computers, aircraft, plastics, etc.). To close the gap between the Soviet Union and the West requires both a resumption of large-scale technological borrowing and the provision of greater incentives to innovation by the Soviet economy itself.

In this new situation, changes in both allocation and organization are essential to improve efficiency and even to maintain the existing level of efficiency. It is not directly demonstrable that industrial efficiency is hampered by a relatively low standard of living (the Soviet average real wage in industry is no more than a third that of the United States, but industrial labor productivity is over half the U.S. level). But in any case political and social pressures have dictated a shift in resources towards consumption. Such a shift requires a much greater output of food; and in agriculture it is very probable that the low return to the peasant for the output of the collective farm held down productivity. And certainly, as the economy has grown, the highly centralized planning structure has become clumsier and less workable.

Here we summarize the principal changes made in 1953–77 in the allocation of resources (i.e., in economic policy) and in economic organization, and two other proposed changes.

Allocation of Resources

1. The share of national resources received by agriculture has been very greatly increased. The proportion of total Soviet capital investment allocated to agriculture increased from 11–12 percent in the late 1930s and in 1946–50, to 15.4 percent in 1961–65 and 19.9 percent in 1971–75. The increase in comparable prices was from 1.13 billion rubles annually in 1946–50 to 23.5 billion rubles in 1975. The prices paid by the state for agricultural products were also very substantially increased after Stalin's death. The money incomes of collective farmers rose from 5 billion rubles in 1950 to 26 billion rubles in 1975.

2. The development of agriculture in turn made possible a more rapid increase in the production of the food and light industries, which use agricultural raw materials. Between 1928 and 1950, the output of producer goods increased much more rapidly than that of consumer goods. Since 1950, the gap between their growth rates has been much narrower.

3. There has been a significant shift in the distribution of income. The incomes of peasants have increased much more rapidly than those of the urban population. Within the urban population, there has been a process of levelling-up: the minimum wage has been increased, wage-differentials have been narrowed, and social benefits such as pensions have been substantially increased.

4. Nevertheless, the priorities have not been reversed. It seems certain, however the measurement is done, that a higher proportion of GNP is allocated to net investment than in the United States, and that a higher proportion of this investment is allocated to the producer goods industries. Very substantial resources have also continued to be allocated to the defense industries. With a much smaller GNP than the United States and a technologically less advanced economy, the USSR has been endeavoring to equal the quantity and quality of U.S. weapons. At a time of rapid advance in technology (missiles, aircraft, nuclear weapons) this has been a great strain on Soviet resources.

Organization

Attempts to improve the Soviet planning process have followed two main lines simultaneously: (1) improvements in central planning; (2) attempts to decentralize.

1. *Improvements in central planning.* Central decision making has undoubtedly tended to be more carefully thought out, and to become more logical and consistent.

In the mid-1950s long-term technological decisions were reconsidered, and a bold policy of technical change was embarked upon. Thus oil was given preference over coal, and the transfer of the railways to diesel power was undertaken; this reversed previous policy. The development and manufacture of prefabricated reinforced concrete components and other building materials was given preference over traditional materials like brick and timber. Great efforts were made to modernize the chemical industry.

Efforts to bring about rapid technological change continued in the 1960s and the 1970s, and plans for new technology were given greater weight in the planning process. In the past ten years, borrowing of Western technology has greatly expanded. In 1975 imports of Western machinery were more than four times as large as in 1965, and were concentrated on a few major industries. Many more licensing agreements for Western know-how have also been signed. But machinery imports are still a much smaller percentage of total investment in machinery in the USSR than in the United States.

Much more attention has been devoted in central planning decisions to economic arguments and economic criteria. The criteria to be used in investment decisions have received much attention in the literature. In 1960, a standard formula for measuring the so-called recoupment period on investment was adopted (the recoupment period is the inverse of the rate of return):

$$\frac{I_1 - I_2}{C_2 - C_1} \leqq R.P.$$

where I_1 and I_2 are the investment alternatives being compared and C_1 and C_2 are the costs of production in the two alternatives, and R.P. is the maximum permissible period in which the investment may be recouped. The R.P. varied by industry, from 4–5 years in light industry (i.e., a rate of return of 20–25 percent) to 16–17 years in electric power (i.e., a rate of return of about 6 percent). In 1969, it was decided, with some important exceptions, that the return on investment should be measured by a single rate of return for the whole economy. This was a significant development. Although calculations based on the formula are often ignored in planning practice, and the formula itself is in any case very crude, the approval of a single rate of return reflected much greater concern at the highest levels of government with economic criteria than at any time since the 1920s.

A stumbling block to consistent macroeconomic decision making in the traditional system was the inconsistency of the prices in which goods were valued. Investment decisions, and indeed all multiproduct decisions, have to be discussed not in physical terms but in value terms. As we have seen, Soviet prices were an inadequate indicator of real costs. They did not include a capital charge, and therefore capital-intensive production was relatively undervalued. They did not vary with the scarcity or abundance of the goods. The rent element for use of natural resources was absent or inconsistent. And the price incorporated a profit markup which was more or less arbitrary. Rule-of-thumb adjustments were made by the central planners, but decisions were clumsy and often inaccurate.

In the past ten years or so, important changes have been made in the structure of prices. In the major reform of the prices of producer goods in 1967, a small capital charge (6 percent of the value of capital assets) was included in costs; differential rents were charged in several extractive industries; and the profit markups included in prices were made much more consistent among and within industries. The prices of electric power, oil, and coal were substantially increased in order to eliminate subsidies. Higher prices for goods of higher quality were introduced much more widely. In 1969, with further adjustments in 1974, an elaborate procedure for fixing prices on new products was devised, with the objective of arriving at prices which split the economic gain from the new products in such a way that producers were encouraged to manufacture them and users to purchase them. From the point of view of central planning, all these changes make industrial prices more consistent. The prices of producer goods remain an unsatisfactory instrument for planning, however, both because many inconsistencies remain and because they do not reflect the relative abundance or scarcity of the product. In 1977, a prominent Gosplan official proposed that prices of producer goods should be raised by the producers, within fixed limits, if the goods were scarce and lowered if they were in surplus. In the same year, the retail prices of various scarce consumer goods were officially increased—a significant step towards more rational prices by a government which has always tried to avoid price increases on consumer goods.

While the prices of industrial goods have thus tended to reflect economic inputs more accurately, the government has been unwilling to increase the retail prices of basic foodstuffs, even though, with the increased incomes of the farmers, costs have risen greatly. This is primarily a political decision. (Increases of basic food prices in Poland resulted in large-scale popular unrest in 1970 and 1976, and in the USSR are believed to have resulted in riots in 1962.) While subsidies for industrial goods have been reduced or eliminated, subsidies for agricultural goods are now very large. (Such subsidies are not, of course, unknown in other countries, and tend to favor those with lower wages, who spend a higher proportion of incomes on food.)

We return below to the question of prices in connection with attempts to decentralize the planning system.

Another line of approach to the improvement of central planning has been to attempt to improve decision making at the center by using mathematical methods and computers. Mathematical methods are frequently used for production scheduling (for example, in the steel industry) and to reduce transport costs (for example, for truck traffic in Moscow). In determining long-term plans for particular industries, the planners frequently make use of optimization techniques to determine the location and size of plant. More elaborate national and regional input-output tables are constructed in the USSR than in any other country; but these are mainly *ex post* tables, and the crucial material balances (physical budgets) are still mainly prepared by rule-of-thumb methods. In general, mathematical methods are used to assist existing procedures and make them work more efficiently.

2. *Attempts at decentralization.* Four major attempts have been made by the Soviet government since 1953 to devolve some of the decision-making powers of the central authorities. All those attempts have been conducted within the framework of the physical planning system, rather than involving a substantial increase in the market sector of the economy.

    a. 1954–56: "Step-by-step" decentralization. The Gosplan Council of Ministers central organization attempted to shed some of its powers by reducing the number of indicators in the national output, supply, and capital investment plans. Thus product groups, for which output targets were laid down, were made more aggregative. The intention was that each ministry, possessing more flexibility itself, would devolve some of its authority to its departments (the *glavki*), which in turn would increase the decision-making powers of economic units (the enterprises).

    The reform was on the whole unsuccessful. Ministries failed to pass down their powers to the factory. Instead, they tended to use their increased authority to bind their own "empires" more closely together. At the same time, the reduction in the number of central output targets (success indicators) revealed clearly a dilemma inherent in administrative planning. The enterprise is required to maximize its output in terms of the output targets. If the targets are broad or loose, it will try to follow the "easiest" course within the target. If the target is merely for "tons of nails shorter than 2 inches" the factory will try to produce all $1\frac{9}{10}''$ nails, because this is easiest. If it is for "numbers of nails," the factory will try to produce all $\frac{1}{2}''$ nails. But if the target is set in terms of $\frac{1}{2}''$, $1''$, $1\frac{1}{2}''$, and $1\frac{9}{10}''$ nails, there will be overcentralization. If the target is set in terms of gross value of output, the factory will maximize its use of materials and semifabs and minimize the net value it adds to each product. And so on.

    b. 1957–65: Regionalization. In 1957, industry was "regionalized": the industrial ministries were abolished, 104 regions were set up, and all factories in each region were put under the regional economic council. However, much of the central administrative machinery was retained, particularly the sales organizations which control product-mix; and in the early 1960s agencies for each industry were reestablished, with research organizations attached. What emerged was thus a mixture of area-by-area and industry-by-industry control. This probably gave the factory manager greater effective power, if only because he no longer had one unambiguous boss. It also led to the break-up of the ministerial "empires" and a more effective consideration of regional factors in central decision making. But it proved very difficult to carry out national plans for particular industries, and above all economic administration became very much more complicated.

c. 1965–: The Kosygin reforms. The reforms introduced by Kosygin in 1965 and implemented in the next few years contained two main elements. First, they abandoned the attempt at regional organization and returned to control by industrial ministries. Secondly, they introduced radical changes in success indicators and incentives, with two major objectives: to increase the powers of factory management, and to replace the traditional methods of planning via output targets by more sophisticated methods involving economic calculation. The changes were very complicated. The most important measures were as follows:

(1) The importance of profits as a success indicator was greatly increased. Profits retained by factories were larger, and the proportion was higher for planned profit (if achieved) than for actual profit, so as to discourage firms from trying to keep their plan targets low. The previous small Factory Fund was replaced by three much larger Economic Incentive Funds, all formed partly or wholly from retained profits: the Production Development (i.e., Investment) Fund, the Social-Cultural Measures and Housing Fund, and the Material Rewards (i.e., Bonus) Fund. The Material Rewards Fund was the most important means of changing the behavior of factory management and professional staff, as henceforth it formed the main source for their bonuses.

(2) Various measures were adopted to encourage efficient use of capital investment. A small interest charge was paid from profits on the fixed and working capital stock of the factory, usually 6 percent of their value. A higher proportion of capital investment was financed by interest-bearing loans rather than budget grants. More investment on the initiative of the enterprise was permitted, primarily financed from the Production Development Fund.

(3) The powers of the factory management to determine the way in which it spends the total allocation for wages were increased. The manager could himself divide up the total allocations between classes of employee. He could, for instance, reduce the total number of persons employed in order to increase the proportion of highly skilled workers.

(4) The main global indicator of output became "actually marketed production" rather than "gross production." It was intended that this would force factories to produce goods for which there was a high demand.

However, the main physical indicators were retained, including both the plan of supplies in physical terms, and the itemization of output in physical terms in the national economic plan. Kosygin merely expressed the hope that the degree of detail would be gradually reduced.

Twelve years have now elapsed since the 1965 reform. Its most important effect has undoubtedly been to increase the importance of profits, and of economic calculation generally, in the behavior of all levels of the Soviet economic administration, including factory managements. In financial plans, profits have increased in importance in relation to capital investment, costs, and turnover tax (see Figure 4 above). Between 1965 and 1975 the proportion of profits retained by enterprises increased from 30 to 44 percent in the economy as a whole, and from 29 to 43 percent in industry. In industry, the various Incentive Funds have increased considerably.

The Material Rewards Fund is substantial. Bonuses to engineering and technical workers (including managers) in industry, paid mainly from the Fund, were 31.7 percent of their average earnings in 1970, and this Fund increased more rapidly than total Incentive Funds between 1970 and 1975 (by 52 against 31 percent). While the size of their bonuses is not the sole basis on which managers and engineers take their decisions, it is an important one, and the principles determining the size of the Fund and its allocation are likely to influence management behavior strongly. In practice, the size of bonuses is determined by a complicated formula, varying by industry, but with profit usually having the most weight, and marketed production a close second.

The 1965 reform has brought about a significant modification in the old planning process, in which output plans in physical terms overwhelmingly predominated, modified by cost requirements. (A first step towards this modification was taken as early as 1959, when cost reduction partly replaced output as the criterion for distributing bonuses to managers and engineers.) The very complexity of the indicators now used is a reflection of the burning desire of the authorities to control the planning process in a more sophisticated way, and with a looser rein.

But the reform has failed in one of its major objectives. It has failed to move away from administrative planning and to devolve economic powers to the factory to any substantial extent. The main reason for this is, of course, that the level of profits earned by the factory, in spite of the price reforms described earlier, is still a most inaccurate indicator of the preferences of either the planners or the consumers. Prices of producer goods, as we have seen, do not vary with supply and demand, and the complex arrangements for pricing new products have not provided adequate incentives to factories to risk the temporary loss of output and profit which is always incurred by innovation. The weakness of the incentives to innovation is indicated by the small size and slow growth of the bonuses for creating and introducing new technology. New types of plans have therefore been introduced at the national level—especially for quality of products, and for new products and processes—and transmitted to the factories; and various ad hoc indicators have been introduced for special purposes. The physical allocation of supplies still covers 97 percent of all supplies. As the continuation of the sellers' market reveals, the change of indicator from "gross production" to "marketed production" has not made much difference. Only a very small part of capital investment is determined by the factories themselves. The Production Development Fund was responsible for only about one-ninth of capital investment in 1975, and it expanded much more slowly than the Material Rewards Fund between 1970 and 1975.

In short, Soviet planning after the 1965 reform became much more complicated as well as much more concerned with economic efficiency. But it has remained administrative planning.

d. 1973–: The associations (ob"edineniia). In a further endeavor to improve the economic mechanism, and to increase the influence of economic incentives, associations are replacing the existing administrative units at every level of the industrial hierarchy below the ministry. This further reform is being superimposed on the 1965 reform, and is intended to be compatible with it. (It was tried out with a few ministries and many groups of factories before 1973.) The existing production departments of ministries (the *glavki*) are being replaced by a larger number of industrial associations, which will be financed not from the budget but from the profits of their constituent factories. The associations will be given some powers at present in the hands of the ministries, and their dependence on the profits of their factories is intended to increase their interest in efficient performance. At the enterprise level, factories are being grouped into *production associations;* these are also intended to acquire greater powers. In science-based industries, research and development facilities have been integrated with factories into *science-production associations.*

It is too early to assess the results of the 1973 reform, which is not to be completed until 1980. The rearrangement of production into more logical units may well in itself improve efficiency. But it may be safely predicted that the 1973 reform, like the 1965 reform, will not fundamentally change the economic mechanism because it does not involve a substantial change in planning indicators or in prices.

Proposed Changes

Two more radical approaches to economic reform were also proposed in the early 1960s.

The first, amounting in essence to "market socialism," was rejected, and now reappears only in cautious suggestions that prices should be adjusted to balance supply and demand. In the more radical versions of market socialism, much discussed in Eastern Europe and partly put into practice in Yugoslavia, the required scale of prices would be reached by permitting state enterprises to compete on a market. The central planners would restrict themselves to controlling the general level of investment, and to intervening in order to ensure that the market was as nearly perfect as possible. The principal economic objection to this solution is that it would incorporate into the planned economy most of the disadvantages of modern capitalism, in a situation in which the imperfections of the market would be more considerable than in a privately-owned economy. In Yugoslavia, substantial economic growth has in fact been accompanied by large-scale unemployment, and the economy would be in deep crisis if substantial numbers of Yugoslav workers had not gone abroad to work. There is no doubt, however, that many powerful Soviet officials also object to market socialism because they oppose in principle the drastic reduction of control by the center over the allocation of resources. Developments in Czechoslovakia seemed to them to demonstrate that market socialism would be accompanied by the disruption of the Soviet political system.

The second radical approach to reform involves the extensive application of mathematical methods and the computer. Computers make it possible to examine the properties of a very large number of economic variables. With the aid of appropriately designed mathematical models, economic processes can be simulated on the computer so that plan variants can be tested for feasibility and consistency. The core of the method is that objective functions are set up which indicate what is to be maximized or minimized within a system of constraints. The functions yield a system of imputed values (efficiency prices or shadow prices), and these for the problem concerned are the consistent system of prices which, as we have seen, the nonmathematical proposals (apart from market socialism) lacked.

Soviet mathematicians and mathematical economists believe that this technique can be applied to the planning of the entire economy. The economy would be divided for planning purposes into a number of blocs or subsystems (both by area and by sector). For each bloc an appropriate programming model would attempt to optimize subgoals consistent with and integrated with the overall national goals, which would in turn be incorporated in a macro-model for the economy as a whole. For each bloc, a set of shadow prices would emerge which would indicate its "best" economic behavior in the planning period. A measure of decentralization is inherent in the system. The elements in each subsystem would be free to move so as to optimize their subgoals within constraints obtained from the larger bloc of which the subsystem formed a part.

A requirement for the efficient working of the new system would be the establishment of a consistent computerized system of information flows. All economic information (for instance, all inputs and outputs) would need to be classified by a unified system for the entire economy, so that data could be processed in forms suitable for feeding into the planning models on which the system is intended to be based.

Some aspects of this proposed reform are being implemented. The establishment of computerized management systems in factories and ministries has been under way in practice since the early 1960s. In 1971 the Soviet government gave strong support to the establishment of a unified State Automated System for the Collection, Storage, and Processing of Data for National Economic Planning, Management, and Accounting (OGAS).

But so far, in spite of much activity, the developments fall far short of the proposals of the mathematical economists. While computerized information systems have been and are being established in many ministries, nothing approaching a compatible unified information system on a national scale has yet emerged. And it has not yet been decided to what extent, if at all, the planning mechanism and planning indicators will be reformed when (or if) OGAS is working satisfactorily.

Two crucial issues are involved. One is the type of planning indicators which will be developed. Can prices calculated from the optimal plans based on data derived from OGAS be used as the sole indicator, so that each Soviet economic unit can be instructed to maximize its profits? In the light of Western studies of the behavior of the private firm, it seems likely that the Soviet firm cannot be expected to behave as though maximizing profits were its sole goal. As part of the restructuring of planning, an appropriate and as yet unknown system of incentives would be needed to ensure that decisions are executed—a system of incentives as powerful as the profit motive, the fear of bankruptcy, and the spur of competition in capitalist economies. The second unresolved issue is the eventual relationship between the computerized information system OGAS and the central planning process. Can means be found to translate government goals into preference functions which would state the goals in meaningful quantities? At present, they are stated in terms of a long series of targets for investment goods, intermediate goods, and final consumption goods. These targets, as we saw earlier, are reached both for five-year and for annual plans as the result of a long bargaining process, and reflect both the need to overcome expected bottlenecks and the major investment projects and priorities which the government intends to encourage. To optimize the achievement of these targets is only to maximize the achievement of a network of decisions reached by a rule-of-thumb process. The alternative is to persuade the politicians to reformulate their goals in more general or more operational terms. A satisfactory outcome would obviously be achieved only, if at all, as a result of a long and difficult dialogue between the politicians and the mathematically-trained planners. One element in this dialogue would have to be the extent to which the preference functions of the planning models should incorporate the preferences of the individual consumer. Some Soviet and East European economists would be prepared to go a very long way in the direction of consumer sovereignty. Others have suggested that zones of state influence, individual influence, and mixed influence would need to be determined. One considerable weakness of present Soviet discussions is that they have paid relatively little attention to techniques such as cost-benefit analysis which are needed in order to bring social and other noneconomic factors more consistently into the considerations of planners and politicians. The rationale of economic policy making has not been carefully considered, and hence goals remain inconsistent or ill-defined. Unless these issues are resolved, the unified information system (if it is completed) will supply data for a modified form of the present system of administrative planning, rather than providing a basis for more radical reorganization.

Results and Prospects

Although the organizational changes have not been fundamental and major attempts at reform are incomplete, have the changes so far, together with the shifts in resource allocation, resulted in satisfactory economic performance? The major strengths and weaknesses of the Soviet economy in recent years can be briefly summarized:

Strengths

1. At a macroeconomic level, the economy has been remarkably stable. GNP, industrial production, agricultural production (with some bad years), and the standard of living have all grown consistently. In contrast, capitalist economies have been subject to serious economic fluctuations and, recently, to a lengthy depression involving inflation and large-scale unemployment.

2. Agricultural production, the great failure of the period of rapid industrialization, has more than doubled since 1953, and food production per head has risen substantially.

3. Industrialization has continued. It should be borne in mind that in 1953, according to the OECD definition, the Soviet Union was not yet an industrialized country.[1] It developed sufficiently to be classified as industrialized only in the second half of the 1960s. Throughout the period from 1953 to 1975, urbanization and industrialization continued. The urban population increased from 43 to 60 percent of the total; and the number of persons employed in industry increased from 17.6 to 34.1 million—a larger increase in absolute terms than in 1928–53. Civilian industrial production in 1975, according to a recent U.S. estimate, was five times as large as in 1953.

4. Defense capacity in relation to that of the United States has apparently been maintained. While the sophistication of Soviet weapons continues to be behind that of the United States (in some cases the lag has increased), it is generally believed that the substantial increase in the quantity of Soviet military production has compensated for this; and some observers hold that the United States' overall lead has been reduced.

Weaknesses

1. The annual rate of growth of gross industrial production has fallen, according to official Soviet figures, from 12 percent in 1953 to 6.5 percent in 1975. The rate of growth of agricultural production has also declined since the very rapid spurt of the mid-1950s. A lower rate of growth might be expected in view of the switch from extensive industrialization (in which

---

[1] Industrial OECD countries are defined as those in which 70 percent or more of the labor force and 85 percent or more of GNP can be attributed to manufacturing and services.

additional inputs of labor account for a substantial proportion of increases in output) to intensive industrialization (in which increases in labor productivity account for nearly all increases in output). But the extent of this deceleration of growth is alarming to the Soviet authorities, because the industrial growth rate is now no higher than that of Germany and France in prosperous years, and considerably lower than that of Japan.

2. The technological gap between the Soviet Union and the advanced capitalist countries has, on the whole, not diminished substantially in the past 15 or 20 years, in spite of the allocation of substantial resources to research, development, and innovation, and in spite of substantial increases in imports of new technology from the West.

The long-term Soviet goal of overtaking the advanced capitalist countries "in an economic and a technological respect" (Stalin, November 1928) has thus somewhat receded in the past decade or so, in terms of both the quantity of production and its technological level; and at least one capitalist country, Japan, has outstripped the Soviet Union in both respects.

Much discussion, so far inconclusive, has taken place among Western economists about the reasons for the deceleration of Soviet industrial growth. It is obviously partly due to the decline in the rate of increase of both capital and labor inputs into Soviet industry. This in turn is due partly to the absorption of surplus labor from the countryside; partly to the switch of resources from the producer goods industries to agriculture and to consumer needs; and partly perhaps to a substantial increase in the skilled manpower and scarce resources devoted to defense since the late 1950s. Is it also due to inefficient use of resources, due to the centralized planning system, as compared with the market economies? Attempts to use production functions to measure Soviet efficiency, and changes in efficiency over time, and to compare the results with other countries, have so far been inconclusive. It is not even entirely certain that the Japanese economy is more efficient than the Soviet economy, as the Japanese economy does not divert substantial resources to defense. There is no doubt, however, that the Soviet leaders themselves are dissatisfied both with the efficiency with which resources are used, and with the level of innovation in Soviet industry.

Great issues are at stake. The Soviet economic system proved able to cope with the first stages of industrialization. Will it be able, with modifications, to deal equally well with the problems of economic growth and technological change in a more advanced industrial society, or will it prove to result in an economy which is economically stable, but develops slowly and shows little technological initiative? Future planning reforms in the Soviet Union and in the East European economies will attempt to reverse recent trends, while maintaining the major features of the present economic mechanism. Whether they succeed or not, there can be no doubt that the future economic organization of every country, and of the world economy, must involve a combination of central planning (without which space exploration, for example, would be impossible) with the decentralization of minor economic decisions, presumably through the market. Soviet successes and failures, carefully examined, provide rich material to assist us in deciding the mixture of planning and the market which we should seek to establish.

17

AN ORGANIZATIONAL MODEL
OF COMMAND FARMING*

Jerzy F. Karcz

The agricultural sector in Communist centrally planned economies is characterized by "command farming," in which farms receive detailed, invariably ambitious, and often unrealistic quotas for
deliveries to state procurement agencies, ordinarily at low prices. In
this way, the state seeks to obtain agricultural production for urban
consumption, industrial inputs, and perhaps export, at terms of trade
unfavorable to the rural population. Collectivization and administrative interference in farm operations are among the methods used to
enforce these difficult plan assignments, which are intended both to
expand output and marketings and to make agriculture contribute to
capital formation in industry. However, the unintended consequences of this approach include lack of specialization, labor shortages, low factor productivity, and stagnation of output.

In this article, Karcz analyzes these relationships in a formal
organizational model based on his extensive studies of Soviet and
East European agriculture. He explains why and how command
farming emerged in the USSR, the extent to which it was adopted in
Eastern Europe, how it operates, and what its weaknesses are.

INTRODUCTION

As a friend of mine remarked privately, signs of "red agrarianism" could
recently be observed on the East European scene as the socialist governments introduced a plethora of reforms designed to improve the perfor-

---

* Copyright 1969 by Jerzy F. Karcz. Reprinted by permission, with the omission of
some footnotes. Jerzy F. Karcz was Professor of Economics at the University of California, Santa Barbara.

mance of their agricultural sectors. In themselves, such policies are vivid testimony to the dissatisfaction with the performance of socialist agricultures.

"Red agrarianism" might or might not be too strong a term, but what we are unquestionably witnessing is a movement away from a particular set of institutions and mechanisms coordinating the economic activity within the agricultural sectors of command economies. It is in this latter sense that the term "command farming" is used here as a convenient shorthand expression, designed to describe a system first introduced in the USSR in the early thirties.

Socialist agriculture has been the subject of a very large research effort on the part of western specialists, and numerous analytical contributions have been made by the late Naum Jasny and Lazar Volin, as well as by Alec Nove, Nancy Nimitz, and others too numerous to mention here. Within the last few years, several economists have also constructed a number of abstract theoretical models, designed to describe the behavior of a cooperative enterprise (in some cases, indeed, the Soviet *kolkhoz*) on the basis of the usual restrictive assumptions. Simultaneously, the work of Gregory Grossman, Benjamin Ward, David Granick, and Robert W. Campbell has vastly increased our understanding of the working of the Soviet-type command economy (hereafter called only the "command economy").[1]

One method which appears to be particularly useful for a study of command farming is that used by Granick in his pioneering organizational model of Soviet industrial planning.[2] It is the great advantage of this method that it brings out clearly the interplay of various functional and dysfunctional aspects of Soviet industrial planning. This makes it possible to identify precisely the key relationships and to pinpoint those that are of special importance in assessing the impact of various reforms, including the "new economic systems."

Granick's analysis proceeds in terms of two conflicting models of the industrial sector, beginning with the fundamental (or command) model

---

[1] Gregory Grossman, "Notes for a Theory of the Command Economy," *Soviet Studies*, vol. 15, no. 2 (October 1963), pp. 101–23; Benjamin Ward, "The Firm in Illyria: Market Syndicalism," *American Economic Review*, vol. 48, no. 4 (September 1958), pp. 566–89; Benjamin Ward, *The Socialist Economy* (New York: Random House, Inc., 1967); Evsey D. Domar, "The Soviet Collective Farm as a Producer Cooperative," *American Economic Review*, vol. 56, no. 4 (September 1966), part 1, pp. 734–57; David Granick, "An Organizational Model of Soviet Industrial Planning," *Journal of Political Economy*, vol. 67, no. 2 (April 1959), pp. 109–30; David Granick, *Soviet Metal-Fabricating and Economic Development* (Madison, Wis.: University of Wisconsin Press, 1966); Walter Y. Oi and Elizabeth M. Clayton, "A Peasant's View of a Soviet Collective Farm," *American Economic Review*, vol. 58, no. 1 (March 1968), pp. 37–59.

[2] Granick, "An Organizational Model of Soviet Industrial Planning." A revised and enlarged version is found in Chapter 7 of his *Soviet Metal-Fabricating and Economic Development*.

that has for prolonged periods of time dominated the subsidiary *khozraschet*[3] or market model. While the antinomy between market and command is relevant for the study of any sector of the command economy, it is the interplay between market and command mechanisms that is a characteristic feature of command farming. Consequently, we make no basic distinction between the two types of models, but attempt to incorporate both types of mechanisms into the single construct.

We follow Granick in many other respects as well. Thus, we use most of his key operating features, with only minor adjustments. Our objectives (O) are designed only as objectives for the agricultural sector, and they are viewed as emerging from certain key features of the Soviet environment (E). Within the latter, we specify separately only a few key features; others are aggregated for the sake of brevity within a catchall category of "Peculiar Characteristics of the Command Economy" (E_4). Our mechanisms (M) are partly market and partly command. We also use a separate variable to describe the primary and auxiliary production units (PU), which are not necessary in Granick's model. Finally, our undesirable consequences (UC) are labelled as such primarily from the standpoint of their impact on the agricultural sector. Most of these consequences, however, are the result of certain economic phenomena operating spontaneously, or in an unplanned manner, subject to the constraints imposed by other operating features. The responses (R) are also those of the sector as a whole.

All of the other *caveats* listed by Granick (hybrid nature of the model, neglect of positive responses, etc.) also apply here. Finally, it seems in order to underline the fact that we do not address ourselves—except briefly in the final section—to the issue of alternative methods of agricultural organization within the context of rapid industrialization, although we believe that this kind of analysis provides additional insight into this important question.

THE EMERGENCE OF COMMAND FARMING

A schematic representation of command farming is shown in Figure 1, which closely follows Granick's presentation of his fundamental model. The specification of the various variables is best understood in terms of the peculiar background of command farming.

As Grossman has pointed out, "command economies do not arise spontaneously." Nor does command farming. The key feature (E_1) from this standpoint is the decision on the overall economic objective of rapid growth, with priority given to heavy industry (it being understood that other sectors absorb the shocks). Scarcity of capital (E_2) combined with

---

3 Editor's note: Literally, "economic calculation" or "economic accountability."

FIGURE 1
Graphic Representation of Command Farming

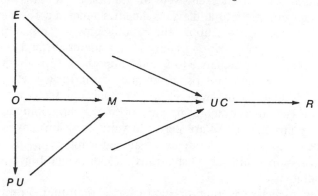

Each feature of the model is dependent on, or related to, that which is enclosed in parentheses underneath its specification.

Objectives (O)
O_1 Growing Marketings
O_2 Contribution of Agriculture to Capital Formation
O_3 Increase in Output through Changes in Technology and Production Functions
O_4 Collectivization of Agriculture
O_5 Rational Allocation of Resources

Production Units (PU)
PU_1 Collective Farm
PU_2 Household Plot
PU_3 State Farm
PU_4 Machine Tractor Station

Undesirable Consequences (UC)
UC_1 Failure to Specialize
    (M_1, M_2, M_3, M_5)
UC_2 Capital Intensity
    (O_4, PU_1, PU_2, E_4)
UC_3 Interdependence of Private and Socialized Sector
    (PU_1, PU_2, PU_3, M_3)
UC_4 Impact on Labor Supply
    (M_4, O_3)
UC_5 Uneven Farm Performance
    (M_1, M_2, M_3, M_5)
UC_6 Faulty Indicators
    (O_1, O_2, O_4, M_5)

Environment (E)
E_1 Industrialization at High Rate with Emphasis on Heavy Industry
E_2 Capital Scarcity
E_3 High Income Elasticities of Demand
E_4 Peculiar Characteristics of the Command Economy at Large

Mechanisms (M)
M_1 Procurement System
    (O_1, O_2, O_4)
M_2 Agricultural Planning
    (E_4, O_3, M_1)
M_3 Administrative Interference
    (O_1, O_3, M_1, M_2)
M_4 Agricultural Incentives
    $(PU_1, PU_2, PU_3, O_2, M_5, M_6)$
M_5 Farm Prices
    (O_2, O_3, M_4)
M_6 Taxation
    (O_2, M_4)
M_7 Credit
    (O_5, M_4)

Responses (R)
R_1 Low Factor Productivity
R_2 Output Tends to Stagnate
R_3 Pressure for Reform

the low rate of saving and the inability to attract foreign capital meant that reliance had to be placed exclusively on domestic capital formation. In turn, the high growth rate and rising incomes increased the demand for agricultural marketings to supply the rapidly growing urban population with food, light industry with agricultural raw materials, and the demand of the state for foreign exchange to finance imports of capital goods. Thus, the objectives of a high and rising volume of marketings (O_1) and the objective of a high saving ratio in the agricultural sector (O_2) follow directly from the environmental features of Soviet development. We may add at this point that these are perfectly valid contributions of the agricultural sector to the development of any growing economy (although their relative priority and the mechanisms through which they are achieved are not at all identical).

A related objective is that of increasing agricultural output through changes in agricultural production functions and the increase in new technology (O_3). This was to operate in part through economies of scale, and a by-product of this objective was the release of labor to industry. This objective is influenced primarily by the high rate of industrial growth (E_1), but is further accentuated by E_4, operating here as demand for labor on the part of industrial enterprises, searching for slack in order to maintain their ability to fulfill changing (or rising) production targets.

The introduction and maintenance of collectivization serve as the next objective (O_4). It has always been an ideologically appealing solution. To the extent that it could activate the economies of scale, it could also be thought of as a derived or secondary objective designed to assist in the performance of the objectives of greater farm output and marketings.

Collectivization of Soviet Agriculture

Recently, considerable light has been shed upon this subject by the researches of Professor Moshe Lewin.[4] At the time when the basic questions of the rate and the nature of industrialization were being debated and resolved, the Soviet agricultural sector consisted primarily of individual peasant households, which had just about completed the process of recovery from the ravages of foreign and domestic war (and, we may add, the policies of War Communism). It was simultaneously trying to adjust its production structure to the signals provided by changes in government price and fiscal policies. As I have shown elsewhere,[5] such

---

[4] M. Lewin, "The Immediate Background of Soviet Collectivization," *Soviet Studies,* vol. 17, no. 2 (October 1965), pp. 162–97, and *Russian Peasants and Soviet Power* (Evanston, Ill.: Northwestern University Press, 1968).

[5] Jerzy F. Karcz, "Thoughts on the Grain Problem," *Soviet Studies,* vol. 18, no. 4 (April 1967), pp. 399–434.

policies during the years 1926–28 were not at all consistent with the objective of rapid industrialization. Failure to make the necessary adjustments in time led to the famous "grain procurement crisis" in the fall of 1927 that virtually eliminated exportable surpluses and threatened supply of the urban population and the whole fabric of the development plan.

Government response took the form of compulsory extraction (repeated again a year later). These policies—a counterpart of the procurement methods under War Communism—proved effective enough (as they usually are in the short run). Their effectiveness appears to have persuaded Stalin and his supporters to adopt a policy of rapid collectivization, never envisaged in the First Five-Year Plan. In this sense, then, it is possible to view collectivization and the eventual emergence of command farming as being "so to speak pushed by the logic of events, with the transformation lubricated rather than propelled by ideological tenets."[6] But once the drive began, it became an objective in its own right, and the results had to be presented later in a favorable light in disregard of any inconvenient facts.

The collectivization which did occur was thus a function of the policy to increase state procurements (rather than total marketings) at any price and might be called properly a part of the policy of collecting "the agricultural surplus." It is not always recognized that this gave rise to some interesting policy developments in intersectoral relationships and an accompanying theoretical discussion.

On the practical level, so-called contract deliveries were used to implement objectives dealing with the volume of marketings and the contribution to capital formation. But the contracts also specified terms of trade as well as the various conditions of production (use of inputs, timing of operations, etc.). Of course, in this chaotic period the latter provisions were seldom carried out, but deliverable produce was collected, resulting frequently in deprivation of farms of seeding stock as well as a considerable part of consumption requirements. Efforts were made to reduce the use of money; cash advances to farmers were first limited, then in 1930 completely eliminated and replaced by advances in kind. Sales of consumer goods were tied to the delivery of products. It might be significant that at about this time the Commissariat of Trade was renamed that of Supply.

On a theoretical plane, several Soviet economists assumed that the end of the New Economic Policy and "the victory of socialism in the countryside" made possible a shift to an absolute command economy,[7] in which

---

[6] Grossman, "Notes for a Theory of the Command Economy," p. 107.

[7] Grossman's term. See also P. J. D. Wiles, *The Political Economy of Communism* (Cambridge, Mass.: Harvard University Press, 1962), pp. 67–68.

allocation of goods and services as well as of resources is carried out exclusively by orders. These developments were viewed as representing a significant step within the organized process of production towards the disappearance of distribution as a link between production and consumption. Market incentives in production were to be replaced by direct supply of producer as well as consumer goods to the ultimate user.

It would be premature to conclude that the directors of the system tried to introduce an absolute command economy within a given time period. Still, steps leading in that direction were being taken in agriculture.[8] In any event, this policy was short-lived, and by mid-1932 there were many signs of retreat from such positions.

The major reason for the retreat lay in the distorted and overoptimistic view of the responses and motivation of households in the absolute command economy.[9] As is well known, Soviet collectivization was carried out in a rapid, brutal, though often haphazard manner. The erratic and discriminatory collection of procurement was accompanied by failure of the "supply" apparatus in the countryside. The extent of outward migration was without precedent: by 1932 agricultural employment declined by about 20 percent. Many were forced to leave, but many others must have left for the greater relative personal security in the city. Such as they were, the meager ration supplies might have seemed greater than the uncertainties of collectivization that often encompassed even the chicken and the cow.

Indeed, the year 1932, when many key decisions were made on the continuation of the general pattern of industrialization and the introduction of key features of command farming, was characterized by very mixed results. The Five-Year Plan was declared fulfilled and the industrialization program survived. But gross national product (in 1937 prices) declined below the level of 1931, and similar trends are shown by a reconstructed index of final industrial production. Agriculture seemed to be at the brink of disaster. Livestock holdings (which by one method of measurement accounted for about one-sixth of the 1928 capital stock) declined drastically. This was one factor responsible for the increase in grain marketings. Average farm marketings in 1928–32 were 7 percent below 1928, and per head of urban population the decline came to 25 percent; by 1932, the situation had worsened. Farm draft power declined by 28 percent. While sown area increased by 19 percent, the official index of output shows a decline of 14 percent, and a western calculation of

---

8 Frequent complaints about violations of economic accountability in industry suggest something of this sort in that sector too, but there is always a shift to more direct controls in periods such as this.

9 On this, see Ward, *The Socialist Economy*, p. 140.

agriculture's contribution to the national product indicates a decline of 28 percent.[10]

Since the system of command farming that did emerge represents a mixture of command and market mechanism and incentives, it should be viewed as a compromise, designed to achieve a better compliance with the overall objectives of the state. Here we should emphasize the decision to continue the pattern of Soviet industrialization (E_1) and the related phenomenon of high income elasticities of expenditures (on food) (E_3). This is partly the result of the relative neglect of the production of consumer goods and services, and partly of the absence (or the insignificant size) of payments for medical care, housing, and education.

Chief Characteristics of Production Units

The most typical production unit has been the collective farm conforming to the provisions of the 1935 charter. Its most important characteristics are production in accordance with the state plan of agricultural production and distribution of output according to the rules of the charter. Under this, the state has had a priority claim on part of the output (see below). Production expenses, tax and insurance payments, and allocations to investment funds all had to be met before remuneration of farm members, which was thus made a residual. The collective farm (PU_1) is hence a very special cooperative.

An important by-product of the collective farm is its private sector. This consists of household plots to which each member is entitled within prescribed limits and where a limited number of animals may be kept. In view of their importance, these plots are labelled here as a separate production unit (PU_2); as our model is intended to cover Eastern Europe, we include here also the farms of individual peasants. (As completely separate units, they are now important only in Yugoslavia and Poland.)

Like the collective, a state farm produces in accordance with the production plan, but it has always paid wages to its workers, and (unlike the collective) has always controlled directly all machinery used in production, particularly tractors. Our definition of state farm (PU_3) includes a variety of other similar production units.

The last production unit has been auxiliary in nature to the collective farm. Machine tractor stations (MTSs) (PU_4) concentrated all heavy machinery and much of the scarce trained labor in the early period of Soviet collectivization. In the USSR, they were abolished in 1958, when

---

[10] See the data in Richard Moorsteen and Raymond P. Powell, *The Soviet Capital Stock, 1928–1962* (New Haven, Conn.: Yale University Press, 1966), p. 361; Powell's essay in *Economic Trends in the Soviet Union*, ed. Abram Bergson and Simon Kuznets (Cambridge, Mass.: Harvard University Press, 1963), p. 178; and Naum Jasny, *The Socialized Agriculture of the USSR* (Stanford, Calif.: Stanford University Press, 1949), p. 458.

machinery was transferred to the collectives. They survive to a limited extent (service of financially weak collectives) in other socialist countries of Eastern Europe.

Introduction of Command Farming in Eastern Europe

The special production units of command farming (with the obvious exception of individual peasants) have been adopted in East European socialist countries in very special circumstances. The influence of environmental characteristics played a major role after the introduction of rapid industrialization plans. No East European country attempted to copy the exact pattern of Soviet collectivization, for reasons that were partly political and partly economic. After the seizure of power, all Communist governments conducted land reforms to eliminate privately owned large-scale holdings. These reforms tended to neutralize the political influence of large and powerful peasant parties, but they made it awkward to proceed immediately with massive collectivization. Moreover, large-scale disinvestment in livestock was one of the direct consequences of rapid Soviet collectivization. That cost could seemingly be avoided by gradual collectivization, and the Soviet experience with command farming during the thirties might have suggested that many if not most of the objectives could be fulfilled in a satisfactory manner by gradual collectivization.

Initial collectivization drives in Bulgaria and Yugoslavia occurred in the early postwar period, but the first major effort came in the latter country in 1948–49. At about the same time, collectivization campaigns began in other socialist countries. In general, several milder, intermediate forms of collectives (including, e.g., distribution of income in part in proportion to the contributed land and/or capital) were used, though the Soviet prototype remained the ultimate objective. Progress was decidedly uneven, as it was interrupted by numerous attempts to "decompress" command farming by increasing the effectiveness of market incentives. This was particularly true after 1953 within the framework of the "New Course" policies. In 1953, Yugoslav collectives were disbanded, and this also occurred in Poland in 1956. Though socialization of agriculture remains the ultimate formal goal in both countries, there has been no attempt to use outright compulsion to date. Elsewhere, however, the process of collectivization was eventually resumed. By 1965, in Eastern Europe the socialized sector of collective and state farms (but excluding household plots) included the following percentages of total arable land in each country: Bulgaria, 89; Czechoslovakia, 93; East Germany, 95; Hungary, 87; Poland, 14; Rumania, 87; and Yugoslavia, 15.[11]

---

[11] U.S. Department of Agriculture, Economic Research Service, *The Europe and Soviet Union Agricultural Situation: Review of 1966 and Outlook for 1967* (Washington, D.C., 1976), p. 133.

Thus, the impact of command farming in Eastern Europe was not quite the same as in the USSR. In the former, the operation of command farming was linked for a considerable period of time to the introduction of collectivization. On the other hand, efforts to correct many of the undesirable consequences occurred more promptly. These two phenomena are, of course, interrelated. But all of the mechanisms, as well as the undesirable consequences, are to be found here as well.

Mechanisms of Command Farming

We now pass to the examination of the ways in which objectives of command farming have been implemented within the framework of the adopted production units. Our first three mechanisms are clearly of the command variety, but others represent a mixture of command and market elements, with the proportion varying at different stages of development and decompression.

The main key mechanism of command farming has been the system of state procurements of agricultural products. This is related first to the objective of increasing the volume of farm marketings (O_1) as well as to that of raising agriculture's contribution to capital formation (O_2). In both instances, reliance is placed on state rather than other procurement in order to concentrate the extracted produce—and savings—in the hands of the state for purposes of centrally determined distribution and final use. To the extent that individual peasant farming still operates, the system of procurements has also been used as a mechanism designed to accelerate the implementation of collectivization (O_4).

The chief characteristic of the procurement system is the use of compulsory delivery quotas. In the early period of industrialization (and until the early fifties in the case of the USSR), these deliveries were paid for at low, virtually nominal prices that remained unchanged in spite of the rapidly rising level of retail prices of industrial and other consumer goods. So long as MTSs existed as a main source of capital inputs in the collective farm sector, the system was supplemented by payments in kind by the farms for services rendered by these stations. In the early stages of command farming, a system of above-quota purchases (at considerably higher prices) was also introduced, with the objective of increasing the volume of output acquired by the state or other organizations. Because a typical Soviet or East European farm unit is a multiproduct enterprise, the system was eventually extended to all the important farm products. Following the Soviet example, technical crops continued to be procured under the contract delivery system, but the environment in which delivery contracts were negotiated did not in any way eliminate the element of compulsion. Since premiums were paid for above-quota deliveries, a double price system also applied here. Prices paid in quota and above-quota deliveries were set centrally by the state.

The obligations to deliver were considered quite firm, and enforcement was assured through the provision that underfulfillment of quota deliveries increased the obligations in the succeeding years. In the USSR, the system also applied to individual household plots of the collective farmers until 1957.

The system of two types of deliveries was eventually abolished in the Soviet Union as well as all East European countries (with the exception of Poland, where compulsory deliveries still exist at very low rates). The obligation to sell a certain amount of output to the state continued to operate—though the number of quotas was somewhat reduced, particularly within the framework of the application of new economic systems to agriculture.[12]

Procurement quotas were at first determined centrally. Subsequently, the need to decentralize was felt in this area as well, and various local administrative agencies were given the right to vary the quotas within a given region. In the USSR, quotas were first imposed on planned sown areas or per head of livestock on hand. Since farms tried to avoid the tax involved in compulsory deliveries by attempting to avoid expansion of acreage or of herds, quotas were ultimately set on the "per hectare basis." This was also done in Eastern Europe in the postwar period.

The second key mechanism is that of agricultural planning (M_2). This is in part the manifestation of the centrally planned nature of the command economy as a whole (E_4), but it is also related to certain other objectives. To the extent that rapid changes were desired in the production structure (e.g., the expansion of cotton sowings in the USSR), the setting of direct output and sown area targets appeared to be advisable and may thus be related to our objective (O_3). Moreover, given the volume of procurement quotas, it also seemed preferable to make sure that what had to be delivered (at nominal prices) would, in fact, be first produced. Finally, the low professional qualifications of farm managers in the early stages of command farming may well have called for greater supervision by higher (and presumably more qualified) outside agencies.

The upshot was a great proliferation of targets of all kinds. These included area to be sown under particular crops, the size and composition of livestock herds, indicators of productivity, the use of equipment (primarily in state farms, where targets were set on the basis of technological efficiency), dates and quality indicators for the performance of certain operations, etc. The supply of many construction materials—other than those

---

12 See Jerzy F. Karcz, "Certain Aspects of New Economic Systems in Bulgaria and Czechoslovakia," in *Agrarian Policies and Problems in Communist and Non-Communist Countries,* ed. W. A. Douglas Jackson (Seattle, Wash.: University of Washington Press, 1971), pp. 178–204.

produced locally—was subject to allocation quotas, and overhead capital investment (such as irrigation facilities) was also planned centrally. Many indicators were at one time approved by the Council of Ministers itself.

The resulting administrative difficulties can only be branded as formidable, especially when planning of this sort was applied to individual peasant farms (as was at one time the case in East Germany and Czechoslovakia). Examples are often cited of instances when the procurement plans exceed output targets.

Beginning with the USSR in 1955 (the innovation spread rapidly throughout the bloc), this type of planning was abolished, and farms were formally allowed to plan their own output on the basis of firm procurement targets that continued to be assigned to individual farms. In practice, however, procurement planning of this type can be fully as effective as output planning, especially when procurement targets encompass such basic products as milk, meat, and grain. (Interviews with farm officials suggest that roughly 90 per cent of the structure of sowing can be determined by the joint impact of five or six procurement quotas. The number was usually greater.[13])

It should be noted that certain key indicators were not planned for prolonged periods of time. Thus, no calculations were made of collective farm production costs until the early fifties. Given the existence of payments in kind and payment to labor out of residual income, such calculations would have been very difficult anyway. Given the high rate of taxation in kind through compulsory deliveries, they were moreover "outright embarrassing."[14] And it took roughly another decade (somewhat less in Bulgaria) before calculations of net income of collective farms became common.

The mechanism of agricultural planning is closely related to the third command mechanism of administrative interference (M_3). It is now readily apparent that most key decisions were made by administrative agencies which were not directly involved in farm operations. Many of these officials performed narrowly defined functions and sought to fulfill only their own particular goals. The interference of procurement officials into operational decision making was always considerable, and they seldom inquired into the long-range consequences of their decision for individual farms. In general, administrative officials entrusted with important decision-making powers were not given any incentives to increase the productivity of farm units.

The really significant interference came, of course, from the Party apparatus, particularly at the lowest administrative level. Their desires to enforce existing regulations, or to enhance the welfare of farms in their districts, was generally subordinated to that of gaining approval of their

---

[13] This is explored at greater length in my paper cited in footnote 12.

[14] The expression was used by Nancy Nimitz.

immediate (or the highest) superiors. It was also true that the task of discovering what the superiors were seeking to maximize at any one time was not always easy, in spite of the priority given to the objective of maximizing procurements and contributions to capital formation. This was particularly true in the Soviet Union, where major measures of farm policy were all too often implemented in the form of campaigns that often resulted in great reductions in both the production possibilities of farms and the individual welfare of farm members. Among the examples that could be mentioned are corn campaigns under Khrushchev, the extension of unirrigated cotton acreage into the Ukraine, sugar beets in Siberia, and the like.

Administrative interference at various levels has often been deplored, although the "right kind of involvement in farm affairs" has equally often been praised. Such formulations create a built-in incentive for violation of standing rules of the game, and we were not surprised to learn that practices of detailed output planning persisted for many years after 1955. The extent of such interference (to which there is no equivalent in industry) is perhaps best explained in terms of the relative ranking of agricultural objectives by various officials (with O_1 and O_3 being given a priority) and a desire to "improve" upon the functioning of the procurement system and agricultural planning (M_1, M_2). A more fundamental reason could be found in the deep distrust of peasantry that dates back to the early years of Soviet power and to peasant resistance to collectivization (O_4).[15]

Given the existence of a free market for consumer goods (apart from periods of rationing), material incentives are in the main used to allocate labor. The nature of these incentives in state farms (PU_3) is straightforward enough, given the existence of guaranteed wages (supplemented by income of plots). In the collective farm sector (PU_1), however, the problem is much more complex. The farm itself, designed primarily as an instrument of forced saving (O_2), cannot serve as a provider of sufficient incentives to assure its members a reward that is adequate to assure a required supply of effort. Thus, the structure of incentives becomes particularly distorted. In the USSR during 1937, fully one-quarter of the total receipts from state procurements accrued to the producers of cotton. For less specialized farms, the household plot (PU_2) became the main source of income, particularly as the legalization of free market sales of farm products—at high prices (M_5)—offered a major opportunity to many to acquire cash. In the thirties, cash income from Soviet collectives never accounted for more than one-quarter of the total household money income from such distributions and sales on the collective farm market. More recently, the corresponding figure is approximately 50 percent. In Czechoslovakia, the share of total (cash and kind) income from the plot in total

15 On this, see Alec Nove, "Incentives for Peasants and Administrators," in *Soviet Agricultural and Peasant Affairs*, ed. Roy D. Laird (Lawrence Kan.: University of Kansas Press, 1963), pp. 51–68.

income of the collective farmer reached a peak of 43 percent, and declined to about 30 percent in 1966.

But the issue is more complex. The private plot economy depends to a very considerable extent on the provision of feed from the socialized sector (mainly through distribution in kind, but more recently also through sales at low prices). There was thus always *some* incentive to supply work to the socialized sector, but on several occasions command mechanisms (minimum number of days per year, restriction of plot size, etc.) were also employed to reinforce this tendency—which is somewhat weakened by the fact that periods of peak activity in the two sectors coincide.

Two more aspects of incentives deserve brief mention. One is the difficulty of retaining such qualified trained personnel as is available on farms; both the resistance to sufficient income differentials and the pull of the city are very hard to overcome. Again, especially in the Soviet Union, use has been made of administrative measures to keep the specialist on the farm.[16] The other refers to various attempts to stimulate participation and to improve the quality of work through extensive use of premiums. This has an unfortunate tendency to introduce a considerable amount of uncertainty into the structure of rewards.[17]

Reference has already been made to the existence of a double price system in state procurements (until the reforms of 1958–60). If free market prices are included, a producing unit might have been faced with three different prices (M_5) for an identical product. As is explained in detail by Morris Bornstein,[18] the low delivery price served as an instrument of forced saving (O_2), while the above-quota price and the free market price were meant to provide incentives for greater supply of effort (M_4) and an increase in production (O_3). It was, however, the average realized price that influenced the total revenue of the collective farm and thus the cash incentives it could offer to members. As it turned out, even under the regime of strict output and procurement planning, average farm prices were not totally deprived of their allocational effect.

As we just noted, a single system of procurement prices is now the rule. Its introduction was beset by two distinct difficulties. First, because various governments (Soviet in 1958, Czechoslovak in 1959, Bulgarian in 1962) were apparently reluctant to give up the existing channels of capital accumulation, many price reforms were enacted under the constraint that allo-

16 Cf. the decree of April 24, 1962, translated in the *Current Digest of the Soviet Press*, vol. 14, no. 16 (May 16, 1972), pp. 16–17.

17 Karl-Eugen Wädekin, *Privatproduzenten in der sowjetischen Landwirtschaft* (Köln: Verlag Wissenschaft und Politik, 1967), pp. 121–34. [A translation has been published as *The Private Sector in Soviet Agriculture*, trans. by Keith Bush and ed. George F. Karcz (Berkeley: University of California Press, 1973)—Editor.]

18 Morris Bornstein, "The Soviet Price System," *American Economic Review*, vol. 52, no. 1 (March 1962), pp. 80–88.

cation of resources to agriculture should not be altered. This combined with the lack of any appropriate criteria for setting agricultural prices, failed to make production of many—primarily animal—products "profitable" (in the sense of covering production costs). Second, it also proved difficult to eliminate other distortions in the structure of procurement prices, such as the persistent undervaluation of grains.

Two other mechanisms deserve brief mention. One is agricultural taxation (M_6), functioning in the collective farm sector through the income tax on the collectives and in the private sector through a variety of what we can here call agricultural (at times straight land) taxes. The purpose of this taxation was to supplement the contribution of agriculture to domestic capital formation (O_2) exacted by the taxation in kind accomplished through the operation of the procurement and price systems. The second is agricultural credit (M_7), the use of which has varied a great deal from one country to another. It has been considerably greater in East European countries than in the Soviet Union, where advances from procurement organizations were relied upon to cover short-term needs for working capital, and where long-term credits were fairly insignificant in relation to internal financing.

UNDESIRABLE CONSEQUENCES

The first undesirable consequence from the standpoint of the agricultural sector has been its failure to specialize (UC_1). This is directly traceable to the operation of the procurement system (M_1) and agricultural planning (M_2), strengthened by administrative interference (M_3) and bolstered by the operation of farm prices (M_5).

One of the basic difficulties lay in the determination of the correct size of delivery quotas. As compulsory deliveries (including MTS payments) reached the level of about 90 percent of total sales—this was the case for grain in the early 50s in Poland and Czechoslovakia, and in the USSR almost throughout Stalin's reign—it proved impossible to avoid excessive assessments on many farms. This was aggravated by the tendency of quota-distributing agencies to "plan safely" for the fulfillment of regional quotas by allocating quotas to a larger number of farms than would be necessary under average harvest conditions. Since most products were subject to some sort of compulsory procurement, many advantages that could be realized from economies of scale were often dissipated. Worse yet, weak farms were often forced to deliver seed stocks of reasonable quality and later received seed grain of lower quality. On the other hand, more efficient farms were often assigned larger quotas (in a legal or illegal manner). Examples of "specialized farms" receiving quotas for 30 products were not at all uncommon.

While the procurement system did tend to freeze the structure of production at the existing level, it also stimulated production of certain types of produce in an artificial manner. In East European countries, larger and more efficient peasant farms were deprived of their own feed (this also occurred in the USSR), while weaker and less prepared farms were forced into livestock production, using feed purchased from the government at somewhat privileged prices. This kind of "pump priming" of grain often called for additional investments and resulted in high-cost production of animal products. The extent to which this was harmful is best revealed by the consideration that for all the countries of the socialist bloc, feed balances were insufficient to supply recommended feed rations. In 1964, feed requirements in Czechoslovakia were covered only to the extent of 85 percent in terms of grain units and 70 percent in terms of protein content. In 1962–64, the overall supply of Bulgarian collective farm animals with concentrated feed fell 30–35 percent short of requirements.

Quota-distribution procedures had yet another and equally adverse effect. Since no wheat quotas were usually set for mountainous areas, it suddenly became profitable to shift from rye to wheat production in spite of lower yields. The reason was that the total revenue from wheat sales (all at the higher above-quota prices) exceeded that from rye, which had a much lower average price because of the relatively high quotas for deliveries at the low quota-price. For the same reason, hog production (often on the basis of imported feed) tended to displace cattle in mountainous areas, and the production of sheep was drastically reduced in the nonblack soil areas of the RSFSR.

The effect of detailed output planning on specialization (with the exception of a few specialized crops, such as cotton) tended to work in the same direction. In 1966–67, when output was planned only through procurement targets, every single farm I visited in Czechoslovakia would have introduced fairly drastic changes in its production structure in the absence of obligations to sell.

Command farming also turned out to be quite capital intensive (UC_2). This is in part related to collectivization (O_4) and the operation of the kind of production units that are used in command farming (PU_1, PU_2). As indicated earlier, initial farm power losses in the Soviet Union had first to be replaced by mechanized power; indeed, total agricultural capital stock in the USSR towards the end of the thirties was about the same as it had been in 1928. Collectivization also results in a high demand for structures, primarily to house the collectivized livestock. Many of these structures, however, contribute little to current production, and their impact on productivity is observable only with a considerable lag. At the same time, of course, investment in machinery is likely to be relatively lower, if—as can be expected—total allocations of capital to agriculture are limited by the demands of the other sectors of the economy.

In the Soviet case, the share of agriculture in total investment in the national economy during the prewar plan period was close to 15 percent (and never declined below 10 percent, even in wartime). Currently, it reached a peak of 22.5 percent in 1966–67. In 1953–63, Bulgaria placed about 28 percent of its gross investment in agriculture and forestry. The corresponding figures are 18 percent for Hungary and Rumania and 16 percent for Czechoslovakia.[19]

These consequences of the introduction of command farming reduce the *net* contribution of the agricultural sector to capital formation, and conflict with the stated (and legitimate) objective of agriculture's contribution to industrialization (O_2). At first glance, they may be interpreted as a once and for all expenditure, but the problem is more complex. Capital-output ratios in socialized agricultures have been rising very considerably in recent years.

This is partly the result of inefficient use of such capital inputs as are made available to individual production units. The Soviet experience with the operation of machine tractor stations is vivid testimony to this effect: the task of coordinating their activities with those of collective farms could not be solved efficiently. State farms too, operating in a manner similar to that of state industrial enterprises with no explicit capital charges, tended to use this factor wastefully. In general, coordination of agricultural investments has been poor. This has been the case in the field of construction (in the early sixties, there was no housing for 20–25 percent of Bulgarian collective farm cows, calves, or sows). The ultimate impact of costly investments in irrigation facilities was frequently reduced because of failure to provide complementary drainage facilities. Finally, existing machinery stocks could not be used to capacity, given the shortage of spare parts and repair facilities that resulted from certain particular characteristics of the operation of the command economy in industry (E_4).

The adopted system of incentives and farm prices characteristic of command farming (M_4, M_5), as well as the existence of its special production units (PU_1, PU_2, PU_3), resulted in a close interdependence of the private and the socialist sector in socialist agricultures, particularly in that of the USSR (UC_3). This is analyzed in great detail in an important book by Karl E. Wädekin.[20] We have already referred to the high contribution of household plot production to total incomes of collective farm members, and it is proper to say that they bore much of the burden of assuring a minimum—though not always adequate—supply of labor for the socialist sector. But this is not all. A special type of the division of labor also occurred in production of crops as well as animal products, with the private sector concentrating, e.g., on the production of potatoes and the socialized

[19] Maurice Ernst, "Commentary," in *Soviet and East European Agriculture*, ed. Jerzy F. Karcz (Berkeley: University of California Press, 1967), p. 409.

[20] Wädekin, *Privatproduzenten in der sowjetischen Landwirtschaft*, chap. v.

on that of grains, feed, and the technical crops. The main source of income from household plots was thus largely dependent upon supplies of feed from the socialized sector. In turn, the latter frequently acquired large numbers of young cattle from the private sector. Even today, the contribution of household plots to supplying the urban (and nonagricultural rural) population with foodstuffs is very considerable.

Private production on household plots, however, has always been suspect on ideological grounds. Various spontaneous attempts to limit the scope for private production in agriculture necessarily affected adversely total production as well. If—as happened in the USSR in 1959 through 1964—such limitations were applied on a national scale, these adverse effects were even more pronounced.

Command farming also affected adversely the composition, and in some instances the size, of the collective farm labor force (UC_4). This impact has varied substantially not only among the various countries of the European socialist bloc, but also regionally within a single country. Disparities of income levels for fairly comparable occupations, especially among the more trained and specialized agricultural workers, have been fairly high. These disparities were further reinforced by the usual "pull" of urban amenities, which proved particularly strong for those villagers with university or other specialized training. Obviously, incentives in agriculture (M_4) were a prime cause of this phenomenon. The situation was at times aggravated by attempts to link the size of professional reward to plan fulfillment (or the volume of production) and the resulting irregularity in *paid* (as opposed to planned) wages or rewards. All kinds of programs have been suggested to deal with this phenomenon, but no satisfactory solutions appear to be in sight. This is particularly inconsistent with the stated objectives of intensifying agricultural production, modernizing production methods, and introducing better technology (O_3).

In certain areas of the USSR, East Germany, and Czechoslovakia, the labor supply problem is much more severe. For here the flight from the land has operated with particular force and affected not only the supply of specialists but that of less qualified labor as well. The resulting age and sex structure of the farm labor force is particularly unsatisfactory. In the collective farm sector, the mobility of labor between farms is not very high. At present, it even appears that labor supplies might be inadequate precisely in some areas with major land improvement programs.

This problem is also related to another peculiar phenomenon (to which there is a counterpart in industry): the uneven performance of individual farm units (UC_5). Given the partly unplanned and often the random impact of the procurement system (M_1), and the uncertain influence of agricultural planning and administrative interference (M_2, M_3), it was often a matter of chance alone whether a given production unit found itself among the "leading" or among the "lagging" farms. These disparities were further reinforced by the impact of the system of farm prices (M_5). The number of such "lagging" farms is relatively large: in Hungary, 40 percent of collectives are currently classified by this category.[21] Elsewhere, their number has been diminished either by conversions to state farms or by mergers with more prosperous neighbors. Thus, command farming tended to promote the coexistence of a "subsistence" and a "commercial" sector in agriculture, a phenomenon that is also found in many market-oriented agricultural systems (including that of the United States).[22] To the extent that weak farms merely performed a function of social assistance in providing minimum living standards to individuals who could not be absorbed by other sectors of the economy, this would not be a serious problem. However, in some socialist countries this is no longer the case.

In the particular conditions of command farming, uneven farm performance gave rise to other undesirable phenomena. To some extent, it contributed to the distortion of information by providing faulty signals to top decision makers (UC_6), perpetuating the impression that the existing income and performance disparities within the farming sector were due merely to managerial incompetence and testifying to the existence of large "internal reserves" (production potential) on weaker farms. But given the persistently high state demand for farm products and the absence of market mechanisms for the reallocation of factors of production within the sector, the state was unable to renounce its claims on a part of the output of these weak farms.

Over the years, we have therefore witnessed the emergence of special, but generally partial, programs to improve the condition and the production possibilities of weak farms. This gave rise to what socialist economists call the process of "secondary redistribution," under which resources initially extracted by the state through the system of farm prices or taxes are redirected to the weaker part of the agricultural sector. In practice, this amounts to the subsidization of weaker farms by their more fortunate counterparts, with adverse effects on incentives, internal capital formation, and the ability to obtain off-farm inputs. It is the opinion of most Czechoslovak economists that such assistance programs have not achieved their goals, but have contributed to the rise of production costs (or a slower rate of their reduction). This was particularly true when the assistance took the form of conversion to state farms, where production costs (except for Bulgaria and Rumania) have been considerably higher than those for the collective farm sector.

Moreover, the coexistence of two sectors in command farming further

---

[21] Fred E. Dohrs, "Incentives in Communist Agriculture: The Hungarian Models," *Slavic Review*, vol. 27, no. 1 (March 1968), p. 29.

[22] Cf. Wyn F. Owen, "The Double Development Squeeze on Agriculture," *American Economic Review*, vol. 56, no. 1 (March 1966), p. 64.

accentuated the already strong pressure for administrative interference and detailed planning of output and agro-technical measures. From what I have been able to observe on the spot, the effect of detailed supervision on incentives—one of the key factors involved—is often the opposite of what is required.

A special feature of command farming has been its tendency to generate faulty signals to various kinds of decision makers (UC_6). Priority of marketings and of the extraction of forced savings (O_1, O_2), the unfortunate tendency to stress the superiority of collectivized agriculture (O_4), and the political climate all combined to distort the flow of information available at various strata of authority.

At the level of the production unit, the chief casualty has been the collective farm, where meaningful cost calculations were prohibited for a considerable period of time, and where the structure of production was largely —if not completely—determined by many planning indicators imposed from above. Collective farm management was further forced to strike an uneasy balance between the provision of minimum incentives (in cash or in kind) to farm members and the fulfillment of procurement quotas or other success indicators. If the former were not forthcoming, there would be an adverse impact on labor supply. If the latter were not fulfilled, reprimands, other punishment, and dismissal would follow. There thus appeared a natural search for some slack and an all too frequent necessity to violate *some* regulation. But this only increased the scope of administrative interference (M_3), and further reduced the scope for autonomous decision making. On balance, however, the tendency was to emphasize short-term results to the detriment of long-run trends in productivity. Given the high rate of turnover in the administrative and the Party apparatus, the same tendency also operated in various "above-enterprise" agencies.

Although an unbelievably large amount of statistical reporting took place, emphasis was primarily placed on series that indicated satisfactory performance of socialist agriculture. While the indicator of "gross cash revenue" was used to represent overall results of collective farm activity, it eventually became clear (in both Czechoslovakia and the USSR) that it misrepresented trends in total gross output of that sector. Similarly, allocations of cash to "indivisible funds" were often used as an indicator of internal accumulation in collectives. Recent Czechoslovak data show that this series differed markedly from trends in the more meaningful series on internal accumulation of cash and kind, which moved in the opposite direction from allocations to indivisible funds after 1959. Finally, the official series seriously understates the share of agriculture in the national product. Whether or not this tendency toward misleading statistics affected major policy decisions at the highest level in all countries must still remain conjectural. But a claim has been made in Czechoslovakia that it did delay a shift of resources to agriculture for about three years prior to 1964. Under the circumstances, it is likely that the top decision makers were at least partly misled by their own statistical agencies.

The overall impact of the mechanisms and the undesirable consequences of command farming are clear enough: the agricultural sector as a whole appears to operate far short of its production possibilities frontier. Its first response then is that of low joint factor productivity (R_1), a conclusion substantiated by such calculations as are presently available for the USSR during the 30s and for Czechoslovakia in the postwar period.[23]

This does not necessarily mean that the imposition of command farming cannot lead to an increase in output. As is well known, Soviet farm output during the thirties recovered rapidly from the low reached in 1932–33. But as the rate of growth of marketings outstripped that of output, and as trends in farm income became less favorable toward the end of the decade, output began to stagnate. A similar tendency appeared in the USSR towards the end of the postwar recovery period (1949–52), and in virtually all East European countries by 1953. It would then appear that the tendency of output to stagnate (apart from recovery from unusual troughs) is a second response (R_2) under command farming.

It should be noted the emergence of R_2 probably went unnoticed in the USSR (exception must be made for such economists as V. G. Venzher) in the particular political climate of the Great Purge and the approach of World War II. In general, little attention has been devoted there to the study of the *total* impact of command farming on the performance of the agricultural sector. (For reasons that cannot be explored here, economic model-building in socialist countries is only a recent development.) It is thus likely that the full effect of command farming was not really recognized for a considerable period of time. This is why a Polish economist, in discussing the application of the procurement system, could say with justification that practitioners of command farming often find themselves in the position of the sorcerer's apprentice.

The tendency of output to stagnate and other undesirable consequences do generate a pressure for systemic reform (R_3), and recent history of communist agricultures provides ample evidence to that effect. However, the complex interrelationships that we have discussed above, as well as the impact of partial reforms introduced in the USSR and Eastern Europe, do suggest that the responsiveness of command farming to partial reforms is sluggish. For example, in the Soviet case in 1958–64, there was improvement of incentives without a corresponding increase in input supplies, and greater formal farm autonomy was accompanied by rising procurement goals and restrictions on the private sector.

Recently, the decompression of command farming has taken the form of "new economic systems" in agriculture, accompanied by corresponding

---

[23] D. Gale Johnson's, Douglas Diamond's, Gregor Lazarcik's, and my own.

reforms (of varying degree of novelty) in the industrial sectors of the economy. Most of these reforms center on many key variables in our model. They stress greater farm autonomy in decision making, reduce the number (or the size) of procurement quotas, emphasize the allocative function of prices (by introducing many reforms that clearly point in the right direction), increase the importance and improve the conditions of bank credit, and attempt to use taxation rather than prices to achieve the desired intersectoral transfer of resources. Much attention has also been given to the improvement of incentives by raising the level of remuneration on the collective farms (USSR, Bulgaria, Czechoslovakia), or introducing various share-cropping practices within the collective farm sector (Hungary). Finally, efforts are being made to provide numerous agricultural services that have hitherto been sadly neglected as well as to improve the volume and the conditions of the supply of off-farm inputs.

It is still too early to say whether these efforts will succeed without further institutional and policy reforms (and the outlook does not seem too bright in the aftermath of the invasion of Czechoslovakia). We ought to point out, however, that balance-of-payments considerations, as well as continuing growth of state demand for farm products, suggest that great attention should be paid to the impact of recent changes in agricultural planning practices as well as of administrative interference. In times of stress, the tendency has always been to apply these mechanisms with greater strength, and there are many subtle ways in which farm operations may be influenced by outside organizations.

CONCLUSION

A brief concluding statement is in order on the overall effectiveness of command farming within the context of economic development as such. Soviet experience, as well as that of some East European countries with relatively abundant availability of labor, suggests that command farming, or similar policies, might be used to assist the development of the economy in the early stage of rapid industrialization. The great danger lies in the fact that command farming, as such, tends to provide signals for turning points in economic policy only with a considerable delay and in a distorted manner. There is, of course, no guarantee that these signals will be interpreted correctly or that they will lead to the implementation of proper policies that deal simultaneously with a wide range of variables. Given the high capital intensity of command farming, which reduces considerably the contribution of agriculture to domestic capital formation, and its adverse or at best dubious productivity trends, it would seem appropriate to explore alternative institutional arrangements and agricultural systems.

In the light of the above, command farming does not appear to be an appropriate agricultural system for accelerating the rate of growth of an economy (such as the Czech) which is not characterized by relative abundance of labor.

Nor is it likely to be a satisfactory arrangement for countries that cannot afford to give first priority to increasing marketings because of the initially low level of per capita production. As is suggested by the experience of Mainland China with its own version of command farming, emphasis must be placed on raising productivity. In turn, the Japanese experience indicates that alternatives to command farming may yield superior results both for the economy as a whole and for its agricultural sector.

18

FOREIGN TRADE BEHAVIOR OF CENTRALLY PLANNED ECONOMIES*

Franklyn D. Holzman[1]

The foreign trade of centrally planned economies differs from that of market-oriented economies in a number of important ways, as a result of the nature of the centrally planned economic system. Typically, the foreign trade of such an economy is characterized by a high degree of autarky, inconvertibility, bilateralism, and discrimination—which in turn are attributable to such features of the economy as physical planning, ambitious targets, irrational price structures, disequilibrium exchange rates, and state trading.

In this comprehensive article, Holzman systematically analyzes how and why centrally planned economies conduct their foreign trade, and the resulting problems of inconvertibility, bilateralism, discrimination, dumping, and the inapplicability of most-favored-nation tariff treatment.

The earliest comprehensive and still relevant analysis of foreign trade in a centrally planned economy (CPE) can be found in Alexander Gerschen-

* Excerpted by permission from *Industrialization in Two Systems: Essays in Honor of Alexander Gerschenkron,* ed. Henry Rosovsky (New York: John Wiley & Sons, Inc., 1966), pp. 237–65. Copyright by the President and Fellows of Harvard College. Franklyn D. Holzman is Professor of Economics at Tufts University.

[1] Many ideas for this paper developed while I was a consultant to the United Nations in 1963. My ideas were clarified in discussion there with Sidney Dell, Rudolf Nötel, Nita Watts, Stein Rossen, Juri Ryska, and Valery Naborov. I am also indebted to Joseph Berliner, Richard Caves, Herbert Levine, Charles Kindleberger, Egon Neuberger, and Raymond Vernon for comments on an early draft. The views reflected in the paper are my own and should not necessarily be atrributed to any of the above individuals or organizations with which they are connected. Finally, I am indebted for financial assistance to the American Council of Learned Societies.

kron's *Economic Relations with the USSR.*[2] In large part, the present paper constitutes an extension of his work.

Traditionally, the foreign trade behavior of centrally planned economies has been characterized by a notoriously high degree of autarky, currency inconvertibility, bilateralism, and discrimination. Although these phenomena occur also in trade among capitalist nations, they do not constitute its "normal" features. Not only are the capitalist deviations from uncontrolled trade of lesser significance, but the issues they raise often differ from those raised by East European trade controls. This is primarily because of the impress on the foreign trade mechanism of certain unique characteristics of the centrally planned economies.

An attempt will be made in this paper to show the effects of central planning on foreign trade practices. In Section I the special characteristics of centrally planned economies that influence their foreign trade will be briefly described. Next, in Section II, it will be shown how they, together with some other relevant factors, affect foreign trade behavior. . . .

I. CHARACTERISTICS OF CENTRALLY PLANNED ECONOMIES

We outline below certain characteristics of centrally planned economies which affect their foreign trade behavior. Some of these characteristics (and the foreign trade behavior resulting) should not be viewed as absolutely necessary to central planning, nor are they present to the same degree in each of the centrally planned economies. They are included because they have been relevant in most East European nations until the present time.

"Irrational" Internal Cost and Price Structures and Disequilibrium Exchange Rates

The prevalence of "irrational" costs and prices in the centrally planned economies is almost universally acknowledged and needs little elaboration. Basically, these are the result of: (*a*) extensive use of differential sales taxes and subsidies to implement certain internal policies;[3] (*b*) the Marxist failure fully to account in the cost structure for rent, interest, and depreciation; and (*c*) insensitivity of prices to supply-demand forces.

Another well-known feature of these economies is the prevalence of disequilibrium exchange rates. Those, of course, are of negligible practical

---

[2] This brief monograph was published in New York in 1945 by the Committee on International Economic Policy in cooperation with the Carnegie Endowment for International Peace.

[3] Such as, for example, a high rate of investment and military expenditures (large sales tax), or encouragement of new types of capital equipment (subsidies).

importance anyway, because of the direct controls used to plan and implement foreign trade.[4]

Autarky

The desire for self-sufficiency in those commodities produced at a comparative disadvantage motivates all nations to some extent, thereby reducing the possible volume of world trade. The nations with centrally planned economies appear to be more strongly motivated in this direction than capitalist economies, for the following well-known reasons. First, because of the complicated input-output interrelationships among intermediate products, most of which are directly allocated, central planners try to avoid heavy dependence of the domestic economy on foreign supplies and, thus, to insulate it from the vagaries, both imaginary and real, of the world market.[5] Second, all nations endeavor to achieve a certain degree of self-sufficiency for reasons of military security—to diminish the risks of economic warfare. Owing to this universal desire, countries where all industry is nationalized are likely to reduce trade to a greater extent than those in which a large part of economic activity is in private hands.[6, 7] Under capitalism, competition exists naturally and protection requires an explicit act by the government; under central planning as it is presently practiced, protection is the rule unless the government makes an explicit decision to allow imports to replace domestic production. Third, the autarkic bias of centrally planned economies may possibly be enhanced by their irrational price systems; in fact, it is often very difficult for the planners to decide what they should trade. These are serious impediments to trade.

---

[4] Whether exchange rates are in equilibrium is of little importance, of course, given the prevalence of irrational prices. Under the latter condition, unrestricted trade at the equilibrium exchange rate cannot be relied upon to benefit the domestic economy (see below).

[5] This view is not restricted, in the centrally planned economies, only to international trade but has its counterparts in domestic trade. In the Soviet Union, for example, one of the major reasons for the 1957 reorganization was the fact that the ministries and enterprises developed autarkic policies which led to excessive cross-hauling (within ministries) and an inordinately low level of subcontracting by enterprises. After the reorganization, regional autarky (*mestnichestvo*) was adopted by individual *sovnarkhozy* [regional economic councils] and created similar problems. The reasons for the local exhibitions of autarkic behavior are somewhat different from that at the international level. Lack of dependability in the former case is due primarily to difficulties with the internal direct-allocation supply system and to the managerial incentive system.

[6] This factor operates to curtail Eastern trade with the West much more than intra-bloc trade. Along these same lines might be mentioned the desire of many nations to industrialize at any cost rather than submit to comparative advantage even when long-run comparative advantage suggests less industrialization. Rumania is a case in point.

[7] The strategic controls imposed by Western nations on trade with the East also contribute somewhat to the low level of East-West trade, although much less so now than in the past decade.

State Trading

It has been said that ". . . economic planning of the type practiced in Russia is not feasible without the use of a foreign trade monopoly. . . ."[8] Whatever the reasons, foreign trade is nationalized in the centrally planned economies and is usually conducted by combines which function as agents of the state. This has at least three major consequences for foreign trade behavior.

First, among the Eastern nations, foreign trade is conducted primarily to obtain essential imports. Exports are considered not as an end in themselves but as a means to finance the necessary imports.[9] This view of the foreign trade process seems natural enough since the CPE nations, typically pursuing overfull employment policies (see below), can hardly be interested in mere employment effects of exports. If, notwithstanding this, some of the CPE nations have led intensive export promotion campaigns, it was because of the balance-of-payment pressures generated by rapid growth (see below), that is, ultimately, to pay for rising imports. In the West, the level of exports is just as (if not more) important a goal as the level of imports. Some individual traders export, others import, with gains to the economy, presumably reflected in private profits, in either case.

Second, the centrally planned economies take a barter-type approach to foreign trade and view exports and imports as interdependent. Profitability is assessed primarily with respect to overall "terms of trade" rather than on the basis of profit on each individual transaction. This is a consequence of the import orientation of trade (above) as well as of "irrational" internal prices, and of the predisposition, inherited from internal planning, to operate in categories of physical allocations.

Third, because foreign trade is run by a state monopoly, tariffs are basically redundant; trade is controlled by implicit import and export quotas. The decisions to trade are made directly by the government, often without the mediation of price comparisons. In the absence of such explicit decisions, trade will not take place, a reaction equivalent to that achieved by employing prohibitive quotas. By comparison, in capitalist nations profitable opportunities for trade may be pursued unless the government makes an explicit decision to the contrary. Such decisions may be implemented by tariffs, quotas, or exchange controls.

---

8 Alexander Gerschenkron, *Economic Relations with the U.S.S.R.* (New York: Committee on International Economic Policy, 1945), p. 18. It should be noted that the character of the state trading could be substantially changed if internal planning practices were "liberalized."

9 "Russia exports solely in order to obtain the wherewithal for payments for imports. In this sense, she is likely to live up to the classical doctrine of foreign trade and to reject the tenets of mercantilism. This, no doubt, sounds paradoxical, but is undeniable. From the Russian point of view exports are a loss and not a gain." (Ibid., p. 47.)

Overfull Employment Planning

An important aspect of the centrally planned economies has been their tendency, not unlike that of capitalist nations during wartime, to over-commitment of resources. The resulting excess demand by consumers for final products and by enterprises for factors and intermediate products expresses itself as either open or repressed inflation. Moreover, the strained plans lead to sellers' markets and to a relative lack of concern for the quality of output,[10] including goods for export. Although overfull employment planning is presently less pervasive than it was in earlier years, it still persists.

Quantity Targeting

Generally, enterprises have as their major goals output targets stated in physical or value terms rather than other so-called success indicators such as profits, cost reduction, and so forth. This, together with the fact that most intermediate products are directly allocated, reinforces the tendency noted just above for management to be less concerned with "quality" than it otherwise might.

Rapid Economic Growth

Rapid economic growth is the overriding goal of the centrally planned economies, one in which they have achieved signal successes. The process of growth usually, though not always, generates import requirements more naturally and easily than exportable items.

Method of Balances

Supply and demand for most intermediate products are balanced quantitatively by direct controls in the East European nations. This procedure, known as the "method of balances," is used because central allocation rather than the market performs the task of distributing essential industrial supplies.

This concludes the brief survey of various characteristics of centrally planned economies which have an impact on foreign trade behavior. Some (the first three) are more important for our purposes than others, but they are all included for completeness.

II. FOREIGN TRADE BEHAVIOR

We turn now to foreign trade behavior. The most important and interesting are the related problems of inconvertibility and bilateralism, which

---

[10] Quality here refers to all characteristics of a commodity, including delivery.

will be treated first. Others, discussed below, have to do with discrimination, most-favored-nation (MFN) clauses, monopoly power, and dumping.

Inconvertibility

Currency convertibility in its commonly used meaning refers to the right or possibility of the holder of a currency to exchange it for gold or for "hard" currencies. Limitations are placed on convertibility when a currency is in excess supply on foreign exchange markets or, what amounts to the same, when other currencies or gold are in excess demand by the holders of the currency in question. Among capitalist nations such limitations on convertibility are likely to be put in force if a currency is overvalued, owing to inflation or to more fundamental structural factors. With overvaluation, there is a tendency for imports to exceed exports. Usually, nonresidents are allowed to convert current earnings of the currency in question into their own currencies; balance is maintained by restricting imports, that is, by placing limits on convertibility for residents.[11]

Why are the currencies of the centrally planned economies, say, the ruble, inconvertible? Before the revaluations of 1961 most, if not all, East European currencies were overvalued. Overvaluation, although a sufficient condition for inconvertibility under capitalism, is neither necessary nor relevant, given the foreign trade institutions and practices of the centrally planned economies. So long as internal prices are disorderly and world prices are used as the basis for trade, and the composition and volume of trade are determined by direct controls and administered by a foreign trade monopoly, the exchange rate remains merely an accounting device. Its changes have no effect on trade. Thus, for instance, the substantial devaluations of April 1936, and January 1961, both of which brought the ruble into rough equilibrium in a purchasing power parity sense,[12] had no discernible impact on the volume, composition, or manner in which Soviet trade is conducted.

---

[11] Under extreme circumstances, nonresidents may be denied convertibility into their own currencies, particularly on capital account. Whether nonresidents are allowed to transfer the currency in question to residents of third countries depends on the degree of overvaluation with respect to all other currencies. Usually, conversion is allowed into "softer" but not into "harder" currencies or into gold. At present, any bloc currency is probably equally "soft," relative to the major Western currencies, since general convertibility prevails in the West. On the other hand, my guess is that some bloc currencies are less desirable than others in intrabloc trade although "which" and "by how much" are impossible to say under the present institutional arrangements.

[12] By this we mean that the foreign trade prices (that is, world prices) of goods exported and imported are, on the average, approximately equal to the domestic prices of the same goods at the given exchange rate. Given the controls which exist over Soviet trade, this appears to be the only operational definition of exchange rate equilibrium which is possible. Equilibrium, under this definition, may deviate substantially from "true" equilibrium, of course.

Currency inconvertibility in centrally planned economies is in part a reaction to balance-of-payment pressures and the lack of sufficient foreign exchange reserves. Yet, although these factors (related to rapid growth, overfull employment planning, inadaptability of exports, and repressed inflation) might partly justify the prohibition against converting domestic currency into foreign exchange by residents, they can hardly be adduced to explain the existing convertibility restrictions on nonresidents. Typically, the Soviet bloc laws do not permit nonresidents to convert domestic currencies into foreign exchange or gold, nor do they even allow them to accumulate such currencies.[13] These extreme legal restrictions on convertibility (to be explained below) obviously reduce the demand for bloc currencies. Their effect, additionally weakening the international financial standing of the bloc nations, has been superimposed on other factors discouraging the potential nonresident demand for bloc currencies. Clearly, even if foreigners were allowed to accumulate rubles, for example, their demand for Soviet currency would be blunted by circumstances always present under central planning.

First, there would be the considerable uncertainty on the part of nonresidents regarding the possibility of purchasing goods with bloc currencies. Nonresidents are quite limited in the scope of possible purchases from the East European nations, not because the latter do not have a large fund of exportables but because most commodity flows are directly planned and it is difficult to buy items not earmarked for export (implicit trade controls). That is to say, within the existing system of allocation, foreign holders of, say, rubles, are not allowed much, if any, opportunity to compete for goods with Soviet enterprises and domestic consumers. Their difficulties might be additionally increased by the fact that trade negotiations are usually conducted with special foreign trade organizations subordinate to the foreign trade monopoly rather than directly with producing or distributing enterprises. This substantial limitation on purchases by nonresidents is aptly called by Oscar Altman "commodity inconvertibility," in contrast with "currency inconvertibility."[14]

Second, uncertainty generated by inaccessibility of bloc exportables is compounded by the irrationality of internal pricing and the overvalued exchange rates which make it difficult to determine in advance of negotia-

---

[13] Exceptions to this rule occur in the use of temporary imbalances in bilaterally balanced trade relationships as well as according to provisions in some bilateral agreements for payment in gold or convertible currency if imbalances exceed prescribed limits for a period of time.

[14] Oscar Altman, "Russian Gold and the Ruble," *International Monetary Fund Staff Papers*, vol. 7, no. 3 (April 1960), pp. 430–31. Note that "commodity convertibility" essentially means absence of restrictions on exports. The term "free trade" on the other hand is typically used to denote absence of restrictions on imports, though in theory it encompasses exports as well.

tions the prices at which goods may be bought or sold. The foreign trade prices, therefore, usually deviate considerably from domestic prices and are, as a "first approximation," based on "world prices." Although this practice largely eliminates the overvaluation problem and may, additionally, reduce somewhat the uncertainty (due to irrational internal prices) in the case of simple standardized commodities, the prices of complex products remain quite conjectural. Finally, uncertainty as to the "value" of a ruble is still further increased by factors mentioned above concerning the quality, delivery, and general unadaptability of exports to foreign markets.[15] To sum up, from the point of view of nonresidents, bloc currencies are not only inconvertible in the usual sense, but also undesirable because of the substantial uncertainties regarding their exchangeability for goods.

Owing to the significance and uniqueness of "commodity inconvertibility" of bloc currencies, it is impossible to explain its existence and implementation without discussing the foreign trade monopolies of centrally planned economies.

First, and most important, since central planning is implemented primarily by direct allocation of resources, the planners deem it necessary to insulate the flows of products from external disruption. This is accomplished by the foreign trade monopoly by prohibition of foreign-held ruble balances and by inconvertibility of rubles into other currencies as well as commodities.

Second, when internal prices are not "rational" as indicators of the relative values of goods to the planners or in terms of some measure of "real costs" (for reasons discussed earlier), free trade (commodity convertibility) cannot be allowed (nor can the foreign trade monopoly be dispensed with) because it would lead to a pattern of trade disadvantageous to the centrally planned economies and productive of large gains for their Western trading partners.

*　　*　　*　　*　　*

Let us sum up these conclusions in another way. Given the irrationality of internal prices, resident convertibility (free imports) cannot be allowed because it will lead to large-scale importation of commodities which have relatively high prices but which, in fact, may be more cheaply produced at home (for example, many consumers' goods). On the other hand, strict controls over exports, discouraging potential ruble holdings by foreigners, must be maintained lest nonresidents compete in domestic markets for goods which, owing to subsidies or some other costing quirk, have a low price but, in fact, are expensive to produce. Nonresident "free" expenditure within the bloc countries cannot be allowed, because it may involve

---

[15] One might also mention here that Western governmental controls and consumers' resistance to imports from the bloc countries have similar effects on the "value" of their currencies.

losses to their domestic economies. As noted earlier, the bloc nations do not grant convertibility rights to nonresidents except in the special instance when the swing credit limits of a bilateral agreement are exceeded. Moreover, foreigners are usually prohibited from accumulating bloc currencies, whether within or outside the centrally planned economies. The only exception to this prohibition is that made for temporary imbalances within the rigid framework of bilateral trade agreements. Presumably, this is because the availability of bloc currencies to outsiders might lead to large discounts in world currency markets, something the East European planners undoubtedly wish to avoid.[16]

In the case of Western nations with inconvertible currencies, nonresidents are encouraged to hold, or spend, the "inconvertible" currency—the problem is that they don't want to. The centrally planned economies are in the peculiar position of being unable to try to boost their exports, thereby improving the position of their currency, by allowing nonresidents freely to import from them.[17]

---

[16] It might be argued that the bloc nations could avoid the pricing uncertainty problem by pricing net of sales taxes and subsidies or that they could circumvent the internal price problem by simply agreeing to buy or sell freely at world prices. Although it is true that the pricing predicament is somewhat overstated by the consumer-producer goods dichotomy in the text, it is also true that sales taxes and subsidies are not the only reasons for irrational prices in the bloc countries (see Section I). If it were, the bloc countries would undoubtedly have solved by this time the intrabloc pricing problem and would no longer have to rely on the embarrassing solution of using world prices in their trade. The many articles which have been published in the East European journals on how to choose commodities for foreign trade are a tribute to the intractability of the problem. A recent Soviet source makes the following commentary: "Wholesale prices, as is known, do not reflect with adequate completeness and precision the socially-necessary labor outlays for the manufacture of goods. Prices of means of production are mainly below value while the prices of many consumer goods are above value. Moreover, the prices of goods within each of these departments also diverge from their value. Thus, numerically-equal outlays of social labor as expressed in different prices. The use of such wholesale prices in internal trade leads to a certain violation of the equivalence of exchange. *That is why, in our opinion, the internal wholesale prices now in force cannot be utilized for forming a new system of prices in trade between the socialist countries* (italics in original). Otherwise the prices of the world socialist market would have the same shortcomings as the internal wholesale prices and would not reflect the outlays of socially necessary labor. In view of the fact that the composition of exports and imports of countries is not the same, trade at such prices would bring about an unjustified redistribution of the national income. States in which the share of goods with prices below value is higher for exports than for imports would turn over part of their national income to countries with a bigger share of exports at prices above value."

As for world prices, they are at present clearly an uneasy expedient. For one thing, there are few, if any, homogeneous commodities. In addition, even in those instances in which commodities appear to be virtually homogeneous, it turns out that different prices are quoted from place to place and from month to month. The concept "world price" is largely an abstraction for the purpose at hand. Finally, even if there were "world prices," they would not always be relevant for pricing bloc products because of the differing comparative advantage (supply-demand) conditions within and without the bloc.

[17] The problem of freeing trade and establishing convertibility with disequilibrium prices is the foreign trade counterpart of the internal problem of decentralizing and using the profit motive without rationalizing the price structure.

Bilateralism

The percentage of bilaterally conducted trade is higher in the centrally planned economies than in either the Western industrial or the developing nations. Moreover, it is higher now than it used to be in the same economies during the 1930s when they were still in the capitalist orbit. Intrabloc trade is more bilateral than East-West trade. Institutionally, the high degree of bilateralism is accomplished by means of annual and long-term trade and payment agreements which attempt, within limits and after taking account of credits, to keep trade between the two participating countries in balance over the period in question. These agreements are implemented, of course, by direct governmental controls over the level and composition of imports and exports.

The centrally planned economies recognize the advantages of multilateralism and have even taken some tentative steps toward increasing its scope in intrabloc transactions. Why, despite that very recognition, bilateralism is still so strongly adhered to can be attributed to currency inconvertibility and the factors behind it discussed above. Since no nation is willing to hold balances in rubles, *levs*, and so forth, payments of the centrally planned economies must be balanced insofar as they are unable to produce gold or develop export surpluses with convertible currency nations.

A second factor leading to bilateralism is the tendency among bloc countries to strive for overall payments balance (especially among themselves), and therefore, erroneously, for bilateral balance (see below). The main reason for the attempt to achieve overall balance has to do with the already discussed view that exports are not an end in themselves but simply a means of financing imports. To the extent that trade policy is guided by such considerations, there is a tendency to strive for an overall payments balance, in the first place, and there is no strong incentive to develop an overall export surplus. Next, imports are confined by controls to the amount which can be financed currently through exports, previous policies of not developing export surpluses having produced no large foreign exchange reserves. Consequently, like all nations under balance-of-payments pressures (owing to rapid growth, difficulties in adapting to export markets, and so forth), centrally planned economies resort to the ultimate adjustment of payments by limiting imports to the level of possible exports.

Now, the necessity or desire to achieve overall balance does not logically require bilateral balancing by nation. Among capitalist nations, however, it has been observed that nations with export marketing problems sometimes resort to bilateral balancing agreements to absorb each other's second-line exportables. The propensity to do so is much stronger among the planned economies. In fact, it is difficult to see how a substantial degree of multilateralism could be achieved by these economies, simultaneously with the desired overall balance. The twin objectives are accomplished imperfectly under capitalism via the automatic operation of price, income, and capital flow adjustment mechanisms that do not function under central planning. The easiest way to achieve overall balance in the latter case is undoubtedly by planning for a high degree of bilateral balance.

Envision the difficulty of planned multilateralism with overall balance. Suppose country A trades with B, C, and D. Overall balance can be achieved by relatively simple balancing with each nation. This is not to say that bilateral balancing is easy, for it undoubtedly requires considerable negotiation and, on the part of one or both partners, either some uneconomic trading or the foregoing of some profitable trading. On the other hand, suppose A runs a surplus with B. This means that A (B) goes into negotiations with C and D requiring a net deficit (surplus) equal to the surplus (deficit) with B (A). But there may be no particular reason why C and D should want to run surpluses with A exactly to offset deficits with B. Under planning, where prices are misleading and only the relatively few goods specifically earmarked for export or import can be traded, nations may be loath to accept a surplus (deficit) with another nation because of the subsequent difficulty of buying (selling) more than can be sold to (bought from) third countries. This, in effect, is equivalent to a situation in which the various inconvertible currencies have different values to different holders. If interest conflicts occur along these lines, there is no economic adjustment mechanism to resolve them. An administrative reconciliation, if any, would undoubtedly involve a substantial reduction of profitable trade and/or addition of unprofitable trade. The problems are likely multiplied as the number of nations in the system increases. (In a system with economic adjustment mechanisms, the problems would probably be lessened as the number of nations increased.)

A third factor encouraging bilateralism is the opportunity that bilateral agreements offer the economically stronger nations (often, in this context, the nation least dependent on the trade in question) to improve the terms of trade. This possibility may motivate the Soviet Union, at least, to trade bilaterally with its smaller partners.

Fourth, the tendency toward bilateral balancing in foreign trade may be strengthened by carryover from the general use of an analogous technique, the "method of balances," in internal commodity planning.

Finally, some of the nonbloc nations with which the centrally planned economies trade prefer bilateral arrangements because of balance-of-payments problems. Even if a centrally planned economy were prepared to trade on a multilateral basis, it would be forced into bilateral trade by such trading partners.

Foreign Trade Discrimination

A basic objective of the Western trading community has been to achieve trade without discrimination. In the foreign trade usage discrimination means that one not buy in the lowest—or sell in the highest—price markets.[18] To the extent that restrictions (tariffs, quotas) are applied to trade, the objective is to have them applied equally to all nations, that is, in a nondiscriminatory manner. Foreign trade discrimination may be motivated by either economic or political factors; discussion will proceed from the former to the latter.

Inconvertibility and bilateralism have almost inevitably involved the introduction of apparently discriminatory controls by capitalist nations; the situation is similar in the case of the centrally planned economies. Western nations discriminate against their trade partners *via* exchange controls and explicit commodity and/or country import quotas. The centrally planned economies achieve the same results by implicit controls which are the outcome of implementing planning decisions regarding the volume, content, and direction of trade.

Among Western nations, where inconvertibility has often been due to overvaluation, serious questions have been raised whether those apparently discriminatory practices observed have in fact really constituted true discrimination.[19] Suppose, as was the case after World War II, that the British pound was overvalued with respect to the U.S. dollar, but not with respect to the Greek drachma. Suppose also that, at going exchange rates, Greek tobacco was more expensive than American tobacco. If the British bought Greek rather than American tobacco, they could be accused, under current conventions, of not buying in the cheapest market, hence of discriminating. It could be argued, however, that if one takes into account the overvaluation of pound and drachma vis-à-vis dollar, Greek tobacco is actually cheaper to the British than American tobacco, and that the apparent discrimination is an illusion resulting from the maintenance of unrealistic pegged exchange rates. It could also be argued that adherence to the ideal of nondiscriminatory application of quotas and exchange controls under these circumstances would unduly and unfairly reduce the volume of trade.

Can discrimination by the centrally planned economies be rationalized on similar grounds? The answer is a hesitant yes, hesitant because the reason is somewhat different. As we have seen, inconvertibility of bloc currencies cannot substantively be attributed to overvaluation in a "purchasing power parity" sense. In fact, by adopting world prices as a first approximation in their foreign trade negotiations, the CPEs are in effect adopting implicit exchange rates which are, in the purchasing power parity sense, "equilibrium" rates.

---

[18] The term price is taken here to include all commercial considerations. In contrast with foreign trade discrimination, monopolistic price discrimination means using market power to buy cheaper and sell dearer than the competitive price. See this writer's "Discrimination in International Trade," *American Economic Review*, vol. 39, no. 6 (December 1949), pp. 1234–44.

[19] That is, not buying in the cheapest and selling in the dearest markets.

On the other hand, however, one could interpret the various uncertainties, mentioned earlier, which are responsible for inconvertibility, as indications of a discounted value of currency. Presumably, there is some discount rate at which foreigners would be willing to hold rubles, *levs*, and so forth, if allowed to.[20] Or, more realistically, one might say there is a price (interest rate, terms of trade) at which foreigners could be prevailed upon to adapt themselves to large-scale, bilaterally balanced trade with bloc nations. The extensive trade of the centrally planned economies with each other at the expense of trade with nonbloc nations, then, may be attributed in part at least, not to discrimination but to the unwillingness of nonbloc nations to adapt themselves, without a charge, to large-scale trade with the centrally planned economies, under the CPE ground rules. To the extent that there is trade between West and East, it is conducted largely according to the former's ground rules—multilaterally, with imbalances settled in convertible currencies or gold.[21]

The extraordinarily large amount of foreign trade discrimination which does exist between East and West[22] is ascribable not primarily to the economic factors just discussed but to politically strategic factors. Both the centrally planned and the Western nations are guilty of politically motivated trade discrimination. Important special instruments of such discrimination are: (*a*) the controls by the United States and COCOM nations over so-called strategic exports to the centally planned economies as well as (*b*) the strong preferences[23] for direct intrabloc trade among the centrally planned economies. The chances for growth of political discrimination are greater in the centrally planned economies than in the Western nations because of nationalization of trade resulting in closer interconnection between political and economic decisions. The interconnection is inevitably less intimate where the conduct of trade is largely in the hands of private enterprise. Finally, it is worth noting that if dis-

---

[20] There may not be an exchange rate which would eliminate the currency discounts —that is, reduce the interest rate in question to zero—since the discount is not entirely due to overvaluation.

[21] If bloc exchange rates were operational, rather than merely accounting devices, then because of the discount on bloc currencies, prices in intrabloc trade would tend to be higher than prices in East-West or West-West trade. In fact, as we have seen, bloc trade is conducted at world prices regardless of the exchange rate, and under these circumstances, the potential discount on bloc currencies cannot easily be isolated statistically. The actual statistical picture shows bloc exports to the West at lower prices and imports from the West at higher prices than those prevailing in intrabloc trade. This is believed the result largely of Western discrimination against and controls over trade with the East. See this writer's articles in the *Review of Economics and Statistics*, vol. 44, no. 2 (May 1962) and no. 4 (November 1962); and in *Soviet Studies*, vol. 17, no. 1 (July 1965).

[22] The evidence for this is that today's intrabloc trade amounts to almost three fourths of the trade of these nations (Eastern Europe), whereas their mutual trade amounted to only about one fourth of the total before World War II.

[23] These have substantially weakened in the past few years.

crimination results from the formation of preferential trade areas and customs unions in the West, it usually takes the form of differential tariffs. The CPEs, on the other hand, implement their "customs union" by implicit quotas. Whereas it is possible for outsiders, if they can surmount tariff barriers, to buy or sell within a Western customs union, it is much more difficult for the outsider, regardless of cost-advantage or need, to break into the planned intrabloc trade.

MFN Clause Tariff Problems[24]

The nations of Eastern Europe customarily request MFN treatment on tariffs in their trade with the West. In return, they purport to reciprocate. The usefulness of such reciprocal guarantees has been questioned in the West ever since the late 1920s when the USSR revived its trade with Europe. The question is of considerable importance today because so much of the increase in world trade and reduction in trade discrimination comes about through the mutual lowering of tariff barriers in which the MFN clause plays an obvious role.

The basic difficulty faced by the CPE nations in adapting to the MFN clause on tariffs is quite obvious. Whereas in the West the mutual cutting of tariffs provides a free market price criterion of the appropriate change in volume and distribution of trade, in the centrally planned economies the decisions (a) to import or not to import and (b) from whom to import,[25] are made quantitatively by quotas that are implicit in the planning process. It is well known that sensitivity to price is in this case much lower than in capitalist countries. It is also worth noting that regardless of the level of tariff, in a centrally planned economy,[26] imported commodities are ordinarily sold at the same price as comparable domestically produced goods. Differences between the "import price plus cost of distribution plus tariff" and the price of the comparable domestically produced goods are equalized by offsetting taxes or subsidies. When the planners have finally decided to import a commodity, tariffs have no impact on final domestic price—nor is the domestic price necessarily affected (in the short run, at least) by the decision to increase through imports the availability of a commodity. Last, but not least, import decisions continue to be

---

[24] The effect of the most-favored-nation clause is to place on the conceding state the obligation to grant to the nationals and goods of the beneficiary state, either in general or in certain specified respects, the treatment accorded or in future to be accorded to the nationals and goods of the state receiving most favorable treatment in the territory of the conceding state.

[25] The decision "from whom to import" is probably less centralized than the one dealing with "what and how much to import" in bloc trade with the West. The foreign trade combines are often told to buy or sell such and such commodities but are left to themselves to seek the best market.

[26] Not all of the centrally planned economies have, or have had, tariffs.

largely "quantitative"; tariffs cannot be allowed to assume their usual market functions so long as exchange rates are in disequilibrium and the relationship between internal prices and costs of production is distorted.

During the past few years, the Soviet Union and Hungary have introduced new double-column tariffs with the clear purpose of providing bargaining weapons against discriminatory treatment by EEC and EFTA. Those nations which do not grant the Soviet Union and Hungary MFN treatment will pay duties according to the higher of the two tariff schedules, all others according to the lower. The foreign trade combines presumably will have an incentive to shift their purchases to countries which receive the lower schedule of duties, because both their profits and the premiums based on these profits are reduced by imports from the higher tariff countries.[27] It may appear that granting MFN status under these double-column tariffs is equivalent to granting MFN status under free market conditions, but in fact it is not. First, it is unlikely that the extensive planned bilateral intrabloc trade would be disrupted or altered for small price differentials, which may develop in favor of Western nations as a result of granting the latter MFN status. Second, for reasons already mentioned, the lowering of a tariff would have no effect on the decisions "how much" and "what" to import—that is, competition with domestic suppliers would not be allowed. The only possible effect of the new system, then, would be to redistribute trade among a nation's Western trading partners.

Monopoly Power

The conduct of trade by state organizations inevitably introduces elements of monopoly power into foreign trade. Monopolistic market power is, of course, often exercised by capitalist trade concerns, for example, those connected with petroleum and aluminum. The major objection to monopoly power in international trade is that it may lead to an unequal distribution of the gains from trade. This consequence of monopoly power has usually been accepted by the market economies as an undesirable, but natural and inevitable concomitant of trade conducted by private enterprise. Objections raised with respect to state trading reflect the conviction that state traders have much more power to drive a hard bargain than private monopolists. This, however, is not necessarily true. As in the case of private traders, the power of the state trader is determined by his share in the world market, the importance of the commodity in his domestic

---

27 That is to say, ". . . profits are calculated on the basis of the value of their deliveries of imported goods to domestic distributing, etc., enterprises at the uniform domestic price of those goods *minus* the foreign exchange cost of their imports together with any duty payable on them. . . ." (United Nations, Economic Commission for Europe, *Economic Bulletin for Europe*, vol. 14, no. 1 [1962], p. 53).

market, etc.—that is, it depends on the assorted relevant "elasticities." In the case of wheat, for instance, the state trader may have relatively little power, in the case of aluminum, relatively much—and in either commodity, possibly neither more nor less power than a private trader.

In bilateral agreements between East and West, the bargaining power of the East is strengthened by another institutional factor already mentioned. The CPEs are more interested in imports than exports—the latter are viewed as a necessary evil. On the other hand, Western nations are just as interested in maintaining the level of exports. This has led to temporary and unplanned surpluses of West with East during the course of bilateral agreements. Under these circumstances, the burden of achieving balance largely falls on the Western nation which does not want to extend credit.[28] This may involve accepting in payment goods which are of lower priority and higher price than are available elsewhere in the world market.

Dumping: Definition and Identification

Dumping is usually defined as selling abroad at a lower price than at home. When the commodity is not sold domestically and therefore has no home price, "domestic cost of production" or "export price in third markets" is sometimes substituted. The Soviet Union has been accused of dumping in Western markets a number of times, first in the early 1930s, particularly in regard to grain, and again more recently in regard to aluminum, tin, glass, and so forth.[29] That the Soviet Union and other state traders have the power to dump[30] is unquestioned. Whether the above criteria of dumping are proper for a centrally planned economy (of the sort described above) is a more difficult question.[31]

First, to the extent that the currencies of the centrally planned economies have been or are substantially overvalued by official exchange rates, comparison of domestic and export prices is a misleading criterion of dumping. Under these circumstances, exports must be nominally subsidized. The nominal losses on exports are matched, of course, by larger nominal profits on imports.

Second, as noted above, relative domestic prices in the centrally planned

---

28 The provision in many of these bilateral agreements for payment in gold or convertible currency in case the imbalance persists or exceeds certain limits prevents this factor from assuming larger proportions than it otherwise would.

29 The East European nations have been forced to sell fairly systematically below world prices in Western markets in the postwar period because of real or imagined inferiority of Eastern goods, for political reasons, and so forth.

30 That is to say, they have sufficient monopoly power to separate the various markets in which they sell as well as to prevent the reimport of goods. They can also easily subsidize losses on dumping out of the general treasury.

31 For an excellent discussion of dumping, see Gerschenkron, *Economic Relations with the U.S.S.R.*, pp. 45 ff.

economies reflect subsidies and sales taxes introduced to satisfy domestic fiscal and other requirements. Here again, comparison of domestic and export prices is a misleading criterion of dumping even when exchange rates are not overvalued.

Third, the centrally planned economies, following the labor theory of value, have a different concept of "cost of production" from that of the West. This makes the use of "cost" an imperfect substitute for "price" in assessing dumping. The problem can be exemplified by commodities like petroleum whose "cost" does not include the quantitatively important categories of rent and interest. Yet, a fairly strong case can be made, in connection with dumping, for accepting the labor theory view of "cost" prevalent in the East. To begin with, when all commodities are so valued, the resulting generally lower price level is compensated for by the commensurately higher value of the equilibrium exchange rate. Next, the configuration of relative prices that emerges from this kind of cost accounting may be treated in the same category as the differences in relative prices which exist between nations as a consequence of different preference structures. Like differences in consumers' tastes, the permanent and basic differences in ways of evaluating "cost" may be accepted as parameters of the world trading system.

Fourth, and in many ways most difficult to deal with, is the fact that export and import decisions are not independent of each other as in capitalist economies; instead, state monopolies view exports as payment for imports.[32] The connection is especially close in bilateral agreements.[33] Thus, for example, a state trader who sold a commodity at one half of domestic cost could hardly be accused of "true" dumping, if the foreign exchange earned were used to import goods purchased at one third of domestic cost. A nominal financial loss on exports would be in this case more than offset by the financial gain on imports.[34]

Although this approach may seem fair from the point of view of the CPEs, it fails to take account of the rationale behind antidumping legislation.[35] A major purpose of antidumping legislation is to prevent the disruption of domestic markets and loss of domestic production facilities as a result of what might be termed unfair competition. If one's markets and

---

[32] On this point Gerschenkron (*Economic Relations with the U.S.S.R.*, p. 46) writes: ". . . What on the face of it looked like a case of dumping reveals itself on closer scrutiny as a normal application of the principles of international specialization. . . ."

[33] However, in my view, it would probably not be possible to link specific exports and imports.

[34] It is this view of the trade process which has enabled the centrally planned economies to maintain overvalued exchange rates and still engage in a reasonable volume of trade.

[35] The centrally planned economies would, of course, welcome Western dumping. Their major foreign trade objective is to get as good terms of trade as possible, and they have no fear of market disruption.

production facilities are lost in (fair) competition with a truly lower cost producer, one can expect, in return, assured imports at lower prices. If, however, a foreign supplier sells below domestic price because of temporary surplus or in an attempt to break into a market, the low price is not likely to be maintained and the disruptive effect is without compensating benefits. CPE exports offered at a loss in order to reap a large profit on imports would seem to fall into the second category; they would not necessarily reflect a stable comparative advantage position. They are, therefore, potentially "disruptive" and should not be allowed.

Finally, systematic data on the prices, taxes, and subsidies to commodities exported by the centrally planned economies are not easily available. Consequently, an evaluation of dumping charges is difficult, if not impossible, regardless of the criterion used.

*   *   *   *   *

19

ECONOMIC REFORM IN
EASTERN EUROPE*

Morris Bornstein[1]

This selection provides a comprehensive analysis and evaluation of efforts to change the economic systems of socialist centrally planned economies in Eastern Europe. Part I explains the pressures for economic reform and the opposition to it. Part II examines some fundamental issues in designing reforms and compares the main alternative approaches. Part III discusses the nature and extent of changes in key aspects of the economic system, including administrative organization, determination of outputs and inputs, performance indicators and incentives, investment, prices, and foreign trade. The article concludes by considering the chief reasons for the retreat from systemic reform, and the search for other ways of improving economic performance.

This essay analyzes the origin, nature, and outcome of economic reform in the last decade in the planned economies of Eastern Europe. This group includes Albania, Bulgaria, Czechoslovakia, the German Democratic Republic (GDR), Hungary, Poland, and Romania. The study does not deal directly with reforms in the USSR or Yugoslavia. However, the USSR and Yugoslavia are considered indirectly, in regard to their influence on reforms in the countries mentioned.

Because its focus is on the process of systemic change, the essay dis-

* Reprinted from *East European Economies Post-Helsinki* (A Compendium of Papers Submitted to the Joint Economic Committee, 95th Cong., 1st sess.) (Washington, D.C.: U.S. Government Printing Office, 1977), pp. 102–34.

[1] This study is part of a research project at The University of Michigan Center for Russian and East European Studies funded by a grant from the Rockefeller Foundation. The author wishes to thank the Foundation for its support and Dennis A. O'Hearn for his assistance in research.

cusses major reform issues, forces, and measures common to most of the seven nations. It does not examine each country's experience separately, although important similarities and differences among countries are noted. Detailed accounts of reforms in particular nations may be found in other studies.[2]

I. THE REFORM MOVEMENT

The economic reform movement was an effort to change the traditional "command economy" model of comprehensive central planning and administrative control established in the USSR in the 1930s and introduced into Eastern Europe after World War II. The reform movement can therefore best be understood by considering the nature and results of this traditional model, the pressures for change, and the sources of resistance to change.[3]

The Traditional Soviet Model

The chief features of the traditional model include the following: (1) All significant means of production outside agriculture were nationalized. (2) In agriculture, the dominant pattern was collectivization, involving nominally cooperative ownership under close state control. (However, the collectivization drive was abandoned in Poland in 1956.)

(3) In the hierarchical system of economic organization, decision making was concentrated near the top. The different levels bargained about production assignments and the allocation of resources to meet them. Inter-enterprise relationships were determined "vertically" through the respective administrative hierarchies, rather than "horizontally" through the market. (4) Production and its disposition were planned in detail in physical units (as well as value terms). (5) To enforce these ambitious plans, the means of production were rationed—materials by administrative orders; labor by controls over the size (and sometimes the distribution) of wage expendi-

---

[2] For example, see George R. Feiwel, *Growth and Reforms in Centrally Planned Economies: The Lessons of the Bulgarian Experience* (New York: Praeger Publishers, 1977), on Bulgaria; Michael Keren, "The New Economic System in the GDR: An Obituary," *Soviet Studies*, vol. 24, no. 4 (April 1973), pp. 554–87, on the GDR; *Reform of the Economic Mechanism in Hungary*, ed. István Friss (Budapest: Akadémiai Kiadó, 1969), and *Reform of the Economic Mechanism in Hungary: Development 1968–71*, ed. Ottó Gadó (Budapest: Akadémiai Kiadó, 1972), on Hungary; Janusz G. Zielinski, *Economic Reforms in Polish Industry* (London: Oxford University Press, 1973), on Poland; Iancu Spigler, *Economic Reform in Rumanian Industry* (London: Oxford University Press, 1973), on Romania; and country chapters in *Plan and Market: Economic Reform in Eastern Europe*, ed. Morris Bornstein (New Haven, Conn.: Yale University Press, 1973), and *The New Economic Systems of Eastern Europe*, ed. Hans-Hermann Höhmann, Michael Kaser, and Karl C. Thalheim (London: Hurst, 1975).

[3] *Plan and Market*, pp. 2–8.

tures; and capital by allocation of investment funds, construction materials, and machinery and equipment.

In turn, (6) prices were set administratively at high levels in the hierarchy and infrequently changed. Industrial wholesale prices were fixed on a cost-plus basis, with the aim of enabling most branches of industry to earn revenues sufficient to cover current (but not also capital) expenditures and show a small profit. Retail prices, often including a large element of excise taxes, were supposedly set near market-clearing levels, but they were frequently too low, as shown by persistent shortages. Agricultural procurement prices were low relative to retail prices for the same commodities and to prices for industrial inputs into agriculture, and various controls were needed to enforce procurement quotas. (7) Money was "passive" at least in the production sector: the flow of funds was adjusted by taxes, subsidies, and credit to implement the allocation of resources and goods previously made in physical terms. (8) Managerial and worker incentives stressed the fulfillment and overfulfillment of quantitative production targets.

Finally, (9) unrealistic exchange rates and a complex structure of taxes and subsidies separated domestic from foreign prices. Foreign trade was conducted by special export-import firms. Producing enterprises had no direct contacts with foreign customers or suppliers, and their interest in foreign trade was weak.

This model was originally applied in the USSR in the 1930s to achieve rapid industrialization and military power in a large but relatively backward country with considerable supplies of unskilled labor and extensive natural resources. The aim was to secure rapid growth and drastic structural change, despite the economic and social costs, through the comprehensive mobilization of labor and capital under centralized administrative direction. However, it was much less relevant to the circumstances of the much smaller East European countries in the late 1940s—and even to those of the USSR itself by the 1950s.

At the end of World War II, Czechoslovakia and the GDR were already industrialized by European standards. They had little surplus agricultural labor which could be shifted to industry, and their populations were accustomed to central European, not Soviet, living standards. Poland and Hungary were less industrialized, but still more advanced than the Balkan countries, which had larger underutilized agricultural labor forces. More important, all of these countries are much smaller than the USSR and lack both its varied resource endowment and its potential internal market for large-scale production. Therefore, they are inherently much more dependent on foreign trade. Hence, the Soviet pattern of rapid development of heavy industry (for which some of the East European countries lack even the basic natural resources), at the expense of international specialization based on comparative advantage, did not fit the circumstances and needs of the East European countries.

The harmful consequences of the imposition of the traditional Soviet model became evident relatively soon and sharply in the more developed countries of the area, such as the GDR, Czechoslovakia, Poland, and Hungary, although later and less acutely in the less advanced countries like Romania and Bulgaria. Overcentralization of decision making, excessively detailed planning and rigid materials allocation procedures, the suppression of local initiative, unsound price structures, and overambitious targets led to visible waste and inefficiency. Shortages of both producer and consumer goods were chronic, while stocks of unwanted goods accumulated. Lacking adequate material inputs and incentives, the agricultural sector performed especially poorly. The low quality and technological lag of manufactured goods limited the possibilities for sale both within the Council for Mutual Economic Assistance (CMEA) bloc and on the world market—making them "soft" goods in comparison with "hard" goods such as agricultural products, raw materials, and fuels.

Despite continuing high rates of investment, the accustomed high growth rates of national product and labor productivity began to decline by the late 1950s or early 1960s, depending upon the country. Throughout the area, capital productivity was falling as a result of investment programs which stressed the highly capital-intensive branches, devoted a large share to structures rather than machinery and equipment, failed to apply up-to-date technology, and dispersed investment over many projects, leading to long delays before new capacity was completed and production from it began.[4]

Pressures for Reform[5]

Thus, by the early 1960s, a growing number of economists had begun to perceive and to express the need for economic reform, as part of a shift from a more centralized economic system in the "extensive" phase of economic development to a less centralized system in the "intensive" phase. This formulation was politically convenient because it enabled them to argue the need for change without as such condemning the traditional system, with which the Communist party leadership was so intimately involved. Instead, it was claimed that different conditions called for a different system of economic planning and management.

In the "extensive" phase, they asserted, the chief aims of "economic construction" had been to alter the structure of the economy drastically

---

[4] Gertraud Seidenstecher, "Capital Finance," chap. 11 in The New Economic Systems.

[5] This analysis deals with pressures for economic reform. For an appraisal of pressures for political and cultural reforms, see Vladimir V. Kusin, "An Overview of East European Reformism," Soviet Studies, vol. 28, no. 3 (July 1976), pp. 338–61.

and rapidly—to industrialize, to urbanize, to adjust to changes in territory resulting from World War II, to develop backward regions, and to reshape the content and geographical orientation of foreign economic relations. The methods chosen for these tasks were socialization of the means of production, a sharp increase in the rate of investment, rapid expansion of the industrial labor force, and revision of the pre-socialist income distribution.

In contrast, in the "intensive" phase, reform advocates observed, the emphasis of economic policy was no longer on rapid structural change, as much as on smaller, marginal changes in the composition of output, technology, etc. With a slowdown in the rate of growth of the labor force, capital deepening rather than capital widening became important. Greater efficiency in the use of limited inputs was essential. Finally, in the consumer sector, for many goods a shift had occurred from a sellers' toward a buyers' market, as a result of the rise in living standards and the availability of stocks.

Thus, they concluded, the economic system should be modified to deal with the new conditions of the "intensive" phase. More decisions should be made at lower levels in the hierarchy, on technical-economic rather than political grounds. However, to be sound, such decentralized decisions must be guided by more rational prices and by more appropriate performance indicators. Product mix and product characteristics should respond more closely to customer demand—for consumer goods as well as producer goods, and especially for exports. The coercion and ideological appeals used to mobilize resources in the extensive phase should yield to more emphasis on incentives to promote the efficient production of the correct output. Finally, they advocated a new approach to foreign trade, recognizing its importance as a source of innovation in technology and products, as a means of competition to discipline highly-concentrated domestic producers, and as a way to obtain economies of scale beyond the capacity of the internal market.

Discussion of the need for reform and of specific reform proposals was aided by political "de-Stalinization" after 1956, which permitted freer discussion of new ideas in the economic sphere and the inflow of information from abroad.[6] The latter brought both greater awareness of economic growth and living standards in Western Europe, and greater understanding of the operation of regulated market economies, in contrast to the "anarchic" capitalist economies depicted in orthodox Marxian writings. Thus, what was previously considered an issue of principle—for example, central formulation of detailed enterprise production plans—became a

---

[6] For a thorough analysis of the political aspects of economic reforms, see Andrzej Korbonski, "Political Aspects of Economic Reforms in Eastern Europe," chap. 1 in *Economic Development in the Soviet Union and Eastern Europe*, vol. 1: *Reforms, Technology, and Income Distribution*, ed. Zbigniew M. Fallenbuchl (New York: Praeger Publishers, 1975).

matter of technique, to be evaluated on its merits. As a result, it was possible to propose "mixed" economic models in which the central authorities could continue to control the main lines of economic development (including income distribution and foreign trade) through macroeconomic planning and monetary-fiscal measures, while permitting more enterprise autonomy in microeconomic decisions in response to market forces.

Resistance to Reform

The political leadership was slow to recognize both the need for change and the form it should take. In the first place, it was reluctant to believe that the economic system itself, rather than the incompetence of individual officials, was responsible. In some cases, shortcomings in the statistical system failed to disclose the facts and causes of declining economic performance promptly and accurately. Reform was also opposed on ideological and philosophical grounds: Reliance on the market was deemed inconceivable in a socialist economy, because "socialism" was held to involve not only collective ownership of the (principal) means of production but also central planning of investment, output, prices, and distribution. Capital and land charges, production for profit, and emphasis on material incentives were condemned as incompatible with socialism. The official ideology of the "solidarity society" denied any conflict between group interests. In contrast, reform proposals recognized the separate interests of firms, workers, and consumers, and recommended the market as the mechanism for reconciling them.

Reforms were also opposed by policy makers on somewhat more pragmatic grounds. (1) Some feared that the proposed systemic changes would mean loss of central (Party) control over the main directions of economic development. Whereas central planning could assure the priority development of those sectors deemed most important to the national welfare, decentralized decision making by autonomous enterprises in response to market forces could lead to the diversion of resources from investment, military programs, and civilian collective consumption to supplying goods and services for personal household consumption. (2) Because centrally planned economies typically operate under conditions of repressed inflation and administrative allocation (rather than price rationing) of many goods, more influence for market forces could bring open inflation (as in Yugoslavia). This would in turn affect the distribution of income and popular attitudes toward the regime. (3) At the same time, unemployment could occur or increase, as enterprises laid off excess workers in response to a shift from output maximization to profit maximization, to more autonomy in the use of wage funds, or to the curtailment of budget subsidies. Also (4), reducing the artificial separation between the domestic economy and foreign trade, by linking domestic and foreign prices through more realistic exchange rates, could lead to higher domestic prices for imports, on the one hand, and make the production of exports less attractive, on the other. In short, some opposition to reform was based on an assessment of the risk and uncertainty attached to both the benefits and the costs of reform, including the problems involved in the transition from the old system to a new one.

Various interest groups resisted reforms. The Party apparatus and the ministerial bureaucracy believed they would lose power as enterprises obtained more freedom to make decisions in response to market forces—in place of the traditional system of joint supervision of enterprises by higher administrative agencies and by parallel Party organizations. In turn, some managers who were successful under the traditional system were not enthusiastic about reforms which called for them to become independent, cost-conscious entrepreneurs selling products in a competitive buyers' market—i.e., to become "businessmen" instead of production engineers.

For their part, workers were concerned about the impact on their real incomes of changes in wages and prices associated with reform. New incentive schemes might increase the money incomes of managerial and technical personnel and more-skilled workers relative to less-skilled workers. Retail prices might be increased, because the "rationalization" of the price system might reduce or eliminate subsidies for some consumer goods and services. Also, the curtailment of unprofitable production and greater freedom for managers over the enterprise wage fund and labor force might lead to at least frictional and perhaps even structural unemployment, despite a national macroeconomic policy of full employment.

Finally, economic reforms were opposed on the ground that liberalization in the economic sphere might spread, threatening the paramount role of the Communist party in national life. Freer discussion of alternatives in the economic sphere might lead in turn to demands for open discussion of cultural, social, and even political issues. Economic reforms imply some diffusion of power, first to enterprise management, but subsequently to the population through reliance on the market for guidance on the composition of at least part of the national output. It was feared that professionals in other fields might also seek greater autonomy in their activities, and that the population might be tempted to express its views on matters (such as living standards, housing policy, the length of the workweek) hitherto reserved to top policy makers.

II. REFORM DESIGN

In view of these conflicting pressures, the designers of reform proposals had to face and resolve several important issues, including the choice between systemic and policy changes, the nature of the "decentralization" of decision making to be sought, and the strategy for implementing reforms.

Systemic versus Policy Changes

It is important to distinguish between changes in economic policy and changes in the economic system since they may represent alternative paths to improving the performance of the economy.[7]

Economic policy involves, for example, decisions on the rates of growth of major components of national product, such as consumption, investment, and military programs; the distribution of investment by sectors and branches of the economy and also by regions of the country; the school-leaving age, the retirement age, and the length of the work week; the relationship of changes in money wages and in retail prices; and the composition and geographical direction of foreign trade.

Thus, for instance, economic performance could—without systemic changes—be improved by economic policy decisions which allocated the same (perhaps even a smaller) amount of investment differently among industries, changed the mix between capital-intensive and labor-intensive technologies, or raised labor force participation rates by altering the entry or retirement ages.

In contrast, modification of the economic system entails a redistribution of decision-making authority regarding various questions among the participants (central planning agencies, ministries, enterprises, workers, households). Corresponding changes in the flow of information used in decision making are commonly required. Also, to get the new decision-making structure to strive for the goals of the system designers, changes in performance indicators and incentives are often necessary.[8]

Hence, systemic changes seek to improve the economy's performance by such measures as transferring from ministries to firms authority and responsibility for decisions on the composition of output, the use of labor inputs, or the nature of new investment (at least below a specified ceiling amount). In turn, to provide firms the information needed for sensible decisions on these questions, prices may be revised to reflect more closely the relative scarcities of inputs and outputs. Finally, the dominant criterion for evaluating enterprise performance may be changed from output or sales to profit, and managerial incentives in the form of bonuses and promotions accordingly related to profit

However, while it is possible to distinguish analytically between policy

---

[7] Antoni Chawluk, "Economic Policy and Economic Reform," *Soviet Studies,* vol. 26, no. 1 (January 1974), pp. 98–100.

[8] The elements of decision making, information, and motivation are discussed in detail in Tjalling C. Koopmans and John Michael Montias, "On the Description and Comparison of Economic Systems," chap. 2 in *Comparison of Economic Systems: Theoretical and Methodological Approaches,* ed. Alexander Eckstein (Berkeley: University of California Press, 1971); and Egon Neuberger and William Duffy, *Comparative Economic Systems: A Decision-Making Approach* (Boston: Allyn & Bacon, 1976), chaps. 4–6.

and systemic changes, they are often linked in practice. First, altering important features of the economic system is in fact a major economic policy decision—about the appropriate mechanisms for determining the bill of goods, allocating resources and distributing income, and perhaps even about property rights. Second, changes in the economic system may be regarded as the best means to accomplish some policy decisions. For instance, to implement a decision to expand exports of manufactured goods to Western market economies, it may be necessary both to give producing enterprises the right to conduct directly (rather than through intermediary foreign-trade enterprises) at least some aspects of export sales, and also to assign realistic domestic prices to exports for use in calculating sales revenue, profits, and managerial bonuses.

Nonetheless, the distinction between policy and systemic changes proved a useful one for economic reform advocates, because they could claim to address themselves to improving the systemic mechanism to implement policy, without challenging the Party's exclusive right to determine policy.

Concepts of "Decentralization"

Several different conceptions of "decentralization" of decision making appeared in the debates over economic reform.

The "administrative decentralization" approach involved partial devolution of authority over selected decisions from higher to lower tiers within the administrative hierarchy—for instance, from the ministry to the intermediate "association" level or even to the actual producing enterprise. Its intent was to "rationalize" the existing scheme of administering the economy, by transferring to lower levels some of the more detailed decisions regarding the composition of output, on the one hand, and production methods, on the other. The lower levels could make more sensible and more timely decisions on these aspects—though subject to constraints in the form of centrally set global output assignments and input authorizations. This shift would also reduce the burden of decision making at higher levels, freeing them to concentrate on their nondelegable responsibilities regarding investment, location, living standards, foreign economic policy, etc.

In contrast, the "economic decentralization" approach envisioned a greater role for domestic and foreign market forces—and concomitantly a smaller voice for central planning and administrative control—in determining the composition of output, the allocation of resources, and even the distribution of income. Enterprise activities would be coordinated through direct "horizontal" market links, rather than a "vertical" administrative command chain. Supply and demand, operating through more flexible domestic prices, which in turn would be related to world market prices, would guide decisions on outputs and inputs. Profit—the "synthetic" indicator simultaneously encompassing all aspects of enterprise activity—could then become the appropriate measure of a firm's contribution to the economy, and the basis for rewarding its personnel.

In short, the "economic decentralization" approach contemplated a move toward a socialist regulated market economy. The state authorities would still control the "main directions and proportions" of the economy through macroeconomic policy decisions and instruments (taxes, subsidies, credit) to promote growth and maintain stability of the price level and employment. They would also provide collective consumption and intervene to deal with externalities. But within this regulatory framework, "the market," not "the plan," would guide the microeconomic decisions of enterprises about what to produce and how to produce it.

These two concepts of "decentralization" concern what powers should be transferred *to* firms from central planning agencies and ministries. A third approach to decentralization involved devolution of authority *within* firms—through a shift from "one-man management" (according to the Soviet principle of *edinonachalie*) by a state-appointed manager to genuine "mass participation" in decision making by workers along the lines of the Yugoslav model. Some reform advocates regarded self-management as the logical completion of the process of decentralization.

Implementation Strategy

Should reform measures—once selected—be introduced in phases, or all together? In selected units on an experimental basis, or across the entire economy? Subject to continuous adjustment, or with a promise of stability? Each of these issues will be discussed briefly.

1. *Phased versus Simultaneous Introduction.* Should different reform measures—for example, concerning performance indicators, authority regarding the output mix, foreign trade rights, and so forth—all be implemented at the same time, or should they be introduced separately in a particular sequence over several years?

Supporters of the phased approach pointed out that some reforms, such as a change from gross output to sales as an enterprise performance indicator, could be adopted immediately, while other measures, particularly price reforms, would take a long time (years rather than months) to prepare. Also, a phased approach was claimed to be less disruptive, permitting enterprises to adjust to one new responsibility before undertaking another.

In contrast, opponents of the phased approach argued that meaningful and successful reform required the simultaneous introduction of an integrated package of mutually supporting measures affecting planning methods, performance indicators, incentives, and prices. Otherwise, a change in only one or some of these aspects of the economic system could yield little improvement and could even prove counterproductive. For instance, if firms gained more power to determine the composition of output without facing new prices more nearly reflecting scarcities, decentralized decision making by individual enterprises might well produce an even less suitable assortment than that generated by the admittedly imperfect decisions of central planning agencies—which at least had a broad economy-wide perspective that partially compensated for the deficiencies of misleading prices.

2. Experimentation versus Commitment. Should reform measures— whether phased or simultaneous—be "tested" by applying them for a trial period only to a selected group of enterprises, or should they be adopted uniformly across the economy (perhaps with the exception of cooperative agriculture)?

The first school held that it was logical and "scientific" to determine the feasibility of reform measures by trying them first in a "pilot" group of ministries and enterprises. In the light of the results obtained, the Party could then decide whether to modify some of the reform measures and whether to extend them to other units and eventually the entire economy.

Critics questioned what could be learned from such experiments. First, they would yield atypically favorable results if—as usually contemplated— the "pilot" group comprised not a representative sample of enterprises but rather a set of the most efficient enterprises, enjoying modern equipment, the best management, and priority in the allocation of materials and machinery. Second, how could any selected "pilot" group of firms truly operate on the new system if the rest of the economy—including their suppliers and customers, and the prices of inputs and outputs—were not also "reformed"?[9] Finally, how long should an experiment run? Presumably, it should be long enough to show convincingly the results of the new arrangements. But scheduling experiments of several years' duration could easily constitute a delaying tactic intended to postpone further implementation of the reform package.

3. Adjustments versus Stability. Should reform measures be continuously evaluated and modified as soon and as often as experience showed any changes to be necessary? This approach has the advantage of flexibility —conceding the possibility of error, and making corrections promptly as required.

Or should reform measures be "stable," so economic agents can have time to learn how to perform their new roles and to accept them? Frequent changes in "ground rules" can weaken confidence in, and commitment to, reforms. For example, this would occur if enterprise managers found that, after they had "mobilized internal reserves" in order to increase profits, the

---

[9] The point is neatly illustrated by a popular Hungarian example about a hypothetical proposed reform of the traffic system in Great Britain from driving on the left to driving on the right. In this case, the "experimentalists" advocate testing the merits of the new system by at first switching only buses to the right, while all other vehicles continue on the left.

central authorities raised profits taxes, preventing managers from using the additional funds for bonuses as they had expected.

Reform Models

This essay does not present a detailed comparison of the original reform "blueprints" of the individual countries in regard to each of the various possible measures. First, such comparisons are available in several earlier studies.[10] Second, and more important, these blueprints soon became outdated, as many important features were not implemented fully or at all.

Instead, in the light of the issues identified in the preceding sections, we may briefly characterize the various national reform blueprints by grouping them into two broad categories: "partial" or "minor" vs. "comprehensive" or "major" reforms. This classification is analytically useful and appropriate for the purpose of this essay, but it unavoidably disregards some interesting, and in some respects substantial, differences among nations in each group.

As in the USSR, a "partial" reform approach was chosen by Albania, Bulgaria, the GDR, Poland, and Romania. It stressed "administrative" decentralization, though in many respects only to an intermediate "association" level between the ministry and the enterprise. It included phased introduction of reform measures, selective experiments, and an inclination toward early revision. The detail of enterprise plan targets was reduced, managers gained more control over the use of the wage fund, and some decentralized investment by firms was promised. Sales and profit became more important performance indicators, with bonuses linked to them. Selected producing units received the right to engage directly in foreign trade, within their global plan assignments. Producer (wholesale) prices were revised to reflect costs more closely, but were not expected to balance supply and demand—a task still assigned to administrative allocation, though now to be performed in some cases at a lower hierarchical level.

In contrast, the more "comprehensive" reform blueprints in Czechoslovakia and Hungary accepted a considerable degree of "economic" decentralization, and the Czech (but not the Hungarian) reform also called for workers' self-management of enterprises. The various reform measures were to be introduced simultaneously in Hungary (though phased in Czechoslovakia), and applied to all firms. "Parameters" (or "regulators") such as taxes and subsidies were to be left unchanged for at least several years, to

---

10 For example, Michael Kaser and J. Zielinski, *Planning in East Europe: Industrial Management by the State* (London: The Bodley Head, 1970); Morris Bornstein, "East European Economic Reforms and the Convergence of Economic Systems," *Jahrbuch der Wirtschaft Osteuropas* (*Yearbook of East-European Economics*), Band 2 (Munich: Günter Olzog Verlag, 1971), pp. 262–63; and Frederic L. Pryor, *Property and Industrial Organization in Communist and Capitalist Nations* (Bloomington, Ind.: Indiana University Press, 1973), chap. VII.

provide a stable environment for enterprise decisions on production and investment. Reform included abolition of obligatory targets for enterprises, distribution of supplies by the market mechanism, designation of profit alone as the key performance indicator, and direct participation by firms in foreign trade. In turn, to provide appropriate signals to guide enterprises' exercise of their new rights, reform of the price system involved not only closer correspondence of prices with costs but also an effort to make prices more flexible and more reflective of scarcity, through progressive decontrol of centrally fixed prices.

III. RETREAT FROM REFORM

Despite the long period (usually two–four years) devoted to working out national economic reform blueprints, none of them was fully implemented. In some cases, key changes were never put into effect. In others, reform measures were introduced but then formally revoked. wholly or partly. Finally, some aspects of reforms survived in name only, as they were subsquently effectively abridged by offsetting recentralizing actions.

The first section below examines experience in implementing the chief reform measures. The second section then analyzes the major factors responsible for the retreat from economic reform.

Implementation Experience

Although the countries in the area differed in the way and extent to which reform blueprints were implemented, some common patterns can be identified in regard to the principal reform measures. These include (1) administrative reorganization, (2) output plan assignments, (3) allocation of supplies of material inputs, (4) use of labor, (5) investment, (6) price formation, (7) performance indicators, (8) incentives, (9) foreign trade, (10) workers' participation in decision making, (11) agriculture, and (12) the scope of the private enterprise sector. Experience regarding each aspect will be discussed briefly.

1. Administrative Reorganization. National reform blueprints based on "administrative" decentralization were reluctant to devolve much authority down to the enterprise and thus the market. Instead, they chose a compromise solution under which certain powers were to be transferred from the ministry, not to the enterprise, but only to an intermediate hierarchical level. The "main administrations" within ministries were renamed "associations" and changed from purely administrative organs, financed by budget grants, to "business organizations" on "economic accountability" status. This status, following the Soviet concept of *khozraschet,* involves separate financial accounts, meeting expenses from sales revenue, partial financing from repayable bank credits, and profit as a performance indicator and basis for bonuses. The association was thus a hybrid: a combined administrative unit and business entity—receiving targets for outputs, inputs, and investment from the ministry, and distributing disaggregated plan assignments to its component enterprises, in pursuit of sales and profit.

Thus, in the GDR the VVB were formed in 1958 from the main administrations, and in 1964 were put on economic accountability status, with performance indicators and inventives similar to those of enterprises. In 1968, some enterprises were further integrated vertically into "combines." In Bulgaria, the association was made the basic business unit: all plan targets, input allocations, budget grants, and credits were channeled to it, and it was responsible for plan fulfillment by its subordinate enterprises. In Poland, the consolidation movement went farther with the creation in 1973 of "big economic organizations" (WOG) combining large multiplant enterprises, vertical complexes, and associations.

(There was no similar reorganization in Hungary, where industry was already highly concentrated after a reorganization in 1963 which preceded economic reform. About 800 state industrial enterprises—half with over 5,000 workers each—produce over 90 percent of total industrial output. This concentration permits ministries to exercise effective control over enterprises directly, without an intermediate association level.)

However, even the promised limited devolution of authority from the ministry to the association was not realized in practice, as the experience of the Romanian "centrals" vividly illustrates.[11] After a short and small experiment with 10 of these associations, a total of 200 were established in 1969, involving both horizontal and vertical integration. In some cases the central was set up as a single large enterprise combining a number of previously independent firms whose identity was lost. In other cases the latter remained as distinct divisions of the central. Finally, in some instances both the central and the component enterprises had separate economic accountability status and individual managements. Within the framework of plan assignments from the ministry, the new centrals were supposed to draw up plans for their member plants; allocate materials and investment funds; sell the output, with the right to direct contacts in foreign trade; and redistribute profits among component units. It soon became clear that ministries would not permit centrals to exercise these rights. From the outset ministries intervened in the day-to-day operations of the centrals and in their instructions to member enterprises, which had to report (formally and informally) to the ministries. The only real autonomy of the centrals proved to be in scheduling production among their plants. In 1972, most of the rights of the centrals were formally rescinded, and in 1974 their number was reduced to 102, to facilitate close control by the ministries.

2. Output Plans. The "comprehensive" approach of Hungary (and

---

[11] Spigler, *Economic Reform in Rumanian Industry*, chaps. 3 and 4; and David Granick, *Enterprise Guidance in Eastern Europe: A Comparison of Four Socialist Economies* (Princeton, N.J.: Princeton University Press, 1975), chap. 4.

Czechoslovakia) abolished centrally set output targets for enterprises. They were instead to determine the level and composition of their output for themselves, in pursuit of profit and in the light of customers' demands, prices, and costs.

In the "partial" reforms of other countries, ministries continued to set global output targets for producers. But in most cases, the concept of output was changed from gross value of output to actual sales of finished products to customers. In addition, the "partial" reforms usually called for less ministerial specification of the "assortment" or product-mix within the assigned global total.

However, the actual increase in enterprise autonomy was much less than promised. First, as explained in the preceding subsection, in many cases the association still worked out detailed output plans for enterprises. Second, central planning agencies and ministries assigned associations and enterprises binding targets for various high-priority consumer, producer, investment, or export goods which the higher levels knew the producing units would find it unprofitable to make and sell at the prevailing distorted, nonscarcity prices. Finally, producers received "informal," but irresistible, guidance in "direct discussions" between state officials and enterprise executives about the latter's responsibility "in the public interest" to produce specified quantities of designated goods despite the adverse effects on their sales revenue, profits, and bonus funds.[12]

3. *Distribution of Material Inputs.* Allocation of raw, semifinished, and finished materials; fuels; and machinery and equipment and parts for them has traditionally been regarded as the fundamental "lever" of central control over the economy—determining what shall be produced, where, how, and for whom. Moreover, with producer goods prices based chiefly on cost and neglecting demand, administrative rationing logically supplants price rationing of scarce supplies. As a result, in centrally planned economies material inputs have long been distributed through a two-step process, involving (a) aggregate "balances" to equate total sources and total uses for thousands of items, and (b) quantitative quotas for each consuming firm.

Yet in practice it has proved extremely difficult and burdensome for central agencies and ministries, remote from both suppliers and customers, to plan accurately the flows of thousands of items among thousands of firms—and to change these allocations promptly and correctly in response to new output assignments or to under- or overfulfillments of plans.

---

12 Cf. Zbigniew M. Fallenbuchl, "The Polish Economy in the 1970s," in *East European Economies Post-Helsinki* (A Compendium of Papers Submitted to the Joint Economic Committee, 95th Cong., 1st sess.) (Washington, D.C.: U.S. Government Printing Office, 1977), p. 845, on Poland; and M. Tardos, "Enterprise Independence and Central Control," *Acta Oeconomica* [Budapest], vol. 15 (1975), nos. 3–4, pp. 277–91, and T. Bauer, "The Contradictory Position of the Enterprise under the New Economic Mechanism," *Co-existence*, vol. 13, no. 1 (April 1976), pp. 65–80, on Hungarian experience.

Hence, the "administrative" decentralization approach to economic reform was sympathetic to proposals to preserve the principle of administrative, rather than price, allocation of materials, but to transfer to lower hierarchical levels the responsibility for many less important and/or more detailed commodity balances. However, although some reform blueprints accepted this idea, it either was not implemented or did not survive long, as the experience of Romania and the GDR, respectively, illustrate.

In Romania, the reform directives provided for a reduction in central planning of supplies and the transfer, from ministries to associations and enterprises, of authority to distribute output. But these decentralizing measures were never carried out. Instead, central control of supply was tightened, and a new ministerial-level agency was established to perform it.[13]

In contrast, in the GDR devolution actually occurred but was subsequently revoked. In 1963, the last year before the introduction of the "New Economic System" (NES), out of 5,192 commodity balances, 1,188 were prepared at the highest hierarchical level (by the State Planning Commission and the National Economic Council) and only 605 by associations and enterprises. In 1967, at the height of the NES, out of 6,045 balances, 138 were drawn up at the top and 5,728 by associations and enterprises. However, in response to supply problems arising from taut planning, beginning in 1972 recentralization occurred in two forms. First, formal authority for compiling many balances (the exact number is unclear) was shifted back up to ministries and the State Planning Commission. Second, they were given the responsibility to "confirm" balances initially prepared by lower levels.[14]

As part of "economic" decentralization in Hungary, for all but a very few products administrative allocation was to be eliminated and firms freed to distribute output on the basis of contracts negotiated between suppliers and customers in a market framework. Thus the National Board for Materials and Prices (NBMP) was to be concerned overwhelmingly with adjusting prices rather than allocating materials. But in practice much more central control over supply was exercised. At first, it was accomplished chiefly through informal "guidance" to enterprises by planning agencies and ministries expressing their concern about "equilibrium of the market." Subsequently, an Intersectoral Committee for Price Setting and and Product Marketing, chaired by the head of the NBMP, was established to advise on output, inventories, and distribution of both domestic production and exports and imports.[15]

---

[13] Spigler, *Economic Reform in Rumanian Industry*, chaps. 2 and 3.

[14] Keren, "The New Economic System," pp. 559–60 and 582–86.

[15] B. Csikós-Nagy, *Kereskedelmi Szemle*, vol. 16 (1975), no. 12, pp. 1–5; abstracted as "New System of Product Marketing," *Abstracts of Hungarian Economic Literature*, vol. 5 (1976), no. 6, pp. 149–51.

4. *Labor and Wages.* With minor exceptions,[16] East European economies do not allocate labor administratively but instead rely upon differential wages in a labor market to place workers (in the light of their training) in particular occupations, branches of industry, firms, and geographical locations. These labor markets are usually "tight" because ambitious development plans maintain a high level of aggregate demand and because enterprise managers respond to taut plans by trying to acquire "excess reserves" of labor. In these conditions, the central authorities are typically concerned about labor shortages; a tendency for actual earnings to rise faster than official wage scales are raised; and the possibility of wider differentiation of income, by occupation and employing firm, than is considered tolerable in an "egalitarian" socialist society. To deal with these problems, the authorities set wage rates and then attempt to control firms' use of labor by regulating the wage bill rather than the number and kind of workers as such.

In no country of the area did the economic reform blueprint call for decentralization of authority to fix wage rates. Rather, in order to carry out a comprehensive and consistent revision of wage schedules, the power to set wage rates was often further centralized by transferring it from branch ministries to an economy-wide commission. In most of the countries, these revisions had three aims: (*a*) changing work norms to increase the share of basic wages (and reduce the share of bonuses) in total earnings; (*b*) altering (usually narrowing but sometimes widening) wage differentials by occupation, skill, and industrial branch; and (*c*) a limited shift from piece rates to time rates.

In contrast, economic reform did bring some loosening of control over the enterprise's wage bill and use of labor.[17] Previously, the ministry usually specified both the total wage bill and the average wage—which, along with centrally set wage rates, severely constrained the enterprise's freedom to determine the total number of workers and their composition.

In the "partial" reforms, the ministry still planned the wage bill—but no longer also the average wage—of the association or the enterprise. In some countries, for instance the GDR, the wage bill was stated as an absolute sum, on the basis of planned output or sales. On the other hand, under the scheme introduced in Poland in 1973, the wage bill is not specified directly but is determined indirectly as a percentage of value added. For every percentage point of increase in value added over the previous year, the enterprise is entitled to increase its wage bill by a fraction (usually 0.6–0.7) of one percent. Thus, the ministry designates not the wage bill

---

[16] For example, new university graduates in certain fields, such as medicine or primary education, whose initial placement is in rural areas.

[17] For a detailed comparison of particular countries, see Jan Adam, "Systems of Wage Regulation in the Soviet Bloc," *Soviet Studies,* vol. 28, no. 1 (January 1976), pp. 91–109.

itself but rather (a) the performance indicator determining it, and (b) the "normative" connecting the two.

In contrast, in the more "comprehensive" Czech and Hungarian reforms, the central authorities were no longer to determine enterprise wage bills but were instead to try to control labor use by regulating only the average wage paid by the enterprise. Thus, in the light of the output program it chose, the enterprise was to decide its labor inputs—subject to constraints in the form of (a) centrally set wage rates and (b) an enterprise income tax levied in relation to the increase in the average wage.

For example, the abortive Czech reform at first included a two-part stabilization tax. One part was aimed at regulating wages and provided that if average wages increased compared to the previous year, the enterprise was liable for a tax equal to 30 percent of the additional wage payments. The second part sought to regulate employment, stipulating that if the number of employees rose, the enterprise owed in tax a sum equal to the wages paid to the new employees. However, this control of enterprise wage payments and employment through taxation was soon reinforced by a scheme of coefficients linking permitted increases in average wages to increases in labor productivity. Furthermore, these coefficients were differentiated by branches and even individual enterprises. Finally, in 1970 ministries returned to specifying enterprise wage bills on the basis of planned sales.

In Hungary, an increase in the average wage of the enterprise depended on the increase in gross income (wages plus profit) per employee. For every percentage point increase in gross income per employee, the average wage could be increased by 0.3 percent, provided that the enterprise could pay a tax (out of its bonus fund) equal to 50 percent of increased wage costs. These coefficients were uniform for all firms in Hungary, in contrast to the differentiation of coefficients by branches and enterprises in Czechoslovakia. However, the Hungarian authorities soon found that this average wage regulation scheme led to intra- and inter-enterprise wage differences which caused serious dissatisfaction among less skilled production workers. As a result, in 1974 a new wage schedule was adopted centrally for 108 "key trades," to be applied across the economy. It was intended to narrow the range between lower and upper limits in the various occupations from the prevailing 60–80 percent to about 30 percent. And in 1976 the central authorities resumed the regulation of enterprise wage bills as well as average wage levels.

Thus, even in the most liberal reform, the enterprise does not have the freedom to hire the workers it considers necessary, and pay them what it believes they are worth, in the light of their contributions to sales and profit.

5. Investment. Reformers advocated some decentralization of decision making regarding investment, as well as related changes in methods of financing it. They hoped thereby to increase the "effectiveness" of investment by altering its distribution among products and firms, and among types (buildings, equipment, inventories); by lowering building costs; by finishing investment projects faster and reducing the backlog of uncompleted investment in process; and by thus more quickly introducing into production "embodied" technological progress involving investment in new methods and products.[18]

Reform proposals called for devolving some authority for selecting, designing, and carrying out investment projects from central planning agencies and ministries to associations and enterprises. The higher levels in the administrative hierarchy would still retain responsibility for big, non-recurring projects of national significance, but now permit the actual producing units to decide investments involving replacement, expansion, and modernization.

These enterprise-determined investments would be financed from three sources: depreciation allowances, profits, and bank credit. Total depreciation allowances should be increased, by raising depreciation rates and by revaluing upward the capital stock to which the higher rates were applied. Of the total amount of depreciation allowances, enterprises would retain a larger share (and transfer to central agencies a smaller share) than before. Next, reform blueprints typically included schemes for the distribution of profit among taxes, bonus funds, reserve funds, and funds destined for "productive" and "nonproductive" (e.g., housing) investment by the firm. Finally, enterprises would borrow at interest from the banking system, not only for working capital as previously, but also for fixed investment in buildings and equipment.

Most countries in the area did not implement to any significant degree changes in either the locus of investment decision making or the methods of finance. The central authorities feared that enterprises' interest in investing—to expand output, sales, profits, and wage funds—would increase the existing strain on the capacity of construction firms and on supplies of building materials and productive equipment. In addition, they doubted whether the prevailing nonscarcity prices of outputs and material inputs would guide decentralized investment decisions in the correct directions.

Therefore, the retained profits available for decentralized investment were strictly limited, often by profits taxes differentiated by firm. Second, the amount and distribution of bank credit for enterprise investments were closely controlled by direct quantitative rationing, rather than by altering interest rates. Since most decentralized investments could not be financed entirely from retained profits but needed also bank loans (and even budget grants as well), the availability of the latter conditioned the use of the former. Finally, through their control of the material supply system, the central authorities prevented enterprises from translating the nominal

---

[18] On investment problems, see Seidenstecher, "Capital Finance."

purchasing power of funds from retained profits and depreciation allowances into actual command over construction services, materials, and equipment.

Hungary at first did permit firms to undertake decentralized investments from profits and bank credits, but the resulting spurt of enterprise spending on investment caused severe shortages of construction materials and serious inflationary pressure, and central control—particularly through the banking system—was soon reasserted. Thus, statements that enterprises decide over half of total investment are misleading, since these "enterprise decisions" are in fact guided formally and informally by the central authorities.

6. Prices. Reform blueprints included two rather different types of changes in the price system: (*a*) extensive revisions of centrally-set (nonagricultural) prices, though essentially within the traditional cost-plus framework; and (*b*) partial decontrol of prices in an effort to increase price flexibility in response to market forces. The first approach was carried out, though sometimes with great delay, in all of the countries. The second was proposed in Hungary, Czechoslovakia, and Bulgaria but implemented (partially) only in Hungary.

The revisions of producer prices involved changes both in the coverage of cost and in the basis for the profit markup added to cost to obtain the price. Most countries revalued fixed assets, to get more realistic depreciation charges. With the exception of Romania, they also introduced some kind of capital charge—either as an element of cost or in the form of a special tax to be paid out of the profit markup above cost. However, the several countries differed in regard to (*a*) the size of the capital charge, (*b*) whether it was differentiated by branches and enterprises, (*c*) whether it was calculated on the depreciated or the undepreciated value of assets, and (*d*) whether it applied to inventories as well as fixed capital (and if to both, whether at the same rate). Finally, in Hungary (as in the USSR) rental payments for some natural resources were adopted.

Preceding the reforms, there had been a long debate in most countries about whether the profit markup should be calculated as a percentage of (*a*) the wage fund, (*b*) production cost (as previously), or (*c*) capital. In addition to these "single-channel" methods, a compromise "two-channel" method related part of the profit markup to the wage fund and another part to capital. Following the Soviet example,[19] the East European countries chose the variant relating the profit markup to capital—a scheme sometimes called "prices of production" following the use of this term by

---

[19] See Morris Bornstein, "Soviet Price Policy in the 1970s," in *Soviet Economy in a New Perspective* (A Compendium of Papers Submitted to the Joint Economic Committee, 94th Cong., 2d sess.) (Washington, D.C.: U.S. Government Printing Office, 1976), pp. 21–25.

Marx in *Capital*, Vol. III—although they did not establish a single, uniform rate of profit in relation to assets for every branch of industry.

However, although profitability was now calculated in relation to assets by branch, this principle could not be carried down to separate products, because it was impossible to determine the amount of assets involved in the production of each item. Hence, the prices of individual products were still formed by adding a profit markup to cost, though with the aim that the sum of profits so derived should yield the desired branch profitability rate in regard to capital. Profitability rates in relation to cost continued to vary widely by product, making some items in the firm's "assortment" much more "advantageous" to produce than others. Also, since price was related to the branch average cost of production, profitability of the same item varied widely by firm, from high profits for low-cost producers to low profits or losses for high-cost firms.

Moreover, because they were set essentially from the supply side, largely neglecting demand (with some exceptions, such as substitute fuels), these prices did not reflect relative scarcities and thus permit the elimination of administrative allocation of materials and equipment. Finally, the widespread revision of producer prices was carried out with little or no alteration in final retail prices to consumers—since changes in the latter, if not offset by changes in wages and transfer payments, would have caused great popular dissatisfaction, as Polish experience has shown.

Thus, little progress was made in eliminating subsidies, on the one hand, and widely varying tax rates on the other. The force of prices in guiding production was therefore limited: if the enterprise could not cover planned costs from planned sales revenue—with both assigned to it by its hierarchical superior—the enterprise had to be assured a subsidy to cover the difference. Widespread use of taxes and subsidies continued to separate both the levels and the structures of producer prices and consumer prices. Hence, the influence of final consumer demand upon production remained weak.

The GDR reform tried also to introduce "dynamic" prices (analogous to "stepped" prices in the USSR). As costs fell and profitability rose, the price of a product was to be reduced. At first, the responsibility for initiating these price cuts was delegated to the VVB (association) level. But experience showed that the VVB had little interest in pursuing price cuts which reduced profits, and responsibility for changes was recentralized three years later.

To increase the flexibility of the price mechanism, reformers in some countries advocated a multi-category scheme of price control. (*a*) "Fixed" prices would be established centrally at a specific level. (*b*) Some prices would be set centrally only as "maximum" prices, with sellers allowed to charge less. (*c*) On other items, the central authorities would fix ceiling and floor prices, but permit sellers to adjust prices between these "limits."

Finally, (d) "free" prices would be determined by direct negotiations between seller and buyer. The long-term objective was to decontrol prices gradually by shifting them from more tightly to less tightly regulated categories.

In Bulgaria, a three-tier scheme (of fixed, limit, and free prices) was officially espoused during the reform debate, but the reform guidelines actually approved in 1968 did not include this approach. In Czechoslovakia, the multi-category principle was formally adopted, but not implemented before the intervention by Warsaw Pact forces in 1968 halted the reform movement.

In Hungary, a four-category scheme was cautiously implemented in 1968.[20] The bulk of raw materials were put in the "fixed" and "maximum" categories. Over three fourths of inter-producer sales of finished goods were formally placed in the "free" category, but control of these prices was effectively exercised through the close regulation of the prices of the raw and semifinished materials constituting inputs into finished goods, and through supervision of wage expenditures at all levels of production. Agricultural procurement prices remained under close control also. Because a relatively stable retail price level is a cornerstone of Hungarian economic policy, all key items of mass consumption were assigned to the tighter control categories, and only about one fourth of household consumption expenditures (chiefly fashion items and imported goods) were put in the "free" price category.

At the time of the 1968 reform, its designers hoped (a) that the share of the "limit" and "free" categories in total sales would steadily increase; (b) that prices in the "maximum" and "limit" categories would often be below the ceiling; and (c) that in the "free" category supply and demand forces would lead to price decreases as well as increases. However, after 1968 none of these hopes was realized to a significant degree, because of inflationary pressures of domestic and foreign origin. Whereas in 1968 it was expected that the share of the "free" category in consumer expenditures would rise from about 23 percent in 1968 to about 50 percent in 1975, the actual 1975 figure has been estimated at only 35–38 percent. Moreover, various forms of official guidance of "free" prices were introduced, including rules for cost calculation and guidelines for distinguishing "fair" from "unfair" levels of profit above costs so calculated. Hence, little devolution of control over price formation has actually occurred in Hungary.

7. Performance Indicators. In centrally planned economies, enterprises

---

[20] Morris Bornstein, "Price Formation Models and Price Policy in Hungary," chap. 9 in *The Socialist Price Mechanism*, ed. Alan Abouchar (Durham, N.C.: Duke University Press, 1977), and P. G. Hare, "Industrial Prices in Hungary," parts I and II, *Soviet Studies*, vol. 28, no. 2 (April 1976), pp. 189–206, and no. 3 (July 1976), pp. 362–90.

have multiple performance indicators, which may be grouped into three categories according to their scope or breadth. (*a*) The narrowest indicators are those referring to an individual productive activity of a firm, such as the output of a particular item, or the introduction of a specific new production process. (*b*) Somewhat broader are "partial synthetic" indicators expressed in value terms and covering one entire aspect of enterprise operations, like total output, total sales, or total costs. (*c*) The broadest indicator of all is profit, the residual which reflects all decisions regarding outputs and inputs (and, over a longer time horizon, investment as well). The thrust of reform proposals was to reduce the number of indicators by placing more emphasis on broader indicators.

First, its hierarchical superior should no longer judge enterprise performance by the fulfillment of assignments for such narrow facets of activity as the extent of subcontracting, the growth of labor productivity, the level of inventories, or the introduction of a new machine.

Second, the traditionally dominant indicator of gross value of output should be replaced by sales or value added, because they more nearly represent what society wants from the firm. Gross value of output includes production for the enterprise's own use, such as building repairs and manufacture of replacement parts for machinery; the change (positive if an increase, negative if a decrease) in unfinished production; and the change (positive or negative) in inventories of finished goods. In contrast, sales refers to the dispatch of finished goods to customers. Finally, some reformers considered the most appropriate indicator to be value added (or net output)—usually calculated as the difference between sales and the cost of materials, interest charges, and other payments to entities outside the firm—because it showed the enterprise's contribution to the national income.

Although profit appeared the ideal "comprehensive" performance indicator to some reformers, most recognized that socialist firms could not become true "profit centers" in the sense described in Western management literature. Because centrally set prices did not (even after "price reforms") reflect relative scarcities, the central authorities would not let enterprises single-mindedly pursue profit by adjusting outputs and inputs in the light of those prices. Rather, at most, firms could strive for a kind of "constrained" profit maximization, subject to (maximum or minimum) restrictions which superior agencies imposed on enterprise output, inputs, and investment. Hence, profit could be made a more important performance indicator than previously, but not the sole indicator to the exclusion of some measure of output—gross, sold, or net.

Thus, gross output remained the chief success criterion in Romania, sales was adopted in the GDR, and value added chosen in Poland. In Hungary, with the abolition of central assignment of obligatory plan targets for enterprises, profit nominally became the only performance indicator. But in practice, as explained above, formal and informal supervision of enterprise output level and composition, input use and wages, and prices effectively limits how enterprises can earn profit, as well as its disposition once earned.

8. Incentives. It is the task of the incentive structure to motivate enterprise personnel to strive for good performance in regard to the indicators chosen and the quantitative targets for each indicator in a particular production period. Communist societies have long used both "moral" and "material" incentives for this purpose. "Moral" incentives can appeal to an individual's genuine wish to do whatever is best for society, as this is defined by the state authorities, or to the less unselfish desire for a reward in the form of public recognition and social prestige. In contrast, "material" incentives include both more money income, to be spent on the market (or saved), and material rewards available through nonmarket channels, such as preference in the allocation of housing or access to special stores not open to the general public. Although appeals to moral incentives continue in the educational system and the media, the East European countries (like the USSR) in practice rely overwhelmingly on material incentives to motivate workers and managers—in contrast to the People's Republic of China, where moral incentives (and coercion) have a much greater role.

The actions of individual workers seldom can affect the overall performance of the firm. Therefore, East European incentive systems for workers typically award bonuses for successful or exceptional execution of particular tasks at the workplace, such as economizing on the use of scarce materials or meeting new quality standards, or for adopted suggestions on "rationalizing" production methods. These bonuses traditionally have come from a special portion of the enterprise wage fund, and this practice was retained in most reform proposals, although in Romania bonus payments to workers come out of profits.

The reforms were more concerned with bonuses for managerial personnel, whose individual decisions directly and strongly affect enterprise results regarding output, cost, and profit. Managerial bonus schemes have several elements: (*a*) the performance indicators whose targets must be fulfilled to qualify for bonuses, (*b*) a schedule of coefficients stating what results for each indicator will earn what amount of money for the bonus fund, (*c*) the source of money for the bonus fund, and (*d*) how the bonus fund is distributed among eligible employees.[21]

The most striking feature of East European bonus schemes is their complexity in the first and second respects. Because enterprises typically have not one but many performance indicators (for reasons explained above), bonuses must in some way reward good results for each indicator. This

---

[21] See Granick, *Enterprise Guidance*, for a detailed discussion of managerial bonus systems in Romania, the GDR, and Hungary.

may be accomplished directly by establishing separate bonuses for each performance indicator, with the respective coefficients or amounts reflecting the relative importance of the different indicators (e.g., sales vs. profit) in the eyes of the firm's hierarchical superior. Or it may be done indirectly through the use of side-conditions, by making the bonus for one indicator contingent upon fulfillment of the plan for another indicator which does not nominally offer a bonus. For example, a bonus due for sales performance may be paid only if the firm has also fulfilled its export assignments, for which no explicit bonus is provided.

The source of funds for managerial bonuses is usually a portion of retained profit, rather than the wage fund as in the case of bonuses for workers. In the GDR and Romania, however, managers may also receive bonuses from special ministerial funds. Such bonuses are paid not according to explicit formulas related to plan fulfillment, but rather on the basis of a more subjective evaluation by the ministry of managerial performance and thus (like promotion) can reward managers who respond properly to "informal" guidance from above.

Reformers advocated establishing incentive structures which were uniform across enterprises (at least within a particular branch of industry) and stable for a number of years. The first feature would bring the management of leading firms higher bonuses than their counterparts in less successful enterprises. The second feature would encourage managers to reveal "reserves" by reducing their fear that when sales or profit rose the bonus coefficients would be changed to prevent managers from reaping the fruits of their efforts.

However, in practice in most countries bonus schemes were not made uniform but instead were tailored by the ministry to its view of the particular circumstances of the individual enterprise or association, with the aim of preventing bonuses in stronger units from becoming too large relative to those in weaker units. In addition, despite assurances that "normatives" for payments to bonus funds would remain unaltered, they were changed frequently and even retroactively. Managers are not likely to have confidence in a system in which the "rules of the game" are changed not only during, but even after, the game. Finally, in Hungary, where a common formula for determining the size of the bonus fund was applied to all enterprises, the maximum possible size of managerial bonuses was reduced sharply after workers expressed their resentment at the effect of bonuses in widening income differentials between managerial personnel and production workers.

9. *Foreign Trade.* In the traditional prereform system, foreign exchange rates were usually quite arbitrary. Producing firms sold exports to, and bought imports from, special foreign trade enterprises at domestic prices completely divorced from the prices at which the foreign trade enterprises dealt with their customers and suppliers abroad. A complex set

of highly differentiated taxes and subsidies, handled through a "price equalization fund," covered differences between the domestic prices of goods and the nominal national equivalent of the foreign trade price obtained by converting it into local currency at the arbitrary exchange rate. In these circumstances, producing firms generally had little interest in foreign trade, which their superiors therefore specified for them in detailed plans.

In regard to foreign trade, reform proposals emphasized two related aspects: closer links between domestic and foreign prices, and some decentralization of decision making to producing units.[22] First, more realistic exchange rates should relate the general levels of domestic and world prices, while a reduction in taxes and subsidies on individual products should align the domestic price structure more closely to the world price structure. Then proceeds from exports and payments for imports could be accurately represented in enterprise accounts, directly affecting their sales, costs, and profits. Second, associations and/or enterprises should be given more authority to determine at least the composition of export production and also the right to negotiate directly with foreign firms, rather than through the intermediary of foreign trade enterprises subordinate to the ministry of foreign trade.

In most countries in the area, both types of proposals were partially implemented, though in different ways and to varying degrees.

Official exchange rates generally were not affected. Instead, shadow exchange rates (often euphemistically called "adjustment coefficients," "foreign trade multipliers," or "direction coefficients") were introduced, usually with separate rates for the world market ("dollar") area and the CMEA ("ruble") area. Enterprises producing for export, or purchasing imports, now included these transactions in their financial accounts at the "foreign price equivalent," i.e., the foreign price translated into the national currency at the appropriate shadow rate.

However, in view of the domestic cost level and structure, full application of this new method of evaluating exports and imports would have led to large profits on some items and heavy losses on others and would have drastically altered the profitability of entire firms in fulfilling their assigned foreign trade plans. Hence, wide use of taxes and subsidies, differentiated by product and/or by enterprise, continued. Also, it was expected that these shadow exchange rates would be adjusted from time to time to reflect changes in the relationship of the domestic and foreign price levels. But this policy instrument was not used flexibly and promptly. For example, in Hungary, the authorities did change the "foreign trade multipliers" to reflect the devaluation of the dollar in 1971, but they were subsequently

---

[22] Alan A. Brown and Paul Marer, "Foreign Trade in the East European Reforms," chap. 5 in *Plan and Market*; and Harriet Matejka, "Foreign Trade Systems," chap. 14 in *The New Economic Systems*.

unwilling to revalue the forint enough to compensate for inflation on the world market beginning in 1973. Instead, they intervened further with export taxes and subsidies.

In most countries of the area, at least some producing units gained more contact with foreign customers or suppliers. For example, foreign trade enterprises were integrated into the new associations in Bulgaria, and into associations or industrial ministries in Romania. In the GDR, the network of foreign trade enterprises handling exports was reorganized so that each VVB association would have to deal with only one foreign trade enterprise, instead of several.

Such administrative changes can make it easier for producers to adjust specifications of exports to customers' requirements and to identify which imported machines best meet their needs. But the quantities to be traded, and the prices involved, are usually determined not by the association or enterprise itself but by the branch ministry and/or the ministry of foreign trade—particularly in regard to trade with CMEA countries, which is arranged in high-level bilateral agreements covering quantities and prices.[23] Thus enterprises still receive foreign trade assignments, and their discretion is usually limited to decisions on some aspects of the assortment, within the specified global total.

10. Workers' Participation in Decision Making. Communist countries have long had formal mechanisms for worker participation in decision making, both through trade union channels and through factory councils. Political speeches often call for workers to take an active role in the formulation, as well as the implementation, of enterprise plans. However, in practice workers seldom have had any significant influence on enterprise decision making—except in Yugoslavia under the system of "self-management" of enterprises introduced over 20 years ago.[24]

Only the Czech reform blueprint included genuine worker control of firms, though differing in important respects from the Yugoslav scheme.[25] Workers' management was implemented in some enterprises for a short period before the intervention of Warsaw Pact forces in 1968. Then it was terminated because it was viewed as a serious threat to Party control over the economy.

---

[23] M. Tardos, Acta Oeconomica [Budapest], vol. 11 (1973), no. 4, pp. 369–80; abstracted as "The Need for Direct Relations among Production Enterprises and Problems in Their Formation in Trade Turnover among CMEA Countries," Abstracts of Hungarian Economic Literature, vol. 4 (1976), no. 6, pp. 78–80.

[24] Standard sources on "self-management" in Yugoslavia include Yugoslav Workers' Selfmanagement, ed. M. J. Broekmeyer (Dordrecht, Holland: Reidel, 1970); Ichak Adizes, Industrial Democracy: Yugoslav Style (New York: Free Press, 1972); Jan Vanek, The Economics of Workers' Management: A Yugoslav Case Study (London: Allen & Unwin, 1972); and Howard M. Wachtel, Workers' Management and Workers' Wages in Yugoslavia (Ithaca, N.Y.: Cornell University Press, 1973).

[25] Ludek Rychetnik, "Two Models of an Enterprise in Market Socialism," Economics of Planning, vol. 8 (1968), no. 3, pp. 216–31.

11. Agriculture. Economic reforms in Eastern Europe in the late 1960s primarily concerned the nonagricultural sectors, with only secondary attention to agriculture. The main approach to improving economic performance in agriculture was through policy measures rather than systemic changes. The latter involved chiefly organizational aspects.[26]

There were no striking organizational changes comparable to decollectivization of agriculture in Poland in 1956. Instead, administrative and producing units in agriculture were reorganized in various ways. (a) In Bulgaria and Hungary the separate ministries of agriculture and food industry were merged. (b) Farm size was altered by combining smaller farms into larger ones in Hungary and the GDR, and by dividing larger farms into smaller ones in Romania. (c) Greater horizontal integration was accomplished by grouping farms into associations in Hungary, Poland, and Czechoslovakia, while the GDR stressed vertical integration. Bulgaria sought both horizontal and vertical integration by forming agroindustrial combines including farms and processing plants.

In most countries the government tried to boost agricultural output by various economic policy measures, such as raising prices and adjusting taxes and subsidies; increasing supplies of machinery, fertilizer, and other industrial inputs; and revising farmer compensation schemes to strengthen incentives. But farms still receive targets for sales to state procurement agencies, and the availability of off-farm inputs is controlled by state supply agencies.

12. Private Sector. To meet consumer demands which state enterprises cannot satisfy, most East European countries permit various small private business activities, such as household plots of farmers, shops of watchmakers and tailors, family-run restaurants or bakeries, and the ownership and rental of private houses and apartments. The scope of this private sector changed relatively little as a result of the reforms.

In agriculture, restrictions on private plot activity were reduced in Bulgaria and Hungary by raising limits on livestock holdings and increasing supplies of feed and tools.

In the nonagricultural sectors, Romania eased restrictions on the amount of labor which private businesses could hire and also promoted private housing construction.

Hungary initially encouraged the growth of the private sector by allowing expanded activity by private artisans and widespread moonlighting by skilled workers, and also permitted agricultural cooperatives to start handicraft and light industry ventures. But by 1971 complaints about "profiteering," "money grubbing," and "materialism" led to higher taxes on private artisans, restrictions on moonlighting and ancillary nonagricultural opera-

---

[26] Jerzy F. Karcz, "Agricultural Reform in Eastern Europe," chap. 6 in *Plan and Market*; and Ivan Lončarević, Eberhard Schinke, and Miklós Géza Zilahi-Szabó, "Farming," chap. 13 in *The New Economic Systems*.

tions of farms, new limits on real estate ownership, and new taxes on land transactions and private rentals.[27]

Most recently, at the end of 1976, Poland undertook to stimulate private artisan activity by increasing the availability of materials and business premises, raising the ceiling on the number of hired workers per firm, reducing taxes, and extending social security and medical care benefits to private businessmen.

Reasons for Retrenchment

Thus, the general pattern in Eastern Europe has been one of retreat, as the official reform blueprints—themselves less ambitious than the proposals of reformers—were at best only partially implemented. This section examines some of the principal reasons for retrenchment, including (1) interest group opposition, (2) internal inconsistencies among the reform measures, (3) excessive tautness (insufficient slack), (4) Soviet influence, and (5) developments in the world economy.

1. Opposition. Only in Czechoslovakia (before the 1968 invasion) and in Hungary was the Party leadership strongly behind economic reform. Elsewhere in the area the Party leaders had only a diffident, ambivalent commitment to reform. In these circumstances, the staffs of the Party and government bureaucracies, fearing (correctly) that genuine reform would reduce their power, successfully impeded the execution of the relatively modest reforms. On the one hand, they urged caution, delay, and experiment in carrying out reforms. On the other, they recommended revision, curtailment, and reversal when the opportunity arose because contradictions among reform measures were perceived, because it proved difficult to achieve ambitious plans, because the example and advice of the USSR suggested a conservative approach, or because developments in the world economy were unfavorable.

In Hungary, where reform went much farther than in the other countries, a major reason for the interruption of the momentum of reform in 1972 appears to have been the discontent of the urban blue-collar working class over the implications of reform for income differentiation and job security. The urban proletariat resented the faster rise in peasant incomes, the size of managerial bonuses, widening interenterprise earnings differentials from profit-sharing, and the ability of skilled workers like mechanics and electricians to obtain large secondary incomes from moonlighting. Less skilled manual workers were also alarmed by public discussions of the desirability of "removing brakes" on the further implementation of the reform by "eliminating unprofitable production" and "restructuring" pro-

---

[27] The main issues are discussed in Walter D. Connor, "Social Consequences of Economic Reforms in Eastern Europe," chap. 3 in *Economic Development in the Soviet Union and Eastern Europe*, vol. 1: *Reforms*.

duction and employment. The authorities responded to the workers' concern by partial recentralization. They raised money wages for manual workers from central funds (rather than enterprise resources, as the reform provided), increased the powers of planning and price control bodies, put the 50 largest industrial firms under formal ministerial supervision, and tightened the regulation of enterprise investment.

2. Internal Inconsistencies. Reform blueprints typically suffered from internal contradictions, because some aspects essential for the successful operation of other aspects were not carried out in the correct way or at the right time. For example, performance indicators were altered to emphasize profit but output plans continued to require firms to produce some products at a loss. Or enterprises were permitted to retain profits for decentralized investment, but the materials allocation system was not relaxed to enable firms to acquire investment goods. As a result, various reform measures failed to yield the hoped for results—which strengthened the hands of opposition groups and either impeded the further implementation of reform or even reversed it.

The most critical dimension of reform from this viewpoint is the price system, because it should link various facets of decision making by providing a comprehensive and mutually consistent expression of relative values for use in evaluating alternatives in production, consumption, and investment. In the reforms of all the countries, fundamental deficiencies in the price system made it impossible to carry out successfully the changes which reformers sought in planning, allocation of materials, labor and wage regulation, performance indicators and incentives, and investment.

As explained above, the central authorities continued to set producer goods prices as the sum of the planned branch average cost of production plus an arbitrary profit markup. But because such prices seldom reflected relative scarcities, the central authorities logically were unwilling in practice to abolish administrative allocation of material inputs and to eliminate obligatory enterprise targets for outputs and inputs. The authorities correctly feared that enterprise managers—motivated by material incentives to strive for good performance in terms of sales, value added, and/or profit calculated in these prices—would be likely to produce different output levels and mixes, using different input levels and mixes, than the authorities considered necessary. Nor could enterprises, and banks, decide what were the socially most desirable investments. Instead, to obtain the production and investment they wanted, the central authorities not only adjusted prices by a complex system of taxes and subsidies, but also continued to specify output assignments for, allocate machinery and materials to, control wages and labor use in, and determine investment by, associations and enterprises.

3. Tautness. A "taut" plan is one whose fulfillment requires great exertion (and/or luck), whereas its opposite, a "slack" plan, can be achieved without special effort. In East European economies the central authorities commonly strive for taut plans for two related reasons: the desire to achieve rapid growth and structural change, and the belief that administrative pressure on enterprises is the best (or only) way to secure maximum performance from them.

However, some slack is essential to carry out reforms. Changes in administrative organization, planning methods, performance indicators, and incentives are bound to be disruptive until ministry and association officials, enterprise managers, and workers understand and adapt to them. During the transition period, economic performance in terms of output, sales, cost, and profit may not improve, and may even worsen. This is more likely to occur if reserves of materials, machinery, consumer goods, and convertible currencies have not been built up before the reform—to deal with foreseeable and unforeseeable difficulties in implementing sweeping new arrangements.

Keren has carefully analyzed the effect of tautness (slack) on the fate of economic reform in the GDR.[28] During the first four years of the New Economic System (NES) in 1964–68, the performance of the economy improved in regard to the rates of growth of national product and exports, the structure of net product, the balance between supply of and demand for consumer goods, and the reduction in the build-up of unfinished construction. This occurred because of a change in planning strategy from tautness to slack as well as because of the introduction of changes in organization, planning, and management.

But when the GDR authorities returned to taut plans in 1969–70, recentralization occurred in various respects, essentially terminating the NES in fact, if not formally. Whereas responsibility for preparing material balances could be delegated to associations and enterprises when plans were slack, tauter plans meant that superior organs had to handle more balances. This would happen even without formal recentralization, because an overcommitted balance at a lower hierarchical level inevitably led to appeals to higher levels by users whose allocations had been cut. Tight balances also caused the reshuffling of planned flows and abrogation of contracts—causing a return to "contracts based on balances" (and flows decided from above), rather than "balances based on contracts" (and flows determined by enterprises themselves). Further, taut plans altered the effective performance indicators and incentives, by inducing neglect of cost, profits, and quality in the attempt to fulfill output assignments, and by encouraging managers to amass reserves of labor, materials, and production capacity to prepare for the higher plan targets expected in the future under the "ratchet principle." Finally, taut plans altered the influence of the price system on production. A taut plan for a sector puts a large premium on its capacity

---

[28] Keren, "The New Economic System," pp. 570–72 and 581–82.

and raises shadow quasi-rents and marginal costs high above normal average costs (on which prices are based). Therefore, the tauter the plan, the less will prices convey scarcity information and guide profit-seeking firms correctly in their choice of inputs.

Polish experience also shows that reform measures seldom can survive conditions of stress. According to the Polish economist Kleer, reform involved reduction in the number of directive indicators handed down from higher to lower levels, but—

> these were not irreversible changes. When, for whatever reason (a poor harvest, difficulties in foreign trade, excessive investment, etc.), difficulties were heightened, the rights granted were "withdrawn." This was revealed in a growing number of commands in the form of directives or at least informational directives, allocation of raw materials and semifinished goods, greater wage discipline, etc.[29]

4. Soviet Influence. The USSR has influenced economic reforms in Eastern Europe in several ways: (*a*) through the example of its own reform, (*b*) through intervention in Czechoslovakia in 1968, and (*c*) through its efforts to coordinate production, investment, and trade in CMEA.

a. The "minor" or "partial" reform countries followed the lead of the USSR in regard to reform discussions, reform blueprints, and the pattern and degree of implementation in many (though not all) respects.[30]

This is illustrated by the similarity of the GDR's NES to the Liberman proposals in the USSR. The latter advocated devolving responsibility for smaller decisions to lower hierarchical levels, while retaining at the top control over more important decisions—by giving enterprises more freedom of maneuver within a centrally determined plan, on whose fulfillment bonus payments depended. The very publication of the Liberman discussion in the USSR beginning in 1962 was seen as a green light for a similar debate in the GDR, and many details of the NES mirrored specific Liberman proposals.[31]

But as the limited scope of economic reform in the USSR became

---

[29] Jerzy Kleer, *Ekonomista* [Warsaw], 1973, no. 1; trans. "Economic Reforms in the Socialist Countries in the Sixties," *Eastern European Economics*, vol. 13, no. 1 (Winter 1974–75), pp. 11–12.

[30] On the Soviet experience, see, for example, Gertrude E. Schroeder, "Recent Developments in Soviet Planning and Incentives," in *Soviet Economic Prospects for the Seventies* (A Compendium of Papers Submitted to the Joint Economic Committee, 93rd Cong., 1st sess.) (Washington, D.C.: U.S. Government Printing Office, 1973), pp. 11–38; Jan Adam, "The Incentive System in the USSR: The Abortive Reform of 1965," *Industrial and Labor Relations Review*, vol. 27, no. 1 (October 1973), pp. 84–92; and Alice C. Gorlin, "Industrial Reorganization: The Associations," in *Soviet Economy in a New Perspective*, pp. 162–88. The establishment of the association link in the administrative hierarchy, discussed by Gorlin, is one aspect in which the USSR appears to have been influenced by East European practice.

[31] Keren, "The New Economic System," pp. 555–56.

clear, the East European countries (with the exception of Hungary, and of Czechoslovakia through 1968) followed the conservatism of the Soviet reform in regard to such critical aspects as the price system, obligatory plan indicators, central control over supply allocation and thus investment, and regulation of enterprise wage funds.

b. Through the intervention of Warsaw Pact forces in Czechoslovakia in 1968, the USSR made clear that it would not tolerate an economic reform in Eastern Europe (outside Yugoslavia) which gave market forces a dominant role in guiding the economy, introduced workers' management, and substantially weakened the Party's control of economic, political, and social life.

Although the Hungarian reform was also of the "comprehensive" type, it proved acceptable to the USSR because it excluded workers' management, retained the unified Party's leading role in society, and assured the primacy of the USSR and other CMEA countries in Hungary's external political and economic relations.

c. Thus, the USSR evaluated economic reform in Eastern Europe in terms of the implications for Soviet political and economic control of the area. The USSR believes it is easier to achieve the bilateral and multilateral production, trade, and investment relations it desires in CMEA (1) if member countries' internal planning and management systems are essentially similar, and (2) if these similar systems involve little devolution of decision making, since decentralization would make it more difficult to negotiate and implement CMEA agreements.[32]

5. Developments in the World Economy. When a nation experiences disturbances in its foreign economic relations—for example, inflation in countries supplying imports or recession in countries buying exports—there is usually a centralized response, in the form of adjusting exchange rates, exchange controls, tariffs, import quotas, and internal taxes and subsidies. Thus, adverse developments in the world economy can be expected to retard or reverse decentralizing economic reforms.

In most of Eastern Europe, economic reforms had stalled before the expansion of East-West relations early in the 1970s made these nations more vulnerable to inflation and recession in the world market—which occurred following the Arab oil embargo in 1973 and the subsequent OPEC-dictated increases in oil prices.

However, these developments did affect the course of reform in Hungary and Poland. In Hungary, the New Economic Mechanism (NEM) of 1968 had assumed a stable world market—not one in which rapid import price rises outstripped export price increases, leading to a severe deterioration in the terms of trade, first with developed and less developed

---

[32] For a detailed discussion of these issues, see Peter Marsh, "The Integration Process in Eastern Europe, 1968 to 1975," *Journal of Common Market Studies*, vol. 14, no. 4 (June 1976), pp. 311–35.

market economies in 1973–74 and then within CMEA in 1974–75. The authorities had to face the conflict between their desire for approximate stability in domestic producer and consumer prices, on the one hand, and the reform's principle that changes in external markets should affect enterprises' production and use of inputs through changes in prices. The authorities chose the former alternative, resorting to large subsidies and export taxes to preserve the prevailing pattern of enterprise activities. As a result, according to a leading Hungarian economist, contrary to the intent of the reform, "the enterprises were interested in successful negotiations with the state organs responsible for taxes and subsidies rather than in adaptation to market tendencies."[33]

In Poland, inflation on the world market was a major cause—along with internal inconsistencies and excessive tautness—of the retrenchment in Gierek's reforms. On the one hand, foreign inflation raised import prices, but because of the political importance of price stability, import prices rises were mostly offset by large increases in subsidies. On the other hand, to induce organizations to produce for export, the reform had included the principle of calculating a firm's exports at so-called realization prices directly related, through foreign exchange coefficients, to the actual prices in foreign currencies. Hence, higher prices in foreign markets raised the amount of sales, value added, the wage fund, and other enterprise funds. To prevent firms from enjoying windfall increases in these funds due not to their efforts but to changes in the world market, "normatives" for allocating money to these funds were reduced, and part of the funds was frozen or transferred to the control of ministries.

IV. CONCLUSIONS

The reform movement in Eastern Europe emerged because of dissatisfaction with the nature and results of the traditional Soviet-type economic system installed in the area after World War II. The struggle between pro- and anti-reform forces varied by country and led to different reform blueprints, incorporating diverse concepts of "decentralization" and dissimilar implementation strategies.

Throughout the area, there was a retreat from reform—earlier, faster, or farther in some countries than others. The reasons included interest group opposition, internal inconsistencies, insufficient slack, Soviet influence, and developments in the world economy. Only Hungary now has a significantly different economic system, although formal and informal central intervention in the Hungarian economy is much greater than intended when the NEM was introduced in 1968.

As a result, it is not possible to determine whether and how much eco-

---

33 M. Tardos, "Impacts of World Economic Changes on the Hungarian Economy," *Acta Oeconomica* [Budapest], vol. 15 (1975), nos. 3–4, p. 287.

nomic reform—in the sense of comprehensive mutually consistent decentralizing systemic changes—can improve economic performance. In most countries, economic reform was not really carried out, or at best was implemented partially for a short period, while internal economic policies—regarding plan tautness or living standards—and the external environment were changing.[34]

The problems of unsatisfactory growth rates, balance of payments difficulties, lagging technological progress, and popular discontent with living standards continue throughout the area. In their search for ways other than systemic change to improve economic performance, the regimes of these countries have turned their attention to foreign trade and investment.

Through expanded East-West economic relations, stemming from Soviet-U.S. "détente," the East European countries (like the USSR) hope to import Western machinery and equipment, licenses for processes, and in some cases consumer goods—in order to expand output, stimulate technological progress, increase exports, and satisfy demands of their populations. However, these hopes are constrained by the inability to increase hard-currency exports fast enough. At first, the gap was covered by Western credits, but outstanding indebtedness is now large—particularly for Poland but also for other countries—and servicing the debt absorbs a large and rising portion of export earnings. Hence, these countries are especially interested in "industrial cooperation" agreements with Western firms which include selling at least part of the output to hard-currency countries.

Some systemic reform may be helpful or even necessary to take full advantage of Western machinery and technology and to expand exports to pay for them. For example, changing the price system to reflect scarcities more accurately and valuing exports and imports at the proper domestic equivalent of their foreign prices would lead to more sensible central decisions on the composition of exports and imports and the pattern of investment. These measures could also induce firms to increase the quantity and quality of exports and to economize on the use of imports—provided that performance indicators and incentives were adapted to give adequate and assured rewards to the personnel of firms accomplishing these difficult tasks.

However, given the current and prospective balance of payments situations of these countries, the central authorities are likely to retain close control over hard-currency exports and imports, as well as negotiations with foreign banks for credits and with foreign firms for joint ventures. Thus, little devolution of authority over these matters to enterprises and associations is probable.

Furthermore, the East European economies will remain heavily in-

---

[34] On problems in evaluating the effects of economic reform, see Zielinski, *Economic Reforms in Polish Industry*, pp. 298–308.

volved in CMEA, both because of Soviet pressure and because their ability in the short- or medium-term to restructure their economies toward more trade with the West is limited. Also, after their sobering experience with fluctuations in prices and quantities on the world market since 1973, they appreciate more keenly the advantages provided by the stability of CMEA trade agreements. But, as explained above, integration in CMEA discourages economic reforms, which differentiate the member countries' economic systems and give enterprises autonomy which complicates fulfillment of centrally-negotiated agreements.

Thus, expanded trade and investment relations with the West and with CMEA are viewed more as alternatives than as companions to internal economic reforms.

20

CHINA'S INDUSTRIAL SYSTEM*

Thomas G. Rawski

The Soviet "model" of central planning to mobilize resources for rapid industrialization was adopted in China after the Communists attained power in 1949. However, this model was modified in China both for ideological reasons, such as Mao's emphasis on "self-reliance," and for pragmatic reasons, such as fragmentation of the backward Chinese economy into local and regional markets. Thus the administration of the economy was much more decentralized in China than in the Soviet Union. Another striking difference concerns incentives. In the Soviet Union (and Eastern Europe), differences in labor income are accepted as necessary for allocation and incentive purposes. But differences in final real income are reduced by (1) transfer payments, which decrease differences in total money income, and (2) the provision of services such as health care through non-market channels, to make the distribution of real income less unequal than the distribution of money income. In the Chinese approach, work for the good of society, rather than personal material gain, is stressed, and strong efforts are made to prevent the emergence of a technical-managerial class.

In this article, Rawski explains how the Soviet scheme of central planning was adapted to Chinese conditions, and how the system has actually operated in practice in China. He concludes that on the whole China has been successful—through administrative control, rather than market guidance—in mobilizing resources, expanding output, and changing its structure.

---

* Reprinted from *China: A Reassessment of the Economy* (A Compendium of Papers Submitted to the Joint Economic Committee, 94th Cong., 1st sess.) (Washington, D.C.: U.S. Government Printing Office, 1975), pp. 175–98, with the omission of charts and references to foreign-language sources. Thomas G. Rawski is Associate Professor of Economics at the University of Toronto.

I. INTRODUCTION

China's achievements in such diverse areas as nuclear weaponry, satellite technology, rural electrification, chemical fertilizer production, and, most recently, petroleum development illustrate the significance of industrial advance since 1949. Although the paucity of statistical information leads to differences among various estimates of industrial growth, all observers agree that output of factories, mines, and utilities has advanced at a rapid, though decelerating pace since 1949. My own studies indicate that in terms of 1952 prices, the average annual growth rate of industrial gross output value since 1952 falls within the range of 12 to 14 percent.[1] China's achievements compare favorably with industrial performance in other large developing nations such as Brazil and India, particularly since these countries have enjoyed freer access to foreign assistance, expertise, and technology than has the People's Republic.

This impressive record raises many questions about the nature and evolution of industrial planning and factory management in the People's Republic. Who formulates annual plans? What relations exist among workers, factory executives, and economic planners? What changes have occurred in industry since the 1950s? Could China benefit from the type of economic reforms which have recently appeared in the European socialist countries? This essay approaches these issues by discussing the origins of China's industrial system, its evolution since the early 1950s, and the efficiency of industrial operations.[2]

II. THE SPREAD OF STATE CONTROL AND PRODUCTION PLANNING

China's system of industrial planning was not born overnight. The spread of central economic control was a gradual process, and it is only

---

[1] Thomas G. Rawski, "Chinese Industrial Production, 1952–1971," *Review of Economics and Statistics*, vol. 55, no. 2 (May 1973), pp. 169–81. The use of a later price base would lower the estimated growth rate, but changing from gross to net output would raise it. For alternative estimates of industrial growth, see Robert Michael Field, "Civilian Industrial Production in the People's Republic of China: 1949–74," in *China: A Reassessment of the Economy* (A Compendium of Papers Submitted to the Joint Economic Committee, 94th Cong., 1st sess.) (Washington, D.C.: U.S. Government Printing Office, 1975), pp. 146–74.

[2] Previous studies of China's industrial system include Audrey Donnithorne, *China's Economic System* (London: Allen & Unwin, 1967); Kang Chao, "Policies and Performance in Industry," ch. 9, and Dwight H. Perkins, "Industrial Planning and Management," ch. 10, in *Economic Trends in Communist China*, ed. Alexander Eckstein and others (Chicago: Aldine Publishing Company, 1968); Barry M. Richman, *Industrial Society in Communist China* (New York: Random House, 1969); and Christopher Howe, *Wage Patterns and Wage Policy in Modern China, 1919–1972* (Cambridge, Eng.: Cambridge University Press, 1973).

with the ratification of China's First Five-Year Plan (FFYP) in mid-1955, over two years after its formal beginning in January 1953, that we can begin to speak of an integrated industrial system and policy rather than collections of ad hoc production orders and investment projects.

As the victorious Red armies swept southward in 1949, China's new leaders sought to revitalize industry under a Soviet-inspired system of state ownership, central planning, and responsive enterprise leadership. Expropriation of enterprises formerly administered by the Kuomintang government placed leading producer enterprises, including Japanese-built plants, in government hands. In the consumer sector, compulsory procurement contracts maintained state control over privately owned factories until they were nationalized in 1956.

In the sphere of planning and management, however, the paucity of expert personnel and of reliable information severely limited the rate of progress. Unavoidable initial confusion was heightened by the regime's determination to begin new construction without waiting for normal production to resume at plants which had escaped severe wartime damage. As thousands of workers were added to industry's payrolls, the competing demands of rebuilding, innovation, and expansion piled new strains on an already overextended corps of skilled and experienced personnel.[3]

Faced with the impossibility of asserting close control over an industrial sector which soon included 10,000 state enterprises, several million employees and thousands of construction projects, Peking concentrated its initial efforts on key commodities, enterprises, and regions. As one area, product, or unit developed adequate managerial competence, economic administrators directed their energies elsewhere.

Growing control was most evident in the iron and steel sector, where rationalization was facilitated by the small number of firms and by the technology of metallurgy, which permits unskilled workers to perform a variety of duties under the direction of a few trained engineers. First priority went to the iron and steel works at Anshan, China's premier industrial facility, and to the nearby steel center at Pench'i. Chinese managers developed forms of teamwork which reduced the importance of individual skills. Captured Japanese personnel prepared detailed manuals which enabled ordinary shophands to work without close supervision. Imaginative innovations enabled even the least trained workers to operate delicate machinery.

Rapid increases in output, labor productivity, and the accuracy of production plans followed these reforms. By 1952, the authorities could turn their attention to smaller steel plants at Chungking, Talien, Tayeh, T'angshan and elsewhere, which suffered from disorganization, poor quality

---

[3] The Shanghai Machine Tool Plant lost 60 percent of its technical staff during 1953–54, while the East China Bureau of the Ministry of Heavy Industry transferred 70 percent of its technical cadres to construction units at about the same time.

control, neglect of maintenance, and other elementary problems already eliminated at Anshan and Pench'i. Once again, reforms led to rapid improvements in performance.

In the machinery industry, creation of a system combining detailed central planning with competent and responsive enterprise management proved far more difficult. In comparison with metallurgy, engineering is characterized by numerous producers, a complex and shifting output mix, and a technology which requires a series of technically exacting operations including design, casting, forging, machining, assembly, and inspection for thousands of different machine parts. In trying to develop planned machinery production, Chinese officials confronted technical conditions which had been "a source of great difficulty" to American mobilization plans during the First World War.[4]

As in steel, economic planning began with key products, regions, and enterprises. Again, outstanding progress was reported in the Northeast (formerly Manchuria), but the national picture was not bright. A 1954 editorial noted that enterprises outside the control of the First Ministry of Machine-building (FMMB), the authority responsible for major products of civilian machinery, lacked unified direction; eliminating their tendency toward "blind development" would take "a long time."

Even within its restricted scope of operation, the ministry found it difficult to prepare prompt, comprehensive, and accurate plans for the 91 firms under its control. A 1953 directive spoke of "utter confusion" in planning, technical and supply work, inspection, and maintenance. Frequent delays and changes in production plans continued in subsequent years. As late as 1957, the FMMB was singled out for criticism and urged to "balance its supply in a well-coordinated and unified way and work out an overall plan of production."

Chronic tardiness, shifting targets, and complaints that plans were based on unreliable estimates and conjectures arose from weaknesses at the factory level as well as in Peking. Preoccupied with daily demands of production, construction, labor training, and technical reform, factory officials could spare little attention for the task of compiling and transmitting the economic and technical data essential for smooth functioning of the planning system.[5]

Elsewhere, progress toward a Soviet-inspired plan system fell between the extremes represented by steel and machinery. Textiles and chemicals were two sectors in which detailed data comparing different factories en-

---

4 Bernard M. Baruch, *American Industry in the War* (New York: Prentice-Hall, 1941), p. 278.

5 To cite one of many examples, a 1956 investigation discovered that officials at Chinan No. 1 Machine Tool Plant could not answer questions about the quantity of fixed capital, the turnover period for working capital, the number of machines in the plant, or the volume of output per ton of raw materials.

abled planners to pinpoint technical difficulties from an early date. Construction, on the other hand, remained intractable, with reports of delays, slipshod budgeting, disorganization, and cost overruns persisting throughout the 1950s.[6] As in the case of machinery, these problems arose in part from the nature of the industry: The unique features of each of many construction projects hamper close control of this sector in any economy.[7]

Despite these variations the FFYP years saw the gradual development of a hierarchy of economic control stretching from Peking to the factory floor. The industrial ministries were increasingly able to translate centrally determined policies into effective action at the microeconomic level. The emerging system of industrial administration, which has survived without fundamental change to the present, is the subject of the following section.

III. THE INDUSTRIAL SYSTEM OF THE 1950s

China's industrial organization is a hybrid combining major features of Soviet institutions introduced during the 1950s with later modifications made in response to changing economic and political conditions. At the top stands the State Council, which holds formal responsibility for promulgating economic targets for all sectors. Once ratified by the State Council, economic plans carry the force of law, and failure to fulfill them is, technically speaking, illegal. In fact, detailed planning takes place in the State Planning Commission, which works in cooperation with the State Economic Commission, the State Statistical Bureau, the State Construction Bureau, the People's Bank and other economic agencies subordinate to the State Council.

The State Council approves output plans for major commodities and value targets for various branches of industry. These norms are transmitted to the central government's industrial ministries—for coal, metallurgy, chemicals, textiles, etc.—which divide tasks and resources among constituent enterprises to ensure fulfillment of their portions of the national plan. Despite a gradual decentralization process beginning in 1957, which has transferred direct control of many industrial enterprises to the provinces and localities, this chain of authority has been an important feature of industrial administration since the creation of the first industrial ministries in 1952.

The fundamental unit of industrial activity is the enterprise. Each

---

[6] Problems abounded even at key projects built with Soviet aid. The cost of enlarging Shenyang's No. 1 Machine Tool Plant, for example, turned out to be five times the initial estimate.

[7] Commenting on the American scene, David Novick and others, *Wartime Production Controls* (New York: Columbia University Press, 1949), p. 287, report that "no phase of industrial and civilian mobilization for war was the subject of as extended discussion and as consistently bad administration as was construction."

enterprise is headed by a director or manager. In addition to the technical functions of procurement, production, and sales work, directors enjoyed broad latitude over personnel and wage matters during the FFYP years. This system of "one-man management," based on Soviet practice, was subsequently challenged, and executive authority partially transferred to enterprise branches of the Communist Party. Party control reached a peak during the Great Leap Forward (1958–60), declined during the early 1960s, and may have rebounded under the Revolutionary Committees which have assumed nominal control of enterprise operations in the wake of the Cultural Revolution (1966–68).

The chief obligation of the firm, and of the managers and Party personnel occupying key posts, is to carry out the annual economic plans issued by the State Council and other organs of the central government. Despite periodic changes in the list of norms and in their relative importance, plan targets have always included figures for sales value and physical output of major commodities; financial quotas involving wages, costs, and profit; and subsidiary requirements concerning input coefficients, research, and innovation. Enterprises may also receive additional assignments such as expanding productive capacity, training workers for other firms, and meeting special orders outside the current plan.

Enterprise plans typically emerge from consultations between factory executives and ministry officials. The center prepares preliminary drafts on the basis of overall policy objectives and the detailed information collected from below. Enterprise directors, and more recently workers, normally have an opportunity to discuss these draft plans and to suggest revisions before the final version is adopted. This bargaining process provides ample scope for enterprises to resist excessive output targets or to request additional materials, labor, or equipment before accepting difficult assignments.

This summarizes the institutional framework of Chinese industry. Producers are subordinate to a dual network of control by government and Party organizations (now complicated by the increasing role of provincial and local governments and their industrial and planning bureaucracies). Industrial units are charged with carrying out economic plans, but participate actively in their formulation. Within the enterprise, authority is shared among professional managers, engineers, Party personnel, and worker organizations. The relative strength of these groups is not constant, but has shifted with changes in the political and economic climate.

In theory, the aim of this planning system is to furnish each unit with precisely enough equipment, materials, labor, and working capital to allow plans to be met if all resources are deployed with maximum economy. If achieved, this goal of making each input a bottleneck for every unit maximizes output at the microeconomic level and simultaneously exposes the incompetence of managers who fail to meet the targets for their units.

Chinese economic planning, however, falls far short of the ideal. Especially in the early years, planners lacked the detailed studies of average and marginal input-output coefficients needed to anticipate the effect of changing the resource mix allotted to each enterprise. Even for sectors which consume only a few basic raw materials, the persistence of large differences among firms and over time in such technical data as the coke required to smelt one ton of pig iron makes it difficult to forecast movements of actual, let alone potentially attainable relations between supplies and output.[8] In addition, the accumulation of technical and managerial skills may cause further unpredictable shifts in input-output ratios. These limits to the exactness of industrial planning apply with added force in more complex sectors. The plethora of established, new, and modified machinery products, for instance, makes it virtually impossible to determine capital-output ratios or materials requirements with any degree of precision.

Under these circumstances, Chinese industrial planning is necessarily a heavy-handed operation which can only aim to achieve rough consistency between input supplies and output targets for individual enterprises. This was particularly evident during the 1950s, when the inevitable confusion of early planning attempts was heightened by China's weak data base and by the paucity of trained and seasoned personnel.[9] Coupled with governmental determination to push for rapid industrial growth, these conditions led to frequent inconsistency between targets and resources.

When resources fall short of requirements, sharp conflict arises between industrial units and the state. The center's planning agencies and industrial ministries expect producers to complete all aspects of their plans with resources assigned them. Victims of egregious supply breakdowns and planning errors can hope for a sympathetic hearing in Peking, but in general, the state has no choice but to insist on the fundamental soundness of economic plans and to interpret noncompliance as evidence of managerial incompetence. Any other course would quickly destroy economic discipline.

*   *   *   *   *

To maintain the fabric of national plans as well as their own career prospects, factory executives must maximize the probability that plans can be met even with unexpected shifts in the balance between output targets and means of production. In their effort to reduce the chance of failure, factory leaders embark upon a search for slack in their operating plans. This

---

[8] Variations of up to 19 percent in unit coal consumption among three groups of thermal power plants [were reported]. At one steelworks, average monthly consumption of metal per ton of steel ingot fluctuated by over 20 percent between May and December 1953.

[9] These problems are analyzed in Cho-ming Li, *The Statistical System of Communist China* (Berkeley: University of California Press, 1962), part 1.

slack or excess capacity may consist of eliminating or relaxing certain plan targets or of increasing the volume of available resources.

Since all targets are compulsory and major inputs are, with few exceptions, limited to quotas furnished by the state, the creation of slack inevitably entails deception and concealment, and often outright illegalities on the part of enterprise directors, engineers, accountants, and Party officials.

This search for slack is not a random process. When confronted by inability to fulfill all targets, Chinese officials at all levels have tended to focus their efforts on quotas dealing with the total value of production and the quantity of physical output. Quality, cost, balance among product types, and preparations for future production are of distinctly secondary importance, and are often neglected in the interest of guaranteeing the planned flow of output.

Disproportionate attention to output volume is deeply rooted in the Soviet system of economic planning adopted in China during the 1950s. The fundamental goal of "material balance planning" is to insure supplies of predetermined quantities of commodities needed at various points for current production, investment, consumption, and export. The primacy of output volume follows directly from this foundation. If sufficient quantities of goods are produced, the intended recipients of the missing products cannot meet their obligations, and the resulting disruption will reverberate through the entire economy. If, on the other hand, quantity targets are met by skimping on quality or variety, customers have little cause for complaint. Their task of meeting ambitious targets with less than ideal resources is not unusual in an economy perpetually straining to squeeze more output from limited means.

In any system based on physical commodity flows, leaders must be willing to accept high costs to avoid delay.[10] If these costs become unbearable, a general reduction in the pace of growth is needed. But so long as the pressure to raise output remains intense, exhortation alone will not suffice to direct managerial attention toward cost, quality, assortment, and other desirable, but secondary criteria.

These matters offer little mystery to Chinese economists:

> Since the general indices of our government's plans and statistics are based on quantities, attention has thus been concentrated on these with little or no regard to quality in the distribution of missions and conducting of examinations on the part of responsible organizations on the upper level.

---

[10] The rationality of paying heavily for promptness is a major theme of Robert C. Repetto, *Time in India's Development Programs* (Cambridge, Mass.: Harvard University Press, 1971). U.S. defense procurement uses systems "in which the control of time is often achieved at large costs in performance and money." See Carl Kaysen, "Improving the Efficiency of Military Research and Development," *Public Policy*, vol. 12 (1963), p. 254.

With Peking's eyes riveted on quantity, factory officials must follow suit. Frequently disputes between managers and inspectors reveal the institutional grounds for neglecting quality:

> Factory manager Chao demanded that inspector Li certify rejects to enable the plant to meet its output quota. Li refused. Chao then appointed Li assistant shop chief and ordered him to see that the plan was fulfilled. Li immediately changed his tune and demanded that the rejects be certified, but another conscientious inspector refused to give in and Chao's plan failed.

Rigidly enforced output quotas encourage a cycle of alternate slack and "storming" or "shock work" which is difficult to break. At the beginning of a new plan period, holidays and equipment repairs postponed during the hectic rush to complete the previous plan divert resources from current production, as does the need to replenish depleted stocks of materials and spares. When attendance, inventories, and equipment return to normal, it is already necessary to begin rushing to fulfill the next output target. As late as 1971, People's Daily took space to commend a Shanghai machinery plant for the seemingly exceptional feat of having "changed the situation of 'working slowly at the beginning of the year and working intensively at the year-end.' "[11]

Innovation is another frequent casualty of the drive to raise output. Research and experimentation require the attention of engineers and skilled workers whose services are also needed to maintain high levels of output. Complaints that "many enterprise leaders who are very concerned about plan fulfillment pay little attention to new product work" fall on deaf ears as long as quantity rules supreme. Conflict between research and production persists. In 1971 at Shanghai's Hungch'i Shipyard,

> under the conditions of the urgency of the task of production, there were some people, including some members of the basic level revolutionary committee, who said, "The task of production is already so heavy, where is there time for carrying out innovation?" There were even some who said, "The task of production is a 'hard target,' but the task of scientific research is a 'soft target.' "

In addition to selective neglect of targets, the firm can also lighten its task by increasing its stock of productive resources. Vertical integration and excess inventory accumulation illustrate this type of behavior.

With suppliers focusing their attention on raising output volume, it is not surprising to find numerous complaints of tardy deliveries, defective products, poor quality, incorrect specifications, and cost overruns in Chi-

---

[11] American government agencies, universities, and other organizations with rigid fiscal years experience similarly wasteful year-end rushing to disburse funds. John P. Miller, *Pricing of Military Procurements* (New Haven, Conn.: Yale University Press, 1949), p. 25, cites a typical example.

nese publications. Inspectors blamed the poor performance of Shenyang's Heavy Machinery Plant on tardy delivery of wooden molds. Tientsin's Power Machinery Works received overweight, overpriced, and defective forgings. Even the army found that its cranes failed to meet specifications and were dangerous to operate. Worst of all, suppliers behaved most selfishly precisely when their cooperation was most urgently needed—in the tense weeks preceding the close of annual and quarterly plan periods.

Under these conditions, managers seek to limit the reliance of their enterprises on outside suppliers by increasing the degree of vertical integration. From the firm's viewpoint, the benefits of integration are nearly costless. Investment funds, if available, bear no interest—only depreciation is charged; and even if integration raises production costs, quirks of China's accounting system may allow profit to rise simultaneously.[12]

Captive repair shops are especially prized. A well-stocked machine shop can repair defective equipment received from outside or retool existing machinery without major investment allocations. In addition, an underutilized repair shop and its staff provide a reserve capacity to be mobilized at year-end or to impress Peking with unscheduled output increases during periodic "production and economy" drives.

The articulation of the transport and exchange mechanism which accompanies industrialization implies that working capital needs, like integration, will decline as the economy advances. As in the case of integration, however, the levels of circulating funds observed in Chinese industry often exceed technical requirements. Industrial units use excess working funds to hoard labor, to finance unauthorized fixed investments, and to maintain stockpiles of finished goods and semifabricates.[13] The most significant use of these funds, however, is to support widespread stockpiling of raw materials in excess of current requirements.

To build illegal stockpiles, managers "play it safe" by basing material requisitions on inflated input coefficients and concealing the resulting accumulation of inventories. In 1953, Anshan [iron and steel works] required 1.05 tons of metal to smelt one ton of steel ingot, but reported figures of 1.07 and 1.09 in the production and supply plans for that year. Elsewhere, "insurance" of 2–6 percent was commonly added to supply requisitions.

Despite institutional reforms and repeated inspections which rarely fail to unearth hidden stocks, demand continues to be swollen by the fictitious claims of would-be hoarders, with the result that scarcities of industrial supplies are worsened, and at times perhaps created by efforts to accumulate illicit inventories.

This system of organization and the deviations which it generates will

---

[12] Absence of interest charges on fixed capital is asserted by Donnithorne, *China's Economic System*, p. 437, and seems implicit in descriptions offered to recent visitors.

[13] [One Chinese source] describes a survey of 175 enterprises under six ministries which revealed excess working capital averaging 21.1 percent of actual requirements.

make familiar reading to students of Soviet industry. In fact, Soviet co-operation and advice failed to shield the Chinese from any of the major problems of plan implementation which have plagued industry in the USSR. Weak quality control, neglect of innovation, excessive integration, stockpiling, and other problems appeared as nearly exact replicas of the prewar Soviet situation.[14]

Studies of industry in the European socialist countries attribute these difficulties to a short-term, output-oriented managerial philosophy which results from rapid turnover of executive personnel and from their pursuit of substantial monetary premiums awarded for meeting certain plan targets.[15] But in China, similar management problems have appeared even though executive bonuses and mobility are far less important than in the USSR.[16] In explaining these common tendencies, we must therefore focus on the quantitative framework of industrial planning and on the tautness between targets and resources, characteristics shared by socialist industry in Europe and China, rather than on the personal circumstances of industrial executives.[17]

IV. REFORMING THE INDUSTRIAL SYSTEM

By 1957, Chinese industrial personnel had outgrown earlier naive expectations that Soviet institutions, advanced technology, and massive investment could rapidly eliminate all obstacles to industrialization. Reforms were needed, and with eight years of experience, the Chinese felt prepared to strike out on their own. As Mao Tse-tung observed:

> In economic work, dogmatism primarily manifested itself . . . in heavy industry and planning. Since we didn't understand these things and had

---

[14] See David Granick, *Management of the Industrial Firm in the U.S.S.R.* (New York: Columbia University Press, 1954), and Joseph S. Berliner, *Factory and Manager in the U.S.S.R.* (Cambridge, Mass.: Harvard University Press, 1957).

[15] Abram Bergson, *The Economics of Soviet Planning* (New Haven, Conn.: Yale University Press, 1964), ch. 5; János Kornai, *Overcentralization in Economic Administration: A Critical Analysis Based on Experience in Hungarian Light Industry* (Oxford: Oxford University Press, 1959), p. 122. David Granick, *The Red Executive: A Study of the Organization Man in Russian Industry* (Garden City, N.Y.: Doubleday, 1960), p. 112, cites studies of the 1930s showing that under 15 percent of Soviet managers held their posts for as long as five years.

[16] In 1966 Richman found that 58 of 74 persons at or above the level of shop chief had held their posts for at least four years (*Industrial Society*, p. 299). Bonuses for Chinese executives never approached Soviet levels, and even the extent to which Chinese managers and engineers were eligible to receive premiums is not clear. See Dwight H. Perkins, *Market Control and Planning in Communist China* (Cambridge, Mass.: Harvard University Press, 1966), p. 121; Donnithorne, *China's Economic System*, pp. 208–10; Howe, *Wage Patterns*, pp. 121–27.

[17] Similar emphasis appears in David Granick, *Soviet Metal-fabricating and Economic Development: Practice vs. Policy* (Madison, Wis.: University of Wisconsin Press, 1967).

absolutely no experience, all we could do in our ignorance was to import foreign methods. . . . Now the situation has changed.[18]

Economic writers showed a growing awareness of industrial interdependence and of the resulting need to extend economic analysis beyond the broad aggregates discussed in the FFYP. The reality of technical and marketing difficulties at even the newest Soviet-built plants pinpointed the need to improve demand forecasting, an area almost entirely neglected before 1957.[19] Without careful microeconomic analysis, introduction of advanced production techniques often created undesirable side effects.

At the same time, growing information and technical resources made it possible to identify industrial problem areas and take concrete remedial steps. The progress of China's statistical system could be seen in the pages of newspapers and economic journals, which now used detailed comparisons of costs, materials consumption, quality, waste, inventories, and productivity to ask "what is advanced, who is backward?" A newly emerging professional inspectorate, increasingly well trained and equipped, carried this approach to the factory floor.

Technical difficulties exposed by factory inspectors or visiting investigation teams were now referred to a growing array of research and design institutes attached to industrial ministries, universities, and enterprises. Lack of experience and equipment initially confined many units to elementary inquiries, and some were attacked as paper organizations incapable of conducting research and existing only "because the ministry said so." Even so, reports of independent Chinese achievements in these years are not without merit, especially with regard to modifications needed to operate Soviet processes and equipment in China and in areas such as ferrous castings in which Soviet methods produced poor results.

This confluence of deepening economic insight, a growing data base and rising technical capacity naturally inspired a wide variety of proposals for improving industrial operations. These suggestions, many of which were implemented during 1957, focused on a general tightening-up of the planning process (e.g., eliminating tardy plan formulation); added emphasis on product quality, customer service, and interunit cooperation; restraints on the growth of accumulation; higher priority for coastal and small-scale industry; and sectoral investment shifts favoring raw materials and agricultural support production.[20]

---

18 *Mao Tse-tung Unrehearsed*, ed. Stuart Schram (Harmondsworth, Eng.: Penguin Books, 1974), pp. 98–99.

19 Officials at the new Soviet-aided Loyang Bearing Works complained that steel producers were not only unable to supply needed materials, but in some cases were unaware of the new plant's existence. Similar problems arose at other new plants, including Anshan's Seamless Tube Mill, Wuhan Steel Corp., Shenyang No. 1 and No. 2 Machine Tool Plants, Ch'angch'un No. 1 Motor Vehicle Works, and Harbin Electric Meter Plant.

20 Many of the proposals are described in Jan S. Prybyla, *The Political Economy of Communist China* (Scranton, Pa.: International Textbook Company, 1970), ch. 7.

These timely changes were swept away by the Great Leap Forward of 1958–60, a succession of campaigns which obliged industry to concentrate almost exclusively on raising output volume. Central controls over funds, manpower, and materials dissolved. Within enterprises, technicians, inspectors, and managers were shunted aside in favor of less conservative leaders who pushed for bold acceleration of production.

Despite long-run benefits from the research efforts and expanded industrial participation of these years, the Leap's overall impact on industry was strongly negative, as uncoordinated pursuit of higher output accentuated weaknesses already apparent in factory operations.

By 1960, the partial breakdown of normal planning and reporting procedures had greatly increased the need for industrial consolidation. To this was added the twin blows of Soviet technical withdrawal, which left key investment projects unfinished and threatened to disrupt supplies of petroleum and military goods, and of consecutive poor harvests, which signaled the need to sharply increase industry's support of agriculture. The demand shifts resulting from these setbacks transformed an unavoidable adjustment process into a crisis in which industrial collapse became a genuine possibility.

As the magnitude of these difficulties became clear, specialists temporarily eclipsed by Mao Tse-tung's personal intervention in economic decision making gradually reasserted control over industrial administration. This group, whose supporters seem to have included such prominent individuals as Liu Shao-ch'i, Chou En-lai, Teng Hsiao-p'ing, Po I-po, Li Hsien-nien, Li Fu-ch'un, T'ao Chu, and Sun Yeh-fang, instituted reforms which went far beyond the changes proposed in 1957. Their policies, which began to appear as early as 1959 and were forcefully applied beginning in 1961, are summarized in the famous and controversial "Seventy Articles Concerning Industrial Enterprises and Mines."[21]

The "Seventy Articles" required enterprises to submit detailed information on their capital stock, inventories, and productive capacity; to curtail unauthorized construction, recruitment, and sales; and to develop programs for monitoring finance, resource consumption, productivity, cost, and quality—all signs of a new determination to exercise firm central control over industry. Emphasis on the "system of responsibility assumed by the factory superintendent under the leadership of the Party committee"; the authority of specialist personnel in the fields of inspection, stock-taking and finance; and the instruction that political "study time should be cut down as far as possible"—all showed that Party personnel and political activity were to serve the needs of current production, rather than vice-versa.[22]

---

[21] A summary of this unpublished document appears in *Documents of Chinese Communist Party Central Committee, September 1956–April 1969* (Kowloon: Union Research Institute, 1971), vol. 1, pp. 689–93.

[22] Ibid. The Party journal *Red Flag* emphasized that "technical problems must be decided on mainly by the technicians."

The authors of the new policies did not shrink from drastic measures. Unproductive resources were summarily dismissed from industry. Unqualified workers who had obtained factory positions during the Great Leap were ordered back to farming.[23] As monetary controls tightened, firms strugged to reduce costs and to avoid the injunction that "except with special instructions . . . losing concerns . . . should stop operation."[24]

The most important change was Peking's reversal of its earlier emphasis on output maximization. The new orders stipulated that "products that are not up to standard shall not be allowed to leave the factory."[25] The party journal *Red Flag* reiterated this directive adding that "products that fail to come up to the quality standards . . . should not be included in the output index."

Instructions to raise product quality had, of course, come from Peking before and had been widely ignored. This time, however, enterprises soon discovered that the center meant business. Tough enforcement was much in evidence. Some units were forced to suspend operations until quality standards could be met.[26] Efforts by Talien's High Pressure Valve Works to attribute substandard output to defects in the plant's equipment brought a curt rebuff from provincial and municipal authorities who ruled that unless the ministry's standards were met, output "would not be examined and accepted." Management finally promised to "adhere resolutely to the principle that accessories not conforming with standards should not be assembled, and final products not conforming with standards should not leave the factory."

Similar confrontations occurred throughout industry. Inspectors pulled no punches: at Shanghai, high waste rates in iron castings were "due to the incompetence of the technical management." Once again, products "which have not been inspected are not allowed to go out of the factory. This regulation is being strictly enforced."

With customers now expected to scrutinize incoming shipments for quality defects and even to send "representatives to the relevant production factories where they would take care of the inspection of products about to be delivered," producers found themselves obliged to heed the requirements of purchasing organizations. Visits to customers gave production personnel a vivid understanding of the importance of quality.

---

[23] The number of workers and officials at the Shihchingshan Iron and Steel Plant rose from 12,000 in February 1958 to 52,000 in July 1960, but was reduced to about 31,000 by 1964. See M. Gardner Clark, *The Development of China's Steel Industry and Soviet Technical Aid* (Ithaca, N.Y.: New York State School of Industrial and Labor Relations, Cornell University, 1973), pp. 17, 124.

[24] *Documents*, vol. 1, p. 689.

[25] *Documents*, vol. 1, p. 691.

[26] Thomas G. Rawski, "The Growth of Producer Industries, 1900–1971," in *China's Modern Economy in Historical Perspective*, ed. Dwight H. Perkins (Stanford, Cal.: Stanford University Press, 1975), p. 229.

Employees of one Shanghai firm who had never seen their products in operation were dispatched to the mines to observe at first hand the damage wrought by their own inferior workmanship. Within three years, successful reforms had catapulted the same unit into national prominence as a cost and quality leader among manufacturers of pneumatic tools.

These are not isolated examples. The considerable achievements of China's industries since 1960, a period in which imports comprised a small, and until recently, declining portion of available supplies of producer goods, could not have occurred without a general restructuring of managerial priorities.[27] Increased industrial support for agriculture, completion of projects abandoned by Soviet technicians, and massive output expansion in petroleum, chemical fertilizer, electronics, weapons, and other comparatively new industries involved thousands of enterprises and millions of workers. Progress in each of these fields presupposed careful attention to specification and workmanship which, as we have seen, was often absent prior to 1960.

The regional pattern of industrial advance lends further support to this view. If added investment were the chief source of recent industrial gains, older industrial centers which were excluded from the investment boom of the 1950s should be conspicuously absent from the cutting edge of technical advance.[28] In fact, the opposite is true. Technological leadership rests in China's older industrial centers, particularly Shanghai.

Shanghai is very much the hub of Chinese industry. Its preeminence is widely recognized, and the list of commodities in which Shanghai producers are national pacesetters runs the entire gamut of manufacturing. Machine tools, diesels, steel, bicycles, computers, cable, pumps, sewing machines, mining equipment, machinery for petroleum and fertilizer plants, transformers, and a wide range of consumer manufactures are among the areas in which, as one newspaper headline put it, "The Nation Looks to Shanghai for Production Experiences."[29]

As qualitative considerations took on added importance in appraising

---

[27] After allowing for inflation, the U.S. Central Intelligence Agency, *China: Foreign Trade in Machinery and Equipment Since 1952* (Washington, D.C., 1975), p. 6, estimates China's 1973 machinery imports to have been 1.4 percent above the 1957 level and 31 percent below the average for 1958–60. At the same time, *Peking Review*, no. 48 (1972), p. 17, reports that domestic output of machinery (probably including military hardware) rose by 1,200 percent between 1957 and 1971 alone.

[28] Data compiled by Nicholas R. Lardy and myself indicate that Shanghai, which turned out 19 percent of national industrial output in 1957, received only three of more than 150 Soviet-aided projects and a mere 2.5 percent of overall investment outlays during 1953–57. Tientsin fared no better, gaining only a 7 percent increase in its machine tool stock during 1953–57, years in which gross fixed investment in industry amounted to over double the 1952 capital stock.

[29] For further discussion, see Thomas G. Rawski, "Problems of Technology Absorption in Chinese Industry," *American Economic Review*, vol. 65, no. 2 (May 1975), pp. 383–88.

industrial performance, older units substituted experience for capital equipment and outstripped newer enterprises to a degree which could not have occurred under the "output-first" rules of the 1950s. As one Chinese writer observed, with their "skilled veteran workers and experienced technical persons" and superior interenterprise cooperation, another legacy of the past, "old industrial bases and old enterprises . . . find it easier to tackle . . . complicated technical problems than new enterprises and new industrial bases."

With the planning system in disarray after a three-year lapse in central control, this shift toward new priorities was necessarily gradual, with reinstatement of expert personnel often a necessary preliminary. At the important Yung-li-ning Chemical Works, for example,[30]

> In arranging work for the technical workers, the factory leaders pay attention to exert the special skills of these workers, so that they can apply what they have learned . . . the deputy head of the education section, who has special experiences in the control of technical materials . . . is now, based on his special knowledge and the needs of technical work developments, transferred back to the control of technical materials.

Lower-level opposition to the reversal of Great Leap initiatives may explain the delayed response of some units to new instructions: T'aiyuan Chemical Works did not begin efforts to eliminate financial losses until late 1962, and neither quality upgrading at Shenyang No. 1 Machine Tool Works nor financial reforms at Peking's Boiler Works began until 1963.

One sign of growing compliance was the confidence with which Peking supported wage and bonus systems based on individual piece rates. In December 1961, Anshan's No. 2 Steel Plant reported that "at the grand judgment at the end of the month, based on the accumulated units for each individual, (the leadership) determines the grades of superiority and awards them each with different grades of material rewards."[31] Since past experience had shown that these policies gave workers an incentive to raise output at the expense of quality, they would not have been brought forward unless factory officials and shop chiefs were prepared to enforce the desired stress on quality rather than volume.

As qualitative concerns took root throughout industry, Peking showed a growing willingness to substitute indirect evaluation in place of detailed regulation of production, investment, resource allocation, and research. The advantage of this system, which lent credence to subsequent allegations that economic policy had "placed profit in command" was described as follows:

---

[30] See also Stephen Andors, "Factory Management and Political Ambiguity, 1961–63," *China Quarterly*, no. 59 (July–September 1974), pp. 435–76.

[31] See also Howe, *Wage Patterns*, pp. 122–23, and Andors, "Factory Management," pp. 57–59.

whether or not an enterprise returns its loan to the bank . . . is a very good yardstick for measuring its operations management and economic accounting. If an obstacle has been encountered at any of the links of production and circulation, it will be reflected here. Such a method of inspecting . . . an enterprise *is simple and direct and can provide clues to many complicated economic problems.*[32]

At the same time, one can discern a modest shift toward regional, local, and enterprise autonomy. One sign of this is the vigorous expansion of small rural industries, often financed and directed at the county level and below, which began around 1964 and has continued to the present.[33] These enterprises now account for a significant share of overall industrial output (possibly 10–15 percent), and have contributed substantially to the expansion of certain industries, especially chemical fertilizer and cement. Local financing and marketing insure that managers of small plants will strive to maintain adequate standards of quality and profitability. Their ability to do so is enhanced by the results of research efforts begun during the Great Leap, by the accumulation of production experience and by increased flows of specialized equipment and personnel from the urban industrial sector.

Research is another area in which the center has allowed a gradual dispersion of authority. After several years in which priorities were closely circumscribed by Peking, enterprises were urged to develop independent programs of applied research based on the combined skills of technicians and ordinary shop hands.

Continuing a trend begun with the downward transfer of some industrial enterprises to the provinces and municipalities in 1957–58, provinces and localities seem to have acquired a share of the planning and supervision tasks formerly assigned to industrial ministries and the State Planning Commission. In supply work, for example, regional and local government agencies now take an active role in resource allocation by organizing distribution conferences and managing commodity banks.[34]

These measures partially offset the inherent weaknesses in China's industrial system discussed above. The quality problem, for example, is under attack from both sides of the marketplace. Small plants, many developed on local initiative, now serve rural customers where the products of large factories are unsuited to their needs either because of inadequate variety (farm machinery) or inordinately high standards (iron and steel, cement). The removal of these responsibilities from the tasks assigned to large enterprises allows these units to divert human and material resources to the

---

[32] Emphasis added.

[33] For further discussion see Jon Sigurdson, "Rural Industrialization in China," in *China: A Reassessment of the Economy*, pp. 411–35.

[34] Richman, *Industrial Society*, pp. 712–20. I am indebted to Professor Bruce L. Reynolds for more recent information on this subject.

innovative and quality goals stressed by the center. As improved methods for allocating materials lessen the chance of inconsistency between targets and resources, enterprises can reduce the time and effort spent on accumulating "insurance" in the form of surplus materials and capacity.

Limited decentralization thus relieves some of the obvious "system costs" of a planned economy while allowing continued central direction of what the Chinese term the "commanding heights" of industry. The ubiquitous presence of the People's Bank, which participates in most significant transactions and seems responsible solely to the center, is itself sufficient to insure Peking's ultimate control over industrial operations at all levels. Continued supervision is also implicit in reports of frequent contact between central and lower-level personnel and in the regular submission of provincial, local, and enterprise plans for Peking's scrutiny and approval.

V. RECENT DEVELOPMENTS

The Cultural Revolution (1966–68) brought bitter attacks on post-Leap economic policies, incidentally providing further evidence of their widespread implementation. As we have seen, complaints that industrial leaders had "taken the capitalist road" by emphasizing production, profit, and material incentives at the expense of "making revolution" were not without foundation. Beginning in December 1966, youthful Red Guards and other protest groups were allowed into industrial units to combat capitalist tendencies among their personnel and management.

The new revolutionaries met with forceful opposition at all levels of industrial administration. Perhaps because the anarchistic tendencies of the insurgents stirred memories of the near-disastrous aftermath of the Great Leap, there was continuous pressure to limit the extent of disruption and to maintain some semblance of industrial normality.[35]

These efforts did not prevent sporadic disruptions of production and temporary displacement of managers, accountants, and engineering personnel. Provincial reports indicate that overall industrial output fell by 14 percent between 1966 and 1968, but in the following year production already surpassed the 1966 peak by 14 percent.[36] As industry gradually returned to normal, it became evident that radical initiatives had failed to dislodge the incumbent industrial leadership and that policy would continue to develop along lines established during the early 1960s.

Chinese of all political persuasions are well aware that the complexity of industrial operations makes it increasingly difficult to dispense with the

---

[35] Some evidence of this is in Thomas G. Rawski, "Recent Trends in the Chinese Economy," *China Quarterly*, no. 53 (January–March 1973), pp. 26–27.

[36] Based on data compiled by Robert M. Field, Nicholas R. Lardy, and John P. Emerson.

services of expert personnel. It is therefore not surprising to find that reinstatement of disgraced specialists began as early as 1967. As one editorial
entitled "Bring Back the Industrial Experts" put it:

> The design of products . . . drawing up of technical specifications . . .
> trial-making of new products . . . technical innovation . . . scientific re-
> search, et cetera, require the participation of the engineers and tech-
> nicians. . . . Without the engineers and technicians taking part in these
> activities, the level of . . . management of an enterprise cannot be
> heightened.

Except for a few who are "unwilling to serve socialism," politically deviant
experts are not to be spurned: they can be remolded on the job.

These views, which echo principles articulated 10 years earlier, are much
in evidence at the microeconomic level. The Communist Party committee
of Talien's Steel Mill found that "the essential management personnel
were too much reduced" during the Cultural Revolution, and reacted by
increasing the number of professional managers and returning recently appointed worker-managers to the production line. Fushun's Coal Research
Institute offers special encouragement to intellectuals "trained in the old
schools." Politicization of specialist functions is excoriated in unusually
harsh terms:

> We often encounter . . . comrades in financial work . . . who chant
> slogans about giving prominence to proletarian politics and speeding up
> socialist construction. But they could not give an answer when asked how
> much money a certain project would require, when the project could be
> completed for production, and how its economic effect could be developed
> to the fullest extent.

The impressions of recent visitors to the People's Republic reinforce
documentary evidence of continuity in industrial policy. Barnett finds
that[37]

> Chinese Communist cadres make it very clear that central authorities
> again exercise effective and extensive overall control over the economy.
> One obtains the impression . . . that even though major annual targets
> are supposed to be set through a process that begins with proposals "from
> the bottom," in reality the crucial decisions about the most important
> targets are handed down "from the top."

Meisner's study of the Shenyang Transformer Factory supports this view:
after semiannual consultations in Peking, the plant receives a plan which
"specifies quantity, quality, variety, cost relationships, labor productivity,
profits, and funding" and "also determines the total number of workers
and the total amount of the wage bill."[38] Visitors to Peking's No. 1 Ma-

---

[37] A. Doak Barnett, *Uncertain Passage: China's Transition to the Post-Mao Era*
(Washington, D.C.: Brookings Institution, 1974), p. 139.

[38] Mitch Meisner, "The Shenyang Transformer Factory—A Profile," *China Quarterly*, no. 52 (October–December 1972), p. 721.

chine Tool Plant received an account of plan formulation little different from descriptions published in industrial journals of the mid-1950s.[39]

Similarly, Joan Robinson finds that new industrial hiring "has to be sanctioned by the Planning Commission." As for regional autonomy, "the province carried the proposals of all its enterprises to the Planning Commission," evidently to secure approval, and "every province has put in schemes of investment and the center has to ration them out." The "rules of management" in industry include such familiar provisions as "no defective goods shall be allowed to leave the factory" and "there must be strict accounting." These rules are not new, but "were drawn up much earlier" although now implemented in a new spirit.[40]

Central authority is most evident in the crucial sphere of finance. As in the 1950s, Peking determines the level of provincial and municipal expenditures through a system of revenue sharing which transfers large sums from Shanghai and other advanced regions to less developed areas.[41] At the enterprise level, budgets are authorized at the center and supervised by the People's Bank. According to Cassou, "all financial needs relating to industrial investments are directly controlled by the state budget" and "the People's Bank rigorously controls the financial situation of an enterprise."[42]

All this indicates an absence of major policy shifts in the wake of the Cultural Revolution. As can be seen from Premier Chou En-lai's report on government work submitted to the National People's Congress held in January 1975, growth continues to occupy a leading position in the constellation of Chinese industrial objectives, but expansion is now limited by the requirement that major effort be directed toward complementarity, raising standards, and technical development.[43] Instead of concentrating on short-term increases in its own rate of expansion, the primary objective of the 1950s, China's industry has broadened its objectives, and now seeks to meet the needs of all sectors, including itself, for current inputs and future growth.

---

[39] "Collective Notes of the First Friendship Delegation of American Radical Political Economists to the People's Republic of China" (Ann Arbor, Michigan, 1972, processed), p. 18.

[40] Joan Robinson, *Economic Management in China* (London: Anglo-Chinese Educational Institute, 1973), pp. 20, 24, 25, 33.

[41] Ibid., p. 27. On revenue sharing, see Nicholas R. Lardy, "Economic Planning in the People's Republic of China: Central-Provincial Fiscal Relations," in *China: A Reassessment of the Economy*, pp. 94–115.

[42] Pierre-Henri Cassou, "The Chinese Monetary System," *China Quarterly*, no. 59 (July–September 1974), pp. 561, 564.

[43] "Excerpts from Address by Chou to the Congress in Peking," *New York Times*, January 21, 1975, p. 12.

VI. EFFICIENCY

To what degree has the industrial system described in the preceding pages enabled China to attain her major economic objectives of rapid growth, structural change, technological modernization, and military self-sufficiency? Given the resources and skills at their command, could the Chinese have achieved better results with different forms of industrial organization and management?

In a dynamic economy such as China's, these questions of efficiency cannot be answered in terms of a few summary statistics. What is needed is a careful comparison of Chinese and foreign performance in a number of areas related to overall efficiency. The following pages represent only a preliminary effort in this direction.

We begin with Paretian efficiency, which measures the performance of economies in which resources, technology, tastes, and income distribution do not change. Under these conditions, a configuration of outputs, inputs, and consumption is efficient in the Pareto sense if raising the output or consumption of any product by any economic agent necessitates reduced output or consumption elsewhere in the system.

Economic theorists have shown that Paretian efficiency cannot be attained unless each economic unit attaches the same relative values to all commodities and services. We have already seen, however, that this requirement is often violated in China's industry. Product quality, vertical integration, and inventories provide clear-cut evidence of deviations from the Paretian ideal.

Central planners, factory managers, quality inspectors, and customers do not impute identical relative values to standard and defective products. An enterprise struggling to meet its annual output target may regard minor defects in workmanship as costless, a viewpoint which customers are unlikely to share. Excessive vertical integration also appears nearly costless to the firm, which pays no interest on its fixed capital. From a national perspective, however, the costs of maintaining underutilized manufacturing facilities in a capital-scarce environment are obvious. Hoarding creates similar difficulties. Some units may be forced to reduce output for lack of materials which are in short supply only because some users have managed to conceal reserves of these items. Again, it is evident that aggregate output could rise if existing resources were properly distributed.

These examples leave no doubt that full Pareto efficiency is not achieved in Chinese industry. But is China's system more or less efficient than industry in other countries? Since departures from the Pareto ideal are as difficult to measure as they are easy to detect, there can be no simple answer to this question.

In fact, no economy can approach the Paretian ideal. Numerous studies indicate that the search for growth and profit often leads American and

European firms to deceive customers and public officials, hoard scarce resources, neglect quality, invest irrationally, and generally pursue microeconomic gain to the detriment of macroeconomic welfare. Organizational parallels between Western corporations and industry in the socialist bloc suggest similar degrees of economic inefficiency.[44] Bernard Baruch's conclusion regarding the extent of Paretian inefficiency, written in 1921, remains valid today:

> experience . . . has clearly demonstrated that there are many practices in American industry which cost the ultimate consumers in the aggregate enormous sums without enriching the producers.[45]

Industrial inefficiency is also common in the developing world. The combination of extensive trade barriers and elephantine rationing of foreign currency found in many countries creates domestic sellers' markets for industrial products and leads manufacturers in the direction of poor quality, neglect of innovation, hoarding, and systematic efforts to deceive and manipulate government agencies.[46] Elsewhere, inflation lowers the real cost of capital toward or even below the zero level observed in China, and provides familiar incentives for excessive integration and mechanization.[47]

Despite the existence of inefficiency in the industrial sectors of nonsocialist nations, both advanced and backward, the organizational uniformity of Chinese industry leads to the presumption that departures from the Paretian ideal are more severe under Chinese (or Soviet) institutions than with relatively heterogeneous systems of management and control. Even if individual Chinese firms create no more inefficiency than their foreign counterparts, the rigidity typified by the requirement that each unit fulfill its plan on the same date leads to uniform deviations which are compounded into quantitatively significant national economic problems.

In a nonsocialist economy, the inertia of one producer may be undone by the alert intervention of profit-seeking entrepreneurs. But in China, the drive for plan fulfillment provides a common source of microeconomic deviation which, despite the beneficial impact of recent reforms, tilts the whole industrial sector toward inefficiencies of which excessive integration and stockpiling provide only two examples.

Paretian efficiency, however, cannot tell the whole story about any real

---

[44] As Ely Devons puts it, "When one reads about the behavior and problems of the firm in Russia, what is striking is the similarity, not the contrast, with the problems and behavior of firms in England or the United States" (*Papers on Planning and Economic Management* [Manchester, Eng.: Manchester University Press, 1970], p. 85).

[45] Baruch, *American Industry*, p. 71.

[46] Bela Balassa, "Growth Strategies in Semi-Industrial Countries," *Quarterly Journal of Economics*, vol. 84, no. 1 (February 1970), pp. 24–47, and Jagdish N. Bhagwati and Padma Desai, *India, Planning for Industrialization* (London: Oxford University Press, 1970), provide numerous examples.

[47] Balassa, "Growth Strategies," pp. 32, 45.

economy. The Pareto concept explicitly assumes fixed and immutable technical relations between inputs consumed and commodities produced: an implicit relationship between society's resource stock and the actual level of factor utilization also lurks in the background. Leibenstein has emphasized the artificiality of these postulates, arguing that an economy typically operates along a socially determined production frontier which is separated from the higher, technically determined frontier to a degree which depends on such factors as the length and pace of the work day, the level of competition, and the extent of managerial familiarity with production processes.[48] To this insight we should add that the location of the technical frontier itself depends on the extent to which society chooses to direct available resources into productive activity.

Both arguments imply that efficiency must reflect not only movements along a single production frontier (as in the Paretian case) but also the degree to which actual production approaches a limit defined by technical rather than social norms. "X-efficiency" is the term which Leibenstein uses to describe the latter criterion.

China's comparative performance in the realm of X-efficiency appears unusually strong. We know that whatever its defects, China's industrial system generates strong and continuous pressure for higher output. The growth of production occupies a central position in Chinese managerial objectives analogous to the primacy of profit in the "satisficing" mentality of Western corporations.

In any society, awareness of the risks of supply disruption and concern for professional reputations make managers err on the side of conservatism in estimating productive capacity. But in China, hesitant managers are bombarded with demands for better results and reports of other units' success in overcoming obstacles to improved performance. Closer to home, enterprise Party committees and worker groups agitate against conservatism and force management toward fuller disclosure of potential than could be achieved in direct negotiations with Peking.

As a result, Chinese industry displays a "ratchet effect" which operates not to maintain prices, but to prevent increases in unit consumption of labor and materials. Since wide differences in technical levels create large inter-plant cost variations in most industries, emphasis on physical indicators permits greater comparability and hence sharper competition among units than would a more general cost criterion. Again, public discussion identifies leaders and spurs laggards to improve their performance.

Internal opposition to higher X-efficiency is absent or subdued in China. Trade unions are more likely to promote higher output than to campaign for on-the-job leisure. Although goldbricking undoubtedly exists, individual workers have much to gain by revealing productivity-enhancing suggestions to their superiors. Inventive workers can earn national recognition and

---

[48] Harvey Leibenstein, "Allocative Efficiency Versus 'X-efficiency,'" *American Economic Review*, vol. 56, no. 3 (June 1966), pp. 392–415.

Party membership; monetary rewards and general approbation accrue to workers who demonstrate enthusiasm and creativity on the job.

Finally, China has abolished barriers to the free circulation of technical information which restrict the level of X-efficiency in the West. Instead of spending large sums to guard trade secrets from rivals, leading manufacturers conduct training schools for workers from less-advanced units. A comprehensive system of spare-time education, technical conferences and inter-plant visits disseminates basic knowledge and spreads the latest innovations throughout industry.

All these measures contribute to reducing the gap between realized and potential output with fixed resources. In addition, Chinese policy has vigorously attacked the problem of mobilizing resources to achieve maximum expansion of the technological production frontier. General measures in this direction, including a high and rising investment rate, employment of seasonally idle rural labor, active recruitment of females into the labor force, and major advances in education and public health are all well known. Exploitation of marginal resource deposits by small rural industries and fixing industrial prices in accordance with average rather than marginal costs, a tendency apparent in U.S. military procurement during World War II, provide further examples of policies which raise the degree to which available resources are utilized in production.[49]

Except for a relatively small number of industries involved in vigorous price competition and rare instances of commodity shortage, the peacetime economies of the industrial West cannot match the strong and continuous pressure for improved X-efficiency which is a daily feature of China's industrial scene. The recent oil contretemps, for instance, showed that "with little or no effort, American industries of all descriptions . . . can save at least 10 percent of the energy they used to consume."[50] At the same time, European firms are believed to incur excessive wage costs of 20–30 percent.[51] It is difficult to believe that surpluses of this magnitude can be found in Chinese consumption of raw materials, the dominant cost component in most sectors of industry.

---

[49] On the American side, one is struck by Miller's claim that "the adoption of the negotiated contract in place of . . . formal competitive bidding represented the greatest single step in the development of procurement policies during the war," even though "industry inevitably has the upper hand in these negotiations because of its superior information and the existence of a seller's market in war." See Miller, *Pricing of Military Procurements*, pp. 84–85, 44, which also notes (p. 13) that war contracts were extended to small firms "even though a price differential . . . might be necessary."

[50] Gene Smith, "A Number of Energy-Reduction Methods Help U.S. Companies Save More than 10 Percent," *New York Times*, March 4, 1974, p. 45.

[51] *New York Times*, February 1, 1974, p. 40. The informant for this story, a management consultant, also asserted that industrial efficiency varies inversely with the strength of price competition: oil, computer, tobacco, beer, and cosmetic firms show the worst performance, while textile producers who "have to be pretty hardnosed to survive" do best.

Similar results would probably emerge from comparisons of China and other developing nations. Inventory data from several dozen major enterprises in India and China, for example, show that Indian firms typically require much more working capital for inventories alone than Chinese firms use for all purposes.[52]

In view of these considerations, it does not seem unreasonable to conclude that Chinese industry probably achieves a degree of X-efficiency which is not normally observed in nonsocialist economies. China's system displays a clear advantage in terms of mobilizing resources for productive use. At the same time, managers are strongly motivated to squeeze the most from available resources by raising output, lowering unit input coefficients, and sharing information. Lacking organized strife within enterprises or secrecy between them, Chinese workers and their leaders appear able to approach industry's technical production frontier more closely than could be expected elsewhere.

Finally, we must touch upon the dynamic aspects of Chinese performance. The presence or absence of either type of static efficiency—Paretian or X-efficiency—tells nothing about an economy's responsiveness to shifts in priorities or in the underlying parameters and constraints imposed by nature and by domestic or international politics. Here, too, China's record appears strong.

With its "command economy" characteristics, China's industry has successfully adjusted to a series of major and discontinuous shifts in allocation and demand: swift growth of the rate of investment after 1949; sudden expansion of the military demand for producer goods after 1960; and in the past 15 years, a continuing shift toward agricultural support activities.

The utility of administrative control over key resources in times of large and rapid shifts in allocation is accepted wisdom among Western economists, whose broad preference for the market system is waived during wartime.[53]

Western economists also agree that the market fails to direct sufficient resources into areas which combine great technical uncertainty with high cost and long gestation periods.[54] This is why we accept a monopsony-

---

[52] Indian data from Bhagwati and Desai, *India*, p. 167; Chinese data from Nai-ruenn Chen, *Chinese Economic Statistics* (Chicago: Aldine Publishing Company, 1967), p. 282.

[53] After setting out to criticize the direct controls implemented in the United States during World War II, Tibor Scitovsky, Edward Shaw, and Lorie Tarshis are forced to conclude that, especially in military-related goods, "the pricing system would not allocate goods adequately" in a future national emergency. See their *Mobilizing Resources for War: The Economic Alternative* (New York: McGraw-Hill Book Company, 1951), p. 207.

[54] Kenneth Arrow, "Economic Welfare and the Allocation of Resources for Invention," in *The Economics of Technological Change*, ed. Nathan Rosenberg (Harmondsworth, Eng.: Penguin Books, 1971), p. 169.

oligopoly relation between government and major defense suppliers despite the copiously documented propensity of this system to produce undesirable side effects which closely resemble the "system costs" found in Chinese and Soviet industry.[55]

Many of China's producer industries regularly engage in innovative tasks which from their perspective involve uncertainties no less serious than those faced by U.S. aerospace contractors. For these industries—and the list must include important elements of the machinery, chemical, metallurgy, petroleum, and defense sectors—China's choice of an allocative framework based on intensive negotiation between government and suppliers should be readily comprehensible to market-oriented Western economists.

Direct international comparison of the adjustment and innovative characteristics of industry is difficult. However, the experience of the 1960s has certainly demonstrated that Chinese industry is capable of meeting urgently required shifts in demand when recourse to imports is not possible. Although no crisis encountered by other large developing nations has placed similar pressures on their domestic industries, available evidence suggests that neither Brazil nor India, for example, could generate a stronger response to a major economic setback than was demonstrated by the Chinese in the wake of the Great Leap Forward.

VII. CONCLUSION

China's system of planned socialist industrialization aims at rapid transformation of the economy by mobilizing resources to raise output for investment and defense as well as for consumption. Consumer preferences, including individual desires for leisure both on and off the job, occupy a distinctly subordinate position in the constellation of official goals.

In light of these objectives, our evaluation of performance in China's post-1949 industrial system must be broadly favorable. The preceding survey has shown that reliance on administrative rather than market control over resource allocation has contributed to China's achievement in raising the level, changing the structure and compressing the real cost of industrial output. This finding draws support from favorable comparisons of industrial growth in China and in other large industrial latecomers, and also from the revealed preference of the industrial democracies for nonmarket distribution of essential resources in wartime, when resource mobilization and rapid structural change replace consumer welfare as primary national goals.

---

[55] See Frederic M. Scherer, *The Weapons Acquisition Process* (Boston: Division of Research, Graduate School of Business Administration, Harvard University, 1964), which refers specifically to the Soviet parallel on pp. 211 ff.

We have also found that, despite its successes, Chinese industry remains far from ideally efficient, especially in Paretian terms. Emphasis on quality objectives, limited decentralization, increased attention to profit and cost criteria, and the "ratchet effect" of state and Party pressure for constant improvement in industrial operations have raised the minimum performance floor beneath which enterprises can expect swift official criticism, but recent news reports show that excessive attention to output volume, hoarding, unwillingness to innovate, and other malpractices have not disappeared from China's industrial scene.

The presence of these and other forms of resource leakage from productive tasks is not unique to China. Any system has its own built-in waste— the effects of pollution, commuting, and product differentiation come to mind in the American case—and it is difficult to argue that these costs are higher in China than elsewhere.[56]

In China's case, the remaining hardcore inefficiencies are much easier to detect than to remedy. Hoarding, for example, could be curtailed by combining stringent control of working funds, random inventory checks, and harsh, well-publicized punishment of violators. But without major reforms in the whole system of allocating and distributing materials, reduced inventories would raise the chances of supply-linked disruptions throughout industry, and might lower rather than raise output. The administrative and financial cost of the changes needed to maintain smooth production could easily outweigh the more obvious gains from liquidating excessive stockpiles.

This finding provides a typical illustration of the theory of the second-best, which teaches that correcting one among many inefficiencies may do more harm than good. The history of Soviet economic reform proposals as well as American defense procurement shows that even marginal institutional shifts may conceal a crossfire of analytic complications. This lends authority to the suggestion that in China, too, simple and seemingly beneficial reforms might set off complex interactions which could interfere with the basic goals of growth and structural change.

It is entirely possible that with their relatively static product mix, modest growth rates, and markets which show signs of becoming less homogeneous as personal incomes rise, China's consumer industries could benefit from a substantial shift toward market-linked methods of allocation. But in the dominant producer sector, the continuing prominence of ambitious targets, technical uncertainty, and unpredictable demand suggests that, as in the past 25 years, fundamental institutional change holds little prospect for improving the performance of China's industrial system.

---

[56] On the concept of built-in costs, see Simon Kuznets, *Economic Growth of Nations: Total Output and Production Structure* (Cambridge, Mass.: Harvard University Press, 1971), pp. 75–98; also E. J. Mishan, *The Costs of Economic Growth* (London: Staples Press, 1967).

21

THE COMMUNE SYSTEM IN THE PEOPLE'S REPUBLIC OF CHINA*

Frederick W. Crook

The commune is one of the most important economic institutions in China. It not only produces and markets agricultural output, but also is involved in water resources, construction, and transportation projects; manages local industrial plants manufacturing producer and consumer goods; and furnishes health, education, and police services.

This detailed study—based on over 1,400 reports on individual communes—provides a careful analysis of the establishment, organization, and operation of the commune system. It discusses in turn the activities of the commune as a whole and of each of its component units—the brigade, the team, and the household. Crook explains the scheme of income distribution and its implications for incentives. He concludes with an appraisal of the factors affecting the degree of decentralization of decision making in the commune system.

I. INTRODUCTION

China's commune system consists of four parts: commune, brigade, team, and household. This system, born in the optimistic fervor of the Great Leap Forward in 1958, was reduced to a skeleton during the lean years from 1959 to 1962, but has developed greatly in the past 12 years.

Currently, China has 50,000 communes, about 25,000 less than the

* Excerpted by permission from *China: A Reassessment of the Economy* (A Compendium of Papers Submitted to the Joint Economic Committee, 94th Cong., 1st sess.) (Washington, D.C.: U.S. Government Printing Office, 1975), pp. 366–410. Frederick W. Crook is an economist in the U.S. Department of Agriculture.

number in existence in 1963. Essentially the commune level functions as the basic unit of local government. This level is charged with the responsibility of procuring grain, collecting taxes, providing public security, and reporting statistics and information to higher levels. In addition, it formulates specific production plans for its subordinate units after adapting policies received from higher levels to local conditions. The commune also provides leadership for the management of water resources, construction, afforestation, and transportation projects which require the direction and control of a large organizational unit. Moreover, it manages local industries which produce consumer and producer goods for local consumption.

Brigades currently are estimated to number about 750,000. The brigade is the final link in the long chain of government and Party control systems. It is the institution charged with overseeing the work of production teams. The brigade has coercive power through its ability to nominate officials which lead teams. The Chinese Communist Party Branch in the brigade is responsible for inculcating socialist ideals in team officials and members. Moreover, brigades can influence team behavior because of the inputs, such as electricity, water, and farm machinery, they control and the social services, such as health and education, they deliver to or withhold from teams.

Production teams are estimated to number about 5 million. The team continues to be the most important formally organized unit in the commune system. This semiautonomous unit makes the final decisions regarding the production of goods and the distribution of income. It is the unit which bears the burden of calculating profits or losses. Most of the grain and foodstuffs grown in teams is consumed by member households with only a portion marketed. Aside from the household, no other institution in China so deeply affects every major aspect of the lives of China's rural population.

Finally, households are estimated to number about 167 million. The household takes the responsibility for disciplining and motivating its labor force, and for distributing income to its individual members. Households continue to cultivate private plots from which come most of China's vegetables, poultry, and hogs.

Regarding similarities and differences in the commune system in various regions of China, two different patterns are evident. On the one hand, communes in various parts of the country have basically similar organizational structures, ownership patterns, and methods of distributing income. On the other hand, communes in different parts of the country vary greatly regarding numbers of brigades, teams, households, population, arable land, level of mechanization, and income.

The persistence of the team as the basic unit and similarities in organization and ownership patterns of contemporary communes with those in 1962 tend to mask important changes which have taken place in the past

12 years at commune and brigade levels. These levels provide more services, control more inputs, have better trained cadres and stronger Party organizations than they did in 1962. Indeed, there has been ideological pressure in the Party to abolish the team and amalgamate households directly into brigades, bringing agriculture one step closer to ultimate socialization. This pressure, understandably, has been supported by poorer teams desiring to increase their share of collective income. However, pressure to change the status of teams has been arrested by the newly passed 1975 Constitution which specifically sustains the continued functioning of these units. Moreover, the requirements of China's labor intensive agriculture necessitate a unit similar to the team in size and organization, which can effectively manage and motivate the farmers of China to produce the foodstuffs needed for this country's huge and growing population.

The purpose of this paper is to describe communes as they exist and function at the present time, and to briefly analyze economic coordination and decision-making processes in the commune system. The scope of the paper is limited to the four levels of commune system in China's economy: i.e., the rural people's commune (RPC); the production brigade (PB); the production team (PT); and the household. Its major focus concerns the economic affairs, especially relating to agricultural production, of the units in the commune system, but of necessity some attention must be paid to education, politics, and health care as well. The study is limited to the 12-year period from January 1963 to December 1974.

In the early 1960s, within six to seven years after the establishment of the communes, there were a series of excellent studies on these institutions by Professors Barnett, Donnithorne, Myrdal, Pelzel, and others. Several of these, including those by Barnett, Myrdal, and Pelzel, involved an in-depth study of one agricultural unit, either a commune, brigade, team, or village.

This paper attempts to give a more nationwide perspective on the commune system in rural China. Primary and secondary source materials were used to collect information on commune organizations and related topics such as education, health, and marketing. The study rests primarily, however, on information gathered from approximately 1,400 individual reports on communes scattered over the broad expanse of China.

Thus while updating information gathered in the 1960s, this study should also allow for some analysis of regional variations and compilation of more aggregate data on the institutional structure of rural China.

Section II of the paper provides background information on the commune system as it was first organized in 1958 and as it was restructured from 1959 through the end of 1962. Section III outlines the main features of the commune system as it exists today and briefly describes the major changes which have occurred in the system since 1962. Section IV completes the discussion by presenting tentative ideas regarding (a) the coordination of economic activities of the separate parts of the commune system; (b) the constraints within which the production team, the most important unit in Chinese agriculture, makes economic decisions; and (c) prospects for change in the commune system in the next five years.

II. ORGANIZATION AND RESTRUCTURING OF COMMUNE SYSTEM, 1958–1962

Rural People's Communes were first organized in 1958 during the Great Leap Forward to resolve a number of problems in China's countryside. Tensions developed between collective farms (Advanced or Higher Agricultural Producers' Cooperatives) organized in 1956 and local hsiang governments regarding responsibilities and functions.[1] Chinese leaders found it difficult to improve both collective farm and hsiang administration at the same time because of the very limited numbers of well-trained persons in rural areas. Small-sized collective farms which were not directly controlled by the Party were felt by some Party leaders to be incapable of maximizing economic growth and initiating social and technological changes at the local level. Moreover, these small-sized production units were thought incapable of generating additional income to bridge the widening gap between rural and urban areas. Party leaders wanted to improve their control in rural areas and curb capitalist tendencies among the peasants. They wanted to create an environment in which a new kind of socialist person could be nurtured without contamination of strong material incentives, private plots, and feudal customs and practices.

The Central Committee of the Chinese Communist Party issued the "Resolution on the Establishment of Communes in Rural Areas" on August 29, 1958, which led to the establishment of 26,000 communes by the end of the year. The resolution stated that the basis for establishing communes was the development of an "overall and continuous leap forward in agricultural production in the whole country and the growing elevation of the political consciousness of the 500 million peasants." The resolution declared that the small-sized collective farm ". . . with a few score or a few hundred households is no longer suited to the demand of the developing situation."

Communes were designed to integrate all aspects of rural life including agricultural, subsidiary, and light industrial production; politics and administration; social services such as education, health, and welfare; transportation and communication; finance and commerce; water conservation and basic construction; and military affairs. The commune, roughly comparable in size to the hsiang in terms of households, replaced the hsiang as the basic administrative unit in rural China. With their larger size,

---

[1] Prior to the formation of communes, China's rural administrative structure consisted of two levels, the hsien or county, and several subordinate units called hsiang.

communes were expected to mobilize underutilized factors of production, especially the labor force, to contract capital projects and to increase production and income.

Communes also were expected to accelerate the building of socialism and the gradual transition to communism.[2]

The production brigade and production team, which corresponded in size to the former collective farm and its production brigades, formed the middle and lower administrative levels of the commune. Attempts were made to reorganize households, the traditional basic unit in rural China, by providing communal living and eating quarters and distributing income directly to individuals rather than to household heads. Nonmaterial rather than material work incentives were stressed. Income was distributed partly on the basis of need through the supply system which guaranteed such things as food, clothing, shelter, and health care; and partly on the basis of labor through the payment of monthly money wages based on each farmer's wage rate per day and the number of days worked.

Communes organized as described above encountered numerous difficulties by December 1958. In fact, very few communes actually operated communal mess halls and nurseries, and for many communes the wage-supply system lasted only a few months. These difficulties have been well documented in works already published and it should be sufficient at this point to briefly outline the main problems and indicate the major organizational changes which took place.[3]

Unlike the previous major agricultural changes of land reform and collectivization for which considerable experience was gained prior to full implementation, the Party organized communes rapidly without benefit of much prior experience.

Accounting and statistical systems failed to provide decision makers with information needed to make economic plans. Decision makers themselves were not prepared to operate such large institutions, especially with regard to managing agricultural production.[4] Expected organization economies through centralization of functions at the commune level did not materialize for some important functions such as the allocation of the labor force, and accumulation of capital. Prof. G. W. Skinner suggested

[2] For more detailed discussions regarding the establishment of communes, see A. Doak Barnett, *Cadres, Bureaucracy, and Political Power in Communist China* (New York: Columbia University Press, 1967), pp. 313–38; and Audrey Donnithorne, *China's Economic System* (New York: Praeger Publishers, 1967), pp. 43–64.

[3] See Kenneth R. Walker, "Organization of Agricultural Production," in *Economic Trends in Communist China*, ed. Alexander Eckstein, Walter Galenson, and Ta-chung Liu (Chicago: Aldine Publishing Co., 1968), pp. 440–52; and T. A. Hsia, *The Commune in Retreat as Evidenced in Terminology and Semantics* (Berkeley: Center for Chinese Studies, Institute of International Studies, University of California, 1964).

[4] See Frederick W. Crook, "Rural Labor Recordkeeping in China, 1962–1970" (unpublished report, U.S. Bureau of the Census, Washington, D.C., 1971).

in several important articles published in 1964–65 that newly organized communes encountered difficulties because they were not properly aligned with traditional rural institutions which had been shaped by decades and perhaps even centuries of rural marketing customs and practices.[5]

Work incentives reached a nadir in communes with the reduction of, and in some cases the elimination of, private plots and with the emphasis on nonmaterial incentives. Farmers saw little correlation between work done and payment for work in the wage-supply system. Furthermore, commune administrators did not appropriately reward farmers in villages which, either through efficient management or favorable endowments of fertile soil and water supplies, were much more productive than farmers in neighboring villages. Incentives declined for farmers in the more productive villages when they found the fruits of their labor, which had been fairly and honestly won, being distributed to other villages. Moreover, the formation of communes put additional strain on both cadres and farmers already weary of constant change for a decade, that is, land reform, collectivization, and finally communization. These difficulties plus poor weather led to declines in production which prompted Chinese leaders to reorganize communes.

In the space of four years, from spring 1959 to winter 1962, communes underwent two reforms. Beginning in spring 1959 and continuing throughout the year, communes began to make the brigade the basic unit of account. A three-level ownership system was instituted which made the brigade the most important production unit in the commune system. Most of the means of production were to be owned and controlled by the brigade and minor portions were to be controlled by the commune and teams.

Experience proved that the brigade also was too large a unit to effectively manage and motivate farmers. The labor-intensive nature of agricultural production in China required that commune institutions pay particular attention to the management, allocation, and motivation of the labor force. In the end it was found that small-sized teams of 20–30 households could best manage and motivate the rural labor force, and, beginning in 1961, teams were made the basic unit. Teams were given ownership and control over most of the agricultural means of production. Economic decisions were implemented at the team level, and teams distributed income and calculated profits or losses.

Instead of centralizing all functions at the commune or brigade level, the commune system was reorganized so that functions requiring large-scale management were aligned with institutions having the capability to most effectively manage that function. Functions such as coordination of production, control of water, agricultural extension, and certain kinds of health activities were allocated to the commune. Small-sized water con-

5 See G. W. Skinner, "Marketing and Social Structure in Rural China," *Journal of Asian Studies*, vol. 24, no. 3 (May 1965), p. 394.

servation projects, primary education (after 1968) and certain kinds of subsidiary production were allocated to the brigade. The function of managing the labor force to raise the bulk of China's agricultural crops was given to the team. Finally, certain functions, such as the raising of specific kinds of livestock, were allocated to households.[6]

By the end of 1962, incentives increased with the return of private plots and the reestablishment of material rewards. The closer correlation between pay and work done was achieved through the rejuvenation of the old collective farm labor day-work payment system.[7]

A December 1962 interview with an average farm family regarding its relationship with these rural institutions during the preceding 13-year period, would reveal that the family had first joined a seasonal mutual aid team which, in time, was merged with an adjacent team to form a permanent mutual aid team. The household next joined a semisocialist agricultural producers cooperative (APC) which in 1956 was merged with other APCs to form a collective farm. In fall 1958 the family's collective farm became a brigade in the newly formed commune. From the family's point of view, their earnings came initially from the commune, which was the basic accounting unit. Then in 1959 they received income from their brigade which had become the unit of account. Finally, the small neighborhood team became the unit of account in 1961. For a single family, specific dates can be pinpointed regarding changes in structure, but for the country as a whole it is well to remember that these changes occurred over a month, season, or even a year's time. Likewise, the number of communes increased gradually from 26,000 in 1961 to 74,000 in 1963.

* * * * *

III. THE COMMUNE SYSTEM SINCE 1962

There appear to be three distinct trends regarding change in the commune system in the past 12 years.[8] On the one hand, the main features of the system, the ownership patterns, incentive systems, and organizational

---

6 Prof. Joan Robinson was one of the first scholars to see the distribution of various functions to the four basic units. See Joan Robinson, "Organization of Agriculture," in *Contemporary China,* ed. Ruth Adams (New York: Vintage Books, 1966), pp. 221–34.

7 Charles Hoffman, *Work Incentive Practices and Policies in the People's Republic of China, 1953–1965* (Albany, N.Y.: State University of New York Press, 1967).

8 This portion of the paper rests on three types of information. The first is the work done by Professors Barnett, Myrdal, Pelzel, Vogel and others. Their information was gathered first-hand in China, or was gained from Chinese refugees. This information, however, is limited primarily to the period 1962–65, prior to the Cultural Revolution (1966–69). The second source is the 1,400 reports on communes gleaned from Chinese news releases of the past 12 years. Finally, the third source is more general information gathered from the Chinese press regarding commune structure, organization, and functions, but not dealing with specific communes.

structures are much the same as they were 12 years ago. On the other hand, in the past 12 years, much change has occurred filling out the basic systems laid out in 1962. Important changes include: the establishment of revolutionary committees during the Cultural Revolution; increased industrial and subsidiary production activities; establishment of a rural health system; improvement in the rural education system; improved rural mechanization through construction of an electrification network, and the establishment of tractor stations and shops to manufacture and repair farm machinery; expansion of the agricultural extension system, and improvement in scientific experiment work in rural areas; greater involvement in managing the retail trade of the supply and marketing cooperatives; and the establishment of a rural broadcasting system. Finally, the third change concerns the fact that the number of communes was reduced about one third from about 74,000 in 1963 to about 50,000 in 1973.

The discussion of each of the four units in the commune system will be organized as follows. First, as appropriate, size, organization, and ownership patterns in communes, brigades, teams, and households will be discussed. A review of the 1,400 reports revealed that most units had remarkably similar organizational structures. However, the size of the units in terms of arable land and population varied greatly from one commune to another. Consequently an effort will be made first to describe what might be called an average unit, and then, as is appropriate, regional variations will be discussed. Second, activities and functions undertaken by each of the four units will be discussed. Here an attempt will be made to clarify: (1) which activities and functions are undertaken by each unit; (2) which functions are undertaken solely by one unit; and (3) which functions are shared. Generally, three kinds of activities or functions will be discussed: (1) administrative activities—government, Party, and military; (2) production activities—agriculture and industry; (3) service activities—health, education, and agricultural extension.

Third, and finally, relationships between units will be discussed. Relationships among units in China's rural economy can be described as: (1) those relations between a unit in the commune system and an institution outside the system; (2) those relations between a superior and a subordinate unit in the system; and (3) those horizontal relations between units at the same level in the commune system. Where appropriate, income distribution will be discussed as an important part of the connection between units.

Commune Level

Size and Organization.   Communes at present are estimated to number about 70,000.

*   *   *   *   *

The average commune in 1970 had about 2,900 households, 13,000 persons, and 5,400 labor force units. The average commune for 1970 was not greatly different from an estimate made of the average commune in 1974. The average commune in 1974 had 15 production brigades and 100 production teams. It contained about 3,346 households with a population of about 14,720 persons, and had about 2,033 hectares (5,024 acres) of arable land.

The number of brigades and teams varied widely from one commune to another. Some localities reported communes had organized only production brigades which had no production teams. A commune in Honan Province which had both brigades and teams reported the largest number of brigades at 38. A commune in Kwangtung Province reported the largest number of production teams at 558.

*   *   *   *   *

Functions and Activities at Commune Level

Administration. Commune, government, and Party entities continue to cooperate together to provide a unified administration for commune functions. As before, communes continue to have congresses (meetings of members or meetings of member representatives) which elect the commune chairman, deputy chairman, and members of the management committee. Since the publication of the 1975 Constitution, these people's congresses of rural people's communes are now considered to be "local organs of state power" which are to be elected every two years.

Management committees function as quasi-official local governments with various departments. The normal functions of the management committee were disrupted temporarily in some communes during the Cultural Revolution in 1966–69 when revolutionary committees were established. These committees integrated Party cadres, military persons, workers, and peasants to plan, coordinate, and manage the commune. The committees blurred the lines demarcating government and Party institutions. Since the Cultural Revolution, however, the "revolutionary" committees have been separated from Party institutions and have taken over the functions of the old commune management committees. Once again there is a distinction between government and Party institutions. The 1975 Constitution changed the name of the commune management committee, which functioned for many years as a quasi-official government institution, to revolutionary committee and stipulated that the new committee is to be the permanent organ of the commune people's congress and, at the same time, to serve as the local people's government. Commune revolutionary committees are accountable to the commune people's congress and the revolutionary committees at the hsien (county) level.

Committees of the Chinese Communist Party continue to be centered at the commune level and they continue to be the most important institution of power in the countryside. These committees interpret policy decisions made in Peking, adapt policies as necessary to local conditions, and insure that policies and production plans are implemented. As was the case in 1962–65, responsible persons continue to hold two jobs, one in the Party and the other in the commune management committee. For example the deputy secretary of the Party Committee of the Hsin Tien Commune in Fukien Province also serves as the director of the commune's military affairs department. One indication that the commune Party secretary continues to be the top local leader concerns the fact that when domestic and foreign correspondents visit communes, more often the Party secretary addresses them than the commune chairman.

Both Party and commune officials have offices in the commune headquarters which might be located in an old abandoned temple, a landlord's villa, a store, or even a group of new office buildings. These commune centers are usually located in one of the large villages within the commune, or in one of the old market towns serving the community.

In addition to their many other duties, Party leaders at the commune level exercise control over the commune level militia organization, as the Party Secretary or deputy secretary often functions as a political commissar in the militia unit. The military affairs section of a commune management committee also receives direction from hsien level military authorities. Militia regiments or battalions are usually organized at the commune level and are responsible for giving direction and training to subordinate company and platoon units. Militia units function primarily to provide public security in the commune. Additional duties include serving as a firefighting force, as a rescue and relief force in natural disasters, and as shock troops in carrying out dangerous or difficult water conservation or agricultural production assignments.[9]

The commune congress, management (revolutionary) committee, and Party committee work together to govern the commune and to coordinate its economic activities. Government administrative services provided by the commune include collecting taxes, maintaining public security, collecting data and writing official reports, and preserving and enhancing the growth of socialism. Commune administrative organs receive state plans from higher levels and allocate production targets to subordinate units. They work with lower levels to make realistic plans and then encourage lower units to fulfill the targets.

These entities promote and exercise control over commune industries. They also manage large-scale water conservation projects. Finally, these organs coordinate the production and service activities which will be dis-

---

[9] For additional reading on the militia, see *Government of Communist China*, ed. George P. Jan (San Francisco: Chandler Publishing Company, 1966), pp. 535–42; and John Gittings, *The Role of the Chinese Army* (London: Oxford University Press, 1967).

cussed below. In general these institutions function today much the same as Professors Barnett and Donnithorne described in their work on commune systems for the period 1962–1965.[10]

Production. The commune level engages in agricultural as well as industrial production, though it does not produce a significant portion of basic agricultural commodities because the team owns and controls most of the labor and land. Commune agricultural production is limited mainly to activities such as fishing, forestry, animal husbandry, and cultivation of fruit orchards.

Communes are far more important with respect to the development of rural industries. Most well known of course were their attempts during the Great Leap Forward to use farmers to produce grain from fields and steel from backyard furnaces. As has been well documented, the backyard blast furnaces produced low-quality high-cost steel. The shutdown of the small furnaces was dramatic and well-remembered. What has not been so well publicized is that in the past 12 years communes have been quite successful in developing a host of rural industries.

A survey of the materials collected for this study indicates that the following industries are most often found at the commune level: grain processing (rice and flour) mills; farm implement construction and repair shops; edible oil presses; and brick, tile, and lime kilns. More specialized regional industries based on local natural resources, crops, and animals include hydroelectric generation; processing of hemp and cotton; dairy; timber; stone quarries and small coal mines; sugar-cane presses; and production of cement. Less widespread among communes are industries such as chemical plants, boatbuilding shops, fruit canneries, starch and paper factories. Also light industrial and consumer products such as light bulbs, shoes, firecrackers, and porcelain and jewelry for export are produced in commune factories.

Tractor stations once again are being established at the commune level. According to Professor Donnithorne, stations were transferred from county levels to communes in 1958–59, but because of a lack of trained staff, management difficulties, and lack of funds, these stations reverted back to the county level in 1960–62.[11]

Evidence collected for this study suggests that, especially since 1969, communes have begun to establish their own tractor stations. It was not possible to learn from the data given what proportion of communes had tractor stations. The evidence, however, clearly suggests that a greater number of communes have farm machinery construction and repair shops than tractor stations.

---

[10] Barnett, *Cadres*, pp. 339–63, and Donnithorne, *China's Economic System*, pp. 43–64.

[11] Donnithorne, *China's Economic System*, p. 60.

Increasing numbers of communes surveyed in the late 1960s and early 1970s cited the use of electrical power in grain, fiber, and oilseed processing, and in pumping water. Some communes have built their own small hydroelectric generating stations. The existence of tractor stations, machine shops, and electrical systems at the commune level should not give the reader the impression that Chinese agriculture is highly mechanized, as these stations and shops at present are a thin veneer spread over an immense agricultural area. Nevertheless, great progress has been made and the new generation of young Chinese farmers are learning to use mechanical tools which will increase their productivity.

It also would be incorrect to leave the impression that China's countryside consists of 70,000 mini-Pittsburghs. Rural industry such as grain, fiber, and edible oil processing has gone on in China for centuries. Travelers from more industrialized countries sometimes describe China's countryside as lacking mechanization and modern industry. What has changed in the last decade is that the commune system has allocated resources and technical skills to rural industries, and these now are applying mechanical power and machinery to old jobs, and some new industries have been added. Also the commune system enables managers to mobilize underemployed labor during slack farming seasons to work in some of these rural industries.

Services. As far as service functions are concerned, communes today continue to have responsibility for health services. Since 1962 and particularly since the beginning of the Cultural Revolution, communes have worked diligently to implement Chairman Mao's dictum, "in health work, put the stress on the rural areas." In 1973, Peking claimed that "nearly" every commune in the country had a clinic.

About one third of these clinics are funded by the state and the remaining two thirds by communes. Half of China's professional medical workers are reported to be working in these clinics. Clinics differ regarding numbers of beds, services, and equipment available to patients. The more fortunate have more than 20 beds, 10 "doctors" and 10 nurses, provide surgical services and have X-ray equipment. Clinics at commune levels direct the functions of brigade-level health stations and the activities of the "barefoot doctors." Clinics also direct birth control efforts and public health programs.[12]

The rural health system is not without problems, i.e., finding trained personnel and funds to support the program.[13] Despite these problems, however, Chinese farmers for the first time in history are now able to receive some medical attention. Granted that the treatment provided may

---

[12] See Robert M. Worth, "Health and Medicine," in *China: A Handbook*, ed. Yuan-li Wu (London: David and Charles, 1973), pp. 657–68.

[13] See David M. Lampton, "Trends in Health Policy," *Current Scene* [Hong Kong], vol. 12, no. 6 (June 1974), pp. 1–8.

be less than satisfactory, some treatment is a vast improvement over the previous lack of medical care.

Commune Departments of Culture, Education, and Welfare continue to be responsible for the education system which includes secondary and special schools at the commune level and primary schools at the brigade level.[14]

During and after the Cultural Revolution commune members were encouraged to take control of, fund, and manage existing schools and to organize various kinds of schools to fit the needs and resources of the local community. In the past 12 years progress has been limited by the dearth of well-trained teachers and funds. In spite of its failings, however, the commune education system has given an increasing number of Chinese young people a chance to obtain a basic education.[15]

Agricultural extension programs were generally available only in advanced communes at the beginning of the period, according to Professor Donnithorne.[16] A survey of communes and literature since the mid-1960s, however, suggests that most communes now have active extension programs, and possess demonstration or experimental farms.

The commune, aided strongly by the state, continues to provide rural marketing services. These services include sales of consumer goods to farmers; sales of producer goods to brigades and teams; and purchase of goods produced by units in the commune system.[17] Two categories of goods are purchased by the state. First-category goods consist of the rationed commodities of grain, cotton, and edible oilseeds. Production teams producing rationed goods in excess of their needs are required to sell a fixed percentage of these goods to state purchasing stations at state-controlled prices. In addition, the state rewards those teams producing goods above their own needs and above their procurement quotas by offering to purchase their excess products at higher than normal prices.

Second-category goods consist of items not rationed but nevertheless in demand for domestic consumption and needed for export to earn foreign exchange, such as pigs, poultry, eggs, nuts, and fruit. Purchases of second-category goods are made for the state by supply marketing cooperatives. These cooperative institutions are operated strictly according to procedures outlined by the state. In some areas cooperatives seem to be organized to serve the brigades and teams of several communes.

---

14 Barnett, *Cadres*, p. 354.

15 See Marianne Bastid, "Economic Necessity and Political Ideals in Educational Reform during the Cultural Revolution," *China Quarterly*, no. 42 (April–June 1970), pp. 16–45; and Peter J. Seybolt, "The Yenan Revolution in Mass Education," *China Quarterly*, no. 48 (October–December 1971), pp. 664–69.

16 Donnithorne, *China's Economic System*, p. 60.

17 Donnithorne, *China's Economic System*, chap. 11.

Cooperatives purchase goods on the local market, which is controlled by the commune administration, and they make contracts with brigades, teams, and households to supply products. Supply and marketing cooperatives, also, are the main channels through which producer and consumer goods move to the ultimate consumer. Commune centers often have a cooperative retail store. Goods warehoused at commune levels are distributed to branch stores at brigade levels.

Communes also regulate the scope and functions of rural markets. First-category rationed goods are prohibited from entering the market. Second-category goods, however, enter the market, where supply and marketing cooperatives purchase locally produced eggs, fruit, and nuts, and farmers exchange goods produced on their private plots.

Credit and banking services at the commune level are provided by branches of the People's Bank and by credit cooperatives. The county-level People's Bank controls the operations of its branch banks. These branch banks serve as the guardians of state interest in communes, as the bank monitors the financial transactions of commune accounts held by the bank, and analyzes commune management, productive capacity, and financial records to determine the credit worthiness of the commune in responding to commune applications for production loans.

Credit cooperatives are not strictly state institutions, as indeed they are cooperatives organized at the commune level by private citizens. They are managed by politically reliable poor and lower middle peasants. Former landlords and rich peasants are excluded from holding office. In practice, credit cooperatives function under the guidance and direction of the People's Bank. In recent years reports from China indicate large numbers of rural households now have savings accounts. Initially credit cooperatives were to function primarily to make consumer loans available to households temporarily short of cash. However, since 1966, credit cooperatives have been called on to make production loans available to brigades and teams. For example, a recent news report from China indicated that 12 percent of credit co-op loans were extended to farm families and 88 percent were granted to teams, brigades, and communes.

In addition, most communes in the past 12 years have established a rural wired-broadcast network. The commune broadcast station receives programs via wireless from provincial radio stations. These programs, along with locally produced news, weather, music, and entertainment programs, are broadcast daily through wire lines running to loudspeakers at brigade and team centers and in the homes of most households.[18]

Relationships between Commune and Other Levels.   Commune leaders continue to look to county government and Party leaders for guidance,

---

[18] Elizabeth F. Crook and Frederick W. Crook, "Wired Broadcasting in the People's Republic of China," *Western Electric*, vol. 25, no. 6 (July–August 1973), pp. 26–31.

target plans, and authority to approve certain actions. As was the case in 1963, communes today continue to have institutions located within their boundaries over which they do not exercise full control. Among these institutions are government-controlled high schools, branches of the People's Bank, supply and marketing co-ops, tax offices, grain depots, state purchasing stations, and machine tractor stations.[19] Commune cadres work very closely with officers in these institutions to coordinate policies and programs.

Regarding economic and commercial transactions, communes arrange contracts with state-owned factories to produce various items. For example, the Hsu-hang commune made light bulbs on contract for a Shanghai factory, and communes near Peking supply vegetables to the Peking Municipal Vegetable Corporation. Communes also make contracts with state institutions to supply labor force units. For example, the state-owned Sha-tze-kang Tree Nursery Farm in Kiangsi Province employed workers from nearby communes to care for the seedlings.[20]

The second class of relationships are those between the commune and its subordinate units. Leaders in the various departments assist their counterparts at brigade and team levels to make and to carry out production plans. Communes send cadres to give ideological and technical training to backward brigades and teams. Commune officers receive periodic reports from brigade and team officers and hold periodic meetings with them.

The third class of relationships are those between individual communes. Communes cooperated with each other to reclaim land from the sea, build hydroelectric power stations, run fertilizer plants, and construct irrigation systems. Four communes in one case cooperated together to overcome a drought condition. Brigades in one commune were compensated by three other communes when the brigades' crops were sacrificed as ditches were dug across brigade land to bring water to save the parched crops in the many other brigades in the other communes.

Communes obtain their income from the sale of products made by commune-owned shops and factories to state institutions and to other communes, to its own brigades and teams, and to commune members. Commune-owned tractors, operators, and machines are rented out to brigades and teams. Commune-owned hydroelectric plants sell electricity to brigades, teams, and households. Some communes also own some farmland and timberland which is rented to brigades and teams. Communes also charge for services they perform, such as the use of veterinary stations, repair of agricultural machinery, and the transportation of goods. Income

[19] Chu Li and Tien Chieh-yun, *Inside a People's Commune: Report from Chi Yi Ling* (Peking: Foreign Languages Press, 1974), p. 101.

[20] Rewi Alley, *Travels in China, 1966–1971* (Peking: New World Press, 1971), p. 289.

from these enterprises is used to defray operating costs, wages, purchase of materials, and taxes.

*   *   *   *   *

Brigade Level

Production brigades have a much more important role in the commune system today than they did in 1963. When communes were restructured in 1961–62 and production teams were made the basic unit of ownership and account, some brigade cadres voiced the opinion that their unit had become a transportation and communication center and they, in turn, had become mere propagandists and collectors of grain and taxes.

Since 1963, however, the Party and government have looked to the brigade with its Party Branch and militia unit to manage and control the political, social, and economic life in rural areas. In general, the brigade is the lowest level at which Party institutions are organized. At the beginning of the period, brigades had to rely more on normative and coercive controls to manage rural life.[21] However, with the development of social services at the brigade level and with the growth in rural industry, the brigade now has resources at its disposal which semiautonomous production teams cannot now afford to ignore.

Size and Organization. Production brigades are estimated to number about 750,000. On the average, a brigade has approximately 7 production teams, about 220 households, and roughly 980 persons. On the average, a brigade cultivates about 136 hectares (336 acres). At the brigade level, one finds the brigade congress, the management committee (revolutionary committee), the Party branch, the political "evening school," the militia company or battalion, primary schools, a medical station, and brigade-run industries.

While most brigades have production teams, some communes have made the brigade the basic unit of ownership and account. This action was laudable by ideological standards, in that it represented one step nearer the goal of eventual elimination of collective ownership and the establishment of socialist ownership or ownership by all the people. Only in advanced units, where ideological and economic conditions permitted and where the masses "willed it," were brigades permitted to become the basic unit of account and ownership. Tachai, the famous model unit from Shansi Province, is a brigade which has no teams and is a basic unit. Nonetheless, as far as could be determined from the reports on communes examined for this study, nearly all brigades have teams and are not basic units. Indeed

---

[21] Robert J. Birrell, "The Centralized Control of the Communes in the Post 'Great Leap' Period," in *Chinese Communist Politics in Action*, ed. A. Doak Barnett (Seattle: University of Washington Press, 1969), pp. 400–443.

Article 7 of the new constitution states that generally brigades are not to be made the basic accounting unit.

* * * * *

Functions and Activities at Brigade Level

Administration. Brigades are structured today much the same as they were in 1958. Members in brigade congresses continue as before to elect a preselected slate of officers for chairman and members of the management committee or revolutionary committee as the case may be.

While not all brigades have Party branches, a survey of reports since the beginning of the Cultural Revolution suggests that the great majority now have them. Party membership has grown in this period and Party organizations have been strengthened since the period began. The Party branch secretary continues to be the most important leader at the brigade level. Party branch leaders today hold concurrent positions in brigade management (revolutionary) committees, as was the case at the beginning of the period.[22]

Another index of the brigade's increasing importance is the fact that in the past few years more brigades have obtained headquarters buildings. These buildings house offices for members of the brigade's management committee and Party branch. They also provide space for the credit cooperative, the branch store of the supply and marketing cooperative, and various brigade industries. These headquarters, usually located in the largest village within the boundaries of the brigade, seem to have become an increasingly important center of rural life.[23]

Depending upon size, a production brigade may have a militia company or a battalion.[24] Often the head of the militia unit is also the chief of the security section of the brigade's management committee. This fact highlights once again the concurrent holding of jobs in different organizational systems and stresses the fact that one of the militia's most important functions is public security.[25] Militia units have important economic functions as well, such as fighting forest fires and reclaiming land.

Moreover, militia units have the special function of mobilizing the masses to work on corvee labor-type projects. They seem to be the activists who go to the worksites illustrating to their fellow brigade members that the work can and will be done. Furthermore, they are called on to do difficult and sometimes dangerous tasks on construction work. For example, the commander of a brigade militia unit in Hunan Province led a group of

---

[22] Barnett, *Cadres*, p. 361.
[23] Alley, *Travels*, pp. 336–37.
[24] Ibid.
[25] Alley, *Travels*, pp. 135–39.

workers to drill holes and set off explosive charges to construct an irrigation ditch alongside a steep cliff. Brigades function today much as they did in 1963.[26] They serve as an intermediary, collecting reports from teams and sending them to the commune, and, in turn, passing instructions and policies from the commune to the teams. The brigade receives state plan targets, compulsory state procurement (grain) quotas, and schedules for delivering grain taxes, and then works out plans with its teams to achieve these targets. Brigades continue to mobilize the rural labor force to build roads, canals, and water conservation projects. Brigades, of course, continue to manage their own enterprises and cooperate with teams to manage joint enterprises. Since the Cultural Revolution, brigades have shouldered the burdens of managing rural health services and primary schools, and have some responsibility for supervising state-managed supply and marketing branch stores.

Production. Like the commune level, brigades do not produce a significant portion of basic agricultural commodities because teams manage most of the labor and arable land. Brigades, however, do undertake certain agricultural production functions. They often engage in swine production, i.e., raising boars and brood sows to produce piglets which are sold to teams and households.

Brigades also operate orchards, fish ponds, and fishing boats, and manage timberland. For example, one brigade in a mountainous region in Anhwei Province afforested 1,300 hectares (3,212 acres), operated a tree nursery, and supervised a timber mill.

Although statistical information is not currently available to indicate trends, many reports on the commune system give the strong impression that the past 12 years have seen considerable growth in brigade-level industry. This industry generally is of a smaller scale, requiring less capital, labor inputs, and technical skills than those run by the commune.

The most frequently mentioned brigade-level industries were grain, fiber, and edible oil processing, and farm equipment repair shops. Specialized regional industries frequently mentioned in the reports include mining, tea curing, and crushing of sugar cane. Industries not as widespread as the preceding, but still rather common include food processing plants producing bean curd and noodles; kilns manufacturing bricks, tiles, and lime; and shops weaving native materials to make gunny sacks, straw mats, hemp rope, and wicker baskets. Among the more unusual industries reported at the brigade level were weaving and knitting cloth, manufacturing paper, generating hydroelectric power, and operating an inn.

Services. Service activities provided by brigades have expanded greatly since 1963. Some improvements occurred in brigade-level health and edu-

---

[26] Barnett, *Cadres*, pp. 372–73.

cation services from 1963 to 1965. During and after the Cultural Revolution, however, great efforts were made to improve these services.

Most brigades in China now have health stations staffed by part-time health workers. Brigade health workers receive training from commune clinics, from special training courses at the county level, and from People's Liberation Army medical teams.[27] Health workers earn part of their living by earning work points laboring in agriculture.[28] For their health services, the brigade gives them a subsidy to bring their income level up to the average earnings in the brigade. These paramedics render simple treatment to farmers, refer more serious cases to commune clinics, work on public health problems, and teach health classes in primary schools.[29] Both Western and traditional Chinese treatments and medicines are used in treating patients.

About half of the brigades in the country now have cooperative medical systems.[30] Persons in the brigade can become cooperative members of the system by paying a small fee (1 yuan per year). For every person who subscribes, the brigade makes a small contribution (0.10 yuan) which it draws from its welfare fund. Patients pay a small fee (0.5 yuan) per visit to the health stations. However, difficulties in recruiting and training personnel and finding adequate funds are problems which are yet to be resolved.

Brigades continue to be responsible for running primary schools.[31] As before, the brigade's Party branch committee person for propaganda continues to be responsible for managing the schools. The achievements of China's rural education efforts prior to the Cultural Revolution have been chronicled elsewhere.[32] As far as could be judged from the research materials gathered for this report, the system seems to have continued to improve in the past six or seven years.

During the Cultural Revolution, and especially since 1968, poor and lower middle peasants in brigades have been mobilized to manage primary schools. If there is a limited number of spaces in school, then poor and lower middle peasants presumably decide whose children will attend. The move to make poor and lower middle peasants responsible for primary schools could also be an attempt by government to make the system more responsive to rural needs. At present, the primary emphasis of education is to train workers who will increase rural production, not migrate to the

---

27 Alley, *Travels*, pp. 164–65.

28 One labor day equals ten work points. See below for more details regarding the meaning of labor days and work points.

29 Alley, *Travels*, pp. 164–65.

30 Lampton, "Trends in Health Policy," p. 4.

31 See Barnett, *Cadres*, pp. 386–88.

32 The Editor, "Educational Reform and Rural Resettlement in Communist China," *Current Scene* [Hong Kong], vol. 8, no. 17 (November 1970), pp. 1–8; and The Editor, "Recent Developments in Chinese Education," *Current Scene* [Hong Kong], vol. 10, no. 7 (July 1972), pp. 1–6.

cities, as has occurred so frequently in developing economies. In fact, educated youths from urban areas are being used as teachers in these primary schools. Other teachers include the head of the militia unit, brigade accountants, paramedics, and agricultural technicians. These teachers, far from being elevated beyond the rural population, are now being paid in work points and receive only the average local income of the farmers they serve.

Brigade-run schools charge tuition fees, as brigade incomes generally cannot fully support operation of the schools. Some brigades give land for students and teachers to work to help support the school and others encourage classes to engage in subsidiary production activity to help support their education.[33]

Regarding marketing services, supply and marketing cooperatives often have branches at the brigade level. These branches receive direction from the headquarters of the supply and marketing cooperative, and from the brigade management committee and Party branch. Especially since the Cultural Revolution, local inhabitants have increased their voice in managing these branches. These branch stores stock small quantities of producer goods and function to supply farmers with manufactured daily necessities of life, such as needles, thread, and rubber shoes. The stores also purchase category 2 goods, pigs, fruit, and handicraft items for the state from brigades, teams, and households.

Branches of credit cooperatives are located at brigade centers. Households put their excess funds in savings accounts in these branches, and can obtain consumption loans from the cooperative, if sanctioned by the proper authorities. From the evidence currently available it was not possible to determine if brigades and teams had their financial accounts with branch credit cooperatives or with branches of the People's Bank at the commune level.

Connections.   While commune level connections with institutions outside the commune system were expected, similar relations between brigades and outside institutions were not expected, but nonetheless may not indicate a degree of autonomy, as they may have been required to obtain approval from the commune level before engaging in the kinds of activities explained below. For example a brigade in Hopeh Province processed hog bristles for the Shihchiachuang Animal Products Co. A state farm in Kwangtung Province paid cash to a brigade which mobilized its labor force to construct fields for the farm. A brigade near Chengtu agreed to supply labor force units for use by a transport and storage company. A brigade near Peking signed a contract to supply vegetables to a specific marketplace. Foreign trade departments approached brigades in Hopeh to process goods for export.

---

[33] Alley, *Travels,* pp. 268–69.

The connections between brigade and team are of great importance because the brigade is the last link in the chain of institutions which bind the Party and government to the basic production unit in rural China. The best plans and policies from Peking tend to miscarry if there is poor exchange between brigade and teams. We know that state plans, policies, procurement targets, and tax quotas are passed from brigades to teams. We do not know precisely how this is accomplished, nor how brigades motivate or lead teams to implement policies and meet targets. Much to the chagrin of researchers, there seems to be an inverse relationship between the importance of these subjects and the quantity of research material available.

Moreover, of the small amount of information obtained, more of it concerned how brigades ought not to work with teams than how they actually did work with teams. Brigades selected for criticism usually violated the rights of teams. For example, one brigade in Liaoning mobilized the labor force of all teams to construct a reservoir regardless of whether teams would benefit from the project or not. Members of those teams not benefitted by the reservoir lagged behind in their work on the project. They began to work diligently only when the brigade, following the principle of "exchange at equal value," began to compensate the laborers for their work.

Regarding the interconnections between individual brigade-level units, the famous Sha Shih Yu (Sand Stone Gulch) Brigade in Hopeh Province provides a good example of cooperative activity. A neighboring brigade gave its consent for the Sand Stone Gulch Brigade to drill an irrigation well in one of its fields. Less neighborly feelings were generated in two brigades, also in Hopeh Province, when children of one brigade killed an animal belonging to a second brigade. The brigades were not on speaking terms until amends were made and the animal lost was replaced.[34] Commercial transactions also occurred between brigades in which hatching eggs and draft animals were exchanged for cash.

Team Level

In the past 12 years, the production team has lost some of its importance because of the growth of industry and services at the commune and brigade level. Nevertheless, aside from the family, the production team today is still, by far, the most important institution in rural China.

The team is the organization in which families first come in contact with an institution organized by the Party and government. It is the institution which controls most of the means of production in China's countryside. It is the unit which takes final responsibility for most of the economic decisions made in rural areas. It is in the context of the teams that

---

[34] Alley, *Travels*, p. 144.

individuals are mobilized to work in the fields. Motivation originates in these organizations, which calculate profit or loss and which distribute income to members, the collective, and the state. Most of the grain and foodstuffs in China are raised and consumed within the confines of this unit. No other institution in China so deeply affects every major aspect of the lives of China's rural population.

Unfortunately source materials collected generally yielded much less information about this important unit than regarding communes and brigades. Chinese authors seem much more willing to discuss the latter than they do to describe the organization, activities, and functioning of teams.

Size and Organization.   Production teams are estimated to number about 5 million. On the average a team has about 33 households (approximately 145 persons) and cultivates roughly 20 hectares (49 acres). Because of the lack of data on teams, it is not possible to highlight differences in team size from province to province, and differences between rural and suburban teams. Some teams were as large as the average brigade; for example, one team in Hopeh had 196 households (985 persons).[35] On the other hand, some teams had as few as 11 households and 50 persons and some specialized teams had almost no arable land at all. For instance, one team near Shanghai had only 1.9 hectares (4.7 acres).

Functions and Activities at Team Level

Administration.   In the past 12 years team organization has not changed significantly. As before, team members periodically elect an approved slate of officers, a team and a deputy team leader, and a management committee. In addition to the above officers, teams have an accountant or a work point recorder, a militia platoon leader, a sparetime wired broadcast repairman, and a custodian to care for the team's tools, animals, and granary.

With the evidence currently available, it is difficult to measure the strength of Party organization and influence at the team level. Reports were found indicating some teams in communes did not have any Party members or organized Party cells. For example Chia-ting County, in formulating a six-year agricultural development plan, stipulated in article 29 that "Party groups (cells) should be set up in most of the production teams."

The fact that cells were to be organized is evidence that, in 1974, most teams in this suburban Shanghai county did not have cells. Assuming half of China's 28 million Party members live at the basic level, and there are ten members per commune and eight members per brigade, there then would be slightly more than one Party member per team.[36] Some Party members holding positions at commune and brigade levels live at the team

---

35 Alley, *Travels*, pp. 157–58.

36 "Press Communique of the Tenth National Congress of the Communist Party of China," in *The Tenth National Congress of the Communist Party of China* (*Documents*) (Peking: Foreign Languages Press, 1973), pp. 77–85.

level, lending Party influence to this level. Generally speaking, however, most teams appear not to have organized Party cells. If a team has a Party member, he usually concurrently has an important position such as team or deputy team leader, a phenomenon parallel to that found at brigade and commune levels.

Production and Services. Most of the income generated in production teams comes from growing crops: grain, cotton, oilseeds, fruit, vegetables, and other crops. Some income also comes from raising livestock, especially hogs, and catching fish. From materials collected for this report, it appears that production teams on the average had much less subsidiary production activity than brigades or commune levels. Individual teams reported activities such as earning money through transportation of goods, making straw sandals[37] and mats,[38] fodder cutting, and beekeeping.

Connections. As was the case with brigades, team connections with institutions outside the commune system may not indicate team autonomy because teams may have cleared activities with brigade and commune levels. Examples of these activities include the making of a contract between a team and an agricultural institute in which team laborers did some of the work on the experimental farm. A team in Hopeh Province hired tractors from the county level tractor station to plow its fields. Teams in Liaoning Province worked with foreign trade departments to select, grade, pack, and deliver apples for export. A team in Kiangsu Province made an agreement with a supply and marketing co-op in a different county to make raincoats.

Regarding the connections between teams, some teams cooperated together to manage joint enterprises. In these enterprises, teams invested resources, supplied the labor force, and shared costs and benefits in proportion to their level of ownership. References to these enterprises occurred more frequently in the mid-1960s than in recent years. Of course, teams competing for scarce resources produced tensions. For example several teams in Kiangsu Province shared a rice threshing machine. When one team failed to cooperate properly in its use, the team was criticized at a brigade level meeting in which all the teams were present.

The most important connections team leaders had to worry about were those related to income distribution in which the team had the responsibility to allocate income to the state, the collective (team), and to households. Income distribution and motivation of individuals are greatly affected by the structure of the commune system. Teams are small-sized collective farms in which farmers pool their land, labor, and capital for purposes of production and agree to be remunerated by dividing the profits (the residual income left after payment of expenses and taxes) among

37 Alley, *Travels*, pp. 475–78.

38 Shahid Javed Burki, *A Study of Chinese Communes* (Cambridge, Mass.: Harvard University Press, 1969), pp. 100–101.

themselves. Because the collective owns the means of production instead of the state, the team is not strictly a socialist institution.[39]

Collective ownership requires that farm families themselves assume responsibility for production risks. In theory, expenses and deductions could be equal to production, leaving no residual income to be distributed to farmers. Moreover, because teams are not state-owned, state labor regulations do not apply, and team members do not have guaranteed wages and related fringe benefits as do state farm employees and factory workers. Furthermore, because of labor discipline in the commune system, members are not allowed the freedom of independent farmers. Obviously, motivation is important in a system in which farmers are required to assume responsibility for risk taking, have no guaranteed wage, and do not have the freedom of individual proprietors.

Team members are motivated to work through a combination of material and nonmaterial incentives. Nonmaterial incentives include labor discipline codes, selecting and honoring "model" farmers for outstanding work, and inducing teams to engage in friendly competition with each other, the winners to be awarded medals, red flags, or other symbols of achievement. These types of incentives were employed through the period under study and continue to be an important element in motivating farmers to work. In spite of all the rhetoric stressing the importance of nonmaterial incentives in the socialist education movement, the Cultural Revolution, and the movement to criticize Lin Piao and Confucius, few teams give nonmaterial incentives the importance they had during the Great Leap Forward described in Section II above. While nonmaterial incentives are expected to become preponderant in the long run, when material rewards will be minimized or eliminated, in the short run the value of material incentives has been respected.

Material incentives have provided the force which has induced farmers to produce from team fields. Many factors affect these incentives, but all factors cannot be treated in equal detail because of the paucity of data. For example, while it is well understood that a farmer's incentives can be raised by reducing the prices he has to pay for tools and fertilizer, it was not possible to obtain precise information on input prices teams paid for such items in the past 12 years. In the past few years articles in newspapers in China say input prices to teams have decreased 50 percent from 1952 to 1973, but no details were given as to the base from which the reductions were made. Similarly, incentives to farmers can be increased by raising the price the state pays teams for the goods it purchases. Some news articles recently reported procurement prices for agricultural and subsidiary products were raised by over 60 percent from 1952 to 1973.

Furthermore, incentives to farmers can be affected by the availability

---

[39] "Socialist" institutions are those in which the means of production are owned by "all the people," i.e., the state.

and prices of consumer goods farmers can purchase with their earnings. Once again little information was found on this topic. The impression gained from the reports on communes is that more consumer goods are available to farmers now than at the beginning of the period. Finally, incentives to farmers can be affected by whether teams allow households to work private plots. Private plots and private production activity of households will be discussed below in the section on households.

Some of the most important factors in the material incentives system are those which (1) determine the relative share of income distributed to the state, the team, and the household; and those which (2) determine the amount of income to be allocated to individual households.

With the lack of information it is not possible to provide a detailed account of the shares allocated to the state, the team, and households. It is important, however, to understand the processes involved in income distribution. To highlight important facets of the income distribution process, an example will be employed. The mechanics of distribution can be seen operating in the example, and the example will provide a general outline of how the shares of income are distributed. After the income distribution system has determined the residual income to be distributed, work payment systems actually allocate the residual income to individual households.

For the purpose of illustration, the average teams discussed above with 33 households, 145 persons, and 20 hectares will be used as a model team. The team's grain production is estimated to be 70 metric tons, and its income from all sources is calculated in terms of grain at 80 metric tons. At the end of the accounting period, income generated in the team is allocated to three entities: the state, the team, and the households.

The state figures prominently in team income distribution because, as has been mentioned previously, teams deliver grain to state tax stations to pay their agricultural taxes and they deliver prescribed quantities of grain, cotton, and edible oil seeds to state procurement stations. Since 1955, the government has implemented a system in which areas producing a surplus of goods are required to sell their excess products to the state at fixed prices and the state bears the burden of rationing grain, cotton cloth, and edible oil to the population. Through planning and the accumulated performance of teams, the government has come to expect certain teams to deliver annually a set quantity of grain under this system. The quantities goods to be purchased are calculated as follows. Officials determine the productive capacity of the team's land to be 70 metric tons of grain. Next they calculate the consumption needs of the team as follows:

1. 34.8 metric tons or 49.7 percent of grain production should be set aside to provide each of the 145 persons in the team with a grain ration of 240 kg. per person.

2. 2.45 metric tons or 3.5 percent of the grain should be reserved for seeding next year's grain fields.
3. 4.2 metric tons or 6 percent of the grain should be allocated as fodder for livestock.
4. 3.5 metric tons or 5 percent of the grain should be reserved by the team to pay its agricultural taxes.

The supply of grain is then compared with the team's consumption needs. If the supply is greater than team needs, the team is declared a grain-surplus team and the state has the prerogative of purchasing up to 90 percent of the quantity in excess of needs. Assume that our model team produces as expected at its normal rate of 70 metric tons. When this amount is compared with the team's consumption rate of 44.95 metric tons, the team is declared a grain surplus team. The state can then purchase 90 percent of 25.05, or 22.55, metric tons. The state purchases this grain at a price which it fixes.

At this step in the process of income distribution, the team has fulfilled its obligations to the state. The team has delivered to the state 3.5 metric tons as agricultural tax and another 22.55 metric tons as a compulsory grain delivery. The team is left with 76.50 metric tons of grain which consists of 53.95 metric tons of actual grain on hand and the value of 22.55 metric tons of grain sold to the state.

The team is the next entity to claim its share of gross income. The team lays claim to about 30 percent of the income, or 24 metric tons of grain to pay for production expenses. Another half a ton of grain (0.5 metric ton) is allocated to the team leaders and bookkeepers to remunerate them for the time they had to attend meetings and to do business for the team and could not earn labor days. About 10 percent of the team's gross income, or 8 metric tons, is put into the team's capital accumulation fund and used to pay off principal and interest on production loans or to purchase machinery. The team's welfare fund receives 2 percent of the income (1.6 metric tons), which is used to help take care of the old, sick, and indigent and to help pay medical and education fees for some members of the team. These deductions total 34.1 metric tons and account for 43 percent of the team's income.

After the state and the team receive their respective shares of the income, the residual is distributed to households. The state's 3.5-metric-ton deductions plus the team's 34.1-metric-ton deductions leave a balance of 42.4 metric tons, which consists of 19.85 metric tons of actual grain on hand and the value of 22.55 metric tons of grain sold to the state. In our average team the households receive 53 percent of the gross income they generated.

How the residual 42.4 metric tons of grain is distributed to households greatly affects incentives. In theory, teams can distribute income to households using one of three payment systems: (a) On the basis of population (egalitarian); (b) on the basis of need (communist); and (c) on the basis of labor contributed to production (socialist). Evidence collected for this study reveals that teams, almost without exception, employed the work payment system (socialist) which correlated work done with income received. More specifically teams utilized the labor-day work payment system. In this system, the amount and quality of work done are measured, and farmers are credited with labor days which serve as their claims on the expected profits, i.e., the residual income of the team. At the end of the agricultural year the number of labor days credited to all farmers and staff of the team are totaled and divided into the amount of residual income to obtain the value of one labor day. If our average team credited its members with 15,865 labor days, then the value of one labor day would be 2.67 kg. (42.4 metric tons divided by 15,865 labor days). Thus if members of a household earned 480 labor days, the household would receive 1,282 kg. of grain as its income for the year, or 480 labor days times 2.67 kg.

An important part of the labor-day work payment system is the measurement of work done by farmers. Seven methods were used to measure work done: equality, assessment, fixed-rate fixed-assessment, fixed-rate flexible-assessment, piece-rate, labor contracts to individuals and households, and labor-production contracts to households.[40] These work measurement methods had been employed in agricultural producer cooperatives, collective farms, and communes prior to 1962 and continued to be used in the period from 1963 to 1974.

A close examination of the operation of these measurements reveals two points: (1) Some methods were employed less frequently than others; and (2) those methods which were utilized frequently tended to provide for an egalitarian distribution of income among households in the team.

Among the less frequently used methods were the piece-rate, labor contracts, and labor-production contracts to households. Teams failed to use the piece-rate because of the difficulties involved in calculating labor norms and because of the difficulties team leaders and bookkeepers had in measuring the work completed and in calculating the labor days due each person. In the labor-production contract to household method, households were assigned responsibility for cultivating a fixed area of land or husbanding a fixed number of animals. The team guaranteed them a certain number of labor days for completing production targets and held out the promise that households could retain a fixed percentage of output in excess of the production target. While this method was used up to 1965 and did provide powerful incentives to farmers, the method also encouraged capitalist practices and so endangered the commune system that teams

---

[40] For a detailed account of the functioning of these work measurement methods, see Frederick W. Crook, *An Analysis of Work Payment Systems Used in Chinese Mainland Agriculture, 1956 to 1970* (Ph.D. dissertation, Fletcher School of Law and Diplomacy, 1970; Ann Arbor, Mich.: University Microfilms, no. 72–2226, 1972).

were forbidden to use it after 1965. In the labor contract work measurement method, teams made contracts with individuals or households to complete tasks, within a given time period, at a stated quality, in return for a predetermined number of labor days. This method was employed more than the labor-production contract method, but nonetheless was used sparingly because it also was thought to encourage capitalist-like behavior.

Work measurement methods which were employed and which tended to provide for an egalitarian distribution of income were the equality, assessment, and the two fixed-rate methods. In the equality method, the same number of labor days were issued to all those members who arrived for work; farmers not attending work received no labor days.[41] In the assessment method, a meeting was held in which members assessed each other's work for a day or a period of time and determined the number of labor days each should receive. In the fixed-rate fixed-assessment method, members were classified into grades according to their level of work skill and capacity to work. Basic labor points were attached to each grade. At the end of each workday, those who worked simply received their basic labor points as work points (1 labor day is equivalent to 10 work points). After initially assessing grades, the actual work done was not assessed. The fixed-rate flexible-assessment method was established in the same manner as the method above. In contrast to the former, however, an assessment meeting was held and work done by members was evaluated. Thus, even if a strong member had a fixed grade of 12 basic labor points, if he failed to do an adequate job in the minds of his team members, his work points for the day could be reduced.

The egalitarian tendencies of the quality method are obvious, but present in the other methods as well. Social pressures apparently worked when teams convened meetings to assess members' work or to fix basic labor points. The results of these meetings show that while there was a distribution of basic labor points or work points, the distribution was made within a rather narrow band. For example, instead of fixing basic labor points for young strong workers at 20 and elderly weak workers at 4, the differences were 10 for the strong and only 6 for the weaker members.

The tendency for teams to distribute incomes on an egalitarian basis does not mean that incomes in the commune system or rural areas are the same. While team members are willing to share income on a more egalitarian basis with their close neighbors, and relatives, they do not seem to be as willing to share income with their compatriots in nearby teams.

Team and per capita income levels were found to vary from region to region, and even within the same brigade. Many factors account for these

---

[41] The equality work measurement method should not be confused with the egalitarian payment system noted above. In the latter, income was divided equally among all members regardless of whether they worked or not. In the former, only those who worked received payment.

differences. Foremost is the fact that the team is the basic unit of account, and hence any differences in factors of production tend to be reflected in differences in levels of income. The fertility of farmland in China varies from place to place just as fertility levels vary in any country. Farmers living in a team located in the fertile Pearl River Delta in South China are likely to have higher incomes than farmers living in dry upland Shansi Province. Farmers living in teams which supply high-value vegetables and fruits to urban centers tend to have higher incomes than farmers living in teams in isolated mountainous regions.

Other factors accounting for differences in team income levels include: (1) management and bargaining skill of team leaders; (2) the quantity and quality of capital investments made in the team area before and after communes were organized; (3) nearness of transportation routes to market products and to obtain supplies of inputs; (4) state investment in fertilizer plants, water conservation projects, and hydroelectric power generating stations; and (5) skills acquired by the labor force.

Households

Households currently number about 167 million and on the average have about 4.4 persons and 1.9 labor force units per household. As before, most households are allowed to engage in a limited amount of private sideline activity and cultivate private plots. Some areas discouraged these activities in the past 12 years, but Article 7 of the new constitution gives commune members the opportunity to farm small plots of land for their own use and to engage in limited sideline production activities, provided that the collective economy in the commune system remains predominant.

Private subsidiary production of households includes such things as tending fruit trees and selling fruit; weaving mats, bags, and baskets; making rope and bamboo articles. Households also collect firewood for sale, and in one case panned for gold in a mountain stream.

Households continue to work private plots and raise hogs and keep poultry as they did prior to 1963. Some teams, however, reported households had no private plots.[42] Nevertheless, most households in rural China probably have a private plot. In most teams 5 percent of the arable land is allocated for private plots. On the average each household is allowed to cultivate about 300 square meters of land, which is a plot of land about 57 feet square.

*　　*　　*　　*　　*

Fruits and vegetables from private plots and the private raising of hogs and poultry continue as before to provide farm families with foods required

---

[42] Alley, *Travels*, pp. 143–45.

for a balanced diet.[43] As before, income generated in private production activity is an important supplement to total household income: At least 5 percent and probably about 10 percent of total household income comes from private plots, since about 5 percent of the arable land is in private plots and households raise high-value chickens and pigs, fruits, vegetables, and cash crops such as tobacco and castorbean seed.

Sales of privately raised vegetables, hogs, and poultry provide households with an important source of cash income. As before, households gain some security from working in private production activity, because it is an activity in which they can control the final output, in contrast to their work in collective production in which the final outcome is the result of the labor and decisions of many other people. Manure from privately raised hogs and poultry continues to be an important source of fertilizer for collective fields. Finally, households continue to be China's most important source of supply for vegetables, rabbits, poultry, and hogs.

In summary, households receive income from three sources. First, labor force units in households earn income by laboring in team fields and brigade and commune shops. Second, members of households receive some income from brigades, communes, and the state in the form of social services, as these institutions provide some subsidies to hospitals, clinics, and schools. Third, households earn income by producing handicraft items, by working at odd jobs, and by growing crops and rearing animals on their private plots. The vast majority of household income comes from cashing in labor days earned working in team fields or on team projects.

A limited amount of per capita and household income data was collected from the 1,400 reports. There were not sufficient income data to illustrate changes in income through time nor were there data to highlight differences in income levels among teams, brigades, communes, counties, and provinces. With the limited number of reports, the best that can be done is to show per capita income differences between North and South China, and differences in income levels between persons residing in rural and suburban teams. While most reports did not provide clear explanations of income data, it is likely that the data were based on residual income distributed to members, and did not include income from private production activity. Also it is likely that the value of the health and education benefits consumed by members likewise is not included in per capita income data.

It is well to note that the per capita income figure for each category was obtained by summing up all the income data through time and by dividing by the total number of reports. Luckily, reports containing information on income were quite evenly distributed throughout the whole period

---

[43] Kenneth R. Walker made these same points in his definitive work on private plots prior to 1963. See his *Planning in Chinese Agriculture: Socialization and the Private Sector, 1956–1962* (Chicago: Aldine Publishing Co., 1965), p. 41.

of study. Hence if the trends of increase in the incomes of various regions did not differ greatly, some general patterns of per capita income can be shown as follows:

Annual Per Capita Income on Chinese Communes (Yuan)

	North China	South China
All communes	141.3	154.8
Rural communes	116.4	134.5
Suburban communes	241.0	170.8

Individuals working in suburban communes generally earned considerably more income, 27 percent in the South and 107 percent in the North, than persons in corresponding rural areas. Note should be made that only a limited number of observations were found for suburban communes in North China, making it difficult to give great weight to the comparison between income levels in that category and other areas in China. Commune members in rural areas in South China generally earned 16 percent more than those in the North. Likewise, farmers in both rural and suburban communes in South China earned an average of 10 percent more than those in the North. Regarding differences between North and South, the pattern of income distribution noted in this study is consistent with that found by Professor Buck in his survey of the Chinese agricultural economy in the period 1929–33.[44]

IV. ECONOMIC COORDINATION AND DECISION MAKING IN THE COMMUNE SYSTEM AND PROSPECTS FOR CHANGE

Because the team is the basic production unit, the key question with regard to decision making in the commune system relates to the degree of autonomy at this level. To what extent are the team's decisions primary and to what extent guided? What are the factors leading toward the integration of the team into the state planning system and what are the factors which encourage its autonomy? What are the pressures that any given team leader must face as he plans for the economic well-being of this unit?

First, there are a series of pressures which combine to make the team organization a fairly autonomous decision-making unit and which limit, to some extent, the degree of flexibility in state planning. There are, for in-

---

[44] John Lossing Buck, *Land Utilization in China* (Nanking: University of Nanking, 1937; New York: Paragon Book Reprint Corporation, 1964), pp. 46, 286, 305, and 470.

stance, physical constraints on state planning possibilities. Factors such as soil, climate, topography, the availability of water, and crop rotation patterns insure that many teams grow the same crops year after year. State directives might influence some of the alternatives, but the production pattern of many teams is predetermined by such physical constraints.

Second, there are what can be termed "social constraints" on higher-level decision making. The team leader, who actually makes the crucial production decisions, is torn, in a sense, between his obligation to state production goals, as handed down through commune and brigade levels, and his responsibility to his team to maximize its income. It is important to note that he is not an "outsider" brought in to administer state plans, but is an integral member of the team. His decisions affect his own income and that of his close friends and relatives. He is an intermediary between the state, on one hand, and neighboring households on the other. He must cater to the former while continuing to work and live with the latter. Any analysis of decision making in the commune system must recognize the divided loyalties of the team leader and the careful balancing of priorities which must exist at this basic level.

Along with physical and social constraints, there are institutional constraints on the degree of influence higher-level officials have on the team. Of all the factors leading toward autonomy at the team level, perhaps the most important concerns the fact that the team is the unit of account. In a sense it resembles the private firm in a capitalist society. It is responsible for its own profitability. Thus team members are not paid by the state. If they are influenced to make erroneous production decisions by higher levels, they suffer the loss in income. Thus they are less tractable than if they were state employees.

In addition, the team distributes income among its members. It operates under a type of "honor system" in its payments of grain tax and in its deliveries of grain purchases to the state, much the same as a firm in the United States is obligated to pay its taxes. Police powers can be invoked but not in every individual case. If the state is occupied with other campaigns, then a relaxation of control at the top occurs and the mobilization of pressure at the team level becomes more difficult.

Finally the state itself has recognized the importance of the team in agricultural production and has imposed restrictions on the intervention of higher levels into the affairs of this basic unit. For instance, a commune or brigade can no longer take labor force units arbitrarily out of the teams for its own projects (such as occurred numerous times during the Great Leap Forward period). The three principles which are to govern the interrelations between levels are (1) volunteerism, (2) mutual benefit, and (3) exchange at equal value. All three principles serve to protect the team from overzealous cadres at higher levels commandeering their resources and disrupting their production processes.

In sum, there seems to be a willingness at very high levels to recognize the productive value of the team and to protect its autonomy (*a*) by making it the unit of account; and (*b*) by establishing administrative barriers to higher-level interference in its affairs. This fact, and the physical and social factors listed above, combine to insure a high degree of autonomy for the team.

However, there are developing institutions and services at the commune and brigade levels which increasingly involve the team in coordination and planning activities at these levels and consequently limit its autonomy. First, although the typical team leader is probably not a member of the Communist Party, he has undoubtedly been influenced by Party doctrine with regard to agricultural collectivization and the building of socialism in the countryside. He is also aware of the great potential for intervention in his affairs by Party and militia leaders. Moreover, he knows that he must obtain the necessary agricultural inputs to maximize production. These are, to a large extent, controlled by state entities and by the commune and brigade organizations. If he is not responsive to higher-level planning, he may find himself without the necessary fertilizer, machinery, or even electricity to carry on his production functions.

He is also aware that credit facilities are controlled by the state. It is unlikely that recalcitrant teams are given first priority when investment loans are decided upon. Then, too, he knows that excellent employment opportunities are sometimes available in commune- and brigade-level industries if cooperation with these units is forthcoming on his part.

Finally, he is keenly aware of the important services controlled by higher levels, such as health, education, and transportation facilities. He is undoubtedly interested in insuring maximum utilization of these services for his team members.

All of these factors—respect for national goals and fear of massive state power, need for agricultural inputs, and desire to utilize higher-level credit and service facilities—encourage the team leader to comply with state agricultural planning.

During the last 12 years, the team has been the basic unit of Chinese agriculture. There is likely to be no important change in this regard for the next five years. Chinese agriculture is labor-intensive and the team is the best-sized unit for organizing and mobilizing the labor force to perform the myriad of tasks involved in this type of agriculture.

There has, however, been significant growth in influence from the brigade and commune levels simply by virtue of the additional agricultural inputs and services provided by these levels. If the regime wished to make the brigade the unit of account, it would be in a better position to do so now than it was during the Great Leap Forward period. A generation of peasants have now matured under the commune system. (An 8-year-old in 1959 is 24 in 1975 and able to assume responsibilities within the system.)

It is, indeed, a familiar structure to the great majority of rural families. In addition, there are better managerial skills available at the commune and brigade levels now than in 1959–61.

However, it is the judgment of this researcher that the team will remain the primary unit for the near future. The new constitution envisions no change in the present structure of agricultural organization. Indeed, there is little incentive to change the system, as agricultural production, so necessary to the regime's long-term plans, has fared well under the present arrangement.

*   *   *   *   *

part V

Selected Aspects of Economic Systems

The following selections compare different economic systems from several standpoints. The first article examines enterprise management in the United States and the Soviet Union, as a key feature illuminating their respective economic systems. The next selection discusses unemployment in different economic systems. Selections 24 and 25 analyze inflation in the OECD countries and Eastern Europe, respectively. The last essay is a multidimensional comparison of East and West Germany.

Management

In every economic system, enterprise management has important functions of planning, coordination, administration, control, and supervision. However, the scope and character of these functions—management's responsibilities and powers—vary with the nature of the economic system.

In a capitalist market economy, management is free to adjust both outputs and inputs in pursuit of profits. In Lange's theoretical model of market socialism, managers are instructed to choose input combinations and output levels which lead to the most economical production of the socially optimal output, regardless of whether profits or losses result. In Yugoslav market socialism, however, enterprises follow the capitalist approach of adjusting outputs and inputs in pursuit of profit. In contrast, in a centrally administered economy, management's task is to fulfill the detailed plan fixed for the enterprise by the central authorities. Managers are expected to produce the scheduled output with the authorized inputs. The profit resulting from the sale of output is likely to be of subordinate importance. Thus, both management's assignment and its freedom to accomplish it vary with the economic system in which it operates. At the same time, it is interesting to note that essentially the same incentives—job security, promotion, and, especially, salary and bonuses—motivate management in all of these economic systems.

The following selection, comparing managerial incentives and decision making in the U.S. and Soviet economies, illustrates these points.

22

MANAGERIAL INCENTIVES AND DECISION MAKING: A COMPARISON OF THE UNITED STATES AND THE SOVIET UNION*

Joseph S. Berliner

Berliner points out the major differences and similarities between the U.S. and Soviet economies in managerial incentives and decision making. Since American managers operate in a much different economic environment, their problems and therefore their practices differ from those of Soviet managers. But in those aspects of economic life in which the two economies are somewhat alike, American and Soviet managers behave in much the same way.

The assignments, powers, and problems of enterprise managers differ notably in the two economies. In the U.S. firm, profit is the main criterion of managerial performance. The Soviet manager, on the other hand, is expected to achieve (or surpass) a number of plan targets which are sometimes mutually exclusive. In the sellers' market of the Soviet economy, managers are usually more concerned with the acquisition of inputs than with the disposition of output. The opposite is true in the U.S. economy, where the biggest problem of management under normal conditions is marketing, rather than purchasing. Thus, the energy spent by the Soviet firm on obtaining materials is devoted by the American firm to selling and advertising.

At the same time, the two economies rely on essentially similar incentives to motivate managers toward whatever is defined as good

* Reprinted from *Comparisons of the United States and Soviet Economies* (Papers Submitted by Panelists Appearing before the Subcommittee on Economic Statistics, Joint Economic Committee, 86th Cong., 1st sess.) (Washington, D.C.: U.S. Government Printing Office, 1959), part I, pp. 349–76. Joseph S. Berliner is Professor of Economics at Brandeis University.

performance. In both economies there are conflicts of interest between the owners of the enterprise and the hired professional managers who run it. And in both countries managers may engage in various illegal or evasive practices when they believe their interests conflict with existing laws and regulations.

The rewards in income and prestige in the United States and Soviet economies are such that a larger proportion of the best young people in the USSR turn to careers in heavy industry, science, and higher education, whereas in the United States a larger proportion of the best talent flows into such fields as heavy or light (consumer goods) industry, finance, commerce and trade, law, medicine, etc. Higher education, particularly technical, is more of a prerequisite for the attainment of a top business career in the Soviet Union than in the United States.

The principal managerial incentive in Soviet industry is the bonus paid for overfulfillment of plan targets. The incentive system is successful in the sense that it elicits a high level of managerial effort and performance. But it has the unintended consequence of causing managers to engage in a wide variety of practices that are contrary to the interests of the state. Managers systematically conceal their true production capacity from the planners, produce unplanned types of products, and falsify the volume and quality of production. In the procurement of materials and supplies they tend to order larger quantities than they need, hoard scarce materials, and employ unauthorized special agents who use influence and gifts to ease management's procurement problems. The incentive system causes managers to shy away from innovations that upset the smooth working of the firm.

Since American managers operate in a different economic environment, their problems and therefore their practices differ from those of Soviet managers. But in those aspects of economic life in which the U.S. economy approximates the operating conditions of the Soviet economy, American managers develop forms of behavior similar to those of Soviet managers. The separation of management and ownership characteristic of the modern corporation leads to conflicts of interest between managers and stockholder-owners, and management's pursuit of its own interest leads to activities similar to those of the Soviet manager striving to defend his interests against those of the owner-state. The spread of legislation constricting the freedom of operation of the American firm leads to the evasion of laws and regulations characteristic of the Soviet economy, though on a larger scale there. Finally, under wartime conditions the burgeoning of government controls and the dominant role of the government as customer alter the operating conditions of the U.S. economy in such ways that it closely approximates some of the normal operating conditions of the Soviet economy. The change is accompanied by black-market operations, hoarding, quality deterioration, and the use of influence, practices which are normal in the peacetime Soviet economy.

MANAGERIAL INCENTIVES AND RECRUITMENT

The most important decision a manager has to make is made before he ever becomes a manager; namely, the decision to prepare for a managerial career. The factors influencing this decision are of vital importance for our industrial society. Imagine the consequences if no one aspired to become a manager, or if young people chose management only as a last resort, or if other careers were so attractive that management got only the last pickings of each year's crop of youngsters. It might therefore be appropriate to begin with some reflections on the incentives that the United States and the USSR offer their young people to choose a managerial career rather than some other.

The factors motivating young people to choose one or another occupation are probably not vastly different in the two countries. Family tradition is often decisive; many a youngster chooses a career simply because he wishes to be like his father (or mother). Special talents such as those of the artist, or early conceived deep interests, like the boy who must be a scientist, account for the career choices of some others. But most teenagers have no clear idea of what they would like to be. It is with respect to these youths that it is most interesting to speculate upon the incentive-pulls that the two systems offer for the choice of one career or another.

Education and Career Choice

The role of higher education in career choice is different in the two nations. Higher education is very much more of a prerequisite for the prestigious, high income occupations in the USSR than in the United States. To be sure, the person with a high school education or less has an increasingly difficult time entering the managerial ladder of the large American corporation. But in such fields as trade, commerce, construction and in small business in general, the opportunities are still vast for a financially successful career. College, and education in general, is not of decisive importance. And the brute fact is that a college diploma can always be obtained somewhere in the United States, with very little effort or ability, by just about anyone who can pay the tuition and write a semiliterate paragraph. Those who don't aspire to a managerial position or who fail to make the grade can, as workingmen, nevertheless enjoy a standard of living that is the envy of the world. The point is that the young American who is not inclined toward academic work need not feel that he is out of the competition for our society's best rewards.

This is not true in the USSR. A number of conversations with young Soviet people have convinced me that to be a "worker" is something devoutly to be shunned by most young people who have reached the high school level. There are at least two reasons for this attitude, which seems so anomalous in a "worker's state." The first is the enormously high prestige that Russian (and European) culture has always placed upon the "intelligent," the learned man, the man who works with his mind instead of his hands. The Soviet regime has striven hard to make manual labor respectable, and it undoubtedly has succeeded in endowing the worker with a social position relatively much higher than before the revolution. But the young person who has reached the educational level at which he can choose between being a worker or an "intelligent" would, other things being equal, choose the latter without question.

Other things are not equal, however. In particular, the income possibilities of a worker are far smaller than those of a college graduate, and this is the second reason for the desperate, and sometimes pathetic, drive for a higher education. Of course, a person must have reached the high school level before he can even begin to think about choosing between the career of a worker or an "intelligent." The steady annual expansion in the high school population has had the effect of presenting ever-increasing numbers of young people with the choice, and few of them would freely choose to be workers. If the expansion of the school population had continued, giving more and more young people the opportunity to avoid being workers, it would have raised serious problems for the recruitment of the labor force. The radical reform of the education system by Khrushchev was undoubtedly motivated, in part, by the wish to avoid that problem.

Thus, the undesirability of a career as a worker has intensified the desire for higher education. Add to this the fact that there is no private enterprise, no small business in which a man could pull himself out of a worker's status and reach a position of prestige and income comparable to the self-made American businessman. I do not wish to state that the door is completely closed. By dint of hard work, ability, and certain other qualities, a Soviet citizen without the college diploma can from time to time rise to an important position in some economic hierarchy. But his chances are about as good as those of an equivalent person in a progressive American corporation. And the young person evaluating the importance of higher education understands this.

Finally, the Russian teenager who decides he has to get a college diploma has very few easy ways out. He can't buy his way into college, as the American student can if he has the money. There are no private colleges that can set whatever standards they wish. To be sure there are instances of bribery or influence, but they are certainly the exception. If the Soviet student wants a college diploma very badly, he has to work hard to gain admission and to be graduated. The very intensity of the drive for education, and the competition of many applicants for the limited number of admissions, permits the high schools and colleges to maintain high standards of performance. Moreover the colleges are financially independent of student tuitions; not only are there no tuitions but most of the students earn stipends. The consequence is that the typical Soviet student works harder and has to meet higher standards of performance than the typical American student. The standards are different in the two countries, of course, because of differences in the philosophy of education. But there is no doubt that study is a much more serious business for the young Soviet student than for the American.

One final note on education and incentives. The quality of the managerial (and technical) manpower of a nation depends on the proportion of the population comprising the pool from which the managers are drawn. That is, if half the population were for some reason excluded from the pool, the quality of the managers would be lower than if the whole population comprised the pool. Both nations suffer in this respect from the fact that rural educational facilities are poorer than urban, which reduces the pool of the potential college group. Since the Soviet rural population is larger percentagewise than that of the United States, and since their rural educational facilities are probably relatively worse than ours, they suffer more than we from this loss. But there are other ways in which our pool is curtailed more than the Soviet. First is the fact that the private cost of education keeps a substantial portion of our talented young people in the lower income groups out of college. I admit that this fact puzzles me. With our network of free state universities and with a fairly abundant scholarship program, I don't fully understand why any competent student who really desired it could not get a college education. It is my impression, however, that systematic studies generally show that we are losing an unfortunate number of young people from higher education for financial reasons. If this is so, we are worse off than the Soviets in this respect, for their education is absolutely free, and most students of any merit earn stipends besides. Lower income young Soviet people may nevertheless be unable to go off to college if the family needs their earnings. A young Soviet woman told me, in reply to my question, that this was why she never went on to college. She is not a very good illustration of my point, however, for she went on to say that she really wasn't very smart anyhow.

The second group that is largely lost from America's pool of potential managerial manpower is the Negro and some other racial minorities. It may well be that the proportion of college graduates among some of the Soviet national minorities is smaller than for the Slavic nationalities; I have seen no data on this. But I would doubt that their loss from racial discrimination is as large as ours.

The third and largest group lost from our pool comprises exactly half our population—the female half. Sex discrimination certainly exists in the

Soviet economy, probably more in management than in science and technology. But undoubtedly the female population enlarges the pool of technical and managerial manpower much more in the USSR than in the United States. The difference in the role of women in the two countries must, I think, enter into the balance I am trying to strike, but it is not a subject on which I would recommend that your committee consider writing corrective legislation. For one thing it is not perfectly clear which way sex discrimination works in the United States. Women discriminate against working about as much as jobs discriminate against women.

Let me summarize briefly this discussion of the relationship of education to career choice. Education, and particularly higher education, is more important in the USSR than in the United States as the gateway to a prestigious and highly remunerative career. Competition is keener for higher education, the cost of education to the individual is less, and the standards of admission and performance are higher in the USSR. Both nations lose part of the potential pool of managerial talent, the USSR because of its large rural population, the United States because of financial burdens and racial and sex discrimination.

Competition among Careers

How does a managerial career compare with the attractiveness of other careers in the two nations? The young American not dedicated to some particular field, but motivated by a roughly equal desire for prestige and money, might select some field such as law, medicine, business, or engineering. He would decidedly not go into education or science. An equivalent young Soviet person would make a somewhat different choice. He would certainly not select law, which has been assigned a most humble role in Soviet society. Nor would he select medicine, for while the prestige is high, the income is low. On the other hand, higher education or science would be an excellent choice. The very title of "Professor" or "Scientific Worker" would assure him one of the highest places of honor in the society. And an outstanding career in either of those fields would assure him an income ranking in the upper 10 percent or perhaps even 5 percent (data are hard to come by) of the population. The difference in the economic and social position of the scientist and teacher in the two countries is of fundamental importance in the matter of career recruitment.

The American who decides to choose a career in the business world has a much wider range of choice than his Soviet counterpart. A great variety of fields offer roughly equivalent rewards in prestige and incomes: advertising, accounting, finance, commerce, trade, sales, light manufacturing, heavy industry. Of all these fields, it is only the latter that would exert a great pull on the young Soviet person. For 40 years the government and party have hammered home the central role of heavy industry, children are instilled with an admiration of technology, and heavy industry has been endowed with an aura of glamour that exceeds even our American fascination with technology. The ideological cards are stacked, in varying degree, against all other branches of the economy. In keeping with the ideology, the prestige and income possibilities in heavy industry are decidedly greater than in the other branches.

Not only will the student be attracted to heavy industry, but he is likely to choose engineering as his path of entry into whatever branch of heavy industry he selects. He would be attracted to engineering for the educational reasons discussed above. Engineering is, moreover, the most direct line of approach to a managerial career.

The Soviet engineering graduate will find his first job opportunities rather different from those of his American counterpart. If he is at the top of his class, the best offers will come from the research institutes, with top starting salaries and opportunities for graduate work. The poorer students will find lower paying jobs in industry. In the United States the situation is quite the reverse. The most successful students will be snapped up by recruiters from the large corporations, with the best starting salary offers. Some of the top students will, to be sure, spurn the attractive job offers and go on to further graduate work, but I suspect that many of those who go immediately into graduate work are the men who didn't get the good job offers. To be sure, many of the top American students who join the corporations are put immediately into research and development, but as many of them will be working on new passenger car or dishwasher design as will be working on electronic development and automation technique. The Soviet researcher is more likely to be working on the latter than the former.

The young Soviet engineer who goes into industry starts at the bottom of the managerial ladder, as chief of a production shop, or the design or maintenance departments of the enterprise. As new job opportunities develop, he faces the choice of continuing in direct production or taking one of the staff jobs in the enterprise, such as the planning department. If he stays in production proper, his career path may lead to chief engineer of an enterprise or to one of the higher economic agencies. If he moves into staff work, his career may lead to the directorship of an enterprise or of one of the higher organs. Either career leads to the pinnacle of Soviet management.

The paths that are least likely to lead to top management are finance or sales. I would guess the proportion of top management in the United States who started in such fields as finance and sales is much larger than in the USSR. There are no "colleges of business administration" in the Soviet Union. The ambitious youngster who wants to work for the top of the Soviet business world studies engineering, not personnel and marketing.

Summarizing, industry in the United States has to compete with a wide variety of other branches of economic activity for its share of the best potential managerial talent. In the USSR the values and the rewards are concentrated in relatively fewer fields, and industry is far more attractive than most others. Science and higher education, which scarcely compete with industry in the United States, are strong competitors of industry in the USSR. Among the various branches of industry, in the United States the light and consumer goods industries compete very effectively for both managerial and engineering talent. In the USSR light and consumer goods industries are much less attractive than heavy industry. And finally the nature of industrial recruitment is such that technical education is much more important as part of the training of a would-be manager in the USSR than in the United States.

My conclusion is that heavy industry, science and higher education attract, by and large, a better and more competent crop of young people in the USSR than in the United States. Moreover, the competition for education is keener in the USSR, so that they get a more rigorously trained (trained in different ways, to be sure) corps of managerial, engineering, scientific and university personnel. On the other hand, such branches of the economy as sales, advertising, finance, trade and commerce, light industry, and law attract a much more competent group of people in the United States than in the USSR. Most of the outstanding people in these fields in the United States would, if they were Soviet citizens, have enjoyed successful careers in heavy industry, science, technology, or higher education. There is, after all, nothing startling in this conclusion. It is but another way of saying that each society gets what it pays for.

MANAGERIAL INCENTIVES AND DECISION MAKING

Material Incentives

The incentives that attract people into management are not necessarily the same incentives that motivate managers to do their jobs and do them well. What are the goals of the manager? What are the considerations that impel him to make one decision rather than the other?

The moving force of our economic system is the pursuit of private gain. The worker chooses the higher paying job, the businessman accepts the more profitable contract, the investor buys the higher interest security. The usual exceptions must of course be made; the laws must be obeyed, public opinion may sometimes require that one decision be made rather than another, people make wrong decisions, a short-run loss may be accepted for a longer term gain. But by and large—"other things being equal," as the economist likes to say—it is private gain that determines economic decisions.

The Soviets have at various times experimented with other forms of incentive, for it did not as first seem quite appropriate that a Socialist economy should stress private gain. But practicality won out over dogma, and private gain has for the last 25 years been the keystone of the managerial incentive system. To be sure, we still find references to various social incentives such as Communist enthusiasm. But we are also reminded that while enthusiasm is well and good, communism, as Lenin used to say, must be built "not directly on enthusiasm but with the aid of enthusiasm born out of the great revolution; [communism must be built] on private interest, on personal incentive, on businesslike accounting." Moreover, the incentive of private gain will be with us for a long time. According to the eminent labor economist E. Manevich, it will not disappear until the day of general overabundance arrives, until the differences between country and city are eliminated, and until the differences between mental and manual labor vanish. We are safe in saying that for the next several decades at least, private gain will be the central economic incentive in both economic systems.

The form that material incentives take is of some importance. For the American businessman it is clearly profit. If you ask why did he take on this contract rather than that, why did he order this machine rather than that, why did he ship by truck rather than train, the answer would normally be, "because it's cheaper that way," or what comes to the same thing, "because he would make more money that way."

For the private businessman managing his own business, profit is clearly the guide to his actions. But most American business is not managed in this way. The men who actually run the firm are salaried managers, hired by the stockholders' representative body, the board of directors. The profit of the business does not belong to the manager but to the stockholder-owners. The fact is that the private interest of the manager need not necessarily coincide with that of the stockholder. In order to bring the manager's private interest into closer coincidence with that of the owners, most corporations have instituted some kind of bonus system, on the assumption that if the manager has a direct stake in the profit of the enterprise, his decisions are more likely to be those that will earn more profit.

In fashioning an incentive system for its managers, the Soviet government faced a problem similar to that of the American corporation. For all Soviet enterprises are run by salaried managers. If the Soviet manager's income consisted solely of his salary, it was conceivable that his private interest would not coincide at all points with the interest of the government. Accordingly a considerable variety of supplementary bonuses are available to the managerial staff. The bonuses are designed to motivate managers to make those decisions that the government considers to be in its own interest.

* * * * *

But incentive for what? This is surely the crucial question. For we can readily imagine an incentive which was extremely successful in motivating action, but action of an undesirable kind. The test of an incentive is therefore not only its motivating power, but the extent to which it leads to the desired kind of decision.

Before proceeding to the relationship of incentives to decision making, let me clarify the sense in which I use the term incentive. By incentive I mean that consideration which explains why one decision was made rather than another. If a young person decides to find employment in the electrical machinery industry rather than in the furniture industry, the difference in basic salaries in the two industries may well have been the decisive consideration. In this case salary is the effective incentive. But once in the job, the salary does not vary according to whether one operating decision is made rather than another. When the manager decides to put one order into production ahead of another, or to substitute one material for another, it is not his salary he is thinking about. It is usually the size of the month's bonus that will depend on the decision taken. It is in this sense that the bonus is the principal incentive in the operational decisions of the Soviet enterprise.

Production Decisions

Two generations ago people debated the question of whether a socialist economy could possibly work. History removed that question from the agenda. The last generation changed the question to whether the Soviet economy could work at all efficiently. That question has also been answered. These hearings would not otherwise be taking place. My discussion takes for granted that the Soviet economy is reasonably efficient and that the question at issue is how efficient.

There is little doubt that the system of managerial incentives, broadly viewed, has created a corps of managers dedicated to their work and responsive to the production demands made upon them. Like their American counterparts, they are deeply involved in their work, they worry about production quotas, they demand results from their labor force. As hired managers, they are aware that if their performance is not satisfactory, there are always other persons spoiling for a chance at their jobs. I have no way of knowing whether the intensity of managerial life is greater in the USSR than in the United States; in both countries there are variations from industry to industry. But there are two reasons why industrial life probably proceeds at a faster tempo in the USSR than here. The first is that the absence of free trade unions makes it difficult for workers to resist pressure for intense operation. The second is that industry is under constant exhortation from government and party for ever-increasing levels of production.

But the question as indicated above is not whether management is motivated to work hard. It is rather whether the incentive system motivates them to do what the state wishes them to do; whether, in other words, they get as much mileage out of their effort as they might get.

One of the most interesting conclusions of the study of Soviet managerial incentives is that the bonus system is directly responsible for motivating management to make a variety of decisions contrary to the intent and the interests of the state. The decisions to be described go far back in the history of the Soviet economy and have resisted countless efforts by the government to eliminate them. Most of them have survived the great organizational changes in industrial organization of the past several years. They are clearly deeply rooted in the soil of Soviet economic organization.

First, consider the matter of the reporting of information. In a planned economy it is vital that the central planners have as accurate information as possible about the productive capacity of enterprises. The bonus system, however, acts as a prevailing motivation for managers to understate their real production capacity. The reason is that the most important of the bonuses available to managers depends on the extent to which the production target of the enterprise is overfulfilled. If the manager honestly reports his full production capacity, and if for some reason something goes wrong in the course of the month, then he and his staff will lose that month's bonus. It is safer therefore to report a smaller capacity than really exists, in order that the production target will be kept low enough to allow for emergencies. The Russians call this "insurance" or "security." The consequence is that the planners can never be sure that their plans are based on accurate figures. The government is aware of the problem: "This is fully understandable," writes a Soviet economist, "because the lower the plan, the greater the opportunity to fulfill and overfulfill it. . . ."

Because the higher state agencies cannot trust management's reporting of its productive capacity, various techniques have been fashioned for setting targets high enough to force the firms to operate as close as possible to capacity. One of these techniques is the arbitrary increase of targets over last year's production. As a prominent state planning commission economist put it, "they take as the base magnitude the level of production achieved during the preceding period and raise it by some percentage or other." Sometimes this technique helps flush out the manager's "hidden reserves," but in other cases the arbitrary increase in targets leads to impossibly high tasks. Indeed, the spirit of planning is reflected in the systematic use of high targets as a device for keeping managers working at as fast a tempo as possible. In the past targets have been set so high (deliberately, one suspects) that one third of all enterprises failed to fulfill their annual plans. . . . The intense pace of plant operation has its distinct advantage from the state's point of view: it elicits from management a high level of effort that might not be forthcoming if the plans were set at a more modest level. But the price paid by the state is the manager's effort to defend his enterprise by concealing his full capacity.

When the target has been set, the manager's bonus depends on the success with which he fulfills it. Most of the firm's production does indeed follow the lines laid down in the plan. But when the end of the month rolls around and, as often happens, production is far short of meeting the month's target, then managers turn to a host of time-tested techniques of meeting—or seeming to meet—the targets. In certain types of production, such as metals, the target is expressed in tons; in such cases the manager might order his shops to curtail the production of relatively lightweight products (special and quality metals) and to throw more men and materials into the production of the heavier products. In textile production we read that the practice of setting targets in "running meters" (that is, in measures of length, without regard to width) causes managers to overproduce narrow-width cloth and underproduce broad width. In firms with a considerable variety of products, the production targets are expressed in value units—so many millions of rubles of production. In such cases managers tend to overproduce those products that have high fixed prices (all prices are fixed): they may deliberately use more expensive materials in order to drive up the value of production. These are some of an endless variety of ways in which managers "violate the planned assortment of production" —to use the official expression of disapproval.

How widespread are these practices? We really don't know. From time to time individual managers are publicly excoriated for such practices, and figures are published to show how widely the planned assortment of production has been departed from. But these may well be extreme cases, and it would be unwise to generalize from them. Occasionally, however, the results of special studies are published, and they give us some idea of the magnitude of the problem. The state planning commission recently released the results of a survey of the production practices of 63 enterprises. Of the total production by these enterprises in excess of the plan targets, only 43 percent consisted of the basic products normally produced by them; 26.5 percent consisted of "products not included in the plan when it was originally confirmed," 20 percent consisted of "other production," and 7 percent consisted not of finished products but of an increase in semifabricated parts and goods-in-process. While these data are not precisely in the form in which we would want them, they do provide a good indication of managers' tendency to produce those products that are best from their own enterprises' point of view, rather than those products that the state would most wish to have produced.

Two other consequences of the bonus system (and the pressure of high targets) should be noted. One is the simple falsification of reported production. "Thus, for example," we read in a Soviet article, "if the plan is fulfilled 99 percent, the managerial and engineering personnel receive no bonus. But if the enterprise fulfills the plan 100 percent, they receive bonuses of from 15 to 37 percent of their salary." Quite a lot of money hinges on that last percentage of production, and it is no wonder that management may succumb to the temptation to "fudge" the report a bit in order to earn the bonus. Again, the techniques of covering up for falsely reported production are myriad. To cite only one, production is "borrowed" from next month. That is, production that is expected to occur next month is reported as having been produced this month. If things go well next month, the "borrowed" output is "repaid"; if not the manager may get into trouble.

More serious than falsification, however, is the deterioration of the quality of production. The poor quality of much of Soviet consumer goods production is well known. In other types of production the danger of detection is greater, and quality standards are less readily violated. But the explanation of management's tendency to shave on quality is the same: the high production targets are so often not attainable, and the manager wants to keep his job. Much of the quality shaving is of a kind that is not easily detected: fewer stitches in the garment, fewer screws in the piece, greener lumber in the building, more impurities in the metal. But if the pressure is keen enough, more extreme forms of quality deterioration will be adopted.

Summarizing, the bonus system is an effective device for eliciting a high level of managerial effort, but in the context of excessively high production targets, it induces management to make certain types of decisions that are contrary to the intent of the state. The production of unplanned products, the concealment of production capacity, the falsification of reports, and the deterioration of quality are the unintended consequences of the system of managerial incentives.

Procurement Decisions

The high level of production targets is but half the problem facing the Soviet manager. The other half is the perpetual shortage of materials and supplies. In order to get the greatest possible production from the available stocks of materials and supplies, the state employs a variety of devices to minimize the use of materials in production and inventory. Undoubtedly these devices have served to control wasteful use of resources, and they have also helped channel the flow of resources in the direction most desired by the state. But they have been self-defeating to some extent for they have forced managers to make certain kinds of decisions which frustrate the intent of the state.

The core of the matter is that managers simply don't trust the planning system to provide them with the supplies and materials they need in the right quantity and quality, and at the right time. . . . For all important materials the manager must still obtain an allocation order from his home office, which must in turn get the allocation order from the republican or all-union planning commission.

Thus, we still read of the "existing complicated system of obtaining allocation orders, under which every enterprise must submit detailed requistions to Moscow a long time before the new planning quarter is to begin." Because plans are not always finally set at the time the planning period is to begin, enterprises sometimes start with "advance allocations," that is, temporary allotments of resources designed to keep them operating until the final allocation orders are available. . . . Perhaps even more serious than the complex supply planning system is the large percentage of enterprises that regularly fail to fulfill their plans, or fulfill them by producing the wrong products or substandard products. Since the production of these enterprises constitutes the planned supplies of other enterprises, the supplies of the latter are delayed or simply not available. Perhaps enough has been said to explain why "managers of enterprises did not have confidence in the possibility of getting their materials on time and having them delivered to the factory by the supply depot's trucks."

What does the manager do to make sure he gets his supplies? Just as he "secures" his production plan by attempting to conceal the existence of some production capacity, so he "secures" the flow of supplies in various ways. He overorders, in the hope that if he doesn't get all he ordered, he may at least get as much as he needs. He also orders excessively large amounts of some supplies in order to be able to buy directly from the producer, instead of having to go through the maze of jobbing depots. A survey of 15 Moscow enterprises showed a 10.4 percent overordering of metals for just this reason. Sometimes management's boldest efforts to obtain supplies are unsuccessful: ". . . over 300,000 construction workers undergo work stoppages daily because of the absence of materials at the workplace." In other cases their padded requisitions are accepted and they receive more than they need of some materials. The consequence is the piling up of hoards of supplies of all kinds, one of the most enduring problems of Soviet industrial organization. The government has waged a long-standing war against hoarding. One of the weapons by which it attempts to hold hoarding within bounds is the use of quotas of working capital; that is, for its annual production program the enterprise is allowed to keep on hand at any one time no more than so many tons of coal, so many board feet of lumber, so many rubles worth of inventory. These quotas must be negotiated between enterprise and government, and the enterprise's interest demands that they be set as high as possible. The mutual attempt at outguessing the other leads to a familiar bureaucratic game: ". . . enterprises try to 'justify' and obtain as large quotas of working capital as possible. The financial agencies, aware of this, strive on the other hand to reduce the quotas of working capital." This kind of planning is hardly calculated to lead to the establishment of the optimal quotas. It is more likely that some quotas will be too large and some too small.

The most interesting of the techniques used by managers to "secure" their supply of materials is the employment of special supply expediters called *tolkachi*, or "pushers." The table of organization does not provide for this occupation, yet so great is the need that firms manage somehow to employ these people. The chief job of the expediter is to make sure that his enterprise gets the materials it needs and when it needs them. Accordingly he spends most of his time on the road, visiting his enterprise's suppliers, handing out little gifts here and there to assure that his orders are well handled, picking up supplies of one kind or another that his firm may be able to use or trade for other goods. Much of their activity is associated with the black market, that is, obtaining materials for which no allocation order has been issued. This may be done either by wrangling an allocation order out of a reluctant government official by one means or another, or by persuading an approachable enterprise official to sell him the things he needs without an allocation order.

Some *tolkachi* take up permanent residence in the city in which the chief suppliers are located, and only occasionally return to their home firms for consultations. To keep the record clean, they are carried on the books as "senior buyer" or "supply agent." If they are known to be particularly adept at their jobs, they may be asked by other firms to represent them. Nothing is known of their incomes, but there is no doubt that they earn many times their base pay. And they fully earn it, both because of the vital nature of their work, and because the risks they take make them vulnerable to prosecution.

How widespread is the use of these expediters? Again, we catch only occasional hints of their prevalence. The most recent outburst against them reports that the number of *tolkachi* who annually visit the typical large enterprise runs into the thousands, and their expenses into hundreds of thousands of rubles. These, however, are only the reported expenses. More often than not their expenses are not reported as such but are concealed under such rubrics as "exchange of technical information," or "contract negotiations." Our latest informant, who is a senior investigator for the State Control Commission of the USSR, is of the opinion that despite continued official criticisms of the use of expediters, their number has actually been increasing. One of the reasons he adduces is interesting. In 1956, along with a wave of measures designed to give more freedom to plant managers, an order was issued relieving managers of the need to report in detail on all minor expenditures. Travel expenditures were among the items exempted. The measure had the unintended effect of encouraging the increased use of expediters.

The economic effect of the use of expediters is difficult to assess. There is no doubt that they are of vital importance to individual enterprises, but from the national point of view much of their activity involves merely the transfer to one fortunate enterprise of resources that otherwise would have gone to another. Since the higher priority enterprises have less need for expediters, the chances are that the net effect of their activity is to cause more resources to flow to lower priority enterprises at the expense of higher priority ones. On the credit side, however, their wide knowledge of sources of supply, of who has what to sell, is of some importance, and they do arrange for the movement of supplies that otherwise would have lain idle in one plant while another had need for it. In short, the expediter possesses a certain kind of knowledge that may be as important to economic organization as the knowledge of the engineer or the machinist. The planning system is able to direct the bulk of the nation's resources with reasonable effectiveness, but substantial quantities of materials and equipment elude the main stream of planning. How to get these resources back into the system is a problem that has exercised Soviet economists for a long time.[1]

In summary, the incentives that motivate managers to strive for the fulfillment of their production targets are the same incentives that motivate them to evade the regulations of the planning system. Because of the tightness of the supply system, which is deliberately engineered by the state, managers are compelled to defend their enterprises' position by overordering supplies, by hoarding materials and equipment, and by employing expediters whose function it is to keep the enterprise supplied with materials at all costs, legal or otherwise. The very planning system that serves to channel most of the nation's resources in directions desired by the state, serves also to misdirect a substantial volume of resources toward uses that are contrary to the wishes of the state.

Investment Decisions

If one were to ask what feature of the Soviet economic system accounts most of all for the rapid rate of growth, the answer would undoubtedly be the high rate of capital formation. The question at issue is whether it is as high as it might be, other things being equal. An examination of the system of managerial incentives will provide part, though by no means all, of the answer to this central question.

Management has a direct interest in obtaining new capital. It adds to productive capacity, and it is good for the record to show steady increases in production. Moreover fixed capital is provided to the enterprise as a free grant by the state, with no interest charge. The problem, therefore, has not been one of inducing management to accept more machines; it has rather been one of dissuading management from ordering too many machines. Far back in Soviet economic history one can find expressions of the problem similar to that recently uttered by Khrushchev in connection with the dissolution of the agricultural machine-tractor stations:

---

[1] Recently there have been numerous suggestions that enterprises and economic regions publish catalogs of the commodities they produce and the surplus materials and equipment they would like to sell. The expediters are rather like walking catalogs.

The machine-tractor stations accept any machine whether they need it or not. They don't grow flax, but they take flax-growing equipment. They don't grow cabbage, but they take cabbage-planting machines. Consequently many machines are not used for years and hundreds of millions of rubles worth of state resources are frozen.

The reason enterprises accept any piece of equipment they can get their hands on is similar to that discussed above in connection with materials hoarding. One can never tell when he may need just that kind of machine and not be able to obtain it. If one has a chance to get it now, order it by all means. It may come in handy some day for trading in return for something one might be able to use more readily. And above all, there is no charge for holding the equipment; there is no interest payment, and if the machine is not used there is no depreciation charge either. Hence there is everything to gain and nothing to lose by holding on to as much machinery and equipment as one can obtain.

How to induce managers to take a less cavalier view of capital has been a long-standing concern of economists. They look with some nostalgia at the effectiveness of the profit motive under capitalism in this respect. An eminent Soviet economist put it this way recently:

> In order to increase his profit as much as possible, the capitalist strives to use his equipment to the fullest extent possible, and in no case will he buy a machine that he doesn't need at the moment, since every surplus machine slows down the turnover of his capital and reduces his profit. For the same reason he strives to keep his inventories down to the very minimum and to market his finished products as quickly as possible.

Recent economic literature contains a number of suggestions of ways in which Soviet managers might be induced to order only that amount of capital needed for production purposes. One of the more interesting is a proposal advanced by the author quoted above. He suggests that profit be calculated not as a ratio to total production cost (as has always been done), but as a ratio to value of invested capital. In this way the enterprise with too much idle capital will show a lower rate of profit, and profit is one of the principal indicators of overall performance. The suggestion is interesting because it proposes that return on capital be used as a criterion of performance, a rather "bourgeois" notion. It should not, however, be thought that the proposal envisages reliance on the "profit motive" as we know it. Profit is an important indicator of the efficiency of plant operation, but the firm does not "own" its profit, although it shares in the profit in a minor way. As a personal incentive, profit is relatively unimportant in Soviet industry, certainly by comparison with the bonus.[2]

---

2 Editor's note: As a result of Soviet recognition of these problems, reforms were adopted in 1965 under which interest is now charged on the enterprise's capital, profitability is calculated in relation to capital, and the enterprise retains a larger share of its profits.

If the incentive system motivates managers to overorder and hoard equipment, the situation is quite the reverse with respect to technological innovation. Concern over managerial resistance to innovation is of long standing, but it has come to the fore in recent years in connection with increased emphasis on automation and modernization of plant and equipment. The reasons for managers' tendency to drag their feet in introducing new products or production techniques are well understood by Soviet economists:

> The explanation is, first of all, that the introduction of new technology involves certain risks and requires a considerable expenditure of time; secondly, after new technology has been introduced, more difficult plan targets are set and consequently there is less opportunity for fulfilling them and receiving bonuses.

When a manager has a well-running plant, when the workers have learned their jobs and have become experienced in using the existing equipment, he is reluctant to upset the cart by trying something new. A new production line means trouble. Production bugs have to be eliminated, workers have to be retrained, time is lost, and spoilage is high. The chances are that plans will be underfulfilled and the precious bonuses lost, particularly in view of the tendency for plan targets to be raised to the rated capacity of the new equipment. It is courting disaster to try new things. If the old machines are wearing out, it is safer to repair or even rebuild them rather than introduce the more complicated new models. Outlays on the rebuilding of old machines often exceed the price of a new modern machine.

There is another reason why managers shy away from innovation. Even if the potential gains from new technology are great, it usually takes a number of years before they are realized. But it is Soviet policy to shift managers around from plant to plant every few years. Therefore managers have a strictly short-run point of view. Why take on all the headaches of introducing a new line when one is not likely to be around to enjoy whatever benefits may eventually accrue? Capital investment policy is by its very nature a matter of long-term planning, and therefore does not commend itself to the short-run horizon of management.

How does the state combat managerial resistance to innovation? One technique is direct pressure. Pressure exerted on and by their own superiors explains much of the innovation that does occur. Enterprise managers may drag their feet for a long time, but when the direct order comes down that the new automatic line must be installed in the next six months, it is eventually acted upon. Pressure is also exerted through the Communist Party; if the Party officials in the enterprise are under direct orders from Moscow that automation must be accelerated, they are in a position to force the manager to move faster than he otherwise might. Such pressures are important, although it must be noted in passing that both the manager's bosses and local Party people often try to shield the enterprise from such pressures. They are as dependent for their careers upon successful plan fulfillment as are the plant managers themselves.

Direct orders from above are one way of getting management to innovate. But innovation would proceed more rapidly if managers could be made to wish to innovate, instead of waiting until they are forced into it. The literature of the past few years is full of suggestions on how this can be accomplished. It is suggested, for example, that attractively high prices be set on new machines, in order to stimulate the producers of those machines to put them into production more rapidly. While this measure might ease the financial strain on the innovating firm, it will not remove the risk that the production plan may be sacrificed. And production is much more vital to the success of the enterprise than finance.

More to the point are the suggestions that the bonus system be employed as an incentive for innovation. Soviet economists seem to have enormous confidence in bonuses as a device for getting management to wish to do what the state wishes them to do. But how to adapt the bonus system to this purpose is more difficult. In the course of years a variety of special bonuses have been introduced for one purpose or another, in addition to the major bonus that comes from fulfillment of the production plan. There are special bonuses available for economizing certain critical materials, for reducing the volume of goods-in-process, for conserving fuel, for increasing labor productivity, for keeping the plant clean, for reducing the volume of spoilage, for operating the plant without stoppages, for winning "socialist competitions," and many others.[3]

This dilution of the bonus system may actually weaken its power as an incentive. If the special bonuses are small, they will not be very effective. If they are large they may detract effort from what is, after all, the main objective of the state: fulfillment of the production plan. For it is interesting to note the evidence that the relative size of the bonus for this or that special purpose often determines the manager's decision to concentrate on this or that objective. There are two types of innovation: relatively small measures such as organizational improvements or inexpensive alterations, and the more dramatic large-scale changes in production techniques. The former are included in the overall enterprise plan each year, under the name of the plan of organizational and technical measures (Orgtekhplan). It happens that there are certain bonuses available for the design and introduction of the large-scale innovations, but none for the fulfillment of the Orgtekhplan. The consequence is that research and managerial personnel concentrate on the large items and pay little attention to the small ones, even though the latter could result in great savings with relatively

---

[3] Not all these types of bonus are available to the director himself, but they are available to different groups of managerial personnel.

little cost and effort. Thus the very potency of the bonus as an incentive militates against its use for too many special purposes which may compete with each other.

To conclude this discussion, the unreliability of the supply system and the absence of a charge for the use of capital motivate management to order more fixed capital than they need and to hoard machines and equipment. This tendency deflects a certain amount of currently produced capital goods from being put directly into production in their best uses. On the other hand, the incentive system discourages management from taking the risks associated with innovation. Direct orders from above lead to a substantial volume of innovation, and in many cases management may consider certain forms of innovation to be to their interest. The provision of special bonuses for innovation, if they were large enough to compete with the production plan bonus, might help provide an incentive for innovation, and much of the current discussion in the Soviet Union seems to point to this as the next phase.

SOME COMPARATIVE OBSERVATIONS

The preceding section has shown that Soviet managers are motivated to make a variety of decisions that are contrary to the interest of the state. Since the state's interest is paramount in the Soviet scheme of things, we may properly conclude that the incentive and decision-making system is "relatively inefficient," or "less than perfectly efficient." Let me caution the reader once more against inferring from this that Soviet managers do not do a good job. They do. There is no doubt that their system works well. If I have chosen to concentrate on the "pathology" of Soviet management, the purpose was not to create the impression of ineffectiveness, but to illuminate the gap that every economy shows between the actual and the ideal.

A comparison of Soviet and American management will help drive the point home. No one doubts that American management does a good job. But it would be fatuous to allege that it operates with perfect efficiency. An exploration of the inevitable gap between the actual and the ideal in the case of American management will help to place the corresponding gap in the USSR in proper perspective.

A comparison of Soviet and American management is difficult for a curious reason; namely, we don't know enough about the more intimate aspects of American managerial practice. A moment's thought will make the reason clear. The American firm is a private enterprise in the full sense of the word. Its internal affairs are no one's business but its own. No one has the right to pry except with special cause. To be sure, the laws of the land have, over the years, required enterprises to disclose more and more of their private affairs to public and governmental perusal. But large sectors of the enterprise's internal operations are protected from the eyes of curious outsiders.

One of the most striking differences in the conduct of American and Soviet management is precisely in this matter of privacy. The Soviet enterprise is a public enterprise in the fullest sense of the word. It has no right to conceal its operations from any officially recognized agent of the state. And a great range of such agents have been deliberately endowed by the state with the obligation of keeping close watch on management and disclosing any irregularities or sources of inefficiency that come to their attention. These agents include the "home office" of the firm (the ministry), the state bank, the local governmental body, the central government's State Control Commission, the Finance Department (the tax collector), the local Communist Party boss and his staff, the Party secretary of the enterprise itself, and indeed just about anyone in the enterprise who enjoys the extracurricular activity of attending meetings to discuss the affairs of the enterprise (the *aktiv*).

If we can imagine an American business executive suddenly placed in charge of a Soviet firm, it is this public character of the enterprise which above all would drive him to distraction. It means that any government official can at any time demand to examine any aspect of the firm's operations he wishes to, that at any time the manager can be called on the carpet by the local Party boss to explain a charge by an irate customer, that any member of his staff (perhaps bucking for his job) can write a letter to *Pravda* exposing him for having made an irregular deal on some supplies, that any scatterbrained worker who wants to "get his picture in the papers" can rise at a public meeting that the director is obliged to attend and compel the director to explain why he hasn't yet installed the new assembly line. The point is that the result of this authorized prying often finds its way into the published Soviet economic and political literature, which gives us an insight into the more intimate operations of the Soviet firm that we cannot have in the case of the American firm. But in view of this committee's expressed interest in comparisons of the United States and Soviet economies, I have attempted certain comparisons below which appear to be highly suggestive.

Managers and Owners

The original form of modern business organization was the small firm in which the owner was also the manager. The owner-manager was responsible to no one but himself for his business decisions, and his interest as manager could not conflict with his interest as owner. The development of the modern giant corporation, however, has led to that separation of management and ownership first elaborated in the work of Berle and

Means.[4] Under the new conditions the private interests of the hired managers (and the controlling group) need no longer coincide at all points with the interests of the stockholder-owners. This is precisely the relationship between the hired Soviet manager and the owner-state.

Berle and Means concluded from their study that "the controlling group, even if they own a large block of stock, can serve their own pockets better by profiting at the expense of the company than by making profits for it."[5] This is precisely what Soviet managers do when they produce unplanned commodities that are advantageous to their firms but not to the state, when they overorder and hoard commodities, and when they resist innovation. Because of the differences between the two economic systems, we should expect that the precise forms that the owner-manager conflict takes would be different in the USSR and the United States. In the United States they are to be found in such decisions as the awarding of subcontracts, the accounting of profit in such way as to benefit the claims of the controlling group, the awarding of bonuses and other benefits to management, and in dividend payment policy. In the Soviet enterprise, the accountant is of crucial importance in handling the books of the enterprise in such ways as make the best possible case for the manager; it is he, for example, who figures out the best way to distract the state's attention from the large expenditures on *tolkachi*. The accounting techniques are, of course, different in the United States; they involve "the charging or the failure to deduct depreciation; charging to capital [account] expenses which properly should be charged against income account; including nonrecurrent profits as income though their real place is in surplus; and the creation of 'hidden reserves.' "[6]

A major difference between the Soviet firm and the American firm is that in the last analysis profit remains the criterion of managerial performance in the latter, whereas the Soviet manager is evaluated by a number of criteria that are sometimes mutually exclusive. Both systems have attempted to bring managerial interests into harmony with owner interests by some sort of profit-sharing system. In the Soviet case, it is clear that profit plays a very minor role, compared with bonuses, as a managerial incentive. In the United States the manager shares directly in profit to a very limited extent, and often follows other goals in his decisions. "The executive not infrequently tends to look upon the stockholders as outsiders whose complaint and demand for dividends are necessary evils . . ." concluded one American student of management.[7] In like fashion the

[4] Adolph A. Berle, Jr., and Gardiner C. Means, *The Modern Corporation and Private Property* (New York: The Macmillan Co., 1945).

[5] Ibid., p. 122.

[6] Ibid., pp. 202–3, 335.

[7] Robert A. Gordon, *Business Leadership in the Large Corporation* (Washington, D.C.: The Brookings Institution, 1945), p. 309.

Soviet manager often begins to feel like the "boss" and resents the intrusion into "his" affairs by the state, which after all is the owner. I have described above some of the ways in which the Soviet manager promotes the interest of "his" enterprise by means contrary to the interests of the owner-state. In the American corporation the forms are somewhat different. ". . . profits are reinvested in the business for the sake of bigness and to protect the company, and the interests of the stockholders may be given second place to the business leader's conception of what is best for the firm itself." Executives manifest a "general unwillingness to liquidate unsuccessful enterprises" and thus put themselves out of jobs, however consistent liquidation might be with the interests of the stockholders.[8] The dramatic growth of corporate self-financing in recent years has strengthened the power of management to expand their own enterprises without having to go through the "test of the marketplace" for capital.

It was observed earlier that the desire for "security" and for what the Russians call a "quiet life" motivates a wide variety of managerial decisions such as concealing production capacity and resisting technological innovation that might rock the boat. Students of American management have also noted the change from the adventurous business tycoons of earlier days to a more professionalized managerial climate in which "greater emphasis is placed on education, training, and a scientific approach, and less on rugged, venturesome, and frequently heedless individualism. The desire for security seems to have increased, and the concomitant of a growing emphasis on security is a diminishing desire for adventure for its own sake."[9] There is indeed a remarkable parallel to this development in the change in the character of Soviet managers. There would have been a great affinity between the industrial empire builders of 19th-century America and the Soviet directors of the first two decades of the Soviet regime. Those directors were often men of little education who came out of the romantic conflict of revolution, who dreamed great dreams of building an industrial nation and who created an ethos of bold plans and adventurous undertakings. The old Commissar of Heavy Industry, Sergei Ordzhonikidze, would have understood the spirit of the ironmonger, Andrew Carnegie, and the man who built the great ZIL automotive works (now named after him) had the drives and the dreams of the bicycle mechanic, Henry Ford.

Time, and Stalin's purges, removed most of those old-timers and their place has now been taken by Soviet-educated young men born not of revolution but of bureaucracy. Organizations seem to develop "organization men" types, whether the organization happens to be Communist or capitalist. An American reporter visiting with a group of Communist

[8] Ibid., p. 309.
[9] Ibid., p. 311.

intellectuals reports that one of them had badgered him with questions about David Riesman's book, *The Lonely Crowd*. "The Communist had read Riesman's book and has been fascinated by it—not, he said, because of its application to life in the United States but because of what he maintained was its extraordinary relevance to the present conditions of life in the Soviet Union."[10] It is not, on reflection, very surprising that the job of running an industrial bureaucracy should place a common stamp on men of otherwise different backgrounds. The same would probably apply to the running of a large city or a large university.

Managers and the Laws

We have found that the Soviet manager is often compelled to evade regulations or even break laws. Part of the explanation is simply that there are so many laws. If a Chicago manaufacturer fails to ship an order to a New York firm, and ships it instead to another Chicago firm, he has nothing to fear but the ire of the New York firm. But if a Kiev manufacturer fails to ship an order to a Moscow firm and ships it instead to another Kiev firm, he has injured a state enterprise and is subject to administrative action, a fine, or even criminal prosecution. If an American firm sells a substandard generator, it may lose money or business. But if a Soviet firm sells a substandard generator, the director may go to prison. Thus, even if Soviet managers acted exactly as American managers do, we should expect to find more illegal or evasive activity in the Soviet Union than in the United States.

With the growing complexity of our society, more and more legislation is enacted to protect the public from potential abuses. With the growth of such legislation, managers find their activities more and more circumscribed by laws and regulations. The Soviet manager apparently treats such legislation rather lightly when it conflicts with the interests of his firm (and his career and pocketbook). How does American management react when confronted by a spreading web of restrictive legislation?

It is not easy to find out very much about American managerial practice in this respect. Unlike the Soviet press, which throws its pages open to reports of the irregular activities of managers in order to warn others, the American press is likely to shy away from this kind of reporting. Moreover the private nature of American business keeps this sort of activity from coming to light as easily as it might in Soviet industry. Nor is it the sort of thing that businessmen are inclined to talk about very readily. If it is true that a businessman would more readily be interviewed on his private sex life than on his private business activity, then we should require the late Dr. Kinsey to help provide the answers to the extent of unlawful or quasi-lawful business activity.

---

[10] *The New Yorker*, April 6, 1955, p. 52.

Prof. E. H. Sutherland, the eminent American criminologist and sociologist, made a bold attempt to investigate the phenomenon he refers to as "white-collar crime." His study is based on the decisions of a limited number of courts and administrative commissions against the 70 largest industrial-type corporations in the country. In the period 1935 to 1944 these 70 corporations were convicted 585 times for such practices as restraint of trade, misrepresentation in advertising, patent and copyright infringements, unfair labor practices, granting of rebates, and a few others.[11] The average was 8.5 convictions per corporation. These data provide some idea of the extensiveness of such practices but they clearly understate the magnitude for a variety of technical reasons. Sutherland's conclusion is that "a great deal of scattered and unorganized material indicates that white collar crimes are very prevalent."[12]

The point I wish to make is that when American management finds itself in a position approximating that of Soviet management it tends to react in ways similar to those of its Soviet counterparts. Sutherland's unique study notes many aspects of American managerial practice that are astonishingly similar to those one might find in the literature on Soviet management. "These crimes are not discreet and inadvertent violations of technical regulations. They are deliberate and have a relatively consistent unity."[13] It is in precisely this way that the Soviet manager deliberately misappropriates earmarked funds or decides to shave on the quality of production. There is evidence that the Soviet manager, aware of the fact that "everybody does it" and that the investigating agencies have restricted budgets, counts on the law of averages (and his own superior shrewdness) to get away with it. So a member of the Federal Trade Commission wrote that "about the only thing that keeps a businessman off the wrong end of a Federal indictment or administrative agency's complaint is the fact that, under the hit-or-miss methods of prosecution, the law of averages hasn't made him a partner to a suit," and "Samuel Insull is reported to have remarked during his trial that he had only done what all other businessmen were doing."[14]

Similarities in managerial practice are paralleled by similarities in attitude to such violations, and toward the administrative agencies enforcing the laws and regulations. The Soviet manager does not think it is "wrong" to use influence to obtain materials unlawfully, or to fudge his reports to the government. Success is the important thing, and if you are successful you can get away with all sorts of violations. There is evidence that the Soviet manager feels contemptuous of government planners and of party

11 Edwin H. Sutherland, *White Collar Crime* (New York: Dryden, 1949), p. 26.
12 Ibid., p. 10.
13 Ibid., p. 217.
14 Ibid., p. 218.

hacks who try to tell him how to run his business but who themselves had "never met a payroll." Sutherland's picture of American management's attitudes contains strains of the same kind.

> The businessman who violates the laws which are designed to regulate business does not customarily lose status among his business associates. Although a few members of the industry may think less of him, others admire him. . . . Businessmen customarily regard government personnel as politicians and bureaucrats, and the persons authorized to investigate business practices as "snoopers."[15]

In the first section of this paper, it was pointed out that a managerial career carries a great deal of prestige in the Soviet Union and attracts a large number of the better students. These youngsters have been raised in Soviet schools and have absorbed the incessant propaganda of the Communist regime. Many of them enter industry as green novices fresh from school, filled with high ideals about building the socialist fatherland and working for the common welfare. One wonders about the process by which the naive, idealistic young Komsomol member is transformed into the hard-headed manager who knows all the angles for survival in the Soviet business world. Numerous incidents such as the following provide a key to the answer. A young Soviet chemist had been assigned to the quality control department of his enterprise. He was quite pleased with himself when his test showed that a sample of production, which had previously been declared acceptable by his laboratory chief, turned out to contain an excess of phosphorus. He reported the "error" and expected to get a bonus for it. Instead, his boss obtained a new sample, gave it to an outside chemist for analysis, and submitted a report showing that the batch of production was acceptable after all. The young chemist protested, was transferred to another shop, and was finally fired on trumped-up charges.

What happens to such young people? Some never quite get the point and remain ordinary engineers in the plant. Others learn to adapt themselves after a few buffetings and, when they decide to play the game according to the real ground rules, begin to rise in the managerial hierarchy.

It is interesting to note that Sutherland's interviews with American businessmen turned up accounts rather similar to that narrated above. His explanation of the process by which the naive American youngster is initiated into the business of selling used cars, settling insurance claims, covering up irregularities in clients' accounts—indeed, toning down the results of chemical analysis—helps explain the process of transformation of the young Komsomol member:

> In many cases he is ordered by the manager to do things which he regards as unethical or illegal, while in other cases he learns from others who

---

[15] Ibid., p. 220.

have the same rank as his own how they make a success. He learns specific techniques of violating the law, together with definitions of situations in which those techniques may be used. Also he develops a general ideology. This ideology grows in part out of the specific practices and is in the nature of generalization from concrete experiences, but in part it is transmitted as a generalization by phrases such as "we are not in business for our health," "business is business," and "no business was ever built on the beatitudes." These generalizations . . . assist the neophyte in business to accept the illegal practices and provide rationalizations for them.[16]

Summarizing, the economic world in which the Soviet manager operates compels him to engage in a variety of illegal or evasive practices. Since the Soviet business world is enmeshed in a much greater web of laws and regulations than the American, the Soviet manager finds his interest in conflict with the laws and regulations more often than his American counterpart. But when American managers' interests conflict with the laws, they too are prepared to take the chance of violating them. Both American and Soviet managers justify their actions by an attitude of contempt for governmental controls and investigating personnel, and by a hardheaded view that "business is business" and "everybody does it." Young people in both systems who wish to achieve managerial prominence have to learn to play the game according to the rules or disqualify themselves from the tough competition for the top.

Managers and Overfull Employment

Many of the peculiarities of Soviet management spring from the fact that the economic system works under conditions of perpetual overfull employment. By "overfull" employment I mean a condition in which there are not merely as many jobs as employables (as under full employment), but the demand for labor far exceeds the available supply. The same applies to other factors of production: materials, equipment, and commodities in general are demanded in far greater volume than the current rates of production. The ability of the Soviet government to maintain, through the planning system, a condition of permanent overfull employment is one of the greatest economic assets of the regime. We err when we interpret evidence of shortages in the Soviet economy as signs of economic weakness; they are rather indications that the economic engine is racing with the throttle wide open.

But just as an engine does not work at its maximum efficiency when it is working at its maximum capacity, so the Soviet economy pays a certain price for the advantages of overfull employment. It is the perpetual shortages of supplies that account in large measure for the losses due to overordering and hoarding. The hunger for goods by both firms and consumers

---

[16] Ibid., p. 240.

encourages the deterioration of quality. The "sea of ink" associated with materials allocations, price fixing, priorities, and all the rigamarole of a controlled economy nurtures the spread of the *tolkach* and the use of influence for personal gain.

The normally functioning American economy does not confront our managers with this kind of problem. Hoarding makes no sense when materials are in adequate supply. Competition and consumer resistance force the quality of production up to standard. The role of influence is narrowly circumscribed when the bureaucratic machinery of government controls is removed. The biggest problem of American managers under normal conditions is marketing, not purchasing. The energy spent by the Soviet firm on obtaining materials is spent by the American firm on selling and advertising.

Thus, the major differences between the practice of American and Soviet management are to be ascribed to the differences in the economic environment. The interesting question is, How do American managers behave when placed in an environment that approximates that of the Soviet manager? The obvious test case is war. During World War II the national emergency forced us into a state of overfull employment. Along with this came the total immersion of government into economic life, with a great burgeoning of materials allocation, price fixing, cost-plus contracting, and a prevailing shortage of supplies.

It is interesting to note that the rate of growth of production during the war rose to levels rivaling the current rates of Soviet economic growth. The implication of this fact is important; it means that there is no magic in the Soviet economic system. Our economy could grow as rapidly as the Soviet economy does if our people would consent to being pushed around as totally as the Soviet people are.

But like the Soviet economy, we paid for our high rate of production in various forms of waste. One of the first consequences of the introduction of materials controls was the rise of the black market. The only full-scale study of the black market, to my knowledge, confirmed what many people felt to be the case at the time:

> During the war at least a million cases of black market violations were dealt with by the Government. Illegal profits ran into billions of dollars. Business interests and Government vied with one another in estimating the seriousness of the black market; business estimates, curiously, often being higher than those of the Government. Such extensive conniving in the black market in illegal prices and rationed commodities took place among so many businessmen, ordinary criminals, and even the average citizen that serious questions might be raised as to the moral fiber of the American people.[17]

---

[17] Marshall B. Clinard, *The Black Market* (New York: Rinehart & Co., Inc., 1952), p. vii.

To understand the position of the Soviet manager, we must realize that the American black market flourished at a time when the nation was fighting for its life and public indignation acted as a restraint. But if the economic controls that led to violations could not be justified by a national emergency, they would be thought of as just irritating obstacles, as so many hurdles that the resourceful manager must overcome as part of the risks of the game. There is good evidence that the Soviet manager takes just this amoral attitude toward economic controls, and it is therefore quite understandable that the evasion of controls would be more widespread.

The high quality of American production in normal times is a byword in international markets. But the effect on the economy of shortages was similar to that in the Soviet economy. One of the techniques used by Soviet managers is to represent lower quality merchandise as of higher quality, and to sell it at the higher price. In the United States during the war—

> upgrading was one of the most difficult violations to detect, particularly where no professional investigator was available who could appraise the grade or where there were no State or Federal grades stamped on the commodity.[18]

The reports of government investigators read like some of the indignant letters of complaint we read in the Soviet press; men's shorts made of cheesecloth, water-resistant baby's pants which permit a third of a glass of water to leak through after one laundering—

> if you pick up a board by both ends without breaking it in the middle, it's No. 1 Select—

testified an American businessman.[19]

One of the features of Soviet managerial life which helps protect the manager is the feeling of "mutual support" among various officials whose fortunes depend on the success of the enterprise. The Communist Party secretary doesn't report the manipulations of a successful director because the Party benefits from the success of the enterprise; the people in the "home office" (the Ministry) are reluctant to fire a director who violates the laws in order to get the materials his plant needs, for while the next director may be more law-abiding, he may not succeed in fulfilling his plan. This tendency to maintain a solid front against authority is a source of great irritation to the government, which periodically inveighs against it but has not been able to eradicate it. A similar sense of common front prevailed among groups of businessmen.

> Nothing better illustrates the degree of organization and consensus among businessmen than their reluctance to testify against each other. . . .

---

18 Ibid., p. 224.
19 Ibid., p. 45.

Some businessmen felt that the trade would disapprove of behavior that might undermine the solid front against the Government as well as interfere with supplies.[20]

One of the major differences in the position of management in the two countries is the nature of the penalty for failure. Under ordinary conditions the unsuccessful manager loses his job. But the Soviet manager faces many more situations in which the action necessary to get the job done carries with it the threat of criminal action. Indeed, whenever the Soviet government has found some managerial practice too damaging to its interests and too intractable to the normal sanctions, it has turned to the criminal courts. Immediately after the death of Stalin the punishment for economic transgressions was relaxed, but the new regime was not able to continue operating without the courts. One of the severest economic problems following the decentralization of industry was the tendency toward "localism": that is, each economic region tended to favor the plants in its "own" region, and would discriminate against plants in other regions. When all exhortation failed, the government had to turn to the law. Today, a manager who fails to honor the orders of plants outside his own region is subject to "administrative action, fines, or even criminal punishment."

Financial penalties, such as fines, have rarely proved successful as restraints on Soviet managerial behavior. American managers seem to have reacted the same way to the fines imposed for black-market violations. "They don't hurt anybody." "It just comes out of profits, like a tax." "They make so much money on the black market they can afford to pay steep fines." But imprisonment was another matter." Jail is the only way; nobody wants to go to jail." "A jail sentence is dishonorable; it jeopardizes the reputation." This would not be quite the same in the case of the Soviet manager. At least during Stalin's lifetime some of the best people served their time in jail, and it definitely did not destroy their reputation among their neighbors; although the neighbors might be wary of associating with them. One has the impression that large numbers of Soviet managers feel the chances are fair that some day they will do their stretch, hopefully for a minor transgression.

The wartime economy of shortages injects the government into business life not only as an agency of control but also as the largest customer of many firms. In the Soviet case we have noted the importance of the *tolkach*, the expediter, the peddler of influence. We might note in passing that the economic system of Nazi Germany, in which government had also assumed a dominant role, also gave rise to this chap. The Germans called him the "contact man." As described by an American student of the German economy:

---

[20] Ibid., pp. 306–7.

To influence the powerful agencies of control, however, he [the German businessman] has good use for what might suitably be called a private relations department. Under the Nazi system of control of business by an absolute government, the contact man, or graft, or both, take the place of the public relations executive.

The contact man is primarily a political figure. His job is to pull wires. He knows the influential members of the all-pervading Nazi Party in a position to bring pressure successfully to bear upon the men in charge of controlling agencies. . . . Two types of contact man are known to be used: one is an independent agent whom the businessman hires, or attempts to hire, whenever necessary; the other is carried on the payroll of the business in a more or less permanent capacity.[21]

The words might well have been writtin about the Soviet economy. In that sector of the U.S. economy in which government plays a dominant role as customer, the symbols of the mink coat or Dixon-Yates, depending upon one's political persuasion, come to mind. "Washington," wrote Senator Paul Douglas, "is indeed full of lawyers and 'representatives' whose primary commodity is 'influence.' "[22] The techniques of the American influence-peddler differ little from those of his colleagues in the Soviet or Nazi economy. Gifts and *quid pro quo* favors are standard among Soviet *tolkachi*. Another way in which Soviet enterprises manage to exert influence is to have one of "their" men placed in other organizations that can be of use, rather like the unusually high employability in industry of retired military personnel. During the war the problem was particularly acute because of our government's desperate need for skilled managerial personnel, many of whom were on loan from corporations with which the government placed contracts. But the use of influence is not confined to government-business relations, as Senator Douglas pointed out in his critical defense of the ethics of government personnel:

As a matter of fact, the abuses which have been exposed and properly denounced in the field of Government are quite widespread practices in private business. Thus the "padding" of expense accounts is so common that they are often referred to as "swindle sheets." Purchasing agents and buyers frequently exact toll from those who seek to sell them, and their Christmas presents and other perquisites appreciably increase their income. Business managers and directors think nothing of awarding contracts, insurance, and underwriting privileges on the basis of friendship and relationship rather than the quality and prices of the goods and services supplied. All this is taken as a matter of course in private business, although it obviously increases costs and intercepts gains which should go to stockholders and consumers.[23]

---

21 L. Hamburger, *How Nazi Germany Has Controlled Business* (Washington, D.C.: The Brookings Institution, 1943), pp. 94–95.

22 Paul H. Douglas, *Ethics in Government* (Cambridge, Mass.: Harvard University Press, 1952), p. 56.

23 Ibid., p. 25.

While gifts, payoffs, and bribery play their role in the Soviet scheme of things, the subtler and much more pervasive technique of influence is known as "blat." To have good blat with someone means that one has an "in"; one can always count on him for a favor because of friendship or family ties or some other relationship of confidence. Blat may be used to obtain everything from a new apartment to a carload of coal. The prominent British observer, Edward Crankshaw, has called blat the most significant word in contemporary Russia.[24] The way in which the American equivalent of blat is cultivated is described in one final quotation from Senator Douglas:

> Today the corruption of public officials by private interests takes a more subtle form. The enticer does not generally pay money directly to the public representative. He tries instead by a series of favors to put the public official under such feeling of personal obligation that the latter gradually loses his sense of mission to the public and comes to feel that his first loyalties are to his private benefactors and patrons. What happens is a gradual shifting of a man's loyalties from the community to those who have been doing him favors. His final decisions are, therefore, made in response to private friendships and loyalties rather than to the public good.[25]

Summarizing, many of the differences between Soviet and United States managerial behavior spring from differences in the economic climate in which they operate. The stress on quality and appearance, the drive for innovation and technological development, and the interest in cost reduction reflect the force of competition and the buyers' market. Such similarities as have been observed in managerial behavior spring from features of the economic environment that are common to the two systems, such as large-scale organization and the intrusion of government into the economy. Under wartime conditions our economy takes on more of the features of normal Soviet economic life, and the consequence is that our managers adopt more of the normal practices of Soviet management.

---

[24] *New York Times Magazine*, June 3, 1951, p. 35.
[25] Douglas, *Ethics in Government*, p. 44.

Unemployment

Unemployment is recognized to be a common and sometimes serious problem in capitalist market economies. On the other hand, it is often claimed that socialist planned economies avoid unemployment because of the combination of socialism's concern for its citizens' well-being and central planning's ability to assure high aggregate demand. The following article discusses the nature and causes of unemployment, and policies to limit it, in the two systems.

23

UNEMPLOYMENT IN CAPITALIST REGULATED MARKET ECONOMIES AND IN SOCIALIST CENTRALLY PLANNED ECONOMIES*

Morris Bornstein[1]

This selection provides a concise comparison of capitalist regulated market economies (CRMEs) and socialist centrally planned economies (SCPEs) in regard to types of unemployment, on the one hand, and antiunemployment measures, on the other. It points out that although seasonal, frictional, and structural unemployment occur in SCPEs, they do not have cyclical unemployment problems comparable to those in CRMEs. However, for various systemic reasons, "open" unemployment is likely to be smaller, but "disguised" unemployment larger, in SCPEs than in CRMEs.

The comparative economic systems literature commonly distinguishes two major types of economic systems—capitalist regulated market economies (CRMEs) and socialist centrally planned economies (SCPEs).

CRMEs have several key characteristics. (1) Most of the means of production are privately owned. (2) Market forces chiefly determine the level of economic activity, the rate of growth, the composition of output, and the distribution of income. But (3) the government intervenes in the economy in various ways to deal with problems of growth, monopoly, in-

---

* Reprinted by permission from *American Economic Review*, vol. 68, no. 2 (May 1978), pp. 38–43, with the omission of references to foreign-language sources.

[1] This paper draws on a research project at the University of Michigan Center for Russian and East European Studies funded by a grant from the Rockefeller Foundation. I wish to thank the Foundation for its support; Dennis A. O'Hearn for his assistance in research; and Robert F. Dernberger, Philip Hanson, and Harold M. Levinson for valuable comments.

flation, unemployment, income distribution, etc. The CRMEs include, for example, the United States, Canada, Western Europe, Japan, and Australia.

In SCPEs, on the other hand, (1) most means of production are collectively owned, and (2) a large administrative bureaucracy attempts to direct resource allocation and income distribution through comprehensive and detailed planning. However, (3) the market mechanism is used to distribute the labor force among planned jobs, and to distribute the planned supply of consumer goods among households, which exercise consumer choice in the expenditure of their money incomes on available goods at prevailing prices. Among the SCPEs are the USSR, most East European countries, and the People's Republic of China.

This paper compares the two systems in regard to types of unemployment and antiunemployment measures.[2] The experience of particular countries, such as the United States or the USSR, is mentioned by way of illustration, but it is not suggested that they are prototypical or ideal examples of their respective economic systems. There are interesting differences in regard to unemployment among the CRMEs and among the SCPEs, arising from differences in the level of economic development, the structure of the economy, the demographic composition of the labor force, and social and institutional arrangements. But space limitations preclude discussion of such intragroup differences.[3] Also, lack of relevant data for the SCPEs prevents reliable statistical comparisons of unemployment rates in the two systems.[4] Finally, the paper does not consider unemployment in a third type of economic system—a socialist regulated market economy—because the sample of countries (Yugoslavia) is too small to permit sound generalizations about systemic characteristics transcending particular national circumstances.

I. TYPES OF UNEMPLOYMENT

Unemployment may be analyzed in terms of its origin or its form. The first approach is more common but the second is perhaps more illuminating in comparing economic systems.

---

[2] Such comparisons were first discussed in Alfred E. Oxenfeldt and Ernest van den Haag, "Unemployment in Planned and Capitalist Economies," *Quarterly Journal of Economics*, vol. 68, no. 1 (February 1954), pp. 43–60; and F. D. Holzman, "Comment," and Oxenfeldt and van den Haag, "Reply," vol. 69, no. 3 (August 1955), pp. 452–64.

[3] For the CRMEs, see, for instance, Joyanna Moy and Constance Sorrentino, "An Analysis of Unemployment in Nine Industrial Countries," *Monthly Labor Review*, vol. 100, no. 4 (April 1977), pp. 12–24.

[4] For a valiant attempt, see P. J. D. Wiles, "A Note on Soviet Unemployment on U.S. Definitions," *Soviet Studies*, vol. 23, no. 4 (April 1972), pp. 619–28.

Origin

In CRMEs four kinds of unemployment are commonly identified. *Seasonal* unemployment arises from regular seasonal fluctuations in the demand for and supply of labor. On the demand side, seasonal variations in labor requirements are common, for instance, in agriculture, construction, and vacation resort activities. On the supply side, the school calendar affects the labor force participation of young people. *Frictional* unemployment involves those seeking their first jobs and those between jobs after quitting or being dismissed. *Structural* unemployment occurs when people are unable over a long period to find work, because of a lack of skills or a shortage of jobs in their particular labor market areas, although national aggregate demand may be high. Finally, *cyclical* unemployment results from a general decline in business activity, with a subsequent recovery leading to reemployment.

In CRMEs, seasonal and frictional unemployment are considered part of the normal process by which the market mechanism adjusts production to demand. Thus a seasonally-adjusted frictional unemployment rate of, say, 3–4 percent of the labor force could be considered compatible with "full employment." On the other hand, cyclical and structural unemployment have more serious economic and social consequences and more urgently require corrective government action.

SCPEs acknowledge seasonal unemployment as inevitable due to natural factors, such as agricultural production cycles, and institutional arrangements, like the academic calendar. In turn, some frictional unemployment is expected so long as new entrants into the labor force can choose their first jobs, workers are free to quit, or enterprise managers are permitted to dismiss unsatisfactory or surplus workers. But authorities in SCPEs often complain about job changes on the initiative of workers—stressing the costs to the economy in lost production during periods of unemployment, in low productivity when workers begin new jobs, and in retraining programs.

In SCPEs, structural unemployment is regarded as evidence of deficiencies in planning, which is supposed to balance the supply of and demand for labor through accurate estimates of the labor force and correct decisions on training programs, technological progress, location of new capacity, and relative wages. This is an extremely difficult task,[5] and in the USSR, for instance, structural unemployment has persisted in certain regions and among women in smaller cities and rural areas.[6]

In contrast, SCPEs do not show the recurrent pattern of cyclical unemployment common in CRMEs. The reasons include the SCPEs' "taut"

[5] Gertrude Schroeder, "Labor Planning in the USSR," *Southern Economic Journal*, vol. 32, no. 1 (July 1965), pp. 63–72.

[6] O. Latifi, *Pravda* (April 20, 1977), p. 2: trans. *Current Digest of the Soviet Press*, vol. 29, no. 16 (May 18, 1977), pp. 24–25.

planning for ambitious growth targets and their measures to insulate the domestic economy from external shocks.[7] Aside from harvest variations, fluctuations in economic activity in SCPEs result primarily from changes in growth rates of investment and output, without periodic recessions in which workers are laid off.[8]

Form

The distinction between "open" and "disguised" unemployment in some ways parallels the more familiar conrtast between "open" and "repressed" inflation. The openly unemployed are seeking jobs but cannot find them. Disguised unemployment—or underemployment—occurs when workers have jobs but are underutilized (1) because they wish full-time jobs but can get only part-time work; (2) because their full-time jobs do not use all their skills and training; or (3) because, though employed full-time in jobs matching their qualifications, their productivity is low.

The first kind of disguised unemployment—part-time work when full-time jobs are sought—is more common in CRMEs than in SCPEs. In the latter, part-time work is more often a way to draw into the labor force pensioners, housewives, and others not available for full-time jobs.

The second category—work below skill level—occurs in both systems because training opportunities and choices are not correctly matched with (future) employment possibilities, information on vacancies is imperfect, or mobility is limited.

The causes of low productivity may include late delivery of materials, equipment breakdowns, poor organization of production, low output norms, weak incentives due to the level and structure of compensation, and hoarding of labor by enterprise management. All of these may be found in both CRMEs and SCPEs, but space limitations permit discussion only of labor hoarding, about which recent literature has shown some interesting similarities between the two systems.

In SCPEs such hoarding is explained by the combination of the "ratchet" principle in planning, tight labor market conditions, and restrictions on the dismissal of redundant workers. The first makes management expect that already ambitious production assignments will be "jacked up" continually in future periods. The second makes it believe that it may be difficult to replace workers who quit or to hire additional workers authorized for the extra output. Therefore, management wants a pool of "reserve" workers on the payroll, not because they are needed now but because

---

[7] Franklyn D. Holzman, "Soviet Central Planning and Its Impact on Foreign Trade Behavior and Adjustment Mechanisms," in *International Trade and Central Planning: An Analysis of Economic Interactions,* ed. Alan A. Brown and Egon Neuberger (Berkeley: University of California Press, 1968), pp. 280–311.

[8] Alexander Bajt, "Investment Cycles in European Socialist Economies: A Review Article," *Journal of Economic Literature,* vol. 9, no. 1 (March 1971), pp. 53–63.

they are likely to be required, but perhaps unavailable, in the future. Finally, there may be restrictions of law or custom on management's ability to discharge unneeded workers.[9]

Labor hoarding also exists in CRMEs when labor input is not adjusted fully to changes in output. Inaccurate sales forecasts can cause "unplanned" hoarding. Conscious "planned" hoarding occurs because of legal commitments, indivisibilities in production, morale considerations, transaction costs in firing and hiring, and expectations of future changes in demand.[10] The Japanese version is sometimes called "permanent employment."[11]

Thus, a comparison of unemployment in CRMEs and SCPEs must consider both the open and the disguised forms. One may hypothesize that central planning's effort to mobilize resources for rapid growth and socialism's ideological commitment to the "right to work" tend to hold open unemployment in SCPEs below the levels observed in CRMEs. At the same time, these two factors may lead to more disguised unemployment in SCPEs than in CRMEs.

Unfortunately, the statistical data to test such hypotheses are lacking. However, the relative importance of the two forms of unemployment may be inferred from the focus of policy discussions and antiunemployment measures in the two systems. In CRMEs, the chief concern is with open unemployment, while SCPEs pay much more attention to underemployment. Thus, SCPEs stress that "full employment" means not only (1) that there is a job for everyone who wants one, but also (2) that labor should be allocated rationally across the economy and (3) that it should be used efficiently inside the enterprise. Similarly, whereas the concept of "labor reserve" has been applied in the United States to refer to potential workers currently outside the labor force,[12] in the USSR it encompasses as well "hidden" or "internal" reserves in the labor input of the employed but underutilized.

II. ANTIUNEMPLOYMENT MEASURES

In turn, the two systems differ in their approach to reducing unemployment.

---

[9] George R. Feiwel, "Causes and Consequences of Disguised Industrial Unemployment in a Socialist Economy," *Soviet Studies*, vol. 26, no. 3 (July 1974), pp. 344–62; Joseph S. Berliner, *The Innovation Decision in Soviet Industry* (Cambridge, Mass.: M.I.T. Press, 1976), pp. 165–67.

[10] Stuart McKendrick, "An Inter-Industry Analysis of Labor Hoarding in Britain, 1953–72," *Applied Economics*, vol. 7, no. 2 (June 1975), pp. 101–17; K. G. Knight and R. A. Wilson, "Labor Hoarding, Employment, and Unemployment in British Manufacturing Industry," *Applied Economics*, vol. 6, no. 4 (December 1974), pp. 303–10.

[11] Robert E. Cole, "Permanent Employment in Japan: Facts and Fantasies," *Industrial and Labor Relations Review*, vol. 26, no. 1 (October 1972), pp. 615–30.

[12] Christopher G. Gellner, "Enlarging the Concept of a Labor Reserve," *Monthly Labor Review*, vol. 98, no. 4 (April 1975), pp. 20–28.

CRMEs

In CRMEs there are two types of constraints on antiunemployment measures. At the micro level, society is loath to impose restrictions on the freedom of workers to choose and quit jobs and on the freedom of firms to determine the amount and kind of labor input. At the macro level, it is widely believed that a reduction in unemployment will be accompanied by an increase in inflation. Thus, policy makers try to determine a "tolerable" rate and composition of unemployment. Efforts to reduce unemployment include (1) job creation, (2) matching the unemployed with job vacancies, and (3) reducing the size of the "labor force" desiring employment.

In CRMEs the conventional approach has been to create jobs in the private sector by stimulating aggregate demand through expansionary monetary policies, tax cuts, and increases in government purchases of goods and services. More recently, some CRME governments have subsidized part of private firms' wage costs to induce them (a) to maintain the employment of workers who would otherwise be laid off or (b) to hire additional workers from the unemployed.[13] Finally, additional (temporary or permanent) public sector jobs can be established at the national, regional or local levels.[14]

The matching of unemployed workers with existing or newly created job vacancies is attempted through placement services, retraining, relocation assistance, and area development schemes.

The unemployment rate can also be decreased by reducing the size of the "labor force" wishing paid employment. Labor force participation of the "old" can be cut by lowering the retirement age and by raising pensions so fewer "retirees" seek work. In turn, the entry of the "young" into the labor force can be delayed by extending compulsory secondary education and by increasing tuition and maintenance subsidies for postsecondary training. Finally, as in West Germany for example, the number of foreign "guest workers" can be cut to expand employment opportunities for citizens.

In addition, the effects of unemployment on household income may be at least partially offset by unemployment insurance schemes and welfare programs.

SCPEs

In SCPEs the attainment of the political leaders' goal of full mobilization of labor resources is constrained by the extent of workers' freedom to

---

[13] John Burton, "Employment Subsidies—the Cases For and Against," *National Westminster Bank Quarterly Review* (February 1977), pp. 33–43.

[14] Michael Wiseman, "Public Employment as Fiscal Policy," *Brookings Papers on Economic Acitivity*, 1976, no. 1, pp. 67–104.

quit—much greater in Eastern Europe than in the People's Republic of China—as well as by the inability of planning agencies to control enterprise operations and regulate labor markets exactly as they wish. But the inflation-unemployment tradeoff is regarded with much less concern than in CRMEs. The SCPEs are more confident about their ability to curtail inflationary pressure by tax and credit measures or to repress it by comprehensive price controls.

In SCPEs jobs are created by ambitious development plans implemented by detailed administrative orders, government expenditure programs, and an accommodating monetary policy. The socialist character of the economy resolves the issue of public vs. private sector employment overwhelmingly in favor of the former—with the private sector usually limited to subsidiary agriculture, handicrafts, and selected personal services. Explicit wage subsidies to public enterprises are the exception rather than the rule. But firms attempt to cover the cost of surplus labor by negotiating larger wage bills in their annual plans and by securing higher prices from central agencies, which usually set prices to cover planned branch average cost plus a profit markup on it.

For matching workers with job vacancies, SCPEs emphasize training programs, and organized mass recruitment for new towns. Although employment bureaus are useful for the latter, the official attitude toward them in SCPEs is ambivalent. The authorities fear that such bureaus may not only help in centrally planned labor placement, but may also facilitate (1) enterprises' efforts to build up "reserve" labor pools and (2) "unplanned" labor turnover at the initiative of workers. Thus, in the USSR for instance, these bureaus are supposed to screen all requests for workers and reject those inconsistent with an enterprise's labor plan, and one indicator of the bureaus' performance is how long workers stay in the jobs in which they are placed.

In SCPEs the relocation of workers to new areas is difficult. One factor is social and cultural obstacles to mobility similar to those in CRMEs. Also, housing shortages are widespread and persistent because of investment plans' neglect of infrastructure. Furthermore, the high participation rate of married women in the labor force requires suitable jobs for both spouses in the new city. Thus, except where location decisions are determined by natural factors like mineral deposits, it has usually proved more feasible to place new capacity in labor surplus areas than to relocate workers.

The SCPEs regard unemployment insurance as unnecessary and indeed harmful. A high level of aggregate demand is supposed to assure enough jobs for all. Furthermore, when a worker is no longer needed by a firm, because of changes in output assignments or production methods (for example, mechanization or automation), the management is expected or even legally obligated (1) if possible to reassign him, with retraining if necessary, inside the enterprise; or (2) to arrange for placement in another firm in the same area. Therefore, the authorities consider that unemployment is voluntary, rather than involuntary, and that compensation for it is not only unjustified but could extend the unemployment period by financing a longer job search. A similar view may be found in the recent discussion in the United States about the disincentive effects of unemployment compensation.[15]

III. CONCLUSION

Contrary to some official claims, unemployment does occur in SCPEs— because of nature, workers' freedom of job choice, and imperfect planning. Although seasonal, frictional, and structural unemployment exist in SCPEs, they do not have cyclical unemployment problems comparable to those in CRMEs. However, the distinction between open and disguised unemployment—alternative forms of inefficiency—is important. In SCPEs a high level of aggregate demand due to ambitious national plans can create a labor shortage at the macro level, while there are labor surpluses at the micro level as a result of the firm's reaction to taut plans and tight labor markets.

These differences are in turn reflected in the emphasis of antiunemployment measures in the two systems. CRMEs stress job creation, with controversy over the shares for the private and public sectors. The CRMEs maintain income and support the job search of the unemployed through unemployment compensation. In the SCPEs, the authorities consider unemployment compensation unnecessary and detrimental, and they try through demanding plans to mobilize "internal" labor reserves of the employed but underutilized.

---

[15] This discussion is summarized in Gary S. Fields, "Direct Labor Market Effects of Unemployment Insurance," *Industrial Relations*, vol. 16, no. 1 (February 1977), pp. 1–14; and Arnold Katz and Joseph E. Hight, "The Economics of Unemployment Insurance—A Symposium," *Industrial and Labor Relations Review*, vol. 30, no. 4 (July 1977), pp. 431–37.

Inflation

Capitalist market economies and socialist planned economies differ in important ways in regard to the causes' and control of inflation.

Selection 24 explains the inflationary problems of Western Europe, North America, and Japan—arising from excess-demand and cost-push forces, augmented by expectations, and transmitted through international economic relations. The authors show why it is very difficult to devise a satisfactory combination of policy measures to reduce inflation.

Selection 25 examines the sources and forms of inflationary pressure in East European centrally planned economies, the approaches to controlling inflation, and their consequences. The author also suggests some lessons possibly applicable in other economic systems.

24

TOWARDS FULL EMPLOYMENT AND PRICE STABILITY*

*Paul McCracken, Guido Carli, Herbert Giersch,
Attila Karaosmanoglu, Ryutaro Komiya, Assar
Lindbeck, Robert Marjolin, and Robin Matthews*

*Industrialized capitalist market economies have experienced serious
problems of unemployment and inflation in the 1970s. This selection,
summarizing a detailed report by eight internationally known economists, asks and undertakes to answer three key questions: (1) What
went wrong and why? (2) What should be the objectives of economic policy over the next ten years? (3) In view of the constraints,
what policy options are, in fact, available?*

*Their analysis stresses the complexity and interrelationships of the
problems and the potential solutions. In the light of the particular
circumstances of each country, policy makers must carefully choose a
mix of many measures in an effort to regulate effective demand, control inflation, decrease unemployment, promote investment, improve
the operation of markets, and reduce barriers to foreign trade. At the
same time, because the industrialized market economies are so closely
integrated through international trade and capital movements and*

* Reprinted by permission from Organization for Economic Co-operation and De-
velopment (OECD), *Towards Full Employment and Price Stability: A Report to the
OECD by a Group of Independent Experts* (Paris: OECD, 1977), pp. 11–33. Paul
McCracken is Professor of Business Administration at The University of Michigan;
Guido Carli, President of Confindustria (Italy); Herbert Giersch, Director of the In-
stitute for World Economics at Kiel University; Attila Karaosmanoglu, Director of De-
velopment Policy at the International Bank for Reconstruction and Development;
Ryutaro Komiya, Professor of Economics at the University of Tokyo; Assar Lindbeck,
Director of the Institute for International Economic Studies at Stockholm University;
Robert Marjolin, former Vice President of the Commission of the European Economic
Community; and Robin Matthews, Master of Clare College, Cambridge University.

exchange rate adjustments, close coordination of national policies is essential.

INTRODUCTION

In the quarter of a century following World War II, the industrial world enjoyed growth to an extent unprecedented in economic history. In part, this was due to the process of postwar reconstruction, rapid and widespread technological progress, stable supplies of raw materials and energy, and the rise in volume of international trade. This potential for rapid growth would not have been realised, however, had it not been for the favourable economic climate created by governments—first by their assumption of responsibility for the achievement of high employment, and second through their commitment to economic integration in the framework of an open multilateral system for international trade and payments.

During recent years, by contrast, the industrial economies have experienced substantial slack in the use of their productive potential, and both unemployment and inflation remain disquietingly high in all but a few countries. Adjustment among the industrialized countries to the new situation created by large OPEC financial surpluses has been unsatisfactory. And there is some danger that the edifice of free trade, so carefully built, may begin to disintegrate.

In the light of these developments, public confidence in the ability of governments to manage the economy has waned, and belief in the likelihood or even desirability of continuing economic growth in the industrialised world has weakened.

This is the background against which this report seeks answers to the three fundamental questions:

What went wrong and why?

What are the objectives of, and constraints on, policies over the next ten years or so?

What are the broad policy options open to us?

Present economic conditions are obviously abnormal in terms of capacity utilisation, inflation and international payments equilibrium. Hence an important part of our policy prescriptions is addressed to the problem of reestablishing a more satisfactory situation on all three counts—which it is imperative to achieve within the next few years. But we also seek to lay down some guidelines for maintaining a more enduring expansion of output, employment and real incomes, without running into similar problems again, once that objective has been reached.

In view of the abnormal starting point, and our related concern with the deterioration of performance regarding growth, employment and prices, as well as with the instability of expectations, we devote considerable attention to demand management and other policies with a more short-term focus. We do not reject or neglect the role that longer-term policies must play to achieve less inflationary growth and continuous adaptations of economic and social structures, institutions, and behaviour patterns. But, at the same time, we believe that by following more stable and predictable demand management policies, governments can make a major positive contribution to a steady improvement of the performance of our economies, including the stabilization of expectations and the rebuilding of confidence. To restore confidence is, perhaps, the most important though least tangible facet of the task facing governments.

The report concentrates on the experience and problems of the major OECD countries, while making generalisations for the "OECD area" as a whole. Economic integration within the area has reached a stage where it is the sum total of policy actions and consequent economic impulses that dominates events in all but the largest of the member countries. It is obvious, however, that our generalisations concerning what went wrong and what should be done need to be interpreted with caution in the light of specific circumstances when applied to individual countries.

WHAT WENT WRONG?

Going back to the 1960s, in the United States, failure adequately to finance the war in Vietnam and major new social programmes through higher taxes led to increasing excess demand, despite monetary restraint. In Europe demand fluctuated around a high level, and towards the end of the decade price inflation accelerated following a series of wage explosions and labour market disruptions. All these led to restrictive policies and the 1970–71 downturn on both sides of the Atlantic. That recession, however, did not eliminate the higher inflation that had become a central concern by the end of the 1960s. Moreover, the attempt to maintain the parity of the dollar in the face of years of deteriorating competitiveness, which had led to loss of confidence in the dollar, massive United States external payments deficits, and a rapid increase in liquidity elsewhere, led ultimately to the breakdown of the pegged-exchange-rate system.

1972 was election year in an unusually large number of OECD countries. Memory of labour market unrest—and, indeed, of social and political unrest more generally—was probably still strong in some countries. Thus, even though major wage increases were still working their way through the system, there were thought to be good domestic reasons for a strong shift to expansionary policies in 1971, and this continued into 1972. But part of the explanation for the pursuit of such expansionary policies lay in the absence of the normal balance-of-payments constraints on the monetary policy of deficit countries during the progressive breakdown of the pegged-exchange-rate system and the large United States deficits on current and capital account which preceded and accompanied it. There would have been a strong upswing in 1972–73 anyway, but because of these external events more expansionary action was taken than would otherwise have been the case and, especially, more of it took the form of *monetary* expansion.

It was the excessive rate of monetary expansion which accounts for the typically speculative features of the subsequent boom. The price of real estate, gold, and other traditional havens of nervous capital in inflationary times soared. Hedging and speculation in commodities developed for stock-building purposes but also as a store of value in an uncertain world. On this situation was superimposed a series of agricultural harvest failures.

The 1972–73 boom was exacerbated by the fact that bottlenecks appeared relatively earlier than expected. In some basic industries inadequate investment in earlier years had resulted in insufficient capacity to meet the surge of demand. More generally, the problem lay not so much in the absolute level reached by demand, as in the *speed* of its increase. A scramble for inventories led to shortages even in sectors where labour and physical capacity were no more stretched than in earlier booms. Prices of food, raw materials, and industrial products all increased disproportionately compared with earlier upswings. International linkages also played a crucial role. Demand expansion in individual countries that would not have been excessive in isolation became so when demand was rising rapidly elsewhere.

One reason why the 1974–75 recession was so severe was that, when the oil crisis came, the world economy was already beginning to respond to restrictive policies put in place in 1973. To these policies was added the massive, though somewhat delayed, contractionary impact of the unspent OPEC oil revenues. The continued pursuit of strongly restrictive policies after the oil price rise was a controversial decision, but in most countries there was no practicable alternative, given that the OPEC decision set off a resurgence of speculative behaviour and a major new price-wage spiral. The impact of these policies, however, was greater than expected.

The recovery which began in the middle of 1975 was intended to be moderate but sustained. It has so far proved rather fragile. An equally striking aspect, which still prevails as we write, was that although inflation rates dropped nearly everywhere, they remained highly divergent as between countries.

What lessons can be learned from this experience? There has been a severe deterioration in the short-run trade-off between activity and inflation. In the late 1960s and into the early 1970s this partly reflected changes in wage-bargaining and price-setting behaviour resulting from growing confidence in governments' ability to ensure full employment, declining fears of unemployment and insolvency, the rapid rise in public expenditure, and more aggressive income-bargaining. At the same time, the level of recorded unemployment corresponding to a given level of capacity utilisation increased as a result of the changing composition of the labour force—and possibly—of more generous unemployment compensation in some countries. This further worsened the apparent trade-off between unemployment and inflation.

But in the last few years this deterioration was sharply accelerated by a series of shocks—the harvest failures and explosive rise in oil prices—which together accounted for a considerable part of the price acceleration from 1972 to 1974. This was compounded by overly-expansionary fiscal and monetary policies followed by most countries, in part induced by events surrounding the move to a more flexible exchange-rate system. In contrast to the 1960s, this bout of inflation originated less in labour markets and more in product markets, both national and international. In particular, the very general and rapid increase in monetary aggregates contributed significantly to the build-up of demand pressures and stubborn inflationary expectations.

Taken by themselves, neither the shocks nor the policy errors might have led to greater disruption than was experienced, for example, at the time of the Korean War. But the combination of the two was decisive, and their legacy is still with us in the form of adverse expectations about inflation, employment, and growth.

This does not mean that demand management is no longer effective in reducing inflation. Although less favourable, the strikingly close correlation between inflation in the OECD area and demand pressures 12–18 months earlier has continued to hold. Inflation has slowed down from a peak of about 15 percent to about 8 percent as demand pressures have eased and the exogenous factors which caused most of the earlier acceleration have ceased or been reversed. Restrictive demand management policies are decidedly effective against the type of inflation in product markets we have been experiencing. Moreover, without significant restraint of demand the wage-price spiral would not have slowed down; on the contrary, the rate of inflation would have risen further.

Adverse expectations born of recent experience will be with us for some time. But there is no fundamental reason why, in more favourable circumstances and with improved policies, they cannot be reversed. As "expectational" inflation subsides, however, we may find that there has been an acceleration of the inflation that can broadly be attributed to competing claims and malfunctioning of market mechanisms—which was apparent at the end of the 1960s, but was then obscured by the various striking developments just described.

To sum up, the immediate causes of the severe problems of 1971–75 can largely be understood in terms of conventional economic analysis. There have been underlying changes in behaviour patterns and in power relationships internationally and within countries. But *our reading of recent history is that the most important feature was an unusual bunching of unfortunate disturbances unlikely to be repeated on the same scale, the impact of which was compounded by some avoidable errors in economic policy.* The continuing legacy of 1971–75 makes for unusual difficulties in framing policies for the years immediately ahead. We reject, however, the view that existing market-oriented economic systems and democratic political institutions have failed. What is needed is better use of existing instruments of economic policy, and better functioning and management of existing market mechanisms.

THE DESIRABILITY AND FEASIBILITY OF GROWTH

Continued economic growth in the industrialized countries, providing for a reasonable rate of expansion in the available supply of goods and services, remains an essential objective. It is needed to satisfy people's aspirations for a rising standard of living and to provide adequate employment opportunities.

Although economic growth has costs—which in conventional national accounting either appear perversely as benefits (i.e., as output), or are not counted at all—it is positively correlated with welfare. And growth makes it easier to change the pattern of resource allocation and output so as to achieve such collective goals as protection of the environment, improvement of the quality of life, and assistance to the disadvantaged. *There is little point in pursuing the fastest possible economic growth at all costs. But reasonably rapid growth remains an appropriate objective.*

The major qualification to this statement lies in issues concerning the distribution of income—both nationally and internationally. From one point of view, economic growth can help the redistribution of income by providing the support for increased assistance programmes and by opening up new opportunities for employing underprivileged groups and for trading with developing countries. Beyond a certain point, however, conflicts may arise in any economic system between equality and efficiency. We believe that such conflicts can normally be reconciled in the light of the preferences existing in each country and in each period, with the reservation that—in an integrated world economy—the margin of manœuvre of individual countries is constrained by an international "demonstration effect," coupled with the threat of capital flight and brain drain.

As regards the international dimension of the problem, we reject the argument that growth in the developed countries must slow down so as to provide room for growth in the Third World. Because of the scope for productivity increase in both the industrial and developing countries, growth of the world economy should not be regarded as a zero-sum game involving a struggle for a fixed amount of world resources. But the international dimension does require a *pattern* of growth in the developed world that helps growth in the developing countries based on increasing their exports, and on the flow of real resources to them in the form of capital exports. This can be achieved on a basis which is to the mutual benefit of both the industrialised and developing countries. At the same time, the terms of trade are likely to shift in favour of countries—many developing, some developed—with large resources of certain raw materials and land; this process should not be resisted.

As we get richer, demand may gradually shift towards leisure and things such as personal services which cannot be mass-produced. This is already happening; as it does, there will be a slowdown of growth as presently measured—but not necessarily of the increase of welfare.

Is growth likely to be restricted importantly by a major break in the trend of supply potential? We do not find the arguments behind this suggestion convincing, even though in most countries a complete return to previous trend rates appears unlikely. In our view, *growth over the next decade or so will be limited not so much by constraints of a physical or technological kind as by the need to overcome the present economic and social stresses and imbalances of which inflation is one of the main symptoms.*

The supply of labour in the industrialized countries of the OECD is likely to rise somewhat more slowly in the future. Demographic trends, changing attitudes towards migration, and a lower outflow from agriculture are the main reasons involved, counter-balanced to some extent by a further rapid rise of female participation rates. These changes in the aggregate supply of labour should not have much impact on real income per head, and their significance is rather that they imply some loss of flexibility in the adjustment by the labour force to changes in the pattern of demand.

The crucial component of growth is, and will remain, the development of labour productivity. There may be reason to be concerned by the declining trend in research and development expenditures and, more importantly, by the risk that if pessimism concerning future profits and corporate cash flow persists, both investment in the research and development of new techniques and the exploitation of existing technological opportunities will be inhibited. We are more agnostic as to the risk of a slowdown in productivity brought about by future sectoral shifts from high to low productivity sectors and to sectors where the rate of growth of productivity is low, or by a possible exhaustion of economies of scale. Productivity growth in the postwar period owed much to the rapid expansion of international trade, permitting much greater specialisation and the realisation of substantial scale economies. There may be less opportunity for future progress along this line by the further expansion of trade among the industrialised countries, but this could be offset by increasing trade with developing countries.

We do not find doomsday predictions about the exhaustion of depletable natural resources, over any reasonable time horizon, to be persuasive.

Changes in relative prices should, in due course, produce the necessary shifts in output, recycling, substitution, and saving. But *serious short-term problems could emerge for prices because of inelastic output or supply interruptions.* In the field of energy, the resource cost of reducing dependence on a small number of suppliers of oil appears now to be much higher than was thought a few years ago. We also note with some concern that after 1990 there may be increasing problems of overall oil supplies, and that because of very long lead times difficult decisions concerning development of alternative energy sources will need to be taken in the next few years.

As far as OECD countries are concerned, it is unlikely that food supply will constitute a constraint on future growth, but there is a risk that the recent instability in the world markets for agricultural products will continue and could even increase in magnitude. As regards industrial raw materials, the available evidence suggests that there will be no generalized supply problems or disruptive price increases over the next few years, on the assumption of a moderate and steady growth path for OECD demand and output. But present information on investment intentions suggests that in the early 1980s productive capacity for some industrial raw materials might become insufficient, given the present combination of political uncertainties and unstable market conditions.

In brief, *we see nothing on the supply side to prevent potential output in the OECD area from growing almost as fast in the next five to ten years as it did in the 1960s, and we repeat that we find reasonably rapid growth desirable.* Whether it is achieved will depend heavily on our ability to obtain a desirable level and structure of final demand and the accompanying distribution of income without arousing disruptive conflicts which exacerbate inflation. Expectations and aspirations which rise more rapidly than the available economic capacity entail competing claims that can be difficult to resolve in a satisfactory—noninflationary—way. Looking further ahead, we see a risk, if appropriate policies are not followed, that growth in the 1990s could be constrained by a shortage of energy.

TOWARDS FULL EMPLOYMENT AND PRICE STABILITY

The Aims of Policy

The fundamental aim of policy is to return to reasonable rates of growth and high levels of employment. In our view this cannot be achieved unless the inflation problem is also solved. Recent events have left behind a legacy of adverse expectations. People expect much higher rates of inflation than in the earlier postwar period, and are less confident about the future growth of output and employment. The initial conditions for the return to full employment and price stability are not favourable.

In these circumstances, governments are right to aim at *a progressive return to full employment and price stability*. What is needed is a moderate but sustained expansion initially less rapid than would otherwise be desirable, during which memories of recent inflation fade, and confidence in rising sales and employment is restored. This will also provide time for the investment and industrial restructuring needed after a severe recession and the substantial changes in relative prices that have occurred.

A strongly front-loaded recovery would have led to an early resurgence of inflation. This would have undermined confidence in the sustainability of the recovery and inhibited the necessary investment. Governments would have been forced to adopt restrictive policies, leading to a new recession and even higher levels of unemployment quite probably already in 1977 or 1978. Because of the unfortunate experience of recent years, a given increase in demand is more likely to generate inflation and less likely to stimulate investment than would have been the case in the past. These are thus risks in trying to proceed either too fast or too slowly.

The aim should be an expansion of demand somewhat greater than the growth of potential supply. We believe that a period of sustained increases in real incomes and employment is a reasonable prospect, with growth rates for real GNP averaging around 5.5 percent a year for the OECD area as a whole over the five years from 1975 to 1980.

It will be difficult to combine rising employment and capacity utilization with a further reduction in the rate of inflation. Higher output will reduce overhead costs and ease distributional conflicts; but against this, rising demand will tend in time to lead to upward pressures on costs and prices. To bring inflation progressively down to an acceptably low level will therefore require skilful and determined use of monetary and fiscal policy, and, where appropriate, prices and incomes policy.

It is not because of demand pressures in labour markets—where conditions are generally slack—that there is a need to avoid a sharp expansion of demand. It is because despite the existing large margins of spare capacity an overly rapid *rate of increase* in demand would lead to a resurgence of the kind of anticipatory inflationary behaviour in commodity and product markets—feeding back on labour markets—which characterised the 1972–73 boom.

There can be no complacency about the consequences of prolonged unemployment on regional, racial, and other social tensions and, in time, on attitudes to work and to society in general. As compared with a strong front-loaded recovery, followed by an early recession, what is involved is accepting, reluctantly, a less rapid reduction of unemployment now, in order to achieve lower levels of unemployment later on. The correctly-judged recovery track is one which will *minimise average unemployment over the recovery period as a whole*.

We reject the view that inflation might offer a way of resolving the underlying conflicts which produced the inflation in the first place. Recent experience has shown only too clearly how inflation tends to feed on itself as money illusion disappears and people act in anticipation of further increases. Inflation is unfair to the weak and unorganised; it inhibits growth through undermining the efficiency of the economic system and creating uncertainty. Accelerating inflation cannot be lived with, and, once it has begun, escape from it is far from painless. The aim should be to bring down the rate of inflation below the point at which it tends to accelerate, and is not so rapid or variable as to impair the role of money as a standard of value.

Our second main policy recommendation applies not only to the recovery but also to the period after return to high levels of employment. We believe that, in future, governments should make it clearer when framing, explaining and executing their policies that *they will not—and, in the end, cannot—pursue policies which will permit or accommodate high rates of inflation.*

The route to sustained full employment lies in recognising that governments cannot guarantee full employment regardless of developments in prices and wages. During the course of the great postwar expansion, those responsible for price-setting and wage-bargaining increasingly behaved as if there was no way in which they could price themselves out of markets or out of jobs. The 1974–75 recession has been a painful revelation, but it also provides a new opportunity. If ways can be found of keeping alive the lesson learned—that inflationary behaviour inevitably leads in the end to loss of sales and loss of jobs—it should be possible to achieve higher levels of employment, lower rates of inflation and more sustained rates of growth.

Such a policy of not accommodating high rates of inflation should be built around some or all of the following: publicly announced targets for the growth of the monetary aggregates; a fiscal policy geared to a budget target designed to avoid giving an inflationary stimulus over the medium term; a prices and incomes policy designed to clarify the kind of price and wage behaviour consistent with achieving and maintaining full employment; and measures to reward or penalise those who conform to guidelines for prices and incomes or fail to do so. Exchange-rate policy may also have a useful role to play; for small open economies, pegging the exchange rate to that of a large stable economy may help to lower their inflationary trend. The right mix of policies will vary between countries according to their circumstances: these include the strength of the government and its constituent organs, the status and prestige of the central bank, and the central organisations of employers and labor.

The difficulty of carrying out such a policy will depend on the degree to which wage and price decisions are monopolised and politicised, on the country's past history of inflation and unemployment, on the degree of social homogeneity—or lack of it—on the existence or otherwise of deep political divisions, and so on. This points to the importance of any action which can be taken to strengthen competition. Under unfavourable circumstances, however, a policy of nonaccommodation based on a broad macroeconomic approach may still leave a situation in which either or both inflation and unemployment remain at unacceptably high levels. There may then be no alternative to policies which involve more detailed intervention in the process of price and income determination with all the difficulties and dangers this involves.

Better Demand Management Policies

The government's control over public revenue and expenditure, and over interest rates and the supply of money and credit have a central role to play in promoting economic growth and containing inflation.

At the present time, the authorities should aim to steer demand along the relatively narrow path consistent with achieving a sustained recovery. The lower limit is set by the need for a rate of expansion sufficient to encourage a recovery in investment, both through spreading overhead costs and improving profit margins, and through creating expectations of the need for additional capacity in the reasonably near future. The upper limit is set by the point at which a rapid increase in aggregate demand would re-ignite inflationary expectations.

Under these conditions a relatively *active* demand management policy may be needed, involving a succession of injections of purchasing power over a period of months or even years, while at the same time standing ready to begin withdrawing stimulus as soon as endogenous forces gather momentum. But in view of the difficulties in identifying new trends, the fallibility of forecasts, and the delays before action is taken and has its impact, policy should also be *cautious*, in the sense that when there is an apparent need to change course, there should be a presumption against taking all the expansionary or restrictive action apparently required in one go. Governments should be ready to act reasonably promptly, but should also try to manage demand more steadily by a process of successive approximation.

As more healthy expectations concerning inflation and growth gradually emerge, it should be increasingly possible and preferable for the authorities to frame monetary and fiscal policies in the light of medium-term requirements and leave correction of minor deviations of aggregate demand from the desired course to built-in stabilizers designed to reinforce such self-correcting forces as exist in the economy. Discretionary action will, of course, remain necessary to deal with significant disturbances.

Governments can and should help to promote healthier expectations about inflation and growth by giving greater emphasis to the need for consistency between the short-term management of demand and the medium-term objectives of economic policy. *By being set more explicitly into the medium-term framework, demand management policies should become steadier and more predictable.*

Monetary Policy. Monetary policy normally affects inflation through its impact on decisions to spend or save, and hence through the pressure of demand on the economy. But, as was very apparent during the 1972–73 boom, monetary policy can more particularly have an impact on prices through specific narrow channels such as real estate and commodity markets. With inelastic supply and easy credit, sharp price rises can easily be initiated in these markets and feed on themselves, with pronounced effects on general inflationary expectations, and hence on wage bargaining and pricing decisions elsewhere in the economy.

The mistakes which led to the excessive monetary expansion of 1971–72 were in part related to the events surrounding the breakdown of the adjustable-peg system of exchange rates. But they also arose from a failure to appreciate the full implications of the explosive rise in inflationary expectations, particularly as regards the interpretation of movements in nominal interest rates, and the fact that monetary phenomena often have their main impact on the real world only after quite a long lag.

We believe that the *public announcement of targets for the rate of growth of the money supply* may provide one of the best ways of giving concrete expression to the government's intention not to accommodate high rates of inflation. In present circumstances, the aim should be to reduce these targets progressively over time as inflation is brought down to acceptably low levels.

Economic and political realism suggests that there will be occasions when the authorities fail to meet their monetary target. Most of us, therefore, believe that this approach should be pursued in a pragmatic and moderately flexible way, with, for example, an upper and lower limit, rather than a fixed point, for the permissible rate of monetary expansion. Too much flexibility, however, could discredit this approach altogether.

There are other reasons why the monetary authorities should give somewhat more weight to trends in the monetary aggregates and less to interest rates than has generally been the emphasis in the past. At times of diminishing money illusion, fluctuations in inflationary expectations translate rather directly into unpredictable changes in nominal interest rates. Basing the operations of the monetary authorities on target rates of interest is then likely to be more misleading and risk greater deviations from desired policy outcomes than would use of monetary aggregates as a target. Moreover, if attention is focused too much on interest rates, the government's vested interest as a borrower itself can impart an expansionary bias to monetary policy.

There is no inherent reason why the functional relationship determining the demand for money should yield a one-for-one relationship between changes in the chosen monetary aggregate and nominal national income. Over the short run the target will need to be adjusted to allow for cyclical and interest-related changes in velocity, and may have to be revised in the event of major exogenous disturbances. Over the longer run there will be secular changes in the demand for those assets counted as part of the money supply. These factors need to be taken into account when establishing targets for individual countries and when trying to compare the stringency of the monetary policies being followed in different countries.

Financing Budget Deficits. The massive monetary expansion of 1971–72 was not essentially caused by the need to finance budget deficits. On the other hand, recent huge deficits resulting from the recession and the need to offset the large financial surpluses of some of the oil-producing countries have generally been financed without excessive rates of monetary expansion. The evidence is that if a government correctly judges the deficit (or surplus) needed to balance out the difference between savings and investment in the private sector, it can be financed without requiring a rate of monetary expansion which would engender inflation later and without raising interest rates so much as to offset the fiscal stimulus through adverse effects on private spending.

There can be practical difficulties, particularly when the public associates large deficits with the likelihood of accelerated inflation. These could be eased by the *issue of index-linked securities by the government.* Continuing efforts are also needed to convince people that budget deficits are not in themselves inflationary, so long as they are no larger than needed to counterbalance an excess of savings in the private sector. Recent experience shows that *monetary control is not necessarily lost in an abnormal recession period and that cautious monetary management is not incompatible with appropriate expansionary fiscal action.*

But as the upswing gathers momentum, the maintenance of overall balance in the economy requires a rapid reduction in the public-sector deficit. If governments are unable or unwilling to bring this about, either inflation ensues, or adherence to a monetary target will lead to a sharp rise in interest rates and private borrowing and private investment will be "crowded out."

Fiscal Policy. Variations in public expenditure and taxation have generally had a predictable impact on economic activity, although the lags have sometimes been unexpectedly and inconveniently long. Fiscal policy failures have been not so much—or, at least, not only—a matter of getting the timing wrong from the point of view of short-term demand management, but rather of a failure to reconcile the need for short-term flexibility with the necessary degree of control over the balance between the growth of public and private expenditure in the medium run.

Governments should establish and publish *medium-term budgetary targets* designed to indicate the underlying budget position such that—at desired levels of output, employment and prices—any difference between private savings and private domestic investment (plus persistent export of domestic savings) is matched by an offsetting and opposite difference between public expenditure and public revenue. They should also provide a regular analysis of *how far deviations of the actual budget out-turn from the target reflect discretionary action rather than automatic stabilizers, and how it is eventually intended to rescind or offset the discretionary anticyclical action that has been taken.*

In making this suggestion, we endorse the ideas underlying the approaches which have been made along these lines in several countries, e.g., the concepts of the "full employment surplus" (United States), the "neutral budget" (Germany), and "structural budget policy" (the Netherlands), without wishing to commit ourselves to any particular technique.

Fitting budgetary targets into regularly revised medium-term projections would provide the required flexibility to adjust the longer-run budget posture to unexpected events and changing public preferences with regard to longer-term economic and social priorities. At the same time, the pursuit of budgetary targets, derived from the position of the public sector in the context of a projected medium-term domestic demand structure and external balance, should help to keep short-run fiscal stabilization policies in line with longer-run economic and social objectives, particularly when combined with medium-term guidelines for public expenditure. The need for firm guidelines to constrain deficit financing will become increasingly important as employment and capacity utilisation rise and the balance between savings and investment swings back sharply in line with more normal propensities to save and invest.

We favour administrative arrangements for controlling public expenditure which, if inflation as it affects public expenditure programmes exceeds the target rate in the course of the budget year, bring automatic pressure to bear on public expenditure in real terms and on wage negotiations in the public sector.

Discretionary fiscal stabilization measures should normally be either temporary or self-liquidating or should take the form of speeding up or slowing down public programmes already agreed upon. Legislating in advance that increases or decreases of taxes will be terminated on a given date can help significantly to shift private expenditures in the way desired. Contrary to conventional wisdom, some countries have been able to achieve a very useful degree of flexibility on the expenditure side. Operating on the expenditure side has a quicker and more certain impact on the economy and, when the need is for restrictive action, has the enormous advantage of not raising costs and prices.

There may be a case for "automating" fiscal policy by *legislative trigger mechanisms which set off tax or expenditure action if, for example, unemployment exceeds a certain figure, or inflation rises above a certain rate.* This extends into the fiscal field the idea of built-in mechanisms to give substance to a policy based on not accommodating high rates of inflation, while at the same time strengthening the automatic stabilizers in the event of deficient demand.

Selective Demand Management Policies. There will frequently be merit in longer-term structural policies for particular sectors or regions. During a recession it is also often tempting to advocate selective policies designed to increase demand in sectors or areas where cyclical unemployment is high. But the more selective such action, the more the government is subject to pressures from individual interest groups. In the most extreme case, a government pursuing a necessarily restrictive demand management policy may find itself bailing out each of the inevitable victims—which is a certain recipe, not for growth without inflation, but for inflation without growth.

Most of us favour, however, quasi-selective action to influence broad categories of demand—business investment, house building, inventories, consumption, etc. The experience of countries which have used temporary fiscal incentives and disincentives for fixed investment, in business as well as house building, is moderately encouraging. We have noted with interest a Swedish scheme for subsidies to production for inventories during a recession. Temporary increases or decreases in indirect taxation can be used to reduce the cyclical instability of private consumption—particularly at times of "stagflation" when reducing indirect taxes can both slow the rise in prices and stimulate demand.

Policies Directly Affecting Employment. At present, when abnormally high rates of unemployment can only be reduced progressively because of the danger of re-igniting inflation, there is a case for policies designed to increase the amount of employment associated with a given increase in aggregate demand. One such policy is additional employment in the public sector. This should normally be temporary, since there is great need to ensure that it is consistent with overall economic and political constraints on the size and growth of government expenditure and employment over the medium run. Programmes introduced in a number of countries whereby, during a fixed period, private sector employers are paid a subsidy for taking on new labour also deserve further study.

We see such policies as an appropriate way of alleviating heavy unemployment—particularly among groups such as school-leavers which are disproportionately hard-hit—in cases where inflation and/or the external situation act as constraints on general expansionary action. This, in turn, implies that such programmes should be limited in scope, since if the situation permitted a major increase in demand it would usually be more appropriate for this to be brought about by general expansionary action.

Better Reconciliation of Competing Claims

Failure to reconcile competing claims in a satisfactory manner can impair growth either directly, by leading to an inappropriate structure of final demand—including, in particular, insufficient productive investment—or, indirectly, by generating inflation.

The Investment Problem.   There is a major question whether sufficient productive investment will be forthcoming to provide the additional capacity and jobs needed to support the return to full employment. A substantial shortfall of investment developed during the recession. At the same time, in many countries investment requirements have increased as a result of demands for environmental protection and in order to achieve greater energy self-sufficiency (though this increase is in part offset by a slower rise in housing demand in some cases). Even where an adequate flow of saving may be assured, the shocks of the recent past have led to widespread pessimism as to whether sufficient investment will be undertaken. Risk premiums have increased. Entrepreneurs are less confident about future sales and profits, less certain about the availability and future costs of energy and raw materials, and more concerned about antipollution or safety regulations and changing attitudes to business.

In addition to these general concerns, there has been, in some countries, a secular rise in the price of labour and other input costs relative to output prices, and reduced flexibility in the adjustment of labour inputs in response to output fluctuations. Because of the low rate of return on capital, there is not enough investment; and what investment takes place is mainly directed to saving labour and reducing other costs rather than expanding capacity and providing additional jobs. As cyclical unemployment falls, a more persistent form of structural unemployment will, on this view, emerge, because of a mismatch between the stock of capital and the supply of labour.

Such a situation can arise from rising labour costs resulting from strong wage bargaining with emphasis on real gains in after-tax incomes, which are not fully passed on into prices because of international competition, price controls, or restrictive demand management policies. Overvalued exchange rates may also play an important role.

There are some differences within our Group on the seriousness of this problem. Not only is the evidence concerning shifts in profitability and capital-intensity equivocal, but it is hard to be sure whether markets have permanently shifted to a higher level of real wage costs. On the basis of the evidence examined, it seems probable that in some cases—the United States, Germany, Italy, the United Kingdom, the Netherlands, and possibly the Scandinavian countries—there may be a reduced willingness to invest associated with reduced profit expectations. But in some other countries, including Canada, Japan and France, it is not clear that there has been any significant, structural change in the level of profitability.

The biggest contribution governments can make to solving these problems is through *success in their efforts to steer their economies back along a medium-term path consistent with steadily rising output and employment and diminishing inflationary expectations.* This would strengthen the incentive to invest by reducing fears of future restrictive policies, produce a substantial cyclical recovery in profits, and facilitate any structural adjustment needed in the relation between labour costs and output prices.

What else can be done? Under present conditions of low capacity utilisation and strong inflationary expectations, a "twist" in the mix towards easy monetary and tight fiscal policies might not do much to stimulate investment and would run the risk of rekindling inflation. An alternative is to increase tax incentives for investment. But where low profitability reflects strong wage pressures, these incentives may well be undermined by further wage increases.

If there is a genuine and persistent investment problem of this kind, the only solution may be to try to reach *a consensus on the need for higher profits and investment among the government, labour and management.* Discussion of the issues involved here could be greatly improved by more widespread use of techniques of *inflation accounting.* This would help those involved in wage negotiations and pricing decisions not to be misled by the distorting effects of past inflation.

The reduced availability of internal funds associated with lower profitability has not, at least until recently, posed any great problem for business investment. The rising level of household savings compensated for the decline in internal financing; intermediation channels worked smoothly to allow enterprises to draw on those savings. But fears have been expressed that the financial limits to this process are being reached as self-financing ratios fall and debt-to-equity ratios rise.

Insofar as this is the case, the solution lies in *improving the flexibility of capital markets*—providing a wider range of financial assets, reducing restrictions on equity investment, and eliminating tax disincentives. Several of us would also support more radical solutions which introduce an "equity" element into wage payments, for example through schemes for *employee participation* where remuneration is partly in the form of share issues and dividends, or profit-sharing.

Public Expenditure. Although the demand for goods and services which are usually provided by the public sector tends to rise as societies get richer, there is considerable evidence that over the last ten years a number of countries went too fast in this direction, with a danger of adverse effects on both their growth and inflation performance. Such dangers can arise because of a squeeze on productive investment and the effects of high rates of tax on incentives to work and take risks. And insofar as wage claims have been formulated more with a view to after-tax incomes, increasing public expenditure matched by higher taxation has in some cases generated "tax-push" inflation even in the absence of general excess demand.

Governments have been right in seeking to establish firmer *guidelines for public expenditure* which act as a "speed limit" indicating the danger point beyond which increases in expenditure are likely to have serious adverse effects on inflation and/or growth. Over the past ten years public expenditure (including transfers) expressed as a percent of GNP has been rising by 0.4 percentage points a year in the OECD area. Most countries which significantly exceeded this average ran into trouble. In the period immediately ahead, the rise in the public expenditure will be constrained by the need to shift resources to investment and (in many countries) to net exports, in the context of a somewhat slower increase in potential output.

In order to improve control over public expenditure, we would generally support *arrangements to eliminate fiscal drag* due to inflation, i.e., the rise in the tax burden which occurs automatically when prices (and hence incomes) rise, while tax allowances and brackets remain fixed in nominal terms. This can be done either by automatic indexation of the various parameters of the income-tax system, or by less rigorous arrangements whereby governments are required to make such adjustments every year unless an explicit decision is taken to the contrary.

We also support the efforts being made to *review priorities and improve the efficiency and effectiveness of public programmes.* Efficient resource allocation in the public sector always involves special problems because of the absence of market discipline and competition. The aim should be to establish more clearly the connection between the demand for particular public services and the price which the community is prepared to pay for them.

Looking somewhat further ahead, there could be a danger of an overreaction against public expenditure. Insufficient public expenditure can also have adverse effects on growth and welfare and, via frustrated expectations, on inflation. This is particularly the case when too much of the brunt of the effort to control public expenditure falls on public investment in economic and social infrastructure, impairing the overall productivity of the economy.

Foreign Sector. The conflict over competing claims within most OECD countries has been accentuated by a deterioration in the terms of trade, following the rise in oil and other commodity prices. In part, this is already being paid for in terms of exports of goods and services, and these will continue to rise as the oil producers increase their capacity to spend their enormously increased revenues.

Looking ahead, the most important external competing claim on the industrialised OECD countries is the commitment to achieve an adequate transfer of resources to the developing countries. We strongly urge early achievement of the international targets for official development assistance. In addition, the necessary transfers should also be achieved by larger capital flows and measures to enhance the purchasing power of developing countries.

For some countries additional claims on resources arise from the fact that their current external balance needs strengthening for reasons unconnected with the oil problem. For countries where, allowing for all these factors, the required shift of resources to the foreign sector is large, it should not be put off too long because it is important that the necessary adjustments be accomplished smoothly without accentuating the wage-price spiral. Otherwise there will be continuing problems into the medium term.

Prices and Incomes Policies. We support the idea that *governments should discuss regularly with the organisations representing business and labour the general evolution of prices and wages to be aimed at over the coming year or so, consistent with achieving or maintaining high employment levels.* Indeed, if governments are going to adopt a policy of not accommodating high rates of inflation, they must be prepared to indicate to those responsible for wage and price determination what kind of behaviour on their part would be consistent with the monetary and fiscal policies the authorities intend to follow.

This idea is not new. What is new is the context within which such discussions take place after a major inflationary recession. Indeed, in quite a number of countries there are signs that attitudes have changed. In pursuing a "concerted action" approach in forms appropriate to their circumstances and institutions, governments should make a major effort to keep alive the lessons which have been learned during this period.

Discussions in connection with the establishment of wage and price guidelines will inevitably involve consideration of most of the other major objectives of economic policy: output, employment, disposable real incomes, profits, income distribution, and so on. They may therefore provide a vehicle for improving, *ex ante*, the reconciliation of competing claims through building up a consensus on certain policy objectives.

If a government adopts this approach it must clearly try to apply the guidelines to the prices and wages for which it itself is responsible. In some cases excessive settlements in the public sector have been an important source of wage inflation. At the same time, however, attempts to "set an example" by low wage increases in the public sector can lead to a serious distortion in the wage structure.

A prices and incomes policy for the private sector becomes both more necessary and more feasible the larger and more strongly centralised are the national organisations representing business and labour. In highly centralised negotiations it is much easier for those involved to see that gains for one party which are not accepted by the others will be eroded by the inflationary process. It also becomes possible for the government to try to influence the outcome by threatening to raise taxes if wage settlements or price increases are excessive, or offering to lower them if they are moderate.

The persistence, ingenuity, and public spirit with which prices and incomes policies have been pursued in a number of countries is certainly impressive. But, at least as far as the larger countries are concerned, we do not find the evidence of any lasting success in terms of lower inflation or higher employment very impressive. We are concerned about certain longer-term dangers involved in this approach and the difficulties involved in establishing and applying guidelines for individual wage and price decisions.

These pitfalls have led to many suggestions for *fiscal or other devices designed to narrow the conflict, at the decentralised level, between the public interest and the self-interest of the parties directly concerned.* Perhaps the most sophisticated device is the French "conjunctural levy," which is designed to penalise excessive increases in unit wages and/or profit margins. These devices are conceptually attractive. Despite the likelihood of administrative complications and difficulties, they deserve further consideration.

There are many difficulties involved in establishing price and wage guidelines applicable to individual cases. In general, *we do not favour policies which involve detailed intervention in the process of price and income determination on a permanent basis.* The benefits obtained in terms of any improvement in the tradeoff between inflation and high levels of employment are outweighed by the costs in terms of the distortions introduced into the economy and the diversion of existing social and political institutions from their natural functions.

In certain extremely difficult circumstances, however, *resort to a wage stop and/or price freeze on a voluntary or statutory basis may be justified as an emergency measure, so long as it is accompanied by appropriate demand management policies.* The primary objective should be to cut into the price-wage spiral and provide the focal point for a significant winding down of inflationary expectations.

In some of the smaller OECD countries, social and political cohesion combined with exposure to strong competitive forces provide the best possible basis for a relatively ambitious prices and incomes policy, and we believe that in a few cases such policies have been moderately successful. But this experience should not be extrapolated to other countries where these conditions are absent.

We support arrangements for the *regular collection and dissemination of information on price developments, together with analysis of how far they conform to norms for noninflationary behaviour.* This can be regarded as much a part of an effective competition policy as a prices and incomes policy. There is an equally good case for *improved information and analysis of trends in both wage and nonwage incomes, before and after taxes,* which should help to clarify the discussion of issues concerned with equality and incentives.

Better Functioning of Markets

Determined government efforts, over a wide range, to eliminate restriction and rigidity and promote competition and mobility would improve the efficiency of macroeconomic policy instruments and make a significant contribution to better price and growth performance. This calls in some areas for the removal of obstacles to a freer play of market forces, in others for action by the authorities to supplement market signals. While we talk about "better" functioning of markets, the problem in many cases is to halt or reverse a tendency towards deterioration in their functioning.

The tendency toward less flexibility in *labour markets* may be one of the main reasons why in recent years the unemployment rate at the peak of the cycle has steadily increased in most countries. Unemployment among youths and women has gone up at the same time as vacancies for adult male labour have increased. Rigidities in the labour market are partly psychological and legal, but are also related to inappropriate wage differentials and the rising costs of hiring and firing labour.

We support traditional labour market policies designed to reduce mismatches between supply and demand for particular categories of labour. Such policies should gradually enable the economy to operate at a higher overall level of demand than would otherwise be possible without encountering labour bottlenecks and strong wage pressures in particular sectors.

Action more directly aimed at *increasing the flexibility of wage structures* is also desirable. Since wages are both incomes and costs, there is a conflict here between equality and efficiency. This can be eased by action to prevent discrimination against particular social groups, and programmes for investment in training and human capital, which can both improve efficiency and reduce inequality. Beyond this, the traditional approach is to let relative wages reflect productivity differentials and to pursue goals of greater equality through tax and transfer policies. Another approach is to allow wage differentials themselves to reflect, at least in part, community attitudes as to the appropriate distribution of income, offsetting resulting imbalances through taxes and subsidies to employers. Both approaches have advantages and limitations. Income redistribution through taxes and transfers has a major role to play, but there are clear limits set by the need to maintain incentives. At the same time, with a greater supply of qualified manpower, it should be possible to tolerate or encourage a gradual trend toward a more egalitarian distribution in primary incomes, perhaps in some cases offsetting any adverse impact on employment through subsidies or other incentives to employers.

More emphasis needs to be given to the needs and capacities of different types of labour in negotiating wage structures and conditions of work. The range of choice between gainful employment and withdrawal from the labour force should be enlarged. Barriers to entry to some occupations should be lowered. In some countries *arrangements for financing social security should be altered to avoid taxing employment so heavily.* There may also be a case for *temporary subsidies to cover part of the cost of taking on new employees.*

If left to themselves, *capital markets* are generally innovative and competitive. Apart from regulations necessary to protect borrowers and lenders, compartmentalisation of financial markets should be reduced and interest rates allowed to reflect market forces. We also recommend the *removal of institutional obstacles to the issue of indexed bonds*. These would reduce uncertainty for borrowers and provide savers with better protection against inflation. Availability of indexed bonds should also help to stabilize prices of other assets, such as land and raw materials, in inflationary periods.

Most of us also believe that *governments themselves should also be prepared to issue indexed bonds*. In countries with sophisticated capital markets, it would not be advisable to present the new asset as a privileged one, limited to some categories of savers and/or made available only in small amounts to each. Instead, indexed government bonds should be just one of the many assets available, with a low real interest rate to test the market.

As regards *product markets*, we are in favour of traditional competition policy. We are concerned about the problem of providing adequate rewards to innovators. In both connections it is important to ensure freedom of entry for both new domestic producers and foreign suppliers.

Perhaps the most promising way of encouraging competition, which would both help to check inflation and promote growth, lies in a sustained effort to *remove tariffs and nontariff barriers to imports, in particular imports from developing countries of manufactures and other products*. This requires vigorous steps to facilitate sectoral adjustment in the industrialised countries. There is also a need to create and maintain conditions favorable to investment and a competitive exchange rate in the developing countries. Economic logic argues strongly for increased capital flows to these countries; this should provide greater impetus to growth in the world economy.

In the light of our analysis of what went wrong, particularly with respect to the inflationary outburst of 1972–74, there is clearly a strong case for action to *reduce the vulnerability of the world economy to shocks*, arising either from interruptions in supply or sharp fluctuations in demand. As regards food, we agree on the desirability of building up *security stocks of cereals*. For industrial raw materials, we support policies designed to *encourage international investment*, consistent with desires of host countries to maintain sovereignty over their resources, and in some cases action to *reduce the instability of commodity prices through buffer stocks*.

More vigorous energy policies are required.   It is essential that full use be made of the market mechanism. Additional measures may be required to provide a firm long-term perspective for energy prices, to encourage research and development in energy production and consumption, and to improve efficiency in energy consumption.

Finally, *environmental considerations* raise serious problems for the functioning of the market mechanism. We support policy instruments, which rely on the price mechanism, to make "polluters pay." In some cases, however, an element of direct regulation may be unavoidable.

The International Dimension

It is only possible to make a provisional assessment of the new more decentralised and flexible international monetary arrangements, featuring widespread floating of exchange rates and an increased role for private financial markets in the provision of international liquidity.

Coordination of Demand Management Policies. To a significant extent, the difficulties of the last five years can be attributed to the fact that, while the economies of the developed and developing world have become so highly synchronised and interdependent, the responsibility for economic policy remains firmly in the hands of independent national entities. This means that there is no way that the economic and political consequences of action taken in the major countries on the rest of the world get fed back to those who took the key decisions, except to the extent that they prove able to act like world statesmen.

Policy makers should communicate and consult with one another as a matter of intelligent self-interest. They should regularly try to form a view as to the need to stimulate or restrain demand in the world economy as a whole. Countries which should take the lead in expanding demand are those with high unemployment, low inflation, favourable balances of payments, large reserves, and good credit-worthiness. The converse obtains if overall restraint of demand is what is required.

There is a need to reduce the present divergent trends of economic performance between OECD countries. This task is greatly complicated by the existence of the collective current deficit with OPEC countries. Some countries have run up debt so massively in recent years that their external credit-worthiness may now be becoming exhausted. It is a matter of some urgency that *a greater share of the oil deficit be borne by countries whose external credit-worthiness is intact.*

Continuation of present trends could undermine confidence, prompt recourse to protectionist trade measures, and lead to a gradual break-up of the open international trade and payments system. The first and essential requirement for halting this trend is *effective domestic antiinflationary policies in the countries with high inflation rates.* The second requirement is that favourably-placed countries which could expand more rapidly without risk of additional inflation should *accept responsibility for maintaining the momentum of the recovery in world economic activity.*

Exchange Rates. Since the move to a more flexible system, exchange rates have tended to move quite closely in line with changes of relative costs and prices—i.e., to depreciate in countries with above-average inflation, and vice versa. In the shorter run, however, rate movements have been comparatively large, owing to the impact of monetary and other developments on equilibrium in international financial markets, and to the slower speed of adjustment in the markets for real goods and services relative to the speed of adjustment in financial markets. And, in the case of a few countries, a tendency toward "over-adjustment" of exchange rates downwards has added to the difficulty of controlling domestic inflationary pressures.

We are *against going back to a formal pegging of exchange rates,* and are also dubious about various proposals to limit exchange-rate flexibility through formal mechanisms. Beyond this, we are uncertain and somewhat divided about the extent to which it is likely to prove necessary or desirable for governments to intervene in the exchange market. The main factor affecting exchange rates cannot be intervention; it is the broad macroeconomic policies being followed by the countries concerned. It is *a mistake to try to resist movements in exchange rates rendered inevitable by changes in relative costs and prices or other factors affecting a country's underlying position on current or capital account.*

At the same time, if the less well-placed countries are to be able to reduce their high inflation rates, their exchange rates must move within a range sufficiently low to provide a significant incentive for changing their production structure towards a more export-oriented economy, but, at the same time, sufficiently high to be compatible—in conjunction with appropriate demand management and other policies—with bringing down the domestic rate of inflation towards that achieved in less inflationary countries.

Since the adjustments in trade and payments flows will take time, these conditions will need to be fulfilled over a period of one, two, or more years. Some of us doubt whether, even if the right policies are being pursued all round, exchange rates will necessarily move within this relatively narrow range in the face of inevitable economic (and political) uncertainties. They therefore believe that in present circumstances there is a case for *contingency planning for more active intervention by governments of various countries in certain exchange markets* to prevent or correct excessive movements of rates.

For certain smaller countries, some members of the Group feel there may be a case for pegging the currency, formally or informally, to that of a major country with a satisfactory price performance. In this way an exchange-rate "norm" can be added to or substituted for monetary, fiscal, and price and incomes norms in a policy of not accommodating high domestic inflation.

There is no easy or simple formula for the management of exchange rates. For some time to come it may be necessary to experiment with a variety of alternative approaches in individual countries, in order to see how the desired blend of flexibility and viscosity can best be achieved. Only time will tell how much collective management will be needed.

International Liquidity. The shift to increased reliance on private lenders for official financing purposes marks the culmination of a secular transformation of the process of liquidity creation. The consequence is that the limits of reserve creation have become ill-defined and fluid, being set more by the private market's judgment of the credit-worthiness of individual countries than by official multilateral evaluation of the policies being followed and the needs of the system as a whole. The international monetary system has taken on some of the characteristics of a domestic credit system without a central bank.

Our concern is not so much with the increase in international liquidity as such, vast though it has been. We are, however, concerned about the extremely uneven accumulation of debt within and outside the OECD area. Access to international financing is, at times, so easy as to tempt governments to postpone needed adjustments, but can then abruptly become difficult as shifts occur in market sentiment regarding individual countries' credit-worthiness. Moreover, limits to the expansion of international financing can become effective only by imposing strains on the monetary system as a whole and the viability of the private financial intermediaries who play such a major role in it.

We do not believe that a solution to these dangers should be sought by trying greatly to restrict the activities of the international financial markets. Rather, the challenge is to manage the supply of liquidity more effectively. There should be *a closer association between private lending and official conditionality.* Private financial institutions should pay more heed to the overall economic situation in borrowing countries. Borrowing countries should be ready to seek advice and help from official multilateral institutions somewhat earlier. There should be *an increase in the amount of official financing available to back up appropriate stabilization programmes and help get through the prolonged period of adjustment to higher oil prices.* And *existing arrangements for supervising the activities of the international markets and for providing lender-of-last-resort facilities in case of real need should be reviewed regularly,* in order to avert the possibility of severe strains on the overall monetary system.

Looking further ahead, what is the likely or desired evolution of the international monetary system as a whole? The present arrangements can perhaps best be described as a market-oriented or "federative" system, where the availability and terms on which external financing can be obtained are determined in individual cases by private institutions, but where for the system as a whole they are determined by the joint product of the monetary policies being followed in the major financial centres. Such a federative system can be viable so long as the authorities responsible for monetary policies in the major countries are prepared to pay sufficient attention to conditions in—and the needs of—the world economy as a whole.

This emphasizes again the need for closer consultation and better co-ordination of demand management policies. The need is not for more meetings or the creation of new international bodies. But the degree to which the world price level as a whole has become sensitive to fluctuations in demand, and the rapidity with which loss of confidence affecting investment, inventories, and consumers' behavior seems to spread out from country to country, underline the fact that close international cooperation is an essential ingredient of a programme directed towards getting back to full employment and price stability.

25

THE CONTROL OF INFLATION:
LESSONS FROM EAST
EUROPEAN EXPERIENCE*

Richard Portes[1]

Centrally planned economies commonly claim that they avoid the inflationary problems of market economies discussed in the preceding selection. The reasons cited include comprehensive price control, incomes policies, the subordination of the financial system to central planning, and the foreign trade monopoly. However, these mechanisms may only repress, rather than eliminate, the inflationary pressures arising from ambitious and imperfect planning. Then, with excess demand at the official prices, there will be widespread shortages, as shown by empty shelves, queues, black markets, and abnormally high saving rates.

In this selection, Portes carefully analyzes inflation in Eastern Europe. He examines official claims of price stability, in the face of strong inflationary forces. He explains the mechanisms for controlling inflation, and their costs. He also evaluates arguments that repressed inflation is substantial. Finally, he suggests a dozen "lessons" from East European experience in the control of inflation.

* Reprinted by permission from *Economica*, vol. 44, no. 174 (May 1977), pp. 109–29, with the omission of tables and the inclusion of some minor revisions by the author. Richard Portes is Professor of Economics at Birkbeck College, University of London.

[1] Discussions with Stan Rudcenko and David Winter and their help with the data have been invaluable. This paper arises out of a project on macroeconomic equilibrium under central planning supported by SSRC (U.K.) grant HR3309. A previous version was presented at the Center for Environmental Studies seminar series on Major Social and Economic Problems of the United Kingdom in the Light of East European Experience, and I have benefited from the comments of the discussants, John Flemming and A. G. Hines. I have also received valuable comments from John Broome. For a paper of this kind, however, it is perhaps especially important to stress my full responsibility for the views expressed as well as for any errors of fact or analysis.

I. INTRODUCTION

Economics is difficult enough, even if one manages to avoid comparative studies in applied economics. Such efforts are inherently unreliable and inconclusive. It is much simpler to model any single set of economic institutions and functional relations, using the data they generate to test hypotheses derived from the model, than to compare two different economic environments with each other in any useful way. With a model, one has an essential extra degree of freedom—one constructs it oneself. In comparative applied economics, however, *everything* is given, and we are reduced to counterfactual hypotheses analogous to those of economic history; e.g., how would a policy directed towards narrowing wage differentials as in the USSR work in some other country?—supposing we do know, more or less, what has actually happened in the USSR.

It is therefore easier to apply the analytical tools of Western economics to the socialist centrally planned economies (CPEs), whatever the data problems and the need to adapt our models, than to seek any comparative lessons. One is especially reluctant to hypothesize the introduction of some CPE institutional pattern into a capitalist mixed economy. In our present circumstances, however, this is perhaps academic self-indulgence. Whether or not we are yet moving towards any "new international economic order," the old one surely has broken down; whether or not we can discern the future outlines of our own domestic economic system, the existing one isn't working very well. To proclaim a "crisis of capitalism"—or of orthodox economics—may be rhetorical excess, but in fact both are being seriously challenged, so far more by events than by new ideas. So it may be useful to put unfamiliar alternatives before a wider public, with a view to evaluating them and drawing implications, both positive and negative, for our own institutions and policies. At least this form of comparative applied economics has some potential value, in contrast with "comparative economic systems," which typically juxtaposes idealized models bearing little relation to actual economies; and it may not be so open to misinterpretation as East-West comparisons of growth rates and efficiency.[2]

I shall deal with the CPEs of Eastern Europe as a group. There are some significant differences between them in economic institutions and levels of development, but all allocate resources centrally in physical terms, and all have similar monetary systems. The USSR stands out for its size, Hungary for its market-oriented "economic reforms" of 1968, which took it partly outside the CPE category. Yugoslavia deliberately rejected central planning over two decades ago, but it is a socialist economy, and its workers' control and inflation justify a brief discussion (Section VIII).

---

[2] See the critique in Philip Hanson, "East-West Comparisons and Comparative Economic Systems," *Soviet Studies*, vol. 22, no. 3 (January 1971), pp. 327–43.

The experience of these countries in controlling inflation might be thought irrelevant to advanced capitalist societies because of their very different political systems, property ownership arrangements, and class relations. This would assume that the essential mechanisms and policy instruments used to control inflation in CPEs were inseparable from the entire socioeconomic system. To evaluate such a view requires a theory of the causes of inflation in advanced capitalist countries. Thus if inflation here results entirely from trade union behaviour, then we can learn nothing from CPEs except to make our unions behave like theirs or find some CPE policy that could neutralize ours. Neither is likely outside a more fundamental transformation of our own system than imagined here. The discussion below imposes no such model of the inflationary process, however, aside from the distinction between impulse and propagating factors in it. Nor shall I go so far as to assess whether any given institutional arrangement or policy tool could be transplanted successfully.

If not irrelevant, the experience of CPEs might be thought uninteresting if they were unsuccessful in controlling inflation, or if success were achieved at an excessive or avoidable cost. On this the reader will form a judgement and may in any case find negative lessons just as informative as positive ones. The object of the exercise however is *not* to evaluate central planning or socialism, or to make overall comparisons of "system performance."

II. THE DATA

The official consumer price statistics for the CPEs show remarkable price stability. We shall ignore the prices of investment goods and intermediate goods and the wholesale prices of consumer goods, looking only at the interface between the productive sector and households: consumer prices and personal incomes. Only here do we find markets in which prices and money flows are active and not fully subordinate to the physical allocation system. Consumer goods prices and wage rates are in general fixed centrally, but in the consumer goods market on the demand side and the labour market on the supply side, household choice is subject to very little administrative constraint.

Whereas there was very considerable open inflation in the USSR up to 1947, from then until 1954 state retail prices were progressively reduced. Most of the other CPEs had some open inflation (and "currency reforms") in the late 1940s and early 1950s, but Bulgaria, Czechoslovakia, and the GDR then followed the Soviet example in reducing prices for several years. Since the mid-1950s, the poorest record is that of Poland, where the consumer price index (CPI) has risen at about 1.5 percent per year.

Even before the major economic policy changes under Gierek, inflationary tendencies were stronger in Poland than in the other CPEs. But inflation at 1 percent per year until 1972 rose to over 4 percent per year in 1972–75, and with *per capita* nominal incomes rising at 12.5 percent in this period, there has been some repressed inflation as well.[3] The abortive attempt to raise food prices sharply in June 1976 was just a symptom of much deeper economic problems.

The stability of the indices is not just an aggregate phenomenon; there has been very little change in individual relative prices over the period. These official indices might nevertheless be misleading. Their coverage is often not clearly defined, and only those for East Germany and Hungary include goods sold on the "free market." This market (*kolkhoz*, or collective farm market), where it exists, is generally small in volume and limited to certain foodstuffs; we return to it later when discussing repressed inflation. Potentially more serious, perhaps, are possible biases or deliberate falsification in reporting or in calculating the indices. Doubtless some transactions in state shops do take place at illegal prices, higher than those fixed centrally, and certainly not reported. The consensus Western view, however, is that this is relatively infrequent, and that the fixed prices themselves are reported accurately. But the statisticians do have disconcerting tendencies to change commodity baskets, base years, and methods of calculation, giving little information about their methodology.

Clever detective work can sort out many of these problems, with little effect on the overall picture. Yet "hidden" price increases may remain. It is often claimed that the quality of consumer goods deteriorates, with significant effects on a quality-corrected price index. But it is difficult to imagine this process *continuing* at any appreciable rate over a long period for any particular good—what would be left, eventually? In any case, the problems besetting *any* attempts at correcting price indices for quality change are severe.[4] A more likely source of bias is the marketing of "new" products at prices unjustifiably higher than the cheaper varieties they displace, which become unavailable but remain in the commodity basket for which the price index is calculated. After 1956, Hungarian statisticians actually estimated the effect of the "hidden" price increases for "new" goods in the

---

[3] See also the econometric evidence suggesting this in Richard Portes and David Winter, "The Demand for Money and for Consumption Goods in Centrally Planned Economies," *Review of Economics and Statistics*, vol. 60, no. 1 (February 1978), pp. 8–18; and in Richard Portes and David Winter, "Disequilibrium Estimates for Consumption Goods Markets in Centrally Planned Economies" (Cambridge, Mass.: Harvard Institute of Economic Research, Discussion Paper no. 612, 1978). For further discussion of recent Polish experience, see Richard Portes, "Inflation under Central Planning," in *The Political Economy of Inflation*, ed. John Goldthorpe and Fred Hirsch (London: Martin Robertson, and Cambridge, Mass.: Harvard University Press, 1978), pp. 73–87.

[4] John Muellbauer, "Household Production Theory, Quality, and the Hedonic Technique," *American Economic Review*, vol. 64, no. 6 (December 1974), pp. 977–94.

1950s (when they were surely more significant than in recent years), and they reported the equivalent of a 1 percent per year increase in the CPI.[5]

"Hidden" price increases—or rising prices on the free market, second-hand markets, or black market—would occur if there were underlying inflationary pressures which central price regulation could not control. But even fully comprehensive, perfectly effective price control cannot ensure that the goods demanded are *available* at the fixed prices. Is there sustained repressed inflation (informal rationing for buyers) on the consumer goods market? Section V below argues that the conventional view that repressed inflation is ubiquitous in CPEs is not supported by empirical evidence. Here we can refer to wage and income data which are relevant in assessing both the reliability of the reported CPIs and the degree of repressed inflation.

It is likely that those who stress queues, hidden price increases, etc., would nonetheless agree from similar casual observation that there *has* been significant growth in *per capita* real disposable incomes in the CPEs since the mid-1950s. A rate of, say, 5 percent per year does not seem a gross overestimate. But this is roughly what the *official* price and income statistics imply, and it is seldom claimed that the official wage and money income data are biased upwards. It would be difficult to argue that living standards haven't at least doubled over the past two decades. This impressionistic evidence is confirmed by direct estimates of consumption based on various quantity series. Thus, even fairly conservative Western recalculations show real *per capita* consumption growing at about 4 percent per year for 1955–67 in Hungary and Poland[6] and at about 4 percent per year for 1955–75 in the USSR.[7] These seem at least as reliable as reports of shortages, quality deterioration, and the like, and would suggest that the official price indices *cannot* be seriously misleading.

In other words, comparing official statistics for *per capita* nominal income growth rates with our impressions and estimates of true real-income growth rates does *not* suggest true rates of consumer price increase that substantially exceed those in the official CPIs. Reasoning in this way, Schroeder and Severin find that "the implicit price index calculated by juxtaposing independent measures of real consumption and Soviet retail

---

[5] Béla Csikós-Nagy, "Anti-Inflationary Policies: Debates and Experience in Hungary," in Centro Studi e Ricerche su Problemi Economico-Sociali (CESES), *Anti-Inflationary Policies: East-West* (Milan: CESES, 1975), pp. 143–63.

[6] Thad Alton, "Economic Structure and Growth in Eastern Europe," in *Economic Developments in Countries of Eastern Europe* (A Compendium of Papers Submitted to the Joint Economic Committee, 91st Cong., 2d sess.) (Washington, D.C.: U.S. Government Printing Office, 1970), pp. 41–67.

[7] Gertrude E. Schroeder and Barbara S. Severin, "Soviet Consumption and Income Policies in Perspective," in *Soviet Economy in a New Perspective* (A Compendium of Papers Submitted to the Joint Economic Committee, 94th Cong., 2d sess.) (Washington, D.C.: U.S. Government Printing Office, 1976), pp. 620–60.

sales in current prices shows an average annual price increase of 1.3 percent over the past 20 years."[8] A similar calculation by Howard[9] gives an estimate of "hidden" inflation at a rate between 0.8 and 1.2 percent per year. Hidden price increases of "several percentage points *annually*"[10] would equal or exceed the rise in money incomes and give no real income increases. This is absurd, and we should therefore ask not why the CPIs rise so slowly, but rather how the planners keep money incomes from rising faster than they do.

III. INFLATIONARY PRESSURES

The performance outlined above has been achieved despite strong underlying inflationary forces in the CPEs. The entire period under consideration has been characterized by rapid structural change and output growth, sustained high investment ratios and "taut planning"[11] throughout the productive sector. All but the last are familiar causes of inflation in developing countries and some developed countries (Japan, Italy). The excess real demand imposed by the planners is specific to CPEs, and it goes by various names in the literature: "planners' tension," "pressure,"[12] "suction."[13] The issue here is how, and to what extent, it may be transmitted from the productive sector to the consumer goods market.

The story of the process by which taut planning supposedly generates inflationary pressures is plausible enough. In principle, the planners try to construct a balanced plan, in particular equating the planned wage bill to the planned supply of consumer goods at current fixed prices. But output plans are typically over-optimistic. This planners' tension is intended to force producers to "mobilize reserves," but even with maximum effort the plan as promulgated is infeasible. To fulfil their output plans, enterprises must use more labour than planned, so actual wage payments exceed the plan. And whereas over-fulfilment of consumer goods output plans may create the increase in supply necessary to match the extra wage disbursements it requires, over-fulfilment of output plans elsewhere does not, and

---

[8] Schroeder and Severin, "Soviet Consumption," p. 636.

[9] David H. Howard, "A Note on Hidden Inflation in the Soviet Union," *Soviet Studies*, vol. 28, no. 4 (October 1976), pp. 599–608.

[10] Gertrude E. Schroeder, "Consumer Goods Availability and Repressed Inflation in the Soviet Union," in *Economic Aspects of Life in the USSR* (Brussels: NATO, 1975), p. 42. Emphasis mine.

[11] Holland Hunter, "Optimal Tautness in Development Planning," *Economic Development and Cultural Change*, vol. 1, no. 4 (July 1961), part II, pp. 561–72; and Richard Portes, "The Enterprise under Central Planning," *Review of Economic Studies*, vol. 36, no. 106 (April 1969), pp. 197–212.

[12] Herbert S. Levine, "Pressure and Planning in the Soviet Economy," in *Industrialization in Two Systems: Essays in Honor of Alexander Gerschenkron*, ed. Henry Rosovsky (New York: John Wiley & Sons, Inc., 1966), pp. 266–86.

[13] János Kornai, *Anti-equilibrium* (Amsterdam: North-Holland, 1971).

therefore creates further pressures. Although wage payments are supposed to be strictly controlled by the banking system, in practice managers can justify above-plan expenditures on wages by pleading the importance of the output plan. Moreover, if planning errors or exogenous shocks (harvest failures, transport and storage problems, delayed investment completions, falling terms of trade) generate shortages of inputs, plan fulfillment for producer goods takes priority; the consumer goods sector is a "buffer," and resources are shifted away from it. Similarly, the ambitions of planners and politicians are reflected in steady pressure to increase investment.

Thus, although plans may be balanced *ex ante*, there is always excess real demand, which is translated into excess money demand for consumer goods. The problem is exacerbated by the excessive use of piece-rate wage systems and some degree of wage drift, which is partly a response to workers' expectations of continuous real-income increases. Since the late 1950s, policy makers have in fact encouraged these expectations. A necessary condition for satisfying them, however, has been growth of agricultural output, which has required redistribution of income towards the peasantry to create incentives (given the deficiencies of agricultural organization). This has in turn increased the political pressures from the urban working class.

This brief summary of the mechanisms that are thought to generate and propagate inflationary pressures in CPEs should indicate how powerful are the forces that anti-inflation policies have had to control. We now consider why and how they have worked.

IV. CONTROL OF INFLATION

Although the control of inflation is not the planners' primary objective, it has none the less been an important desideratum throughout the period, for several reasons. First, some of the East European countries had gone through severe episodes of inflation just after the war, the extreme case being the Hungarian hyperinflation of 1945–46 (at 10^{24}, the worst ever recorded). These and the subsequent currency reforms were painful experiences which left the population highly sensitive to price increases. Subsequently, the longer consumer prices remained stable, the more any apparent increase was resented, to the point where in recent years a "perverse" money illusion has operated. Price changes calculated to compensate each other so as not to reduce the real income of any significant group are in fact *perceived* as increases in the overall price level, and price increases with compensating money wage increases are perceived as reductions in real income. This has inhibited the planners from making any price adjustments at all.

Second, the planners fear the unplanned, "spontaneous" phenomena that open inflation can bring, especially any effects in the politically sensitive area of income distribution. In particular, inflationary pressures that spill over into the *kolkhoz* market can affect the distribution between workers and peasants. Repressed inflation also has political disadvantages: black markets are bad for morale, and queues are highly visible foci for resentment and agitation.

Finally, the monetary planners and central bankers in Eastern Europe are a remarkably conservative, indeed orthodox, group, for whom excess liquidity and "monetary overhang" are anathema. They therefore carry out comprehensive financial planning centered on the planned balance of the population's incomes and expenditures and implemented through a well integrated monetary and fiscal system. The anti-inflationary tools available to them and the structural characteristics of the system on which they can rely go far beyond mere price and income controls.[14]

The banking system is in fact a monobank, a single, combined central and commercial bank with many branches. It can therefore enforce complete separation between the circuits of enterprise money (entries in the monobank's books) and household money (cash and savings deposits). Thus monetary disequilibrium in the enterprise circuit, where money is passive, will have little effect unless it creates household money through wage payments, which the bank controls directly (see below). There is a very restricted range of assets. Enterprises have only their deposit money: they do not issue debt instruments, and they are in principle prohibited from extending trade credit to each other, although payment delays sometimes have this effect. Consumer credit is limited—its opposite is more common, when the authorities require advance deposits in special savings accounts to hold a place on a waiting list for a car or apartment. Some "state savings bonds" were sold to households to absorb liquidity in the 1950s, but this is no longer done.

Thus the planners' control over money and credit is direct and quantitative. They need not worry about regulating the reserves of independent commercial banks, or about the prices and yields of financial assets and their effects on expenditures. There are no reserve or liquidity ratios, no secondary credit expansion or open market operations. Foreign exchange movements have no effect on the domestic monetary system, because the "price equalization subsidy" (*Preisausgleich*) system completely separates domestic from foreign prices and transactions.[15]

Fiscal instruments include direct taxes (income taxes, typically at low and relatively flat rates, and deductions from enterprise profits), a highly

---

[14] See George Garvy, *Money, Banking, and Credit in Eastern Europe* (New York: Federal Reserve Bank of New York, 1966), for a detailed description.

[15] Peter Wiles, "The New Inflation Consists of Too Many Bankers Chasing Too Few Ideas," in CESES, *Anti-inflationary Policies*, pp. 229–46. For further discussion of how the *Preisausgleich* insulates the domestic economy from imported inflation, see Portes, "Inflation under Central Planning."

differentiated structure of turnover taxes and subsidies, and control over the large share of aggregate expenditure which is financed directly from the state budget. All these monetary and fiscal controls, however, are not intended to *affect* real variables, but rather to *adjust* to the planned values of those variables, so as to maintain the proper environment for price and income controls.

The task of a prices and incomes policy is to match aggregate demand and its structure to the planned supply of consumer goods, with due regard to egalitarian objectives and production incentives as well. The enterprise's wage plan is usually a total wage bill or an average wage, and it is enforced by detailed bank supervision of wage fund expenditure. The banks have gradually become more effective in this role, as the absolute priority of the output plan has diminished and permissible wage expenditure has become less related to output plan fulfilment.[16] The rationalization of wage structures around 1960 also helped, by giving a more secure basis to the national job evaluation systems within which individual wage rates are determined.[17]

Consumer prices are fixed individually and changed rarely, only for specific reasons (except for some seasonal foods). Any producer (wholesale) price changes can be absorbed by fiscal measures; i.e., the system of commodity taxes and subsidies allows the maintenance of fixed consumer prices if desired. This will of course affect the state budget, and the financial planners must deal with the repercussions. But a rising aggregate subsidy bill is *not* a sign of inflation, either open or repressed. A given set of consumer prices and quantities may be consistent with various sets of producer prices, turnover taxes and subsidies, and associated financial flows.[18] The planners may change these relationships as costs change without any effect on the balance of supply and demand in the consumer goods market, provided their calculations are correct.

For instance, if foreign prices rise, keeping domestic prices constant by increasing import subsidies and export taxes is not repressing inflation; but rather carrying out a basic function of the foreign trade control system, which is to divorce domestic from foreign prices so the planners may deal with real variables at fixed prices. A deterioration of the terms of trade will indeed affect real variables, but even then, keeping consumer prices constant need not imply repressed inflation; the fall in real income can be met by reducing either money wages or real nonconsumption expenditure. In a

---

[16] Franklyn D. Holzman, "Soviet Inflationary Pressures, 1928–1957: Causes and Cures," *Quarterly Journal of Economics*, vol. 74, no. 2 (May 1960), pp. 167–88; and John P. Farrell, "Bank Control of the Wage Fund in Poland: 1950–1970," *Soviet Studies*, vol. 27, no. 2 (April 1975), pp. 265–87.

[17] Alastair McAuley, "Wage Determination in the USSR" (London: Centre for Environmental Studies, 1976), and United Nations, Economic Commission for Europe, *Incomes in Postwar Europe* (Geneva, 1967).

[18] Robert W. Campbell, "Macroeconomic Models and Central Price-setting in the Soviet Economy," in *Essays in Economic Analysis and Policy*, ed. F. Gehrels and others (Bloomington, Ind.: Indiana University Press, 1970), pp. 253–70.

market economy, a rise in costs or an exogenous shock reducing real income would be directly inflationary and would also *redistribute* real income, perhaps consequently generating further inflationary pressures. CPE planners cannot avoid the initial impulse, but they *can* control both where its impact falls and its income distributional effects. (Indeed, empirical evidence suggests that the planners have *not* used the consumer goods sector as a "buffer" to absorb the main effects of exogenous shocks.[19])

This is just one example of the way in which certain interconnections characteristic of capitalist mixed economies are broken in the CPEs. Such structural differences are particularly significant because of the self-propelling and often cumulative feedbacks in the inflation propagation mechanisms of mixed economies. Thus in the CPEs, the direct link from costs to prices is broken by the product-specific turnover tax and subsidy system, which can insulate consumer prices from increases in costs. The link between prices and expenditures via factor incomes is also broken, since turnover taxes or deductions from profits may be adjusted to draw off into the state budget any net revenues arising out of price increases. There is little direct dependence of personal incomes or funds for investment on profits generated in production and distribution (profit-based incentives introduced in recent "economic reforms" are still quantitatively insignificant, except in Hungary). Nor does excess demand, even for consumer goods, necessarily provoke any response in supply and hence in the demand for labour. The planners may instead choose to absorb it in turnover tax increases (which, while raising prices once-for-all, are clearly deflationary, since the revenues go straight to the budget), or they may increase imports or reduce the rate of growth of money wages. They might also simply allow some repressed inflationary pressure to persist (but see Section V).

We come finally to trade unions. It is doubtless a great help to the planners in CPEs that their trade unions play no significant role in wage determination—that there is no formally organized expression of real income aspirations through collective bargaining. But I believe that the importance of this institutional difference is often exaggerated.[20] For there *is* pressure from urban workers for wage increases, from consumers for higher living standards, from peasants for industrial consumer goods. There *are* ways in which these pressures may be transmitted, and planning is itself a bargaining process in which they are certainly taken into account. The planners' wage and agricultural procurement price policies cannot for long ignore production incentives.[21] The infrequency of (illegal) strikes is matched by the prevalence of slacking and slowdowns when workers are dissatisfied or simply see no material incentive to work harder. Relativity

---

[19] Richard Portes and David Winter, "The Supply of Consumption Goods in Centrally Planned Economies," *Journal of Comparative Economics*, vol. 1, no. 4 (December 1977), pp. 351–65.

[20] E.g., in Wiles, "The New Inflation."

[21] Cf. Poland in the late 1960s—Farrell, "Bank Control."

comparisons do generate some wage drift on the shop floor, and workers are conscious of interenterprise differentials and very sensitive indeed to increases in peasant incomes. As elsewhere, only *upwards* adjustments of nominal incomes are admissible in rectifying perceived distortions of relativities or distributional inequities. The population also clearly expect the continuous annual real income growth to which they have become accustomed since the mid-1950s, and the authorities have made little serious effort in recent years to discourage comparisons with advanced capitalist countries or hinder the development of "consumerism" in all its forms.

Moreover, just as at the highest political level there are those whose interests are served by advancing the causes of the workers or the peasants, so throughout the Party and the planning and industrial bureaucracies tasks are made easier by the ability to grant wage increases. Thus the Ministry of Labour, the Ministry of Finance, and the banking apparatus do face powerful pressures. They may react more slowly to these pressures because they are not expressed institutionally through free collective bargaining with the trade unions, and so the propagation of "cost-inflationary" impulses is delayed. But the planners must eventually respond, regardless of the unions' weakness, or risk creating insupportable social and political tensions. The apparatus of anti-inflationary techniques described here is by no means superfluous.

V. REPRESSED INFLATION

Section II suggested that real consumption standards in Eastern Europe have not lagged much behind money incomes deflated by official consumer price indices. The residual expansion of household money balances might well have been absorbed voluntarily without creating repressed inflationary pressures, especially since at these countries' level of development one expects households to have high income elasticities of demand for real balances (and such balances started from abnormally low levels in the mid-1950s because of the "currency reforms"). Such assertions as "savings deposits have been rising so rapidly" as to indicate "imbalance in the consumer goods market,"[22] and that "the most dramatic indicator of repressed inflation in recent years has been the sharp rise in personal savings,"[23] are common fallacies based on misunderstandings of the relevant savings ratios.[24] The authors quoted are considering, respectively, S/W and $S/\triangle Y$

---

[22] Schroeder, "Consumer Goods," p. 42.

[23] Keith Bush, "Soviet Inflation," in *Banking, Money, and Credit in Eastern Europe*, ed. Yves Laulan (Brussels: NATO, 1973), p. 100.

[24] See the discussion in Richard Portes, "Macroeconomic Equilibrium under Central Planning" (Stockholm: Institute for International Economic Studies, University of Stockholm, Seminar Paper no. 40, 1974), and the econometric evidence in Richard Portes and David Winter, "The Demand for Money."

rather than S/Y or $\triangle S/\triangle Y$ (S = flow of savings, Y = income, W = stock of savings deposits). In fact, savings ratios in CPEs are rather low in comparison with those in advanced capitalist countries. The evidence for the USSR given by Pickersgill [25] clearly supports our view.

One of the authors quoted above has apparently revised her view recently: Schroeder and Severin ask "whether the state has been able to achieve reasonable balance between aggregate money incomes and aggregate money expenditures" and find that "the data . . . suggest that fairly good balance has indeed been achieved on the whole," and that calculations suggest that "saving by Soviet households out of current income is not high by comparison with other countries."[26] Finally, it is interesting that even in Poland, where the control of inflation has been weakest among all the CPEs, data on the "turnover" of savings deposits suggest they may be primarily used as *transactions* balances: the ratio of total withdrawals during a year to total new deposits during that year seldom falls much below 80 percent (it has fallen towards 70 percent just in the past few years, when there clearly *has* been some "forced saving").

None of this, however, is conclusive, and it is undeniably conventional wisdom that CPEs suffer chronically from significant repressed inflation: "That the seller's market does obtain in Soviet-type economies even in 'normal' times, in the household sector as well as in the production sector, is an elementary truth which hardly needs substantiation."[27] We have challenged this received view in recent papers,[28] and our research in this area continues. One must first work out the theory implicit in the orthodox repressed inflation story, so as to determine what would constitute evidence of repressed inflationary pressures; one must then test the resulting hypotheses against CPE data. The evidence so far does *not* confirm the conventional view.

We should expect repressed inflation to have a variety of effects, most of which one would regard as undesirable costs of maintaining fixed prices in conditions of excess aggregate demand: ubiquitous queues and shortages, entailing costs in time and forcing consumers to substitute less desired goods for those that are unavailable; the black markets and spivs which some think are inevitable under central planning; no incentives for sellers

[25] Joyce Pickersgill, "Soviet Household Saving Behavior," *Review of Economics and Statistics*, vol. 58, no. 2 (May 1976), pp. 139–47.

[26] Schroeder and Severin, "Soviet Consumption," pp. 636–38.

[27] Gregory Grossman, "Gold and the Sword: Money in the Soviet Economy," in *Industrialization in Two Systems*, ed. Rosovsky, p. 215.

[28] Portes, "Macroeconomic Equilibrium under Central Planning"; Richard Portes, "Macroeconomic Equilibrium and Disequilibrium in Centrally Planned Economies: A Model for Empirical Implementation" (London: Birkbeck College, Discussion Paper in Economics, no. 45, 1976); Portes and Winter, "The Demand for Money"; and Portes and Winter, "Disequilibrium Estimates."

to satisfy consumers, and hence adverse effects on quality and the assortment of goods; forced savings; disincentive effects on labour supply; and free market prices (where they exist) higher than those in the state shops.

There is abundant anecdotal evidence for some of these phenomena,[29] and of course Western visitors perceive shortages, inferior quality, and low real consumption standards as compared with their own countries. But we cannot quantify newspaper reports and casual observation, and a simple "shortage" of consumer goods does not signify repressed inflation, which may be defined as a situation in which buyers are (informally) rationed: i.e., a shortage *relative to incomes* and consequent *desired* expenditure at given prices. We have discussed "hidden" price increases and the difficulties in measuring them in Section II above. We can however systematically investigate savings behaviour, labour supply behaviour and the free market–state retail price differential. (Taking a quite different approach based on inventory–sales ratios and turnover data, Skurski found that "buyers' market conditions [excess supply] have existed for the majority of nonfood Soviet consumer goods since about 1958."[30])

We have reported elsewhere econometric results on household demand for money and savings behaviour and on the balance between supply and demand in the consumption goods market,[31] and I shall not argue here for our interpretations.[32] Our evidence so far is consistent with the hypothesis that the planners have in fact maintained macroeconomic equilibrium on the consumption goods market for all but a few brief periods during most of the past two decades. The data on the relation between state retail and free market food prices since the mid-1950s in Hungary, Poland, and the USSR are also consistent with this view.

Thus we must remain agnostic on this issue, especially since a distorted *relative* price structure (and other features of CPEs, such as the low number of retail outlets) could account for some of the phenomena often attributed to repressed inflation, particularly when seen in conjunction with the *excess stocks* of many goods which observers also report. But disequilibrium relative prices would be a natural consequence of the techniques of inflation control used in CPEs, as we discuss below. And even if there has been some degree of repressed inflation in the CPEs, against the disadvan-

---

[29] E.g., Bush, "Soviet Inflation," and Schroeder, "Consumer Goods."

[30] Roger Skurski, "The Buyers' Market and Soviet Consumer Goods Distribution," *Slavic Review*, vol. 31, no. 4 (December 1972), p. 818. Other approaches also suggest that queues and related phenomena are due partly to characteristics of the retail distribution sector; see Frederic L. Pryor, "Some Costs and Benefits of Markets: An Empirical Study," *Quarterly Journal of Economics*, vol. 91, no. 1 (February 1977), pp. 81–102; and J. Turcan, "Some Observations on Retail Distribution in Poland," *Soviet Studies*, vol. 29, no. 1 (January 1977), pp. 128–36.

[31] Portes and Winter, "The Demand for Money," and Portes and Winter, "Disequilibrium Estimates."

[32] For my views on labour market behaviour, cf. Portes, "Macroeconomic Equilibrium under Central Planning," which answers Wiles, "The New Inflation."

tages suggested above must be set the possibility that it is still easier to enforce social preferences and control real variables than under *open* inflation. In any case, there is a lot to be said for excess demand if the alternative is serious excess supply.

VI. COSTS OF CONTROLS

It should now be clear that the mechanisms of inflation control in CPEs are pervasive and embedded in the entire structure of the central planning system. Yet we cannot here evaluate the system as a whole, so I consider only the potential costs of centrally fixing prices and wages. Most of these are familiar, but difficult to measure, and I shall therefore dwell only upon points that come specifically out of CPE experience.

We may begin with the loss in static efficiency in the conventional neoclassical sense. Doubts about the size of "dead-weight loss" or the welfare implications of "incorrect" relative prices cannot obscure the obvious high real costs of queues and unsaleable inventories. But some of these may be due to the inadequacies of the distributive network or to the incentive system for sellers. The Hungarian experience in decentralization suggests that relative prices and quantities may not be all that distorted: when price controls were relaxed in 1968 and the incentive system (and much else) changed, a reasonable degree of micro-market equilibrium was quickly established *without* drastic shifts in relative prices. And in CPE labour markets, where the supply side is relatively free from administrative restrictions, the planners managed during the 1950s and 1960s to compress the wage structure (narrow differentials) substantially, without creating great disorder in labour allocation.[33]

Both the consumer price structure and wage relativities in CPEs reflect egalitarian objectives, and CPE experience emphasizes how powerful central price and wage determination can be as a redistributive tool, whatever the cost in efficiency.[34] It is also revealing that the planners felt they needed this tool, despite the redistribution of wealth in the switch from capitalist to socialist property relations.[35]

---

[33] Daniel Hamermesh and Richard Portes, "The Labour Market under Central Planning," *Oxford Economic Papers*, vol. 24, no. 2 (July 1972), pp. 241–58; Janet G. Chapman, "Soviet Wages under Socialism," in *The Socialist Price Mechanism*, ed. Alan Abouchar (Durham, N.C.: Duke University Press, 1977), pp. 246–81; McAuley, "Wage Determination."

[34] For the effects of the Polish consumer price structure in reducing inequality, see John Muellbauer, "Inequality Measures, Prices, and Household Composition," *Review of Economic Studies*, vol. 41, no. 128 (October 1974), pp. 493–504.

[35] In their concern for efficiency and incentives, however, the Hungarian "reformers" appear to have abandoned the use of consumer prices for redistribution. John Muellbauer, "Distributional Aspects of Price Comparisons" (unpublished paper presented at International Economic Association Conference, Urbino, 1976), finds that by 1970 the Hungarian consumer price structure may actually have been less egalitarian than that in the United Kingdom.

A second important cost arises from the insulation of domestic from foreign prices. A highly trade-dependent economy should react to foreign price changes, if only to minimize the cost of procuring desired imports. There is no doubt that their inflexibility here has significantly reduced real incomes in the smaller CPEs, and the inefficiencies of foreign trade have gone so far as to create activities with negative value added similar to those found for some LDCs in the effective protection literature. Yet the planners might argue that, to the extent that relative price changes on foreign markets are short-run phenomena, they ought not to be transmitted to the economy, where they might affect long-run choices. This argument is independent of the advantages of the *Preisausgleich* stressed by Wiles.[36]

Relative price flexibility is not unambiguously beneficial, even if it could be attained without sacrificing stability of the price level. Walrasian general equilibrium theory itself suggests that very rapid price adjustment may be a source of instability for the economic system. Moreover, without recontracting, transactions at "false" short-run prices will lead to inefficiencies. Thus Hubert Henderson's "price prescription . . . [was] that the price should deviate from the long-term norm in the direction of the short-term equilibrium price, but only by a narrow angle."[37] CPEs go to the other extreme, and their fixed prices are not intended to be long-term equilibrium prices. But the average cost price-setting rules they use may get them closer to such prices than we might think.[38] And the planners are supposed to make short-run allocation decisions in physical terms using nonprice data anyway.

There is no doubt, however, that the fixed-price system and CPE enterprise incentives are together a most powerful obstacle to rational investment decisions and technical progress. The desire of CPEs to import Western technology now, and the difficulty they have in diffusing it once they get it, are sufficient evidence of this weakness in the system, a major cause of which is the rigidity and irrationalities of the price system.

The system could perhaps be made more flexible and certainly more rational, however, without sacrificing control of inflation. There is in principle no reason why consumer prices should remain fixed for decades, or why it should take several years to implement a producer "price reform." But more flexible (yet still controlled) prices might require an even larger bureaucracy, and the administrative cost and bureaucratic apparatus of price-fixing are a further major disadvantage. The Hungarian experience, however, where a Price Office of 100 staff seems to exercise fairly effective

36 Wiles, "The New Inflation."

37 Hubert Henderson, "The Price System," *Economic Journal*, vol. 58, no. 232 (December 1948), p. 478.

38 Cf. Abram Bergson, *The Economics of Soviet Planning* (New Haven, Conn.: Yale University Press, 1964); Michael Manove, "Soviet Pricing, Profits, and Technological Choice," *Review of Economic Studies*, vol. 43, no. 3 (October 1976), pp. 413–21.

control,[39] might suggest the cost need not be so great. In the U.S. wartime economy, according to Galbraith,[40] only a few thousand skilled administrators were needed to run the entire system of controls. Perhaps conditions have changed drastically since then, for this would be a trivial addition to our existing civil service bureaucracies.

VII. PROSPECTS FOR INFLATION CONTROL IN CPES

Continued economic growth alone is unlikely to bring endogenous structural changes that would affect the analysis presented so far. We must however ask whether possible "economic reforms" or exogenous forces might do so.

In my own judgment, we should *not* expect significant decentralizing, market-oriented reforms in Eastern Europe in the foreseeable future—the next decade, say. We are more likely to see only further rationalization of the system, technocratically oriented adjustments of the basic central planning framework. If this prediction proves wrong, however, the model for the other countries is likely to be Hungary, and we should therefore briefly consider how Hungary has dealt with inflation since 1968.[41]

It is clear that the reformed system has allowed some increase in the rate of inflation. But we should all be happy with 2.5 percent per year, and it is indeed remarkable in the circumstances. External inflationary pressures have been strong, at least since 1972. "Planners' tension" and pressure for growth have been maintained, operating primarily through investment goods markets; and some of the structural relations characteristic of mixed economies have been re-established, though in attenuated form. Profit-dependent incentives have restored the link between price increases and aggregate demand through personal incomes and decentralized investment funds. Excess demand is transmitted to producers and elicits a supply response, with corresponding pressure on the labour market. Domestic prices are now related to foreign prices, and consumer prices to producer

---

[39] Peter Wiles, "The Control of Inflation in Hungary, January 1968–June 1973," *Economie Appliquée*, vol. 27 (1974), no. 1, pp. 119–47.

[40] John Kenneth Galbraith, *A Theory of Price Control* (Cambridge, Mass.: Harvard University Press, 1952).

[41] Richard Portes, "The Strategy and Tactics of Economic Decentralization," *Soviet Studies*, vol. 23, no. 4 (April 1972), pp. 629–58; Richard Portes, "Hungary: The Experience of Market Socialism," in *The Chilean Road to Socialism*, ed. J. A. Zammit (Sussex: Institute of Development Studies, University of Sussex, 1973), pp. 367–90; Richard Portes, "Hungary: Economic Policy, Performance, and Prospects," in *East European Economies Post-Helsinki* (A Compendium of Papers Submitted to the Joint Economic Committee, 95th Cong., 1st sess.) (Washington, D.C.: U.S. Government Printing Office, 1977), pp. 766–815; Wiles, "The Control of Inflation"; P. G. Hare, "Economic Reform in Hungary: Problems and Prospects," *Cambridge Journal of Economics*, vol. 1, no. 4 (December 1977), pp. 317–33.

prices, although the extent of product-specific taxes and subsidies is much greater than had originally been intended. Indeed, there have been some overall retrenchment and recentralization in the reformed system over the past few years, partly as a reaction to inflationary tendencies. These in turn were to some extent both a cause and a consequence of distributional tensions, which have been the key political issue in the reforms.

Price controls have nevertheless been very successful in the context of the much more flexible price system introduced in 1968. They take a variety of forms: some prices are still centrally fixed, others are subject to maxima or "early warning" requirements, and in many cases the authorities have used differentiated subsidies and taxes to neutralize increases in the foreign prices of imports and exports (until recently they were inexplicably reluctant to revalue the *forint*). On the wage side, centrally-fixed wage plans were replaced by the "tax on wage increases." This has restrained the rate of growth of money wages (to 6 percent per year in 1968–75) despite distributional problems and the more assertive behaviour of the trade unions. There is still excess demand on *producer* goods markets, and this does now matter. But over all, the new Hungarian system has by various means maintained a reasonable control over inflation while allowing more price flexibility, and output growth and productivity performance have been quite good.

Both Hungary and the other CPEs are subject to the same influences operating in world markets as is any Western mixed economy, with the qualification that the CPEs conduct only a third to a half of their total trade outside Comecon. Reformed or not, the CPEs face the same forces that generate "imported inflation" in mixed economies: rising oil prices and, more generally, sharp changes in the terms of trade between primary products and manufactures, as well as the upwards trend in the prices of industrial goods produced by advanced capitalist countries. One might also expect a slowly rising share of East-West exchanges in their total trade (though I am not as convinced of this as most observers) and a continued increase in overall foreign trade dependence, which will motivate a closer relation of domestic to foreign prices.

These forces may result in slightly more consumer price inflation than in the past, although in principle there is no reason why they should. Clearly the planners ought to raise the *relative* price of petrol to domestic consumers, but in practice they have done so by raising its absolute price; similarly with certain foodstuffs, which are substantially underpriced by world market standards. On the other hand, the strength of the system is that it should permit these to be once-for-all increases which need not generate any inflationary spiral. General world inflation need have no effect, for the "price equalization subsidies" (*Preisausgleich*) automatically achieve the accounting equivalent of revaluing the currency.

In all CPEs but Hungary, the *Preisausgleich* and consequent divorce between foreign and domestic prices and monetary phenomena mean that exchange rate changes cannot be used as a balance of payments equilibrating mechanism. This may be bad for the balance of payments, but it is certainly good for the rate of inflation. A deterioration of the terms of trade may induce some consumer price increases, although the required cut in real incomes or investment or government consumption could be achieved by a variety of monetary techniques, depending on where the planners want the impact to fall and the political effects of alternative policies. (Thus even with Hungary's relatively flexible price system and highly open economy, although the terms of trade fell by 14 percent from 1973 to 1975,[42] the total rise in the CPI was kept to 6 per cent.) But that can and should be the end of it, unless their terms of trade *continuously* fall. This seems unlikely—the oil price increase is more a redistribution from the smaller CPEs to the USSR than a change in Comecon's terms of trade with the rest of the world, and the CPEs' main exports to the West are agricultural goods and raw materials.

VIII. YUGOSLAVIA

Worker participation in ownership and control of enterprises has recently been taken seriously as a possibility for institutional change in the West, both by the professional economics literature and in wider, more practical contexts. It has many virtues (principally in combating alienation), but the control of inflation is decidedly not one of them. Yet a widely publicized recent proposal to escape from the United Kingdom's inflation–unemployment dilemma suggests that we "change company law [to give] ownership and ultimate control of enterprises to the people employed by them. They would then have to sink or swim in a market environment. Inflation would subside. Employment would be high."[43]

If comparative applied economics can tell us anything whatsoever, the Yugoslav experience should be a conclusive counterexample. With inflation at almost 15 percent per year since 1963, registered unemployment in 1975 averaged slightly over 10 percent of the resident labour force and a further 800,000 Yugoslav workers (15 percent of the domestic labour force) had to find employment abroad.[44] Any closer examination of the Yugoslav economy supports the analysis of a leading Yugoslav economist: "The decentralization of decision making and workers' management are . . . responsible for the transformation of Yugoslav CPE inflation into a market

---

[42] Portes, "Hungary: Economic Policy."

[43] Peter Jay, *Employment, Inflation and Politics* (London: Institute of Economic Affairs, 1976), p. 34.

[44] Organization for Economic Cooperation and Development (OECD), *Economic Survey: Yugoslavia* (Paris: OECD, 1976).

phenomenon. . . . Only since 1960, and more so since 1963, when enterprises gained autonomy in their wage rate determination, has inflation set in triumphantly."[45] Bajt argues that the essential structural relation in the inflationary process is the link between wages and product markets through workers' involvement in the distribution of profits. A significant element in the wage–push mechanism has been the behaviour of inter-enterprise wage differentials over the business cycle.[46]

IX. LESSONS

Without reiterating in full the warnings in Sections I and II above about the validity of an exercise such as this, I should stress that any interpretation of "lessons" drawn from CPE experience must rest on both a theory of the inflationary process and clearly defined political and economic values. I do believe there is something for virtually everyone, however, in the following main points for consideration and perhaps further research:

1. Workers' control in itself is not the solution to the inflation-unemployment problem in a relatively decentralized, market-oriented economy (Section VIII). Profit-sharing in such an economy is likely to contribute to inflation (cf. Hungary as well as Yugoslavia).

2. Supposing that little serious "hidden" or repressed inflation can be demonstrated for CPEs (Sections II and V), it is clearly possible to run a modern economy under high pressure with rapid growth and virtually no inflation, even with significant foreign trade dependence on an inflating capitalist world.

3. This control over prices can be accompanied by considerable control over the distribution of real income and may indeed facilitate it (Sections IV and VI). And conversely, central planning of income distribution, taking distributional conflict out of the market place, does not eliminate such conflicts but does limit their inflationary consequences.

4. In particular, wage differentials may be significantly compressed (as compared with the wage structure which might evolve without such a conscious egalitarian policy) without excessive disorder in the allocation of labour between alternative employments. There may however be some negative incentive effect in production itself, as well as resistance from the shop floor. (Experience in the United Kingdom, where differentials have also narrowed, appears to suggest similar conclusions.) A national "job

---

[45] Aleksander Bajt, "Yugoslav Experience in Inflation," in CESES, *Anti-inflationary Policies*, pp. 180–81.

[46] For a detailed explanation and econometric evidence, see Aleksander Bajt, "Patterns of Instability in Socialist Economies," in *International Aspects of Stabilization Policies*, ed. Albert Ando and others (Boston: Federal Reserve Bank of Boston, 1975), pp. 357–80.

evaluation" system is feasible (Section VI)[47] and has indeed worked quite well in the CPEs.

5. Consumer price policy can also be an extremely powerful distributional tool (Section VI), and in this role might be a good substitute for high marginal rates of income tax (with their disincentive effects) or wealth taxes (if these are politically or otherwise infeasible).

6. CPE success in controlling inflation is *not* due solely or even primarily to limits on the power and role of the trade unions (Section IV). Distributional pressures and real income growth expectations are significant autonomous inflationary forces, even though they are not primarily expressed through trade union activity.

7. From the viewpoint of inflation control, the degree of articulation and sophistication of our financial and monetary system may be excessive (Section IV). There are considerable potential gains from blocking certain channels of monetary transmission in our macroeconomy.

8. In particular, the control of inflation is greatly facilitated by measures that directly insulate the domestic monetary system from the foreign sector (Section IV).[48]

9. There are advantages for consumer price control in rationalization and concentration in the distributive network.

10. Weakening the link from product markets back to demand, by limiting the dependence of personal incomes and investment funds on profits, is clearly a powerful anti-inflationary tool (Section IV). Its cost is of course to weaken the capital market incentives which are in principle a prime virtue of competitive capitalism (Section VI).

11. The major costs of relatively rigid price and wage controls are the disincentive to technical progress and the bureaucratic apparatus required for implementation; but common impressions of the latter may be exaggerated (Section VI).

12. A "tax on wage increases" on the Hungarian model (Section VII) might be a useful adjunct to inflation control policies in Western conditions, if supported by appropriate aggregative monetary and fiscal policies (the tax is a microeconomic tool) and policies for the distribution of income and wealth.[49]

Doubtless one could suggest further generalizations, but these are enough to be going on. All require extensive qualification, some of which is provided in earlier sections. How much any or all of these statements depend on the transformation of property relations, restriction of political

---

[47] See also McAuley, "Wage Determination."

[48] See also Wiles, "The New Inflation," and Portes, "Inflation under Central Planning."

[49] See the theoretical analysis in Yehuda Kotowitz and Richard Portes, "The 'Tax on Wage Increases': A Theoretical Analysis," *Journal of Public Economics*, vol. 3, no. 2 (May 1974), pp. 113–32.

liberties, and the right to emigrate, etc., is for the reader to judge. It is however clear that the control of inflation does not require that "moral incentives" or "restraint" replace the material incentives which Western societies are unlikely to discard. Yet it is also evident that many of the policies implicit in points 1–12 above are contrary to those with which the OECD countries have been facing the inflationary pressures of the 1970s.

Multidimensional Comparisons

A comparison of the performance of different economies should include many dimensions, and it should distinguish the relative importance of systemic vs. nonsystemic factors in explaining differences in performance.

The following selection provides such a comparison for one of the most appropriate pairs of countries, East Germany and West Germany. It identifies the aspects to be compared, some important conceptual and data problems, and the part inevitably played by the analyst's own judgments.

26

SIMILAR SOCIETIES UNDER DIFFERING ECONOMIC SYSTEMS: THE CASE OF THE TWO GERMANYS*

Paul Gregory
and
Gert Leptin[1]

The authors begin by assessing the reasonability of the assumption that nonsystemic differences between East Germany (the German Democratic Republic, or GDR) and West Germany (the Federal Republic of Germany, or FRG) are relatively small compared to systemic differences. Next they make careful statistical comparisons of the two Germanys' performance in regard to economic growth, productivity, consumption levels, income distribution, and stability of prices and employment. Then they examine the extent to which the GDR and FRG may be considered typical, respectively, of socialist centrally planned economies and capitalist regulated market economies.

* Reprinted by permission from *Soviet Studies*, vol. 29, no. 4 (October 1977), pp. 519–42, with the omission of appendixes, references to foreign-language sources, and some technical footnotes. Paul Gregory is Professor of Economics at the University of Houston, and Gert Leptin is a Professor at the East Europe Institute of the Free University of Berlin.

1 This paper was presented at a joint session of the American Economic Association and the Association for Comparative Economic Studies in Atlantic City, N.J., in September 1976. Professor Gregory worked on this study under the auspices of a Humboldt Foundation Fellowship at the Institute of East European History at the University of Tubingen. We would like to thank Wolfgang Stolper for his valuable comments and Joseph Berliner for suggesting this study. Any errors are to be attributed to the authors.

I. THE VALIDITY OF "ALL OTHER THINGS EQUAL"

Comparative economists welcome the prospect of comparing societies that are alike except for their economic systems. Such contrasts offer the opportunity to isolate the impact of the economic system on economic structure and performance, and this is, after all, what comparative economics is all about. Analysis of economies unlike in both system and socio-economic endowments introduces the difficult methodological problem of differentiating the impact of the system from that of other performance-related factors exogenous to the economic system.

To what extent do economic comparisons of East (GDR) and West (FRG) Germany offer a simple solution to this problem? That is, can one in this case invoke the *ceteris paribus* assumption without undue distortion and thus deal directly with the system's impact on economic performance? The "systems" in question are the state-planned socialist economy of the GDR and the FRG's market-directed economy. We are, of course, not suggesting that both countries are prototypes of the systems they represent (cf. state intervention in the FRG and the retention of some private markets and ownership in the GDR); nevertheless, they are close enough for our purposes. The applicability of *ceteris paribus* to the two Germanys is critical, and we consider first points in its support.

The strongest argument is the common endowment of per capita human capital in the FRG and GDR at the end of the war, a proposition which holds today despite the notable divergences in population and labour force dynamics of the postwar period. This proposition could be documented with a mass of data on education, training, etc., but it should suffice to note that the two Germanys today are essentially inhabited by a homogeneous population.[2] Closely related to (and perhaps inseparable from) the matter of a common population are the shared culture, traditions, tastes, etc., all of which argue for equal "noneconomic" factor endowments. Third, despite some notable structural differences, the two Germanys were among the most modern industrial economies at the outbreak of the war, with particular branches considered to be the world leaders in their fields. The equivalence in the level of economic development in the two areas which were later to become the GDR and FRG is seen in the rough equivalence of per capita incomes and per capita industrial outputs in 1939.[3] The advanced nature of the two German economies persists to the present, as is evidenced

---

[2] We speak here in the most general terms. There are differences in the age structure of population in the two Germanys along with other differences, but such factors must be marginal when compared with the common features of the two populations.

[3] According to figures supplied by Wolfgang Stolper, *The Structure of the East German Economy* (Cambridge, Mass.: Harvard University Press, 1960), p. 418, the ratio of GDR to FRG per capita income in 1936 was 0.98. On the other hand, per capita industrial output in the GDR was 16 percent higher than in the FRG in 1939 [according to another source].

by the structure of output and capital stock (the distributions of which are remarkably similar) and in the advanced structure of exports and imports.

The arguments against the invocation of "all other things equal" are more numerous and must be weighed against the above common features. In considering nonequivalencies, a thorny issue must be confronted, namely, to what extent are they truly *exogenous* to the economic system or are indeed *consequences* of the system? To illustrate, consider a factor which has served to retard GDR economic performance. If this factor is independent of (exogenous to) the economic system, then one must avoid attributing its weakness to the system. But if the factor is an integral consequence of the system, then its weakness should be attributed to the system.

The notably smaller scale of the GDR economy is an obvious exogenous difference. The population of the GDR territory at the end of the war was 18 million, roughly one-quarter that of the combined FRG-GDR territory. Today, it is closer to one-fifth. This difference in scale, with its potential impact on economic performance, is without question exogenous, and must be weighed when evaluating the system's impact on performance. Differences in energy and resource bases are also exogenous and should be "held constant" in performance comparisons. Although it is commonly argued that the GDR resource base is inferior to that of the FRG (owing to the loss of Silesian coal), this matter is not obvious. Population density is lower in the GDR and suggests a more favourable land-population ratio for the GDR. Moreover, although soft coal supplies are lacking, lignite is a relatively abundant fuel and is available for synthetic fuel production and electricity generation.[4] The redefinition of political boundaries and the incorporation of the GDR into the communist bloc did represent a greater disruption of existing trade and production patterns for the GDR and is likely to have necessitated a longer adjustment to the new environment than in the FRG.

Final exogenous factors are the unequal treatment of the two Germanys at the hands of their respective occupation forces, and the unequal wartime destruction of industrial capacity. It has been roughly estimated that demontage and wartime destruction wiped out some 50 percent of GDR and 25 percent of FRG 1943 industrial capacity. Thus, the GDR entered the postwar period with more substantial capacity losses than the FRG.[5] While the GDR economy was saddled in the early postwar period with reparation payments from current production, the FRG benefited from Marshall assistance, receiving some 16 billion marks in credits. On the

---

[4] We are grateful to Wolfgang Stolper for this point.

[5] One may question to what extent the loss of old industrial capacity is necessarily bad insofar as it provides the opportunity to replace older technology with new technology. Moreover, there was a relatively greater build-up of industries in the area of the GDR after 1936, so one might question whether prewar comparisons are appropriate in this instance.

other side, the FRG paid out some 33 billion marks as *Wiedergutmachung* payments,[6] a sum double that of its Marshall Aid receipts. The GDR did not participate in the *Wiedergutmachung* program.

These factors had little to do with the system of state planning introduced into the GDR, but they could conceivably have had a significant impact on postwar economic performance. In fact, one author has argued (incorrectly, we believe) that the postwar performance of the GDR was indeed remarkable (a *Wirtschaftswunder* [Economic Miracle]) in light of these constraints.

These exogenous forces should not be ignored in evaluating FRG–GDR economic performance. Rather, one must consider to what extent they may explain the GDR's contemporary productivity, per capita income, and consumption gaps relative to the FRG. In our view, they all, with the exception of scale, represent largely transitional problems of the immediate postwar period which can be largely held constant by dealing with long-term performance in the postrecovery era. We maintain that scale differences are unlikely to be crucial: there are successful large and small economies, and there seems to be no correlation between per capita income and size. We note, however, that the most successful small economies (Switzerland, Holland, for example) are intensively integrated into the world economy and owe their success to this fact. Under conditions of autarky, which we feel to be systemic to Comecon, size can play a considerable role as can deficient resource endowments. Again, we should note that there are successful resource-poor economies (Japan, for example), but that integration in the world economy appears to be a necessary condition for this success.

Other FRG–GDR differences are less obviously exogenous to the economic system, and are likely to be more important. The GDR's loss of population to the West ("republic flight") between 1945 and August 1961 (ranging from 144,000 to 330,000 per year) left its imprint on postwar GDR development. To some extent, this republic flight was a continuation of the traditional migration pattern of the German empire, strengthened by the strong performance of the postwar FRG economy (and perhaps by unemployment problems in the GDR prior to 1961[7]), but it was also a consequence of the choice of economic system, especially in the composition of this migration. The republic flight was comprised largely of free professions, skilled technicians, and former entrepreneurs. Moreover, over one-half of the refugees during this period were under 25 years of age. In these cases, the GDR economic system itself played a prominent role in prompting this flight through its income distribution policies, housing policies, and discrimination against independent eco-

---

[6] Editor's note: Compensation payments to victims of Nazism.

[7] We are grateful to Wolfgang Stolper for this point.

nomic activity; the ensuing brain and skill drain was costly.[8] It is not possible to separate the republic flight into its exogenous and endogenous elements, but our subjective suspicion is that the latter dominated.

We regard divergences in participation in postwar international trade and capital flows by the FRG and GDR as largely endogenous to the system. The GDR's failure to reach its potential in international trade is evidenced by its documented low ratio of trade volume to GNP, corrected for scale and level of income.[9] Throughout the postwar era, per capita trade volume in the GDR ranged from 50 to 60 percent of that of the FRG,[10] a remarkably low figure in view of the GDR's smaller scale and less varied resource base. This policy must have been costly to growth and productivity performance. First, it suggests a tendency towards autarky in an economy ill-suited for self-sufficiency.[11] Secondly, whereas the FRG at least initially was a recipient of advanced technology, the GDR has served throughout the postwar period as a technology exporter (a lower level of technology, to be sure) within the communist bloc. Also lacking was the pressure of international competition to which the FRG export industries have been subjected—a weakness general to the Comecon countries.

How can one argue that the adoption of the autarky model is an integral part of the planned socialist model? The theoretical arguments have been made before,[12] and they relate to the desire of planners to reduce planning risks (which are raised if foreign suppliers enter the picture), to the absence of standard monetary arrangements for international trade, to the use of distorted accounting prices, and to barter arrangements, all of which reduce international trade volume. As these are all integral parts of the state planning model, it is impossible to separate the low trade volumes from the economic system. The major disadvantages of autarky should therefore be attributed to the system and not to exogenous forces.[13]

As there are arguments both for and against *ceteris paribus*, some subjective weights must be introduced. Our own feeling is that the invocation of *ceteris paribus* is not an undue distortion of reality once *long-term* per-

---

[8] Previous attempts to capture these costs as lost capital formation are unsatisfactory not only because of the statistical materials but also because of the methodology.

[9] Paul Gregory, *Socialist and Nonsocialist Industrialization Patterns* (New York: Praeger Publishers, 1970), p. 120.

[10] These figures are rough approximations, as the GDR figures are cited in valuta marks, whose parity is unknown.

[11] This matter is discussed in some detail in Gregory, *Socialist and Nonsocialist Industrialization Patterns*, chaps. 6 and 7.

[12] In particular, see Franklyn Holzman, "Foreign Trade," in *Economic Trends in the Soviet Union*, ed. Abram Bergson and Simon Kuznets (Cambridge, Mass.: Harvard University Press, 1963), chap. vii.

[13] It may be relevant to distinguish between policies and systems in this instance. For example, Poland and Hungary appear to be examples of CMEA countries which have significantly changed their "policy" regarding trade with the West without altering the economic system. We are grateful to J. M. Montias for this point.

formance is considered and the interrelationships between the system and performance-related factors, especially in the areas of foreign trade and migration, are recognized. We believe that the differential treatment of the two Germanys and the disruptions of the immediate postwar period should have been overcome within a decade. The most convincing *ceteris paribus* argument is the common population of the two Germanys which should have provided the same potential for recovery, holding the impact of the system constant. The disadvantages of integration into the communist bloc should be attributed to general system-related problems, and should not be regarded as exogenous to the system.

II. COMPARISONS OF ECONOMIC SYSTEMS

We have maintained that the application of *ceteris paribus* to the evaluation of GDR–FRG economic performance is not an undue distortion of reality. The problem of evaluating performance, where economic goals differ radically, remains. How goals are established in planned and market economies is not critical here. What is important is that the various economic desiderata—growth, efficiency, "good" income distribution, rising standards of living, environmental quality, stability, etc.—have been weighted differently in the FRG and GDR, and, insofar as the achievement of one goal may mean the sacrifice of another, a multidimensional picture of economic performance must be sketched. Overall evaluations must remain subjective, except in the obvious and rare case where one economy outperforms the other with regard to all conceivable goals.[14]

We provide in this section summary statistics concerning a series of desiderata—growth, efficiency, income distribution, standard of living, stability, and environmental quality—to shed light on the relative performance of the FRG and GDR. Because of the greater availability of comparable statistics after 1960, we shall concentrate on this period, but we also seek to provide information on the entire postwar period where possible. Short-term performance considerations and fluctuations will be avoided, and we provide only aggregative summary statistics to avoid inundating the reader with details. That these aggregations may conceal truly important information is recognized, but this has proved necessary to remain within space limitations.

Economic Growth

The GDR, like its CMEA counterparts, has emphasized rapid economic growth, particularly of industry, as its overriding long-term goal. The growth objective is less well defined in the FRG, where other objectives

---

[14] For a more complete discussion, see Paul Gregory and Robert Stuart, *Soviet Economic Structure and Performance* (New York: Harper and Row, 1974), chap. 10.

(price stability, export growth) have been accorded priority. Given the GDR leadership's intense interest in growth, it is therefore instructive to contrast the long-term growth of the two Germanys. At the outset, we should emphasize that the FRG growth has been exceptional and that to use it as a yardstick for the GDR represents a quite ambitious criterion. The FRG and GDR are among the most successful of the systems they represent, and this fact makes our comparison an interesting one. Yet it raises the issue articulated by Hanson,[15] namely, that it is difficult to generalize from such bi-country comparisons, as both countries may be inferior (superior) to other economies operating under the other system.

In Table 1 we cite growth statistics for the 1960–73 period. The period is selected both on the grounds of data availability and to allow more than sufficient time for adjustment to the disruptions of the early postwar period. The cited GDR aggregates are reconstructions according to Western accounting definitions. Although independently estimated, they still rely heavily on official GDR industrial production indexes, which we believe contain some serious inconsistencies. These inconsistencies suggest some overstatement of GDR growth, while not denying its general rapidity, and that moderate margins of error in the direction of downward adjustment should be applied.[16] For this reason, we attempt to keep our conclusions as general as possible, regarding small growth differentials as statistically insignificant.

The most general conclusion is that the FRG and GDR economies grew at roughly the same rate (identical according to our Table 1 figures) between 1960 and 1973, at a respectable rate of approximately 4.6 percent per annum. Turning to the sector growth rates, we fail to find major FRG–GDR differences. In the GDR priority sector, industry, the calculated growth rates are identical, but in view of our feeling that the GDR rate is overstated it appears that industry grew faster in the FRG. On the other hand, construction grew faster while services grew more slowly in the GDR. Our general conclusion, however, is that the growth performances of the two Germanys between 1960 and 1973 have been remarkably similar, even taking into consideration the inflation of the GDR rate. The most notable distinction is not the trend rate but deviations around this trend. The annual growth rate shows much greater variability in the FRG (ranging from −2.4 to 11.5 percent) than in the GDR (ranging from 3.3 to 6.7 percent). We return to this point in later discussion.

Data for earlier periods are less reliable and less complete, and overall conclusions depend upon whose data one accepts. Reconstructions of FRG

---

15 Philip Hanson, "East-West Comparisons and Comparative Economic Systems," *Soviet Studies*, vol. 22, no. 3 (January 1971), pp. 327–43.

16 One should note that equivalent GNP growth means higher per capita income growth for the GDR, owing to its lower rate of population growth. Between 1960 and 1973, population grew at 0.7 percent annually in the FRG, and it declined at a rate of 0.1 percent annually in the GDR.

TABLE 1

Annual Rates of Growth of Output, Inputs, and Factor Productivity, GDR and FRG, 1960–73

A. GDR (constant 1967 prices)*

	(1) Output	(2) Labour	(3) Capital	(4) Labour Produc- tivity	(5) Capital Produc- tivity	(6) Total Factor Produc- tivity
Industry	5.3	0.2	5.0	5.1	0.2	3.9
Construction	6.4	1.6	9.9	4.7	−3.2	2.7
Agriculture	1.5	−2.8	6.0	4.5	−4.2	2.1
Transport and communication	4.8	0.6	3.4	4.1	1.3	3.5
Trade	4.7	−0.4	5.2	5.2	−0.5	3.7
Services	3.0	1.6	1.7	1.3	−0.1	1.4
GNP	4.6	0.2	4.0	4.4	−0.1	3.4

* Estimates by Herbert Wilkens. In col. 6 labour and capital inputs are combined with weights of 0.75 and 0.25 respectively.

B. FRG (constant 1962 prices)†

	(1) Output	(2) Labour	(3) Capital	(4) Labour Produc- tivity	(5) Capital Produc- tivity	(6) Total Factor Produc- tivity
Industry	5.3 ⎫ 5.2	0.1 ⎫ 0.2	⎫ 6.9	5.2 ⎫ 3.5	⎫ −1.6	⎫ 3.3
Construction	4.4 ⎭	0.4 ⎭	⎭	3.9 ⎭	⎭	⎭
Agriculture	1.8	−4.6	3.3	6.6	−1.5	4.4
Transport and communication	4.2 ⎫	0.3 ⎫		3.9		
Trade	4.0 ⎬4.2	0.2 ⎬1.3	⎬ 5.2	3.8 ⎬ −1.0	⎬1.9	
Services	4.3 ⎭	2.3 ⎭		2.0		
GNP	4.6	0.2	5.9	4.5	−1.2	3.0

† In col. 6 labour and capital inputs are combined with weights of 0.75 and 0.25 respectively.

statistics to conform to GDR statistical definitions, when compared with *official* GDR statistics, suggest a higher annual growth rate for the GDR between 1950 and 1960 (10 percent vs. 8 percent), but such data suffer from the standard weaknesses (judged by Western standards) of CMEA statistical procedures. The pioneering studies by Stolper and others yield a different picture. Between 1950 and 1958 the annual growth of the GDR economy was 6.5 percent, some 0.7 percentage points below the FRG rate. Stolper's comparisons with prewar (1936) production indicate a rather substantial decline in production in the GDR (1950 equals 73 percent of 1936) contrasted with an increase in aggregate production for the FRG (1950 equals 117 percent of 1936).[17]

---

[17] Stolper, *The Structure of the East German Economy*, pp. 418–19.

One common conclusion, however, emerges from the above statistics, namely, that both countries have grown at quite respectable rates between 1950 and 1973 (even after downward adjustment of the GDR figures) and that growth differences between the two economies are quite small. A common pattern of resource allocation is not suggested by this conclusion. If one proceeds to a lower level of aggregation, the more typical features of the socialist industrialization model become apparent: the relative neglect of residential construction, transport and communication, and social overhead investment, and the relatively larger share of heavy industrial branches in total manufacturing output.

Dynamic Efficiency and Patterns of Growth

The search for the sources of this rapid growth in the FRG and GDR necessarily leads one to consider resource allocation policies and the role of technological progress. Looking first at investment rates (Table 2), we find that the GDR figure depends upon the statistical system and prices employed. According to official GDR statistics, the GDR investment rate has been below that of the FRG throughout the postwar era, although the gap has been narrowing in recent years (Panel A, Table 2). On the other hand, recalculations according to Western concepts and in some instances applying West German (or German Reich) prices indicate higher GDR investment rates with the exception of the immediate postwar reconstruction years (Panel B).

These investment rate comparisons indicate quite high (by international standards) investment proportions in both Germanys and that, in general, investment proportions have not been all that different with the exception of the early postwar period. While the GDR investment rate is roughly equivalent to that of the FRG, GDR output and output per capita are well below the FRG (Table 3). Thus the burden of maintaining this

TABLE 2
Investment Rates, GDR and FRG

A. Official Investment Rates in Domestic Prices (excluding inventory investment)

	1960–64	1965–68	1969–72
GDR	14.5	17.7	19.5
FRG	24.2	21.8	22.3

B. Investment Rates (including inventory investment) in Western GNP Definitions

	1950	1955	1967	1974	
GDR	15*	22*	25*	26–28*	(27†)
FRG	24	25	23	23	

* FRG prices.
† GDR prices.

TABLE 3
Absolute Productivity Comparisons, GDR and FRG, 1967:
GDR (in West German Prices) as Percent of FRG

Category of Output	Total	Per Capita	Per Worker
GNP, total	22	78	67
GNP originating in			
Agriculture	41	141	92
Industry, construction, and mining ..	24	84	72
Trade and transport	19	65	59
Services	19	67	66

investment rate appears to be heavier in the GDR. Our comparison suggests, as well, that the GDR investment rate has not been exceptionally high by CMEA standards, and more detailed studies reveal that the composition of this investment in recent years has become more oriented towards housing construction than in the other CMEA countries.

A final brief comment is in order here concerning relative defense burdens in the two Germanys. Although the usual statistical problems limit accurate comparisons, one can nevertheless tentatively conclude that the defense burden as measured by the ratio of defense outlays to GNP has been quite similar in the two Germanys after 1960 and has not been excessive in either area, a factor which has very likely contributed to the impressive growth of both countries.

The pattern of factor (capital and labour) growth was surprisingly similar between 1960 and 1973. We say "surprising" because of divergent trends in population growth, where population declined 4 percent in the GDR and increased by 12 percent in the FRG during this period. Despite these divergent trends in population growth, aggregate labour force growth rates were identical at 0.2 percent per annum (Table 1). The sectoral pattern of labour force growth was generally similar but with some notable differences: the more rapid decline in agriculture, the less rapid increase in service employment, and the more rapid increase in construction in the GDR. Labour force growth was achieved in the GDR, despite declining population, through increases in the labour force participation rates of women and older people, so that now the overall GDR participation rate (about 50 percent) and the female participation rate (84 percent of working-age women) are among the highest in the world.

One also finds similarities in the patterns of capital stock growth. The overall growth of capital stock was more rapid in the FRG (6 percent vs. 4 percent), but the distribution of this growth was similar, although the growth rate of capital was higher in agriculture and lower in transport, communication, trade, and services in the GDR.

With similar aggregate growth rates of outputs and inputs in the two Germanys, the growth of factor productivity will be similar, although slightly higher as measured for the GDR owing to the somewhat slower growth of capital. In both Germanys labour productivity grew per annum at around 4.5 percent and total factor productivity at from 3 percent (FRG) to 3.4 percent (GDR). Capital productivity was negative in both economies, although more negative for the FRG (−1.2 percent) than for the GDR (−0.1 percent). Again, we stress our feeling that the cited GDR output growth statistics are inflated, and this will also affect the productivity calculations. We maintain, however, that downward adjustment of the GDR figures would fail to alter the overall finding of generally similar rates of growth of factor productivity.

Looking at the earlier period we note, according to Stolper's findings,[18] that aggregate labour productivity grew at annual rates of 6 percent (GDR) and 4.5 percent (FRG) between 1950 and 1958. Nevertheless, our overall conclusion remains, namely, that productivity growth in the two Germanys has been similar throughout the postwar period. By international standards, productivity growth has been impressive in both economies.

Absolute Efficiency Comparisons

In order to make some judgements about absolute productivity in the two Germanys, GNP figures in a common set of prices are required. Such estimates have been made by Herbert Wilkens of the Deutsches Institut für Wirtschaftsforschung[19] on the basis of 1967 West German prices for the years 1967 and 1974. Because of the wider margins of error for the 1974 figures, we concentrate here on the 1967 GDR–FRG comparisons (Table 3). Figures for relative capital stocks are not available, so our discussion is restricted to labour productivity comparisons, but one can nonetheless make some judgements about the possible impact of capital on our conclusions.

Concentrating on the GNP comparisons, we see that 1967 GDR GNP in West German prices was 22 percent of the FRG. On a per capita basis, it was 78 percent. On a per worker basis the relative figure is 67 percent, owing to the higher labour force participation rate of the GDR. Thus GDR labour productivity was roughly two-thirds that of the FRG in 1967. In terms of sectoral productivity, the best relative performance was (surprisingly) that of GDR agriculture at 92 percent of the FRG figure, with industry (broadly defined) at 72 percent.[20] This latter figure is in accord with other estimates, which place East German industrial labour productivity around three-quarters that of the FRG. The addition of capital stock

---

18 Stolper, *The Structure of the East German Economy*, p. 421.

19 Editor's note: (West) German Institute for Economic Research.

20 The finding of relatively good agricultural productivity is not consistent with other evidence for specific crops. Yields per acre in the GDR are much lower (with roughly the same factor proportions per man), and other inputs are also generally lower. We are grateful to Wolfgang Stolper for this evidence.

to this analysis would not materially alter this picture. Under the most favourable assumption that capital productivity in the GDR is equal to that of the FRG, the overall productivity figure would be raised from two-thirds to three-quarters. A more likely picture, however, is lower GDR capital productivity, which would require a lowering of GDR relative productivity to less than two-thirds of the FRG.

Estimates of absolute labour productivity for the mid 1950s[21] indicate an aggregate labour productivity for the GDR in 1955 approximately one-half that of the FRG, a finding which is not fully consistent with the labour productivity growth figures cited above, for it suggests a substantial elimination (from one-half to two-thirds) of the differential between 1955 and 1967—a finding not supported by the cited growth of labour productivity. On the other hand, this inconsistency may be explained by index number phenomena, as different price weights are being used in the 1955 and 1967 estimates, and by the fact that the 1955 estimates are based upon more partial data.

Combination of Tables 1 and 2 and Stolper's estimates leads one to the conclusion that, in relation to 1936, the GDR suffered a severe relative loss in labour productivity (a drop from parity to perhaps as low as 50 percent of the FRG according to the Stolper figures). The emergence of this gap is not reflected in official GDR statistics, at least as far as industry is concerned, for GDR industrial statistics indicate similar rates of growth of labour productivity in the two Germanys between 1936 and 1950. We find the Stolper-Wilkens evidence of the existence of a substantial productivity gap, supported by official GDR evidence, convincing. Although this gap may have narrowed between 1955 and 1967, the gap remains substantial (approximately one-third), and it appears to be increasingly difficult to close it further if the 1967 and 1974 experience remains typical.

The basic issue, which these productivity comparisons raise, remains to be confronted. Can the GDR productivity differential be explained by factors exogenous to the economic system? Our subjective opinion, derived from the standard resource allocation model of the centrally planned economies (labour hoarding, nonclearing prices, failure to innovate, satisficing, material stockpiling, autarky, etc.[22]), is that the endogenous element is strong and that contemporary productivity differentials cannot be explained by the legacy of the immediate postwar period. Perhaps the most important endogenous element was the inability of a relatively small and possibly resource-poor economy such as the GDR to integrate itself fully in the world economy. This, combined with internal allocation practices, is likely to explain much of the productivity differential.

[21] Stolper, *The Structure of the East German Economy*, pp. 416–18.

[22] Abram Bergson, *The Economics of Soviet Planning* (New Haven, Conn.: Yale University Press, 1964).

Living Standards

Selected data on relative GDR–FRG living standards are supplied in Table 4. The most aggregative figures on per capita consumption and net monthly wages of households and of income recipients all roughly agree that the GDR living standard (recognizing that these measures are only proxies for living standards) in the late 1960s and early 1970s was between 50 percent and two-thirds that of the FRG. The above figures fail to adjust completely for quality differentials, the inclusion of which we believe would lower the respective GDR ratios, by how much we cannot guess. The two benchmarks from the mid 1950s and mid 1960s (Table 4) indicate a narrowing of the consumption differential, and this is consistent with official GDR statistics. However, other data on the real income of industrial workers suggest a relative decline for the GDR industrial worker between 1960 and 1973.[23] Thus we cannot come to any firm conclusions concerning relative rates of growth of living standards since the 1950s.

Despite its poor showing relative to the FRG, the GDR living standard

TABLE 4
Various Indicators of GDR Living Standards as Percent of FRG*

Indicator	Year	GDR as percent of FRG
1. Private consumption expenditures (in DMW) ..	1955	60
	1967	69
2. Average monthly income of households (net) adjusted for purchasing power differentials in DMO and DMW	1967	59
3. Average monthly income of income recipient adjusted for DMO-DMW purchasing power	1967	59
differentials (industrial workers)	1973	51
4. Per capita consumption of various foodstuffs ...	1973	
Pork		107
Other meat		75
Eggs		85
Milk		117
Fresh fruits		53
Coffee		55
Wine and champagne		78
5. Per capita stock of various consumer durables ..	1972/73	
Cars		32
Motorcycles		73
Radios		95
Televisions		87
Electrical refrigerators		85
Electrical washing machines		84

* DMW and DMO are the West German (FRG) and East German (GDR) mark currencies, respectively.

---

[23] These are Leptin's own calculations of real net incomes of industrial workers in the GDR and FRG.

is none the less impressive by other standards, both in its composition and relative to other CMEA countries. In composition, the GDR performs better relative to the FRG in the area of necessities excluding housing, and less well in the area of nonnecessities including consumer durables. However, we should stress that the stock of consumer durables (row 5) in the GDR is quite impressive both by CMEA and Western European standards, but such comparisons violate the *ceteris paribus* assumption upon which this analysis is based.

Our conclusion therefore is that the contemporary GDR consumption gap is at least in the neighbourhood of one-third. It is difficult to determine whether this gap has narrowed since the early 1950s because of conflicting data, but we would imagine that any narrowing during this period would be, at best, marginal. In fact, a stronger case could be made that the GDR relative living standard has declined. These conclusions are not altered by the inclusion of social services provided by the state, as such services are quite similar per capita in the two Germanys. Thus, starting from a position of parity in 1936, the GDR suffered a substantial decline in consumption *vis-à-vis* the FRG. At best, this gap is being reduced at an almost imperceptible rate.

Income Distribution

The comparison of income distributions in the GDR and FRG raises two conceptual problems. The first is that income from wealth accrues—with only minor exceptions—to the one major property owner, the state, in the GDR, while it accrues to the private and public owners of wealth in the FRG. It is therefore crucial to a meaningful analysis to be able to determine the claims and control which particular individuals or groups in the GDR exercise over this state wealth. Analysis of this issue must rest to a large extent on sociopolitical considerations, with which we as economists are not exceptionally conversant. Thus our analysis must be limited to general observations. The second problem is that the distribution of income in the GDR will not necessarily coincide with the distribution of real goods and services. This is true because a whole series of scarce goods and services are allocated outside the market mechanism (apartments, vacations, travel to the West, etc.) on the basis of social position, productivity, or political criteria. The third problem is one of data availability. For market economies such as the FRG, one does have data on the distribution of income from wages and from wealth for the spectrum of societal groups, while for the CMEA countries one generally has only wage income distribution data for particular groups, in the GDR for workers and employees. Thus one has practically no information about the income of farm families, managers, politicians, academicians, artists, etc., who exercise an important impact on the Western distributions.

TABLE 5
Comparison of the Distribution of Disposable Net Income of
Worker and Employee Households, GDR and FRG, 1960 and 1970

Percent of the Number of Households	Percent of Net Income			
	1960		1970	
	GDR	FRG	GDR	FRG
First quintile	10.4	8.4	10.4	10.7
Second quintile	15.3	12.6	15.8	16.2
Third quintile	19.2	16.4	19.8	19.7
Fourth quintile	23.4	22.8	23.3	22.8
Fifth quintile	31.7	39.8	30.7	30.6
Total	100.0	100.0	100.0	100.0

In Table 5 we cite statistics for the income distribution of worker and employee (*Arbeiter und Angestellte*) families, data which suffer from the conceptual problems raised above. As such families earn income almost entirely from wages and salaries, this comparison sheds light primarily on the distribution of labour income among families, and fails to deal with the broader issue of the distribution of income from wealth for society as a whole. As is evident from Table 5, the distribution of wage and salary income among families was more nearly equal in the GDR in both 1960 and 1970. However, one can also say that the distribution of wage income is not all that different in the two Germanys, suggesting that wage differentiation plays a major role in providing incentives in both countries. This point can also be seen from the close similarity of branch wage differentials in the GDR and FRG.[24] In fact, we believe that the trend towards less inequality between 1960 and 1970 in Table 5 is not the product of a conscious egalitarian policy in either Germany but rather the consequence of autonomous economic processes.

A more comprehensive comparison involving all societal groups would have to consider not only income from consumption but also those components of income which are invested in market economies and thus serve to determine the basic direction of economic growth. In this manner, wealth owners exercise control and influence over the direction of economic activity in market economies well above their influence as consumers. To ensure comparability in this broader sense, one would have to impute some hypothetical income to the lower, middle, and upper leadership of the GDR in order to equate their degree of influence over resource allocation to that of the wealth owners in the FRG. Such an exercise is impossible to carry through; nevertheless, it suggests a method whereby meaningful comprehensive comparisons including the distribution of wealth can be made. The specific issue being raised is: what hypothetical

---

[24] Paul Gregory, "A Model of Socialist Industrial Wage Differentials: The Case of East Germany," *Quarterly Journal of Economics*, vol. 87, no. 1 (February 1973), pp. 132–37.

income would have to be assigned to the GDR leadership in order to give them a control over resource allocation equivalent to that exercised by the totality of wealth owners in the FRG?

Economic Stability

It is our conclusion that the GDR has had greater economic stability throughout the postwar period than the FRG, but that this stability has been purchased at considerable cost. By stability, we refer to the stability of economic growth and to the absence of excessive inflation and unemployment. In our discussion of economic growth, we noted the greater variation of growth in the FRG, which has experienced several recessions in the postwar era. The GDR economy has not had a recession between 1950 and the present, although it has had reductions in growth during the early 1960s and early 1970s. To some extent, the growth of recent years has been at the expense of foreign indebtedness to the West. But the conclusion is obvious: the GDR economy has been less subject to cyclical fluctuations in total output than the FRG.

Both producer and consumer goods prices have grown less rapidly in the GDR than in the FRG from the 1950s to the 1970s, although it is difficult to determine the real rate of producer goods inflation owing to the problem of pricing of "new" commodities. The cost of restraining the rate of inflation of producer goods in the GDR has not been too substantial in terms of allocative inefficiencies, as prices have not played that much of an allocative role anyway. As far as consumer goods are concerned, the official GDR index shows a 10 percent *decrease* between 1955 and 1973. This remarkable result is the consequence of several factors, the first being the acceptance by GDR trade unions of the formula that wage increases should be less than the rate of labour productivity growth. The second is that GDR pricing authorities have been willing to accept disequilibria in particular consumer markets and the disincentive costs thereof. The third factor is that the state has been willing to subsidize certain products and to experience a reduction in turnover tax revenues in cases where wholesale prices of consumer goods have risen (such as food products). Nevertheless, the political and other benefits of consumer price stability have apparently exceeded these costs. The point we would emphasize is that this apparent price stability has been achieved at the price of disguised instabilities (subsidies, nonmarket allocation, etc.), and it is difficult to measure the extent of these instabilities. However, in the GDR case, our impression is that such instabilities have not got out of hand (as in Poland) and do not represent a serious threat to social stability.

Although one cannot estimate the aggregate unemployment rate of the GDR to compare with that of the FRG (which is currently substantial), we believe one can safely conclude that it is minimal by Western standards. The major price of this minimal unemployment, in our opinion, has been disguised unemployment, which again is impossible to measure. During periods of slack economic activity employment remains stable at the macro level and at the micro level less productive individuals do not lose their jobs, and excess labour is hoarded like excess materials. A major price of job security and of the ensured existence of enterprises is that quality is likely to suffer as the failure to produce quality products does not result in a loss of jobs or in the demise of the enterprise. This stability of the employment rate is also an explanatory factor for the stability of the GDR growth rate in that the major component of aggregate value added is wages, which will remain stable owing to the stability of employment.

What are our conclusions, then, concerning economic stability? In general, we conclude that the GDR economy has been stable in terms of growth rate, in that the major component of aggregate value added is stability, disequilibria in consumer markets and disguised unemployment, cannot be measured and have apparently been kept in reasonable check in view of the lack of strong evidence to the contrary. On the other hand, we should note that the FRG economy has been among the most stable of the market economies, and that the price of GDR stability has very likely been a relative loss of productivity and of quality.

Environmental Quality

We cannot hope to deal with this topic and remain within reasonable space limitations. All we can do is to relate our casual impression that although ambitious plans exist in the GDR for the elimination of environmental disruption, only minimal capital expenditures have been made, for the simple reason that capital resources are limited and have had to be devoted to more pressing social and economic needs. It is thus our impression that, both absolutely and relatively, more has been expended and accomplished in the area of providing environmental quality in the FRG than in the GDR. Perhaps this is what one should expect, for the availability of resources for environmental protection tends to be related to the affluence of the society. We would further argue that it may prove more difficult for a state-planned economy to direct resources into environmental quality owing to extreme pressures to maintain the growth rate. As to the more general issue of the "quality of life" in the FRG and GDR, we feel this is an issue well beyond the scope of this study.

III. THE TYPICALITY OF THE GDR-FRG EXPERIENCES FOR PLANNED AND MARKET ECONOMIES

The question of the typicality of the East and West German experiences for state-planned socialism and market economies remains unanswered. The issue of the typicality of the West German experience is well beyond the scope of this inquiry, so we limit our remarks to the GDR.

We should begin by noting that in terms of institutional arrangements for allocating resources the GDR economy is the image of the Soviet economy. On the other hand, there are features of the GDR development process which make it quite different from its Soviet and CMEA counterparts. Some of these features are the consequence of the more advanced stage of economic development of the GDR; others are the result of certain unique features of the GDR. The issue of the atypicality of the GDR economy is relevant for two reasons. The first is that the GDR has been forced to develop without the luxury of forcing industrial growth through the rapid expansion of labour inputs. Thus the experience of the GDR economy may have something to say about the future development prospects of the other CMEA countries when they, as well, exhaust their extensive development opportunities. A second reason for interest is the achievements of the GDR economy noted above, and one would like to find an explanation for its success relative to the other CMEA countries.

Turning now to the matter of the atypical features of the GDR model, we first note the point raised above, namely, the necessity of generating economic growth with a declining population. This necessity forced the GDR authorities, in our opinion, to be more conscious of the role of incentives to ensure not only high participation rates but also the productive use of labour resources. The fact that the GDR investment rate has not been exceptionally high relative to CMEA standards despite higher per capita income, and the fairly ample (by CMEA standards) stock of consumer durables, support this conclusion. Also the distribution of investment resources in the late 1960s and early 1970s in the direction of social overhead capital and apartment construction all indicate an effort on the part of GDR authorities to improve industrial incentives and mobility. The greater toleration of private enterprise in handicraft, retail trade, and agriculture is also indicative of this trend.

An alternative explanation offers itself as well. The proximity and close emotional and family ties with the FRG made it politically and socially impossible to allow too large a gap in living standards to develop. To what extent the apparent greater attention paid to the consumer in the GDR was the consequence of political necessity owing to the presence of the FRG or the need to preserve labour incentives cannot be answered, but both forces are likely to have played important roles.

The special relationship with the FRG may have played other roles as well. The special trade relationship gave the GDR access to the Common Market on a preferential basis, but perhaps more important, in view of the relatively low trade proportions with the West, was the role of information transfers to the GDR from the FRG. As a result of these ties, GDR managers and authorities had more knowledge of prevailing industrial practices and relative prices, which may have provided better information upon which to base their own resource allocation decisions.

IV. CONCLUSIONS

We began this article with a discussion of the validity of the *ceteris paribus* assumption, for we felt this was the crucial issue in GDR–FRG comparisons. Our conclusion was that the *ceteris paribus* assumption could be applied, due primarily to the common level of prewar economic development and to the existence of a relatively homogeneous population in the two Germanys. However, the limits of the *ceteris paribus* assumption were also recognized, and these limits must be broadened if our assumptions concerning the endogeneity of certain negative factors are not accepted. We also noted that the factors exogenous to the system, which would have to be held constant, almost all worked to the disadvantage of the GDR, but were regarded by us as largely transitional factors.

What our empirical analysis revealed is the existence of substantial per capita output, productivity, and consumption gaps for the GDR, where the gaps appear to be wider for consumption than for per capita output and for productivity. Moreover, we found that these gaps do not appear to be narrowing significantly, although there is some contradictory evidence on this point. Throughout the empirical section we were troubled by certain contradictions in the GDR industrial production figures which introduced measurement errors into the aggregate figures. Concerning the priority objective of the GDR, economic growth, we found roughly equivalent rates of growth of output and industry over the postwar period.

We were unable to compare the distribution of income on a comprehensive basis including both wage and wealth income and including all social groups. Rather, our analysis was limited to the distribution of income among worker families. This comparison indicated a slightly less unequal distribution of wage income in the GDR but failed to reveal dramatic differences in the distribution of income. Finally, we argued that the apparently greater stability of the GDR economy in terms of growth, price stability, and employment has led to certain efficiency and quality costs, but that these costs have been kept within manageable limits. On the other hand, we recognized the fact that the FRG economy also has been among the most stable of the major market economies.

So what we appear to have are two quite successful representatives of the two economic systems. They suggest what can be accomplished under specific conditions by each economic system. To what extent are they, then, "typical" of their systems? This question we cannot answer, for lack of a generally accepted criterion of typicality. Our subjective conclusion is that the FRG economy, even after holding the differential experience of the immediate postwar period constant, has "outperformed" the GDR economy. For this conclusion, we rely heavily on the productivity and consumption gaps and the fact that these gaps do not appear to be disappearing over time, and we state quite clearly that we are using our own subjective weights in this matter. We do also recognize the point that the use of FRG economic performance as a measuring rod for GDR performance is indeed a rigorous criterion, and that the GDR has "outperformed" other major market economies in those areas to which we have subjectively attached large weights. It may be more realistic to engage in other comparisons, but then the matter of evaluating the *ceteris paribus* model becomes enormously complex.